W9-BSI-061

Fodor's
ESSENTIAL
HAWAII

Hawaiian Ocean
SURFTECH

WELCOME TO HAWAII

Hawaii overflows with natural beauty. Piercing the surface of the Pacific from the ocean floor, the Hawaiian Islands are garlanded with soft sand beaches and dramatic volcanic cliffs. Long days of sunshine and fairly mild year-round temperatures make this an all-season destination, and the Islands' offerings—from urban Honolulu on Oahu to the luxury resorts of Maui to the natural wonders of Kauai and the Big Island—appeal to all kinds of visitors. Less-developed Lanai and Molokai are quieter, but all the Islands are rich in Hawaiian culture.

TOP REASONS TO GO

★ **Beaches:** Every island claims its share of postcard-perfect strands.

★ **Resorts:** Spas, pools, lavish gardens, and golf courses make relaxing easy.

★ **Pearl Harbor:** This historic memorial site on Oahu is not to be missed.

★ **Napali Coast:** Kauai's jagged emerald-green coast makes an unforgettable excursion.

★ **Whale-Watching:** In winter humpback whales swim right off Maui's shores.

★ **Volcanoes National Park:** On the Big Island you can explore the world's most active volcano.

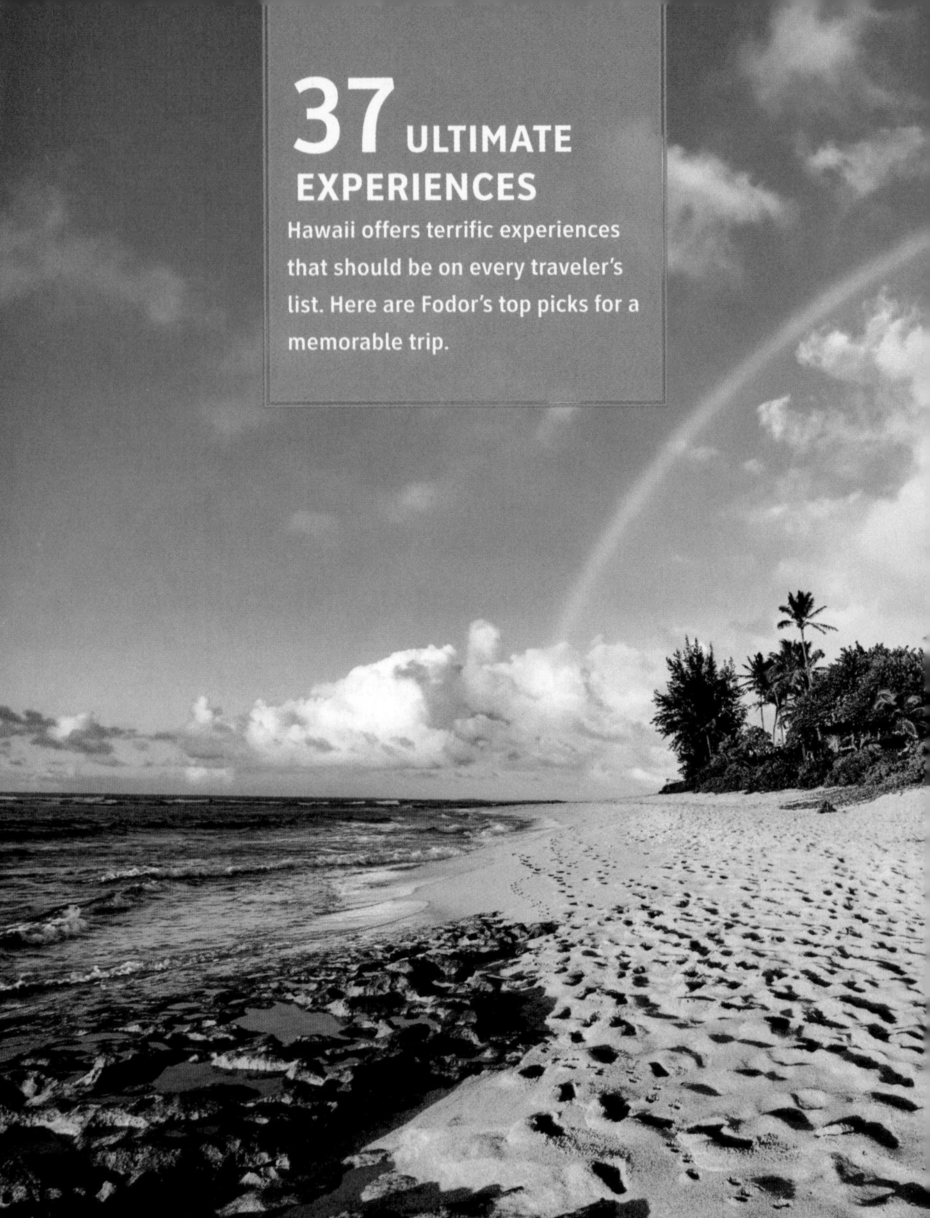

1 Explore Oahu's North Shore

Make a day of it when you head to the North Shore. Start off in Kaneohe and drive up Kamehameha Highway to Haleiwa, stopping along the way at fruit stands, shrimp trucks, beaches, world-famous surfing spots, and scenic overlooks. *(Ch. 2)*

2 Tour a Kona Coffee Plantation

Local farmers love to share their passion for farming genuine Kona coffee with the public and offer free tours. Our favorite is Lion's Gate Farm at mile marker 101 in Honaunau. *(Ch. 4)*

3 Be a Cowboy for a Day

Saddle up and get ready to ride the ranges, cliffs, and trails of the Big Island on horseback. It's one of the best ways to take in the island's beautiful scenery. *(Ch. 4)*

4 Mountain Tubing

A century ago, Lihue Plantation dug waterways to irrigate it's fields. Now you can take a tubing tour via the waterways for a glimpse of Kauai's hidden interior. *(Ch. 5)*

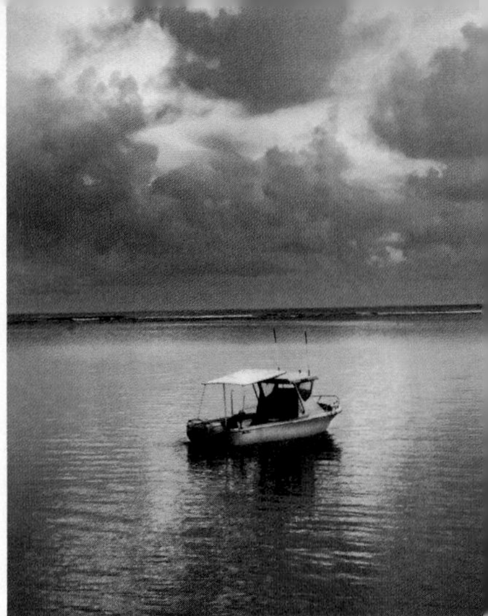

5 Go Deep Sea Fishing

The deep Pacific waters surrounding Kauai are teaming with fish. Charters, most of which depart from Lihue, visit the best spots and provide all the gear. *(Ch. 5)*

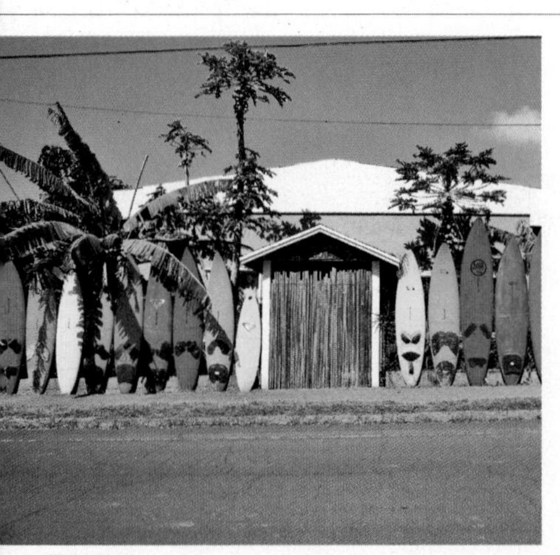

6 Small-Town Charm

Discovered by hippies in the 1970s, Paia continues to be a hip and happening place with galleries, eateries, antique stores, and, of course, surf shops. *(Ch. 3)*

7 Snorkel at Haunama Bay

This nature preserve nestled in a volcanic crater with a vibrant reef is a phenomenal, family-friendly place to see colorful fish and other sea life. *(Ch. 2)*

8 Watch Lava Flow at Hawaii Volcanoes National Park

Witness the primal birth of living land from two eruption sites flowing from Kilauea Volcano, currently the world's most active volcano. *(Ch. 4)*

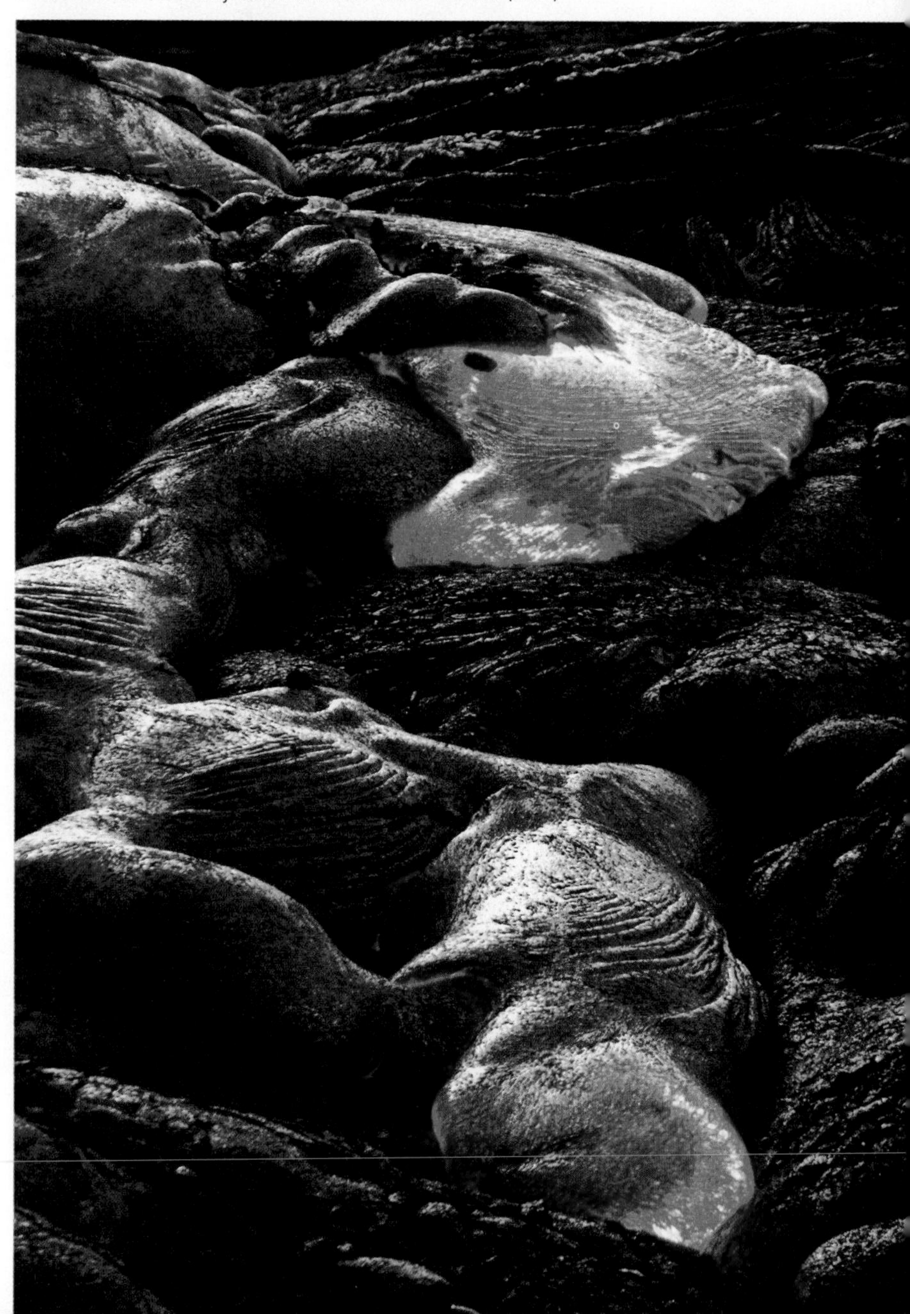

9 Watch for Whales

Humpback whales hang out in the Au'Au Channel off Maui every winter, and boats leaving from Lahaina can be in the midst of these gentle giants within 15 minutes. *(Ch. 3)*

10 Learn to Surf

Waikiki is still a popular spot to try Hawaii's favorite sport, but White Plains has fewer crowds and great conditions for beginner surfers. *(Ch. 2)*

11 Attend a Luau

Guests are treated to Hawaiian-style storytelling, complete with hula dancing, traditional knife dancing, and fire poi ball throwing at traditional luaus.

12 Treat Yourself to Shave Ice at Island Snow in Kailua

Matsumoto's on the North Shore may be the most well-known, but we prefer Island Snow in Kailua. *(Ch. 2)*

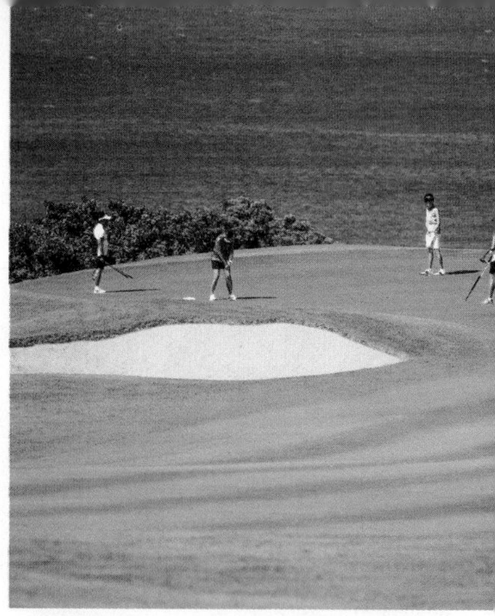

13 Duffer's Paradise

The perfect storm of golf occurs on Maui, where stunning weather, gorgeous views, and amazing course layouts converge. *(Ch. 3)*

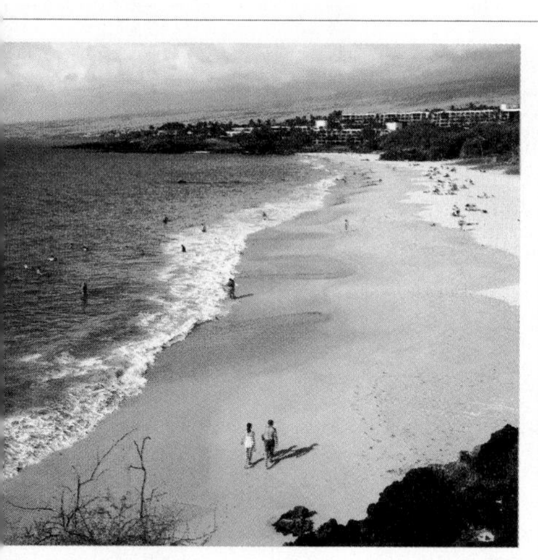

14 Visit a 5-Star Beach

The Big Island's most beautiful beaches, including Anaehoomalu Bay, Hapuna Beach, and Kaunaoa Beach, flank the Kohala Coast. *(Ch. 4)*

15 Visit Sacred Heiaus

Remains of sacred structures of the Kauai kingdom are found in Wailua along Route 580 between the mouth of the Wailua River and Mount Waialeale. *(Ch. 5)*

16 Waimea Canyon Dazzles

A vast canyon on Kauai's west side, this geologic wonder measures a mile wide, more than 10 miles long, and 3,567 feet deep. *(Ch. 5)*

17 Watch the Pros Surf at Waimea Bay

Oahu's Waimea Bay was integral to the early development of big wave surfing. It's still a great place to watch the pros. You'll get the best views during the winter. *(Ch. 2)*

18 Relive History at Pearl Harbor

World War II Valor in the Pacific National Monument preserves four different World War II sites at Pearl Harbor, including the the USS *Arizona* Memorial. *(Ch. 2)*

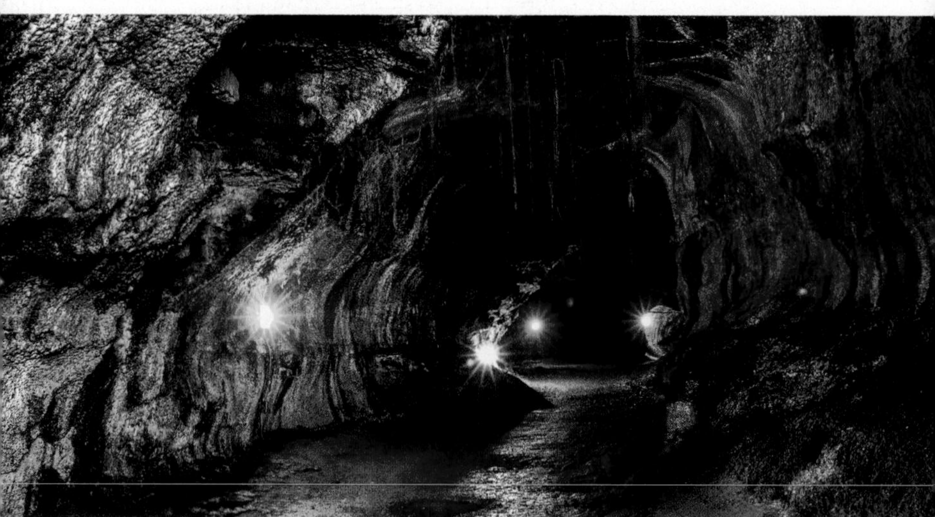

19 Explore Lava Tubes

While the Thurston Lava Tube in Hawaii Volcanoes National Park is convenient, Kula Kai Caverns and Kilauea Caverns of Fire are also fascinating but require expert guides. *(Ch. 4)*

20 Dive the Cathedrals of Lanai

These lava tubes comprise one of Maui's primo diving spots (technically off Lanai) boasting a variety of multicolored fish, eels, turtles, dolphins, and octopi. (Ch. 7)

21 Walk Down to Waipio Valley

This lush, waterfall-laden valley—surrounded by sheer, fluted 2,000-foot cliffs—was once a favorite retreat for Hawaiian royalty. *(Ch. 4)*

22 Have a Plate Lunch

Everyone should try this Hawaii lunch tradition: an entrée with white rice and a scoop of macaroni salad. It's an island favorite and bargain-priced.

23 Visit Iolani Palace

The only royal residence in the U.S. gives you an introduction to Hawaii's monarchy era, which ended with the overthrow of Queen Liliuokalani in 1893. *(Ch. 2)*

24 See the Sunrise

Haleakala National Park's Puu Ulaula Overlook is Maui's highest point and the best place to see the sunrise. *(Ch. 4)*

25 Relax on Poipu Beach

Popular with tourists and locals, uncrowded Poipu Beach has calm waters ideal for snorkeling, and you might just spot an endangered Hawaiian monk seal. *(Ch. 5)*

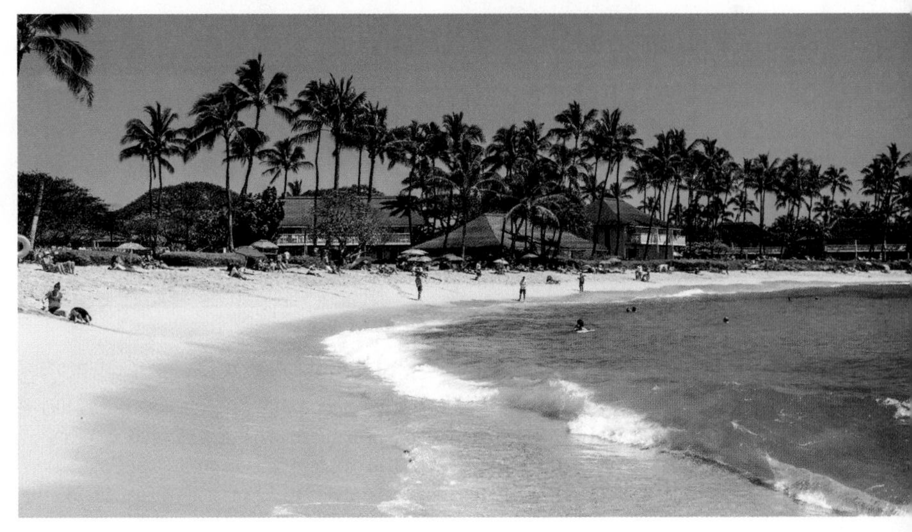

26 Watch a Hula Show

If you want a more traditional, less touristy introduction to hula and Hawaiian music, go to the Kuhio Beach Hula Show on Kuhio Beach. *(Ch. 2)*

27 Snorkel Molokini Crater

Tropical fish thrive at Molokini Crater, a partially submerged caldera about 3 miles off of Maui's southern coast that serves as a fortress against the waves. *(Ch. 3)*

28 The Road to Hana

One of the world's most famous drives, this precarious road has more than 600 curves and crosses some 50 gulch-straddling bridges in just 52 coastline miles. *(Ch. 3)*

29 Helicopter Vistas

Kauai's interior is best seen via helicopter. Tours give access to breathtaking scenery like Waimea Canyon and Waialeale Crater. *(Ch. 5)*

30 Kayaking to Secret Falls

One of Hawaii's few navigable rivers, kayaking Wailua River leads you into a mystical realm of lush rain forests, velvety green mountains, and secret, crystal-clear waterfalls. *(Ch. 5)*

31 Walk Through Waikiki

The best way to people-watch, shop, eat, and sightsee on Waikiki's iconic tourist strip is by foot. *(Ch. 2)*

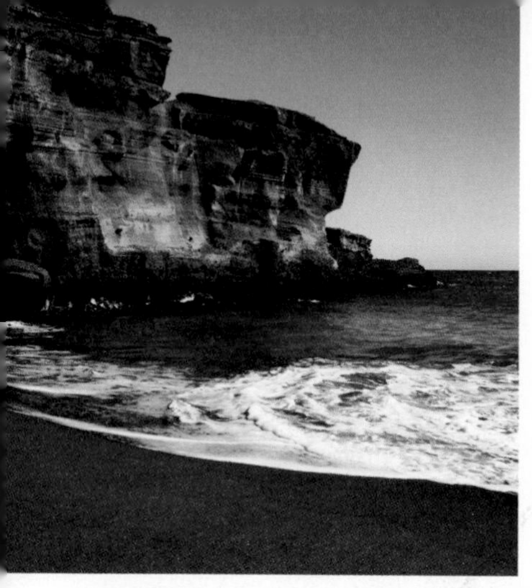

32 Hike to the Green Sand Beach

It's worth the effort to drive to the end of South Point Road and hike to Papakolea Beach. Take lots of water. *(Ch. 4)*

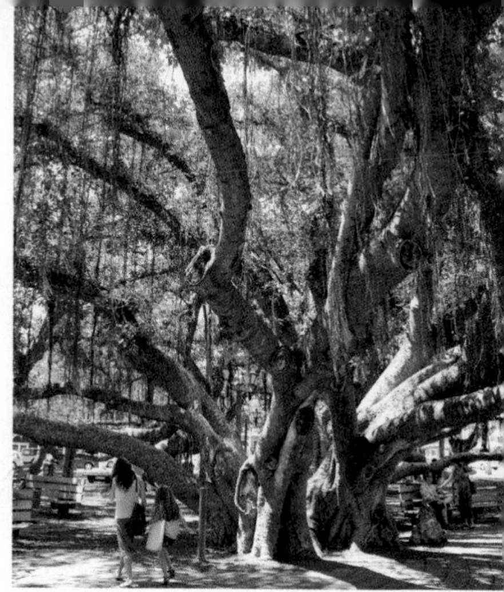

33 Historic Lahaina

Once an active hub for whaling, pineapple, and sugar, Lahaina is a busy downtown with restaurants, shops, and galleries. *(Ch. 3)*

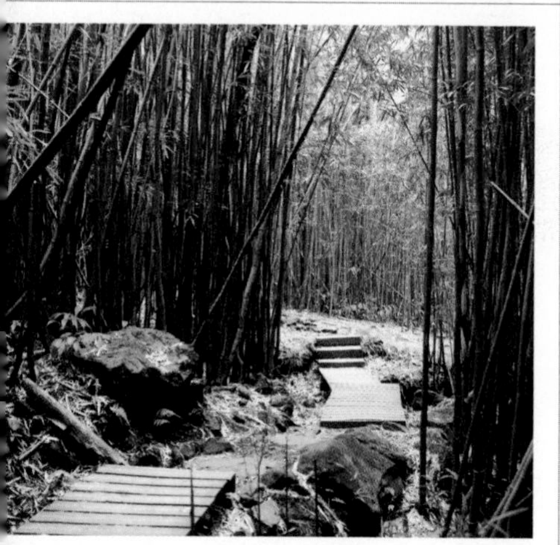

34 Hike a Bamboo Forest

Haleakala National Park's 4-mile round-trip Pipiwai Trail is a dramatic realm of plunging waterfalls, archaic ferns, and an immense bamboo forest. *(Ch. 3)*

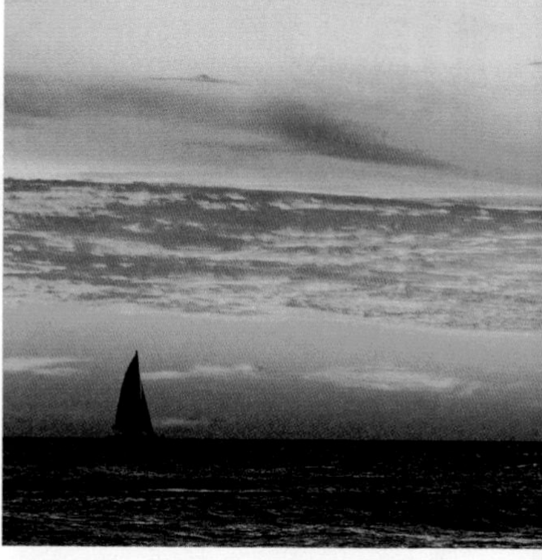

35 Coastal Sunset Sail

Kauai sunsets are sublime, and perhaps the best way to experience that magical hour of the day is by boat, facing stunning Napali Coast. *(Ch. 5)*

36 Stargaz

The sunset and stargaz
center offers free public st

37 Visit Iao Valley

Central Maui's iconic, green-mantled natural spire rises 1,200 feet above a verdant valley; go early in the day before clouds obscure the views. *(Ch. 3)*

ISBN 978–1–64097–084–7

ISSN 2471–9048

Library of Congress Control Number 2018950373

All details in this book are based on information supplied to us at press time. Always confirm information when it matters, especially if you're making a detour to visit a specific place. Fodor's expressly disclaims any liability, loss, or risk, personal or otherwise, that is incurred as a consequence of the use of any of the contents of this book.

SPECIAL SALES

This book is available at special discounts for bulk purchases for sales promotions or premiums. For more information, e-mail SpecialMarkets@fodors.com.

PRINTED IN THE UNITED STATES OF AMERICA

10 9 8 7 6 5 4 3 2 1

CONTENTS

Fodor's Features

CONTENTS

MAPS

ABOUT THIS GUIDE

Fodor's Recommendations

Everything in this guide is worth doing—we don't cover what isn't—but exceptional sights, hotels, and restaurants are recognized with additional accolades. Fodor's Choice ★ indicates our top recommendations. Care to nominate a new place? Visit Fodors.com/contact-us.

Trip Costs

We list prices wherever possible to help you budget well. Hotel and restaurant price categories from **$** to **$$$$** are noted alongside each recommendation. For hotels, we include the lowest cost of a standard double room in high season. For restaurants, we cite the average price of a main course at dinner or, if dinner isn't served, at lunch. For attractions, we always list adult admission fees; discounts are usually available for children, students, and senior citizens.

Hotels

Our local writers vet every hotel to recommend the best overnights in each price category, from budget to expensive. Unless otherwise specified, you can expect private bath, phone, and TV in your room. For expanded hotel reviews, visit Fodors.com.

Top Picks
★ Fodor's Choice

Listings
- Address
- Branch address
- Telephone
- Fax
- Website
- E-mail
- Admission fee
- Open/closed times
- Subway
- Directions or Map coordinates

Hotels & Restaurants
- Hotel
- Number of rooms
- Meal plans
- Restaurant
- Reservations
- Dress code
- No credit cards
- Price

Other
- See also
- Take note
- Golf facilities

Restaurants

Unless we state otherwise, restaurants are open for lunch and dinner daily. We mention dress code only when there's a specific requirement and reservations only when they're essential or not accepted. For expanded restaurant reviews, visit Fodors.com.

Credit Cards

The hotels and restaurants in this guide typically accept credit cards. If not, we'll say so.

EUGENE FODOR

Hungarian-born Eugene Fodor (1905–91) began his travel career as an interpreter on a French cruise ship. The experience inspired him to write *On the Continent* (1936), the first guidebook to receive annual updates and discuss a country's way of life as well as its sights. Fodor later joined the U.S. Army and worked for the OSS in World War II. After the war, he kept up his intelligence work while expanding his guidebook series. During the Cold War, many guides were written by fellow agents who understood the value of insider information. Today's guides continue Fodor's legacy by providing travelers with timely coverage, insider tips, and cultural context.

EXPERIENCE HAWAII

WHAT'S WHERE

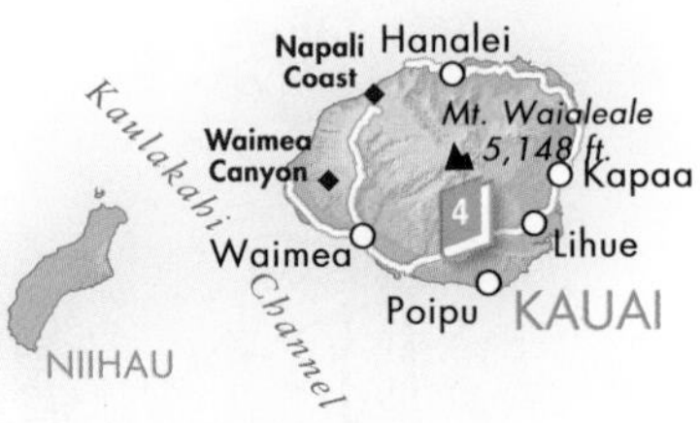

1 Oahu. Honolulu and Waikiki are here—and it's a great big luau. It's got hot restaurants and lively nightlife as well as gorgeous white-sand beaches, knife-edged mountain ranges, and cultural sites, including Pearl Harbor.

2 Maui. The phrase *Maui no ka oi* means Maui is the best, the most, the tops. There's good reason for the superlatives. It's got a little of everything, perfect for families with divergent interests.

3 Big Island of Hawaii. It has two faces, watched over by snowcapped Maunakea and steaming Mauna Loa. The Kona side has parched, lava-strewn lowlands, and eastern Hilo is characterized by lush flower farms, waterfalls, and fresh lava forming daily.

4 Kauai. This is the "Garden Isle," and it's where you'll find the lush, green folding sea cliffs of Napali Coast, the colorful and awesome Waimea Canyon, and more beaches per mile of coastline than any other Hawaiian island.

5 Molokai. It's the least changed, most laid-back of the Islands. Come here to ride a mule down a cliff to Kalaupapa Peninsula; to experience the Kamakou Preserve, a 2,774-acre wildlife refuge; and for plenty of peace and quiet.

6 Lanai. For years there was nothing here except for pineapples and red-dirt roads. In 2012 Oracle billionaire Larry Ellison purchased 98% of the island, and it still attracts the well-heeled in search of privacy, with two upscale resorts, archery and shooting, four-wheel-drive excursions, and superb scuba diving.

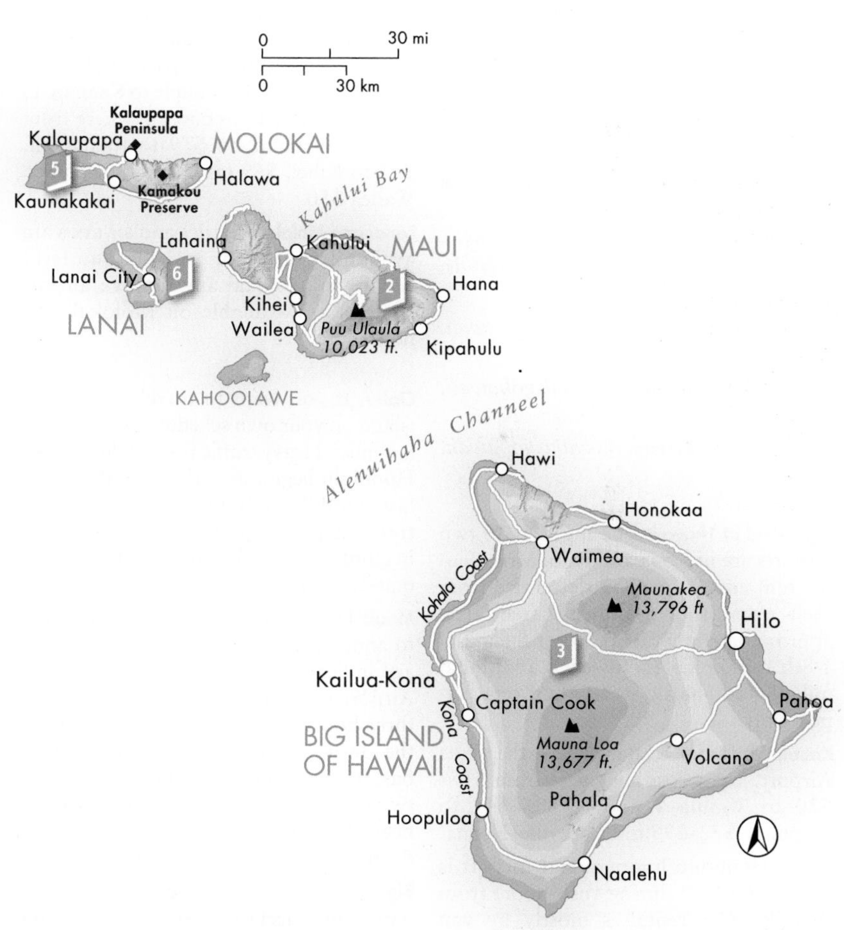

0
30 mi
0
30 km
Kalaupapa Peninsula
Kalaupapa
MOLOKAI
Halawa
Kaunakakai
Kamakou Preserve
5
Kahului Bay
Lahaina
Kahului
MAUI
Lanai City
6
2
Hana
Kihei
LANAI
Wailea
Puu Ulaula 10,023 ft.
Kipahulu
KAHOOLAWE
Alenuihaha Channeel
Hawi
Honokaa
Waimea
Kohala Coast
Maunakea 13,796 ft
Hilo
3
Kailua-Kona
Kona Coast
Captain Cook
Pahoa
BIG ISLAND OF HAWAII
Mauna Loa 13,677 ft.
Volcano
Pahala
Hoopuloa
Naalehu

HAWAII PLANNER

When You Arrive

Honolulu's International Airport is the main stopover for most domestic and international flights, but all of Hawaii's major islands have their own airports and direct flights from the Mainland are more common these days. Flights to the Neighbor Islands leave from Honolulu almost every half hour daily.

Visitor Information

Hawaii Beach Safety. 🌐 *hawaiibeachsafety.com.*

Hawaii Department of Land and Natural Resources. 🌐 *dlnr.hawaii.gov.*

Island of Hawaii Visitors Bureau. ☎ *800/648–2441* 🌐 *www.gohawaii.com/islands/hawaii-big-island.*

Kauai Visitors Bureau. 🌐 *www.gohawaii.com/kauai.*

Maui Visitors Bureau. 🌐 *www.gohawaii.com/islands/maui.*

Oahu Visitors Bureau. 🌐 *www.gohawaii.com/oahu.*

Getting Here

Big Island of Hawaii: The Big Island's two airports are in Kona and Hilo. Most people rent cars or get shuttle service from their resort (not usually for free). The approximate taxi rate is $3 for the initial 1/8th mile, plus $3 for each additional mile. SpeediShuttle serves the Kona Airport only.

Kauai: All commercial flights use the Lihue Airport. Taxis cost anywhere from $17–$20 to Wailua–Waipouli, $35–$41 to Poipu, or $72–$95 to Princeville–Haena.

Oahu: Honolulu International Airport is 20 minutes (40 during rush hour) from Waikiki. Car rental is mostly by van pickup across the street from baggage claim. An inefficient airport taxi system requires you to line up for a taxi wrangler who radios for cars ($40–$45 plus 60¢ per bag to Waikiki). Other options: TheBus ($2.75, one lap-size bag allowed), and the Roberts Hawaii Express Shuttle ($16 per person). Uber and Lyft also serve the airport.

Maui: Most visitors arrive at Kahului Airport in Central Maui and rent a car. If you don't want to drive yourself, SpeediShuttle costs $67 per couple to Kaanapali, $47 to Wailea. Taxis cost anywhere from $20 to Wailuku, to $79 to Kaanapali, $45 to Kihei, $69 to Lahaina, or $50 to Wailea $50.

Lanai and Molokai: Ferries and air taxis are available from Maui to Lanai (no ferry service to Molokai any longer); airport shuttles are available on Molokai, but not Lanai.

Getting Around

Oahu: If you want to travel around the island on your own schedule, renting a car is a must. Heavy traffic toward downtown Honolulu begins as early as 6:30 am and lasts until 9 am. In the afternoon, expect traffic departing downtown to back up beginning around 3 pm until approximately 7 pm.

Maui: Driving from one point on Maui to another can take longer than the mileage indicates. It's 52 miles from Kahului Airport to Hana, but the drive can take three hours. As for driving to Haleakala, the 38-mile drive from the mountain's base to its summit will take you about two hours. Traffic on Maui's roads can be heavy, especially during the rush hours of 6 am to 8:30 am and 3:30 pm to 6:30 pm.

Big Island: It's a good idea to rent a car with four-wheel drive, such as a jeep, on the Big Island. Some of the island's best sights (and most beautiful beaches) are at the end of rough or unpaved roads. Most agencies make you sign an agreement that you won't drive on the path to Maunakea and its observatories. Keep in mind that, while a good portion of the Saddle Road is smoothly paved, it is also remote, winding, and bumpy in certain areas, unlighted, and bereft of gas stations.

Kauai: A rental car is the best way to get to your hotel, though taxis and some hotel shuttles are available. From the airport it will take you about 15 to 25 minutes to drive to Wailua or Kapaa, 30 to 40 minutes to reach Poipu, and 45 minutes to an hour to get to Princeville or Hanalei. Kauai roads can have heavy traffic.

ISLAND DRIVING TIMES	
Oahu: Waikiki to Downtown Honolulu	4 miles/10 mins
Oahu: Waikiki to Honolulu Int'l Airport	12 miles/25 mins
Oahu: Waikiki to Haleiwa	34 miles /45 mins
Maui: Kahului to Wailea	17 miles /30 mins
Maui: Kahului to Kaanapali	25 miles /45 mins
Maui: Kahului to Kapalua	36 miles /1 hr 15 mins
Big Island: Kailua-Kona to Kohala Coast	32 miles /50 mins
Big Island: Kailua-Kona to Hilo	86 miles /2.5 hrs
Kauai: Hanalei to Lihue	32 miles /1 hr 5 mins
Kauai: Lihue to Poipu	13 miles /25 mins

Hawaii's Best Festivals and Events

February: Chinese New Year: Lahaina, Maui, and in Chinatown on Oahu. Waimea Town Celebration: Waimea, Kauai.

March: Prince Kuhio Day Celebration: Lihue, Kauai.

April: Maui County Agricultural Festival: Maui. Merrie Monarch Hula Festival: Hilo, Big Island. East Maui Taro Festival: Hana, Maui. Kona Chocolate Festival: Big Island.

May: World Fire-Knife Dance Championships & Samoa Festival: Polynesian Cultural Center, Laie, Oahu. Maui Onion Festival: Kaanapali, Maui.

June: Hawaiian Slack-Key Guitar Festival: Kahului, Maui. King Kamehameha Hula Competition: Honolulu, Oahu. Flavors of Honolulu: Oahu. Maui Film Festival: Maui.

July: July 4 celebrations: Magic Island, Kailua Beach, and at Pearl Harbor's Schofield Barracks, Oahu. In Honolulu, displays light up the skies.

October: Ironman Triathalon World Championship: Kailua-Kona, Big Island. Halloween festivities: Lahaina, Maui, and Chinatown and Waikiki on Oahu. Plantation Days: Lahaina, Maui.

November: Kona Coffee Cultural Festival: Kona, Big Island. Triple Crown of Surfing: North Shore, Oahu.

HAWAII TODAY

Hawaiian culture and tradition have experienced a renaissance over the last few decades. there's a real effort to revive traditions and to respect history as the islands go through major changes. New resort developments often have a Hawaiian cultural expert on staff to ensure cultural sensitivity and to educate newcomers. Nonetheless, development itself remains the biggest issue for all Islanders, with land prices still skyrocketing, putting popular areas out of reach for locals. Traffic is becoming a problem on roads that were not designed to accommodate all the drivers (particularly on Oahu and Maui), and the Islands' limited natural resources are being seriously tapped while 90% of Hawaii's food and energy are still imported despite government efforts to increase sustainability.

Sustainability

Kauai may be the leader, with regard to sustainability. On some sunny days the Kauai electric grid is more than 95% powered by alternative-energy sources. In fact, Kauai leads the state in alternative energy solutions, including hydro.

Much of Hawaii's open land has historically been used for mono-cropping of pineapple and sugarcane. Those businesses are all but gone on a grand scale. When the Maui Pinapple Company ceased production in 2009, a group of executives began the Maui Gold Pineapple Company with 1350 acres on the slopes of Mount Haleakala, where they still grow pineapples for export and local use.

Oahu is home to many of the restaurants and chefs leading the Hawaii Regional Cuisine food movement, with a focus on fresh, local ingredients. Chefs are expanding and riffing off Hawaiian Regional Cuisine, taking it into new, international, eclectic, and refreshing directions.

Back-to-Basics Agriculture

Emulating how the Hawaiian ancestors lived and returning to their simple ways of growing and sharing a variety of foods have become statewide initiatives. Many locals buy all their fruit and produce from the numerous farmers' markets, which often feature exotic in-season crops at reasonable costs.

The seed of this movement is thriving with various farmers' markets and partnerships between restaurants and local farmers. Localized efforts such as the Hawaii Farm Bureau Federation are collectively aiding the organic and sustainable agricultural renaissance. From home-cooked meals to casual plate lunches or fine-dining cuisine, these sustainable trailblazers enrich the state's culinary tapestry. A recent "explosion" of food trucks on Kauai, Oahu, and Maui offering various cuisines also uplifts the overall quality of life.

Tourism and the Economy

The $17 billion tourism industry represents more than a third of Hawaii's state income. Naturally, this dependency caused economic hardship when the 2008 financial meltdown affected tourists' ability to visit and spend, but the tourism industry has bounced back stronger than ever in 2017, when a record 9.4 million tourists enjoyed the Islands.

One way the industry has changed has been to adopt more eco-conscious practices, as many residents feel that development shouldn't happen without regard for impact to local communities and their natural environment.

The belief that an industry based on the Hawaiians' *aloha* should protect, promote, and empower local culture and provide more entrepreneurial opportunities for local people has become more important to tourism businesses. More companies are incorporating authentic Hawaiiana in their programs and aim not only to provide a commercially viable tour but also to ensure that the visitor leaves feeling connected to his or her host.

The concept of *kuleana,* a word denoting both privilege and responsibility, is a traditional value. Having the privilege to live in such a sublime place comes with the responsibility to protect it.

Sovereignty

Political issues of sovereignty continue to divide Native Hawaiians, who have formed myriad organizations, each operating with a separate agenda and lacking one collectively defined goal. Ranging from achieving complete independence to solidifying a nation within a nation, existing sovereignty models remain fractured and their future unresolved.

The introduction of the Native Hawaiian Government Reorganization Act of 2009 (The Akaka Bill) attempted to set up a legal framework in which Native Hawaiians can attain federal recognition and coexist as a self-governed entity. Still held up in Congress, the bill has faced innumerable challenges through the years, including among Native Hawaiians who disagree about its merits and mission.

Rise of Hawaiian Pride

After the overthrow of the monarchy in 1893, a process of Americanization began. Traditions were duly silenced in the name of citizenship. Teaching the Hawaiian language was banned from schools, and children were distanced from their local customs.

But Hawaiians are resilient people, and with the rise of the civil rights movement they began to reflect on their own national identity, bringing an astonishing renaissance of the Hawaiian culture to fruition.

The people rediscovered language, hula, chanting, and even the traditional Polynesian arts of canoe building and wayfinding (navigation by the stars without use of instruments). This cultural resurrection is now firmly established in today's Hawaiian culture, with a palpable pride that exudes from Hawaiians young and old.

Latest Eruptions

In May 2018, dramatic changes began happening at Kilauea Volcano on the Big Island of Hawaii. The collapse of the Pu'u O'o vent, which has been continuously erupting since 1983, preceded fissure eruptions in a remote neighborhood in Lower Puna, destroying dozens of homes. Meanwhile, back in Hawaii Volcanoes National Park, the lava lake at Halema'u,ma'u began receding quickly, creating ash plumes above the summit and steam explosions. As with any eruption, no one knows how long the eruption in Lower Puna will last, or what will happen at Halema'uma'u Crater. What's important for the visitor to know is that these events are taking place in remote areas. Most of the Big Island is safe from ongoing eruptions at Kilauea. If you are planning a trip to Lower Puna or Pahoa, do your research first before booking your stay since some places are closed and some roads have been covered by lava flows.

CHOOSING YOUR ISLAND

You've decided to go to Hawaii, but should you stay put and relax on one island or try sampling more than one? If all you have is a week, it is probably best to stick to just one island. You traveled all this way, why spend your precious vacation time at car-rental counters, hotel check-in desks, and airports? But, with seven or more nights, a little island-hopping is a great way to experience the diversity of sights and experiences that are packed into this small state. Here are some of our favorite island-pairing itineraries for every type of trip.

Family Travel: Oahu and Maui

If you're traveling with children, Oahu and Maui have the most options.

Why Oahu: Oahu is by far the most kid-friendly island. For sea life, visit the Waikiki Aquarium and Sea Life Park or let the little ones get up close and personal with fish at Hanauma Bay. At Pearl Harbor you can visit an aircraft carrier or, if the kids are at least four, a World War II submarine. Then there's the Honolulu Zoo and a slippery slide–filled water park, not to mention some very family-friendly and safe beaches. *Plan to spend 4 nights.*

Why Maui: Whales! Though you can see whales from any island between November and April, there's no better place than Maui. If your visit doesn't fall during peak whale-watching season, visit the Whalers Village Museum, the Hawaiian Islands Humpback Whale National Marine Sanctuary, or the Maui Ocean Center (to get an up-close look at some of Hawaii's smaller sea creatures). Away from the water, there's the Sugar Cane Train. *Plan to spend at least 3 nights.*

Romance: Maui and Kauai

If you're getting away for seclusion, romantic walks along the beach, and the pampering at world-class spas, consider Maui and Kauai.

Why Maui: You'll find waterfalls, salt-and-pepper sand beaches, and incredible views as you follow the twisting turning Road to Hana. The luxury resorts in Wailea or Kaanapali provide lots of fine dining and spa treatment options. And for those who want to start their day early, there's the drive up to Haleakala to see the sun rise—or for couples who prefer to sleep in, there's the arguably even more spectacular sunset from the summit. *Plan to spend 4 nights.*

Why Kauai: The North Shore communities of Hanalei and Princeville provide the opportunity to get away and indulge in some spectacular beaches, hiking, and helicopter rides. At Princeville you can experience views straight out of *South Pacific* as well as excellent dining and spas at the St. Regis Hotel, while a drive to Kee Beach at the end of the road provides options for pulling over and grabbing a beach, all for just the two of you. *Plan to spend at least 3 nights.*

Golf, Shopping, and Luxury: Maui and the Big Island

For luxurious travel, great shopping, restaurants, and accommodations you can't beat Maui and the Big Island.

Why Maui: The resorts at Wailea and Kaanapali have endless options for dining, shopping, and spa treatments. And, the golf on Maui can't be beat with Kapalua, the Dunes at Maui Lani, and Makena Resort topping the list of spectacular courses. *Plan to spend 4 nights.*

Why the Big Island: In addition to having incredible natural scenery, the Big Island offers world-class resorts and golfing along the Kohala Coast. The Mauna Kea and Hapuna golf courses rank among the top in state while the courses at Mauna Lani Resort and Waikoloa Village allow the unusual experience of playing in and around lava flows. Gourmet dining and spa treatments are readily available at the top resorts and you'll find shopping opportunities at King's Shops at Waikoloa Village as well as within many of the resorts themselves. Or, travel to Hawi or Waimea (Kamuela) for original island boutiques. *Plan to spend at least 3 nights.*

Natural Beauty and Pristine Beaches: The Big Island and Kauai

Really want to get away and experience nature at its most primal? The Big Island is the place to start, followed by a trip to Kauai.

Why the Big Island: Home to 11 different climate zones, the Big Island is large enough to contain all the other Hawaiian Islands. There are countless options for those who want to get off the beaten track and get their hands (and feet) dirty—or sandy as the case may be. See lava flowing or steam rising from Kilauea. Visit beaches in your choice of gold, white, green, or black sand. Snorkel or dive just offshore from an ancient Hawaiian settlement. Or, hike through rain forests to hidden waterfalls. The choices are endless on this island. *Plan to spend at least 4 nights.*

Why Kauai: The Napali Coast is the main draw for those seeking secluded beaches and incredible scenery. If you're interested in hiking to otherwise inaccessible beaches along sheer sea cliffs, this is as good as it gets. Or, head up to Waimea Canyon to see the "Grand Canyon of the Pacific." Want waterfalls? Opaekaa Falls outside Lihue is one of the state's most breathtaking. And there's no better place for bird-watching than Kilauea Point National Wildlife Refuge. *Plan to spend at least 3 nights.*

Volcanic Views: The Big Island and Maui

For those coming to Hawaii for the volcanoes, there are really only two options: the Big Island and Maui.

Why the Big Island: Start by flying into Hilo and head straight to Hawaii Volcanoes National Park and Kilauea Volcano. Plan to spend at least two days at Kilauea—you'll need time to really explore the caldera, drive to the end of Chain of Craters Road, and have some time for hiking in and around this active volcano. While eruptions are unpredictable, helicopter companies can get you views of otherwise inaccessible lava flows. You can also make a visit up to the summit of Maunakea with a tour company. From here you'll see views not only of the observatories (Maunakea is one of the best places in the world for astronomy), but also Kilauea and Haleakala volcanoes, which loom in the distance. *Plan to spend at least 4 nights.*

Why Maui: Though all the islands in Hawaii were built from the same hot spot in Earth's crust, the only other island to have had volcanic activity in recorded history was Maui, at Haleakala. The House of the Sun (as Haleakala is known) has great hiking and camping opportunities. *Plan to spend 3 nights.*

BEST BEACHES

No one ever gets as much beach time in Hawaii as they planned to, it seems, but it's a problem of time, not beaches. Beaches of every size, color (even green), and description line the state's many shorelines.

They have different strengths: some are great for sitting, but not so great for swimming. Some offer beach-park amenities like lifeguards and showers, whereas others are more private and isolated. Read up before you head out.

Oahu

Kailua Beach Park. This is a true family beach, offering something for everyone: A long stretch of sand for walking, turquoise seas set against cobalt skies for impressive photographs, a sandy-bottom shoreline for ocean swimming, and grassy expanses underneath shade trees for picnics.

You can even rent a kayak and make the short paddle to Popia (Flat) Island. This is Windward Oahu, so expect wind—all the better if you're an avid windsurfer or kiteboarder.

Makapuu Beach. Quite possibly Oahu's most breathtaking scenic view—with a hiking trail to a historic lighthouse, offshore views of two rocky islets, home to thousands of nesting seabirds, and hang gliders launching off nearby cliffs.

While the white-sand beach and surroundings adorn many postcards, the treacherous ocean's currents invite experienced body boarders only.

Waimea Bay. This is the beach that makes Hawaii famous every winter when monster waves and the world's best surfers roll in.

Show up to watch, not partake. If the rest of us want to get in the water here, we have to wait until summer when the safe, onshore break is great for novice bodysurfers.

White Plains. This beach is equal parts Kailua Beach Park with its facilities and tree-covered barbecue areas and Waikiki with its numerous surf breaks—minus the crowds and high-rises.

Pack for the day—cooler with food and drink, snorkel gear, inflatables, and body board—as this destination is 35 minutes from downtown Honolulu.

Maui

Makena (Big Beach). Don't forget the camera for this one. A bit remote and tricky to find, the effort is worth it—a long, wide stretch of golden sand and translucent offshore water. It's beautiful, yes, but the icing on the cake is this beach is never crowded. Use caution for swimming because the steep, onshore break can get big.

Napili Beach. There is much to love about this intimate, crescent-shaped beach. Sunbathing, snorkeling, swimming, bodysurfing, and—after a full day of beach fun—startling sunsets. Bring the kids; they'll love the turtles that nosh on the *limu* (seaweed) growing on the lava rocks.

Waianapanapa State Park. The rustic beauty will capture your heart here—a black-sand beach framed by lava cliffs and backed by bright green *naupaka* bushes. Ocean currents can be strong, so cool off in one of two freshwater pools.

Get an early start, because your day's destination is just shy of Hana and requires a short, quarter-mile walk.

Big Island

Hapuna Beach State Recreation Area. It's hard to know where to start with this beach—the long, perfect crescent of sand, the calm, turquoise waters, rocky points for snorkeling, even surf in winter. Just about everyone can find something to love here. With its west-facing views, this is a good spot for sunsets.

Kaunaoa Beach (Maunakea Beach). This is like the big brother, more advanced version of Hapuna Beach with snorkeling, bodysurfing, and board surfing but trickier currents, so be careful. Still, it's worth it. Try them both and let us know which you prefer. For most, it's a toss-up.

Papakolea Beach (Green Sand Beach). Papakolea makes our list, because, really, how often do you run across a green-sand beach? That's right, green. The greenish tint here is caused by an accumulation of olivine crystals that formed in volcanic eruptions.

This isn't the most swimmable of beaches, but the sand, sculpted cliffs, and dry, barren landscape make it quite memorable. A steep, 2-mile hike is required to access the beach.

Punaluu Beach Park (Black Sand Beach). This might as well be called Turtle Beach. Both the endangered Hawaiian green sea turtle and hawksbill turtle bask on the rocky, black-sand beach here.

We prefer to stay dry at this beach—due to strong rip currents—and snap pictures of the turtles and picnic under one of the many pavilions.

Kauai

Haena Beach Park (Tunnels Beach). Even if all you do is sit on the beach, you'll leave here happy. The scenic beauty is unsurpassed, with verdant mountains serving as a backdrop to the turquoise ocean.

Snorkeling is the best on the island during the calm, summer months. When the winter's waves arrive, surfers line up on the outside break.

Hanalei Bay Beach Park. When you dream of Hawaii, this is what comes to mind: a vast bay rimmed by a wide beach and waterfalls draping distant mountains. Everyone finds something to do here—surf, kayak, swim, sail, sunbathe, walk, and celebrity-watch.

Like most north shore beaches in Hawaii, Hanalei switches from calm in summer to big waves in winter.

Poipu Beach Park. The *keiki* (child's) swimming hole makes Poipu a great family beach, but it's also popular with snorkelers and moderate-to-experienced surfers. And while Poipu is considered a tourist destination, the Kauai residents come out on the weekends, adding a local flavor.

Be mindful of the endangered Hawaiian monk seals; they like it here, too.

Polihale State Park. If you're looking for remote, if you're looking for guaranteed sun, or if you're thinking of camping on the beach, drive the 5-mile-long cane-haul road to the westernmost point of Kauai. Be sure to stay for the sunset.

Unless you're an experienced water person, we advise staying out of the water due to a steep, onshore break. You can walk for miles along this beach, the longest in Hawaii.

KIDS AND FAMILIES

With dozens of adventures, discoveries, and fun-filled beach days, Hawaii is a blast with kids. Even better, the things to do here do not appeal only to small fry. The entire family, parents included, will enjoy surfing, discovering a waterfall in the rain forest, and snorkeling with sea turtles. And there are plenty of organized activities for kids that will free parents' time for a few romantic beach strolls.

Choosing a Place to Stay

Condos: Condo and vacation rentals are a fantastic value for families vacationing in Hawaii. You can cook your own food, which is cheaper than eating out and sometimes easier (especially if you have a finicky eater in your group), and you'll get twice the space of a hotel room for about a quarter of the price. If you decide to go the condo route, be sure to ask about the size of the complex's pool (some try to pawn a tiny soaking tub off as a pool) and whether barbecues are available.

Resorts: All the big resorts make kids' programs a priority, and it shows. When you are booking your room, ask about "kids eat free" deals and the number of kids' pools at the resort. Also check out the size of the groups in the children's programs, and find out whether the cost of the programs includes lunch, equipment, and activities.

Ocean Activities

Hawaii is all about getting your kids outside—away from TV and video games. And who could resist the turquoise water, the promise of spotting dolphins or whales, and the fun of body boarding, snorkeling, or surfing?

On the Beach: Most people like being in the water, but toddlers and school-age kids are often completely captivated by Hawaii's beaches. The swimming pool at your condo or hotel is always an option, but don't be afraid to hit the beach with a little one in tow. There are several in Hawaii that are nearly as safe as a pool—completely protected bays with pleasant white-sand beaches. As always, use your judgment, and heed all posted signs and lifeguard warnings.

On the Waves: Surf lessons are a great idea for older kids, especially if Mom and Dad want a little quiet time. Beginner lessons are always on safe and easy waves and last anywhere from two to four hours.

The Underwater World: If your kids are ready to try snorkeling, Hawaii is a great place to introduce them to the underwater world. Even without the mask and snorkel, they'll be able to see colorful fish darting this way and that, and they may also spot turtles and dolphins at many of the island beaches.

Land Activities

In addition to beach experiences, Hawaii has rain forests, botanical gardens, aquariums (Oahu and Maui), and even petting zoos and hands-on children's museums that will keep your kids entertained and out of the sun for a day.

After Dark

At night, younger kids get a kick out of luau, and many of the shows incorporate young audience members, adding to the fun. The older kids might find it all a bit lame, but there are a handful of new shows in the Islands that are more modern, incorporating acrobatics, lively music, and fire dancers. If you're planning on hitting a luau with a teen in tow, we highly recommend going the modern route.

CRUISING THE HAWAIIAN ISLANDS

Cruising has become popular in Hawaii. Cruises are a comparatively inexpensive way to see all of Hawaii, and you'll save travel time by not having to check in at hotels and airports on each island. The limited amount of time in each port can be an argument against cruising, but you can make reservations for tours, activities, rental cars, and more aboard the cruise ship.

The larger cruise lines such as Carnival, Princess, and Holland America offer itineraries of 10–16 days departing from the West Coast of the United States, most with stops at all the major Hawaiian Islands. Some cruise lines, such as Crystal, Cunard, and Disney, include ports in Hawaii on around-the-world cruises. All have plenty on board to keep you busy during the four to five days that you are at sea between the U.S. mainland and Hawaii.

Cruise ships plying the Pacific from the continental United States to Hawaii are floating resorts complete with pools, spas, rock-climbing walls, restaurants, nightclubs, shops, casinos, children's programs, and much more.

Prices for cruises are based on accommodation type: interior (no window, in an inside corridor); outside (includes a window or porthole); balcony (allows you to go outside without using a public deck); and suite (larger cabin, more amenities and perks). Passages start at about $1,000 per person for the lowest class accommodation (interior) and include room, on-board entertainment, and food. Ocean-view, balcony, and suite accommodations can run up to $6,500 and more per person.

Cruising to Hawaii

Carnival Cruises is great for families, with plenty of kid-friendly activities. Departing from Los Angeles or Vancouver, Carnival's "fun ships" show your family a good time, both on board and on shore (☎ *888/227–6482* 🌐 *www.carnival.com*). The grand dame of cruise lines, Holland America has a reputation for service and elegance. Their 14-day Hawaii cruises leave from and return to San Diego, with a brief stop at Ensenada (☎ *877/932–4259* 🌐 *www.hollandamerica.com*). More affordable luxury is what Princess Cruises offers. Although their prices seem a little higher, you get more bells and whistles on your trip (more affordable balcony rooms, more restaurants to choose from, personalized service) (☎ *800/774–6237* 🌐 *www.princess.com*).

Cruising within Hawaii

Norwegian Cruise Lines (🌐 *www.ncl.com*) is the only major operator to begin and end cruises in Hawaii. *Pride of Hawaii* (vintage America theme, family focus with lots of connecting staterooms and suites) offers a seven-day itinerary that includes stops on Maui, Oahu, the Big Island, and Kauai. This is the only ship to cruise Hawaii that does not spend days at sea visiting a foreign port, allowing you more time to explore destinations). Ocean conditions in the channels between islands can be a consideration when booking an interisland cruise on a smaller vessel such as the one operated by **Un-Cruise Adventures** (🌐 *www.un-cruise.com*)—a stately yacht accommodating only 36 passengers. This yacht's small size allows it to dock at less frequented islands such as Molokai and Lanai. The cruise is billed as "all inclusive"—your passage includes shore excursions, water activities, and a massage.

WEDDINGS AND HONEYMOONS

There's no question that Hawaii is one of the country's foremost honeymoon destinations. Romance is in the air here, and the white, sandy beaches, turquoise water, swaying palm trees, balmy tropical breezes, and perpetual sunshine put people in the mood for love. So it goes without saying, that Kauai has also become a popular wedding destination, especially as new resorts and hotels entice visitors, and same-sex marriage is legal. Once the knot is tied, why not stay for the honeymoon?

The Big Day

Choosing the Perfect Place. You really have two choices to make: the ceremony location and where to have the reception. For the former, Kauai boasts stunning beaches, sea-hugging bluffs, gardens, private residences, resort lawns, and, of course, places of worship. As for the reception, there are these same choices, as well as restaurants and even a luau. If you decide to go outdoors, make sure to have a backup plan for inclement weather.

Finding a Wedding Planner. If you're planning to invite more than an officiant and your loved one to your wedding ceremony, seriously consider a Kauai wedding planner who can help select a location, design the floral scheme, and recommend a florist and photographer. They can also plan the menu and choose a restaurant, caterer, or resort, and suggest any Hawaiian traditions to incorporate into your ceremony.

Getting Your License. There's no waiting period in Hawaii, no residency or citizenship requirements, and no required blood test or shots. You can apply and pay the fee online; however, both the bride and groom must appear together in person before a marriage-license agent to receive the marriage license (the permit to get married) at the State Department of Health in Lihue. You'll need proof of age—the legal age to marry is 18. Upon approval, a marriage license is immediately issued and costs $60. After the ceremony, your officiant will mail the marriage certificate to the state. Approximately four months later, you will receive a copy in the mail. For more detailed information, visit 🌐 *marriage.ehawaii.gov.*

Also—this is important—the person performing your wedding must be licensed by the Hawaii Department of Health, even if he or she is a licensed officiant. Be sure to ask.

Wedding Attire. In Hawaii, basically anything goes, from long, formal dresses with trains to white bikinis. For men, a pair of solid-colored slacks with a nice aloha shirt is appropriate. If you're planning a wedding on the beach, barefoot is the way to go.

Local Customs. The most obvious traditional Hawaiian wedding custom is the lei exchange in which the bride and groom take turns placing a lei around the neck of the other—with a kiss. Bridal lei are usually floral, whereas the groom's is typically made of *maile,* a green leafy garland that drapes the neck. Brides often also wear a *lei poo*—a circular floral headpiece.

The Honeymoon

Do you want Champagne and strawberries delivered to your room each morning? A breathtaking swimming pool in which to float? A five-star restaurant in which to dine? Then a resort is the way to go. A small inn is also good if you're on a tight budget or don't plan to spend much time in your room. The lodging accommodations are almost as plentiful as the beaches.

HAWAIIAN CULTURAL TRADITIONS HULA, LEI, AND LUAU

HULA: MORE THAN A FOLK DANCE

Hula has been called "the heartbeat of the Hawaiian people" and also "the world's best-known, most misunderstood dance." Both are true. Hula isn't just dance. It is storytelling.

Chanter Edith McKinzie calls it "an extension of a piece of poetry." In its adornments, implements, and customs, hula integrates every important Hawaiian cultural practice: poetry, history, genealogy, craft, plant cultivation, martial arts, religion, protocol. So when 19th-century Christian missionaries sought to eradicate a practice they considered depraved, they threatened more than just a folk dance.

With public performance outlawed and private hula practice discouraged, hula went underground for a generation. The fragile verbal link by which culture was transmitted from teacher to student hung by a thread. Even increasing literacy did not help because hula's practitioners were a secretive and protected circle.

As if that weren't bad enough, vaudeville, Broadway, and Hollywood got hold of the hula, giving it the glitz treatment in an unbroken line from "Oh, How She Could Wicky Wacky Woo" to "Rock-A-Hula Baby." Hula became shorthand for paradise: fragrant flowers, lazy hours. Ironically, this development assured that hundreds of Hawaiians could make a living performing and teaching hula. Many danced *auana* (modern form) in performance; but taught *kahiko* (traditional), quietly, at home or in hula schools.

Today, decades after the cultural revival known as the Hawaiian Renaissance, language immersion programs have assured a new generation of proficient—and even eloquent—chanters, songwriters, and translators. Visitors can see more, and more authentic, traditional hula than at any other time in the last 200 years.

Like the culture of which it is the beating heart, hula has survived.

Lei *poo.* Head lei. In *kahiko,* greenery only. In *auana,* flowers.
Face emotes appropriate expression. Dancer should not be a smiling automaton.
Shoulders remain relaxed and still, never hunched, even with arms raised. No bouncing.
Eyes always follow leading hand.
Lei. Hula is rarely performed without a shoulder lei.
Arms and hands remain loose, relaxed, below shoulder level—except as required by interpretive movements.
Traditional hula skirt is loose fabric, smocked and gathered at the waist.
Hip is canted over weight-bearing foot.
Knees are always slightly bent, accentuating hip sway.
Kupee. Ankle bracelet of flowers, shells, or foliage.
In kahiko, feet are flat. In auana, they may be more arched, but not tiptoes or bouncing.

BASIC MOTIONS

Speak or Sing

Moon or Sun

Grass Shack or House

Mountains or Heights

Love or Caress

At backyard parties, hula is performed in bare feet and street clothes, but in performance, adornments play a key role, as do rhythm-keeping implements such as the pahu drum and the ipu (gourd).

In hula *kahiko* (traditional style), the usual dress is multiple layers of stiff fabric (often with a pellom lining, which most closely resembles *kapa*, the paperlike bark cloth of the Hawaiians). These wrap tightly around the bosom but flare below the waist to form a skirt. In pre-contact times, dancers wore only kapa skirts. Men traditionally wear loincloths.

Monarchy-period hula is performed in voluminous muumuu or high-necked muslin blouses and gathered skirts. Men wear white or gingham shirts and black pants.

In hula *auana* (modern), dress for women can range from grass skirts and strapless tops to contemporary tea-length dresses. Men generally wear aloha shirts, but sometimes grass skirts over pants or even everyday gear.

SURPRISING HULA FACTS

- Grass skirts are not traditional; workers from Kiribati (the Gilbert Islands) brought this custom to Hawaii.
- In olden-day Hawaii, *mele* (songs) for hula were composed for every occasion—name songs for babies, dirges for funerals, welcome songs for visitors, celebrations of favorite pursuits.
- Hula *mai* is a traditional hula form in praise of a noble's genitals; the power of the *alii* (royalty) to procreate gave *mana* (spiritual power) to the entire culture.
- Hula students in old Hawaii adhered to high standards: scrupulous cleanliness, no sex, daily cleansing rituals, certain food prohibitions, and no contact with the dead. They were fined if they broke the rules.

WHERE TO WATCH

If you're interested in "the real thing," there are annual hula festivals on each island. Check the individual island visitors' bureaus websites at 🌐 *www.gohawaii.com.*

If you can't make it to a festival, there are plenty of other hula shows—at most resorts, many lounges, and even at certain shopping centers. Ask your hotel concierge for performance information.

ALL ABOUT LEI

Lei brighten every occasion in Hawaii, from birthdays to bar mitzvahs to baptisms. Creative artisans weave nature's bounty—flowers, ferns, vines, and seeds—into gorgeous creations that convey an array of heartfelt messages: "Welcome," "Congratulations," "Good luck," "Farewell," "Thank you," "I love you." When it's difficult to find the right words, a lei expresses exactly the right sentiment.

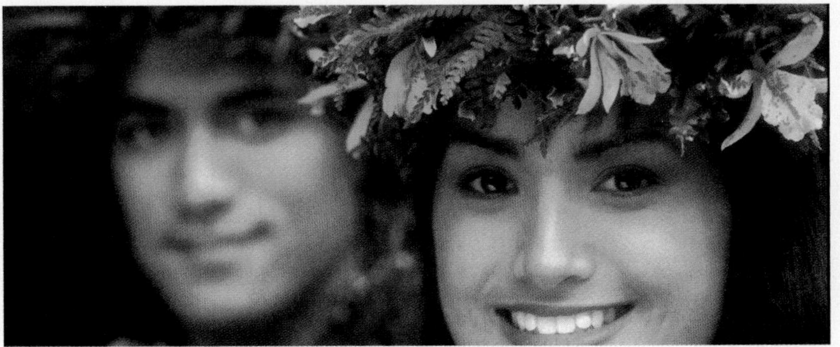

WHERE TO BUY THE BEST LEI

Most airports in Hawaii have lei stands where you can buy a fragrant garland upon arrival. Every florist shop in the Islands sells lei; you can also treat yourself to a lei while shopping for provisions at any supermarket or box store. And you'll always find lei sellers at crafts fairs and outdoor festivals.

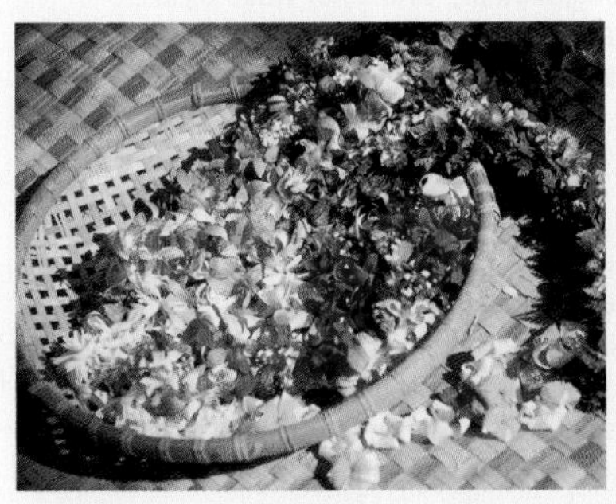

LEI ETIQUETTE

- To wear a closed lei, drape it over your shoulders, half in front and half in back. Open lei are worn around the neck, with the ends draped over the front in equal lengths.
- Pikake, ginger, and other sweet, delicate blossoms are "feminine" lei. Men opt for cigar, crown flower, and ti leaf lei, which are sturdier and don't emit as much fragrance.
- Lei are always presented with a kiss, a custom that supposedly dates back to World War II when a hula dancer fancied an officer at a U.S.O. show. Taking a dare from members of her troupe, she took off her lei, placed it around his neck, and kissed him on the cheek.
- You shouldn't wear a lei before you give it to someone else. Hawaiians believe the lei absorbs your *mana* (spirit); if you give your lei away, you'll be giving away part of your essence.

	**ORCHID** Growing wild on every continent except Antarctica, orchids—which range in color from yellow to green to purple—comprise the largest family of plants in the world. There are more than 20,000 species of orchids, but only three are native to Hawaii—and they are very rare. The pretty lavender vanda you see hanging by the dozens at local lei stands has probably been imported from Thailand.
	**MAILE** Maile, an endemic twining vine with a heady aroma, is sacred to Laka, goddess of the hula. In ancient times, dancers wore maile and decorated hula altars with it to honor Laka. Today, "open" maile lei usually are given to men. Instead of ribbon, interwoven lengths of maile are used at dedications of new businesses. The maile is untied, never snipped, for doing so would symbolically "cut" the company's success.
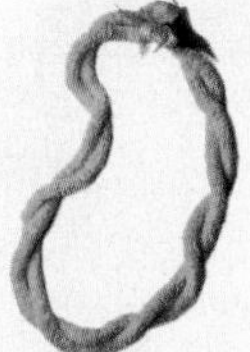	**ILIMA** Designated by Hawaii's Territorial Legislature in 1923 as the official flower of the island of Oahu, the golden ilima is so delicate it lasts for just a day. Five to seven hundred blossoms are needed to make one garland. Queen Emma, wife of King Kamehameha IV, preferred ilima over all other lei, which may have led to the incorrect belief that they were reserved only for royalty.
	**PLUMERIA** This ubiquitous flower is named after Charles Plumier, the noted French botanist who discovered it in Central America in the late 1600s. Plumeria ranks among the most popular lei in Hawaii because it's fragrant, hardy, plentiful, inexpensive, and requires very little care. Although yellow is the most common color, you'll also find plumeria lei in shades of pink, red, orange, and "rainbow" blends.
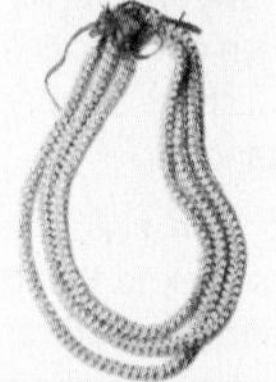	**PIKAKE** Favored for its fragile beauty and sweet scent, pikake was introduced from India. In lieu of pearls, many brides in Hawaii adorn themselves with long, multiple strands of white pikake. Princess Kaiulani enjoyed showing guests her beloved pikake and peacocks at Ainahau, her Waikiki home. Interestingly, pikake is the Hawaiian word for both the bird and the blossom.
	**KUKUI** The kukui (candlenut) is Hawaii's state tree. Early Hawaiians strung kukui nuts (which are quite oily) together and burned them for light; mixed burned nuts with oil to make an indelible dye; and mashed roasted nuts to consume as a laxative. Kukui nut lei may not have been made until after Western contact, when the Hawaiians saw black beads from Europe and wanted to imitate them.

LUAU: A TASTE OF HAWAII

The best place to sample Hawaiian food is at a backyard luau. Aunts and uncles are cooking, the pig is from a cousin's farm, and the fish is from a brother's boat.

But even locals have to angle for invitations to those rare occasions. So your choice is most likely between a commercial luau and a Hawaiian restaurant.

Some commercial luau are less authentic; they offer little of the traditional diet and are more about umbrella drinks, spectacle, and fun.

For greater culinary authenticity, folksy experiences, and rock-bottom prices, visit a Hawaiian restaurant (most are in anonymous storefronts in residential neighborhoods). Expect rough edges and some effort negotiating the menu.

In either case, much of what is known today as Hawaiian food would be as foreign to a 16th-century Hawaiian as risotto or chow mien. The pre-contact diet was simple and healthy—mainly raw and steamed seafood and vegetables. Early Hawaiians used earth ovens and heated stones to cook seafood, taro, sweet potatoes, and breadfruit and seasoned their food with sea salt and ground kukui nuts. Seaweed, fern shoots, sweet potato vines, coconut, banana, sugarcane, and select greens and roots rounded out the diet.

Successive waves of immigrants added their favorites to the ti leaf–lined table. So it is that foods as disparate as salt salmon and chicken long rice are now Hawaiian—even though there is no salmon in Hawaiian waters and long rice (cellophane noodles) is Chinese.

AT THE LUAU: KALUA PORK

The heart of any luau is the *imu*, the earth oven in which a whole pig is roasted. The preparation of an imu is an arduous affair for most families, who tackle it only once a year or so, for a baby's first birthday or at Thanksgiving, when many Islanders prefer to imu their turkeys. Commercial luau operations have it down to a science, however.

THE ART OF THE STONE

The key to a proper imu is the *pohaku*, the stones. Imu cook by means of long, slow, moist heat released by special stones that can withstand a hot fire without exploding. Many Hawaiian families treasure their imu stones, keeping them in a pile in the backyard and passing them on through generations.

PIT COOKING

The imu makers first dig a pit about the size of a refrigerator, then lay down *kiawe* (mesquite) wood and stones, and build a white-hot fire that is allowed to burn itself out. The ashes are raked away, and the hot stones covered with banana and ti leaves. Well-wrapped in ti or banana leaves and a net of chicken wire, the pig is lowered onto the leaf-covered stones. *Laulau* (leaf-wrapped bundles of meats, fish, and taro leaves) may also be placed inside. Leaves—ti, banana, even ginger—cover the pig followed by wet burlap sacks (to create steam). The whole is topped with a canvas tarp and left to steam for the better part of a day.

OPENING THE IMU

This is the moment everyone waits for: The imu is unwrapped like a giant present and the imu keepers gingerly wrestle out the steaming pig. When it's unwrapped, the meat falls moist and smoky-flavored from the bone, looking just like Southern-style pulled pork, but without the barbecue sauce.

WHICH LUAU?

Most resort hotels have luau on their grounds that include hula, music, and, of course, lots of food and drink. Each island also has at least one "authentic" luau. For lists of the best luau on each island, visit the Hawaii Visitors and Convention Bureau website at 🌐 *www.gohawaii.com.*

MEA AI ONO: GOOD THINGS TO EAT.

Laulau

LAULAU

Steamed meats, fish, and taro leaf in ti-leaf bundles: fork-tender, a medley of flavors; the taro resembles spinach.

LOMI LOMI SALMON

Salt salmon in a piquant salad or relish with onions and tomatoes.

Lomi Lomi Salmon

POI

Poi, a paste made of pounded taro root, may be an acquired taste, but it's a must-try during your visit.

Consider: The Hawaiian Adam is descended from *kalo* (taro). Young taro plants are called "keiki"–children. Poi is the first food after mother's milk for many Islanders. Ai, the word for food, is synonymous with poi in many contexts.

Not only that, we love it. "There is no meat that doesn't taste good with poi," the old Hawaiians said.

But you have to know how to eat it: with something rich or powerfully flavored. "It is salt that makes the poi go in," is another adage. When you're served poi, try it with a mouthful of smoky kalua pork or salty lomi lomi salmon. Its slightly sour blandness cleanses the palate. And if you don't like it, smile and say something polite. (And slide that bowl over to a local.)

Poi

E HELE MAI AI! COME AND EAT!

Local-style Hawaiian restaurants tend to be inconveniently located in well-worn storefronts with little or no parking, outfitted with battered tables and clattering Melmac dishes, but they personify aloha, invariably run by local families who welcome tourists who take the trouble to find them.

Many are cash-only operations and combination plates, known as "plate lunch," are a standard feature: one or two entrées, two scoops of steamed rice, one scoop of macaroni salad, and—if the place is really old-style—a tiny portion of coarse Hawaiian salt and some raw onions for relish.

Most serve some foods that aren't, strictly speaking, Hawaiian, but are beloved of kamaaina, such as salt meat with watercress (preserved meat in a tasty broth), or *akubone* (skipjack tuna fried in a tangy vinegar sauce).

MENU GUIDE

Much of the Hawaiian language encountered during a stay in the Islands will appear on restaurant menus and lists of luau fare. Here's a quick primer.

ahi: *yellowfin tuna.*

aku: *skipjack, bonito tuna.*

amaama: *mullet; it's hard to get but tasty.*

bento: *a box lunch.*

chicken luau: *a stew made from chicken, taro leaves, and coconut milk.*

haupia: *a light, pudding-like sweet made from coconut.*

imu: *the underground oven in which pigs are roasted for luau.*

kalua: *to bake underground.*

kimchee: *Korean dish of fermented cabbage made with garlic, hot peppers, and other spices.*

Kona coffee: *coffee grown in the Kona district of the Big Island.*

laulau: *literally, a bundle. Laulau are morsels of pork, chicken, butterfish, or other ingredients wrapped with young taro leaves and then bundled in ti leaves for steaming.*

lilikoi: *passion fruit, a tart, seedy yellow fruit that makes delicious desserts, juice, and jellies.*

lomi lomi: *to rub or massage; also a type of massage. Lomi lomi salmon is fish that has been rubbed with onions and herbs; commonly served with minced onions and tomatoes.*

luau: *a Hawaiian feast; also the leaf of the taro plant used in preparing such a feast.*

luau leaves: *cooked taro tops with a taste similar to spinach.*

mahimahi: *mild-flavored dolphinfish, not the marine mammal.*

mai tai: *potent rum drink with orange liqueurs and pineapple juice, from the Tahitian word for "good."*

malasada: *a Portuguese deep-fried doughnut without a hole, dipped in sugar.*

manapua: *steamed Chinese buns filled with pork, chicken, or other fillings.*

niu: *coconut.*

onaga: *pink or red snapper.*

ono: *a long, slender mackerel-like fish; also called wahoo.*

ono: *delicious; also hungry.*

opihi: *a tiny limpet found on rocks.*

papio: *a young ulua or jack fish.*

poha: *Cape gooseberry. Tasting a bit like honey, the poha berry is often used in jams and desserts.*

poi: *a paste made from pounded taro root, a staple of the Hawaiian diet.*

poke: *cubed raw tuna or other fish, tossed with seaweed and seasonings.*

pupu: *appetizers or small plates.*

saimin: *long thin noodles and vegetables in broth, often garnished with small pieces of fish cake, scrambled egg, luncheon meat, and green onion.*

sashimi: *raw fish thinly sliced and usually eaten with soy sauce.*

ti leaves: *a member of the agave family. The leaves are used to wrap food while cooking and removed before eating.*

uku: *deep-sea snapper.*

ulua: *a member of the jack family that also includes pompano and amberjack. Also called crevalle, jack fish, and jack crevalle.*

2

OAHU

WELCOME TO OAHU

TOP REASONS TO GO

★ **Waves:** Body board or surf some of the best breaks on the planet.

★ **Pearl Harbor:** Remember Pearl Harbor with a visit to the Arizona Memorial.

★ **Diamond Head:** Scale the crater whose iconic profile looms over Waikiki.

★ **Nightlife:** Raise your glass to the best party scene in Hawaii.

★ **The North Shore:** See Oahu's countryside—check out the famous beaches from Sunset to Waimea Bay and hike to the remote tip of the island.

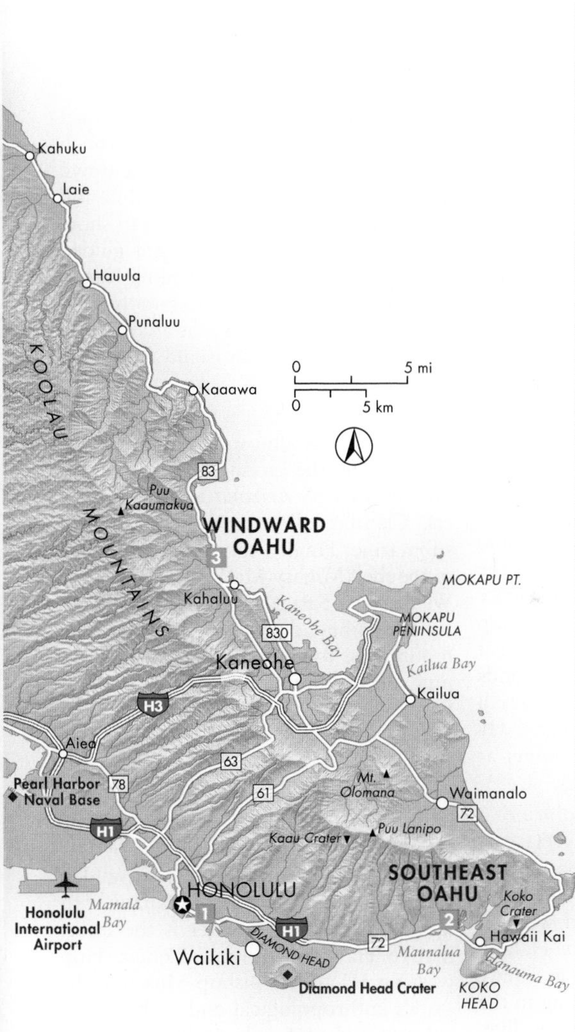

1 Honolulu. The vibrant capital city holds the nation's only royal palace, and the art galleries, hipster bars, and open markets of Chinatown.

2 Southeast Oahu. Honolulu's main bedroom communities crawl up the steep-sided valleys. Also here is Hanauma Bay.

3 Windward Oahu. The neighborhoods at the base of the majestic Koolau Mountains offer a respite from the bustling city.

4 The North Shore. Best known for its miles of world-class surf breaks, this area also boasts farms, restaurants, and hiking trails.

5 Central Oahu. This valley, between the Waianae and Koolau mountains, is an eclectic mix of farms, planned communities, and strip malls.

6 West (Leeward) Oahu. This rugged part of the island is finding a new identity as a "second city."

GREAT ITINERARIES

To experience even a fraction of Oahu's charms, you need a minimum of four days and a bus pass. Five days and a car is better: Waikiki is at least a day, Honolulu and Chinatown another, Pearl Harbor the better part of another. Each of the rural sections can swallow a whole day just for driving, sightseeing, and stopping to eat. And that's before you've taken a surf lesson, hung from a parasail, hiked a loop trail, or visited a botanical garden. The following itineraries will take you to our favorite spots on the island.

First Day in Waikiki

You'll be up at dawn due to the time change and dead on your feet by afternoon due to jet lag. Have a dawn swim, change into walking gear, and head east along Kalakaua Avenue to Monsarrat Avenue toward Diamond Head. Either climb to the summit (about 1½ hours round-trip) or enjoy the view from the lookout. After lunch—there are plenty of options along Monsarrat—take a nap in the shade, do some shopping, or visit the nearby East Honolulu neighborhoods of Moiliili and Kaimuki, rife with small shops and quaint restaurants. End the day with an early and inexpensive dinner at one of these neighborhood spots.

Southeast and Windward Exploring

For sand, sun, and surf, follow H1 east to the keyhole-shaped Hanauma Bay for picture-perfect snorkeling, then round the southeast tip of the island with its windswept cliffs and the famous Halona Blowhole. Watch bodysurfers at Sandy Beach or walk up the trail leading to the Makapuu Point Lighthouse. If you like, stop in at Sea Life Park. In Waimanalo, stop for local-style plate lunch or punch on through to Kailua, where there's intriguing shopping and good eating. Lounge at Lanikai Beach until sunset, then grab dinner at one of the area's many restaurants.

The North Shore

Hit H1 westbound and then H2 to get to the North Shore. You'll pass through pineapple fields before dropping down a scenic winding road to Waialua and Haleiwa. Stop in Haleiwa town to shop, enjoy shave ice, and pick up a guided dive or snorkel trip. On winding Kamehameha Highway, stop at famous big-wave beaches, take a dip in a cove with a turtle, and buy fresh island fruit from roadside stands.

Pearl Harbor

Pearl Harbor is almost an all-day investment. Be on the grounds by 7:30 am to line up for USS *Arizona* Memorial tickets. Clamber all over the USS *Bowfin* submarine. Finally, take the free trolley to see the "Mighty Mo" battleship. If it's Wednesday, Saturday, or Sunday, make the five-minute drive *mauka* (toward the mountains) for bargain-basement shopping at the sprawling Aloha Stadium Swap Meet.

Town Time

If you are interested in history, devote a day to Honolulu's historic sites. Downtown, see Iolani Palace, the Kamehameha Statue, and Kawaiahao Church. A few blocks east, explore Chinatown, gilded Kuan Yin Temple, and artsy Nuuanu with its galleries. On the water is the informative Hawaii Maritime Center. Hop west on H1 to the Bishop Museum, the state's anthropological and archaeological center. And 1 mile up Pali Highway is Queen Emma Summer Palace, whose shady grounds were a royal retreat. The Foster Botanical Garden is worth a visit for plant lovers.

Updated by Tiffany Hill

Oahu is one-stop Hawaii—all the allure of the Islands in a plate-lunch mix that has you kayaking around offshore islets by day and sitting in a jazz club 'round midnight, all without ever having to take another flight or repack your suitcase. It offers both the buzz of modern living in jam-packed Honolulu (the state's capital) and the allure of slow-paced island life on its northern and eastern shores. It is, in many ways, the center of the Hawaiian universe.

There are more museums, staffed historic sites, and guided tours here than you'll find on any other island. And only here do a wealth of renovated buildings and well-preserved neighborhoods so clearly spin the story of Hawaii's history. It's the only place to experience Islands-style urbanity, since there are no other true cities in the state. And yet you can get as lost in the rural landscape and be as laid-back as you wish.

Oahu is home to Waikiki, the most famous Hawaiian beach, as well as some of the world's most famous surf on the North Shore and Hawaii's best known historical site—Pearl Harbor. If it's isolation, peace, and quiet you want, Oahu might not be for you, but if you'd like a bit of spice with your piece of paradise, this island provides it.

Encompassing 597 square miles, Oahu is the third-largest island in the Hawaiian chain. Scientists believe the island was formed about 4 million years ago by three shield volcanoes: Waianae, Koolau, and the recently discovered Kaena. Recognized in mid-2014, Kaena is the oldest of the three and has long since been submerged 62 miles from Kaena Point on Oahu's northwestern side. Waianae created the mountain range on the western side of the island, whereas Koolau shapes the eastern side. Central Oahu is an elevated plateau bordered by the two mountain ranges, with Pearl Harbor to the south. Several of Oahu's most famous natural landmarks, including Diamond Head and Hanauma Bay, are tuff rings and cinder cones formed during a renewed volcanic stage (roughly 1 million years ago).

Koko Head in Hawaii Kai is a volcanic cinder cone near Hanauma Bay.

The northern and eastern sides of Oahu—and on each Hawaiian island—are referred to as the Windward side, and generally have a cooler, wetter climate. The island's southern and western sides are commonly called the Leeward side, and are typically warmer and more arid. The island's official flower, the little orange *ilima,* grows predominantly in the east, but lei throughout the island incorporate *ilima.* Numerous tropical fish call the reef at Hanauma Bay home, migrating humpback whales can be spotted off the coast past Waikiki and Diamond Head from December through April, spinner dolphins pop in and out of the island's bays, and the 15 islets off Oahu's eastern coast provide refuge for endangered seabirds.

Oahu is the most visited Hawaiian island because early tourism to Hawaii started here. It's also the most inhabited island today—69% of the state's population lives on Oahu—due to job opportunities and the island's military bases. Although Kilauea volcano on Hawaii was a tourist attraction in the late 1800s, it was the building of the Moana Hotel on Waikiki Beach in 1901 and subsequent advertising of Hawaii to wealthy San Franciscans that really fueled tourism in the Islands. Oahu was drawing tens of thousands of guests yearly when, on December 7, 1941, Japanese Zeros appeared at dawn to bomb Pearl Harbor. Though tourism understandably dipped during the war (Waikiki Beach was fenced with barbed wire), the subsequent memorial only seemed to attract more visitors, and Oahu remains hugely popular with tourists—especially the Japanese—to this day.

OAHU PLANNER

GETTING HERE AND AROUND

AIR TRAVEL

Honolulu International Airport (HNL) is roughly 20 minutes (9 miles) west of Waikiki, and is served by most of the major domestic and international carriers. To travel to other islands from Honolulu, you can depart from either the interisland terminal or the commuter-airline terminal, located in two separate structures adjacent to the main overseas terminal building. A free Wiki-Wiki shuttle bus operates between terminals.

From the U.S. mainland, Alaska Airlines, American, Delta, Hawaiian, and United are the primary U.S. carriers to serve Honolulu. Southwest plans to add service to Hawaii in late 2018 or early 2019.

CAR TRAVEL

You can get away without renting a car if you plan on staying in Waikiki. But if you want to explore the rest of the island, there's no substitute for having your own wheels. Avoid the obvious tourist cars—candy-color convertibles, for example—and never leave anything valuable inside, even if you've locked the car. A GPS will save you on phone data and guide you through Oahu's sometimes-confusing streets.

If you are renting a car, reserve your vehicle in advance, especially when traveling during the Christmas holidays and summer breaks. This will not only ensure that you get a car but also that you get the best rates. Also, be prepared to pay for parking; almost all hotels in Honolulu (and many outside of Honolulu) charge for parking.

Except for one area around Kaena Point, major highways follow Oahu's shoreline and traverse the island at two points. Rush-hour traffic (6:30–9:30 am and 3:30–6 pm) can be frustrating around Honolulu and the outlying areas. Winter swells also bring traffic to the North Shore, as people hoping to catch some of the surfing action clog the two-lane Kamehameha Highway. Parking along many streets is curtailed during these times, and tow-away zones are strictly enforced. Read curbside signs before leaving your vehicle, even at a meter.

Asking for directions will almost always produce a helpful explanation from the locals, but you should be prepared for an island term or two. Instead of using compass directions, remember that Hawaii residents refer to places as being either *mauka* (toward the mountains) or *makai* (toward the ocean). Other directions depend on your location: in Honolulu, for example, people say to "go Diamond Head," which means toward that famous landmark, or to "go *ewa*," meaning in the opposite direction. A shop on the *mauka*–Diamond Head corner of a street is on the mountain side of the street on the corner closest to Diamond Head. It all makes perfect sense once you get the lay of the land.

Here are some average driving times—without traffic—that will help you plan your excursions.

DRIVING TIMES	
Waikiki to Ko Olina	1 hour
Waikiki to Haleiwa	45 minutes
Waikiki to Hawaii Kai	25 minutes
Waikiki to Kailua	30 minutes
Waikiki to downtown Honolulu	10 minutes
Waikiki to airport	25 minutes
Kaneohe to Turtle Bay	1 hour
Hawaii Kai to Kailua	25 minutes
Haleiwa to Turtle Bay	20 minutes

HOTELS

Most of Oahu's lodging options are in Waikiki, which offers a mix of large and small hotels. Aqua Hotels have several properties that create a boutique feel without the price tag, while the Outrigger chain carries broad appeal for those traveling with kids. *Hotel reviews have been shortened. For full information, visit Fodors.com*

RESTAURANTS

Honolulu is home to some of the world's most famous chefs, from Sam Choy and his down-home cooking to the artistic Roy Yamaguchi. Though there are plenty of glitzy and recognizable names, some of the best cuisine is off Waikiki's beaten path. Look to Kapahulu and Waialae avenues for fantastic hole-in-the-wall sushi joints and local favorites. Chinatown is the spot for not just dim sum but the best of Italian, French, and Cuban dishes. *Restaurant reviews have been shortened. For full information, visit Fodors.com*

WHAT IT COSTS

	$	$$	$$$	$$$$
Restaurants	Under $17	$17–$26	$27–$35	Over $35
Hotels	Under $180	$180–$260	$261–$340	Over $340

Restaurant prices are for a main course at dinner. Hotel prices are for two people in a standard double room in high season. Condo price categories reflect studio and one-bedroom rates. Prices exclude 13.96% tax.

GUIDED TOURS

Guided tours are convenient; you don't have to worry about finding a parking spot or getting admission tickets. Most of the tour guides have taken special classes in Hawaiian history and lore, and many are certified by the state of Hawaii. On the other hand, you won't have the freedom to proceed at your own pace, nor will you have the ability to take a detour trip if something else catches your attention.

BUS AND VAN TOURS

Polynesian Adventure. This company leads tours of Pearl Harbor and other Oahu sights and also offers a circle-island tour by motor coach, van, or mini-coach. ☎ *808/833–3000, 888/206–4531* ⊕ *www.polyad.com* *From $50.96.*

THEME TOURS

Discover Hawaii Tours. In addition to circle-island and other Oahu-based itineraries on motor and mini-coaches, this company can also get you from Waikiki to the lava flows of the Big Island or to Maui's Hana Highway and back in one day. ☎ *808/690–9050* ⊕ *www.discoverhawaiitours.com* *From $42.99.*

E Noa Tours. This outfitter's certified tour guides conduct circle-island, Pearl Harbor, and shopping tours. ☎ *808/591–2561, 800/824–8804* ⊕ *www.enoa.com* *From $29.*

VISITOR INFORMATION

Before you go to Hawaii, contact the Oahu Visitors Bureau (OVB) for a free vacation planner and map. The OVB website has an online listing of accommodations, activities and sports, attractions, dining venues, services, transportation, travel professionals, and wedding information. For general information on all the Islands, contact the Hawaii Visitors & Convention Bureau. The HVCB website has a calendar of local events that will be taking place during your stay.

Contacts **Hawaii Visitors & Convention Bureau.** ☎ *800/464–2924 for brochures* ⊕ *www.gohawaii.com.* **Oahu Visitors Bureau.** ☎ *800/464–2924* ⊕ *www.gohawaii.com/oahu.*

EXPLORING

HONOLULU

Here is Hawaii's only true metropolis, its seat of government, center of commerce and shipping, entertainment and recreation mecca, a historic site, and an evolving urban area—conflicting roles that engender endless debate and controversy. For the visitor, Honolulu is an everyman's delight: hipsters and scholars, sightseers and foodies, nature lovers, and culture vultures all can find their bliss.

Once there was the broad bay of Mamala and the narrow inlet of Kou, fronting a dusty plain occupied by a few thatched houses and the great Pakaka *heiau* (shrine). Nosing into the narrow passage in 1794, British sea captain William Brown named the port Fair Haven. Later, Hawaiians would call it Honolulu, or "sheltered bay." As shipping traffic increased, the settlement grew into a Western-style town of streets and buildings, tightly clustered around the single freshwater source, Nuuanu Stream. Not until piped water became available in the early 1900s did Honolulu spread across the greening plain. Long before that, however, Honolulu gained importance when King Kamehameha I reluctantly abandoned his home on the Big Island to build a stately compound near the harbor in 1804 to better protect Hawaiian interests from the Western incursion.

Two hundred years later, the entire island is, in a sense, Honolulu—the City and County of Honolulu. The city has no official boundaries, extending across the flatlands from Pearl Harbor to Waikiki and high into the hills behind.

The main areas (Waikiki, Pearl Harbor, downtown, Chinatown) have the lion's share of the sights, but greater Honolulu also has a lot to offer. One reason to venture farther afield is the chance to glimpse Honolulu's residential neighborhoods. Species of classic Hawaiian homes include the tiny green-and-white plantation-era house with its corrugated tin roof, two windows flanking a central door and small porch; the breezy bungalow with its swooping Thai-style roofline and two wings flanking screened French doors through which breezes blow into the living room. Note the tangled "Grandma-style" gardens and many *ohana* houses—small homes in the backyard of a larger home or built as apartments perched over the garage, allowing extended families to live together. Carports, which rarely house cars, are the island's version of rec rooms, where parties are held and neighbors sit to "talk story." Sometimes you see gallon jars on the flat roofs of garages or carports: these are pickled lemons fermenting in the sun. Also in the neighborhoods, you find the folksy restaurants and takeout spots favored by locals.

WAIKIKI

Waikiki is approximately 3 miles east of downtown Honolulu.

A short drive from downtown Honolulu, Waikiki is Oahu's primary resort area. A mix of historic and modern hotels and condos front the sunny 2-mile stretch of beach, and many have clear views of Diamond Head. The area is home to much of the island's dining, nightlife, and shopping scene—from posh boutiques to hole-in-the-wall eateries to craft booths at the International Marketplace.

Waikiki was once a favorite retreat for Hawaiian royalty. In 1901 the Moana Hotel debuted, introducing Waikiki as an international travel destination. The region's fame continued to grow when Duke Kahanamoku helped popularize the sport of surfing, offering lessons to visitors at Waikiki. You can see Duke immortalized in a bronze statue, with a surfboard, on Kuhio Beach. Today there is a decidedly "urban resort" vibe here; streets are clean, gardens are manicured, and the sand feels softer than at beaches farther down the coast. There isn't much of a local culture—it's mainly tourist crowds—but you'll still find the relaxed surf-y vibe that has drawn people here for more than a century.

Kapiolani Park lies in the shadow of the Diamond Head crater, which is just beyond the easternmost limits of Waikiki. King David Kalakaua established the park in 1887, named it after his queen, and dedicated it "to the use and enjoyment of the people." Kapiolani Park is a 500-acre expanse where you can play all sorts of field sports, enjoy a picnic, see wild animals and tropical fish at the Honolulu Zoo and the Waikiki Aquarium, or hear live music at the Waikiki Shell or the Kapiolani Bandstand.

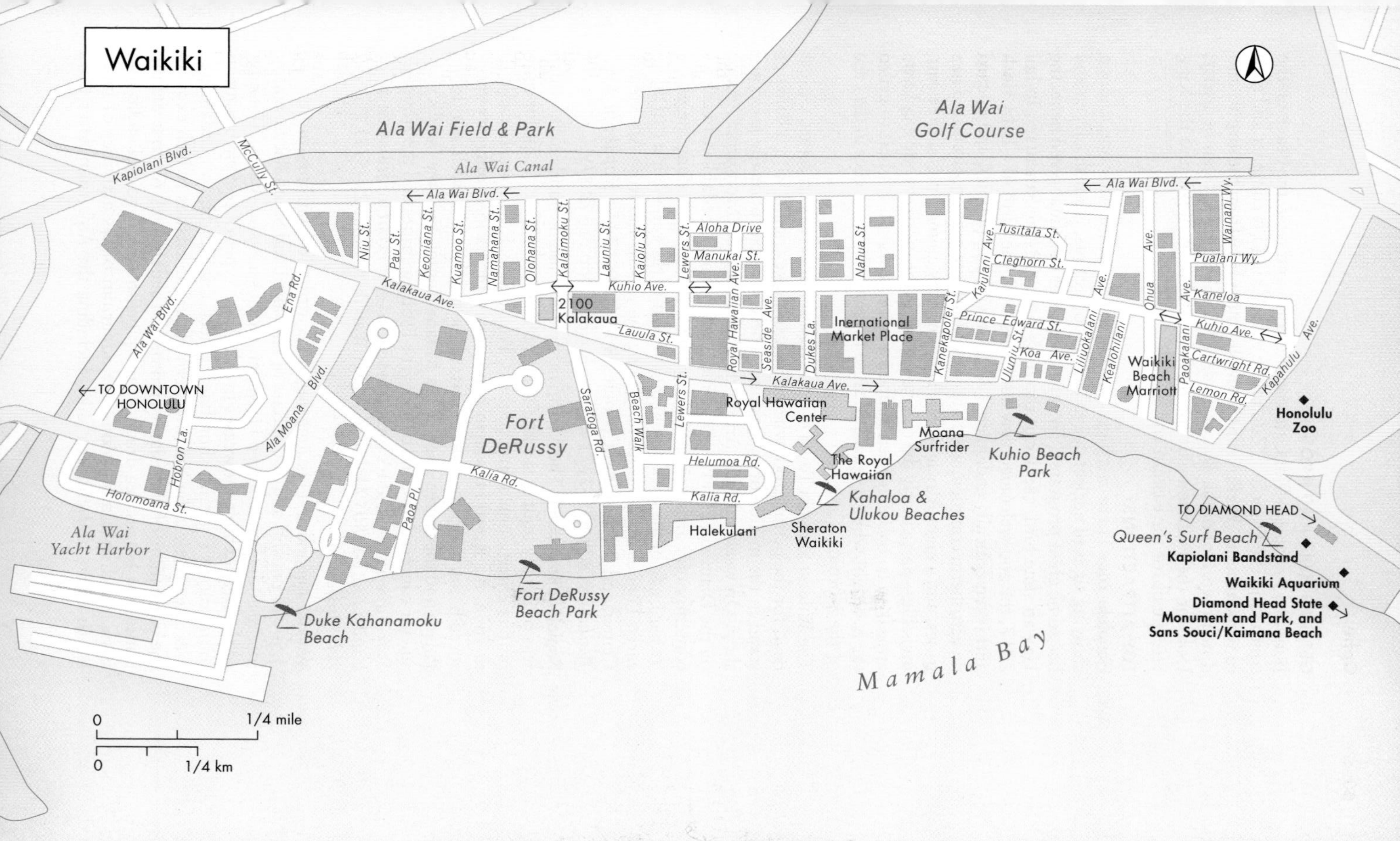

Waikiki
Ala Wai Field & Park
Ala Wai Golf Course
Ala Wai Canal
Kapiolani Blvd.
McCully St.
Ala Wai Blvd.
Niu St.
Pau St.
Keoniana St.
Kuamoo St.
Namahana St.
Olohana St.
Kalaimoku St.
Launiu St.
Kaiolu St.
Lewers St.
Aloha Drive
Manukai St.
Royal Hawaiian Ave.
Seaside Ave.
Dukes La.
Nahua St.
Kuhio Ave.
Kalakaua Ave.
2100 Kalakaua
Lauula St.
International Market Place
Kanekapolei St.
Kaiulani Ave.
Tusitala St.
Cleghorn St.
Prince Edward St.
Uluniu St.
Koa Ave.
Liliuokalani Ave.
Kealohilani
Ohua Ave.
Paoakalani Ave.
Kaneloa
Pualani Wy.
Wainani Wy.
Cartwright Rd.
Lemon Rd.
Kapahulu Ave.
Waikiki Beach Marriott
Honolulu Zoo
Ena Rd.
Ala Moana Blvd.
TO DOWNTOWN HONOLULU
Hobron La.
Holomoana St.
Ala Wai Yacht Harbor
Paoa Pl.
Kalia Rd.
Fort DeRussy
Saratoga Rd.
Beach Walk
Helumoa Rd.
Royal Hawaiian Center
The Royal Hawaiian
Moana Surfrider
Kuhio Beach Park
Kahaloa & Ulukou Beaches
Sheraton Waikiki
Halekulani
Fort DeRussy Beach Park
Duke Kahanamoku Beach
TO DIAMOND HEAD
Queen's Surf Beach
Kapiolani Bandstand
Waikiki Aquarium
Diamond Head State Monument and Park, and Sans Souci/Kaimana Beach
Mamala Bay
0
1/4 mile
0
1/4 km

GETTING HERE AND AROUND

Bounded by the Ala Wai Canal on the north and west, the beach on the south, and the Honolulu Zoo to the east, Waikiki is compact and easy to walk around. TheBus runs multiple routes here from the airport and downtown Honolulu. By car, finding Waikiki from H1 can be tricky; look for the Punahou exit for the west end of Waikiki, and the King Street exit for the eastern end.

TOP ATTRACTIONS

FAMILY **Honolulu Zoo.** There are bigger and better zoos, but this one, though showing signs of neglect due to budget constraints, is a lush garden and has some great programs. To get a glimpse of the endangered *nene,* the Hawaii state bird, check out the zoo's Kipuka Nene Sanctuary. In fall 2017, the zoo welcomed new additions, with the birth of a baby sloth and seven critically endangered African wild dog puppies, and opened an ectotherm complex, which houses a Burmese python, elongated tortoises, and a giant African snail. Though many animals prefer to remain invisible—particularly the elusive big cats—the monkeys and elephants appear to enjoy being seen and are a hoot to watch. It's best to get to the zoo right when it opens, because the animals are livelier in the cool of the morning.

The Wildest Show in Town is a 10-week summer concert series. Or just head for the petting zoo, where kids can make friends with a llama or stand in the middle of a koi pond. There's an exceptionally good gift shop. On weekends, the Art on the Zoo Fence, on Monsarrat Avenue on the Diamond Head side outside the zoo, has affordable artwork by contemporary artists. Metered parking is available all along the *makai* (ocean) side of the park and in the lot next to the zoo—but it can fill up early. TheBus makes stops here along the way to and from Ala Moana Center and Sea Life Park (Routes 8 and 22). ✉ *151 Kapahulu Ave., Waikiki* ☎ *808/971–7171* 🌐 *www.honoluluzoo.org* 🎫 *$19.*

FAMILY **Kapiolani Bandstand.** The Victorian-style Kapiolani Bandstand, which was originally built in the late 1890s, is Kapiolani Park's stage for community entertainment and concerts. Founded by King Kamehameha III in 1836, the Royal Hawaiian Band, today, the nation's only city-sponsored band, performs free concerts at the bandstand as well as at Iolani Palace and the center stage at Ala Moana Center. Visit the band's website for concert dates, and check event-listing websites and the *Honolulu Star-Advertiser*—Oahu's local newspaper—for event information at the bandstand. ✉ *2805 Monsarrat Ave., Waikiki* ☎ *808/922–5331* 🌐 *www.rhb-music.com.*

FAMILY **Waikiki Aquarium.** This amazing little attraction harbors more than 3,500 organisms and 500 species of Hawaiian and South Pacific marine life, including endangered Hawaiian monk seals and sharks. *The Edge of the Reef* exhibit showcases five different types of reef environments found along Hawaii's shorelines. Check out exhibits on endangered green sea turtles, the Northwestern Hawaiian Islands (which explains the formation of the island chain), and jellyfish. A 60-foot exhibit houses sea horses, sea dragons, and pipefish. A self-guided audio tour is included with admission. The aquarium offers activities of interest to adults and children alike, including the Aquarium After Dark

Waikiki and Honolulu, looking west to Diamond Head, as seen from above

program, when visitors grab a flashlight and view fish going about their rarely observable nocturnal activities. ✉ *2777 Kalakaua Ave., Waikiki* ☎ *808/923–9741* 🌐 *www.waikikiaquarium.org* 🎟 *$12.*

DIAMOND HEAD

Besides hiking Diamond Head, visitors will enjoy the eclectic shops and restaurants along Monsarrat Avenue like Diamond Head Market & Grill. Don't forget the amazing *poke* (seasoned raw fish) and other local goodies at Fort Ruger Market, and the Saturday farmers' market at Kapiolani Community College is arguably the best on the island.

Diamond Head State Monument and Park. Panoramas from this 760-foot extinct volcanic peak, once used as a military fortification, extend from Waikiki and Honolulu in one direction and out to Koko Head in the other, with surfers and windsurfers scattered like confetti on the cresting waves below. This 360-degree perspective is a great orientation for first-time visitors. On a clear day, look east past Koko Head to glimpse the outlines of the islands of Maui and Molokai.

To enter the park from Waikiki, take Kalakaua Avenue east, turn left at Monsarrat Avenue, head a mile up the hill, and look for a sign on the right. Drive through the tunnel to the inside of the crater. The ¾-mile trail to the top begins at the parking lot. Be aware that the hike to the crater is an upward ascent with numerous stairs to climb; if you aren't in the habit of getting occasional exercise, this might not be for you. At the top, you'll find a somewhat awkward scramble through a tunnel and bunker out into the open air, but the view is worth it.

Take bottled water with you to stay hydrated under the tropical sun. **■ TIP→ To beat the heat and the crowds, rise early and make the hike**

before 8 am. As you walk, note the color of the vegetation; if the mountain is brown, Honolulu has been without significant rain for a while; but if the trees and undergrowth glow green, you'll know it's the wet season (winter) without looking at a calendar. This is when rare Hawaiian marsh plants revive on the floor of the crater. Keep an eye on your watch if you're here at day's end: the gates close promptly at 6 pm. ✉ *Diamond Head Rd. at 18th Ave., Diamond Head* ☎ *808/587–0300* 🌐 *dlnr.hawaii.gov/dsp/parks/oahu/diamond-head-state-monument* 🎟 *$1 per person, $5 per vehicle (cash only).*

PEARL HARBOR

Pearl Harbor is approximately 9 miles west of downtown Honolulu, beyond Honolulu International Airport.

December 7, 1941. Every American then alive recalls exactly what he or she was doing when the news broke that the Japanese had bombed Pearl Harbor, the catalyst that brought the United States into World War II. Those who are younger have learned about the events of the fateful day, when more than 2,000 people died, and a dozen ships were sunk. Here, in what is still a key Pacific naval base, the attack is remembered every day by thousands of visitors. In recent years, the memorial has been the site of reconciliation ceremonies involving Pearl Harbor veterans from both sides. There are five distinct sights in Pearl Harbor, but only two are part of World War II Valor in the Pacific National Monument. The others are privately operated. It's possible to make reservations for the national park sites at 🌐 *www.recreation.gov*.

Fodor's Choice ★ ***Battleship Missouri* Memorial.** The Japanese signed their Terms of Surrender after World War II on the deck of the USS *Missouri*, which was commissioned in 1944 as the last battleship ever built. In 2017 the battleship underwent a $3.5-million renovation (now complete) to replace rusted steel and repaint its upper decks. It's the biggest preservation effort to the *Missouri* since it was drydocked in 2009 for a $15.5-million top-to-bottom paint job. To begin your visit, pick up tickets online or at the Pearl Harbor Visitor Center. Then board a shuttle bus for the ride to Ford Island. Join a free, guided tour to learn more about the *Missouri*'s long and dramatic history. Near the entrance are a gift shop and a lunch wagon serving hamburgers and hot dogs. ✉ *Pearl Harbor, 63 Cowpens St., Pearl Harbor* ⊕ *You cannot drive directly to the USS Missouri; you must take a shuttle bus from the Pearl Harbor Visitor Center* ☎ *808/455–1600* 🌐 *www.ussmissouri.org* 🎟 *From $29.*

Pacific Aviation Museum. The museum, which opened on Ford Island in 2006, documents the history of aviation in the Pacific during World War II and is housed in hangars 37 and 79, which survived the Japanese attack on Pearl Harbor on December 7, 1941. There are a number of interesting (sometimes interactive) displays, including the plane flown by President George H.W. Bush. You can purchase tickets either at the Pearl Harbor Visitor Center or at the museum itself after you get off the shuttle bus, which departs for the museum and the USS *Missouri* from the Pearl Harbor Visitor Center. ✉ *Ford Island, 319 Lexington Blvd., Pearl Harbor* ⊕ *You cannot drive directly to the museum; you*

Continued on page 69

USS *West Virginia* (BB48), 7 December 1941

PEARL HARBOR

December 7, 1941. Every American then alive recalls exactly what he or she was doing when the news broke that the Japanese had bombed Pearl Harbor, the catalyst that brought the United States into World War II.

Although it was clear by late 1941 that war with Japan was inevitable, no one in authority seems to have expected the attack to come in just this way, at just this time. So when the Japanese bombers swept through a gap in Oahu's Koolau Mountains in the hazy light of morning, they found the bulk of America's Pacific fleet right where they hoped it would be: docked like giant stepping stones across the calm waters of the bay named for the pearl oysters that once prospered there. More than 2,000 people died that day, including 49 civilians. A dozen ships were sunk. And on the nearby air bases, virtually every American military aircraft was destroyed or damaged. The attack was a stunning success, but it lit a fire under America, which went to war with "Remember Pearl Harbor" as its battle cry. Here, in what is still a key Pacific naval base, the attack is remembered every day by thousands of visitors, including many curious Japanese, who for years heard little World War II history in their own country. In recent years, the memorial has been the site of reconciliation ceremonies involving Pearl Harbor veterans from both sides.

GETTING AROUND

Pearl Harbor is both a working military base and the most-visited Oahu attraction. Four distinct destinations share a parking lot and are linked by footpath, shuttle, and ferry.

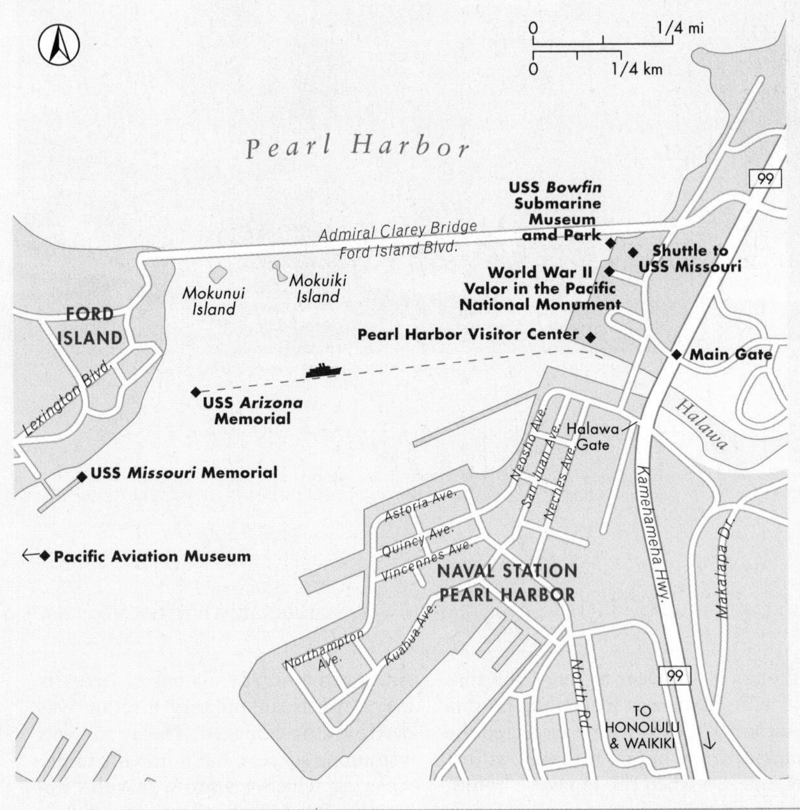

The visitor center is accessible from the parking lot. The USS *Arizona* Memorial itself is in the middle of the harbor; get tickets for the ferry ride at the visitor center. The USS *Bowfin* is also reachable from the parking lot.

The USS *Missouri* is docked at Ford Island, a restricted area of the naval base. Vehicular access is prohibited.To get there, take a shuttle bus from the station near the *Bowfin.*

ARIZONA MEMORIAL

Snugged up tight in a row of seven battleships off Ford Island, the USS *Arizona* took a direct hit that December morning, exploded, and rests still on the shallow bottom where she settled.

The swooping, stark-white memorial, which straddles the wreck of the USS *Arizona*, was designed to represent both the depths of the low-spririted, early days of the war, and the uplift of victory.

A visit here begins at the Pearl Harbor Visitor Center, which recently underwent a $58 million renovation. High definition projectors and interactive exhibits were installed, and the building was modernized. From the visitor center, a ferry takes you to the memorial itself, and a new shuttle hub now gives access to sites that were previously inaccessible, like the USS *Utah* and USS *Oklahoma*.

A somber, contemplative mood descends upon visitors during the ferry ride to the *Arizona*; this is a place where 1,177 crewmen lost their lives. Gaze at the names of the dead carved into the wall of white marble. Scatter flowers (but no lei—the string is bad for the fish). Salute the flag. Remember Pearl Harbor.

☎ *808/422–0561*
🌐 *www.nps.gov/valr*

USS *MISSOURI* (BB63)

Together with the *Arizona* Memorial, the *Missouri's* presence in Pearl Harbor perfectly bookends America's WWII experience that began December 7, 1941, and ended on the "Mighty Mo's" starboard deck with the signing of the Terms of Surrender.

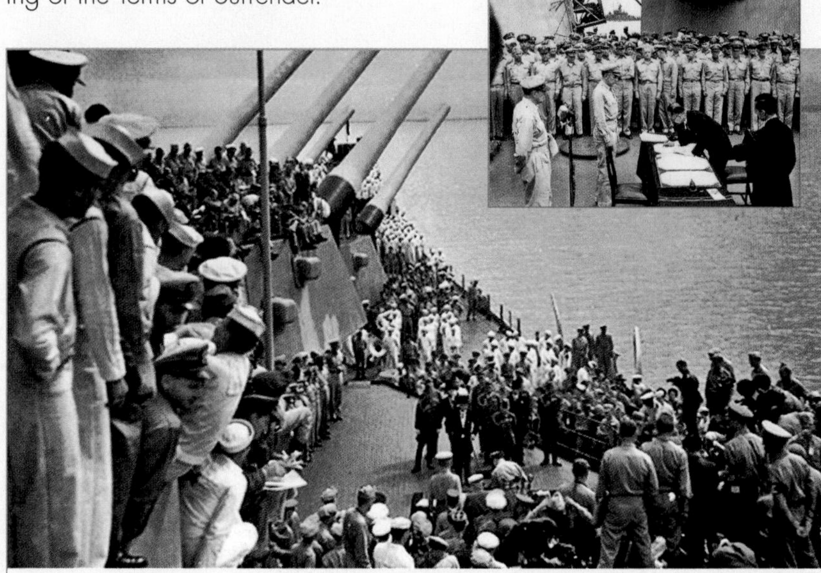

Surrender of Japan, USS *Missouri*, 2 September 1945

In the parking area behind the USS *Bowfin* Museum, board a shuttle for an eight-minute ride to Ford Island and the teak decks and towering superstructure of the *Missouri*. The last battleship ever built, the *Missouri* famously hosted the final act of WWII, the signing of the Terms of Surrender. The commission that governs this floating museum has surrounded her with buildings tricked out in WWII style with quonset huts serving as shaded eating areas for the nearby lunch wagon and a Victory Store housing a souvenir shop and covered with period mottos ("Don't be a blabateur").

■ TIP→ Definitely hook up with a tour guide (no additional charge) or audio tour—these add a great deal to the experience.

The *Missouri* is all about numbers: 209 feet tall, six 239,000-pound guns, capable of firing up to 23 miles away. Absorb these during the tour, then stop to take advantage of the view from the decks. The Mo is a work in progress, with only a handful of her hundreds of spaces open to view.

☎ *808/423–2263* or ☎ *888/877–6477*
🌐 *www.ussmissouri.com*

USS *BOWFIN* (SS287)

SUBMARINE MUSEUM & PARK

Launched one year to the day after the Pearl Harbor attack, the USS *Bowfin* sank 44 enemy ships during WWII and now serves as the centerpiece of a museum honoring all submariners.

Although the *Bowfin* no less than the *Arizona* Memorial commemorates the lost, the mood here is lighter. Perhaps it's the childlike scale of the boat, a metal tube just 16 feet in diameter, packed with ladders, hatches, and other obstacles, like the naval version of a jungle gym. Perhaps it's the World War II-era music that plays in the covered patio. Or it might be the museum's touching displays—the penciled sailor's journal, the Vargas girlie posters. Aboard the boat nicknamed "Pearl Harbor Avenger," compartments are fitted out as though "Sparky" was away from the radio room just for a moment, and "Cooky" might be right back to his pots and pans. The museum includes many artifacts to spark family conversations, among them a vintage dive suit that looks too big for Shaquille O'Neal. A caution: The *Bowfin* could be hazardous for very young children; no one under four allowed.

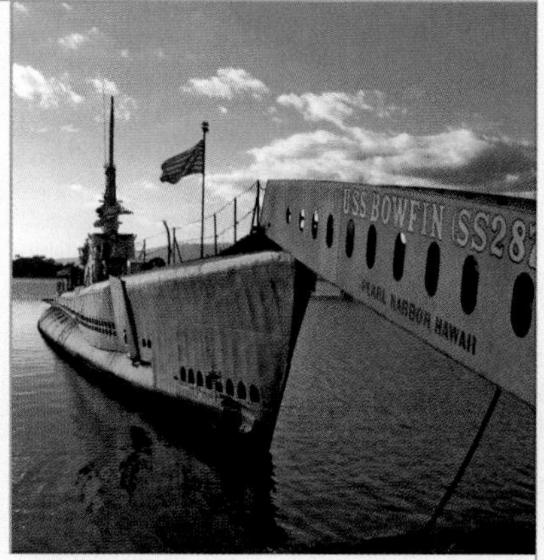

☎ *808/423–1341*
🌐 *www.bowfin.org*

PACIFIC AVIATION MUSEUM PEARL HARBOR

This museum opened on December 7, 2006, as as a tribute to aviation in the Pacific. Located on Ford Island in Hangars 37 and 79, actual seaplane hangars that survived the Pearl Harbor attack, the museum is made up of a theater where a short film on Pearl Harbor kicks off the tour, an education center, a shop, and a restaurant. Exhibits—many of which are interactive and involve sound effects—include an authentic Japanese Zero in a diorama setting, vintage aircraft, and the chance to play the role of a World War II pilot using one of six flight simulators. Various aircrafts are employed to narrate the great battles: the Doolittle Raid on Japan, the Battle of Midway, Guadalcanal, and so on. The actual Stearman N2S-3 in which President George H. W. Bush soloed is housed in Hangar 79. ☎ *808/441–1000* 🌐 *www.pacificaviationmuseum.org* 🎫 $35; an aviator led tour is available for $10.

PLAN YOUR PEARL HARBOR DAY LIKE A MILITARY CAMPAIGN

DIRECTIONS

Take H–1 west from Waikiki to Exit 15A and follow signs. Or take The-Bus route 20 or 47 from Waikiki. Beware high-priced private shuttles. It's a 30-minute drive from Waikiki.

WHAT TO BRING

Picture ID is required during periods of high alert; bring it just in case.

You'll be standing, walking, and climbing all day. Wear something with lots of pockets and a pair of good walking shoes. Carry a light jacket, sunglasses, hat, and sunscreen.

No purses, packs, or bags are allowed. Take only what fits in your pockets. Cameras are okay but without the bags. A private bag storage booth is located in the parking lot near the visitors' center. Leave nothing in your car; theft is a problem despite bicycle security patrols.

HOURS

Hours are 7 am to 5 pm for the visitor center, though the attractions open at 8 am. The *Arizona* Memorial starts giving out tickets on a first-come, first-served basis at 7 am; the last tickets are given out at 3 pm. Spring break, summer, and holidays are busiest, and tickets sometimes run out by noon or earlier.

TICKETS

Arizona: Free. Add $7.50 for museum audio tours.

Aviation: $35 adults, $22 children. Add $10 for aviator's guided tour.

Missouri: $25 adults, $13 children. Add $25 for in-depth, behind-the-scenes tours.

Bowfin: $12 adults, $5 children. Children under 4 may go into the museum but not aboard the *Bowfin.*

KIDS

This might be the day to enroll younger kids in the hotel children's program. Preschoolers chafe at long waits, and attractions involve some hazards for toddlers. Older kids enjoy the *Bowfin* and *Missouri,* especially.

MAKING THE MOST OF YOUR TIME

Expect to spend at least half a day; a whole day is better if you're a military history buff.

At the *Arizona* Memorial, you'll get a ticket, be given a tour time, and then have to wait anywhere from 15 minutes to 3 hours. You must pick up your own ticket so you can't hold places. If the wait is long, skip over to the *Bowfin* to fill the time.

SUGGESTED READING

Pearl Harbor and the USS Arizona Memorial, by Richard Wisniewski. $5.95. 64-page magazine-size quick history.

Bowfin, by Edwin P. Hoyt. $14.95. Dramatic story of undersea adventure.

The Last Battleship, by Scott C. S. Stone. $11.95. Story of the Mighty Mo.

must take a shuttle bus to Ford Island from the Pearl Harbor Visitor Center ☎ 808/441–1000 🌐 www.pacificaviationmuseum.org 🎫 $25.

Fodor's Choice ★ **Pearl Harbor Visitor Center.** The Pearl Harbor Visitor Center reopened after a $58-million renovation and is now the gateway to the World War II Valor in the Pacific National Monument and the starting point for visitors to this historic site. At the visitor center are interpretive exhibits in two separate galleries (*Road to War* and *Attack*) that feature photographs and personal memorabilia from World War II veterans. But there are other exhibits, a bookstore, and a Remembrance Circle, where you can learn about the people who lost their lives on December 7, 1941. Survivors are often on hand to give their personal accounts and answer questions. The visitor center is also where you start your tour of the USS *Arizona* Memorial if you have secured a walk-in or reserved a timed ticket (reserve at 🌐 *www.recreation.gov)* ✉ *World War II Valor in the Pacific National Monument, 1 Arizona Memorial Pl., Pearl Harbor* ☎ *808/422–3399, 877/444–6777 Timed Ticket Reservations* 🌐 *www.nps.gov/valr* 🎫 *Free (timed-entry tickets $1.50).*

USS *Arizona* Memorial. The USS *Arizona*, which was destroyed by a Japanese bomber on December 7, 1941, lies precisely where she sank. A visit to what is now known as the World War II Valor in the Pacific National Monument, begins prosaically—a line, a wait filled with shopping, visiting the museum, and strolling the grounds. You can reserve timed tickets online at 🌐 *www.recreation.gov* and skip the wait, which is advisable since this is one of Hawaii's busiest tourist sights, and tickets do well out. When your tour starts, you watch a short documentary film, then board the ferry to the memorial. At the site, you may scatter flowers in memory of the dead (but no lei—the string is bad for the fish). ✉ *World War II Valor in the Pacific National Monument, Pearl Harbor* ☎ *808/422–3300, 877/444–6777 Timed Ticket Reservations* 🌐 *www.nps.gov/valr* 🎫 *Free (timed-entry tickets $1.50); museum audio tours $7.50. Arrive early for limited same-day tickets.*

USS *Bowfin* Submarine Museum and Park. The USS *Bowfin* claimed to have sunk 44 enemy ships during World War II and now serves as the centerpiece of a museum honoring all submariners. The submarine, which has been preserved as a museum and is privately owned and operated, includes a good audio tour with admission. Children under four are not allowed due to safety considerations. ✉ *11 Arizona Memorial Place, Pearl Harbor* ☎ *808/423–1341* 🌐 *www.bowfin.org* 🎫 *$15 to tour the submarine and museum; $6 to visit the museum only.*

DOWNTOWN

Honolulu's past and present play a delightful counterpoint throughout the downtown area, which is approximately 6 miles east of Honolulu International Airport. Postmodern glass-and-steel office buildings look down on the Aloha Tower, built in 1926 and, until the early 1960s, the tallest structure in Honolulu. Hawaii's history is told in the architecture of these few blocks: the cut-stone turn-of-the-20th-century storefronts of Merchant Street, the gracious white-columned American-Georgian manor that was the home of the Islands' last queen, the jewel-box palace occupied by the monarchy before it was overthrown, the Spanish-inspired stucco and tile-roofed Territorial Era government buildings, and the 21st-century glass pyramid of the First Hawaiian Bank Building.

GETTING HERE AND AROUND

To reach downtown Honolulu from Waikiki by car, take Ala Moana Boulevard to Alakea Street and turn right; three blocks up on the right, between South King and Hotel streets, there's a municipal parking lot in Alii Place on the right. There are also public parking lots in buildings along Alakea, Smith, Beretania, and Bethel streets (Chinatown Gateway on Bethel Street is a good choice). The best parking downtown, however, is metered street parking along Punchbowl Street—when you can find it.

Another option is to take Route 20 or 42 of highly popular and convenient TheBus to the Aloha Tower Marketplace, or take a trolley from Waikiki.

TOURS

American Institute of Architects (AIA) Honolulu Walking Tour. Join an AIA tour to see downtown Honolulu from an architectural perspective, including the restored Hawaii Theatre, city seat Honolulu Hale, Iolani Palace, Kawaiahao Church, and the open-air state capitol. Tours are led by AIA Honolulu members and architects and are offered on the second and fourth Saturday of each month. Advance reservations are required. AIA also offers a companion tour booklet for an additional $5 with the tour, $10 without. ✉ *Honolulu* ☎ *808/628–7243* 🌐 *www.aiahonolulu.org* 🎟 *$15.*

TOP ATTRACTIONS

Fodor's Choice ★ **Iolani Palace.** America's only official royal residence was built in 1882 on the site of an earlier palace. It contains the thrones of King Kalakaua and his successor (and sister) Queen Liliuokalani. Bucking the stereotype of simple island life, the palace had electric lights even before the White House. Downstairs galleries showcase the royal jewelry, and a kitchen and offices restored to the glory of the monarchy. The palace is open for guided tours or self-guided audio tours, and reservations are recommended. ■ TIP→ **If you're set on taking a guided tour, call or book online for reservations a few days in advance.** Tours are available only in the mornings and are limited. The palace gift shop and ticket office was formerly the Iolani Barracks, built to house the Royal Guard. ✉ *364 South King St., Downtown* ☎ *808/522–0832* 🌐 *www.iolanipalace.org* 🎟 *$21.75 guided tour, $14.75 audio tour, $5 downstairs galleries only* ⊗ *Closed Sun. (except for monthly Kamaaina Sun.).*

Kamehameha I Statue. Paying tribute to the Big Island chieftain who united all the warring Hawaiian Islands into one kingdom at the turn of the 18th century, this statue, which stands with one arm outstretched in welcome, is one of three originally cast in Paris by American sculptor T. R. Gould. The original statue, lost at sea and replaced by this one, was eventually salvaged and is now in Kapaau, on the Big Island, near the king's birthplace. Each year on the king's birthday (June 11), the more famous copy is draped in fresh lei that reach lengths of 18 feet and longer. A parade proceeds past the statue, and Hawaiian civic clubs, women in hats and impressive long *holoku* dresses, and men in sashes and cummerbunds, pay honor to the leader whose name means "The One Set Apart." ✉ *417 S. King St., outside Aliiolani Hale, Downtown.*

Kawaiahao Church. Fancifully called Hawaii's Westminster Abbey, this historic house of worship witnessed the coronations, weddings, and funerals of generations of Hawaiian royalty. Each of the building's 14,000 coral blocks was quarried from reefs offshore at depths of more than 20 feet and transported to this site. Interior woodwork was created from the forests of the Koolau Mountains. The upper gallery has an exhibit of paintings of the royal families. The graves of missionaries and of King Lunalilo are adjacent. Services in English, with songs and prayers in Hawaiian, are held each Sunday, and the church members are exceptionally welcoming, greeting newcomers with lei; their affiliation is United Church of Christ. Although there are no guided tours, you can look around the church at no cost. ✉ *957 Punchbowl St., at King St., Downtown* ☎ *808/469–3000* 🌐 *www.kawaiahao.org* 🎟 *Free.*

CHINATOWN

Chinatown's original business district was made up of dry-goods and produce merchants, tailors and dressmakers, barbers, herbalists, and dozens of restaurants. The meat, fish, and produce stalls remain, but the mix is heavier now on gift and curio stores, lei stands, jewelry shops, and bakeries, with a smattering of noodle makers, travel agents, Asian-language video stores, and dozens of restaurants.

The name "Chinatown" here has always been a misnomer. Though three-quarters of Oahu's Chinese lived closely packed in these 25 acres in the late 1800s, even then the neighborhood was half Japanese. Today you hear Vietnamese and Tagalog as often as Mandarin and Cantonese, and there are voices of Japan, Singapore, Malaysia, Korea, Thailand, Samoa, and the Marshall Islands, as well.

Perhaps a more accurate name is the one used by early Chinese: *Wah Fau* (Chinese port), signifying a landing and jumping-off place. Chinese laborers, as soon as they completed their plantation contracts, hurried into the city to start businesses here. It's a launching point for today's immigrants, too: Southeast Asian shops almost outnumber Chinese; stalls carry Filipino specialties like winged beans and goat meat; and in one tiny space, knife-wielding Samoans skin coconuts to order.

In the half century after the first Chinese laborers arrived in Hawaii in 1851, Chinatown was a link to home for the all-male cadre of workers who planned to return to China rich and respected. Merchants not only sold supplies, they held mail, loaned money, wrote letters, translated documents, sent remittances to families, served meals, offered rough bunkhouse accommodations, and were the center for news, gossip, and socializing.

Although much happened to Chinatown in the 20th century—beginning in January 1900, when almost the entire neighborhood was burned to the ground to halt the spread of bubonic plague—it remains a bustling, crowded, noisy, and odiferous place bent primarily on buying and selling, and sublimely oblivious to its status as a National Historic District or the encroaching gentrification on nearby Nuuanu Avenue.

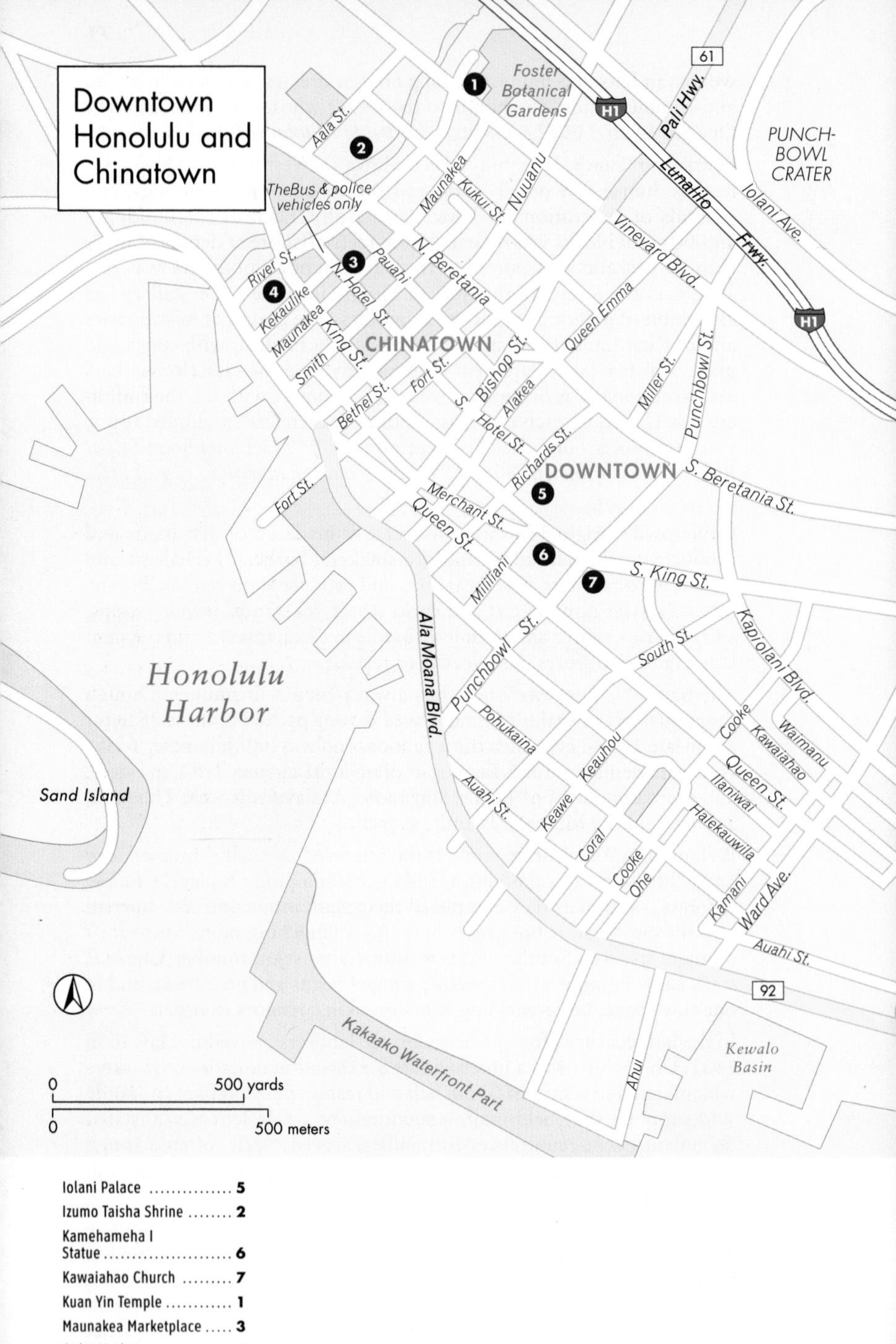

Iolani Palace 5

Izumo Taisha Shrine 2

Kamehameha I Statue 6

Kawaiahao Church 7

Kuan Yin Temple 1

Maunakea Marketplace 3

Oahu Market 4

GETTING HERE AND AROUND

Chinatown occupies 15 blocks immediately north of downtown Honolulu—it's flat, compact, and very walkable.

GUIDED TOURS

Hawaii Food Tours. Come hungry for food writer Matthew Gray's culinary Hole-in-the-Wall Tour through Honolulu, which includes discussion of Hawaiian culinary history and the diversity of the Islands' food culture, along with 15- to 20-plus samples of local favorites as you walk to a variety of ethnic restaurants, markets, and bakeries, including two hours in Chinatown. It's a great way to get a delicious taste of Hawaii's culture. The tour begins at 9 am. Gray also has a North Shore Food Tour, which includes transportation from Waikiki. ☎ *808/926–3663* 🌐 *www.hawaiifoodtours.com* 🎫 *From $139.*

TOP ATTRACTIONS

Izumo Taisha Shrine. From Chinatown Cultural Plaza, cross a stone bridge to the Izumo Taishakyo Mission of Hawaii to visit this shrine established in 1906. It honors Okuninushi-no-Mikoto, a *kami* (god) who is believed in Shinto tradition to bring good fortune if properly courted (and thanked afterward). ✉ *215 N. Kukui St., Chinatown* ✣ *At the canal* ☎ *808/538–7778.*

Kuan Yin Temple. A couple of blocks *mauka* (toward the mountains) from Chinatown is the oldest Buddhist temple in the Islands. Mistakenly called a goddess by some, Kuan Yin, also known as Kannon, is a *bodhisattva*—one who chose to remain on Earth doing good even after achieving enlightenment. Transformed from a male into a female figure centuries ago, she is credited with a particular sympathy for women. You will see representations of her all over the Islands: holding a lotus flower (beauty from the mud of human frailty), as at the temple; pouring out a pitcher of oil (like mercy flowing); or as a sort of Madonna with a child. Visitors are permitted but be aware this is a practicing place of worship. ✉ *170 N. Vineyard Blvd., Chinatown.*

Maunakea Marketplace. On the corner of Maunakea and Hotel streets is this busy plaza surrounded by shops, an indoor market, and a food court. It gets packed every year for the annual Chinese Lunar New Year. ■ **TIP→ If you appreciate fine tea, visit the unpretentious tea counter in the Tea Hut, a curio shop filled with Chinese gifts and good luck charms.** ✉ *1120 Maunakea St., Chinatown* ☎ *808/524–3409.*

Oahu Market. In this market founded in 1904, you'll find a taste of old-style Chinatown, where you might be hustled aside as a whole pig (dead, of course) is wrestled through the crowd and where glassy-eyed fish of every size and hue lie stacked forlornly on ice. Try the bubble tea (juices and flavored teas with tapioca balls inside) or pick up a bizarre magenta dragonfruit for breakfast. ✉ *N. King St., Chinatown* ✣ *At Kekaulike St.*

GREATER HONOLULU

One reason to venture beyond the areas of Honolulu that have a wider range of tourist sights (primarily Waikiki, Pearl Harbor, downtown, and Chinatown) is the chance to glimpse Honolulu's residential neighborhoods. Species of classic Hawaii homes include the tiny green-and-white plantation-era house with its corrugated tin roof, two windows flanking a central door and small porch; or the breezy bungalow with its swooping Thai-style roofline and two wings flanking screened French doors through which breezes blow into the living room. Note the tangled "Grandma-style" gardens and many *ohana* houses—small homes in the backyard of a larger home or built as apartments perched over the garage, allowing extended families to live together. Carports, which rarely house cars, are the island's version of rec rooms, where parties are held and neighbors sit to "talk story." Sometimes you see gallon jars on the flat roofs of garages or carports: these are pickled lemons fermenting in the sun. Also in the neighborhoods, you find the folksy restaurants and takeout spots favored by the islanders.

GETTING HERE AND AROUND

For those with a Costco card, the cheapest gas on the island is at the Costco station on Arakawa Street between Dillingham Boulevard and Nimitz Highway, though the line can sometimes wind into the street.

TOP ATTRACTIONS

Fodor's Choice ★ **Bishop Museum.** Founded in 1889 by Charles R. Bishop as a memorial to his wife, Princess Bernice Pauahi Bishop, the museum began as a repository for the royal possessions of this last direct descendant of King Kamehameha the Great. Today it's the state's designated history and culture museum. Its five exhibit halls house almost 25 million items that tell the history of the Hawaiian Islands and their Pacific neighbors. The complex also features a 16,500-square-foot natural-science wing with a three-story simulated volcano at its center, where twice-daily "lava melt" shows take place, much to the enjoyment of younger patrons. The renovated Pacific Hall (formerly Polynesian Hall) now focuses on the history of the entire Pacific region.

The Hawaiian Hall, with state-of-the art and often interactive displays, teaches about the Hawaiian culture. Spectacular Hawaiian artifacts—lustrous feather capes, bone fishhooks, the skeleton of a giant sperm whale, photography and crafts displays, and an authentic, well-preserved grass house—are displayed inside a three-story 19th-century Victorian-style gallery. The building alone, with its huge Victorian turrets and immense stone walls, is worth seeing. Also check out the planetarium, daily tours, *lauhala*-weaving and science demonstrations, special exhibits, the Shop Pacifica, and the Bishop Museum Café, which serves *ono* (delicious) Hawaiian food by local restaurant Highway Inn. ✉ *1525 Bernice St., Kalihi* ☎ *808/847–3511* 🌐 *www.bishopmuseum.org* 🎟 *$24.95 (parking $5).*

National Memorial Cemetery of the Pacific. Nestled in the bowl of Puowaina, or Punchbowl Crater, this 112-acre cemetery is the final resting place for more than 50,000 U.S. war veterans and family members and is a solemn reminder of their sacrifice. Among those buried here is Ernie Pyle, the famed World War II correspondent who was killed by a Japanese sniper on Ie Shima, an island off the northwest coast of Okinawa. There are intricate stone maps providing a visual military-history lesson. Puowaina, formed 75,000–100,000 years ago during a period of secondary volcanic activity, translates as "Hill of Sacrifice." Historians believe this site once served as an altar where ancient Hawaiians

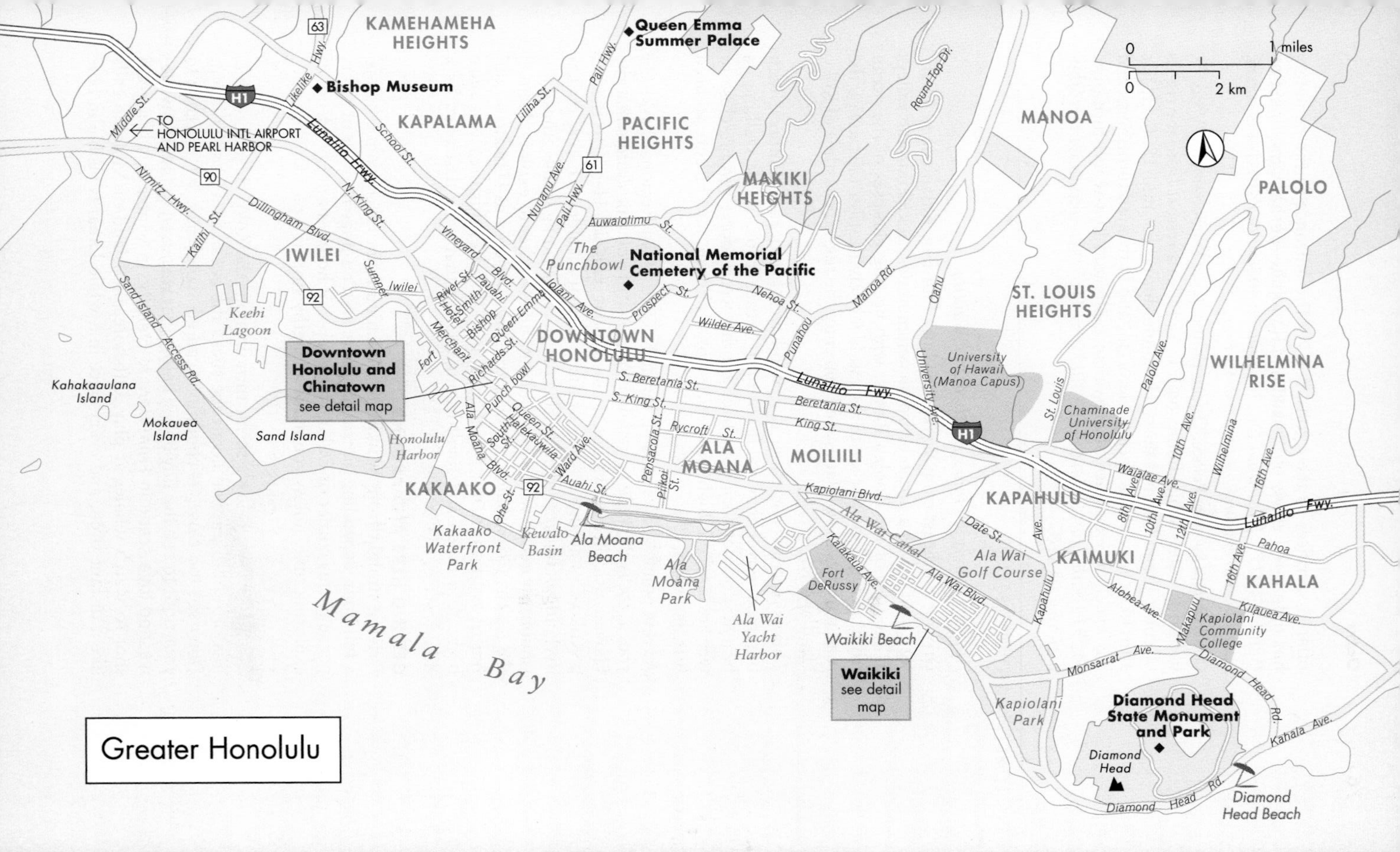
Greater Honolulu
KAMEHAMEHA HEIGHTS
KAPALAMA
IWILEI
PACIFIC HEIGHTS
MAKIKI HEIGHTS
DOWNTOWN HONOLULU
ALA MOANA
MOILIILI
KAKAAKO
MANOA
ST. LOUIS HEIGHTS
WILHELMINA RISE
PALOLO
KAPAHULU
KAIMUKI
KAHALA
Queen Emma Summer Palace
Bishop Museum
National Memorial Cemetery of the Pacific
Diamond Head State Monument and Park
Diamond Head
TO HONOLULU INTL AIRPORT AND PEARL HARBOR
Downtown Honolulu and Chinatown see detail map
Waikiki see detail map
The Punchbowl
University of Hawaii (Manoa Capus)
Chaminade University of Honolulu
Kapiolani Community College
Kapiolani Park
Ala Wai Golf Course
Fort DeRussy
Ala Moana Park
Kakaako Waterfront Park
Ala Moana Beach
Waikiki Beach
Diamond Head Beach
Ala Wai Yacht Harbor
Kewalo Basin
Honolulu Harbor
Keehi Lagoon
Sand Island
Mokauea Island
Kahakaaulana Island
Mamala Bay
Lunalilo Fwy.
Middle St.
Likelike Hwy.
School St.
Liliha St.
Pali Hwy.
Nuuanu Ave.
Nimitz Hwy.
Kalihi St.
Dillingham Blvd.
N. King St.
Sumner
Iwilei
Vineyard Blvd.
River St.
Smith
Pauahi
Hotel
Bishop
Queen Emma
Merchant
Fort
Richards St.
Punch bowl
Ala Moana Blvd.
Queen St.
South St.
Halekauwila
Ward Ave.
Auahi St.
Ohe St.
Iolani Ave.
Auwaiolimu St.
Prospect St.
Nehoa St.
Wilder Ave.
Manoa Rd.
Punahou
Round Top Dr.
Oahu
University Ave.
S. Beretania St.
S. King St.
Beretania St.
King St.
Rycroft St.
Pensacola St.
Piikoi St.
Kapiolani Blvd.
Ala Wai Canal
Kalakaua Ave.
Ala Wai Blvd.
Date St.
Kapahulu Ave.
St. Louis
Paiolo Ave.
Waialae Ave.
8th Ave.
10th Ave.
12th Ave.
16th Ave.
Wilhelmina
Pahoa
Alohea Ave.
Makapuu
Kilauea Ave.
Monsarrat Ave.
Diamond Head Rd.
Kahala Ave.
Sand Island Access Rd.
H1
63
61
90
92
0
1 miles
2 km

offered sacrifices to their gods. ■ **TIP→ The entrance to the cemetery has unfettered views of Waikiki and Honolulu—perhaps the finest on Oahu.** ✉ *2177 Puowaina Dr., Nuuanu* ☎ *808/532–3720* 🌐 *www.cem.va.gov/cem/cems/nchp/nmcp.asp* 🎫 *Free.*

Queen Emma Summer Palace. Queen Emma, King Kamehameha IV's wife, used this stately white home, built in 1848, as a retreat from the rigors of court life in hot and dusty Honolulu during the mid-1800s. It has an eclectic mix of European, Victorian, and Hawaiian furnishings and has excellent examples of Hawaiian quilts and koa-wood furniture. ✉ *2913 Pali Hwy., Nuuanu* ☎ *808/595–3167* 🌐 *www.daughtersofhawaii.org* 🎫 *$10.*

SOUTHEAST OAHU

Approximately 10 miles southeast of Waikiki.

Driving southeast from Waikiki on busy four-lane Kalanianaole Highway, you'll pass a dozen bedroom communities tucked into the valleys at the foot of the Koolau Range, with fleeting glimpses of the ocean from a couple of pocket parks. Suddenly civilization falls away, the road narrows to two lanes, and you enter the rugged coastline of Koko Head and Ka Iwi.

This is a cruel coastline: dry, windswept, and rocky shores, with untamed waves that are notoriously treacherous. While walking its beaches, do not turn your back on the ocean, don't venture close to wet areas where high waves occasionally reach, and be sure to heed warning signs.

At this point, you're passing through Koko Head Regional Park. On your right is the bulging remnant of a pair of volcanic craters that the Hawaiians called Kawaihoa, known today as Koko Head. To the left is Koko Crater and an area of the park that includes a hiking trail, a dryland botanical garden, a firing range, and a riding stable. Ahead is a sinuous shoreline with scenic pullouts and beaches to explore. Named the Ka Iwi Coast (*iwi*, "ee-vee," are bones—sacred to Hawaiians and full of symbolism) for the channel just offshore, this area was once home to a ranch and small fishing enclave that were destroyed by a tidal wave in the 1940s.

GETTING HERE AND AROUND

Driving straight from Waikiki to Makapuu Point takes from a half to a full hour, depending on traffic. There aren't a huge number of sights per se in this corner of Oahu, so a couple of hours should be plenty of exploring time, unless you make a lengthy stop at a particular point.

TOP ATTRACTIONS

Halona Blowhole. Below a scenic turnout along the Koko Head shoreline, this oft-photographed lava tube sucks the ocean in and spits it out. Don't get too close, as conditions can get dangerous. ■ **TIP→ Look to your right to see the tiny beach below that was used to film the wave-washed love scene in *From Here to Eternity*.** In winter this is a good spot to watch whales at play. Offshore, the island of Molokai calls like a distant siren, and every once in a while Lanai is visible in blue silhouette. Take your valuables with you and lock your car, because this scenic location is overrun with tourists and therefore a hot spot for petty thieves. ✉ *Kalanianaole Hwy., Hawaii Kai* ✣ *1 mile east of Hanauma Bay.*

Koko Crater Botanical Gardens. If you've visited any of Oahu's other botanical gardens, this one will be in stark contrast. Inside the tallest tuff cone on Oahu, in one of the hottest and driest areas on the island, Koko Crater Botanical Garden allows visitors the opportunity to see dryland species of plants including baobab trees, cacti, plumeria, and bougainvillea. ✉ *Entrance at end of Kokonani St., near Hawaii Kai Dr., Hawaii Kai* ☎ *808/522–7066* 🌐 *www.honolulu.gov/parks/hbg.html* 🎫 *Free.*

Lanai Lookout. A little over half a mile past Hanauma Bay as you head toward Makapuu Point, you'll see a turnout on the ocean side with some fine views of the coastline. In winter you'll have an opportunity to see storm-generated waves crashing against lava cliffs. This is also a popular place for winter whale-watching, so bring your binoculars, some sunscreen, and a picnic lunch and join the small crowd scanning for telltale white spouts of water only a few hundred yards away. On clear days you should be able to see the islands of Molokai and Lanai off in the distance, hence the name. ✉ *Kalanianaole Hwy., Hawaii Kai* ✣ *Just past Hanauma Bay.*

Makapuu Point. This spot has breathtaking views of the ocean, mountains, and the windward Islands. The point of land jutting out in the distance is Mokapu Peninsula, site of a U.S. Marine base. The spired mountain peak is Mt. Olomana. On the long pier is part of the Makai Undersea Test Range, a research facility that's closed to the public. Offshore is Manana Island (Rabbit Island), a picturesque cay said to resemble a swimming bunny with its ears pulled back. Ironically enough, Manana Island was once overrun with rabbits, thanks to a rancher who let a few hares run wild on the land. They were eradicated in 1994 by biologists who grew concerned that the rabbits were destroying the island's native plants.

Nestled in the cliff face is the **Makapuu Lighthouse,** which became operational in 1909 and has the largest lighthouse lens in America. The lighthouse is closed to the public, but near the Makapuu Point turnout you can find the start of a paved mile-long road (it's closed to vehicular traffic). Hike up to the top of the 647-foot bluff for a closer view of the lighthouse and, in winter, a great whale-watching vantage point. For the more adventurous, at the whale-watching sign on the main path, head down a switchback trail to the Makapuu tide pools below. ✉ *Ka Iwi State Scenic Shoreline, Kalanianaole Hwy., Kaneohe* ✣ *At Makapuu Beach* 🌐 *dlnr.hawaii.gov/dsp/hiking/oahu/makapuu-point-lighthouse-trail.*

Fodor's Choice ★ **Shangri La.** In 1936 heiress Doris Duke bought 5 acres at Black Point, down the coast from Waikiki, and began to build and furnish the first home that would be all her own. She called it Shangri La. For more than 50 years, the home was a work in progress as Duke traveled the world, buying art and furnishings, picking up ideas for her Mughal Garden,

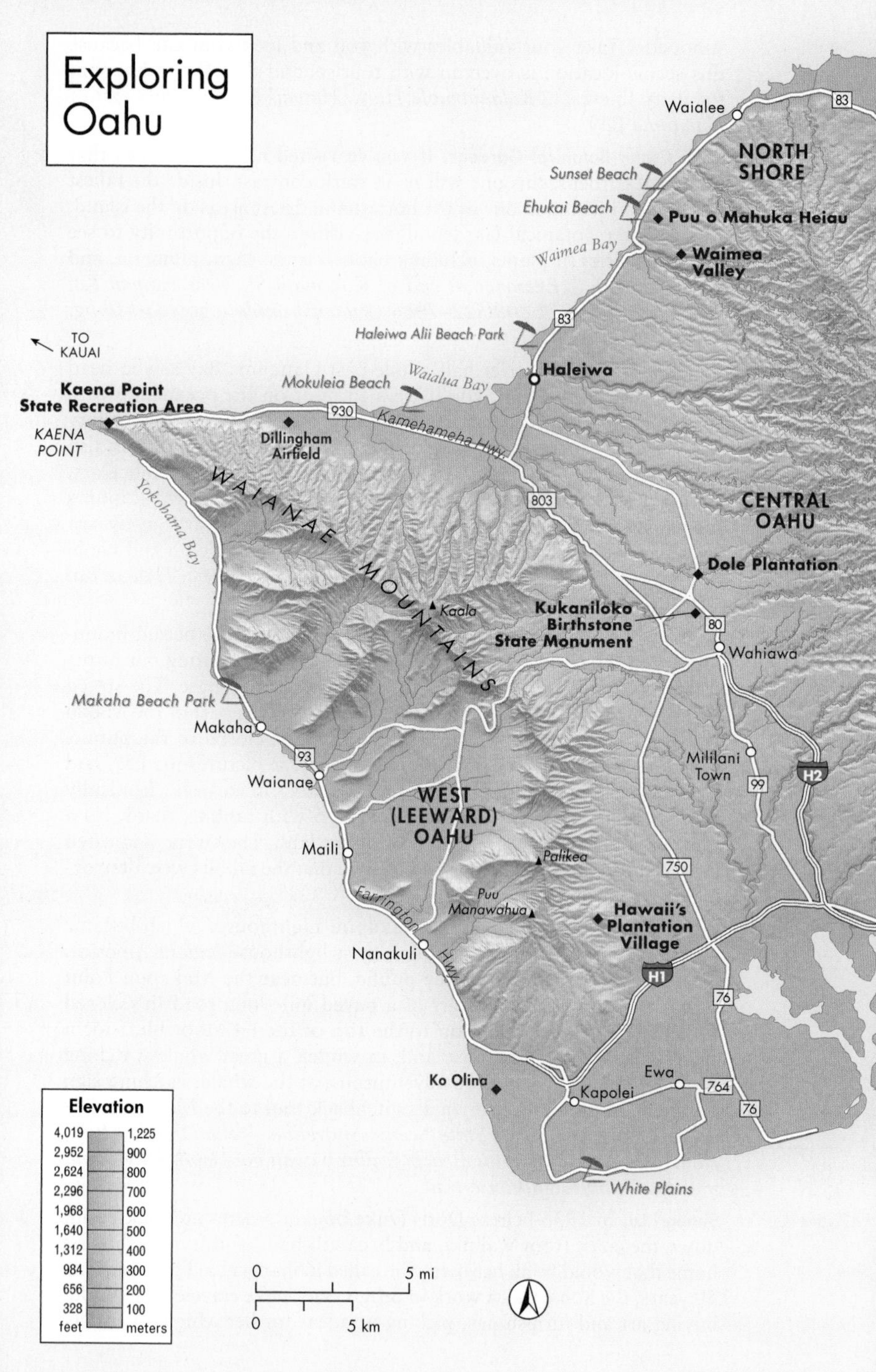
Exploring Oahu
Waialee
83
NORTH SHORE
Sunset Beach
Ehukai Beach
Puu o Mahuka Heiau
Waimea Bay
Waimea Valley
83
Haleiwa Alii Beach Park
TO KAUAI
Haleiwa
Mokuleia Beach
Waialua Bay
Kaena Point State Recreation Area
930
Kamehameha Hwy.
KAENA POINT
Dillingham Airfield
WAIANAE MOUNTAINS
Yokohama Bay
803
CENTRAL OAHU
Dole Plantation
Kaala
Kukaniloko Birthstone State Monument
80
Wahiawa
Makaha Beach Park
Makaha
93
Waianae
Mililani Town
99
H2
WEST (LEEWARD) OAHU
Maili
Palikea
750
Farrington Hwy
Puu Manawahua
Hawaii's Plantation Village
Nanakuli
H1
76
Ko Olina
Ewa
764
Kapolei
76
White Plains
Elevation
4,019
2,952
2,624
2,296
1,968
1,640
1,312
984
656
328
feet
1,225
900
800
700
600
500
400
300
200
100
meters
0
5 mi
0
5 km

PACIFIC OCEAN
Kahuku
Laie
Polynesian Cultural Center
Hauula
Punaluu
KOOLAU MOUNTAINS
Kahana Bay Beach Park
Kaaawa
Kualoa Regional Park
83
Mokolii
Puu Kaaumakua
WINDWARD OAHU
Kahaluu
MOKAPU PT.
MOKAPU PENINSULA
Kaneohe Bay
830
Byodo-In Temple
Trans-Koolau Tunnel
USS Bowfin Submarine Museum and Park
Pearl Harbor Visitor Center
World War II Valor in the Pacific National Memorial
Kaneohe
Kailua Bay
TO MOLOKAI, MAUI AND LANAI
Kailua
Lanikai Beach Park
Pearl Harbor
H3
Aiea
78
Wilson Tunnel
63
Likelike Hwy.
Kailua Rd.
Kalanianaole Hwy.
USS Arizona Memorial
Battleship Missouri Memorial
Pali Hwy.
61
Pali Tunnel
Mt. Olomana
Bellows Beach
Waimanalo Beach Park
Waimanalo
72
MANANA ISLAND (RABBIT ISLAND)
Nuuanu Pali Lookout
Puu Lanipo
Kaau Crater
H1
Pearl Harbor Naval Base
Sea Life Park
Makapuu Beach
Makapuu Point
SOUTHEAST OAHU
HONOLULU
Honolulu International Airport
Mamala Bay
H1
Lunalilo Hwy.
72
Sandy Beach
Hawaii Kai
Koko Crater
Ala Moana Beach Park
DIAMOND HEAD
Maunalua Bay
Halona Blowhole
Hanauma Bay Nature Preserve
Hanauma Bay
Downtown Honolulu and Chinatown see detail map
Waikiki see detail map
Shangri La
KOKO HEAD

for the Playhouse in the style of a 17th-century Irani pavilion, and for the water terraces and tropical gardens. When she died in 1993, Duke left instructions that her home was to become a public center for the study of Islamic art.

To walk through the house and its gardens—which have remained much as Duke left them with only some minor conservation-oriented changes—is to experience the personal style of someone who saw everything as raw material for her art. (The courtyard and pool underwent extensive renovations starting in 2017.) With her trusted houseman, Jin de Silva, she helped build the elaborate Turkish Room, trimming tiles and painted panels to retrofit the existing space (including raising the ceiling and lowering the floor) and building a fountain of her own design. Among many aspects of the home inspired by the Muslim tradition is the entry: an anonymous gate, a blank white wall, and a wooden door that bids you, "Enter herein in peace and security" in Arabic script. Inside, tiles glow, fountains tinkle, and shafts of light illuminate artworks through arches and high windows. In 2014, after years of renovation, Duke's bedroom (the Mughal Suite) opened to the public. This was her private world, entered only by trusted friends.

The house is open by guided tour only and reservations are required. Book your tour as early as possible, as tours fill up very quickly. Tours take 2½ hours including transportation from the Honolulu Museum of Art (*900 S. Beretania St., downtown Honolulu*), where all tours begin. Children under eight are not admitted. ✉ *Hawaii Kai* ☎ *808/532–3853 for Honolulu Museum of Art* 🌐 *www.shangrilahawaii.org or honolulumuseum.org/385-about_shangri_la* 🎫 *Tour $25 ($1.50 fee for online reservations, $2 for phone reservations)* ⏲ *Closed Sun.–Tues. and Sept.*

WINDWARD OAHU

Approximately 15 miles northeast of downtown Honolulu (20–25 minutes by car), approximately 25 miles southeast of downtown Honolulu via Ka Iwi and Waimanalo (35–45 minutes by car).

Looking at Honolulu's topsy-turvy urban sprawl, you would never suspect the windward side existed. It's a secret Oahuans like to keep, so they can watch the awe on the faces of their guests when the car emerges from the tunnels through the mountains and they gaze for the first time on the panorama of turquoise bays and emerald valleys watched over by the knife-edged Koolau ridges. Jaws literally drop. Every time. And this just a 15-minute drive from downtown.

It's on this side of the island where many Native Hawaiians live. Evidence of traditional lifestyles is abundant in crumbling fishponds, rock platforms that once were altars, taro patches still being worked, and throw-net fishermen posed stock-still above the water (though today, they're invariably wearing polarized sunglasses, the better to spot the fish).

Here the pace is slower, more oriented toward nature. Beachgoing, hiking, diving, surfing, and boating are the draws, along with a visit to the Polynesian Cultural Center, and poking through little shops and wayside stores.

GETTING HERE AND AROUND

For a driving experience you won't soon forget, take the H3 freeway over to the windward side. As you pass through the tunnels, be prepared for one of the most breathtaking stretches of road anywhere.

TOP ATTRACTIONS

Fodor's Choice ★ **Byodo-In Temple.** Tucked away in the back of the Valley of the Temples cemetery is a replica of the 11th-century Temple at Uji in Japan. A 2-ton carved wooden statue of the Buddha presides inside the main temple building. Next to the temple building are a meditation pavilion and gardens set dramatically against the sheer, green cliffs of the Koolau Mountains. You can ring the 5-foot, 3-ton brass bell for good luck and feed some of the hundreds of koi, ducks, and swans that inhabit the garden's 2-acre pond. Or, you can enjoy the peaceful surroundings and just relax. ✉ *47-200 Kahekili Hwy., Kaneohe* ☎ *808/239–8811* 🌐 *www.byodo-in.com* 🎫 *$5 (cash only).*

NEED A BREAK

Kalapawai Market. Generations of children have purchased their beach snacks and sodas at Kalapawai Market, near Kailua Beach. A Windward Oahu landmark since 1932, the green-and-white market has distinctive charm. **Known for:** take-out deli sandwiches; good coffee; a great selection of wine. ✉ *306 S. Kalaheo Ave., Kailua* ☎ *808/262–4359* 🌐 *www.kalapawaimarket.com.*

Nuuanu Pali Lookout. This panoramic perch looks out to expansive views of Windward Oahu. It was in this region that King Kamehameha I drove defending forces over the edges of the 1,200-foot-high cliffs, thus winning the decisive battle for control of Oahu. ■ **TIP→ From here, views stretch from Kaneohe Bay to Mokolii ("little lizard," also called Chinaman's Hat), a small island off the coast, and beyond.** Temperatures at the summit are several degrees cooler than in warm Waikiki, so bring a jacket along. Hang on tight to any loose possessions and consider wearing pants; it gets extremely windy at the lookout, which is part of the fun. Lock your car in the pay-to-park lot; break-ins have occurred here (this wayside is in the most trafficked state park in Hawaii). ✉ *Kaneohe* ✣ *Top of Pali Hwy.* 🌐 *dlnr.hawaii.gov/dsp/parks/oahu/nuuanu-pali-state-wayside* 🎫 *Free* ☞ *Parking $3 per car.*

NEED A BREAK

Island Snow. Long a favorite of Windward Oahu residents for its shave ice counter within the clothing store, Island Snow has more recently become known as the place where President Obama and his daughters have gone for the sweet treat when they vacation in Hawaii. Extra fluffy shave ice topped off with local syrup flavors and a milky "snow cap" make this one of the best shave ice stops on the island. **Known for:** fluffy shave ice; extras like adzuki beans; macadamia nut ice cream. ✉ *130 Kailua Rd., Kailua* ✣ *Separate entrance from clothing shop* ☎ *808/263–6339.*

Mokolii. As you drive the Windward and North shores along Kamehameha Highway, you'll note a number of interesting geological features. At Kualoa look to the ocean and gaze at the uniquely shaped little island of Mokolii ("little lizard"), a 206-foot-high sea stack also known as Chinaman's Hat. According to Hawaiian legend, the goddess Hiiaka, sister of Pele, slew the dragon Mokolii and flung its tail into the sea, forming the distinct islet. Other dragon body parts—in the form of rocks, of course—were scattered along the base of nearby Kualoa Ridge. ■ TIP→ **In Laie, if you turn right on Anemoku Street, and right again on Naupaka, you come to a scenic lookout where you can see a group of islets, dramatically washed by the waves.** ✉ *49-479 Kamehameha Hwy., Kaneohe.*

FAMILY **Polynesian Cultural Center.** Re-created individual villages showcase the lifestyles and traditions of Hawaii, Tahiti, Samoa, Fiji, the Marquesas Islands, New Zealand, and Tonga. Focusing on individual islands within its 42-acre center, 35 miles from Waikiki, the Polynesian Cultural Center was founded in 1963 by the Church of Jesus Christ of Latter-day Saints. It houses restaurants, hosts luau, and demonstrates cultural traditions such as hula, fire dancing, and ancient customs and ceremonies. The Hukilau Marketplace carries Polynesian handicrafts. There are multiple packages available, from basic admission to an all-inclusive deal. Every May the PCC hosts the World Fireknife Dance Competition, an event that draws the top fire-knife dance performers from around the world. Get tickets for that event in advance. ■ TIP→ **If you're staying in Honolulu, see the center as part of a van tour so you won't have to drive home late at night after the two-hour evening show.** ✉ *55-370 Kamehameha Hwy., Laie* ☎ *800/367–7060* 🌐 *www.polynesia.com* 🎫 *From $64.95* ⏲ *Closed Sun.*

THE NORTH SHORE

Approximately 35 miles (one hour by car) north of downtown Honolulu, approximately 25 miles (one hour by car) from Kualoa Regional Park (Chinaman's Hat) in Windward Oahu.

An hour from town and a world away in atmosphere, Oahu's North Shore, roughly from Kahuku Point to Kaena Point, is about small farms and big waves, tourist traps, and otherworldly landscapes. Parks and beaches, roadside fruit stands and shrimp shacks, a bird sanctuary, and a valley preserve offer a dozen reasons to stop between the onetime plantation town of Kahuku and the surf mecca of Haleiwa.

Haleiwa has had many lives, from resort getaway in the 1900s to plantation town through the 20th century to its life today as a surf and tourist magnet. Beyond Haleiwa is the tiny village of Waialua, a string of beach parks, an airfield where gliders, hang gliders, and parachutists play, and, at the end of the road, Kaena Point State Recreation Area, which offers a brisk hike, striking views, and whale-watching in season.

Pack wisely for a day's North Shore excursion: swim and snorkel gear, light jacket and hat (the weather is mercurial, especially in winter), sunscreen and sunglasses, bottled water and snacks, towels and a picnic blanket, and both sandals and closed-toe shoes for hiking. A small cooler

DID YOU KNOW?

You can experience authentic Hawaiian culture at the Polynesian Cultural Center on the windward side of the island, including sampling traditional foods such as this Tahitian coconut bread.

The Byodo-In Temple on the windward side of Oahu is a replica of an 11th-century temple in Japan.

is nice; you may want to pick up some fruit or fresh corn. As always, leave valuables in the hotel safe and lock the car whenever you park.

GETTING HERE AND AROUND

From Waikiki, the quickest route to the North Shore is H1 east to H2 north, and then the Kamehameha Highway past Wahiawa; you'll hit Haleiwa in just under an hour. The windward route (H1 east, H3, Likelike or Pali Highway, through the mountains, or Kamehameha Highway north) takes at least 90 minutes to Haleiwa, but the drive is far prettier.

TOP ATTRACTIONS

Haleiwa. Today Haleiwa is a fun mix of old and new, with charming general stores and contemporary boutiques, galleries, and eateries. During the 1920s this seaside hamlet boasted a posh hotel at the end of a railroad line (both long gone), while the 1960s saw hippies gathered here, followed by surfers from around the world. Be sure to stop in at **Liliuokalani Protestant Church,** founded by missionaries in the 1830s. It's fronted by a large, stone archway built in 1910 and covered with night-blooming cereus. ✉ *Haleiwa* ✥ *Follow H1 west from Honolulu to H2 north, exit at Wahiawa, follow Kamehameha Hwy. 6 miles, turn left at signaled intersection, then right into Haleiwa.*

NEED A BREAK

Matsumoto Shave Ice. For a real slice of Haleiwa life, stop at Matsumoto Shave Ice, a family-run business in a building dating to 1910, for shave ice in every flavor imaginable. For something different, order a shave ice with adzuki beans—the red beans are boiled until soft, mixed with sugar, and then placed in the cone with the ice on top. **Known for:** one of the most popular shave ice spots on Oahu; the Masumoto with lemon, pineapple, and

CLOSE UP

Windward Oahu Villlages

Tiny villages—generally consisting of a sign, store, a beach park, possibly a post office, and not much more—are strung along Kamehameha Highway on the windward side. Each has something to offer. In **Waiahole,** look for fruit stands and an ancient grocery store. In **Kaaawa,** there's a lunch spot and convenience store–gas station. In **Punaluu,** get a plate lunch at Keneke's, or visit venerable Ching General Store. Kim Taylor Reece's photo studio, featuring haunting portraits of hula dancers, is between Punaluu and Hauula. **Hauula** has the gallery of fanciful landscape artist Lance Fairly; the Shrimp Shack; Hauula Gift Shop & Art Gallery, formerly yet another Ching Store, now a clothing shop where sarongs wave like banners; and, at Hauula Kai Shopping Center, Tamura's Market, with excellent seafood and the last liquor before Mormon-dominated Laie.

2

coconut syrup; house made adzuki beans. ✉ ***66-111 Kamehameha Hwy., Suite 605, Haleiwa*** ☎ ***808/637–4827*** 🌐 ***www.matsumotoshaveice.com.***

Kaena Point State Recreation Area. The name means "the heat" and, indeed, this windy barren coast lacks both shade and freshwater (or any man-made amenities). Pack water, wear sturdy closed-toe shoes, don sunscreen and a hat, and lock the car. The hike is along a rutted dirt road, mostly flat and nearly 3 miles long, (one way) ending in a rocky, sandy headland. It is here that Hawaiians believed the souls of the dead met with their family gods, and, if judged worthy to enter the afterlife, leapt off into eternal darkness at Leinaakauane, just south of the point. In summer and at low tide, the small coves offer bountiful shelling; in winter, don't venture near the water. Rare native plants dot the landscape and seabirds like the Laysan albatross nest here. If you're lucky, you might spot seals sunbathing on the rocks. From November through March, watch for humpbacks, spouting and breaching. Binoculars and a camera are highly recommended. ✉ *69-385 Farrington Hwy., Waialua* 🌐 *dlnr.hawaii.gov/dsp/parks/oahu/kaena-point-state-park.*

Puu o Mahuka Heiau. Worth a stop for its spectacular views from a bluff high above the ocean overlooking Waimea Bay, this sacred spot is the largest heiau on the island and spans nearly 2 acres. At one time it was used as a *heiau luakini,* or a temple for human sacrifices. It's now on the National Register of Historic Places. Turn up the road at the Pupukea Foodland and follow the road up to the heiau. ✉ *Pupukea Rd., ½ mile north of Waimea Bay, Haleiwa* ✢ *From Rte. 83, turn right on Pupukea Rd. and drive 1 mile uphill* 🌐 *dlnr.hawaii.gov/dsp/parks/oahu/puu-o-mahuka-heiau-state-historic-site.*

FAMILY Fodor's Choice ★ **Waimea Valley.** Waimea may get lots of press for the giant winter waves in the bay, but the valley itself is a newsmaker and an ecological treasure in its own right. The local nonprofit is working to conserve and restore the natural habitat. Follow the Kamananui Stream up the valley through the 1,875 acres of gardens. The botanical collections here include more than 5,000 species of tropical flora, including a superb gathering of Polynesian plants. It's the best place on the island to see native species, such as the endangered Hawaiian moorhen. You can also see the restored Hale o Lono *heiau* (shrine) along with other ancient archaeological sites; evidence suggests that the area was an important spiritual center. Daily activities include botanical walking tours and cultural tours. At the back of the valley, Waihi Falls plunges 45 feet into a swimming pond. ■ **TIP→ Bring your board shorts—a swim is the perfect way to end your hike. Be sure to bring mosquito repellent, too; it can get buggy.** ✉ *59-864 Kamehameha Hwy., Haleiwa* ☎ *808/638–7766* 🌐 *www.waimeavalley.net* 🎟 *$16.*

QUICK BITES

Ted's Bakery. The chocolate *haupia* (coconut pudding) pie at Ted's Bakery is legendary. Stop in for a take-out pie or for a quick plate lunch or sandwich. ✉ ***59-024 Kamehameha Hwy., Haleiwa*** ⊕ ***Near Sunset Beach*** ☎ ***808/638–8207*** 🌐 ***www.tedsbakery.com.***

CENTRAL OAHU

Wahiawa is approximately 20 miles (30–35 minutes by car) north of downtown Honolulu, 15 miles (20–30 minutes by car) south of the North Shore.

Oahu's central plain is a patchwork of old towns and new residential developments, military bases, farms, ranches, and shopping malls, with a few visit-worthy attractions and historic sites scattered about. Central Oahu encompasses the Moanalua Valley, residential Pearl City and Mililani, and the old plantation town of Wahiawa, on the uplands halfway to the North Shore.

GETTING HERE AND AROUND

For Central Oahu, all sights are most easily reached by either the H1 or H2 freeway.

FAMILY **Dole Plantation.** Pineapple plantation days are nearly defunct in Hawaii, but you can still celebrate Hawaii's famous golden fruit at this promotional center with exhibits, a huge gift shop, a snack concession, educational displays, and the world's second-largest maze. Take the self-guided Garden Tour, or hop aboard the Pineapple Express for a 20-minute train tour to learn a bit about life on a pineapple plantation. Kids love the more than 3-acre Pineapple Garden Maze, made up of 14,000 tropical plants and trees. If you do nothing else, stop by the cafeteria in the back for a delicious pineapple soft-serve Dole Whip. This is about a 40-minute drive from Waikiki, a suitable stop on the way to or from the North Shore. ✉ *64-1550 Kamehameha Hwy., Wahiawa* ☎ *808/621–8408* 🌐 *www.doleplantation.com* 🎟 *Plantation free, Pineapple Express $10.50, maze $8, garden tour $7.*

Kukaniloko Birthstone State Monument. In the cool uplands of Wahiawa is haunting Kukaniloko, where noble chieftesses went to give birth to high-ranking children. One of the most significant cultural sites on the island, the lava-rock stones here were believed to possess the power to ease the labor pains of childbirth. The site is marked by approximately 180 stones covering about a half acre. It's a 40- to 45-minute drive from

See colorful wildlife at the Waimea Valley Audubon Center on Oahu's North Shore.

Waikiki. ✉ *Kamehameha Hwy. and Whitmore Ave., Wahiawa* ⊕ *The north side of Wahiawa town.*

WEST (LEEWARD) OAHU

Kapolei is approximately 20 miles (30 minutes by car) west of downtown Honolulu, and 12 miles (20 minutes by car) from Mililani; traffic can double or triple the driving time.

West (or Leeward) Oahu has the island's "second city"—the planned community of Kapolei, where for years the government has been trying to attract enough jobs to lighten inbound traffic to downtown Honolulu—then continues on past far-flung resorts to the Hawaiian communities of Nanakuli and Waianae, to the beach and the end of the road at Keaweula, aka Yokohama Bay.

A couple of cautions as you head to the leeward side: Highway 93 is a narrow, winding two-lane road, notorious for accidents. There's an abrupt transition from freeway to highway at Kapolei, and by the time you reach Nanakuli, it's a country road, so *slow down.* ■ **TIP→ Car break-ins and beach thefts are common here.**

GETTING HERE AND AROUND

West Oahu begins at folksy Waipahu and continues past Makakilo and Kapolei on H1 and Highway 93, Farrington Highway.

Hawaii's Plantation Village. Starting in the 1800s, immigrants seeking work on the sugar plantations came to these Islands like so many waves against the shore. At this living museum 30 minutes from downtown Honolulu (without traffic), visit authentically furnished buildings, original and replicated, that re-create and pay tribute to the plantation era. See a Chinese social hall; a Japanese shrine, sumo ring, and saimin stand; a dental office; and historic homes. The village is open for guided tours only. ✉ *Waipahu Cultural Gardens Park, 94-695 Waipahu St., Waipahu* ☎ *808/677–0110* 🌐 *www.hawaiiplantationvillage.org* 🎫 *$15.*

BEACHES

Updated by Trina Kudlacek

Tropical sun mixed with cooling trade winds and pristine waters make Oahu's shores a literal heaven on Earth. But contrary to many assumptions, the island is not one big beach. There are miles and miles of coastline without a grain of sand, so you need to know where you're going to fully enjoy the Hawaiian experience.

Much of the island's southern and eastern coast is protected by inner reefs. The reefs provide still coastline water but not much as far as sand is concerned. However, where there are beaches on the south and east shores, they are mind-blowing. In West Oahu and on the North Shore you can find the wide expanses of sand you would expect for enjoying the sunset. Sandy bottoms and protective reefs make the water an adventure in the winter months. Most visitors assume the seasons don't change a bit in the Islands, and they would be mostly right—except for the waves, which are big on the South Shore in summer and placid in winter. It's exactly the opposite on the north side, where winter storms bring in huge waves, but the ocean becomes glass-like come May and June.

HONOLULU

WAIKIKI

The 2-mile strand called Waikiki Beach extends from Hilton Hawaiian Village on one end to Kapiolani Park and Diamond Head on the other. Although it's one contiguous piece of beach, it's as varied as the people that inhabit the Islands. Whether you're an old-timer looking to enjoy the action from the shade or a sports nut wanting to do it all, you can find every beach activity here without ever jumping in the rental car.

Plenty of parking exists on the west end at the Ala Wai Marina, where you can park in metered stalls around the harbor for $1 an hour. For parking on the east end, Kapiolani Park and the Honolulu Zoo also have metered parking for $1 an hour—more affordable than the $10 per hour the resorts want. ■ TIP→ **If you're staying outside the area, our best advice is to park at either end of the beach and walk in.**

FAMILY **Duke Kahanamoku Beach.** Named for Hawaii's famous Olympic swimming champion, Duke Kahanamoku, this is a hard-packed beach with the only shade trees on the sand in Waikiki. It's great for families with young children because it has both shade and the calmest waters in Waikiki, thanks to a rock wall that creates a semiprotected cove. The ocean clarity here is not as brilliant as most of Waikiki because of the stillness of the surf, but it's a small price to pay for peace of mind about youngsters. The beach fronts the Hilton Hawaiian Village Beach Resort

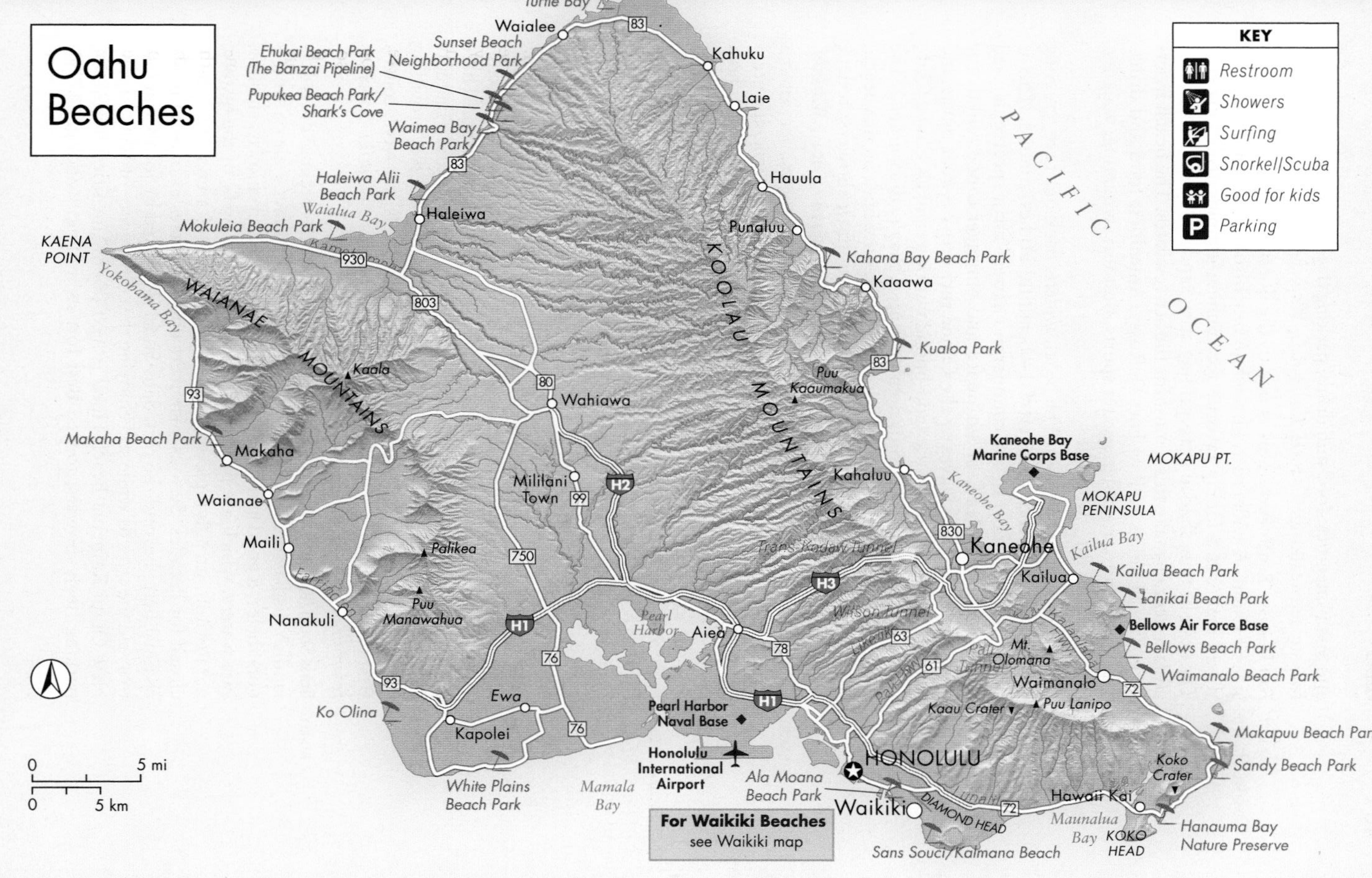

Oahu
Beaches
KEY
Restroom
Showers
Surfing
Snorkel/Scuba
Good for kids
Parking
PACIFIC OCEAN
Turtle Bay
Waialee
Sunset Beach
Neighborhood Park
Ehukai Beach Park
(The Banzai Pipeline)
Pupukea Beach Park/
Shark's Cove
Waimea Bay
Beach Park
Kahuku
Laie
Hauula
Punaluu
Kahana Bay Beach Park
Kaaawa
Kualoa Park
Puu
Kaaumakua
KOOLAU MOUNTAINS
Kahaluu
Kaneohe Bay
Marine Corps Base
MOKAPU PT.
MOKAPU
PENINSULA
Kaneohe Bay
Kaneohe
Kailua Bay
Kailua
Kailua Beach Park
Lanikai Beach Park
Bellows Air Force Base
Bellows Beach Park
Waimanalo Beach Park
Mt.
Olomana
Waimanalo
Puu Lanipo
Kaau Crater
Makapuu Beach Park
Sandy Beach Park
Koko
Crater
Hawaii Kai
Hanauma Bay
Nature Preserve
Maunalua
Bay
KOKO
HEAD
Sans Souci/Kalmana Beach
DIAMOND HEAD
Waikiki
HONOLULU
Ala Moana
Beach Park
For Waikiki Beaches
see Waikiki map
Honolulu
International
Airport
Pearl Harbor
Naval Base
Mamala
Bay
Pearl
Harbor
Aiea
Trans Koolau Tunnel
Wilson Tunnel
Haleiwa Alii
Beach Park
Waialua Bay
Haleiwa
Mokuleia Beach Park
KAENA
POINT
Yokobama Bay
WAIANAE MOUNTAINS
Kaala
Wahiawa
Mililani
Town
Makaha Beach Park
Makaha
Waianae
Maili
Palikea
Puu
Manawahua
Nanakuli
Ewa
Kapolei
Ko Olina
White Plains
Beach Park
0 5 mi
0 5 km
83
930
803
80
99
750
76
93
830
63
61
78
72
H1
H2
H3

and Spa. **Amenities:** food and drink; parking (fee); showers; toilets. **Best for:** sunset; walking. ✉ *2005 Kalia Rd., Waikiki.*

FAMILY Fodor's Choice ★ **Fort DeRussy Beach Park.** This is one of the finest beaches on the south side of Oahu. A wide, soft, ultrawhite beachfront with gently lapping waves makes it a family favorite for running-jumping-frolicking fun. The new, heavily shaded grass grilling area, sand volleyball courts, and aquatic rentals make this a must for the active visitor. The beach fronts Hale Koa Hotel as well as Fort DeRussy. **Amenities:** food and drink; lifeguards; showers; toilets; water sports. **Best for:** swimming; walking. ✉ *2161 Kalia Rd., Waikiki.*

Kahaloa and Ulukou Beaches. The beach widens back out here, creating the "it" spot for the bikini crowd—beautiful bodies abound. This is where you find most of the catamaran charters for a spectacular sail out to Diamond Head, or surfboard and outrigger canoe rentals for a ride on the rolling waves of the Canoe surf break. Great music and outdoor dancing beckon the sand-bound visitor to Duke's Canoe Club, where shirt and shoes not only aren't required, they're discouraged. The Royal Hawaiian Hotel and the Moana Surfrider are both on this beach. **Amenities:** food and drink; lifeguards; parking (fee); showers; toilets; water sports. **Best for:** partiers; surfing. ✉ *2259 Kalakaua Ave., Waikiki.*

FAMILY **Kuhio Beach Park.** This beach has experienced a renaissance after a recent face-lift. Now bordered by a landscaped boardwalk, it's great for romantic walks any time of day. Check out the Kuhio Beach hula mound Tuesday, Thursday, and Saturday at 6:30 (at 6 November–January) for free hula and Hawaiian-music performances and a torch-lighting ceremony at sunset. Surf lessons for beginners are available from the beach center every half hour. **Amenities:** food and drink; lifeguards; showers; toilets; water sports. **Best for:** surfing; walking. ✉ *2461 Kalakaua Ave., Waikiki* ✣ *Go past Moana Surfrider Hotel to Kapahulu Ave. pier.*

FAMILY **Queen's Surf Beach.** So named as it was once the site of Queen Liliuokalani's beach house, this beach draws a mix of families and gay couples—and it seems as if someone is always playing a steel drum. There are banyan trees for shade and volleyball nets for pros and amateurs alike. The water fronting Queen's Surf is an aquatic preserve, providing the best snorkeling in Waikiki. **Amenities:** lifeguards; showers; toilets. **Best for:** swimming; walking. ✉ *2598 Kalakaua Ave., Waikiki* ✣ *Across from the entrance to Honolulu Zoo.*

FAMILY **Sans Souci/Kaimana Beach.** Nicknamed Dig-Me Beach because of its outlandish display of skimpy bathing suits, this small rectangle of sand is nonetheless a good sunning spot for all ages. Children enjoy its shallow, safe waters, which are protected (for now) by the walls of the historic natatorium, an Olympic-size saltwater swimming arena that's been closed for decades. Serious swimmers and triathletes also swim in the channel here, beyond the reef. Sans Souci is favored by locals wanting to avoid the crowds while still enjoying the convenience of Waikiki. The New Otani Kaimana Beach Hotel is next door. **Amenities:** lifeguards; parking (fee); showers; toilets. **Best for:** swimming; walking. ✉ 2776

DID YOU KNOW?

Waikiki Beach stretches from Hilton Hawaiian Village to Kapiolani Park and Diamond Head, and if you surf here you'll be hanging 10 with the best of 'em.

Kalakaua Ave., Waikiki ⊕ Across from Kapiolani Park, between New Otani Kaimana Beach Hotel and Waikiki War Memorial Natatorium.

ALA MOANA

Honolulu proper only has one beach: Ala Moana. Popular with locals, it hosts everything from Dragon Boat competitions to the Aloha State Games.

FAMILY **Ala Moana Beach Park.** A protective reef makes Ala Moana essentially a ½-mile-wide saltwater swimming pool. Very smooth sand and no waves create a haven for families and stand-up paddle surfers. After Waikiki, this is the most popular beach among visitors, and the free parking area can fill up quickly on sunny weekend days. On the Waikiki side is a peninsula called Magic Island, with shady trees and paved sidewalks ideal for jogging. Ala Moana also has playing fields, tennis courts, and a couple of small ponds for sailing toy boats. This beach is for everyone, but only in the daytime; it's a high-crime area, with lots of homeless people, after dark. **Amenities:** food and drink; lifeguards; parking (fee); showers; toilets. **Best for:** swimming; walking. ✉ *1201 Ala Moana Blvd., Ala Moana ⊕ From Waikiki take Bus No. 8 to Ala Moana Shopping Center and cross Ala Moana Blvd.*

SOUTHEAST OAHU

Much of Southeast Oahu is surrounded by reef, making most of the coast uninviting to swimmers, but the spots where the reef opens up are true gems. The drive along this side of the island is amazing, with its sheer lava-rock walls on one side and deep-blue ocean on the other. There are plenty of restaurants in the suburb of Hawaii Kai, so you can make a day of it, knowing that food isn't far away.

FAMILY Fodor's Choice ★ **Hanauma Bay Nature Preserve.** Picture this as the world's biggest open-air aquarium. You go here to see fish, and fish you'll see. Due to their exposure to thousands of visitors every week, these fish are more like family pets than the skittish marine life you might expect. An old volcanic crater has created a haven from the waves where the coral has thrived. There's an educational center where you must watch a nine-minute video about the nature preserve before being allowed down to the bay. ■ **TIP→ The bay is best early in the morning (around 7), before the crowds arrive; it can be difficult to park later in the day.**

Snorkel equipment and lockers are available for rent, and there's an entry fee for nonresidents. Smoking is not allowed, and the beach is closed on Tuesday. Wednesday to Monday, the beach is open 6 am–6 pm (until 7 pm June–August). There's a tram from the parking lot to the beach, or you can walk the short distance on foot. Need transportation? Take TheBus each way from anywhere on the island. Alternatively, Hanauma Bay Snorkeling Excursions runs snorkeling tours to Hanauma Bay, with equipment and transportation from Waikiki hotels. **Amenities:** food and drink; lifeguards; parking (fee); showers; toilets. **Best for:** snorkeling; swimming. ✉ *7455 Kalanianaole Hwy., Hawaii Kai* ☎ *808/396–4229* 🌐 *www.honolulu.gov/cms-dpr-menu/site-dpr-sitearticles/1716-hanauma-bay-home.html* 🎫 *Nonresidents $7.50;*

parking $1; mask and snorkel $12, with fins $20; tram from parking lot to beach $2.25 round-trip.

Sandy Beach Park. Probably the most popular beach with locals on this side of Oahu, the broad, sloping beach is covered with sunbathers there to watch the "Show" and soak up rays. The Show is a shore break that's like no other in the Islands. Monster ocean swells rolling into the beach combined with the sudden rise in the ocean floor causes waves to jack up and crash magnificently on the shore. Expert surfers and body boarders young and old brave this danger to get some of the biggest barrels you can find for bodysurfing. ⚠ **But keep in mind that the beach is nicknamed Break-Neck Beach for a reason: many neck and back injuries are sustained here each year.** Use extreme caution when swimming here, or just kick back and watch the drama unfold from the comfort of your beach chair. **Amenities:** lifeguards; parking (no fee); showers; toilets. **Best for:** body boarding; walking. ✉ *7850 Kalanianaole Hwy., Hawaii Kai* ⊕ *Makai (toward ocean) of Kalanianaole Hwy., 2 miles east of Hanauma Bay.*

2

WINDWARD OAHU

The windward side lives up to its name, with ideal spots for windsurfing and kiteboarding, or for the more intrepid, hang gliding. For the most part the waves are mellow, and the bottoms are all sand—making for nice spots to visit with younger kids. The only drawback is that this side of Oahu does tend to get more rain. But the vistas are so beautiful that a little sprinkling of "pineapple juice" shouldn't dampen your experience; plus, it benefits the waterfalls that cascade down the Koolaus.

Fodor's Choice ★ **Bellows Beach Park.** Bellows is the same beach as Waimanalo, but it's under the auspices of the military, making it more friendly for visitors—though that also limits public beach access to weekends. The park area is excellent for camping, and ironwood trees provide plenty of shade. **■ TIP→ The beach is best before 2 pm. After 2, trade winds bring clouds that get hung up on steep mountains nearby, causing overcast skies.** There are no food concessions, but McDonald's and other take-out fare are right outside the entrance gate. **Amenities:** lifeguards; parking (no fee); showers; toilets. **Best for:** solitude; walking; swimming. ✉ *520 Tinker Rd., Waimanalo* ⊕ *Enter on Kalanianaole Hwy. near Waimanalo town center.*

FAMILY **Kahana Bay Beach Park.** Local parents often bring their children here to wade in safety in the very shallow, protected waters. This pretty beach cove, surrounded by mountains, has a long arc of sand that is great for walking and a cool, shady grove of tall ironwood and pandanus trees that is ideal for a picnic. An ancient Hawaiian fishpond, which was in use until the 1920s, is visible nearby. The water here is not generally a clear blue due to the runoff from heavy rains in the valley. **Amenities:** parking (no fee); showers; toilets. **Best for:** swimming; walking. ✉ *52-201 Kamehameha Hwy., Kaneohe* ⊕ *North of Kualoa Park.*

FAMILY Fodor's Choice ★ **Kailua Beach Park.** A cobalt-blue sea and a wide continuous arc of powdery sand make Kailua Beach Park one of the island's best beaches, illustrated by the crowds of local families who spend their weekend days

For a hopping scene with everything from surfing to volleyball, head to Waikiki Beach.

here. This is like a big Lanikai Beach, but a little windier and a little wider, and a better spot for spending a full day. Kailua Beach has calm water, a line of palms and ironwoods that provide shade on the sand, and a huge park with picnic pavilions where you can escape the heat. This is the "it" spot if you're looking to try your hand at windsurfing or kiteboarding. You can rent kayaks nearby at Kailua Beach Adventures (130 Kailua Rd.) and take them to the Mokulua Islands for the day. **Amenities:** lifeguards; parking (no fee); showers; toilets; water sports. **Best for:** walking; swimming; windsurfing. ✉ *437 Kawailoa Rd., Kailua* ⊕ *Near Kailua town, turn right on Kailua Rd. After the market, cross bridge, then turn left into beach parking lot.*

Kualoa Park. Grassy expanses border a long, narrow stretch of beach with spectacular views of Kaneohe Bay and the Koolau Mountains, making Kualoa one of the island's most beautiful picnic, camping, and beach areas. Dominating the view is an islet called Mokolii, better known as Chinaman's Hat, which rises 206 feet above the water. You can swim in the shallow areas of this rarely crowded beach year-round. The one drawback is that it's usually windy here, but the wide-open spaces are ideal for kite flying. **Amenities:** lifeguards; showers; toilets. **Best for:** solitude; swimming. ✉ *49-479 Kamehameha Hwy., Kaaawa* ⊕ *North of Waiahole.*

Lanikai Beach Park. Think of the beaches you see in commercials: peaceful jade-green waters, powder-soft white sand, families and dogs frolicking mindlessly, and offshore islands in the distance. It's an ideal spot for camping out with a book. Though the beach hides behind multimillion-dollar houses, by state law there is public access every 400 yards. Street parking is available but difficult to find (and prohibited on holiday weekends. ■ TIP→ **Look for walled or fenced pathways every 400 yards, leading to the beach. Be sure not to park in the marked bike/jogging lane**. There are no shower or bathroom facilities here—but you'll find both a two-minute drive away at Kailua Beach Park. **Amenities:** none. **Best for:** swimming; walking; sunrise. ✉ *974 Mokulua Dr., Kailua* ✥ *Past Kailua Beach Park.*

Makapuu Beach Park. A magnificent beach protected by Makapuu Point welcomes you to the windward side. Hang gliders circle above the beach, and the water is filled with body boarders. Just off the coast you can see Bird Island, a sanctuary for aquatic fowl, jutting out of the blue. The currents can be heavy, so check with a lifeguard if you're unsure of safety. Before you leave, take the prettiest (and coldest) outdoor shower available on the island. Being surrounded by tropical flowers and foliage while you rinse off that sand will be a memory you will cherish from this side of the rock. **Amenities:** lifeguards; parking (no fee); showers; toilets. **Best for:** sunrise; walking. ✉ *41-095 Kalanianaole Hwy., Waimanalo* ✥ *Across from Sea Life Park, 2 miles south of Waimanalo.*

FAMILY **Waimanalo Beach Park.** One of the most beautiful beaches on the island, Waimanalo is a local pick, busy with picnicking families and active sports fields. Expect a wide stretch of sand; turquoise, emerald, and deep blue seas; and gentle shore-breaking waves that are fun for all ages. Theft is an occasional problem, so lock your car. **Amenities:** lifeguards; parking (no fee); showers; toilets. **Best for:** sunrise; swimming; walking. ✉ *41-849 Kalanianaole Hwy., Waimanalo* ✥ *South of Waimanalo town center.*

THE NORTH SHORE

"North Shore, where the waves are mean, just like a washing machine," sing the Kaau Crater Boys about this legendary side of the island. And in winter they are absolutely right. At times the waves overtake the road, stranding tourists and locals alike. When the surf is up, there are signs on the beach telling you how far to stay back so that you aren't swept out to sea. The most prestigious big-wave contest in the world, the Eddie Aikau, is held at Waimea Bay on waves the size of a five- or six-story building. The Triple Crown of Surfing roams across three North Shore beaches in the winter months.

All this changes come summer when this tiger turns into a kitten, with water smooth enough to water-ski on and ideal for snorkeling. The fierce Banzai Pipeline surf break becomes a great dive area, allowing you to explore the coral heads that, in winter, have claimed so many lives on the ultrashallow but big, hollow tubes created here. Even with the monster surf subsided, this is still a time for caution: lifeguards are scarce, and currents don't subside just because the waves do.

That said, it's a place like no other on Earth, and must be explored. From the turtles at Mokuleia to the tunnels at Shark's Cove, you could spend your whole trip on this side and not be disappointed.

Ehukai Beach Park. What sets Ehukai apart is the view of the famous Banzai Pipeline. Here the winter waves curl into magnificent tubes, making it an experienced wave-rider's dream. It's also an inexperienced swimmer's nightmare. Spring and summer waves on the other hand are more accommodating to the average person, and there's good snorkeling. Except when the surf contests are going on, there's no reason to stay on the central strip. Travel in either direction from the center, and the conditions remain the same but the population thins out, leaving you with a magnificent stretch of sand all to yourself. **Amenities:** lifeguards; parking (no fee); showers; toilets. **Best for:** snorkeling; surfing. ✉ *59-406 Kamehameha Hwy., Haleiwa* ⊕ *1 mile north of Foodland at Pupukea.*

FAMILY **Haleiwa Alii Beach Park.** The winter waves are impressive here, but in summer the ocean is like a lake, ideal for family swimming. The beach itself is big and often full of locals. Its broad lawn off the highway invites volleyball and Frisbee games and groups of barbecuers. This is also the opening break for the Triple Crown of Surfing, and the grass is often filled with art festivals or carnivals. **Amenities:** lifeguards; parking (no fee); showers; toilets. **Best for:** surfing; swimming. ✉ *66-162 Haleiwa Rd., Haleiwa* ⊕ *North of Haleiwa town center and past harbor.*

Mokuleia Beach Park. There is a reason why the producers of the TV show *Lost* chose this beach for their set. On the remote northwest point of the island, it is about 10 miles from the closest store or public restroom. Its beauty is in its lack of facilities and isolation—all the joy of being stranded on a deserted island without the trauma of the plane crash. The beach is wide and white, the waters bright blue (but a little choppy) and full of sea turtles and other marine life. Mokuleia is a great secret find; just remember to pack supplies and use caution, as there are no lifeguards. **Amenities:** parking (no fee). **Best for:** walking, sunset. ✉ *68-67 Farrington Hwy., Haleiwa* ⊕ *West of Haleiwa town center, across from Dillingham Airfield.*

Fodor's Choice ★ **Pupukea Beach Park/Shark's Cove.** Surrounded by shady trees, Pupukea Beach Park is pounded by surf in the winter months but offers great diving and snorkeling in summer (March through October). The cavernous lava tubes and tunnels are great for both novice and experienced snorkelers and divers. It's imperative that you wear reef shoes at all times since there are a lot of sharp rocks. Sharp rocks also mean that this beach isn't the best for little ones. Some dive-tour companies offer round-trip transportation from Waikiki. Equipment rentals and dining options are nearby. **Amenities:** parking (no fee); showers; toilets. **Best for:** diving; snorkeling; swimming. ✉ *Haleiwa* ⊕ *3.5 miles north of Haleiwa, across the street from Foodland.*

Sunset Beach Neighborhood Park. The beach is broad, the sand is soft, the summer waves are gentle—making for good snorkeling—and the winter surf is crashing. Many love searching this shore for the puka shells that adorn the necklaces you see everywhere. **Amenities:** lifeguards; parking (no fee); showers; toilets. **Best for:** snorkeling; sunset; surfing. ✉ *59 Kamehameha Hwy., Haleiwa* ⊕ *1 mile north of Ehukai Beach Park.*

DID YOU KNOW?

Windward Oahu's Makapuu Beach is protected by Makapuu Point, but currents are still strong so take caution when in the water.

FAMILY **Turtle Bay.** Now known more for its resort (the Turtle Bay Resort) than its magnificent beach, Turtle Bay is mostly passed over on the way to the better-known beaches of Sunset and Waimea. But for the average visitor with average swimming capabilities, this is a good place to be on the North Shore. The crescent-shaped beach is protected by a huge sea wall. You can see and hear the fury of the northern swell while blissfully floating in cool, calm waters. The convenience of this spot is also hard to pass up—there is a concession selling sandwiches and sunblock right on the beach. The resort has free parking for beach guests. **Amenities:** food and drink; parking (no fee); showers; toilets. **Best for:** sunset; swimming. ✉ *57-20 Kuilima Dr., 4 miles north of Kahuku, Kahuku* ✥ *Turn into Turtle Bay Resort, and let guard know where you are going.*

Fodor's Choice ★ **Waimea Bay Beach Park.** Made popular in that old Beach Boys song "Surfin' U.S.A.," Waimea Bay Beach Park is a slice of big-wave heaven, home to king-size 25- to 30-foot winter waves. Summer is the time to swim and snorkel in the calm waters. The shore break is great for novice bodysurfers. Due to its popularity, the postage-stamp parking lot is quickly filled, but it's also possible to park along the side of the road and walk in. **Amenities:** lifeguards; parking (no fee); showers; toilets. **Best for:** snorkeling (in summer); surfing (in winter); swimming (in summer). ✉ *61-31 Kamehameha Hwy., Haleiwa* ✥ *Across from Waimea Valley, 3 miles north of Haleiwa.*

WEST (LEEWARD) OAHU

The North Shore may be known as "country," but the west side is truly the rural area on Oahu. There are commuters from this side to Honolulu, but many are born, live, and die on this side with scarcely a trip to town. For the most part, there's little hostility toward outsiders, but occasional problems have flared up, mostly due to drug abuse, which has ravaged the fringes of the island—generally on the order of car break-ins, not violence. So, in short, lock your car, don't bring valuables, and enjoy the amazing beaches.

The beaches on the west side are expansive and empty. Most Oahu residents and tourists don't make it to this side simply because of the drive; in traffic it can take almost 90 minutes to make it to Kaena Point from downtown Honolulu. But you'll be hard-pressed to find a better sunset anywhere.

FAMILY **Ko Olina.** This is the best spot on the island if you have small kids. The resort area commissioned a series of four man-made lagoons, but, as it has to provide public beach access, you are the winner. Huge rock walls protect the lagoons, making them into perfect spots for the kids to get their first taste of the ocean without getting bowled over. The large expanses of seashore grass and hala trees that surround the semicircle beaches are made-to-order for nap time. A 1½-mile jogging track connects the lagoons. Due to its appeal for *keiki* (children), Ko Olina is popular, and the parking lot fills up quickly when school is out and on weekends, so try to get here before 10 am. The biggest parking lot is at the farthest lagoon from the entrance. There are actually three resorts here: Aulani (the Disney resort), Four Seasons Resort Oahu, and the Ko Olina Beach Villas Resort (which has a time-share section as well). **Amenities:** food and drink; parking (no fee); showers; toilet. **Best for:** sunset; swimming; walking. ✉ *92 Aliinui Dr., 23 miles west of Honolulu, Kapolei ⊕ Take Ko Olina exit off H1 West and proceed to guard shack.*

Makaha Beach Park. This beach provides a slice of local life most visitors don't see. Families string up tarps for the day, fire up hibachis, set up lawn chairs, get out the fishing gear, and strum ukulele while they "talk story" (chat). Legendary waterman Buffalo Keaulana can be found in the shade of the palms playing with his grandkids and spinning yarns of yesteryear. In these waters Buffalo not only invented some of the most outrageous methods of surfing, but also raised his world-champion son Rusty. He also made Makaha the home of the world's first international surf meet in 1954 and still hosts his Big Board Surfing Classic. With its long, slow-building waves, it's a great spot to try out longboarding. The swimming is generally decent in summer, but avoid the big winter waves. The only parking is along the highway, but it's free. **Amenities:** lifeguards; showers; toilets. **Best for:** surfing; swimming. ✉ *84-450 Farrington Hwy., Waianae ⊕ Go 32 miles west of Honolulu on the H1, then exit onto Farrington Hwy. The beach will be on your left.*

FAMILY Fodor's Choice ★ **White Plains Beach Park.** Concealed from the public eye for many years as part of the former Barbers Point Naval Air Station, this beach is reminiscent of Waikiki but without the condos and the crowds. It is a long, sloping beach with numerous surf breaks, but it is also mild enough at shore for older children to play freely. It has views of Pearl Harbor and, over that, Diamond Head. Although the sand lives up to its name, the real joy of this beach comes from its history as part of a military property for the better part of a century. Expansive parking, great restroom facilities, and numerous tree-covered barbecue areas make it a great day-trip spot. As a bonus, a Hawaiian monk seal takes up residence here several months out of the year (seals are rare in the Islands). **Amenities:** lifeguards; parking (no fee); showers; toilets. **Best for:** surfing; swimming. ✉ *Essex Rd. and Tripoli Rd., Kapolei ⊕ Take Makakilo exit off H1 West, then turn left. Follow it into base gates, make left. Blue signs lead to beach.*

WHERE TO EAT

Updated by Powell Berger

Oahu is undergoing something of a renaissance at both ends of the dining spectrum. You can splurge on world-class contemporary cuisine at destination restaurants and explore local flavors at popular, very affordable holes in the wall. Whatever your taste and budget, you'll find places that pique your interest and palate.

You may wish to budget for a pricey dining experience at the very top of the restaurant food chain, where chefs Alan Wong, Roy Yamaguchi, George Mavrothalassitis, Chris Kajioka, and others you've seen on the Food Network and Travel Channel put a sophisticated spin on local foods and flavors. Savor dishes that take cues from Japan, China, Korea, the Philippines, the United States, and Europe, then are filtered through an Island sensibility. Take advantage of the location and order the superb local fish—mahimahi, opakaka, ono, and opah.

Spend the rest of your food dollars where budget-conscious locals do: in plate-lunch places and small ethnic eateries, at roadside stands and lunch wagons, or at window-in-the-wall delis. Snack on a *musubi* (a handheld rice ball wrapped with seaweed and often topped with Spam), slurp shave ice with red-bean paste, or order Filipino pork adobo with two scoops of rice and macaroni salad.

In Waikiki, where most visitors stay, you can find choices from upscale dining rooms with a view to Japanese noodle shops. When you're ready to explore, hop in the car, or on the trolley or bus—by going just a few miles in any direction, you can save money and eat like a local.

Kaimuki's Waialae Avenue, for example, is a critical mass of good eats and drinks. There you'll find an espresso bar, a Chinese bakery, a patisserie, an Italian bistro, a dim-sum restaurant, Mexican food, and a Hawaiian regional-cuisine standout (3660 on the Rise)—all in three blocks, and 10 minutes from Waikiki. Chinatown, 15 minutes in the other direction and easily reached by the Waikiki Trolley, is another dining (and shopping) treasure, not only for Chinese but also Vietnamese, Filipino, Malaysian, and Indian food, and even a chic little tea shop. Kakaako, the developing urban area between Waikiki and Chinatown, also offers a mix of local eateries, upscale restaurants, and ethnic takeout.

Outside Honolulu and Waikiki there are fewer dining options, but restaurants tend to be filled with locals and are cheaper and more casual. Windward Oahu's dining scene has improved greatly in recent years due to the visitors to Kailua and Lanikai beaches, so everything from plate lunches to Latin foods to creative regional offerings can be found there. Across the rest of the island, the cuisine is mainly American—great if you're traveling with kids—but there are a handful of Italian and Asian places worth trying as well.

HONOLULU

There's no lack of choices when it comes to dining in Honolulu, where everything from the haute cuisine of heavy-hitting top-notch chefs to a wide variety of Asian specialties to reliable and inexpensive American favorites can be found.

WAIKIKI

As Honolulu's tourist hub, Waikiki is dense with restaurants. There are notable steak houses and grills in Waikiki as well, serving upscale American cuisine. But thanks to the many Japanese nationals who stay here, Waikiki is blessed with lots of cheap, filling, authentic Japanese food, particularly noodle houses. Plastic representations of food in the window outside are an indicator of authenticity and a help in ordering. It's not uncommon for a server to accompany a guest outside so that the selection can be pointed to.

$$$$ STEAKHOUSE ✕ **dk Steak House.** Honolulu has its share of national-chain steak houses, but D.K. Kodama's local steak house serves steaks free from hormones,

antibiotics, and steroids straight from Oahu's first dry-aging room. **Known for:** addictive potatoes au gratin topped with Maui onions and Parmesan; local flavors, local ownership, and locally sourced produce and select meats; sunset views from outdoor tables. *Average main: $55 Waikiki Beach Marriott Resort & Spa, 2552 Kalakaua Ave., Waikiki 808/931–6280 www.dksteakhouse.com No lunch.*

$$$ AMERICAN FAMILY **Duke's Waikiki.** Locals often take visiting friends and family from the mainland to this popular open-air hotel restaurant for the beachfront setting—it's right in front of the famed Canoes surf break in Waikiki—and bar scene and *pupu* (hors d'oeuvres) more than the food. Named for the father of modern surfing and filled with Duke Kahanamoku memorabilia, it's got a great salad bar and a crowd-pleasing menu that includes fish, prime rib, and *huli huli* (rotisserie). **Known for:** iconic local spot with great views, great bar scene, and perfect location in Waikiki; Duke's on Sunday is so popular musician Henry Kapono wrote a song about it (Duke's on Sunday); bar seating for better service and better prices. *Average main: $28 Outrigger Waikiki on the Beach, 2335 Kalakaua Ave., Waikiki 808/922–2268 www.dukeswaikiki.com.*

$$$$ AMERICAN **Hau Tree Lanai.** Countless anniversaries, birthdays, and family milestones have been celebrated under this spectacular *hau* tree, where it's said that even Robert Louis Stevenson found shade as he mused and wrote about Hawaii. Still today, diners are captivated by the shade, the beach views, the romantic setting, and a menu that delivers everything from eggs Benedict to a sizzling steak. **Known for:** the romantic beach dining spot folks dream about; spectacular views of the beach and water by day and by night; a solid menu, big portions, and attentive service. *Average main: $48 New Otani Kaimana Beach Hotel, 2863 Kalakaua Ave., Waikiki 808/921–7066 www.kaimana.com/hautreelanai.htm.*

$$$$ FRENCH **La Mer.** Looking out on its namesake, La Mer is the most romantic dining room on Oahu, with carved wooden screens setting an elegant art deco–ish tone. The window tables—and most of the restaurant's tables are windowside or very close—open to the fresh air, and sounds of the beach just below are sufficiently captivating that guests often forgive the tired classic haute-cuisine French food. **Known for:** it doesn't get more romantic than this; an impressive wine list and a sommelier to match; a classy bar scene that includes the romance at a less staggering price. *Average main: $142 Halekulani, 2199 Kalia Rd., Waikiki 808/923–2311 www.halekulani.com/living/dining/la_mer No lunch Jacket required.*

$$$$ FRENCH **Michel's at the Colony Surf.** Often called Waikiki's most romantic spot, Michel's is an old-school French favorite on Waikiki's tranquil Gold Coast, where you pay for a spectacular beachside sunset view and classic French fare. Opened in 1962, the place retains a *Mad Men* feel, with lots of wood and stone and bow-tied servers preparing things like steak tartare tableside. **Known for:** the sound of the surf and the intoxicating smell of the islands; classic French cuisine with some local twists; a vibe that steps back in time, in all the right ways. *Average main: $55 Colony Surf, 2895 Kalakaua Ave., Waikiki 808/923–6552 michelshawaii.com No lunch.*

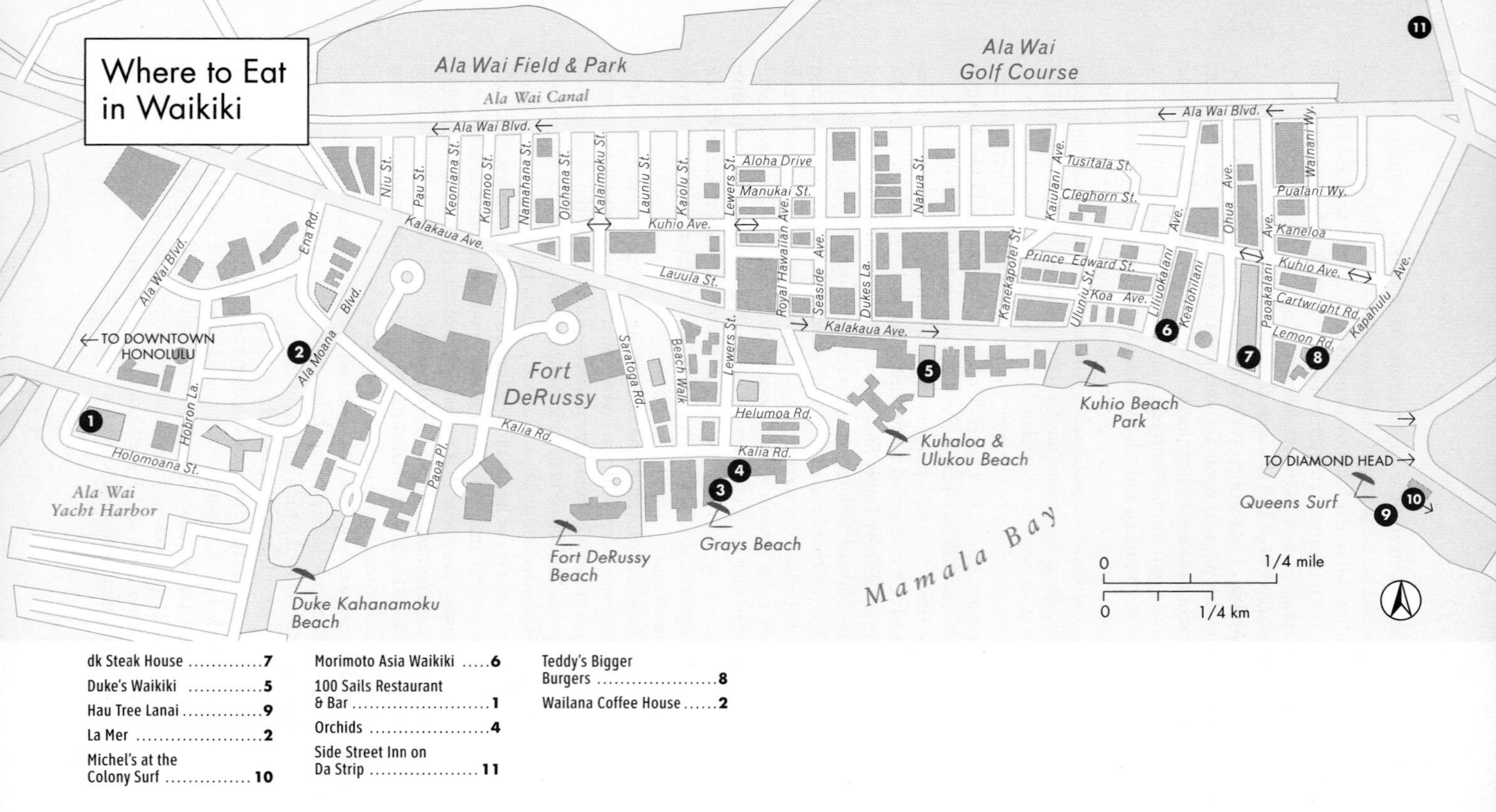

dk Steak House 7
Duke's Waikiki 5
Hau Tree Lanai 9
La Mer 2
Michel's at the Colony Surf 10
Morimoto Asia Waikiki 6
100 Sails Restaurant & Bar 1
Orchids 4
Side Street Inn on Da Strip 11
Teddy's Bigger Burgers 8
Wailana Coffee House 2

$$$$ JAPANESE ✕ **Morimoto Asia Waikiki.** Locals were surprised when chef Masahara Morimoto vacated the Modern for new digs at the renovated and rebranded Alohilani Resort (formerly the Pacific Beach hotel), but loyalists have not been disappointed. The sleek space includes an open-air lanai and gorgeous bar, as well as a dining room designed for entertaining clients or celebrating with friends. **Known for:** attentive service and great food; casual elegance in a lovely spot in Waikiki; new menu with enough to draw loyalists. *Average main: $41 ✉ Alohilani Resort, 2490 Kalakaua Ave., Waikiki ☎ 808/922–0022 🌐 www.morimotoasiawaikiki.com.*

$$$$ ECLECTIC ✕ **100 Sails Restaurant & Bar.** With the top-to-bottom renovations of the Prince Hotel, the former Prince Court (known for its buffet and views) has become the 100 Sails, a new take with the same commitment to great food and great views. Slightly more casual than its predecessor, 100 Sails continues the everything-you-can-imagine buffet tradition (with crab legs and prime rib of course) along with à la carte "small bites." But the chef never loses focus on locally sourced ingredients and knock-out presentation. **Known for:** international buffet for every meal; views and sunsets to rival any other Waikiki location; free valet parking at the hotel. *Average main: $58 ✉ Hawaii Prince Hotel Waikiki, 100 Holomoana St., Waikiki ☎ 808/944–4494 🌐 www.princewaikiki.com/dining/honolulu-american-restaurant/.*

$$$$ SEAFOOD ✕ **Orchids.** Perched along the seawall at historic Gray's Beach, Orchids in the luxe Halekulani resort is open all day—it's a locus of power breakfasters, ladies who lunch, celebrating families at the over-the-top Sunday brunch, and the gamut at dinner. The louvered walls are open to the breezes, sprays of orchids add color, the seafood is perfectly prepared, and the wine list is intriguing. **Known for:** island breezes, ocean sounds, and five-star service and food; great service and even better food; a menu with something for just about everyone. *Average main: $42 ✉ Halekulani, 2199 Kalia Rd., Waikiki ☎ 808/923–2311 🌐 www.halekulani.com/dining/orchids-restaurant.*

$$ ECLECTIC FAMILY ✕ **Side Street Inn on Da Strip.** The original Hopaka Street pub is famous as the place where celebrity chefs gather after hours; this second location is on bustling Kapahulu Avenue, closer to Waikiki. Local-style bar food—salty panfried pork chops with a plastic tub of ketchup; lup cheong fried rice; and passion fruit–glazed ribs—comes in huge, shareable portions. **Known for:** portions that can seemingly feed you for a week; regulars have reserved seats at the bar; diner feel with really good food. *Average main: $20 ✉ 614 Kapahulu Ave., Waikiki ☎ 808/739–3939 🌐 www.sidestreetinn.com ⏲ No lunch.*

$ BURGER ✕ **Teddy's Bigger Burgers.** Modeled after 1950s diners, this local franchise serves classic moist and messy burgers, along with turkey and veggie burgers, as well as chicken breast and fish sandwiches. The fries are crisply perfect, the shakes rich and sweet. **Known for:** messy burgers, great fries, and rich milk shakes; diner-style service, with food to go; dependable quick lunch across the island. *Average main: $11 ✉ Waikiki Grand Hotel, 134 Kapahulu Ave., Waikiki ☎ 808/926–3444 🌐 www.teddysbb.com.*

A typical Hawaiian "plate lunch" usually includes meat along with one scoop of rice and another of macaroni salad.

$ AMERICAN **Wailana Coffee House.** Plenty of local gossip, drama, family feuds, and stories fill the history of Wailana Coffee House, a staple in Honolulu since 1969. Budget-conscious snowbirds, night owls with a yen for karaoke, all-day drinkers of both coffee and the stronger stuff, hearty eaters, and post-clubbing club kids all crowd this venerable, family-run diner and cocktail lounge—which recently underwent a renovation of the dining room and kitchen—at the edge of Waikiki. **Known for:** never changing; always open 24/7/365; karaoke bar and stiff cocktails. *Average main: $12* *1860 Ala Moana Blvd., at Ena Rd., Waikiki* *808/955–1764.*

DOWNTOWN

$ VIETNAMESE **Bac Nam.** Tam and Kimmy Huynh's menu is much more extensive than most, ranging far beyond the usual pho and *bun* (cold noodle dishes) found at many Vietnamese restaurants. Lamb curry, tapioca dumplings, tamarind head-on shrimp, an extraordinary crab noodle soup, and other dishes hail from North and South Vietnam. **Known for:** favorite of neighborhood workers; free parking behind the restaurant; no frills hole-in-the-wall. *Average main: $12* *1117 S. King St., Ala Moana* *808/597–8201.*

$$ AMERICAN **Honolulu Museum of Art Café.** The Honolulu Museum of Art's cool courtyards and galleries filled with works by masters from Monet to Hokusai are well worth a visit and, afterward, so is this popular lunch restaurant. The open-air café is flanked by a burbling water feature and 8-foot-tall ceramic "dumplings" by artist Jun Kaneko—a tranquil setting in the shade of a 75-year-old monkeypod tree in which to eat your salade niçoise (featuring seared coriander-crusted ahi) or fork-tender

CLOSE UP

Honolulu's Food Trucks

Lunch wagons, or food trucks, as they are now known around the country, have been an island staple for plate lunches for decades. With the taco-truck craze and the emergence of social media, Oahu's fleet is growing like crazy. Some make it, some don't, but the variety and array of flavors make them hard to turn down.

You can check the trucks' locations and daily menus on Twitter or Instagram, or try a sampling from more than two-dozen vendors at the monthly Eat the Street food-truck rally. Visit 🌐 *www.eatthestreethawaii.com* for details. Also check out the assortment of trucks that gather for the monthly Honolulu Night Market in Kakaako, the free monthly outdoor film screenings at the iconic IBM building in Kakaako, and the assortment of food trucks that gather at the Wednesday-evening farmers' market at Blaisdell Center or the Saturday-morning market at Ward Village.

Here are some of our favorite lunch wagons:

Elena's (🌐 *www.elenasrestaurant.com*) is an extension of the popular, family-run Filipino restaurant in Waipahu. There are three trucks, in Campbell, Mililani, and the airport area. Try the AFRO, an adobo–fried rice omelet, or the famous *lechón* (roast pork with onions and tomatoes) special.

The Girls Who Bake Next Door (🌐 *www.thegirlswhobakenextdoor.com*) are just that—two friends who love to bake. Their cupcakes, cookies, and other sweet treats show up at events all over Honolulu.

Chubbie's Burgers Burgers and fries, every which way. Sometimes the staff even set up tables and chairs and play some music. 🌐 *www.chubbies-burgers.com*).

Sweet Revenge (🌐 *www.sweetrevengehonolulu.com*) serves up pies of all types, all in the individual size, and all for around $8. Everything from quiche to chicken potpie to s'mores pies and chocolate Twix pies.

filet mignon sandwich with dijon-caper relish. **Known for:** wonderfully chic setting; limited but beautifully prepared menu of soups, salads, sandwiches, and mains; nice spot for Sunday brunch. 💲 *Average main: $17* ✉ *Honolulu Museum of Art, 900 S. Beretania St., Downtown* ☎ *808/532–8734* 🌐 *www.honolulumuseum.org/394-museum_cafe* ⏲ *Closed Mon. No dinner.*

$$$ **JAPANESE** ✕ **Yanagi Sushi.** One of relatively few restaurants to serve the complete menu until 2 am (until 10 pm on Sunday), Yanagi is a full-service Japanese restaurant offering not only sushi and sashimi around a small bar, but also *teishoku* (combination menus), tempura, stews, and grill-it-yourself shabu-shabu. The fish can be depended on for freshness and variety. **Known for:** late hours, making it a favorite among night owls; well-priced combo dinners; a local favorite for sushi. 💲 *Average main: $28* ✉ *762 Kapiolani Blvd., Downtown* ☎ *808/597–1525* 🌐 *www.yanagisushi-hawaii.com.*

2

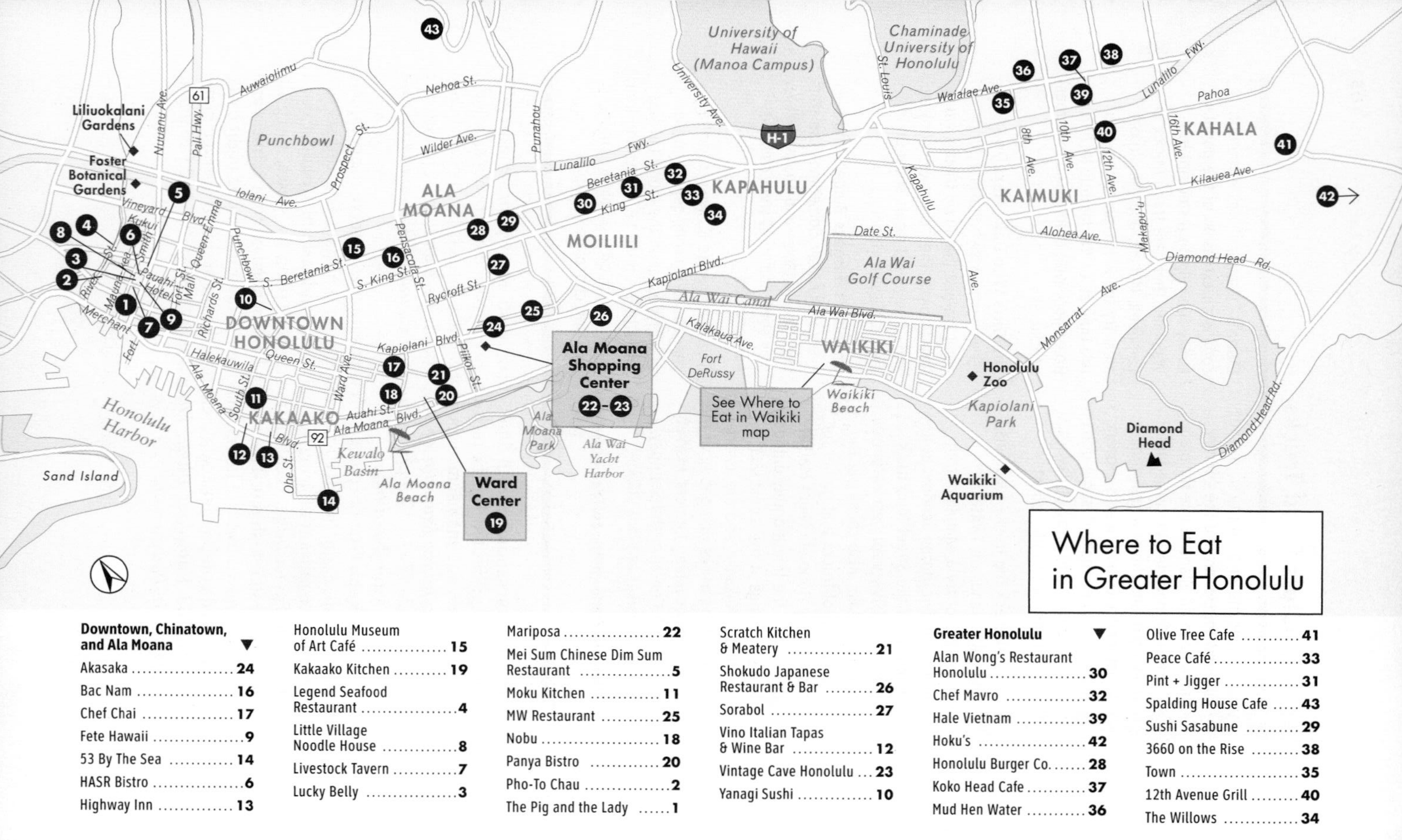

Downtown, Chinatown, and Ala Moana

- Akasaka ... **24**
- Bac Nam ... **16**
- Chef Chai ... **17**
- Fete Hawaii ... **9**
- 53 By The Sea ... **14**
- HASR Bistro ... **6**
- Highway Inn ... **13**
- Honolulu Museum of Art Café ... **15**
- Kakaako Kitchen ... **19**
- Legend Seafood Restaurant ... **4**
- Little Village Noodle House ... **8**
- Livestock Tavern ... **7**
- Lucky Belly ... **3**
- Mariposa ... **22**
- Mei Sum Chinese Dim Sum Restaurant ... **5**
- Moku Kitchen ... **11**
- MW Restaurant ... **25**
- Nobu ... **18**
- Panya Bistro ... **20**
- Pho-To Chau ... **2**
- The Pig and the Lady ... **1**
- Scratch Kitchen & Meatery ... **21**
- Shokudo Japanese Restaurant & Bar ... **26**
- Sorabol ... **27**
- Vino Italian Tapas & Wine Bar ... **12**
- Vintage Cave Honolulu ... **23**
- Yanagi Sushi ... **10**

Greater Honolulu

- Alan Wong's Restaurant Honolulu ... **30**
- Chef Mavro ... **32**
- Hale Vietnam ... **39**
- Hoku's ... **42**
- Honolulu Burger Co. ... **28**
- Koko Head Cafe ... **37**
- Mud Hen Water ... **36**
- Olive Tree Cafe ... **41**
- Peace Café ... **33**
- Pint + Jigger ... **31**
- Spalding House Cafe ... **43**
- Sushi Sasabune ... **29**
- 3660 on the Rise ... **38**
- Town ... **35**
- 12th Avenue Grill ... **40**
- The Willows ... **34**

CHINATOWN

$$ HAWAIIAN ✕ **Fete Hawaii.** Fete slipped into its cozy brick-walled space amid the Chinatown culinary boom in 2016, and it's been packing in regulars ever since. Folks come for the burgers and specials at lunch; for dinner, try one of the pastas, seafood, or to-die-for twice-fried chicken with grits and collard greens. **Known for:** tiny, chic space with a hipster vibe; twice-fried chicken that regulars swear by; craft cocktails and beer. *Average main: $23 ✉ 2 N. Hotel St., Chinatown ☎ 808/369–1390 🌐 fetehawaii.com.*

$$ BISTRO ✕ **HASR Bistro.** This country-style European bistro in the middle of bustling Chinatown brings a fun, playful attitude to fine dining ("HASR" stands for Highly Allocated Spoiled Rotten). Owner Terry Kakazu brings her wine expertise to the restaurant, while executive chef Rodney Uyehara adds his culinary flair to this quaint eatery with lunch sandwiches like the Crabby Melt (a tuna melt but with crab) and dinner specialities like cioppino and Kurobuta pork chop. **Known for:** bistro-style comfort food; live entertainment on weekends; small with lots of charm. *Average main: $25 ✉ 31 N. Pauahi St., Chinatown ☎ 808/533–4277 🌐 www.hasrbistro.com ⏲ Closed Sun. No lunch Mon.*

$ CHINESE ✕ **Legend Seafood Restaurant.** Use your best cab-hailing technique and sign language to make the cart ladies stop at your table and show you their fare at this large, loud Hong-Kong-style dim sum spot. The pork-filled steamed buns, spinach dumplings, taro-and-pork *gok* (bite-size fried balls), and still-warm custard tarts are excellent pre-shopping fortification. **Known for:** loud and chaotic atmosphere (and that's the fun); dim sum that draws in both locals and visitors; breakfast before a busy day. *Average main: $13 ✉ Chinese Cultural Plaza, 100 N. Beretania St., Suite 108, Chinatown ☎ 808/532–1868 🌐 www.legendseafoodhonolulu.com.*

$$ CHINESE ✕ **Little Village Noodle House.** Unassuming and budget-friendly, Little Village is so popular with locals that it expanded to the space next door. The extensive Pan-Asian menu is filled with crowd-pleasers like spicy panfried beef, eggplant with garlic sauce, Singapore rice noodles, honey-walnut shrimp, crispy orange chicken, and dried string beans with pork. **Known for:** the best Chinese food in Chinatown; budget-friendly prices and extensive menu; BYOB. *Average main: $18 ✉ 1113 Smith St., Chinatown ☎ 808/545–3008 🌐 www.littlevillagehawaii.com.*

$$ AMERICAN Fodor's Choice ★ ✕ **Livestock Tavern.** Livestock scores big with its seasonal menu of comfort foods, craft cocktails, and cowboy-minimalist decor. Although meat commands the menu, offerings like burrata, creative salads, and crispy snapper round out the possibilities. **Known for:** nice bar scene with good craft cocktails; a hamburger that draws locals again and again; creative dishes ranging from comfort food to trendy salads. *Average main: $20 ✉ 49 N. Hotel St., Chinatown ☎ 808/537–2577 🌐 www.livestocktavern.com ⏲ Closed Sun.*

$$ ASIAN ✕ **Lucky Belly.** A hip local crowd sips cocktails and slurps familiar noodle dishes with a modern twist at this popular fusion ramen bar. Try the Belly Bowl with smoked bacon, sausage, and pork belly in a savory broth loaded with noodles, as well as the trendy small plates such as pork belly buns, oxtail dumplings, and steak tartare spiced with

Japanese chili powder. **Known for:** huge portions of unique, tasty fusion cuisine; attentive and casual service; hang out for local hipsters and downtown professionals. *Average main: $20 50 N. Hotel St., Chinatown 808/531–1888 www.luckybelly.com Closed Sun.*

$ CHINESE **Mei Sum Chinese Dim Sum Restaurant.** In contrast to the sprawling, noisy halls in which dim sum is generally served, Mei Sum is compact and shiny bright, not to mention a favorite of locals who work in the area. Be ready to guess and point at the color photos of dim sum favorites; not much English is spoken, but the charades pay off when you get your delicate buns and tasty bites. **Known for:** all-day dim sum until 9 pm; not much English spoken, but it will be a social experience; dim sum, but with a more wide-ranging menu. *Average main: $11 1170 Nuuanu Ave., Suite 102, Chinatown 808/531–3268.*

$ VIETNAMESE **Pho-To Chau.** Those people lined up on River Street know where to get bowls of steaming *pho* (Vietnamese beef noodle soup) with all the best trimmings. This divey storefront was the go-to pho spot long before hipsters and foodies found Chinatown. **Known for:** a local institution with long lines; when they run out, they close, regardless of the time; large pho can be easily shared. *Average main: $8 1007 River St., Chinatown 808/533–4549 No credit cards No dinner.*

$$ MODERN ASIAN Fodor's Choice ★ **The Pig and the Lady.** Chef Andrew Le's casual noodle house attracts downtown office workers by day, but by night it becomes a creative contemporary restaurant, pulling in serious chowhounds. Drawing on both his Vietnamese heritage and multicultural island flavors, the talented, playful Le is a wizard with spice and acid, turning out dishes of layered flavor such as "coffee can bread" (which is baked in Café du Monde coffee cans) with chicken-liver paté, Kyoho grapes, and pink peppercorns. **Known for:** masterful fusion mash-up of Vietnamese tastes, spices, and local foods; house-made soft-serve and sorbets, including unexpected flavors; sister location, Piggy Smalls, in Kakaako. *Average main: $20 83 N. King St., Chinatown 808/585–8255 www.thepigandthelady.com Closed Sun.*

KAKAAKO

$$$$ CONTEMPORARY **53 by the Sea.** Housed in a McVilla aimed at attracting a Japanese wedding clientele, this restaurant serves contemporary Continental food that focuses primarily on well-prepared standards you'd find at a reception (crab cakes in lemon puree, mahimahi with a mango beurre blanc, lamb chops in a red wine reduction)—albeit with a million-dollar view of Honolulu, from Kakaako to Diamond Head. Perched at water's edge, with famed surf break Point Panic offshore, 53 by the Sea uses its setting to great advantage—the crescent-shaped dining room faces the sea, so even if you're not at a table nestled against the floor-to-ceiling windows, you have a fine view. **Known for:** views, especially at sunset; odd villa decor that somehow works; wedding chapel on-site in case the mood strikes. *Average main: $50 53 Ahui St., Kakaako 808/536–5353 www.53bythesea.com.*

$ MODERN HAWAIIAN FAMILY **Highway Inn.** Highway Inn serves up what it does best: local favorites like Kalbi ribs, *kalua* (roasted in an underground oven) pork sliders, beef stew, and old-fashioned hamburger steaks. It's a local favorite for breakfast, a great lunch spot, and happening at dinner. **Known for:** local

Hawaiian food done right; near the cruise terminal; the place for poi, lau lau, and other Hawaiian staples you can't get back home. *Average main: $15* *680 Ala Moana Blvd., Kakaako* *808/954–4955* *www.myhighwayinn.com.*

$ MODERN HAWAIIAN FAMILY **Kakaako Kitchen.** Kakaako has grown up around Russell Siu's masterpiece kitchen, where he serves high-quality plate lunches utilizing local, farm-to-table ingredients. Here, you can get a crab-and-avocado salad on toasted ciabatta or deep-fried pork chops topped with caramelized onion gravy and served with two scoops of either brown or white rice, and green salad instead of the usual mayo-laden macaroni salad. **Known for:** fresh, local food with a twist; lunchtime favorite for area workers; brown gravy, a staple on the menu, made from scratch. *Average main: $14* *Ward Village Shops, 1200 Ala Moana Blvd., Kakaako* *808/596–7488* *www.kakaakokitchen.com.*

$$ HAWAIIAN FAMILY **Moku Kitchen.** In the hip SALT complex, Moku's draws locals, including both foodies and families, as well as visitors looking for authentic farm-to-table cuisine in a laid-back, urban setting. It's one of legendary chef Peter Merriman's restaurants. **Known for:** local, farm-to-table menu with something for everyone; impressive list of craft cocktails and beers; live music that can get loud. *Average main: $19* *SALT at Our Kakaako, 660 Ala Moana Blvd., Kakaako* *808/591–6658* *www.mokukitchen.com.*

$$$$ JAPANESE FUSION **Nobu.** Always a local favorite, Nobu's move from Waikiki to the chic Kakaako high-rise Waiea has only made it better. It remains a magnet for visiting celebrities and local bigwigs—and its new location now draws a local after-work crowd to sip cocktails in the open-air bar. **Known for:** casual elegance at serious prices; consistently good and creative cuisine; a bar scene that rarely disappoints. *Average main: $38* *Waiea at Ward Village, 1118 Ala Moana Blvd., Kakaako* *808/237–6999* *www.noburestaurants.com/honolulu* *No lunch.*

$$ ECLECTIC **Panya Bistro.** This easy-breezy café run by Hong Kong–born sisters Alice and Annie Yeung offers a crowd-pleasing menu of contemporary American (salads, sandwiches, pastas) and Asian (Thai-style steak salad, Japanese-style fried chicken, Singaporean *laksa*), served in a disco-tinged space (there's also a full bar). A gourmet pizza chef turns out custom pizzas on the lanai every Thursday night. **Known for:** French-style pastries and cakes; gourmet pizzas cooked on the lanai every Thursday; great spot for breakfast. *Average main: $18* *Hokua, 1288 Ala Moana Blvd., Kakaako* *808/946–6388* *www.panyagroup.com.*

$$ HAWAIIAN **Scratch Kitchen & Meatery.** Tucked into the chic South Shore Market in Kakaako's Ward Village, this former Chinatown spot has moved uptown with its hipster decor, open kitchen, and creative menu. For breakfast, you'll be drawn to milk-and-cereal pancakes; for dinner it's small plates that might include foi gras loco moco or chicken and waffles. **Known for:** locally popular breakfast and brunch; perhaps a bit too much hipster vibe; spicy (and good) chicken and waffles. *Average main: $18* *South Shore Market at Ward Village, 1170 Auahi St., Kakaako* *Entrance on the side of the building, along Queen St.* *808/589–1669* *www.scratch-hawaii.com* *No dinner weekends.*

$$ WINE BAR

✕ **Vino Italian Tapas & Wine Bar.** Vino has a lock on local oenophiles, who make a beeline for this wine bar and restaurant, and neighborhood regulars who gather for pau hana with friends and co-workers. Chef Keith Endo creates his take on contemporary Mediterranean-inspired cuisine, including house-made pastas, jumbo shrimp in a resonant cioppino sauce, and Big Island smoked pork, all paired with wines selected by the nationally recognized sommelier Chuck Furuya. **Known for:** excellent wines, with wine tastings regularly; casual atmosphere with excellent food; house-made pastas, breads, and sausages. *Average main: $25 ✉ Waterfront Plaza, 500 Ala Moana Blvd., Suite 6F, Kakaako ☎ 808/524–8466 ⊕ www.vinohawaii.com ⊙ Closed Mon. No lunch.*

ALA MOANA

$$ JAPANESE

✕ **Akasaka.** Step inside this tiny sushi bar tucked between the strip clubs behind the Ala Moana Hotel, and you'll swear you're in an out-of-the-way Edo neighborhood in some indeterminate time. Don't be deterred by its dodgy neighbors or its reputation for inconsistent service. **Known for:** great spot for before or after concerts at nearby Republik; local favorite; no pretense, nothing fancy. *Average main: $21 ✉ 1646 B Kona St., Suite B, Ala Moana ☎ 808/942–4466.*

$$$ FUSION

✕ **Chef Chai.** This sleek, contemporary dining room on the edge of Kakaako offers an eclectic, fusion mix of seafood, meats, and creative starters and salads. Committed to healthier options, Chef Chai cut back his dependence on butter and cream, creating menu items like a delicious lobster bisque thickened with squash puree, and ahi tartare cones that look like tiny ice-cream cones but taste like sashimi with avo and wasabi. **Known for:** pre- and post-theater crowds from the Blaisdell; creative fusion cuisine melding local flavors with global influences; excellent desserts. *Average main: $30 ✉ Pacifica Honolulu, 1009 Kapiolani Blvd., Ala Moana ☎ 808/585–0011 ⊕ www.chefchai.com.*

$$$ ASIAN

✕ **Mariposa.** Yes, the popovers and the wee cups of bouillon are there at lunch, but in every other regard, this Neiman Marcus restaurant menu departs from the classic model, incorporating a clear sense of Pacific place. The breezy open-air veranda, with a view of Ala Moana Beach Park, twirling ceiling fans, and life-size hula-girl murals say Hawaii. **Known for:** the go-to spot for the local "ladies who lunch" crowd; warm lilikoi pudding cake; lovely interiors reminiscent of Hawaii plantation days. *Average main: $35 ✉ Neiman Marcus, Ala Moana Center, 1450 Ala Moana Blvd., Ala Moana ☎ 808/951–3420 ⊕ www.neimanmarcushawaii.com.*

$$$ HAWAIIAN
Fodor's Choice ★

✕ **MW Restaurant.** The "M" and "W" team of husband-and-wife chefs Michelle Karr-Ueko and Wade Ueko bring together their collective experience (20 years alongside chef Alan Wong, a side step to the famed French Laundry, and some serious kitchen time at comfort food icon Zippy's) to create a uniquely local menu with a decidedly upscale twist. Don't miss the mochi-crusted opakapaka and the garlic steamed onaga. **Known for:** scrumptious desserts (save room); small bar that turns out nice craft cocktails; valet parking only. *Average main: $35 ✉ 1538 Kapiolani Blvd., Suite 107, Ala Moana ✥ Behind the strip shopping center; walk down the side towards the lights in the back ☎ 808/955–6505 ⊕ www.mwrestaurant.com.*

2

$$ JAPANESE

Shokudo Japanese Restaurant & Bar. With a soaring ceiling, crazy red mobile sculpture, contemporary Japanese grazing plates, fruity vodka "sodas," and hungry young people, Shokudo is a culinary house of fun. Whether you go for new-wave fusion dishes such as sushi pizza (a flat, baked square of rice topped with salmon, scallop, crab, and pickled jalapeño), or more traditional noodle bowls and sushi, the food is all good. **Known for:** honey toast for dessert; vibe and decor to keep you entertained; popular, but losing charm for old-timers. *Average main: $21 Ala Moana Pacific Center, 1585 Kapiolani Blvd., Ala Moana 808/941–3701 www.shokudojapanese.com Closed Mon.*

$$ KOREAN

Sorabol. Open 24 hours a day on weekends and until 1 am on weeknights, with a tiny parking lot and a maze of booths and private rooms, Sorabol offers a vast menu encompassing the entirety of day-to-day Korean cuisine, plus sushi. English menu translations are cryptic at best, and the decor is a bit tired and off-putting. **Known for:** late-night dining; simple but good Korean food; inconsistent service. *Average main: $24 805 Keeaumoku St., Ala Moana 808/947–3113 www.sorabolhawaii.com.*

$$$$ CONTEMPORARY Fodor's Choice ★

Vintage Cave Honolulu. One of Oahu's priciest and most exclusive and creative dining options is Vintage Cave, a luxurious, art-filled reinvention of what was once the brick-lined basement of Shirokyua department store. The restaurant now offers two options: the more casual Vintage Cave Café (for mere mortals) and the ultra luxe Vintage Cave Club for those looking for an over-the-top experience. **Known for:** an elaborate dining experience; spectacular art; pampering, decadence, and romance. *Average main: $300 Ala Moana Shopping Center, 1450 Ala Moana Blvd., Suite 2250, Level B, Row D, Ala Moana 808/441–1744 www.vintagecave.com Jacket required.*

MAKIKI HEIGHTS

$ BURGER FAMILY Fodor's Choice ★

Honolulu Burger Co. Owner Ken Takahashi retired as a nightclub impresario on the Big Island to become a real-life burger king. This modest storefront is the home of the locavore burger, made with range-fed beef, Manoa lettuce, tomatoes, and a wide range of toppings, all island-grown—and you can taste the difference. **Known for:** burgers made with the best local ingredients; popular food truck; excellent truffle fries. *Average main: $11 1295 S. Beretania St., Makiki Heights 808/626–5202 www.honoluluburgerco.com.*

$ AMERICAN

Spalding House Cafe. In the exclusive Makiki Heights neighborhood above the city, the Honolulu Museum of Art Spalding House's casual café spills out of the ground floor of the museum onto the lush, expansive lawn with a million-dollar view of the city and Diamond Head. Sit inside when it's hot, grab an outdoor table when the trade winds are blowing. **Known for:** picnic for two on the museum grounds; deviled eggs; BYOB (and no corkage). *Average main: $14 Honolulu Museum of Art Spalding House, 2411 Makiki Heights Dr., Makiki Heights 808/237–5225 www.honolulumuseum.org/12001-spalding_house Closed Mon. No dinner.*

MOILIILI

$$$$ MODERN HAWAIIAN Fodor's Choice ★ **Alan Wong's Restaurant Honolulu.** James Beard Award–winning Alan Wong is the undisputed king of Hawaiian regional cuisine, earning love and respect for his humble demeanor and practice as much as for his food. The "Wong Way," as it's not-so-jokingly called by his staff, includes an ingrained understanding of the aloha spirit, evident in the skilled but unstarched service and creative and playful interpretations of Islands cuisine. **Known for:** well-deserved awards and accolades, which line the walls; island-inspired dishes, especially seafood; bland location (but it's all about the food). *Average main: $43 McCully Court, 1857 S. King St., 3rd fl., Moiliili 808/949–2526 www.alanwongs.com No lunch.*

$$$$ MODERN EUROPEAN Fodor's Choice ★ **Chef Mavro.** George Mavrothalassitis, who took two hotel restaurants to the top of the ranks before opening this well-regarded restaurant in 1998, admits he's crazy. Crazy because of the care he takes to draw out the truest and most concentrated flavors, to track down the freshest fish, to create one-of-a-kind wine pairings, and marry French technique with global flavors and local ingredients. **Known for:** exquisite prix-fixe cuisine; understated location; wine pairings unmatched on Oahu. *Average main: $130 1969 S. King St., Moiliili 808/944–4714 www.chefmavro.com No lunch.*

$ VEGETARIAN **Peace Café.** This tranquil little storefront with a rustic country communal table is a nurturing sanctuary on a fast-food-loving island. Place your order at the counter, serve yourself lemon-infused water from a large glass beverage jar, and wait for your Yogini plate (a mountain of brown rice, beans, greens, and seaweed), soy soba salad, Moroccan chickpea stew, barbecue tempeh sandwich, and other vegan bites. **Known for:** tiny refuge with a devoted clientele; innovative menu; mellow and calming setting. *Average main: $10 2239 S. King St., Moiliili 808/951–7555 www.peacecafehawaii.com No dinner Sun.*

$ ECLECTIC **Pint + Jigger.** Dining trends like the gastro pub are typically late to arrive in Honolulu, but Pint + Jigger was worth the wait. Sit at one of the "beer garden" communal benches or perch at a hightop in this welcoming wood-and-brick room for farm-to-glass cocktails, craft beers, and creative small bites. **Known for:** great craft beer and good cocktails; Sunday morning NFL games (7 am kickoff); convivial vibe, but hit-or-miss service. *Average main: $13 1936 S. King St., Moiliili 808/744–9593 www.pintandjigger.com No lunch weekdays.*

$$$$ JAPANESE **Sushi Sasabune.** Try to get a coveted seat at the counter, and prepare for an unforgettable sushi experience—if you behave. This is the home of Seiji Kumagawa—Honolulu's Sushi Nazi, who prefers that diners eat omakase-style, letting the chef send out his choices of his favorites for the night, each priced individually (prices add up quickly). **Known for:** one of Honolulu's top sushi spots; a strict chef who expects you to follow directions; all sushi priced by the course until you stop. *Average main: $115 1417 S. King St., Moiliili 808/947–3800 Closed Sun. and Mon. No lunch Sat.*

$$$$ HAWAIIAN **The Willows.** Old-time locals come to this buffet-only spot to celebrate things like graduations, showers, and centennials, and it hosts its share of wedding receptions (there's a chapel on-site), not to mention a full

acre of pavilions overlooking a network of ponds (once natural streams flowing from mountain to sea). The Island-style comfort food includes signature chicken-and-shrimp curry (*Joy of Cooking*–style, not Indian), crab legs and lobster claws, along with local favorites such as *laulau* (a steamed bundle of ti leaves containing pork, butterfish, and taro tops), oxtail soup, and kalua pig. **Known for:** particularly lovely grounds; a buffet that seems to never end; dated decor that is somehow still charming in its own way. *Average main: $40* *901 Hausten St., Moiliili* *808/952–9200* *www.willowshawaii.com.*

KAIMUKI

$$ VIETNAMESE

Hale Vietnam. One of Oahu's first Vietnamese restaurants, this neighborhood spot, initially popular with budget-minded college kids, expresses its friendly character with its name: *hale* (hah-lay) is the Hawaiian word for house or home. As Kaimuki has gentrifed, Hale Vietnam has remained an anchor spot, albeit with prices that reflect the changing times. **Known for:** neighborhood staple; friendly, helpful staff who will help first-timers; local family favorite that welcomes kids. *Average main: $17* *1140 12th Ave., Kaimuki* *808/735–7581.*

$ MODERN HAWAIIAN

Fodor's Choice ★

Koko Head Cafe. When Lee Anne Wong, best known as a competitor on the first season of Bravo's "Top Chef," moved to the Islands, foodies waited with bated breath for her first brick-and-mortar restaurant. And this is it: a lively and laid-back café in Kaimuki, where she took the concept of breakfast and flipped it, creating innovative dishes like the miso-smoked pork-and-onion omelet, cornflake French toast with billionaire's bacon and frosted flake gelato, and kimchi bacon cheddar scones. **Known for:** cornflake French Toast; creative cocktail menu; crazy busy weekends. *Average main: $13* *1145c 12th Ave., Kaimuki* *808/732–8920* *www.kokoheadcafe.com* *No dinner.*

$$ HAWAIIAN

Mud Hen Water. The name of this restaurant perched on busy Waialae Avenue is the English translation of *Waialae* (meaning a gathering spot around a watering hole). Chef Ed Kenney (of 12th Avenue Grill fame) explores modern interpretations of the Hawaiian foods he remembers from his childhood: line-caught, local seafood, roasted-beet poke with gorilla *ogo* (seaweed), and opah buried in coals and steamed in banana leaves with local vegetables and coconut cream. **Known for:** constantly changing menu of what's fresh, local, and available; spot where locals and visitors actually mingle; small plates and snacks. *Average main: $17* *3452 Waialae Ave., Kaimuki* *808/737–6000* *www.mudhenwater.com* *Closed Mon. No lunch Tues.–Fri.*

$$$$ MODERN HAWAIIAN

3660 on the Rise. Named for its address on Honolulu's premier Waialae Avenue, this restaurant brought fresh dining to Kaimuki when it opened in 1992, inspiring a neighborhood dining renaissance. Loyalists swear by the New York Steak Alaea (grilled with Hawaiian clay salt), potato-crusted crab cakes, and the signature ahi katsu wrapped in *nori* (seaweed) and deep-fried with a wasabi-ginger butter sauce. **Known for:** local favorite for special occasions; ahi katsu that sets the local bar for this favorite dish; good desserts. *Average main: $38* *3660 Waialae Ave., Kaimuki* *808/737–1177* *www.3660.com* *Closed Mon. No lunch.*

$$ INTERNATIONAL Fodor's Choice ★

✕ **Town.** Town remains a hot spot for Honolulu's creative class and farm-to-table diners, where chef-owner Ed Kenney and his partner Dave Caldiero offer a Mediterranean-eclectic menu ranging from hand-cut pastas and refreshing, composed salads (pastas and salads) to clean preparations of fish and meat (polenta with egg and asparagus or buttermilk panna cotta). The menu is constantly changing, reflecting what's fresh and available. **Known for:** eclectic menu that suits both meat eaters and vegetarians; indoor-outdoor seating; great burger and fries. *Average main: $25 3435 Waialae Ave., Kaimuki 808/735–5900 www.townkaimuki.com Closed Sun.*

$$$ MODERN HAWAIIAN Fodor's Choice ★

✕ **12th Avenue Grill.** A local favorite since the doors opened over a decade ago, this award-winning American brasserie from chef-owner Kevin Hanney keeps surprising loyalists with an expanding menu and lively bar scene.The longtime favorite grilled pork chop is joined on the menu by shwarma-spiced Niihau lamb shanks with house-made yogurt, pan-roasted U-10 Hokkaido scallops with Kaffir-Kahuku corn puree, and beautifully prepared soups, salads, and small plates. The specials are always excellent, and the passion-fruit mochi cake with vanilla-ginger syrup is one of the best desserts in town. **Known for:** Kevin Hanney, who is a local icon; commitment to locally sourced ingredients; innovative craft cocktails. *Average main: $28 1120 12th Ave., Kaimuki 808/732–9469 www.12thavegrill.com No lunch.*

KAHALA

$$$$ ASIAN FUSION

✕ **Hoku's.** Everything about this room speaks of quality and sophistication: the wall of windows with their beach views, the avant-garde cutlery and dinnerware, the solicitous staff, and the carefully constructed Euro-Pacific cuisine. The menu constantly changes, but you can count on chef Wayne Hirabayashi to use fresh, local ingredients (including herbs from the hotel's on-site herb garden) in his innovative dishes that include braised short-rib tempura, salt-crusted rack of lamb with basil pesto, and butter-poached lobster with passion-fruit jus. **Known for:** relaxed elegance in the grande dame of Hawaii's social scene; panoramic views from every table; setting and service that can outshine the food. *Average main: $55 The Kahala Hotel & Resort, 5000 Kahala Ave., Kahala 808/739–8760 www.kahalaresort.com/honolulu_restaurants/hokus Closed Tues. No lunch.*

$ GREEK

✕ **Olive Tree Cafe.** An Iranian Hellenophile owns this bustling, self-serve café that dishes up the best taramasalata, falafel, and souvlaki in town. Stand in line at the counter to order while your companion tries to finagle one of the outdoor tables. **Known for:** seriously good Greek food; unpretentious and somehow still charming; BYOB (borrow their corkscrew). *Average main: $14 4614 Kilauea Ave., Suite 107, Kahala 808/737–0303 No credit cards No lunch.*

SOUTHEAST OAHU

$$$ MODERN HAWAIIAN

✕ **Roy's.** Roy Yamaguchi is one of the 12 founding chefs of Hawaiian regional cuisine, a culinary movement that put Hawaii on the food map back in 1991. Opened in 1988, his flagship restaurant across the highway from Maunalua Bay is still packed every night with food-savvy visitors mixing with well-heeled residents. **Known for:** spectacular sunset views and a tiki torch–lit lanai and bar area; small and large portions available for many dishes; signature menu items like blackened ahi with a cultlike following. *$ Average main: $34 ✉ Hawaii Kai Corporate Plaza, 6600 Kalanianaole Hwy., Hawaii Kai ☎ 808/396–7697 🌐 www.royshawaii.com ⏲ No lunch.*

WINDWARD OAHU

$$$ STEAKHOUSE **Buzz's Lanikai.** Virtually unchanged since owners Bobby Lou and Buzz opened it in 1967, this neighborhood institution opposite Kailua Beach Park is filled with the aroma of grilling steaks and plumeria blooms. Sadly, Buzz has passed on, but you can now enjoy a predinner drink on Stan's Deck, a salute to Bobby Lou's second husband. **Known for:** local institution; the views from the lanai at lunch; excellent fruity beach cocktails. *$ Average main: $35 ✉ 413 Kawailoa Rd., Kailua ☎ 808/261–4661 🌐 www.buzzsoriginalsteakhouse.com.*

$ AMERICAN **Cinnamon's Restaurant.** Known for uncommon variations on common breakfast themes (pancakes, eggs Benedict, French toast, home fries, and eggs), this neighborhood favorite is tucked into a hard-to-find Kailua office park (call for directions). Lunch features local-style plate lunches, which are good, but the main attraction is breakfast. **Known for:** endless variations on pancakes, eggs Benedict, and waffles; cinnamon rolls (of course); long waits. *$ Average main: $14 ✉ 315 Uluniu St., Kailua ☎ 808/261–8724 🌐 www.cinnamons808.com.*

$$ ECLECTIC **Kalapawai Cafe & Deli.** This one-stop Mediterranean-leaning café, wine bar, bakery, and gourmet deli is the creation of the Dymond family, two generations of restaurateurs who have shaken up the Windward food scene with their signature green-and-white market and café. Come in on your way to the beach for a cup of coffee and bagel, and stop back for a gourmet pizza or bruschetta (how does eggplant confit, sweet peppers, honey, and goat cheese sound?) for lunch or a candlelit dinner at night. **Known for:** candlelight dinners and signature dishes by night; good coffee and sandwiches by day; impressive wine list for such a small spot. *$ Average main: $19 ✉ 750 Kailua Rd., Kailua ☎ 808/262–3354 🌐 www.kalapawaimarket.com.*

$$ CHINESE **Pah Ke's Chinese Restaurant.** If you happen to be on the Windward side at dinner time, this out-of-the-ordinary Chinese restaurant—named for the local pidgin term for Chinese (literally translated, this is "Chinese's Chinese Restaurant")—is a good option. Ebullient owner and chef Raymond Siu, a former hotel pastry chef, focuses on healthier cooking techniques and local ingredients. **Known for:** dependable spot for the family; house specials that are usually better than standard menu fare; a big dining room with bright lights and not much atmosphere. *$ Average main: $22 ✉ 46-018 Kamehameha Hwy., Kaneohe ☎ 808/235–4505 🌐 www.pahke.com.*

$$ PIZZA **Prima.** The beautifully blistered pies are cooked in a white-tiled Ferrara kiawe wood-burning oven that you can see in the open kitchen of this bright, light pizzeria with robin's egg–blue Eames shell chairs. This is as Neapolitan as it gets on Oahu, and these are the best pizzas on the island, topped with such ingredients as soppressata, prosciutto,

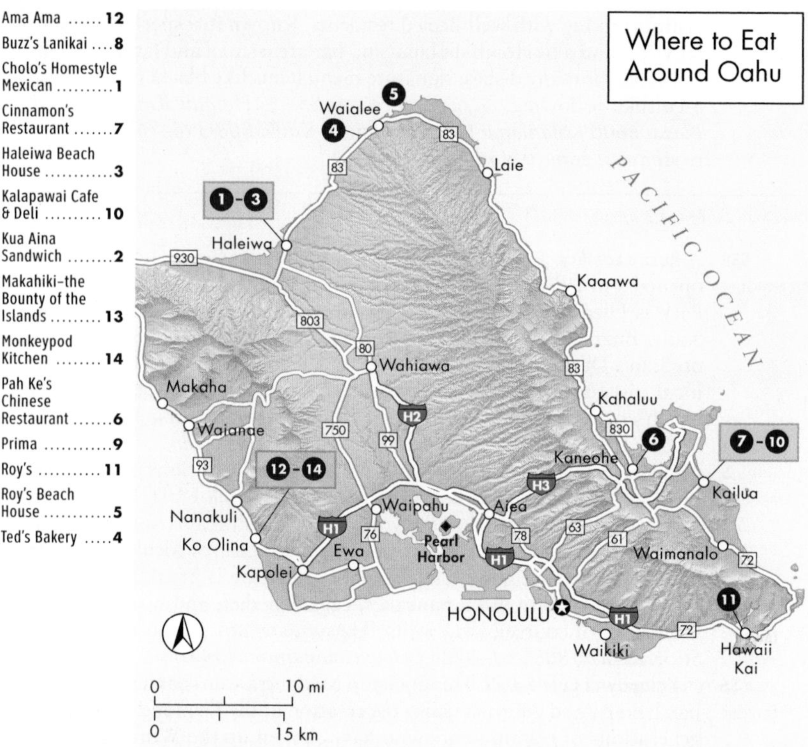

and spicy meatballs, paired with fresh, local produce. **Known for:** a once-hidden gem now discovered; hit-or-miss service; the pizza ... don't worry about the rest. $ *Average main: $18* ✉ *Kailua Foodland Marketplace, 108 Hekili St., Kailua* ☎ *808/888–8933* 🌐 *www.primahawaii.com.*

THE NORTH SHORE

$ MEXICAN **Cholo's Homestyle Mexican.** There are a few institutions on the North Shore that are the area's great gathering places. Foodland (the great grocery store) is one, and the other is Cholo's. **Known for:** excellent sashimi-grade ahi tacos; a good breakfast burrito when you need it; fresh mango margaritas. $ *Average main: $15* ✉ *North Shore Marketplace, 66-250 Kamehameha Hwy., Haleiwa* ☎ *808/637–3059* 🌐 *www.cholos.mx.*

$$ AMERICAN **Haleiwa Beach House.** The newest restaurant on the North Shore, Haleiwa Beach House takes full advantage of its epic views of the water and the glorious building it calls home. Once the local icon Jamesons, this beautifully restored spot puts diners on the lanai, up the spiral wood staircase at the bar, and always within view of the surf and the sounds of the ocean. **Known for:** view and setting that can't be beat; solid, reliable beef, seafood, salads, and kids options; craft beers on draft and

a nice wine list. $ *Average main: $25* ✉ *62-540 Kamehameha Hwy, Haleiwa* ☎ *808/637–3435* 🌐 *www.haleiwabeachhouse.com.*

$ BURGER ✕ **Kua Aina Sandwich.** This North Shore spot has gone from funky burger shack (it first opened in 1975) to institution, with crowds of tourists and locals standing in line to order the large, hand-formed burgers heaped with bacon, cheese, salsa, and pineapples. Frankly, there are better burgers to be had around the island, but this place commands a loyal following who return again and again. **Known for:** a pilgrimage stop on the North Shore surf circuit; tourists by the busload; decent burgers and fries. $ *Average main: $10* ✉ *66-160 Kamehameha Hwy., Haleiwa* ☎ *808/637–6067.*

MALASADAS

Malasadas are a contribution of the Portuguese, who came to the Islands to work on the plantations. Roughly translated, the name means "half-cooked," which refers to the origin of these deep-fried, heavily sugared treats said to have been created as a way to use up scraps of rich, buttery egg dough. A handful of bakeries specialize in them (Leonard's on Kapahulu, Agnes in Kailua, Champion on Beretania); restaurants sometimes serve an upscale version stuffed with fruit puree; and they're inevitable at food trucks, fairs, and carnivals. Eat them hot or not at all.

$$$$ MODERN HAWAIIAN ✕ **Roy's Beach House.** Loyalists of Roy Yamaguchi's iconic spots in Hawaii Kai and Waikiki are thrilled that he's also represented on the North Shore, in this rustic-beam-and-concrete-floor pavilion literally on the sand at Turtle Bay. All the favorites are served at this more beach-casual spot, from the miso butterfish to the beef short ribs, along with a more casual lunch menu. **Known for:** casual, romantic setting right on the beach; Roy's signature dishes; special-occasion celebrations. $ *Average main: $42* ✉ *Turtle Bay Resort, 57-091 Kamehameha Hwy., Kahuku* ☎ *808/293–0801* 🌐 *www.roysbeachhouse.com.*

$ AMERICAN ✕ **Ted's Bakery.** No North Shore trek is complete without a stop at a shrimp truck and a slice of Ted's pie. Sunburned tourists and salty surfers rub shoulders in their quest for Ted's famous chocolate *haupia* pie (layered coconut and dark chocolate puddings topped with whipped cream) and hearty plate lunches—like gravy-drenched hamburger steak and mahimahi. **Known for:** Ted's pies, which seem to show up at every Oahu pot luck; reliable all-day dining; plate lunches. $ *Average main: $9* ✉ *59-024 Kamehameha Hwy., Haleiwa* ☎ *808/638–8207* 🌐 *www.tedsbakery.com.*

WEST (LEEWARD) OAHU

$$$$ MODERN HAWAIIAN ✕ **Ama Ama.** There's nothing "Mickey Mouse" about the food at the fine-dining restaurant of this Disney resort. Add to that the views of the Ko Olina lagoons and Pacific Ocean—and live music by top local performers Friday–Sunday nights—and you have an evening worth the pretty penny. **Known for:** outstanding views and setting; consistently good food; hit-or-miss service. $ *Average main: $40* ✉ *Aulani, a Disney Resort & Spa, 92-1185 Aliinui Dr., Ko Olina* ☎ *808/674–6200* 🌐 *www.disneyaulani.com/dining.*

$$$$ HAWAIIAN FAMILY ✕ **Makahiki—The Bounty of the Islands.** The buffet restaurant at Disney's Aulani resort offers a wide variety of locally produced items, as well as familiar dishes from stateside and the rest of the world. You'll find sustainable Hawaiian seafood, Asian selections, familiar grilled meats and vegetables, and a kids' menu. **Known for:** true reflection of Hawaii; wide array of food to please every member of the family; popular character breakfasts (which book up months in advance). *Average main: $52 ✉ Aulani, a Disney Resort & Spa, 92-1185 Aliinui Dr., Ko Olina ☎ 808/674–6200 ⊕ www.disneyaulani.com/dining ⊗ No lunch.*

$$ HAWAIIAN ✕ **Monkeypod Kitchen.** Local farm-to-table guru Peter Merriman is known throughout Hawaii for his inventive and popular restaurants. Monkeypod at Ko Olina captures his creativity and locally inspired food mantra perfectly. **Known for:** lobster deviled eggs and fresh fish tacos; indoor/outdoor setting; life-changing strawberry cream pie. *Average main: $17 ✉ Ko Olina Resort, 92-1048 Olani St., Kapolei ☎ 808/380–4086 ⊕ www.monkeypodkitchen.com.*

WHERE TO STAY

Updated by Powell Berger

As in real estate, location matters. And although Oahu is just 44 miles long and 30 miles wide—meaning you can circle the entire island before lunch—it boasts neighborhoods and lodgings with very different vibes and personalities. If you like the action and choices of big cities, consider Waikiki, a 24-hour playground with everything from surf to karaoke bars. Those who want an escape from urban life look to the island's leeward or windward sides, or to the North Shore, where the surf culture creates a laid-back atmosphere.

Most of the island's major hotels and resorts are in Waikiki, which has a lot to offer within a small area—namely shopping, restaurants, nightlife—and nearly 3 miles of sandy beach. You don't need a car in Waikiki; everything is nearby, including the Honolulu Zoo and Waikiki Aquarium, the 300-acre Kapiolani Park, running and biking paths, grocery stores, and access to public transportation that can take you to museums, shopping centers, and historic landmarks around the island.

You'll find places to stay along the entire stretch of both Kalakaua and Kuhio avenues, with smaller and quieter hotels and condos at the eastern end, and more business-centric accommodations on the western edge of Waikiki, near the Hawaii Convention Center, Ala Moana Center, and downtown Honolulu.

The majority of tourists who come to Oahu stay in Waikiki, but choosing accommodations in downtown Honolulu affords you the opportunity to be close to shopping and restaurants at Ala Moana Center, the largest shopping mall in the state. It also provides easy access to the airport.

If you want to get away from the bustle of the city, consider a stay on Oahu's Leeward Coast. Consider the Ko Olina resort area, about 20 minutes from the Honolulu International Airport and 40 minutes from Waikiki. Here, there are great golf courses and quiet beaches and coves that make for a relaxing getaway. But you'll need a car to get off the property if you want to explore the rest of the island.

Other, more low-key options are on Windward Oahu or the North Shore. Both regions are rustic and charming, with quaint eateries and coffee shops, local boutiques, and some of the island's best beaches. One of Oahu's premier resorts, Turtle Bay, is located here, too.

HONOLULU

The vast majority of hotels in Honolulu are in Waikiki, but there are also a few in downtown Honolulu and in the Ala Moana area between downtown and Waikiki. Away from the hopping scene of Waikiki or busy downtown, accommodations on the rest of Oahu range from quiet and romantic bed-and-breakfasts and cottages to less expensive hotels that are a great value. There are a few luxury resorts as well, where you'll truly feel like you're getting away from it all.

For expanded hotel reviews, visit Fodors.com.

WAIKIKI

Hotels in Waikiki range from superluxe resorts to the kind of small, beachy places where shirtless surfers hang out in the lobby. It's where the heart of the visitor action is on Oahu. Those traveling with families might want to take into consideration easy access to the beach, restaurants, and other activities, as parking in the area can sometimes be difficult and pricey. For those looking to be slightly removed from the scene, choose accommodations on the *ewa* (western) end of Waikiki.

$$ RENTAL FAMILY **Aston at the Waikiki Banyan.** Families and active travelers love the convenience and action of this hotel, just a block from Waikiki Beach, the aquarium, the zoo, and bustling Kalakaua Avenue. **Pros:** many rooms have great views with kitchens; walking distance to shops, beach, restaurants, and activities; fabulous recreation deck for the entire family. **Cons:** room conditions can vary greatly; no on-site restaurant; sharing hotel with residents. *Rooms from: $200 ✉ 201 Ohua Ave., Waikiki ☎ 808/922–0555, 877/997–6667 🌐 www.astonwaikikibanyan.com 876 suites No meals.*

$ RENTAL **The Breakers.** Despite an explosion of high-rise construction all around it, the Breakers continues to transport guests back to 1960s-era Hawaii in this small, low-rise complex a mere half-block from Waikiki Beach. **Pros:** intimate atmosphere with fabulous poolside courtyard; great location; a throw back to a different era. **Cons:** a bit worn down and dated; parking space is extremely limited (but free); showers only. *Rooms from: $170 ✉ 250 Beach Walk, Waikiki ☎ 808/923–3181, 800/923–7174 🌐 www.breakers-hawaii.com 63 rooms No meals.*

$$$ RENTAL FAMILY **Castle Waikiki Shore.** Nestled between Fort DeRussy Beach Park and the Outrigger Reef on the Beach, this is the only condo hotel directly on Waikiki Beach. **Pros:** right on the beach; great views from spacious private lanai; location near beach and lush park areas. **Cons:** units can vary and some are dated; two-night minimum stay; not all suites have all amenities listed, so remember to ask. *Rooms from: $270 ✉ 2161 Kalia Rd., Waikiki ☎ 808/952–4500, 800/367–5004 🌐 www.castleresorts.com 168 suites No meals.*

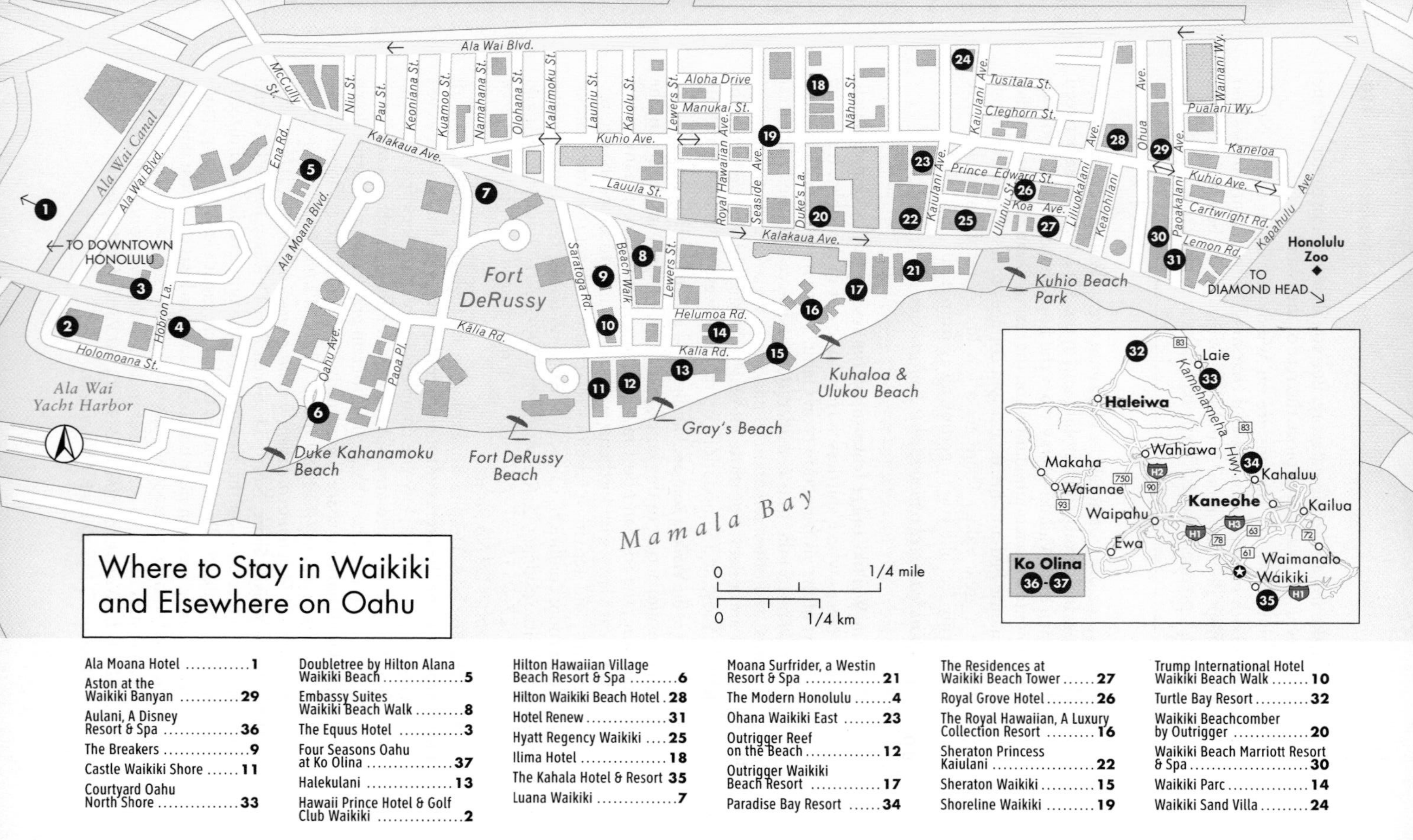

Where to Stay in Waikiki and Elsewhere on Oahu
Ala Moana Hotel 1
Aston at the Waikiki Banyan 29
Aulani, A Disney Resort & Spa 36
The Breakers 9
Castle Waikiki Shore 11
Courtyard Oahu North Shore 33
Doubletree by Hilton Alana Waikiki Beach 5
Embassy Suites Waikiki Beach Walk 8
The Equus Hotel 3
Four Seasons Oahu at Ko Olina 37
Halekulani 13
Hawaii Prince Hotel & Golf Club Waikiki 2
Hilton Hawaiian Village Beach Resort & Spa 6
Hilton Waikiki Beach Hotel . 28
Hotel Renew 31
Hyatt Regency Waikiki 25
Ilima Hotel 18
The Kahala Hotel & Resort 35
Luana Waikiki 7
Moana Surfrider, a Westin Resort & Spa 21
The Modern Honolulu 4
Ohana Waikiki East 23
Outrigger Reef on the Beach 12
Outrigger Waikiki Beach Resort 17
Paradise Bay Resort 34
The Residences at Waikiki Beach Tower 27
Royal Grove Hotel 26
The Royal Hawaiian, A Luxury Collection Resort 16
Sheraton Princess Kaiulani 22
Sheraton Waikiki 15
Shoreline Waikiki 19
Trump International Hotel Waikiki Beach Walk 10
Turtle Bay Resort 32
Waikiki Beachcomber by Outrigger 20
Waikiki Beach Marriott Resort & Spa 30
Waikiki Parc 14
Waikiki Sand Villa 24
TO DOWNTOWN HONOLULU
TO DIAMOND HEAD
Honolulu Zoo
Ala Wai Canal
Ala Wai Yacht Harbor
Fort DeRussy
Duke Kahanamoku Beach
Fort DeRussy Beach
Gray's Beach
Kuhaloa & Ulukou Beach
Kuhio Beach Park
Mamala Bay
Ala Wai Blvd.
Kalakaua Ave.
Kuhio Ave.
Ala Moana Blvd.
Kālia Rd.
Saratoga Rd.
Beach Walk
Lewers St.
Royal Hawaiian Ave.
Seaside Ave.
Duke's La.
Kaiulani Ave.
Kapahulu Ave.
0 1/4 mile
0 1/4 km
Laie
Haleiwa
Kamehameha Hwy.
Wahiawa
Makaha
Waianae
Waipahu
Ewa
Kahaluu
Kaneohe
Kailua
Waimanalo
Waikiki
Ko Olina 36-37

2

WHERE TO STAY ON OAHU

Neighborhood	Local Vibe	Pros	Cons
Honolulu	Lodging options are limited in downtown Honolulu, but if you want an urban feel or to be near Chinatown, look no farther.	Access to a wide selection of art galleries, boutiques, and new restaurants as well as Chinatown.	No beaches within walking distance. If you're looking to get away from it all, this is not the place.
Waikiki	Lodgings abound in Waikiki, from youth hostels to five-star accommodations. The area is always abuzz with activity and anything you desire is within walking distance.	You can surf in front of the hotels, wander miles of beach, and explore hundreds of restaurants and bars.	This is tourist central. Prices are high, and you are not going to get the true Hawaii experience.
Windward Oahu	More in tune with the local experience, here is where you'll find most of the island's B&Bs and enjoy the lush side of Oahu.	From beautiful vistas and green jungles, this side really captures the tropical paradise most people envision when dreaming of a Hawaiian vacation.	The lushness comes at a price—it rains a lot on this side. Also, luxury is not the specialty here; if you are looking to get pampered, stay elsewhere.
The North Shore	This is true country living, with one luxurious resort exception. It's bustling in the winter (when the surf is up) but pretty slow-paced in the summer.	Amazing surf and long stretches of sand truly epitomize the beach culture in Hawaii. Historic Haleiwa has enough stores to keep shopaholics busy.	There is no middle ground for accommodations; you're either in backpacker cabanas or $300-a-night suites. There is also zero nightlife, and traffic can get heavy during winter months.
West (Leeward) Oahu	This is the resort side of the rock; there is little outside of these resorts, but plenty on the grounds to keep you occupied for a week.	Ko Olina's lagoons offer the most kid-friendly swimming on the island, and the golf courses on this side are magnificent. Rare is the rainy day out here.	You are isolated from the rest of Oahu, with little in the way of shopping or jungle hikes.

$$ HOTEL **Doubletree by Hilton Alana Waikiki Beach.** A convenient location—10 minutes' walk from the Hawaii Convention Center—a professional staff, pleasant public spaces, and a 24-hour business center and gym draw a global business clientele to this reliable chain hotel. **Pros:** walkable to the beach and Ala Moana mall; walk-in glass showers with oversize rain showerheads; heated outdoor pool and 24-hour fitness center. **Cons:** a 10-minute walk to the beach; little local flavor; valet parking only. *Rooms from: $209* *1956 Ala Moana Blvd., Waikiki* *808/941–7275* *doubletree3.hilton.com* *317 rooms* *No meals.*

$$$ RESORT FAMILY **Embassy Suites Waikiki Beach Walk.** In a place where space is at a premium, this all-suites resort offers families and groups traveling together a bit more room to move about, with two 21-story towers housing one- and two-bedroom suites. **Pros:** great location next to Waikiki Beach Walk and all its shops and restaurants; spacious and modern rooms; complimentary hot breakfast and evening reception daily. **Cons:** no direct beach access; not steeped in Waikiki charm; property can seem busy and noisy. *Rooms from: $319 ✉ 201 Beachwalk St., Waikiki ☎ 800/362–2779, 808/921–2345 ⊕ www.embassysuiteswaikiki.com 369 suites Free Breakfast.*

$$ HOTEL **The Equus Hotel.** This small, boutique hotel has been completely renovated with a Hawaiian country theme that pays tribute to Hawaii's polo-playing history. **Pros:** casual and fun atmosphere; attentive staff; nicely furnished rooms. **Cons:** busy, hectic area; must cross a major road to get to the beach; limited on-site dining (coffee shop and bar only). *Rooms from: $190 ✉ 1696 Ala Moana Blvd., Waikiki ☎ 808/949–0061 ⊕ www.equushotel.com 67 rooms No meals.*

$$$$ RESORT Fodor's Choice ★ **Halekulani.** The luxurious Halekulani exemplifies the translation of its name—the "house befitting heaven"—and from the moment you step into the lobby, the attention to detail and impeccable service wrap you in privilege at this beachfront location away from Waikiki's bustle. **Pros:** heavenly interior and exterior spaces; wonderful dining opportunities in-house; world-class service. **Cons:** might feel a bit formal for Waikiki; pricey; can seem busy with events and formal gatherings. *Rooms from: $500 ✉ 2199 Kalia Rd., Waikiki ☎ 808/923–2311, 800/367–2343, 844/288–8022 ⊕ www.halekulani.com 453 rooms No meals.*

$$$$ HOTEL **Hawaii Prince Hotel & Golf Club Waikiki.** This slim, renovated high-rise with 538 oceanfront rooms including 57 luxury suites fronts Ala Wai Yacht Harbor at the *ewa* (western) edge of Waikiki. **Pros:** fantastic views from all rooms; elegant and sophisticated; location avoids complicated-to-maneuver Waikiki. **Cons:** no free Internet; no beach access; between weddings and functions, property can seem very busy. *Rooms from: $500 ✉ 100 Holomoana St., Waikiki ☎ 888/977–4623, 808/956–1111 ⊕ www.hawaiiprincehotel.com 538 rooms No meals.*

$$ RESORT FAMILY **Hilton Hawaiian Village Beach Resort & Spa.** Location, location, location: this megaresort and convention destination sprawls over 22 acres on Waikiki's widest stretch of beach, with the green lawns of neighboring Fort DeRussy creating a buffer zone to the high-rise lineup of central Waikiki. **Pros:** activities and amenities can keep you and the kids busy for weeks; stellar spa; Friday-night fireworks. **Cons:** size of property can be overwhelming; resort fee $30 (plus tax) per room per night; parking is expensive ($43 per day for self parking). *Rooms from: $239 ✉ 2005 Kalia Rd., Waikiki ☎ 808/949–4321, 800/774–1500 ⊕ www.hiltonhawaiianvillage.com 4499 rooms No meals.*

$$ HOTEL **Hilton Waikiki Beach Hotel.** Two blocks from Kuhio Beach, this 37-story high-rise, located on the Diamond Head end of Waikiki, is great for travelers who want to be near the action, but not right in it. **Pros:** central location; helpful staff; pleasant, comfortable public spaces. **Cons:** long walk to the beach; very few rooms have views; older property that

shows some wear. *Rooms from: $219 ✉ 2500 Kuhio Ave., Waikiki ☎ 808/922–0811, 888/370–0980 🌐 www.hiltonwaikikibeach.com ⇨ 609 rooms 🍴 No meals.*

$$ HOTEL **Hotel Renew.** Located a block from world-famous Waikiki Beach, this 72-room boutique hotel managed by Aston Hotels & Resorts is a casual but chic change from the big resorts that dominate the oceanfront here. **Pros:** free Wi-Fi; personalized service; close to zoo, aquarium, and beach. **Cons:** no pool; new hotel but older refurbished facility requires constant upkeep; rooms on the small side. *Rooms from: $180 ✉ 129 Paoakalani Ave., Waikiki ☎ 808/687–7700, 877/997–6667 🌐 www.hotelrenew.com ⇨ 72 rooms 🍴 Free Breakfast.*

$$$ RESORT FAMILY **Hyatt Regency Waikiki Resort & Spa.** This large high-rise hotel, where the lively atrium-style lobby is the focal point, is across the street from Kuhio Beach, but there's no resort between it and the Pacific Ocean. **Pros:** public spaces are open; elegant and very professional spa; kid-friendly and close to the beach. **Cons:** in a very busy and crowded part of Waikiki; on-site pool is quite small; can feel a bit like you're staying in a shopping mall. *Rooms from: $300 ✉ 2424 Kalakaua Ave., Waikiki ☎ 808/923–1234, 800/633–7313 🌐 www.hyattregencywaikiki.com ⇨ 1,248 rooms 🍴 No meals.*

$ RENTAL **Ilima Hotel.** Tucked away on a residential side street near Waikiki's Ala Wai Canal, this locally owned 17-story condominium-style hotel is a throwback to old Waikiki, offering large units that are ideal for families. **Pros:** free parking in Waikiki is a rarity; great value; free Wi-Fi. **Cons:** furnishings are dated; 10-minute walk to the beach; no ocean views. *Rooms from: $160 ✉ 445 Nohonani St., Waikiki ☎ 808/923–1877, 800/801–9366 🌐 www.ilima.com ⇨ 98 units 🍴 No meals.*

$ HOTEL FAMILY **Luana Waikiki.** At the entrance to Waikiki near Fort DeRussy is this welcoming hotel offering both rooms and condominium units. **Pros:** coin-operated laundry facilities on-site; sundeck with barbecue grills; free Wi-Fi. **Cons:** no direct beach access; area can be busy and noisy; pool is small. *Rooms from: $175 ✉ 2045 Kalakaua Ave., Waikiki ☎ 808/955–6000, 866/940–2782, 808/441–7774 🌐 www.aqualuanawaikiki.com ⇨ 225 units 🍴 No meals.*

$$$$ RESORT **Moana Surfrider, A Westin Resort & Spa.** Outrageous rates of $1.50 per night were the talk of the town when the "First Lady of Waikiki" opened her doors in 1901; today, this historic beauty—the oldest hotel in Waikiki—is still a wedding and honeymoon favorite with a sweeping main staircase and period furnishings in its historic Moana Wing (and considerably more expensive). **Pros:** elegant, historic property; best place on Waikiki Beach to watch hula and have a drink; can't beat the location. **Cons:** you'll likely dodge bridal parties in the lobby; the hotel now charges a mind-boggling resort fee of $37.70 per room per day; expensive parking ($35/day for self parking across the street). *Rooms from: $400 ✉ 2365 Kalakaua Ave., Waikiki ☎ 808/922–3111, 866/716–8112 🌐 www.moana-surfrider.com ⇨ 796 rooms 🍴 No meals.*

$$$$ HOTEL **The Modern Honolulu.** The lobby of this edgy, slickly designed hotel has the feel of an upscale jazz club, with recessed lighting and bookcases, making this the best hotel pick in Waikiki for urbanites who like the hip, big-city vibe. **Pros:** excellent design; unpretentious but hip feel;

great bars and restaurants. **Cons:** not kid-friendly; on the outer edge of Waikiki; direct beach access a five-minute walk away. *Rooms from: $450 ✉ 1775 Ala Moana Blvd., Waikiki ☎ 808/943–5800, 888/970–4161 🌐 www.themodernhonolulu.com 383 rooms No meals.*

$$ HOTEL **Ohana Waikiki East.** If you want to be in central Waikiki and don't want to pay beachfront lodging prices, consider the Ohana Waikiki East. **Pros:** close to the beach and reasonable rates; decent on-site eateries, including a piano bar; in the middle of the Waikiki action. **Cons:** some rooms with no lanai and very basic public spaces; an older property with signs of wear and tear; limited self-parking at $30/day. *Rooms from: $229 ✉ 150 Kaiulani Ave., Waikiki ☎ 808/922–5353, 866/956–4262, 800/688–7444 🌐 www.ohanahotelsoahu.com/ohana_east 441 rooms No meals.*

$$$ HOTEL FAMILY **Outrigger Reef on the Beach.** What had been a plain but pleasant oceanfront bargain now offers an updated experience in keeping with its prime location, and although the decor and feel may not be to everyone's taste, the staff's aloha and attention to guests' needs bring people back again and again. **Pros:** on the beach; direct access to Waikiki Beach Walk; attentive staff. **Cons:** room decor is dated; views from non-oceanfront rooms are uninspiring; can get pricey compared to the value. *Rooms from: $340 ✉ 2169 Kalia Rd., Waikiki ☎ 808/923–3111, 866/956–4262, 800/688–7444 🌐 www.outriggerreef-onthebeach.com 669 rooms No meals.*

$$$$ RESORT **Outrigger Waikiki Beach Resort.** Outrigger's star property sits on one of the finest sections of Waikiki Beach and is a visitor favorite for its array of cultural activites, live music, dining options, and bar scene. **Pros:** the best beach bar in Waikiki; shopping, activities, and services abound on the property; on-site coin-operated laundry. **Cons:** the lobby feels a bit like an airport with so many people using it as a throughway to the beach; valet parking is $38 per day; the property has aged, which can sometimes be felt in guest-room decor. *Rooms from: $450 ✉ 2335 Kalakaua Ave., Waikiki ☎ 808/923–0711, 808/956–4262, 800/442–7304 🌐 www.outriggerwaikikihotel.com 527 rooms No meals.*

$$$$ RENTAL **The Residences at Waikiki Beach Tower.** You'll find the elegance of a luxury all-suites condominium combined with the intimacy and service of a boutique hotel right on bustling Kalakaua Avenue. **Pros:** roomy suites with quality amenities; great private lanai and views; a recreation deck with something for everyone. **Cons:** no on-site restaurants; you must cross a busy street to the beach; space, amenities, and location don't come cheap. *Rooms from: $499 ✉ 2470 Kalakaua Ave., Waikiki ☎ 877/997–6667, 855/776–1766, 808/670–3999 🌐 www.theresidencesatwaikikibeach.com 140 suites No meals.*

$ HOTEL **Royal Grove Hotel.** Two generations of the Fong family have put their heart and soul into the operation of this tiny (by Waikiki standards), pink six-story hotel that feels like a throwback to the days of boarding houses—an era where rooms were outfitted for function, not style, and served up with a wealth of simple hospitality at a price that didn't break the bank. **Pros:** very economical Waikiki option; lots of character; a throwback to another era. **Cons:** no air-conditioning in some rooms; room decor is dated; no on-site parking. *Rooms from: $100 ✉ 151*

Uluniu Ave., Waikiki ☎ 808/923–7691 🌐 www.royalgrovehotel.com ⇨ 87 rooms 🍽 No meals.

$$$$ RESORT Fodor'sChoice ★ **The Royal Hawaiian, a Luxury Collection Resort.** There's nothing like the iconc "Pink Palace of the Pacific," on 14 acres of prime Waikiki Beach, which has held fast to the luxury and grandeur that defined the hotel since it began hosting the rich and famous in the 1930s. **Pros:** can't beat it for history; mai tais and sunsets are amazing; luxury, history, and a prime location. **Cons:** history is not cheap; you'd better like pink; be prepared to share the luxury with brides and galas. 💲 *Rooms from: $650 ✉ 2259 Kalakaua Ave., Waikiki ☎ 808/923–7311, 866/716–8110 🌐 www.royal-hawaiian.com ⇨ 561 rooms 🍽 No meals.*

CONDO COMFORTS

The local **Foodland** grocery-store chain has two locations near Waikiki (✉ *Market City, 2939 Harding Ave., near intersection with Kapahulu Ave. and highway overpass, Kaimuki ☎ 808/734-6303 ✉ 1460 Beretania St., Honolulu ☎ 808/946–4654*). A smaller version of larger Foodland, **Food Pantry** (✉ *2370 Kuhio Ave., across from Miramar hotel, Waikiki ☎ 808/923–9831*) also has apparel, beach stuff, and tourist-oriented items.

$$$ HOTEL FAMILY **Sheraton Princess Kaiulani.** Starwood's Princess Kaiulani sits across the street from the regal Moana Surfrider, without some of the more elaborate amenities (such as a spa or a kid's club), but with rates that are considerably kinder to the wallet. **Pros:** in the heart of everything in Waikiki, with beach right across the street; Beach Service with chairs, towels, fruit, and water available on the beach; great value for the location. **Cons:** lobby area can feel like Grand Central Station; pool closes at 7 pm; resort fee a whopping $34.55/day, with parking an additional $35/day. 💲 *Rooms from: $310 ✉ 120 Kaiulani Ave., Waikiki ☎ 808/922–5811, 866/716–8109 🌐 www.princess-kaiulani.com ⇨ 1,010 rooms 🍽 No meals.*

$$$$ HOTEL FAMILY **Sheraton Waikiki.** If you don't mind crowds, this could be the place for you: towering over its neighbors on the prow of Waikiki's famous sands, the enormous Sheraton sits right at center stage on the beach. **Pros:** location in the heart of everything; variety of on-site activities and dining options; swimming pools often ranked among the Islands' best. **Cons:** busy atmosphere clashes with laid-back Hawaiian style; pricey resort fee and parking fees; local events routinely fill the ballrooms. 💲 *Rooms from: $515 ✉ 2255 Kalakaua Ave., Waikiki ☎ 808/922–4422, 866/716–8109 🌐 www.sheraton-waikiki.com ⇨ 1,634 rooms 🍽 No meals.*

$$ HOTEL **Shoreline Waikiki.** Situated right on the bustling Seaside Avenue in Waikiki, this 14-story, 1970s-era modernist boutique hotel is another old dame that's been brought back to life as an urban-chic property. **Pros:** great location in the middle of bustling Waikiki; no resort fee; hipster decor a refreshing break from old-style Hawaiiana. **Cons:** if the 1970s aren't your thing, skip it; rooms are small and inconsistent, so ask about the details; pool very small. 💲 *Rooms from: $250 ✉ 342 Seaside Ave., Waikiki ☎ 808/931–2444, 855/931–2444 🌐 www.shorelinehotelwaikiki.com ⇨ 135 rooms 🍽 No meals.*

$$$$ HOTEL **Trump International Hotel Waikiki Beach Walk.** One of the chicest hotels on the Waikiki scene, the Trump has been drawing visitors since it opened in late 2009. **Pros:** beautifully appointed rooms; on the edge of Waikiki so a bit quieter; great views of Friday fireworks and nightly sunsets. **Cons:** must cross street to reach the beach; pricey; small pool often filled with kids. *Rooms from: $550 223 Saratoga Rd., Waikiki 808/683–7777, 877/683–7401 www.trumphotelcollection.com/waikiki 462 rooms No meals.*

$$$$ RESORT **Waikiki Beach Marriott Resort & Spa.** On the eastern edge of Waikiki, this flagship Marriott sits on about 5 acres across from Kuhio Beach and close to Kapiolani Park, the Honolulu Zoo, and the Waikiki Aquarium. **Pros:** stunning views of Waikiki; airy, tropical public spaces; unbeatable location. **Cons:** large impersonal hotel, sometimes confusing to navigate; Kalakaua Avenue can be noisy; pricey parking and resort fee. *Rooms from: $350 2552 Kalakaua Ave., Waikiki 808/922–6611, 800/367–5370 www.marriottwaikiki.com 1,310 rooms No meals.*

$$ HOTEL FAMILY **Waikiki Beachcomber by Outrigger.** Located almost directly across from the Royal Hawaiian Center and next door to the new and revamped International Market Place, the Beachcomber is a well-situated hotel for families as well as those looking for a boutique feel in the heart of the action. **Pros:** Magic of Polynesia live entertainment; airport transportation; no resort fees, free Wi-Fi, and unlimited trolley rides. **Cons:** very busy area in the thick of Waikiki action; a busy property that sometimes shows the wear; valet parking only ($38 per day). *Rooms from: $250 2300 Kalakaua Ave., Waikiki 808/922–4646, 877/317–5756 www.waikikibeachcomberresort.com 496 rooms No meals.*

$$ HOTEL **Waikiki Parc.** In contrast to the stately vintage-Hawaiian elegance of her sister hotel, the Halekulani, the Waikiki Parc makes a contemporary statement, offering the same attention to detail in service and architectural design but lacking the beachfront location and higher prices. **Pros:** modern, consistent, and well-appointed; great access to Waikiki Beach and Beach Walk shopping and dining; lots of activities for the active traveler, including at the Halekulani across the street. **Cons:** no direct beach access; rooms can be small; renovations anticipated in 2018, so check before booking. *Rooms from: $240 2233 Helumoa Rd., Waikiki 808/921–7272, 844/640–0842, 800/422–0450 www.waikikiparc.com 297 rooms No meals.*

HOTEL CULTURAL PROGRAMS

Hotels, especially in Waikiki, are fueling a resurgence in Hawaiian culture, thanks to repeat visitors who want a more authentic island experience. In addition to lei-making and hula-dancing lessons, you can learn how to strum a ukulele, listen to Grammy Award–winning Hawaiian musicians, watch a revered master *kumu* (teacher) share the art of ancient hula and chant, chat with a marine biologist about Hawaii's endangered species, or get a lesson in the art of canoe making. Check with the concierge for daily Hawaiian activities at the hotel or nearby.

$ HOTEL **Waikiki Sand Villa.** Families and those looking for an economical rate without sacrificing proximity to Waikiki's beaches, dining, and shopping return to the Waikiki Sand Villa year after year. **Pros:** fun bar; pool and foot spa great for lounging; economical choice. **Cons:** the noise from the bar might annoy some; 10-minute walk to the beach; street noise from Ala Wai can get loud. *Rooms from: $165 ✉ 2375 Ala Wai Blvd., Waikiki ☎ 808/922–4744, 800/247–1903 🌐 www.sandvillahotel.com 214 rooms No meals.*

ALA MOANA

$$$ HOTEL **Ala Moana Hotel.** A decent value in a pricey hotel market, this well-located and nicely appointed hotel is connected to Oahu's largest mall, the Ala Moana Center, by a pedestrian ramp, and is a 10-minute walk to Waikiki. **Pros:** great value (and no resort fee); rooms are comfortably appointed; quick walk to the beach, convention center, and shopping. **Cons:** outside the heartbeat of Waikiki; some areas and rooms feel dated; large, impersonal hotel. *Rooms from: $269 ✉ 410 Atkinson Dr., Ala Moana ☎ 808/955–4811, 866/488–1396 🌐 www.alamoanahotelhonolulu.com 1,134 rooms No meals.*

KAHALA

$$$$ RESORT FAMILY Fodor's Choice ★ **The Kahala Hotel & Resort.** Hidden away in the upscale residential neighborhood of Kahala (on the other side of Diamond Head from Waikiki), this elegant oceanfront hotel has played host to celebrities, princesses, the Dalai Lama, and nearly every president since Lyndon Johnson as one of Hawaii's very first luxury resorts. **Pros:** away from hectic Waikiki; beautiful rooms and public spaces; heavenly spa. **Cons:** Waikiki is a drive away; in a residential neighborhood, so not much to do within walking distance of hotel; might be too quiet for some. *Rooms from: $495 ✉ 5000 Kahala Ave., Kahala ☎ 808/739–8888, 800/367–2525 🌐 www.kahalaresort.com 338 rooms No meals.*

NORTH SHORE

$$ HOTEL **Courtyard Oahu North Shore.** This property offers reliable and affordable hotel accommodations close to the Polynesian Cultural Center and a short drive to some of the North Shore's most iconic beaches and surfing spots. **Pros:** best bet for North Shore exploring; reliable, modern, and clean; near the beach. **Cons:** a long drive to the rest of Oahu's attractions; no alcohol served in the hotel or nearby establishments; a car is needed, and parking is not free. *Rooms from: $259 ✉ 55-400 Kamehameha Hwy., Laie ☎ 808/293–4900 🌐 www.marriott.com/hotels/travel/hnloa-courtyard-oahu-north-shore 144 rooms No meals.*

$$$ RESORT **Paradise Bay Resort.** Located right on picturesque Kaneohe Bay amidst the junglelike fauna of the windward side, this resort offers apartment-style units ranging from cozy studios to spacious two-bedroom suites with breathtaking views of the majestic Koolau Mountains, and even one stand-alone cottage in a remote area not generally frequented by tourists. **Pros:** local, authentic experience; beautiful views over the bay; pet-friendly (but $25 per night charge). **Cons:** remote location not near most other attractions; neighborhood is a bit run-down; rental car a

necessity (but parking included in $35 nightly resort fee). *Rooms from: $295* *47-039 Lihikai Dr., Kaneohe* *800/735–5071, 808/239–5711* *www.paradisebayresort.com* *46 rooms* *Free Breakfast.*

$$$$ RESORT **Turtle Bay Resort.** Sprawling over 840 acres of natural landscape on the edge of Kuilima Point in Kahuku, the Turtle Bay Resort boasts spacious guest rooms averaging nearly 500 square feet, with lanai that showcase stunning peninsula views. **Pros:** fabulous open public spaces in a secluded area of Oahu; beautiful two-level spa; excellent location for exploring the North Shore. **Cons:** very remote—even Haleiwa is a 20-minute drive; $48-per-night resort fee; 24/7 resort living isn't for everyone. *Rooms from: $360* *57-091 Kamehameha Hwy., Kahuku* *808/293–6000, 800/203–3650, 866/827–5321 for reservations* *www.turtlebayresort.com* *535 rooms* *No meals.*

WEST (LEEWARD) OAHU

$$$$ RESORT FAMILY Fodor's Choice ★ **Aulani, A Disney Resort & Spa.** Disney's first property in Hawaii melds the Disney magic with breathtaking vistas, white sandy beaches, and sunsets that even Mickey stops to watch. **Pros:** tons to do on-site; family-friendly done right; Painted Sky teen spa. **Cons:** a long way from Waikiki; character breakfasts are often sold out (book far in advance); areas and events can get really busy. *Rooms from: $550* *92-1185 Aliinui Dr., Ko Olina* *714/520–7001, 808/674–6200, 866/443–4763* *www.disneyaulani.com* *856 rooms* *No meals.*

$$$$ RESORT **Four Seasons Oahu at Ko Olina.** Oahu welcomed this luxurious new property to Ko Olina with great excitement—the first Four Seasons on the island, with nearly every room and suite in the 17-story hotel offering floor-to-ceiling windows and a private lanai, all with an ocean view. **Pros:** luxurious and exclusive; secluded, even in the Ko Olina complex; amenities and options abound. **Cons:** an hour from Waikiki; luxury doesn't come cheap; it doesn't always measure up to other Four Seasons. *Rooms from: $675* *92-1001 Olani St., in the Ko Olina complex, Kapolei* *808/679–0079, 844/387–0308* *www.fourseasons.com/oahu* *371 rooms* *No meals.*

NIGHTLIFE AND PERFORMING ARTS

Updated by Tiffany Hill

Gone are the days when there was nothing to do in Honolulu at night. Any guidebook that tells you Honolulu isn't for the night owl is outdated. Most nights it's hard to pick which DJ to see at which nightclub, or which art show opening to attend. In fact, many people who arrive in Oahu expecting to find white-sand beaches and nothing else are surprised at such a vibrant nightlife. Bask in the shade of the swaying palm trees, watch the sunset over Waikiki, and dress up, because more and more clubs in Honolulu enforce a dress code.

Posh bars can be found in many of the larger hotels, but venture outside the strip and into places like Chinatown (which virtually explodes with events on the first Friday of each month) and surrounding neighborhoods, and you'll discover comfortable local watering holes. Every night of the week you can find musicians in venues from Kailua to Ko Olina—and everywhere in between.

And if all-night dancing isn't for you, Oahu also has a thriving arts and culture scene, with community-theater productions, stand-up comedy, outdoor concerts, film festivals, and chamber-music performances. Major Broadway shows, dance companies, rock stars, and comedians come through the Islands, too. Check local newspapers—the *Honolulu Star-Advertiser* or *Midweek*—for the latest events. Websites like 🌐 *www.frolichawaii.com* and 🌐 *www.honolulumagazine.com* also have great information.

Whether you stay out all night or get up early to catch the morning surf, there's something for everyone on Oahu.

NIGHTLIFE

Oahu is the best of all the Islands for nightlife. The locals call it *pau hana,* but you might call it happy hour (the literal translation of the Hawaiian phrase is "done with work"). On weeknights, it's likely that you'll find the working crowd, still in their business-casual attire, downing chilled beers even before the sun goes down. Those who don't have to wake up in the early morning should change into a fresh outfit and start the evening closer to 10 pm.

On the weekends, it's typical to have dinner at a restaurant before hitting the clubs around 9:30. Some bar-hoppers start as early as 7, but partygoers typically don't patronize more than two establishments a night. That's because getting from one Oahu nightspot to the next usually requires transportation. Happily, cab services are plentiful, and rideshares like Uber and Lyft give Honolulu a San Francisco feel.

You can find a bar in just about any area on Oahu. Most of the clubs, however, are in Waikiki, near Ala Moana, and in Chinatown, near downtown Honolulu. The drinking age is 21 on Oahu and throughout Hawaii. Many bars will admit younger people but will not serve them alcohol. By law, all establishments that serve alcoholic beverages must close by 2 am, although you might get lucky and stumble into a secret all-night party. The only exceptions are those with a cabaret license, which can stay open until 4 am. ■ TIP→ **Some places have a cover charge of $5–$10, but with many establishments, getting there early means you don't have to pay.**

HONOLULU

WAIKIKI

Addiction Nightclub. Traditional banquettes offer intimate seating for VIP tables, and bottle service lends a New York City nightclub feel at The Modern Honolulu. Red-velvet ropes guide you to the entrance; once inside you can dance to house and hip-hop music under a stunning ceiling installation of 40,000 round lights. But Addiction comes with a price: there's a hefty cover for men, less for women (if you're not on the guest list), and drinks aren't cheap. ✉ *The Modern Honolulu, 1775 Ala Moana Blvd., Waikiki* ☎ *888/244–9925 For reservations* 🌐 *www.addictionnightclub.com.*

Duke's Waikiki. Making the most of its spot on Waikiki Beach, Duke's presents live music everyday. Contemporary Hawaiian musicians like Henry Kapono and Maunalua have performed here, as have nationally known musicians like Jimmy Buffett. It's not unusual for surfers to leave their boards outside to step in for a casual drink after a long day on the waves. The bar-and-grill's surf theme pays homage to Duke Kahanamoku, who popularized the sport in the early 1900s. ✉ *Outrigger Waikiki, 2335 Kalakaua Ave., Suite 116, Waikiki* ☎ *808/922–2268* 🌐 *www.dukeswaikiki.com.*

Hula's Bar and Lei Stand. Hawaii's oldest and best-known gay-friendly nightspot offers panoramic views of Diamond Head by day and high-energy club music by night. Patrons have included Elton John, Adam Lambert, and Dolly Parton. ✉ *Waikiki Grand Hotel, 134 Kapahulu Ave., 2nd fl., Waikiki* ☎ *808/923–0669* 🌐 *www.hulas.com.*

Fodor's Choice ★ **Lewers Lounge.** A great spot for predinner drinks or post-sunset cocktails, Lewers Lounge offers a relaxed but chic atmosphere in the middle of Waikiki. There are classic and contemporary cocktails. Some standouts include Chocolate Dreams (made with Van Gogh Dutch Chocolate Vodka) and the Lost Passion (featuring a rich blend of tequila, Cointreau, and fresh juices topped with champagne). Enjoy your libation with nightly live jazz and tempting desserts, such as the hotel's famous coconut cake. Or just sit back and relax in the grand setting of the luxurious lounge, which is decked in dramatic drapes and cozy banquettes. ✉ *Halekulani Hotel, 2199 Kalia Rd., Waikiki* ☎ *808/923–2311* 🌐 *www.halekulani.com.*

Lulu's Waikiki. Even if you're not a surfer, you'll love this place's retro vibe and the unobstructed second-floor view of Waikiki Beach. The open-air setting, casual dining menu, and tropical drinks are all you need to help you settle into your vacation. The venue transforms from a nice spot for breakfast, lunch, or dinner (happy hour is 3 to 5 pm) to a bustling, high-energy club with live music lasting into the wee hours. ✉ *Park Shore Waikiki Hotel, 2586 Kalakaua Ave., Waikiki* ☎ *808/926–5222* 🌐 *www.luluswaikiki.com.*

Fodor's Choice ★ **Mai Tai Bar at the Royal Hawaiian.** The bartenders here sure know how to mix up a killer mai tai. This is, after all, *the* establishment that first made the famous drink in the Islands. The umbrella-shaded tables at the outdoor bar are front-row seating for sunsets and also have an unobstructed view of Diamond Head. Contemporary Hawaiian musicians hold jam sessions onstage nightly. ✉ *Royal Hawaiian Hotel, 2259 Kalakaua Ave., Waikiki* ☎ *808/923–7311* 🌐 *www.royal-hawaiian.com.*

Moana Terrace. Three floors up from Waikiki Beach, this is a casual, open-air terrace where some of Hawaii's finest musicians play every evening. Order a drink served in a fresh pineapple and watch the sun dip into the Pacific Ocean. ✉ *Waikiki Beach Marriott Resort, 2552 Kalakaua Ave., Waikiki* ☎ *808/922–6611* 🌐 *www.marriott.com.*

RumFire. Locals and visitors head here for the convivial atmosphere, trendy decor, and the million-dollar view of Waikiki Beach and Diamond Head. Come early to get a seat for happy hour (3–5 pm daily). If you're feeling peckish, there's a menu of Asian-influenced dishes.

RumFire also features original cocktails, signature shots, and daily live music. On Friday and Saturday, the bar gets even livelier once local DJs start spinning at 9:30. ✉ *Sheraton Waikiki, 2255 Kalakaua Ave., Waikiki* ☎ *808/922–4422* 🌐 *www.rumfirewaikiki.com.*

Sky Waikiki. This may just be the club Oahu has been waiting for. Sky Waikiki sits 19 stories above the city, just below Top of Waikiki, the strip's iconic revolving restaurant (and is managed by the same company). From the couches on the welcoming open-air lanai, you are treated to nearly 360-degree scenic views of Diamond Head, the Waikiki beaches, and the classic coral Royal Hawaiian hotel. It's one of the best spots to take in a Waikiki sunset. The club inside exudes contemporary-LA chic every night, and resident DJs spin on Friday and Saturday nights. ✉ *Waikiki Trade Center, 2270 Kalakaua Ave., Waikiki* ☎ *808/979–7590* 🌐 *www.skywaikiki.com.*

The Study. It's tricky to find the Study at the Modern Honolulu—it's behind a huge, revolving bookcase in the lobby behind the registration desk. It's an überchic space, with intimate alcoves and oversize sofas that are both hip and inviting. The bar features literary-themed cocktails, like the Huckleberry Finn and the War and Peace. ✉ *The Modern Honolulu, 1775 Ala Moana Blvd., Waikiki* ☎ *808/450–3396* 🌐 *www.themodernhonolulu.com/the-study.*

Tiki's Grill & Bar. Tiki torches light the way to this restaurant and bar overlooking Kuhio Beach. A mix of locals and visitors head here on the weekend to get their fill of kitschy cool. There's nightly entertainment featuring contemporary Hawaiian musicians. Don't leave without sipping on the Lava Flow, or noshing on the famous coconut shrimp. ✉ *Aston Waikiki Beach Hotel, 2570 Kalakaua Ave., Waikiki* ☎ *808/923–8454* 🌐 *www.tikisgrill.com.*

DOWNTOWN

Fodor's Choice ★ **Bar Leather Apron.** The bar at this intimate cocktail spot on the mezzanine of a downtown Honolulu office building seats only six, so you'll want to make reservations to enjoy bespoke cocktails that utilize only the finest liquors and ingredients. Owners Tom Park and Justin Park (no relation) have cultivated a reputation for their E Ho'o Pau Mai Tai made with raisin-infused, five-year-old El Dorado rum, 12-year-old El Dorado, coconut water syrup, spiced orgeat, ohia blossom honey, lime, and absinthe. The bar is closed on Sunday and Monday. ✉ *Topa Financial Center, 745 Fort St., Mezzanine Level, Ste. 127A, Downtown* ☎ *808/524–0808* 🌐 *www.barleatherapron.com.*

Murphy's Bar & Grill. On the edge of Chinatown, this bar has served drinks to such locals and visitors as King Kalakaua and Robert Louis Stevenson since the late 1800s. The kind of Irish pub you'd find in Boston, Murphy's is a break from all the tropical, fruit-garnished drinks found in Waikiki, and it's definitely the place to be on St. Patrick's Day. Its block-party fund-raiser on that day is one of the most popular on the island. On Friday it serves some of the best homemade fruit pies around; they're so good, they sell out during lunch. ✉ *2 Merchant St., Downtown* ☎ *808/531–0422* 🌐 *www.murphyshawaii.com.*

Nocturna Lounge. This is Hawaii's first self-described NextGen lounge, a stylish and sophisticated karaoke and gaming lounge at the Waterfront Plaza. It boasts a full bar, four private suites with state-of-the-art karaoke, and video game consoles around the lounge featuring the latest in social gaming. Play Street Fighter in the open lounge, perfect your moves in Dance Central on the Xbox Kinect in a side room, or wander through the noisy club while sipping one of Nocturna's creative cocktails with names like Princess Peach and Falcon Punch. The crowd isn't as young as you'd expect at a club outfitted with video game consoles—in fact, you must to be at least 21 to enter. ✉ *Waterfront Plaza, 500 Ala Moana Blvd., No. 5D, Downtown* ☎ *808/521–1555* 🌐 *www.nocturnalounge.com.*

CHINATOWN

Downbeat Lounge. This dimly lit but welcoming lounge is the soulful little sister of the trendy all-night Downbeat Diner next door, and owned by the same people. There's live music most nights, so it's a great place to catch one of Oahu's local acts. And it's a diverse lineup, from punk, ska, and indie rock, to bluegrass and folk. The lounge serves craft and draft beers as well as creative cocktails focusing on whiskey and moonshine, such as the Oke Punch made with Okolehau Hawaiian Moonshine. If your late-night Chinatown partying has you hankering for a hamburger, you can also order from the diner's menu. The lounge is closed on Sunday. ✉ *42 N. Hotel St., Chinatown* ☎ *808/533–2328* 🌐 *www.downbeatdiner.com.*

The Dragon Upstairs. In the heart of Chinatown, this cool club—formerly a tattoo parlor, hence the dragon mural—serves up classic cocktails along with loungy jazz performances most nights of the week. You'll hear local vocalists, as well as small combos, in this unique venue upstairs from Hank's Cafe Honolulu. ✉ *1038 Nuuanu Ave., Chinatown* ☎ *808/526–1411* 🌐 *thedragonupstairs.com.*

Encore Saloon. Hawaii isn't a hotbed for quality Mexican cuisine, so when Encore opened in 2016, it was a welcome addition to Chinatown's already buzzing bar and restaurant scene. The mezcal-focused bar also serves good Mexican-inspired food, but its drinks menu is most impressive, offering more than 50 varieties of tequila and mezcal, both of which are distilled from agave. You can also get a traditional margarita here, as well as wine and canned beer. If you're hungry, order the pork carnitas or the chicken mole street-style tacos, which come in sets of two. The bar is closed Sunday. ✉ *10 North Hotel St., Chinatown* ☎ *808/367–1656* 🌐 *www.encoresaloon.com.*

Fodor's Choice ★ **J.J. Dolan's.** This place bills itself as an "Irish pub with New York pizza from two guys in Chinatown." Those two guys are J.J. and Dolan, respectively, the pub's owners. And they know how to make a killer pie. The classics are always on the menu, but J.J. Dolan's daily specials are toothsome and inventive, like its white pie generously topped with smoked salmon, Maui sweet onions, capers, roasted red peppers, and feta. From downtown professionals to local families, these pies are crowd pleasers. The drinks are just as popular as the pizza and reasonably priced by Honolulu standards, making it a favorite among locals. Don't be surprised if you have to put your name on the waiting list come 5 pm. It's closed on Sunday. ✉ *1147 Bethel St., Chinatown* ☎ *808/537–4992* 🌐 *www.jjdolans.com.*

Manifest. With exposed red brick, big skylights, and rotating exhibitions every three months from local photographers and painters, Manifest Hawaii has an artist's loft feel to it. Indeed, graphic designers, artists, and writers who have offices nearby are known regulars. The bar handcrafts quality cocktails such as the Love of My Life (Espolon tequila, Vieux Pontarlier absinthe, orgeat, lemon, and Peychaud bitters) and mules made with vodka, tequila, gin, whiskey, bourbon, or even absinthe. It's even a good "coffice" (coffee shop–office); by day Manifest serves coffee and tea and has free Wi-Fi. ✉ *32 N. Hotel St., Chinatown* 🌐 *www.manifesthawaii.com.*

2

ALA MOANA

Mai Tai Bar. After a long day of shopping at Ala Moana Center, the fourth-floor Mai Tai Bar is a perfect spot to relax. There's live entertainment and happy hour specials for both food and drink. There's never a cover charge and no dress code. To avoid waiting in line, get here before 9 pm. ✉ *Ala Moana Center, 1450 Ala Moana Blvd., Ala Moana* ☎ *808/947–2900* 🌐 *www.maitaibar.com.*

KAKAAKO

Aloha Beer Co. At this cool brewpub, you order everything at the counter and then pick a spot to sit in either the industrial indoor taproom or the casual outdoor area. (There's also an upstairs space, complete with its own speakeasy-style entrance.) With 11 beers on draft, including the Hop Lei IPA, Waimanalo Farmhouse, and Portlock Porter, you can find something to your taste. If you're hungry, there's hearty sandwiches, some made with Oahu-based Pono Pork. ✉ *700 Queen St., Kakaako* ☎ *808/544–1605* 🌐 *www.alohabeer.com.*

Fodor's Choice ★

Bevy. Tucked at the end of a row of new boutiques in Kakaako, Bevy is urban, modern, and furnished with up-cycled materials; its benches are upholstered in denim jeans and the table tops feature flattened wine boxes. But locals in the know go for artisan cocktails created by owner and award-winning mixologist Christian Self, who deftly concocts libations utilizing ingredients such as rye whiskey and Italian green walnut. One happy hour (4–7 pm) bright spot is the $1.50 oyster shooters. The bar is closed on Sunday. (Next door is Bevy Market, Self's foray into the gourmet food market; it's open for lunch.) ✉ *675 Auahi St., Kakaako* ☎ *808/594–7445* 🌐 *www.bevyhawaii.com.*

The Brewseum. This brewpub is a must-visit for imbibers who like a little history with their beer. The charming spot wonderfully combines World War II memorabilia with small-craft brews. On the walls hang 1940s-era telephones that transmit actual archival radio transmissions through their receivers. Overhead, a model freight train chugs around the room, while model bomber planes fly over on a pulley system. There's even an army jeep parked inside—everyone loves to have their photo taken in it. The bar is owned and operated by the Tomlinson family, who treat each patron like *ohana*. The Brewseum has its own label, Home of the Brave Brewing. Each pint comes with complimentary popcorn, or you can order a soft pretzel or a personal pizza. It's closed Sunday and Monday. ✉ *901 Waimanu St., Kakaako* ☎ *808/396–8112* 🌐 *www.brewseums.com.*

Fodor's Choice ★ **Waikiki Brewing Company.** This company not only brews its own quality craft beer but also serves delicious food. Although the original is still operational in Waikiki at 1945 Kalakaua Ave., this second location opened in 2017. The brewery always offers nine beers on tap, including the Skinny Jeans IPA and the Hana Hou Hefe, in which sweet orange peel and strawberry puree are added before fermentation. You can also buy six-packs at the bar to go. What makes this location unique is that the chef smokes meat in-house using local kiawe wood, resulting in tender beef brisket, flavorful pulled pork, juicy bratwursts, and herb-crusted chicken. Any of these would be the perfect pairing for your beer. ✉ *831 Queen St., Kakaako* ☎ *808/591–0387* 🌐 *www.waikikibrewing.com.*

MOILIILI

Fodor's Choice ★ **Pint + Jigger.** This spot has cultivated a regular following with nearby college students and thirtysomethings since its opening by doing two simple, but essential things: making a high-quality cocktail and dishing up polished pub fare. It doesn't hurt that the bar also boasts a rotation of 20 beers, plus one cocktail on tap. Its Scotch egg and stout burger are consistent, while drinks such as the Talventi (rye whiskey, Campari, and cold-brewed coffee topped with house-made vanilla cream) are refreshing and inventive. After your meal, head to the back of the bar for a friendly game of shuffleboard. ✉ *1936 S. King St., Moiliili* ☎ *808/744–9593* 🌐 *www.pintandjigger.com.*

WINDWARD OAHU

Boardrider's Bar & Grill. Tucked away in Kailua Town, Boardrider's has long been the place for local bands to strut their stuff. Look for live music—reggae to rock and roll—every Friday and Saturday night. The space includes a pool table, dartboards, and eight TVs for watching the game. ✉ *201-A Hamakua Dr., Kailua* ☎ *808/261–4600.*

THE NORTH SHORE

Surfer, the Bar. This laid-back bar is located in the Turtle Bay Resort and is a partnership between the hotel and *Surfer* magazine. It's a hip spot for the bar's namesake crowd to unwind, as well as meandering hotel guests. There's live music and Talk Story sessions, where Hawaii's surfing legends regale bar goers with their gnarliest experiences out on the waves. ✉ *Turtle Bay Resort, 57-091 Kamehameha Hwy., Kahuku* ☎ *808/293–6000* 🌐 *www.surferthebar.com.*

PERFORMING ARTS

DINNER CRUISES AND SHOWS

Dinner cruises depart either from the piers adjacent to the Aloha Tower Marketplace in downtown Honolulu or from Kewalo Basin, near Ala Moana Beach Park, and head along the coast toward Diamond Head. There's usually a buffet-style dinner with a local flavor, dancing, drinks, and a sensational sunset. Except as noted, dinner cruises cost approximately $80 to $200, cocktail cruises $40 to $55. Some cruises offer discounts for online reservations. Most major credit cards are accepted. In all cases, reservations are essential. Check the websites for savings of up to 15%.

Atlantis Cruises. The sleekly high-tech *Majestic,* designed to sail smoothly in rough waters, powers farther along Waikiki's coastline than its competitors, sailing past Diamond Head. Enjoy sunset dinners or moonlight cruises aboard the 400-passenger boat, feasting on garlic shiitake teriyaki chicken and the catch of the day. ✉ *Aloha Tower Marketplace, 1 Aloha Tower Rd., Pier 6, Honolulu* ☎ *808/973–1311, 800/381–0237* 🌐 *www.atlantisadventures.com* 🎫 *From $79.*

Ha: Breath of Life. The Polynesian Cultural Center's long-running nightly show, *Ha: Breath of Life,* is a story of love, respect, and responsibility. *Ha,* which means "breath" in Hawaiian, follows the central character of Mana from his birth to the birth of his own child. The performances highlight ancient Hawaiian, Polynesian, Samoan, and Tahitian culture, music, and dance, including fire-knife dancers, and with more than 100 performers. Performances are Monday–Saturday at 7:30 pm. ✉ *Polynesian Cultural Center, 55-370 Kamehameha Hwy., Laie* ☎ *800/367–7060* 🌐 *www.habreathoflife.com* 🎫 *From $89.95.*

Magic of Polynesia. Hawaii's top illusionist, John Hirokawa, displays mystifying sleight of hand in this highly entertaining show, which incorporates contemporary hula and Islands music into its acts. It's held in the Waikiki Beachcomber by Outrigger's $7.5-million showroom. Reservations are required for dinner and the show. Dinner choices range from a ginger sesame glazed chicken dinner to a deluxe steak-and-lobster combo. Walk-ins are permitted if you just want the entertainment. Nightly dinner begins at 5:45, the show at 7 pm. ✉ *Holiday Inn Waikiki Beachcomber Hotel, 2300 Kalakaua Ave., Waikiki* ☎ *808/539-9400* 🌐 *www.robertshawaii.com* 🎫 *Show from $52; show and dinner from $91.*

LUAU

The luau is an experience that everyone, both local and tourist, should have. Today's luau still offer traditional foods and entertainment, but there's often a fun, contemporary flair. With many, you can watch the roasted pig being carried out of its *imu,* a hole in the ground used for cooking food with heated stones.

Luau average around $100 per person—some are cheaper, others twice that amount—and are held around the island, not just in Waikiki. Reservations—and a camera—are a must.

Chief's Luau at Wet 'n' Wild Hawaii. Chief Sielu and his *ohana* (family) perform at Wet 'n' Wild Hawaii waterpark. It's a top-rated luau with everything you'd expect from this island tradition: good food, rhythmic music, and interactive performances. The show ends with a high-energy fire-knife dance. The chef also heads the Fia Fia Luau at the Marriott in Ko Olina. ✉ *Wet 'n' Wild Hawaii, 400 Farrington Hwy., Kapolei* ☎ *877/357–2480* 🌐 *www.chiefsluau.com* 🎫 *From $95.*

Fia Fia Luau. Just after sunset at the Marriott Ko Olina Beach Club, the charismatic Chief Sielu Avea leads the Samoan-based Fia Fia, an entertaining show that takes guests on the journey through the South Pacific. Every show is different and unscripted, but always a good look at Polynesian culture. It's the only recurring show with eight fire-knife dancers in a blazing finale. It's held on Tuesday at 4:30. Admission includes a buffet dinner. ✉ *92-161 Waipahe Pl., Ko Olina* ☎ *808/679–4700*, 🌐 *www.marriott.com/hotels/hotel-information/restaurant/hnlko-marriotts-ko-olina-beach-club* 🎫 *From $105.*

Germaine's Luau. More than 3 million visitors have come to this luau, held about 45 minutes west of Waikiki in light traffic. Widely considered one of the most folksy and laid-back, Germaine's offers a tasty, multicourse, all-you-can-eat buffet. Admission includes the buffet and one drink to three drinks (depending on the package). It's held Tuesday to Sunday at 6. ✉ *91-119 Olai St., Kapolei* ☎ *808/202–2528* 🌐 *www.germainesluau.com* 🎫 *From $85, transportation from $16.*

Paradise Cove Luau. One of the largest shows on Oahu, the lively Paradise Cove Luau is held in the Ko Olina resort area, about 45 minutes from Waikiki (if there's light traffic). Drink in hand, you can stroll through the authentic village, learn traditional arts and crafts, and play local games. The stage show includes a fire-knife dancer, singing emcee, and both traditional and contemporary hula and other Polynesian dances. A finale dance features participation from the audience. Admission includes the buffet, activities, and the show. You pay extra for table service, box seating, and shuttle transport to and from Waikiki—the stunning sunsets are free. It starts daily at 5. ✉ *92-1089 Alii Nui Dr., Ko Olina* ☎ *808/842–5911* 🌐 *www.paradisecove.com* 🎫 *From $97* ☞ *Round-trip Waikiki transportation, $16.*

Fodor's Choice ★ **Polynesian Cultural Center Alii Luau.** Although this elaborate luau has the sharpest production values, there is no booze allowed (it's a Mormon-owned facility in the heart of Laie—Mormon country). It's held amid the seven re-created villages at the Polynesian Cultural Center in the North Shore town of Laie, about a 1½-hour drive from Honolulu. The luau—considered one of the most authentic on the island—includes the *Ha: Breath of Life* show that has long been popular with both residents and visitors. Rates vary depending on activities and amenities that are included (personalized tours, reserved seats, or table service, for example). Waikiki transport is available. It's held Monday–Saturday at 5. ✉ *Polynesian Cultural Center, 55-370 Kamehameha Hwy., Laie* ☎ *808/293–3333, 800/367–7060* 🌐 *www.polynesia.com* 🎫 *From $119.95.*

SHOPS AND SPAS

Updated by Chris Oliver

Eastern and Western traditions meet on Oahu, where savvy shoppers find luxury goods at high-end malls and scout tiny boutiques and galleries filled with pottery, blown glass, woodwork, and Hawaiian-print clothing by local artists. This blend of cultures is pervasive in the wide selection of spas as well. Hawaiian *lomilomi* and hot-stone massages are as omnipresent as the orchid and plumeria flowers decorating every treatment room.

Experience one of Hawaii's most spectacular luau at the Polynesian Cultural Center.

Exploring downtown Honolulu, Kailua on the windward side, and the North Shore often yields the most original merchandise. Some of the small stores carry imported clothes and gifts from around the world—a reminder that, on this island halfway between Asia and the United States, shopping is a multicultural experience.

If you're getting a massage at a spa, there's a spiritual element to the *lomilomi* that calms the soul while the muscles release tension. During a hot-stone massage, smooth rocks, taken from the earth with permission from Pele, the goddess of volcanoes, are heated and placed at focal points on the body. Others are covered in oil and rubbed over tired limbs, feeling like powerful fingers. For an alternative, refresh skin with mango scrubs so fragrant they seem edible. Savor the unusual sensation of bamboo tapped against the arches of the feet. Indulge in a scalp massage that makes the entire body tingle. Day spas provide additional options to the self-indulgent services offered in almost every major hotel on the island.

HONOLULU

There are two distinct types of shopping experiences for visitors: vast malls with the customary department stores and tiny boutiques with specialty items. Three malls in Honolulu provide a combination of the standard department stores and interesting shops showcasing original paintings and woodwork from local artists and craftsmen. Shoppers who know where to look in Honolulu will find everything from designer merchandise to unusual Asian imports.

Possibilities are endless, but a bit of scouting is usually required to get past the items you'll find in your own hometown. Industrious bargain hunters can detect the perfect gift in the sale bin of a slightly hidden store at every mall.

You'll find that shops stay open fairly late in Waikiki. Stores open at around 9 am and many don't close until 10 or even 11 pm.

WAIKIKI

CLOTHING

Newt at the Royal. Newt is known for high-quality, handwoven Panama hats and tropical sportswear for men and women. ✉ *The Royal Hawaiian Hotel, 2259 Kalakaua Ave., Waikiki* ☎ *808/923–4332* 🌐 *www.newtattheroyal.com.*

GIFTS

Sand People. This little shop stocks beach-inspired, easy-to-carry gifts, such as fish-shaped Christmas ornaments, Hawaiian-style notepads, frames, charms in the shape of flip-flops (known locally as "slippahs"), soaps, kitchen accessories, and ceramic clocks. There's another branch in the Waikiki Sheraton, one in Kailua, as well as three each on Kauai and Maui. ✉ *Moana Surfrider, 2369 Kalakaua, Waikiki* ☎ *808/924–6773.*

JEWELRY

Philip Rickard. The heirloom design collection of this famed jeweler features custom Hawaiian jewelry, particularly its Wedding Collection often sought by various celebrities. The jewelry is made in many different gold colors and platinum, which feature the scrolling patterns, enameled names, and inlays of traditional Hawaiian jewelry. ✉ *International Market Place, 2330 Kalakaua Ave., Level 1, Banyan Court, #105, Waikiki* ☎ *808/924–7972* 🌐 *www.philiprickard.com.*

SHOPPING CENTERS

T Galleria Hawaii. Hermès, Cartier, Michael Kors, Dior, and Marc Jacobs are among the shops on the Waikiki Luxury Walk in this enclosed mall, as well as Hawaii's largest beauty and cosmetic store. The third floor caters to duty-free shoppers only and features an exclusive Watch Shop. ✉ *330 Royal Hawaiian Ave., Waikiki* ☎ *808/931–2700* 🌐 *www.dfs.com/en/tgalleria-hawaii.*

Royal Hawaiian Center. An open and inviting facade has made this three-block-long shopping center a garden of Hawaiian shops. There are more than 110 stores and restaurants, including local gems such as Fighting Eel, Honolulu Home Collection, and Koi Honolulu. Check out tropical Panama hats at Hawaiian Island Arts or offerings at Island Soap & Candleworks, while Royal Hawaiian Quilt offers handmade Hawaiian quilts, pillow covers, kitchen accessories, and more. Nine restaurants round out the dining options, along with the Paina Lanai Food Court, complimentary cultural classes, plus a theater and nightly outdoor entertainment. ✉ *2201 Kalakaua Ave., Waikiki* ☎ *808/922–0588* 🌐 *www.royalhawaiiancenter.com.*

2100 Kalakaua. Tenants of this elegant, town house–style center known as Luxury Row include Chanel, Coach, Tiffany & Co., Yves Saint Laurent, Bottega Veneta, Gucci, Hugo Boss, Miu Miu, and Montcler. ✉ *2100 Kalakaua Ave., Waikiki* ☎ *808/922–2246* 🌐 *www.luxuryrow.com.*

INEXPENSIVE LOCAL SOUVENIRS

Hawaii can be an expensive place. If you are looking to bring someone a gift, consider the following, which can be found all over the island:

Try the coconut peanut butter from **North Shore Goodies**. Just when you thought peanut butter couldn't get any better, someone added coconut to it and made it even more delicious.

If you are a fan of plate lunches, **Rainbow Drive In** has T-shirts with regular orders—"All rice," "Gravy all over," "Boneless"—printed on them. They come packed in an iconic plate lunch box.

Relive your memories of tea on the Veranda by purchasing Island Essence Tea, created by the **Moana Surfrider**.

Harvested from a salt farm on Molokai, **Hawaii Traditional Salts** come in a variety of flavors, including black lava, Cabernet, balsamic, and classic. They're colored to match their flavor, so they are beautiful as well as tasty.

Foodland makes insulated cooler bags that are decorated with uniquely local designs that go beyond tropical flowers and coconuts. Look for the pidgin or poke designs.

Made with all-natural, local ingredients, like kukui-nut oil, local flowers, herbs, even seaweed, indigenous bar soap is available online or in stores, like **Blue Hawaii Lifestyle**.

Waikiki Beach Walk. This open-air shopping center greets visitors at the west end of Waikiki's Kalakaua Avenue with 70 locally owned stores and restaurants. Get reasonably priced, fashionable resort wear for yourself at Mahina; find unique pieces by local artists at Under the Koa Tree; or buy local delicacies from the Poke Bar. Or you can browse Koa and sandalwood gifts at Martin & MacArthur in the nearby Outrigger Reef Hotel. The mall also features free local entertainment on the outdoor-fountain stage at least once a week. ✉ *226 Lewers St., Waikiki* ☎ *808/931–3591* 🌐 *www.waikikibeachwalk.com.*

DOWNTOWN

HOME DECOR

Robyn Buntin Galleries. Chinese antiques, Japanese art, Buddhist sculptures, and important works by Hawaiian artists are among the international pieces sold here as well as jewelry and an extensive selection of prints. The gallery has more than 7,000 items available online. ✉ *Robyn Buntin Gallery, 848 S. Beretania St., Downtown* ☎ *808/523–5913* 🌐 *www.robynbuntin.com.*

CHINATOWN

GALLERIES

Louis Pohl Gallery. Stop in this gallery to browse modern works from some of Hawaii's finest artists. In addition to pieces by resident artists, there are monthly exhibitions by local and visiting artists. ✉ *1142 Bethel St., Chinatown* ☎ *808/521–1812* 🌐 *www.louispohlgallery.com.*

KAKAAKO

CLOTHING

Anne Namba Designs. This designer combines the beauty of classic kimonos with contemporary styles to make unique pieces for career and evening. In addition to women's apparel, she designs a men's line and a wedding couture line. ✉ *324 Kamani St., Kakaako* ☎ *808/589–1135* 🌐 *www.annenamba.com.*

ALA MOANA

BOOKS

Na Mea Hawaii. In addition to Islands-style clothing for adults and children, Hawaiian cultural items, and unusual artwork such as Niihau-shell necklaces, this boutique's book selection covers Hawaiian history and language, and offers children's books set in the Islands. ✉ *Ward Village, 1200 Ala Moana Blvd., Ste. 270, Ala Moana* ☎ *808/596–8885* 🌐 *www.nameahawaii.com.*

CLOTHING

Reyn Spooner. This clothing store is a good place to buy the aloha-print fashions residents wear. Look for the limited-edition Christmas shirt, a collector's item manufactured each holiday season. Reyn Spooner has eight locations statewide and offers styles for both men and children. ✉ *Ala Moana Shopping Center, 1450 Ala Moana Blvd., Ala Moana* ☎ *808/949–5929* 🌐 *www.reynspooner.com.*

FOOD

Honolulu Chocolate Company. To really impress those back home, pick up a box of gourmet chocolates here. Choose from dozens of flavors of Hawaii, from Kona coffee to macadamia nuts, dipped in fine chocolate. ✉ *Sheraton Waikiki, 2255 Kalakaua Ave., Ala Moana* ☎ *808/931–8937.*

Longs Drugs. For gift items in bulk, try one of the many outposts of Longs, the perfect place to stock up on chocolate-covered macadamia nuts—at reasonable prices—to carry home. ✉ *Ala Moana Shopping Center, 1450 Ala Moana Blvd., 2nd level, Ala Moana* ☎ *808/941–4433* 🌐 *www.alamoanacenter.com/en/directory/longs-drugs-789.html.*

GIFTS

Blue Hawaii Lifestyle. The Ala Moana store carries a large selection of locally made products, including soaps, honey, tea, salt, chocolates, art, and CDs. Every item, in fact, is carefully selected from various Hawaiian companies, artisans, and farms, from the salt fields of Molokai to the lavender farms on Maui to the single-estate chocolate on Oahu's North Shore. A café in the store serves healthy smoothies, panini, tea, and espresso. ✉ *Ala Moana Shopping Center, 1450 Ala Moana Blvd., Ala Moana* ☎ *808/949–0808* 🌐 *www.bluehawaiilifestyle.com.*

HAWAIIAN ARTS AND CRAFTS

Hawaiian Quilt Collection. Traditional island comforters, wall hangings, pillows, bags, and other Hawaiian-print quilt accessories are the specialty here. There are also two locations in Waikiki hotels and one on Waikiki Beach Walk. ✉ *Ala Moana Shopping Center, 1450 Ala Moana Blvd., Ala Moana* ☎ *808/946–2233* 🌐 *www.hawaiian-quilts.com.*

Na Hoku. If you look at the wrists of *kamaaina* (local) women, you might see Hawaiian heirloom bracelets fashioned in either gold or silver and engraved in a number of Islands-inspired designs. Na Hoku sells traditional and modern jewelry in designs that capture the heart of the Hawaiian lifestyle in all its elegant diversity. ✉ *Ala Moana Center, 1450 Ala Moana Blvd., Ala Moana* ☎ *808/946–2100* 🌐 *www.nahoku.com.*

SHOPPING CENTERS

Ala Moana Shopping Center. The world's largest open-air shopping mall is five minutes from Waikiki by bus. More than 350 stores and 60 restaurants make up this 50-acre complex, which is a unique mix of national and international chains as well as smaller, locally owned shops and eateries—and everything in between. Thirty-five luxury boutiques in residence include Gucci, Louis Vuitton, Christian Dior, and Emporio Armani. All of Hawaii's major department stores are here, including the state's only Neiman Marcus and Nordstrom, plus Macy's, Target, and Bloomingdales. To get to the mall from Waikiki, catch TheBus line 8, 19, 20, 23, 24 or 42; a one-way ride is $2.50. Or hop aboard the Waikiki Trolley's Pink Line for $2 each way; it comes through the area every 10 minutes. ✉ *1450 Ala Moana Blvd., Ala Moana* ☎ *808/955–9517* 🌐 *www.alamoanacenter.com.*

Ward Village. Heading west from Waikiki toward downtown Honolulu, you'll run into a section of town with five distinct shopping-complex areas; there are more than 135 specialty shops and 40 eateries here. The Ward Entertainment Center features 16 movie theaters, including a state-of-the-art, 3-D, big-screen auditorium. For distinctive Hawaiian gifts, such as locally made muumuu, koa-wood products, and Niihau shell necklaces, visit Martin & MacArthur and Na Mea Hawaii. Twin Islands sells clothing for adults and children representing the laid-back lifestyle of Hawaii. Take TheBus line 19, 20, or 42; fare is $2.50 one-way. Or hop on the Waikiki Trolley Red Line; it comes through the area every 40 minutes. There also is free parking nearby and a valet service. ✉ *1050-1200 Ala Moana Blvd., Ala Moana* ☎ *808/591–8411* 🌐 *www.wardvillageshops.com.*

MOILIILI

JEWELRY

Maui Divers Design Center. For a look into the harvesting and design of coral and black pearl jewelry, visit this shop and take a free tour at its adjacent factory near the Ala Moana Shopping Center. ✉ *1520 Liona St., Moiliili* ☎ *808/946–7979* 🌐 *www.mauidivers.com.*

GREATER HONOLULU

CLOTHING

Bailey's Antiques & Aloha Shirts. Vintage aloha shirts are the specialty at this kitschy store. Prices range from $3.99 to several hundred dollars for the 15,000 shirts in stock; thousands of them are used while others come from top designers. The tight space and musty smell are part of the thrift-shop atmosphere. ■ TIP→ **Antiques hunters can also buy old-fashioned postcards, Hawaiian LPs, authentic military clothing, funky hats, and denim jeans from the 1950s.** ✉ *517 Kapahulu Ave., Kapahulu* ☎ *808/734–7628* 🌐 *www.alohashirts.com.*

SHOPPING CENTERS

Kahala Mall. The upscale residential neighborhood of Kahala, near the slopes of Diamond Head, is 10 minutes by car from Waikiki. The only shopping of note in the area is located at the indoor mall, which has more than 100 stores and restaurants, including Macy's, Reyn Spooner, an Apple store, Island Sole footwear, and T&C Surf. Shops include local and national retailers. Don't miss fashionable boutiques such as **Ohelo Road** (☎ *808/735–5525*), where contemporary clothing for all occasions fills the racks. You can also browse local foods and products at Whole Foods. Eight movie theaters provide post-shopping entertainment. ✉ *4211 Waialae Ave., Kahala* ☎ *808/732–7736* 🌐 *www.kahalamallcenter.com.*

WINDWARD OAHU

Fodor's Choice ★ **Bookends.** The perfect place to shop for gifts, or just take a break with the family, this independent bookstore feels more like a small-town library, welcoming browsers to linger for hours. Selling new and secondhand books, the large children's section is filled with toys and books to read. ✉ *600 Kailua Rd., Kailua* ☎ *808/261–1996.*

Fodor's Choice ★ **Global Village.** Tucked into a tiny strip mall near Maui Tacos, this boutique features jewelry, clothing, accessories, gifts, and handcrafted jewelry from the islands and around the globe. ✉ *Kailua Village Shops, 539 Kailua Rd., No. 104, Kailua* ☎ *808/262–8183* 🌐 *www.globalvillagehawaii.com.*

Fodor's Choice ★ **Under a Hula Moon.** Exclusive tabletop items and Pacific home decor, such as shell wreaths, shell night-lights, Hawaiian beach sheets, frames, and unique one-of-a-kind gifts with an Islands influence, define this eclectic shop. ✉ *Kailua Shopping Center, 600 Kailua Rd., Kailua* ☎ *808/261–4252.*

NORTH SHORE

Global Creations Interiors. Look for Hawaiian bath products, pikake perfume, locally made jewelry, island bedding, and a carefully chosen selection of Hawaiian music CDs. Popular gifts include Hawaiian sarongs and Islands-inspired kitchen items. ✉ *66-111 Kamehameha Hwy., No. 901, Haleiwa* ☎ *808/637–1780* 🌐 *www.globalcreationshaleiwa.com.*

The Growing Keiki. Frequent visitors return to this store year after year for a fresh supply of unique, locally made Hawaiian-style clothing for youngsters. ✉ *66-051 Kamehameha Hwy., Haleiwa* ☎ *808/637–4544* 🌐 *www.thegrowingkeiki.com.*

Fodor's Choice ★ **Silver Moon Emporium.** The small boutique carries everything from Brighton jewelry and European designer wear to fashionable T-shirts, shoes, and handbags. Shoppers get attentive yet casual and personalized service. The stock changes frequently, and there's always something wonderful on sale. No matter what your taste, you'll find something for everyday wear or special occasions. ✉ *North Shore Marketplace, 66-250 Kamehameha Hwy., Haleiwa* ☎ *808/637–7710* 🌐 *silvermoonhawaii.blogspot.com.*

WEST (LEEWARD) OAHU

Aloha Stadium Swap Meet & Marketplace. This thrice-weekly outdoor bazaar attracts hundreds of vendors and even more bargain hunters. Every Hawaiian souvenir imaginable can be found here, from coral shell necklaces to bikinis, as well as a variety of ethnic wares, from Chinese brocaded dresses to Japanese pottery. There are also ethnic foods, silk flowers, and luggage in aloha floral prints. Shoppers must wade through the typical sprinkling of used and stolen goods to find value. Wear comfortable shoes, use sunscreen, and bring bottled water. The flea market takes place in the Aloha Stadium parking lot Wednesday and Saturday 8–3, Sunday 6:30–3. Admission is $1 per person ages 12 and up.

Several shuttle companies serve Aloha Stadium for the swap meet for those tourists who don't rent a car, including VIP Shuttle (☎ *808/839–0911*), Reliable Shuttle (☎ *808/924–9292*), and Hawaii Super Transit (☎ *808/841–2928*), with a cost of $20 or less round-trip. The Waikiki Trolley Purple Line also stops at the Swap Meet. For a cheaper but slower ride, take TheBus (🌐 *www.thebus.org*). ✉ *Aloha Stadium, 99-500 Salt Lake Blvd., Aiea* ☎ *808/486–6704* 🌐 *www.alohastadiumswapmeet.net.*

Waikele Premium Outlets. AIX Armani Exchange, Calvin Klein, Coach, and Saks Fifth Avenue outlets anchor this discount destination of around 50 stores. You can take a shuttle from Waikiki for the 30-minute ride to the outlets for $18 round-trip, but the companies do change frequently. Reservations are recommended. ✉ *94-790 Lumiaina St., Waipahu* ☎ *808/676–5656* 🌐 *www.premiumoutlets.com/outlet/waikele.*

SPAS

Excellent day and resort spas can be found throughout Oahu, primarily in the resorts of Waikiki but also downtown and on the North Shore. Individual treatments and day packages offer a wide choice of rejuvenating therapies, some of which are unique to the Islands. Try the popular *lomilomi* massage with kukui-nut oil (*lomi* meaning to rub, knead, and massage using palms, forearms, fingers, knuckles, elbows, knees, feet, even sticks). Add heated *pohaku* (stones) placed on the back to relieve sore muscles, or choose a facial using natural ingredients such as coconut, mango, papaya, ti leaf, Hawaiian honey, or ginger. Many full-service spas offer couples' private treatment rooms, fitness suites, yoga, and hydrotherapy pools.

HONOLULU

WAIKIKI

Mandara Spa at the Hilton Hawaiian Village Beach Resort & Spa. From its perch in the Kalia Tower, Mandara Spa, an outpost of the chain that originated in Bali, overlooks the mountains, ocean, and downtown Honolulu. Fresh Hawaiian ingredients and traditional techniques headline an array of treatments. Try an exotic upgrade, such as reflexology or a Balinese body polish. Or relieve achy muscles with a traditional Thai poultice massage. The delicately scented, candlelit foyer can fill up quickly with robe-clad conventioneers, so be sure to make a reservation. There are spa suites for couples, a private infinity pool, and a boutique. ✉ *Hilton Hawaiian Village Beach Resort & Spa, 2005 Kalia Rd., 3rd & 4th fl., Kalia Tower, Waikiki* ☎ *808/945–7721* 🌐 *www.mandaraspa.com.*

Na Hoola Spa at the Hyatt Regency Waikiki Resort & Spa. Na Hoola is the premier resort spa in Waikiki, with 16 treatment rooms sprawling across 10,000 square feet and two floors of the Hyatt on Kalakaua Avenue. Arrive early for your treatment to enjoy the postcard views of Waikiki Beach. Four packages identified by Hawaii's native healing plants—noni, kukui, awa, and kalo—combine various body, face, and hair treatments; the spa also has luxurious packages that last three to six hours. The Kele Kele body wrap employs a self-heating mud wrap to release tension and stress. The small exercise room is for use by hotel guests only. ✉ *Hyatt Regency Waikiki Resort & Spa, 2424 Kalakaua Ave., Waikiki* ☎ *808/923–1234, 808/237–6330 for reservations* 🌐 *www.nahoolaspawaikiki.com.*

Fodor's Choice ★ **SpaHalekulani.** SpaHalekulani mines the traditions and cultures of the Pacific Islands with massages and body and facial therapies. Try the Samoan Nonu, which uses warm stones and healing nonu gel to relieve muscle tension. The exclusive line of bath and body products is scented by maile, lavender orchid, or coconut passion. Facilities are specific to treatment but may include Japanese furo bath or steam shower. ✉ *Halekulani Hotel, 2199 Kalia Rd., Waikiki* ☎ *808/931–5322* 🌐 *www.halekulani.com/living/spahalekulani.*

The Spa at Trump Waikiki. The Spa at Trump offers private changing and showering areas for each room, creating an environment of uninterrupted relaxation. No matter what treatment you choose, it is inspired by "personal intention," such as purify, balance, heal, revitalize, or calm, to elevate the senses throughout your time there. Don't miss the signature gemstone treatments, which feature products by Shiffa; or treat yourself to a Naturally Yours facial to emerge with younger-looking skin. The Healing Hawaiian Ocean Ritual is one of the most popular massages to begin—or end—your day. ✉ *Trump International Hotel Waikiki, 223 Saratoga Rd., Waikiki* ☎ *808/683–7466* 🌐 *www.trumpwaikikihotel.com.*

ALA MOANA

Hoala Salon and Spa. This Aveda concept spa has everything from Vichy showers to hydrotherapy rooms to customized aromatherapy. Ladies, they'll even touch up your makeup for free before you leave. ✉ *Ala Moana Shopping Center, 3rd fl., 1450 Ala Moana Blvd., Ala Moana* ☎ *808/947–6141* 🌐 *www.hoalasalonspa.com.*

THE NORTH SHORE

Nalu Kinetic Spa at Turtle Bay Resort. Luxuriate at the ocean's edge in this renovated spa on Oahu's North Shore. Try one of the spa's body wraps, including the lilikoi citrus polish using Hawaiian cane sugar and organic lehua honey in its Vichy shower treatment room. Or book a shiatsu massage, which utilizes foot pressure to release soft tissue constrictions and improve circulation. There are private spa suites, an outdoor treatment cabana that overlooks the surf, an outdoor exercise studio, and a lounge area and juice bar. ✉ *Turtle Bay Resort, 57-091 Kamehameha Hwy., Kahuku* ☎ *808/447–6868* 🌐 *www.nalukineticspa.com.*

WEST (LEEWARD) OAHU

Laniwai Spa at Aulani, A Disney Resort & Spa. At this spa, every staff member—or "cast member," as they call themselves—is extensively trained in Hawaiian culture and history to ensure they are projecting the right *mana,* or energy, in their work. To begin each treatment, you select a special pohaku with words of intent, then cast it into a reflective pool. Choose from about 150 spa therapies, and indulge in Kulu Wai, the only outdoor hydrotherapy garden on Oahu—with private vitality pools, co-ed mineral baths, six different "rain" showers, whirlpool jet spas, and more. ✉ *Aulani, A Disney Resort & Spa, 92-1185 Aliinui Dr., Ko Olina* ☎ *808/674–6300* 🌐 *disneyaulani.com/spa-fitness.*

WATER SPORTS AND TOURS

Updated by Trina Kudlacek

From snorkeling on the North Shore to kayaking to small islands off Kailua Beach to stand-up paddleboarding in Waikiki—when you're on Oahu, there's always a reason to get wet. You can swim with native fish in a protected bay, surf waves in an outrigger canoe, take to the skies in a parasail above Diamond Head, or enjoy panoramic views of Waikiki aboard a 45-foot catamaran. Diving into the ocean—whether in a boat, on a board, or with your own finned feet—is a great way to experience Oahu.

But, as with any physical activity, heed the warnings. The ocean is unpredictable and unforgiving, and it can be as dangerous as it can be awe-inspiring. But if you respect it, it can offer you the kind of memories that last well after your vacation.

BOAT TOURS AND CHARTERS

Being on the water can be the best way to enjoy the Islands. Whether you want to see the fish in action or experience how they taste, there is a tour for you.

For a sailing experience in Oahu, you need go no farther than the beach in front of your hotel in Waikiki. Strung along the sand are several beach catamarans that will provide you with one-hour rides during the day and 90-minute sunset sails. Look for $35 for day sails and $49–$120 for sunset rides. ■ TIP→ **Feel free to haggle, especially with the smaller boats.** Some provide drinks for free, some charge for them, and some let you pack your own, so keep that in mind when pricing the ride. Or choose to go the ultraluxe route and charter a boat for a day or week. These run from less than $100 per person per day to over $1,000. *(see Deep-Sea Fishing).*

Hawaii Nautical. With two locations in Waikiki and one on the Waianae Coast, this outfit offers a wide variety of cruise options including guaranteed-sighting dolphin and whale-watching (in season), gourmet dinners, lunches, snorkeling, scuba diving, and sunset viewing. Three-hour cruises, including lunch and two drinks, depart from the Kewalo Basin

Harbor just outside Waikiki. (The company's Port Waikiki Cruises sail from the Hilton Pier off the Hilton Hawaiian Village in Waikiki.) For those interested in leaving from the Waianae Coast, snorkel tours are available from the Waianae Boat Harbor on Farrington Highway (85-471 Farrington Hwy.). Prices include all gear, food, and two alcoholic beverages. The dock in the Waianae Boat Harbor is a little more out of the way, but this is a much more luxurious option than what is offered in Waikiki. Both morning and afternoon snorkel tours include stops for observing dolphins from the boat and visit to a snorkel spot well populated with fish. All gear, snacks, sandwiches, and two alcoholic beverages make for a more complete experience. Pickup in Ko Olina is free. ✉ *Kewalo Basin Harbor, 1125 Ala Moana Blvd., Waikiki* ☎ *808/234–7245* 🌐 *www.hawaiinautical.com* 🎫 *From $97.*

Maitai Catamaran. Taking off from the stretch of sand behind the Sheraton Waikiki, this 44-foot cat is the fastest and sleekest on the beach. There are a variety of tours to choose from, including a sunset sail and a snorkel excursion. If you have a need for speed and enjoy a little more upscale experience, this is the boat for you. ✉ *Sheraton Waikiki, 2255 Kalakaua Ave., Waikiki* ✣ *On the beach behind the hotel* ☎ *808/922–5665, 800/462–7975* 🌐 *www.maitaicatamaran.net* 🎫 *From $39.*

FAMILY **Star of Honolulu Cruises.** Founded in 1957, this company's fleet includes two family-friendly vessels. The 232-foot *Star of Honolulu,* which casts off at Pier 8 in the **Aloha Tower harbor** (*1 Aloha Tower Drive, downtown Honolulu*) offers seasonal whale-watching as well as sunset gourmet dinner cruises with live entertainment. Some cruises even teach you how to string lei, play ukulele, or dance hula. Moored at the **Waianai Boat Harbor** (*85-491 Farrington Hwy., Waianae* 🌐 *www.dolphin-star.com*), the 65-foot *Dolphin Star* catamaran, offers either dolphin-viewing or snorkeling cruises with optional barbecue lunches. Because of its size, this cat provides a comfortable way for three generations of family members to enjoy the water together. Transportation from all hotels on the island can be arranged. ✉ *Honolulu* ☎ *808/983–7827, 800/334–6191* 🌐 *www.starofhonolulu.com* 🎫 *From $34.*

Tradewind Charters. This company's half-day private excursions can include sailing, snorkeling, reef fishing, sunset dinner cruises, or whale-watching excursions and can accommodate from two to 49 people. Traveling on these luxury yachts not only gets you away from the crowds but also gives you the opportunity to take the helm if you wish. The cruises may include snorkeling at an exclusive anchorage, as well as hands-on snorkeling and sailing instruction. All charters are for the full ship. ✉ *Kewalo Basin Harbor, 1125 Ala Moana Blvd., Ala Moana* ☎ *808/227–4956, 800/829–4899* 🌐 *www.tradewindcharters.com* 🎫 *From $495.*

BODY BOARDING AND BODYSURFING

Body boarding (or sponging) has long been a popular alternative to surfing for a couple of reasons. First, the start-up cost is much less—a usable board can be purchased for $30–$40 or can be rented on the beach for $5 an hour. Second, it's a whole lot easier to ride a body board than to tame a surfboard. All you have to do is paddle out to the waves, then turn toward the beach as the wave approaches and kick like crazy.

Most grocery and convenience stores sell body boards. Though these boards don't compare to what the pros use, beginners won't notice a difference in their handling on smaller waves.

Though they are not absolutely necessary for body boarding, fins do give you a tremendous advantage when you're paddling. If you plan to go out into bigger surf, we would also suggest getting a leash, which reduces the chance you'll lose your board. The smaller, sturdier versions of dive fins used for body boarding sell for $25–$60 at surf and sporting-goods stores. Most beach stands don't rent fins with the boards, so if you want them you'll probably need to buy them.

Bodysurfing requires far less equipment—just a pair of swim fins with heel straps—but it can be a lot more challenging to master. Typically, surf breaks that are good for body boarding are good for bodysurfing.

If the direction of the current or dangers of the break are not readily apparent to you, don't hesitate to ask a lifeguard for advice.

BEST SPOTS

Body boarding and bodysurfing can be done anywhere there are waves, but due to the paddling advantage surfers have over spongers, it's usually more fun to go to surf breaks exclusively for body boarding.

Bellows Beach. On Oahu's windward side, Bellows Field Beach has shallow waters and a consistent break that makes it an ideal spot for body boarders and bodysurfers. (Surfing isn't allowed between the two lifeguard towers.) But take note: the Portuguese man-of-war, a blue jellyfishlike invertebrate that delivers painful and powerful stings, is often seen here. ✉ *41-043 Kalanianaole Hwy., Waimanalo.*

Kuhio Beach Park. This beach is an easy spot for first-timers to check out the action. The Wall, a break near the large pedestrian walkway called Kapahulu Groin, is the quintessential body boarding spot. The soft, rolling waves make it perfect for beginners. Even during summer's south swells, it's relatively tame because of the outer reefs. ✉ *Waikiki Beach, between the Sheraton Moana Surfrider Hotel and the Kapahulu Groin, Honolulu.*

Makapuu Beach. With its extended waves, Makapuu Beach is a sponger's dream. If you're a little more timid, go to the far end of the beach to **Keiki's,** where the waves are mellowed by Makapuu Point. Although the main break at Makapuu is much less dangerous than Sandy's, check out the ocean floor—the sands are always shifting, sometimes exposing coral heads and rocks. Always check (or ask lifeguards about) the currents, which can get pretty strong. ✉ *41-095 Kalanianaole Hwy., across from Sea Life Park.*

Sandy Beach. The best spot—and arguably one of the most dangerous—on the island for advanced body boarding is Sandy Beach, located on Oahu's eastern shore. Dubbed one of the most treacherous shore breaks in the nation, the break can be extremely dangerous even when it's small. As lifeguards will attest, there are more neck injuries suffered here than at any other surf break in the United States. It's awesome for

The windward side has many good spots for body boarding.

the advanced, but know its danger before paddling out. ✉ *8800 Kalanianaole Hwy., 2 miles east of Hanauma Bay, Honolulu.*

Waimanalo Beach Park. With the longest sand beach on Oahu's windward side, Waimanalo Bay has a shallow sandbar at the water's edge that provides good waves for body boarding and bodysurfing. It's an ideal break for novices because of its soft waves. Like Walls in Waikiki, this area is protected by an outer reef. And like Bellows, it's favored by the dangerous Portuguese man-of-war. ✉ *Aloiloi St., Waimanalo.*

EQUIPMENT

There are more than 30 rental spots along Waikiki Beach, all offering basically the same prices. But if you plan to body board for more than just an hour, we would suggest buying an inexpensive board for $20–$40 at an ABC Store—there are more than 30 in the Waikiki area—and giving it to a kid at the end of your vacation. It will be more cost-effective for you, and you'll be passing along some aloha spirit in the process.

DEEP-SEA FISHING

Fishing isn't just a sport in Hawaii, it's a way of life. A number of charter boats with experienced crews can take you on a sportfishing adventure throughout the year. Sure, the bigger yellowfin tuna (ahi) are generally caught in summer, and the coveted spearfish are more frequent in winter, but you can still hook them any day of the year. You can also find dolphinfish (mahimahi), wahoo (ono), skipjacks, and the king—Pacific blue marlin—ripe for the picking on any given day. The largest marlin ever caught, weighing in at 1,805 pounds, was reeled in along Oahu's coast.

When choosing a fishing boat in the Islands, keep in mind the immensity of the surrounding ocean. Look for veteran captains who have decades of experience. Better yet, find those who care about Hawaii's fragile marine environment. Many captains now tag and release their catches to preserve the state's fishing grounds.

The general rule for the catch is an even split with the crew. Unfortunately, there are no "freeze-and-ship" providers in the state, so unless you plan to eat the fish while you're here, you'll probably want to leave it with the boat. Most boats do offer mounting services for trophy fish; ask your captain.

Prices vary greatly, but expect to pay from around $65 per person for a spot on a boat with more than 20 people to $2,000 for an overnight trip for up to 6 people. Besides the gift of fish, a gratuity of 10%–20% is standard, but use your own discretion depending on how you feel about the overall experience.

BOATS AND CHARTERS

Maggie Joe Sport Fishing. The oldest sportfishing company on Oahu boasts landing one of the largest marlins ever caught out of Kewalo Basin. With a fleet of three boats including the 53-foot custom *Maggie Joe* (which can hold up to 15 anglers and has air-conditioned cabins, hot showers, and cutting-edge fishing equipment), they can offer a variety of offshore fishing packages. A marine taxidermist can mount the monster you reel in. Half-day exclusives on the 41-foot *Sea Hawk* or the 38-foot *Ruckus* can accommodate up to six people and are the cheapest options for daytime fishing. Charters on the larger *Maggie Joe* can start at a three-quarter day or a full day (but not a half day). ✉ *Kewalo Basin, 1025 Ala Moana Blvd., Ala Moana* ☎ *808/591–8888, 877/806–3474* 🌐 *www.maggiejoe.com* 🎫 *From $190.*

Magic Sportfishing. This 50-foot Pacifica fishing yacht, aptly named *Magic,* boasts a slew of sportfishing records, including some of the largest marlins caught in local tournaments and the most mahimahi hooked during a one-day charter. This yacht is very comfortable, with twin diesel engines that provide a smooth ride, air-conditioning, and a cozy seating area. The boat can accommodate up to six passengers and offers both shared and full charters. ✉ *Kewalo Basin Harbor, 1125 Ala Moana Blvd., Slip G, Ala Moana* ☎ *808/596–2998* 🌐 *www.magicsportfishing.com* 🎫 *From $220 per person for a shared charter; from $1,095 for a private charter.*

Sashimi Fun Fishing. With a luxury 74-foot boat for sport fishing, a 65-footer for bottom fishing, and a 100-foot double-decker boat for dinner cruises, Sashimi Fun Fishing offers a variety of water activities. Choose a midnight shark hunt, head out in search of marlin, bottom fish near shore, or relax and enjoy live entertainment on the *Prince Kuhio's* sunset steak and seafood dinner cruise. Rates can include hotel transportation. ✉ *Kewalo Basin Harbor, 1025 Ala Moana Blvd., Ala Moana* ☎ *808/955–3474* 🌐 *www.808955fish.com or princekuhiocruises.com* 🎫 *From $63 per person for shared trips; $69 for dinner cruises.*

KAYAKING

Kayaking is an easy way to explore the ocean—and Oahu's natural beauty—without much effort or skill. It offers a vantage point not afforded by swimming or surfing, and a workout you won't get lounging on a catamaran. Even novices can get in a kayak and enjoy the island's scenery.

The ability to travel long distances can also get you into trouble. ■ **TIP→ Experts agree that rookies should stay on the windward side.** Their reasoning is simple: if you get tired, break or lose an oar, or just plain pass out, the onshore winds will eventually blow you back to the beach. The same cannot be said for the offshore breezes of the North Shore and West Oahu.

Kayaks are specialized: some are better suited for riding waves while others are designed for traveling long distances. Your outfitter can address your needs depending on your skill level. Sharing your plans with your outfitter can lead to a more enjoyable—and safer—experience. Expect to pay from $35 for a half-day single rental to $139 for a guided kayak tour with lunch. Some kayaking outfitters also rent stand-up paddleboards (⇨ *see Stand-Up Paddling*).

BEST SPOTS

If you want to try your hand at surfing kayaks, **Bellows Field Beach** (near Waimanalo Town Center, entrance on Kalanianaole Highway) on the windward side and **Mokuleia Beach** (across from Dillingham Airfield) on the North Shore are two great spots. Hard-to-reach breaks, the ones that surfers exhaust themselves trying to reach, are easily accessed by kayak. The buoyancy of the kayak also allows you to catch the wave earlier and get out in front of the white wash. One reminder on these spots: if you're a little green, stick to Bellows Field Beach with those onshore winds. Generally speaking, you don't want to be catching waves where surfers are; in Waikiki, however, pretty much anything goes.

The perennial favorite of kayakers is **Lanikai Beach**, on the island's windward side. Tucked away in an upscale residential area, this award-winning beach has become a popular spot for amateur kayakers because of its calm waters and onshore winds. More adventurous paddlers can head to the Mokulua Islands, two islets less than 1 mile from the beach. You can land on Moku Nui, which has surf breaks and small beaches great for picnicking. Take a dip in Queen's Bath, a small saltwater swimming hole.

For something a little different, try the Kahana River on the island's windward side, which empties into the ocean at **Kahana Bay Beach Park**. The river may not have the blue water of the ocean, but the majestic Koolau Mountains, with waterfalls during rainy months, make for a picturesque backdrop. It's a short jaunt, about 2 miles round-trip from the beach, but it's tranquil and packed with rain-forest foliage. Bring mosquito repellent.

EQUIPMENT, LESSONS, AND TOURS

Go Bananas. Staffers make sure that you rent the appropriate kayak for your abilities, and can also outfit your rental car with soft racks to transport your boat to the beach. (Racks are included in the rental fee.) You can rent either a single or double kayak. The store also carries clothing and kayaking accessories and rents stand-up paddleboards. (There's a second location in Aiea, which is closer to the North Shore.) ✉ *799 Kapahulu Ave., Kapahulu* ☎ *808/737–9514* 🌐 *www.gobananaskayaks.com* 🎫 *From $35.*

2

Kailua Beach Adventures. One of the best places for beginners to rent kayaks is Kailua Beach, and Kailua Beach Adventures has an ideal location just across the street. The company offers two- and five-hour guided kayak tours (the longer tour includes lunch, time for kayaking, and time for the beach). More adventurous visitors can rent a kayak (double or single for a half or full day) and venture to the Mokulua Islands off Lanikai. You can also rent snorkeling equipment, stand-up paddleboards, and bikes. (Discounts are given if booked online.) ✉ *Kailua Beach Shopping Center, 130 Kailua Rd., Kailua* ☎ *808/262–2555* 🌐 *www.kailuasailboards.com* 🎫 *From $59 for rental; $139 for tours.*

Twogood Kayaks Hawaii. The outfitter offers kayak rentals (single or double), lessons, and guided tours. Guides are trained in the history, geology, and birds of the area. Fully guided kayak excursions are either 2½ or 5 hours and include lunch, snorkeling gear, and transportation to and from Waikiki. For those who want to create their own itinerary, owner Bob Twogood also offers custom "Elite" tours. ✉ *134B Hamakua Dr., Kailua* ☎ *808/262–5656* 🌐 *www.twogoodkayaks.com* 🎫 *Rentals from $60, tours from $115.*

SCUBA DIVING

Not all of Hawaii's beauty is above water. What lurks below can be just as magnificent.

Although snorkeling provides adequate access to this underwater world, nothing gives you the freedom—or depth, quite literally—as scuba.

The diving on Oahu is comparable with any you might do in the tropics, but its uniqueness comes from the isolated environment of the Islands. There are literally hundreds of species of fish and marine life that you can find only in this chain. In fact, about 25% of Hawaii's marine life can be seen here only—nowhere else in the world. Adding to the singularity of diving off Oahu is the human history of the region. Military activities and tragedies of the 20th century filled the waters surrounding Oahu with wreckage that the ocean creatures have since turned into their homes.

Although instructors certified to license you in scuba are plentiful in the Islands, we suggest that you get your PADI certification before coming, as a week of classes may be a bit of a commitment on a short vacation. Expect to pay around $100 for a two-tank boat dive (provided that you are certified). ■ **TIP→ You can go on short, shallow introductory dives without the certification, but the best dives require it and cost a bit more.**

BEST SPOTS

Hanauma Bay Nature Preserve. On Oahu's southeast shore, about 30 minutes drive east of Waikiki, Hanauma Bay Nature Preserve is home to more than 250 different species of fish, of which a quarter can be found nowhere else in the world. This has made this volcanic crater bay one of the most popular dive sites in the state. It's a long walk from the parking lot to the beach—even longer lugging equipment—so consider hooking up with a licensed dive-tour operator. Preservation efforts have aided the bay's delicate ecosystem, so expect to see various butterfly fish, surgeonfish, tangs, parrot fish, and endangered Hawaiian sea turtles. ✉ *7455 Kalanianaole Hwy., Hawaii Kai* ☎ *808/396–4229* $7.50 per person and $1 parking.

Hundred Foot Hole. Once an ancient Hawaiian fishing ground reserved for royalty, the Hundred Foot Hole is a cluster of volcanic boulders that have created ledges, caves, and a large open-ended cavern perfect for diving. Accessible from shore, this spot near Diamond Head attracts octopus, manta rays, and the occasional white-tip shark. ✉ *Off Diamond Head, Honolulu.*

Mahi Waianae. Hawaii's waters are littered with shipwrecks, but one of the most intact and accessible is the *Mahi Waianae,* a 165-foot minesweeper that was sunk in 1982 off the Waianae Coast. It lies upright in about 90 feet of calm and clear water, encrusted in coral and patrolled by white spotted eagle rays and millet seed butterfly fish. The wreck serves as an artificial reef for such Hawaii aquatic residents as blue-striped snappers, puffer fish, lionfish, moray eels, and octopus. Visibility averages about 100 feet, making this one of the most popular dives on the island. ✉ *Waianae.*

Maunalua Bay. The bay stretches about 7 miles, from Portlock Point to Black Point on Oahu's southeastern shore. Teeming with marine life, this spot has several accessible dive sites of varying difficulty. The shallow-water Turtle Canyon is home to endangered Hawaiian green sea turtles. Fantasy Reef is another shallow dive with three plateaus of volcanic rock lined with coral that is home to fish, eels, and sea turtles. In about 85 feet of water, *Baby Barge* is an easy-to-penetrate sunken vessel encrusted in coral. An advanced dive, the wreck of a Vought F4U Corsair gives you a close-up look at garden eels and stingrays. ✉ *Southeast Oahu.*

Sharks Cove. Oahu's best shore dive is accessible only during the summer months. Sharks Cove, on Oahu's North Shore, churns with monster surf during the winter, making this popular snorkeling and diving spot extremely dangerous. In summer, the cavernous lava tubes and tunnels are great for both novices and experienced divers. Some dive-tour companies offer round-trip transportation from Waikiki. ✉ *Haleiwa.*

Three Tables. A short walk from Sharks Cove is Three Tables, named for a trio of flat rocks running perpendicular to shore. There are lava tubes to the right of these rocks that break the surface and then extend out about 50 feet. Although this area isn't as active as Sharks Cove, you can still spot octopus, moray eels, parrot fish, green sea turtles, and the occasional shark. ✉ *Haleiwa.*

2

EQUIPMENT, LESSONS, AND TOURS

Aaron's Dive Shop. Whether you're diving for the first time or a master diver, this friendly and well-equipped dive shop caters to everyone. Take an "introductory" dive if you're not certified; get certified; or sign up for an offshore day or night dive excursion if you're experienced. In addition to organized group dives, the company's "Dive Concierge" can arrange private charters for those who want a completely customized experience. Snorkelers can go along on many dives as well. ✉ *307 Hahani St., Kailua* ☎ *808/262–2333* 🌐 *aaronsdiveshop.com* 🎫 *From $120 for 2-tank dive.*

Surf 'N Sea. The North Shore headquarters for all things water-related is also great for diving. One interesting perk: upon request, their dive guides can shoot a video of you diving. It's hard to see facial expressions under the water, but it still might be fun for those who want to prove that they took the plunge. Two-tank shore dives are the most economical choice (prices for noncertified divers are higher), but the company also offers boat dives, and in the summer, night dives are available for only slightly more. ✉ *62-595 Kamehameha Hwy., Haleiwa* ☎ *800/899–7873* 🌐 *www.surfnsea.com* 🎫 *From $100 (2-tank shore dives).*

SNORKELING

If you can swim, you can snorkel. And you don't need any formal training, either.

Snorkeling is a favorite pastime for both visitors and residents and can be done anywhere there's enough water to stick your face in. You can pick up a mask and snorkel at a corner ABC store for around $35, including fins, and get going on your own or pay up to $175 for a luxurious snorkel cruise including lunch and drinks. Each spot will have its great days depending on the weather and time of year, so consult with the purveyor of your gear for tips on where the best viewing is that day. Keep in mind that the North Shore should be attempted only when the waves are calm, namely in the summertime.

Make sure you put plenty of sunscreen on your back (or better yet, wear a T-shirt) because once you start gazing below, your head may not come back up for hours.

BEST SPOTS

Electric Beach. On the western side of the island, directly across from the electricity plant—hence the name—Electric Beach is a haven for tropical fish, making it a great snorkeling spot. The expulsion of hot water from the plant raises the temperature of the ocean, attracting Hawaiian green sea turtles, spotted moray eels, and spinner dolphins. Although visibility is not always the best, the crowds are small and the fish are guaranteed. ✉ *Farrington Hwy., 1 mile west of Ko Olina Resort, Kapolei.*

Hanauma Bay Nature Preserve. What Waimea Bay is to surfing, Hanauma Bay in Southeast Oahu is to snorkeling. Easily the most popular snorkeling spot on the island, it's home to more than 250 different species of marine life. Due to the protection of the narrow mouth of the cove and the prodigious reef, you will be hard-pressed to find a place you

Oahu's North Shore has the island's biggest waves as well as some of the best snorkeling—but not at the same time of year.

will feel safer while snorkeling. ✉ *7455 Kalanianaole Hwy., Honolulu* ☎ *808/396–4229 $7.50 per person and $1 parking.*

Queen's Surf Beach. On the edge of Waikiki, Queen's Surf is a marine reserve located between Kapahulu Groin and the Waikiki Aquarium. It's not as chock-full of fish as Hanauma Bay, but it has its share of colorful reef fish and the occasional Hawaiian green sea turtle. Just yards from shore, it's a great spot for an escape if you're stuck in Waikiki and have grown weary of watching the surfers. ✉ *Kalakaua Ave., Honolulu.*

Sharks Cove. Great shallows protected by a huge reef make Sharks Cove on the North Shore a prime spot for snorkelers, even young ones, in the summer. You'll find a plethora of critters, from crabs to octopus, in water that's no more than waist deep. When the winter swells come, this area can turn treacherous. ✉ *Kamehameha Hwy., across from Foodland, Haleiwa.*

EQUIPMENT AND TOURS

Hanauma Bay Snorkeling Excursions. If you're going to Hanauma Bay, you have three options: take a chance with limited parking spaces at the park, take TheBus, or contact Hanauma Bay Snorkeling Excursions. They provide transportation to and from Waikiki hotels, equipment, and instruction on how to use the equipment for a reasonable price that does not include the $7.50 park entrance fee. ☎ *808/306–3393* 🌐 *www.hanaumabaysnorkel.com* 🎫 *From $25.*

Snorkel Bob's. This place has all the stuff you'll need—and more—to make your water adventures more enjoyable. Bob makes his own gear and is active in protecting reef fish species. Feel free to ask the staff about good snorkeling spots, as the best ones can vary with weather and the seasons. You can either rent or buy gear (and reserve it in advance online). ✉ *700 Kapahulu Ave., Kapahulu* ☎ *808/735–7944, 800/262–7725* 🌐 *www.snorkelbob.com* 💵 *Rentals from $38 per wk.*

2

STAND-UP PADDLING

From the lakes of Wisconsin to the coast of Lima, Peru, stand-up paddleboarding (or SUP, for short) is taking the sport of surfing to the most unexpected places. Still, the sport remains firmly rooted in the Hawaiian Islands.

Back in the 1960s, Waikiki beach boys would paddle out on their longboards using a modified canoe paddle. It was longer than a traditional paddle, enabling them to stand up and stroke. It was easier this way to survey the ocean and snap photos of tourists learning how to surf. Eventually it became a sport unto itself, with professional contests at world-class surf breaks and long-distance races across treacherous waters.

Stand-up paddleboarding is easy to learn—though riding waves takes some practice—and most outfitters on Oahu offer lessons for all skill levels starting at about $55. It's also a great workout; you can burn off yesterday's dinner buffet, strengthen your core, and experience the natural beauty of the island's coastlines all at once. Once you're ready to head out on your own, half-day rentals start at $50.

If you're looking to learn, go where there's already a SUP presence. Avoid popular surf breaks, unless you're an experienced stand-up paddle surfer, and be wary of ocean and wind conditions. You'll want to find a spot with calm waters, easy access in and out of the ocean, and a friendly crowd that doesn't mind the occasional stand-up paddleboarder.

BEST SPOTS

Ala Moana Beach Park. About a mile west of Waikiki, Ala Moana is the most SUP-friendly spot on the island. In fact, the state installed a series of buoys in the flat-water lagoon to separate stand-up paddlers and swimmers. There are no waves here, making it a great spot to learn, but beware of strong trade winds, which can push you into the reef.

Anahulu Stream. Outfitters on the North Shore like to take SUP beginners to Anahulu Stream, which empties into Waialua Bay near the Haleiwa Boat Harbor. This area is calm and protected from winds, plus there's parking at the harbor, and surf shops nearby rent boards.

Waikiki. There are a number of outfitters on Oahu's South Shore that take beginners into the waters off Waikiki. Canoes, the surf break fronting the Duke Kahanamoku statue, and the channels between breaks are often suitable for people learning how to maneuver their boards in not-so-flat conditions. But south swells here can be deceptively menacing, and ocean conditions can change quickly. Check with lifeguards before paddling out and be mindful of other surfers in the water.

White Plains. If you've got a car with racks, you might want to venture to White Plains, a fairly uncrowded beach about 27 miles west of Waikiki. It's a long, sandy beach with lots of breaks, and plenty of room for everyone. There are lifeguards, restrooms, and lots of parking, making this a great spot for beginners and those just getting comfortable in small waves.

EQUIPMENT AND LESSONS

FAMILY **Hawaiian Watersports.** Paddle off the shore of picturesque Kailua Beach. This safety-conscious outfitter offers both equipment rentals and 90-minute and 3-hour group or individual lessons. A one-stop shop for water sports, they also offer kiteboarding, surfing, and windsurfing lessons as well as kayak tours and equipment rentals. Discounts are available online if you book ahead. ✉ *171 Hamakua Dr., Kailua* ☎ *808/262–5483* 🌐 *www.hawaiianwatersports.com* 🎫 *Rentals from $29, lessons from $74.*

Paddle Core Fitness. Paddling is a way of life for Reid Inouye, who now shares his passion for the sport with students. (He's also the publisher of *Standup Paddle Magazine.*) His company offers introductory classes as well as fitness programs for serious paddlers. Lessons and workout programs are held in the flat waters of Ala Moana Beach, where there's a designated area for paddling, and you can have either group or private lessons. ✉ *Ala Moana Beach Park, Ala Moana Blvd., Ala Moana* ☎ *808/200–0574* 🌐 *www.paddlecorefitness.com* 🎫 *Workout programs from $25, lessons from $75.*

SUBMARINE TOURS

Atlantis Submarines. This is the underwater adventure for the unadventurous. Not fond of swimming, but want to see what you've been missing? Board this high-tech 64-passenger vessel for a ride past shipwrecks, turtle breeding grounds, and coral reefs. The tours, which depart from the pier at the Hilton Hawaiian Village, are available in several languages. A smaller 48-passenger semisubmersible boat with underwater viewing windows is a bit cheaper than the submarine trip. (Discounts are available if booked online.) ✉ *Hilton Hawaiian Village Beach Resort & Spa, 2005 Kalia Rd., Honolulu* ☎ *808/973–9800, 800/381–0237 for reservations* 🌐 *www.atlantisadventures.com* 🎫 *From $119.*

SURFING

Perhaps no word is more associated with Hawaii than surfing. Every year the best of the best gather on Oahu's North Shore to compete in their version of the Super Bowl: the prestigious Vans Triple Crown of Surfing. The pros dominate the waves for a month, but the rest of the year belongs to folks just trying to have fun.

Oahu is unique because it has so many famous spots: Banzai Pipeline, Waimea Bay, Kaiser Bowls, and Sunset Beach. These spots, however, require experience. Nonetheless, with most dependable sets and access to lessons, Waikiki is still a great place for beginners to learn or for novice surfers to catch predictable waves. Group lessons on Waikiki Beach start at $50, but if you really want to fine-tune your skills, you can pay up to $500 for a daylong private outing with a former pro.

The island also has miles of coastline with surf spots that are perfect for everyday surfers. But remember this surfer's credo: when in doubt, don't go out. If you're unsure about conditions, stay on the beach and talk to locals to get more info about surf breaks before trying yourself.

⚠ If you don't want to run the risk of a confrontation with local surfers, who can be very territorial about their favorite breaks, try some of the alternate spots listed below. They may not have the name recognition, but the waves can be just as great.

BEST SPOTS

Makaha Beach Park. If you like to ride waves, try Makaha Beach on Oahu's west side. It has legendary, interminable rights that allow riders to perform all manner of stunts: from six-man canoes with everyone doing headstands to Bullyboards (oversize body boards) with whole families along for the ride. Mainly known as a longboarding spot, it's predominantly local but respectful to outsiders. Use caution in winter, as the surf can get huge. It's not called Makaha—which means "fierce"—for nothing. ✉ *84-369 Farrington Hwy., Waianae.*

Sunset Beach. If you want to impress your surfing buddies back home, catch a wave at the famous Sunset Beach on Oahu's North Shore. Two of the more manageable breaks are **Kammie Land** (or Kammie's) and **Sunset Point.** For the daring, Sunset is part of the Vans Triple Crown of Surfing for a reason. Thick waves and long rides await, but you're going to want to have a thick board and a thicker skull. Surf etiquette here is a must, as it's mostly local. ✉ *59-104 Kamehameha Hwy., 1 mile north of Ehukai Beach Park, Haleiwa.*

Ulukou Beach. In Waikiki you can paddle out to **Populars,** a break at Ulukou Beach. Nice and easy, Populars—or Pops—never breaks too hard and is friendly to both newbies and veterans. It's one of the best places to surf during pumping south swells, as this thick wave breaks in open ocean, making it more rideable. The only downside is the long paddle out to the break from Kuhio Beach, but that keeps the crowds manageable. ✉ *Waikiki Beach, in front of the Sheraton Waikiki hotel, Honolulu.*

White Plains Beach. Known among locals as "mini Waikiki," the surf at White Plains breaks in numerous spots, preventing the logjams that are inevitable at many of Oahu's more popular spots. It's a great break for novice to intermediate surfers, though you do have to keep a lookout for wayward boards. From the H1, take the Makakilo exit. ✉ *Off H1, Kapolei.*

EQUIPMENT AND LESSONS

Aloha Beach Services. It may sound like a cliché, but there's no better way to learn to surf than from a beach boy in Waikiki. And there's no one better than Harry "Didi" Robello, a second-generation beach boy and owner of Aloha Beach Services. Learn to surf in an hour-long group lesson, a semiprivate lesson, or with just you and an instructor. You can also rent a board here. ✉ *2365 Kalakaua Ave., on beach near Moana Surfrider, Waikiki* ☎ *808/922–3111* 🌐 *www.alohabeachservices.com* 🎫 *Lessons from $50, board rentals from $20.*

Faith Surf School. Professional surfer Tony Moniz started his own surf school in 2000, and since then he and his wife, Tammy, have helped thousands of people catch their first waves in Waikiki. The 90-minute group lessons include all equipment and are the cheapest option. You can pay more (sometimes a lot more) for semiprivate lessons with up

Surfing is an iconic Hawaii water activity; don't miss a chance to take a surfing lesson.

to three people or for private lessons. You can also book an all-day surf tour with Moniz, riding waves with him at his favorite breaks. ✉ *Outrigger Waikiki Beach Resort, 2335 Kalakua Ave., Waikiki* ☎ *808/931–6262* 🌐 *www.faithsurfschool.com* 🎫 *Lessons from $65; board rental from $20.*

Surf 'N Sea. This is a one-stop shop for surfers (and other water-sports enthusiasts) on the North Shore. Rent a short or long board by the hour or for a full day. Two-hour group lessons are offered, as well as surf safaris for experienced surfers, which can last between four and five hours. ✉ *62-595 Kamehameha Hwy., Haleiwa* ☎ *800/899–7873* 🌐 *www.surfnsea.com* 🎫 *Lessons from $85, rentals from $5 per hr.*

WHALE-WATCHING

December is marked by the arrival of snow in much of America, but in Hawaii it marks the return of the humpback whale. These migrating behemoths move south from their North Pacific homes during the winter months for courtship and calving, and they put on quite a show. Watching males and females alike throwing themselves out of the ocean and into the sunset awes even the saltiest of sailors. Newborn calves riding gently next to their 2-ton mothers will stir you to your core. These gentle giants can be seen from the shore as they make a splash, but there is nothing like having your boat rocking beneath you in the wake of a whale's breach.

Wild Side Specialty Tours. Boasting a marine-biologist/naturalist crew, this company takes you to undisturbed snorkeling areas. Along the way you may see dolphins and turtles. The company promises a sighting of migrating whales year-round on some itineraries. Tours may depart as early as 8 am from Waianae, so it's important to plan ahead. The three-hour deluxe wildlife tour is the most popular option. ✉ *Waianae Boat Harbor, 85-471 Farrington Hwy., Waianae* ☎ *808/306–7273* 🌐 *www.sailhawaii.com* 🎫 *From $175.*

GOLF, HIKING, AND OUTDOOR ACTIVITIES

Updated by Cheryl Crabtree

Although much is written about the water surrounding this little rock known as Oahu, there is as much to be said for the rock itself. It's a wonder of nature, thrust from the ocean floor thousands of millennia ago by a volcanic hot spot that is still spitting out islands today. Hawaii is the most remote island chain on Earth, and there are creatures and plants that can be seen here and nowhere else. And there are dozens of ways for you to check them all out.

From the air you can peer down into nooks and crannies in the mountains—where cars cannot reach and hikers don't dare. Whether flitting here and there amid a helicopter's rush and roar, or sailing by in the silence of a glider's reverie, you glimpse sights that few have experienced. Or, if you would rather, take a step back in time and take off from the waters of Keehi Lagoon in a World War II–era seaplane. Follow the flight path flown by the Japanese Zeros as they attempted to destroy Pearl Harbor and the American spirit.

Would you prefer the ground tour, where you and gravity are no longer at odds? Oahu is covered in hiking trails that vary from tropical rain forest to arid desert. Even when in the bustling city of Honolulu, you are but minutes from hidden waterfalls and bamboo forests. Out west you can wander a dusty path that has long since given up its ability to accommodate cars but is perfect for hikers. You can splash in tidal pools, admire sea arches, and gape at caves opened by the rock slides that closed the road. You can camp out on many of these treks and beaches.

If somewhat less rugged and less vigorous exploration is more your style, how about letting horses do your dirty work? You can ride them on the beaches and in the valleys, checking out ancient holy sites, movie sets, and brilliant vistas.

Finally, there is the ancient sport of Scotland. Why merely hike into the rain forest when you can slice a 280-yard drive through it and then hunt for your Titleist in the bushy leaves instead? Almost 40 courses cover this tiny expanse, ranging from the target jungle golf of the Royal Hawaiian Golf Club to the pro-style links of Turtle Bay. There is no off-season in the tropics, and no one here knows your real handicap.

AERIAL TOURS

Taking an aerial tour of the Islands opens up a world of perspective. Look down from the sky at the outline of the USS *Arizona,* where it lies in its final resting place below the waters of Pearl Harbor, or get a glimpse of the vast carved expanse of a volcanic crater—here are views only seen by an "eye in the sky." Don't forget your camera.

Blue Hawaiian Helicopters. This company stakes its claim as Hawaii's largest helicopter company, with tours on all the major Islands and more than two-dozen choppers in its fleet. The 45-minute Oahu tour seats up to six passengers and includes narration from your friendly pilot along with sweeping views of Waikiki, the beautiful Windward Coast, and the North Shore. If you like to see the world from above or are just pinched for time and want to get a quick overview of the whole island without renting a car, this is the way to go. Discounts are available if you book online in advance. ✉ *99 Kaulele Pl., Honolulu* ☎ *808/831–8800, 800/745–2583* 🌐 *www.bluehawaiian.com* 🎟 *From $259.*

Island Seaplane Service. Harking back to the days of the earliest air visitors to Hawaii, the seaplane has always had a special spot in island lore. The only seaplane service still operating in Hawaii takes off from Keehi Lagoon. (It was featured in the film *50 First Dates.*) Flight options are either a twenty-minute or half-hour southern and eastern Oahu shoreline tour or an hour-long island circle tour. Groups can opt for a catered dinner on a floating dock in the lagoon. The Pan Am Clipper may be gone, but you can revisit the experience with this company. ✉ *85 Lagoon Dr., Airport Area* ☎ *808/836–6273* 🌐 *www.islandseaplane.com* 🎟 *From $99.*

Makani Kai Helicopters. This may be the best—if not the only—way to see the beautiful Sacred Falls on the windward side of the island, as the park around the falls was closed to hikers after a deadly 1999 rock slide. Makani Kai flies the helicopter over the pristine waterfall to show you the once-favorite trail that leads to it. Tours can last either a half hour, 45 minutes, or a full hour. Or the more adventurous can book the 50-minute Doors Off tour in the MD-500, the iconic helicopter from the *Magnum PI* TV series. Customized private charters are available for up to six passengers. ✉ *130 Iolana Pl., Honolulu* ☎ *808/834–5813, 877/255–8532* 🌐 *www.makanikai.com* 🎟 *From $170.*

The Original Glider Rides. "Mr. Bill" has been offering piloted glider (sailplane) rides over the northwest end of Oahu's North Shore since 1970. Choose from piloted scenic rides for one or two passengers in sleek, bubble-top, motorless aircraft with aerial views of mountains, shoreline, coral pools, windsurfing sails, and, in winter, humpback whales. Seeking more thrills? You can also take a more acrobatic ride or take control yourself in a mini lesson. Flights run 15–60 minutes long and depart continuously, daily 10–5. Reservations are requested. ✉ *Dillingham Airfield, 69-132 Farrington Hwy., Waialua* ☎ *808/637–0207* 🌐 *www.honolulusoaring.com* 🎟 *From $85.*

Paradise Helicopters. A certified Hawaii Ecotourism Association operator, Paradise offers tours on several islands. On Oahu, the tours depart from two helipads: Kalaeloa (at the Ko Olina resorts on the west side) and Turtle Bay Resort on the North Shore. Kalaeloa options range from a one-hour scenic tour over Diamond Head to a two-hour island circle (daytime and sunset) to specialized trips that focus on WW II history. Turtle Bay choices include several one- to one-and-a half-hour North Shore adventures. ☎ *808/969–7392* 🌐 *paradisecopters.com* 🎫 *From $189.*

GOLF

Unlike on the other Hawaiian Islands, the majority of Oahu's golf courses are not associated with hotels and resorts. In fact, of the island's three dozen–plus courses, only five are tied to lodging; none is in the tourist hub of Waikiki.

Municipal courses are a good choice for budget-conscious golfers but are more crowded and are not always maintained to the same standard as the private courses. Your best bet is to call the day you want to play and inquire about walk-on availability. Greens fees are standard at city courses: walking rate $66 for visitors, riding cart $20 for 18 holes, pull carts $4.

Greens fees listed here are the highest course rates per round on weekdays and weekends for U.S. residents. (Some courses charge non–U.S. residents higher prices.) Discounts are often available for resort guests and for those who book tee times online. Twilight fees are usually offered; call individual courses for information.

WAIKIKI

Ala Wai Municipal Golf Course. Just across the Ala Wai Canal from Waikiki, this municipal golf course is said to host more rounds than any other U.S. course—up to 500 per day. Not that it's a great course, just really convenient. The best bet for a visitor is to show up and expect to wait at least an hour or call up to three days in advance for a tee-time reservation. When reserving, the automated system will ask for an ID code—simply enter your phone number and give that number and your tee time when checking in. The course itself is flat; Robin Nelson did some redesign work in the 1990s, adding mounding, trees, and a lake. The Ala Wai Canal comes into play on several holes on the back nine, including the treacherous 18th. There's also an on-site restaurant and bar. ✉ *404 Kapahulu Ave., Waikiki* ☎ *808/733–7387 for starter's office, 808/738–4652 for pro shop, 808/296–2000 for reservations only* 🌐 *www.honolulu.gov/des/golf/alawai.htm* 🎫 *$66* ⛳ *18 holes, 5861 yards, par 70.*

SOUTHEAST OAHU

Hawaii Kai Golf Course. The **Championship Golf Course** (William F. Bell, 1973) winds through a Honolulu suburb at the foot of Koko Crater. Homes (and the liability of a broken window) come into play on many holes, but they are offset by views of the nearby Pacific and a crafty routing of holes. With several lakes, lots of trees, and bunkers in all the wrong places, Hawaii Kai really is a "championship" golf course, especially when the trade winds howl. Greens fees for this course include mandatory cart. The **Executive Course** (1962), a par-54 track, is the first of only three courses in Hawaii built by Robert Trent Jones Sr. Although a few changes have been made to his original design, you can find the usual Jones attributes, including raised greens and lots of risk-reward options. You may walk or use a cart on this course for an additional fee. ✉ *8902 Kalanianaole Hwy., Hawaii Kai* ☎ *808/395–2358* 🌐 *hawaiikaigolf.com* 🎫 *Championship Course $150, Executive Course $50* ⛳ *Championship Course: 18 holes, 6207 yards, par 72. Executive Course: 18 holes, 2196 yards, par 54.*

WINDWARD OAHU

Koolau Golf Club. Koolau Golf Club is marketed as the toughest golf course in Hawaii and one of the most challenging in the country. Dick Nugent and Jack Tuthill (1992) routed 10 holes over jungle ravines that require at least a 110-yard carry. The par-4 18th may be the most difficult closing hole in golf. The tee shot from this hole's regular tees must carry 200 yards of ravine, 250 from the blue tees. The approach shot is back across the ravine, 200 yards to a well-bunkered green. Set at the windward base of the Koolau Mountains, the course is as much beauty as beast. Kaneohe Bay is visible from most holes, orchids and yellow ginger bloom, the shama thrush (Hawaii's best singer since Don Ho) chirps, and waterfalls flute down the sheer, green mountains above. The greens fee includes a (required) cart. ✉ *45-550 Kionaole Rd., Kaneohe* ☎ *808/236–4653* 🌐 *www.koolaugolfclub.com* 🎫 *$155* ⛳ *18 holes, 7310 yards, par 72.*

Olomana Golf Links. Bob and Robert L. Baldock are the architects of record for this layout, but so much has changed since it opened in 1969 that they would recognize little of it. A turf specialist was brought in to improve fairways and greens, tees were rebuilt, new bunkers added, and mangroves cut back to make better use of natural wetlands. But what really puts Olomana on the map is that this is where wunderkind Michelle Wie learned the game. A cart is required at this course and is included in the greens fee. ✉ *41-1801 Kalanianaole Hwy., Waimanalo* ☎ *808/259–7926* 🌐 *olomana.golf* 🎫 *$50 for 9 holes, $89 for 18 holes* ⛳ *18 holes, 6306 yards, par 72.*

Fodor's Choice ★ **Royal Hawaiian Golf Club.** In the cool, lush Maunawili Valley, Pete and Perry Dye created what can only be called target jungle golf. In other words, the rough is usually dense jungle, and you may not hit a driver on three of the four par 5s, or several par 4s, including the perilous 18th that plays off a cliff to a narrow green protected by a creek. Mt. Olomana's twin peaks tower over the course. **■ TIP→ The back nine wanders deep into the valley, and includes an island green (par-3 11th) and perhaps the loveliest inland hole in Hawaii (par-4 12th).** ✉ *770 Auloa Rd., at Luana Hills Rd., Kailua* ☎ *808/262–2139* 🌐 *royalhawaiiangc.com* 🎫 *$160* ⛳ *18 holes, 5541 yards, par 72.*

Take a helicopter tour for a unique perspective of the island.

NORTH SHORE

Turtle Bay Resort & Spa. When the Lazarus of golf courses, the **Fazio Course** (George Fazio, 1971), rose from the dead in 2002, Turtle Bay on Oahu's rugged North Shore became a premier golf destination. Two holes had been plowed under when the **Palmer Course** (Arnold Palmer and Ed Seay, 1992) was built, while the other seven lay fallow, and the front nine remained open. Then new owners came along and re-created holes 13 and 14 using Fazio's original plans, and the Fazio became whole again. It's a terrific track with 90 bunkers. The gem at Turtle Bay, though, is the Palmer. The front nine is mostly open as it skirts Punahoolapa Marsh, a nature sanctuary, while the back nine plunges into the wetlands and winds along the coast. The short par-4 17th runs along the rocky shore, with a diabolical string of bunkers cutting diagonally across the fairway from tee to green. Carts are required for both courses and are included in the greens fee. ✉ *57-049 Kuilima Dr., Kahuku* ☎ *808/293–8574* 🌐 *www.turtlebaygolf.com* 🎟 *Fazio Course: $115 for 18 holes, $65 for 9 holes. Palmer Course: $165 for 18 holes, $95 for 9 holes* 🏌 *Fazio Course: 18 holes, 6600 yards, par 72. Palmer Course: 18 holes, 7200 yards, par 72.*

CENTRAL OAHU

Royal Kunia Country Club. At one time, the PGA Tour considered buying the Royal Kunia Country Club and hosting the Sony Open here. It's that good. ■ TIP→ **Every hole offers fabulous views from Diamond Head to Pearl Harbor to the nearby Waianae Mountains.** Robin Nelson's eye for natural sight lines and his dexterity with water features add to the visual pleasure. Carts are required and are included in the greens fee. ✉ *94-1509 Anonui St., Waipahu* ☎ *808/688–9222* 🌐 *www.royalkuniacc.com* 🎫 *$60 for 9 holes, $150 for 18 holes* ⛳ *18 holes, 6507 yards, par 72.*

Waikele Country Club. Outlet stores are not the only bargain at Waikele. The adjacent golf course is a daily-fee course that offers a private club–like atmosphere and a terrific Ted Robinson (1992) layout. Robinson's water features are less distinctive here but define the short par-4 4th hole, with a lake running down the left side of the fairway and guarding the green; and the par-3 17th, which plays across a lake. The par-4 18th is a terrific closing hole, with a lake lurking on the right side of the green. Carts are required and are included in the greens fee. ✉ *94-200 Paioa Pl., Waipahu* ☎ *808/676–9000* 🌐 *www.golfwaikele.com* 🎫 *$170* ⛳ *18 holes, 6261 yards, par 72.*

WEST (LEEWARD) OAHU

Coral Creek Golf Course. On the Ewa Plain, 4 miles inland, Coral Creek is cut from ancient coral left from when this area was still underwater. Robin Nelson (1999) did some of his best work in making use of the coral—and of some dynamite, blasting out portions to create dramatic lakes and tee and green sites. They could just as easily call it Coral Cliffs, because of the 30- to 40-foot cliffs Nelson created. They include the par-3 10th green's grotto and waterfall, and the vertical drop-off on the right side of the par-4 18th green. An ancient creek meanders across the course, but there's not much water, just enough to be a babbling nuisance. Carts are required and are included in the greens fee. ✉ *91-1111 Geiger Rd., Ewa Beach* ☎ *808/441–4653* 🌐 *www.coralcreekgolfhawaii.com* 🎫 *$70 for 9 holes, $140 for 18 holes* ⛳ *18 holes, 6347 yards, par 72.*

Ko Olina Golf Club. Hawaii's golden age of golf-course architecture came to Oahu when Ko Olina Golf Club opened in 1989. Ted Robinson, king of the water features, went splash-happy here, creating nine lakes that come into play on eight holes, including the par-3 12th, where you reach the tee by driving behind a Disney-like waterfall. Tactically, though, the most dramatic is the par-4 18th, where the approach is a minimum 120 yards across a lake to a two-tiered green guarded on the left by a cascading waterfall. Today Ko Olina has matured into one of Hawaii's top courses. You can niggle about routing issues—the first three holes play into the trade winds (and the morning sun), as do two consecutive par 5s on the back nine play—but Robinson does enough solid design to make those of passing concern. **TIP→ The course provides free transportation from Waikiki hotels.** ✉ *92-1220 Aliinui Dr., Ko Olina* ☎ *808/676–5300* 🌐 *www.koolinagolf.com* 🎫 *$115 for 9 holes, $225 for 18 holes* ⛳ *18 holes, 6432 yards, par 72.*

HIKING

The trails of Oahu cover a full spectrum of environments: desert walks through cactus, slippery paths through bamboo-filled rain forest, and scrambling rock climbs up ancient volcanic calderas. The only thing you won't find is an overnighter, as even the longest of hikes won't take you more than half a day. In addition to being short in length, many of the prime hikes are within 10 minutes of downtown Waikiki, meaning that you won't have to spend your whole day getting back to nature.

BEST SPOTS

Diamond Head Crater. Every vacation has requirements that must be fulfilled, so that when your neighbors ask, you can say, "Yeah, did it." Climbing Diamond Head is high on that list of things to do on Oahu. It's a moderately easy hike if you're in good physical condition, but be prepared to climb many stairs along the way. Also be sure to bring a water bottle, because it's hot and dry. Only a mile up, a clearly marked trail with handrails scales the inside of this extinct volcano. At the top, the fabled final 99 steps take you up to the pillbox overlooking the Pacific Ocean and Honolulu. It's a breathtaking view and a lot cheaper than taking a helicopter ride for the same photo op. Last entry for hikers is 4:30 pm. ✉ *Diamond Head Rd. at 18th Ave., Diamond Head* ✣ *Enter on east side of crater; there's limited parking inside, so most park on street and walk in* ☎ *808/587–0300* 🌐 *dlnr.hawaii.gov/dsp/parks/oahu/diamond-head-state-monument* 🎫 *$1 per person, $5 to park.*

Fodor's Choice ★ **Kaena Point Trail.** Kaena Point is one of the island's last easily accessible pockets of nature left largely untouched. For more than a quarter century, the state has protected nearly 60 acres of land at the point, first as a nature preserve and, more recently, as an ecosystem restoration project for endangered and protected coastal plants and seabirds. The uneven 5-mile trail around the point can be entered from two locations—Keawaula Beach (aka Yokohama Bay) at the end of Farrington Highway on Oahu's western coastline, or Mokuleia at the same highway's northern coast endpoint. It's a rugged coastline hike without much shade, so bring lots of water and sunscreen (or better yet, start early!). ■ TIP→ **Keep a lookout for the Laysan albatrosses; these enormous birds have recently returned to the area. Don't be surprised if they come in for a closer look at you, too.** ✉ *81-780 Farrington Hwy., Waianae* ✣ *Take Farrington Hwy. to its end at Yokohama. Hike in on old 4x4 trail* 🌐 *dlnr.hawaii.gov/dsp/hiking/oahu/kaena-point-trail.*

Makapuu Lighthouse Trail. For the less adventurous hiker and anyone looking for a great view, this paved trail that runs up the side of Makapuu Point in Southeast Oahu fits the bill. Early on, the trail is surrounded by lava rock but, as you ascend, foliage—the tiny white *koa haole* flower, the cream-tinged spikes of the *kiawe,* and, if you go early enough, the stunning night-blooming *cereus*—begins taking over the barren rock. At the easternmost tip of Oahu, where the island divides the sea, this trail gives you a spectacular view of the cobalt ocean meeting the land in a cacophony of white caps. To the south are several tide pools and the lighthouse, while the eastern view looks down upon Manana (Rabbit Island) and Kaohikaipu islets, two bird sanctuaries just off the

DID YOU KNOW?

Manoa Falls is about 150 feet high and is the gem at the end of a mile-long hike.

coast. The 2-mile round-trip hike is a great break on a circle-island trip. From late December to early May, this is a great perch to see migrating humpback whales. ■TIP→ **Be sure not to leave valuables in your car, as break-ins, even in the parking lot, are common.** ✉ *Makapuu Lighthouse Rd., Makapuu* ✣ *Take Kalanianaole Hwy. to base of Makapuu Point, then look for the parking lot* 🌐 *dlnr.hawaii.gov/dsp/hiking/oahu/makapuu-point-lighthouse-trail.*

Fodor's Choice ★ **Manoa Falls Trail.** Travel up into the valley beyond Honolulu to make the Manoa Falls hike. Though only a mile long, this well-trafficked path, visited by an estimated 100,000 hikers a year, passes through so many different ecosystems that you feel as if you're in an arboretum—and you're not far off. (The beautiful Lyon Arboretum is right near the trailhead, if you want to make another stop.) Walk among the elephant ear ape plants, ruddy fir trees, and a bamboo forest straight out of China. At the top is a 150-foot waterfall, which can be an impressive cascade or, if rain has been sparse, little more than a trickle. This hike is more about the journey than the destination; make sure you bring some mosquito repellent because they grow 'em big up here. ✉ *3998 Manoa Rd., Manoa* ✣ *West Manoa Rd. is behind Manoa Valley in Paradise Park. Take West Manoa Rd. to end, park on side of road or in parking lot for a small fee, follow trail signs* 🌐 *www.hawaiitrails.org/trails/#/trail/manoa-falls-trail/225.*

GOING WITH A GUIDE

FAMILY **Hawaii Nature Center.** A good choice for families, the center in upper Makiki Valley conducts a number of programs for both adults and children. There are guided hikes into tropical settings that reveal hidden waterfalls and protected forest reserves. They don't run tours every day, so it's a good idea to get advance reservations. ✉ *2131 Makiki Heights Dr., Makiki Heights* ☎ *808/955–0100* 🌐 *www.hawaiinaturecenter.org.*

Oahu Nature Tours. Guides explain the native flora and fauna and history that are your companions on their various walking and hiking tours on Oahu. This outfitter offers tours to the North Shore, Diamond Head, and Windward Oahu. The company also offers much more expensive private birding tours, perfect for those interested in spotting one of Hawaii's native honeycreepers. Tours include pickup at centralized Waikiki locations and are discounted if booked online in advance. ☎ *808/924–2473* 🌐 *www.oahunaturetours.com* 🎟 *From $35.*

HORSEBACK RIDING

FAMILY **Happy Trails Hawaii.** Take a guided horseback ride above the North Shore's Waimea Bay along trails that offer panoramic views from Kaena Point to the famous surfing spots. Groups are no larger than 10, and instruction is provided. The rides are particularly family-friendly, and children six and older are welcome. You can take either a 1½- or a 2-hour ride, which includes a 15-minute mini-lesson. Reservations are required. ✉ *59-231 Pupukea Rd., Pupukea* ✣ *Go 1 mile mauka (toward mountain) up Pupukea Rd.; the office is on the right* ☎ *808/638–7433* 🌐 *www.happytrailshawaii.com* 🎟 *$95 for 1½ hrs, $115 for 2 hrs.*

FAMILY **Kualoa Ranch.** This 4,000-acre working ranch across from Kualoa Beach Park on Windward Oahu offers two-hour trail rides in the breathtaking Kaaawa Valley, which was the site of such movie back lots as *Jurassic Park, Godzilla,* and *50 First Dates.* There is an hour-long option, but it doesn't take you into the valley. Instead, this tour takes you to the scenic northern section of the ranch with its WWII-era bunkers. Kualoa has other activities such as bus, boat, and jeep tours, ATV trail rides, canopy zipline tours, and children's activities, which may be combined for full-day package rates. The minimum age for horseback rides is 10. ✉ *49-479 Kamehameha Hwy., Kaneohe* ☎ *800/231–7321, 808/237–7321* 🌐 *www.kualoa.com* 🎫 *$85 for 1 hr, $130 for 2 hrs.*

FAMILY **Turtle Bay Stables.** Trail rides follow the 12-mile-long coastline and even step out onto sandy beaches fronting this luxe resort on Oahu's fabled North Shore. The stables here are part of the resort but can be utilized by nonguests. The sunset ride is a definite must. A basic trail ride lasts 45 minutes and visits filming sites for ABC's *Lost* and the film *Pirates of the Caribbean.* ✉ *Turtle Bay Resort, 57-091 Kamehemeha Hwy., Kahuku* ☎ *808/293–6024* 🌐 *www.turtlebayresort.com/things-to-do/sports-recreation/horse-riding* 🎫 *From $85.*

MAUI

WELCOME TO MAUI

TOP REASONS TO GO

★ **The Road to Hana:** Each curve of this legendary cliff-side road pulls you deeper into the lush green rain forest of Maui's eastern shore.

★ **Haleakala National Park:** Explore the lava bombs, cinder cones, and silverswords at the gasp-inducing, volcanic summit of Haleakala, the House of the Sun.

★ **Hookipa Beach:** On Maui's North Shore, the world's top windsurfers will dazzle you as they maneuver above the waves like butterflies shot from cannons.

★ **Waianapanapa State Park:** Head to East Maui and take a dip at the stunning black-sand beach or in the cave pool where an ancient princess once hid.

★ **Resorts, Resorts, Resorts:** Opulent gardens, pools, restaurants, and golf courses make Maui's resorts some of the best in the Islands.

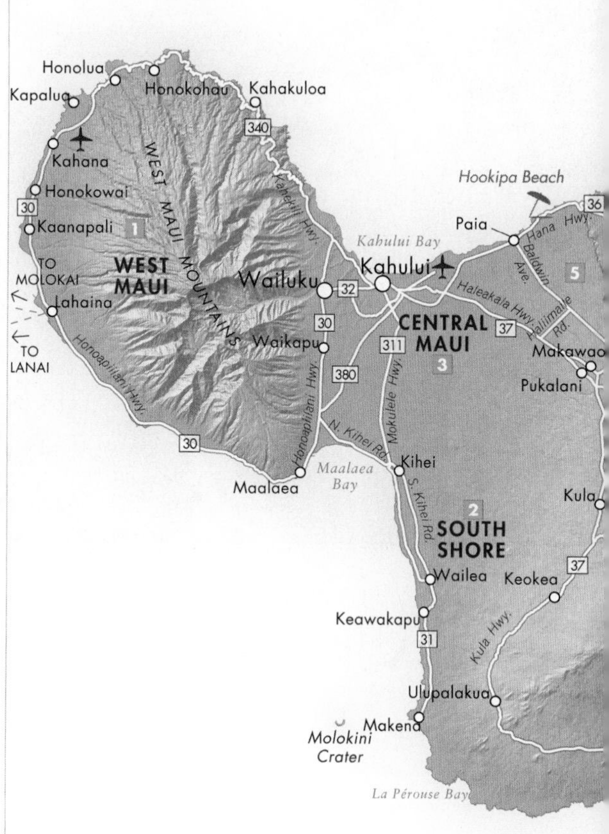

1 West Maui. This leeward, sunny area is ringed by resorts and condominiums in areas such as Kaanapali and Kapalua. Also on the coast is the busy, tourist-oriented town of Lahaina.

2 South Shore. The leeward side of Maui's eastern half is what most people mean when they say South Shore. This popular area is sunny and warm year-round.

3 Central Maui. Between Maui's two mountain areas is Maui's county seat of Wailuku and the commercial center of Kahului (and the airport).

4 Upcountry. Island residents affectionately call the regions climbing up the slope of Haleakala Crater Upcountry.

5 North Shore. The North Shore has no large resorts, just plenty of picturesque small towns like Paia and Haiku.

6 Road to Hana. The island's northeastern, windward side is largely one great rain forest, traversed by the stunning Road to Hana.

GREAT ITINERARIES

Maui's landscape is incredibly diverse, offering everything from underwater encounters with eagle rays to treks across moonlike terrain. Although daydreaming at the pool or on the beach may fulfill your initial island fantasy, Maui has much more to offer. The following one-day itineraries will take you to our favorite spots on the island.

Beach Day in West Maui

West Maui has some of the island's most beautiful beaches, though many of them are hidden by megaresorts. If you get an early start, you can begin your day snorkeling at Slaughterhouse Beach (in winter, D.T. Fleming Beach is a better option as it's less rough). Then spend the day beach hopping through Kapalua, Napili, and Kaanapali as you make your way south. You'll want to get to Lahaina before dark so you can spend some time exploring the historic whaling town before choosing a restaurant for a sunset dinner.

Focus on Marine Life on the South Shore

Start your South Shore trip early in the morning, and head out past Makena into the rough lava fields of rugged La Perouse Bay. At the road's end there are areas of the Ahihi-Kinau Marine Preserve open to the public (others are closed indefinitely) that offer good snorkeling. If that's a bit too far afield for you, there's excellent snorkeling at Polo Beach. Head to the right (your right while facing the ocean) for plenty of fish and beautiful coral. Head back north to Kihei for lunch, and then enjoy the afternoon learning more about Maui's marine life at the outstanding Maui Ocean Center at Maalaea.

Haleakala National Park, Upcountry, and the North Shore

If you don't plan to spend an entire day hiking in the crater at Haleakala National Park, this itinerary will at least allow you to take a peek at it. Get up early and head straight for the summit of Haleakala (if you're jet-lagged and waking up in the middle of the night, you may want to get there in time for sunrise). Bring water, sunscreen, and warm clothing; it's freezing at sunrise. Plan to spend a couple of hours exploring the various lookout points in the park. On your way down the mountain, turn right on Makawao Avenue and head into the little town of Makawao. You can have lunch here, or make a left on Baldwin Avenue and head downhill to the North Shore town of Paia, which has a number of great lunch spots and shops to explore. Spend the rest of your afternoon at Paia's main strip of sand, Hookipa Beach.

The Road to Hana

This cliff-side driving tour through rainforest canopy reveals Maui's lushest and most tropical terrain. It will take a full day to explore this part of the North Shore and East Maui, especially if you plan to make it all the way to Oheo Gulch. You'll pass through communities where old Hawaii still thrives, and where the forest runs unchecked from the sea to the summit. You'll want to make frequent exploratory stops. To really soak in the magic of this place, consider staying overnight in Hana town. That way you can spend a full day winding toward Hana, hiking and exploring along the way, and the next day traveling leisurely back to civilization.

Updated by Lehia Apana, Christie Leon, and Heidi Pool

Those who know Maui well understand why it's earned all its superlatives. The island's miles of perfect beaches, lush green valleys, historic villages, top-notch water sports and outdoor activities, and amazing marine life have made it an international favorite. But nature isn't all Maui has to offer: it's also home to a wide variety of cultural activities, stunning ethnic diversity, and stellar restaurants and resorts.

Maui is much more than sandy beaches and palm trees; it's a land of water and fire. Puu Kukui, the 5,788-foot interior of Mauna Kahalawai, also known as the "West Maui Mountains," is one of Earth's wettest spots—an annual rainfall of 400 inches has sculpted the land into impassable gorges and razor-sharp ridges. On the opposite side of the island, the blistering lava fields at Ahihi-Kinau receive scant rain. Just above this desertlike landscape, *paniolo* (cowboys) herd cattle on rolling fertile ranchlands. On the island's rugged east side is the lush tropical Hawaii of travel posters.

In small towns like Paia and Hana you can see remnants of the past mingling with modern-day life. Ancient *heiau* (platforms, often made of stone, once used as places of worship) line busy roadways. Old coral-and-brick missionary homes now welcome visitors. The antique smokestacks of sugar mills tower above communities where the children blend English, Hawaiian, Japanese, Chinese, Portuguese, Filipino, and more into one colorful language. Hawaii is a melting pot like no other. Visiting an eclectic mom-and-pop shop—such as Makawao's T. Komoda Store & Bakery—can feel like stepping into another country, or back in time. The more you look here, the more you find.

At 729 square miles, Maui is the second-largest Hawaiian Island, but it offers more miles of swimmable beaches than any of its neighbors. Despite rapid growth over the past few decades, the local population still totals less than 200,000.

GEOLOGY

Maui is made up of two volcanoes, one now extinct and the other dormant but that erupted long ago, joined into one island. The resulting depression between the two is what gives the island its nickname, the Valley Isle. West Maui's 5,788-foot Puu Kukui was the first volcano to form, a distinction that gives that area's mountainous topography a more weathered look. The Valley Isle's second volcano is the 10,023-foot Haleakala, where desertlike terrain abuts tropical forests.

HISTORY

Maui's history is full of firsts—Lahaina was the first capital of Hawaii and the first destination of the whaling industry (early 1800s), which explains why the town still has that seafaring vibe. Lahaina was also the first stop for missionaries on Maui (1823). Although they suppressed aspects of Hawaiian culture, the missionaries did help invent the Hawaiian alphabet and built a printing press—the first west of the Rockies—that rolled out the news in Hawaiian, as well as, not surprisingly, Hawaii's first Bibles. Maui also boasts the first sugar plantation in Hawaii (1849) and the first Hawaiian luxury resort (1946), now called the Travaasa Hana.

ON MAUI TODAY

In the mid-1970s savvy marketers saw a way to improve Maui's economy by promoting the Valley Isle to golfers and luxury travelers. The strategy worked well; Maui's visitor count is about 2.6 million annually. Impatient traffic now threatens to overtake the ubiquitous aloha spirit, development encroaches on agricultural lands, and county planners struggle to meet the needs of a burgeoning population. But Maui is still carpeted with an eyeful of green, and for every tailgater there's a local on "Maui time" who stops for each pedestrian and sunset.

MAUI PLANNER

GETTING HERE AND AROUND

AIR TRAVEL

Maui has two major airports. Kahului Airport handles major airlines and interisland flights; it's the only airport on Maui that has direct service from the mainland. Kapalua–West Maui Airport is served by Hawaiian and Mokulele airlines. If you're staying in West Maui and you're flying in from another island, you can avoid the hour drive from the Kahului Airport by flying into Kapalua–West Maui Airport. Hana Airport in East Maui is small; Mokulele Airlines flies twice per day between Kahului and Hana.

Service to Maui changes regularly, so it's best to check when you are ready to book. Alaska Airlines offers nonstop flights from Anchorage, Bellingham, Wash.; Oakland; Portland, Ore.; Sacramento; San Diego; and Seattle. American Airlines flies from Dallas, Los Angeles, and Phoenix. Hawaiian Airlines has nonstop service from Los Angeles, Oakland, Portland, San Francisco, and Seattle; it also offers the only nonstop flight from JFK to Honolulu. United's nonstop flights leave from Chicago, Denver, Los Angeles, and San Francisco. Delta has flights from

Los Angeles, Salt Lake City, and Seattle. Virgin flies nonstop from Los Angeles and San Francisco. In addition to offering competitive rates and online specials, all have frequent-flyer programs that will entitle you to rewards and upgrades the more you fly.

CAR TRAVEL

Should you plan to do any sightseeing on Maui, it's best to rent a car. Even if all you want to do is relax at your resort, you may want to hop in the car to check out one of the island's popular restaurants.

Many of Maui's roads are two lanes, so allow plenty of time to return your vehicle to the airport. Traffic can be bad during morning and afternoon rush hours, especially between Kahului and Paia, Kihei, and Lahaina. Give yourself about 3½ hours before departure time to return your vehicle.

Make sure you've got a GPS or a good map. Free visitor publications containing high-quality road maps can be found at airports, hotels, and shops.

Hawaii residents refer to places as being either *mauka* (toward the mountains) or *makai* (toward the ocean).

Hawaii has a strict seat-belt law. All passengers, regardless of age, in the front and back seat must wear a seat belt. The fine for not wearing a seat belt is $102. Jaywalking is also common, so pay careful attention to pedestrians. Turning right on a red light is legal in the state, except where noted. Your unexpired mainland driver's license is valid for rental cars for up to 90 days.

ISLAND DRIVING TIMES

Driving from one point on Maui to another can take longer than the mileage indicates. It's 52 miles from Kahului Airport to Hana, but the drive will take you about three hours if you stop to smell the flowers, which you certainly should do. As for driving to Haleakala, the 38-mile drive from sea level to the summit will take about two hours. The roads are narrow and winding; you must travel slowly. Kahului is the transportation hub—the main airport and largest harbor are here. Traffic on Maui's roads can be heavy, especially from 6 am–8:30 am and 3:30 pm–6:30 pm. Here are average driving times.

DRIVING TIMES	
Kahului to Wailea	17 miles/30 mins
Kahului to Kaanapali	25 miles/45 mins
Kahului to Kapalua	36 miles/1 hr 15 mins
Kahului to Makawao	13 miles/25 mins
Kapalua to Haleakala	73 miles/3 hrs
Kaanapali to Haleakala	62 miles/2 hrs 30 mins
Wailea to Haleakala	54 miles/2 hrs 30 mins
Kapalua to Hana	88 miles/5 hrs
Kaanapali to Hana	77 miles/5 hrs
Wailea to Hana	69 miles/4 hrs 30 mins
Wailea to Lahaina	20 miles/45 mins
Kapalua to Lahaina	12 miles/20 mins

HOTELS

Maui is well known for its lovely resorts, some of them very luxurious; many cater to families. But there are other options, including abundant and convenient apartment and condo rentals for all budgets. The resorts and rentals cluster largely on Maui's sunny coasts, in West Maui and the South Shore. For a different, more local experience, you might spend part of your time at a small bed-and-breakfast. Check Internet sites and ask about discounts and packages. *Hotel reviews have been shortened. For full information, visit Fodors.com.*

RESTAURANTS

There's a lot going on for a place the size of Maui, from ethnic holes-in-the-wall to fancy oceanfront fish houses. Much of it is excellent, but some of it is overpriced and touristy. Choose menu items made with products that are abundant on the island, including local fish. Local cuisine is a mix of foods brought by ethnic groups since the late 1700s, blended with the foods Native Hawaiians have enjoyed for centuries. For a food adventure, take a drive into Central Maui and eat at one of the "local" spots recommended here.

WHAT IT COSTS

	$	$$	$$$	$$$$
Restaurants	Under $18	$18–$26	$27–$35	Over $35
Hotels	Under $181	$181–$260	$261–$340	Over $340

Restaurant prices are the average cost of a main course at dinner or, if dinner is not served, at lunch. Hotel prices are the lowest cost of a standard double room in high season or, for rentals, the lowest per-night cost for a one-bedroom unit in high season. Prices do not include 13.42% tax.

VISITOR INFORMATION

The Hawaii Visitors and Convention Bureau (HVCB) has plenty of general and vacation-planning information for Maui and all the Islands, and offers a free official vacation planner.

Information Maui Visitors Bureau. 🌐 *www.gohawaii.com/islands/maui.*

EXPLORING

Updated by Lehia Apana

Maui is more than sandy beaches and palm trees. Puu Kukui, the 5,788-foot interior of the West Maui Mountains, also known as Mauna Kahalawai, is one of Earth's wettest spots—annual rainfall of 400 inches has sculpted the land into impassable gorges and razor-sharp ridges. On the opposite side of the island, the blistering lava fields at Ahihi-Kinau receive scant rain. Just above this desertlike landscape, *paniolo* (Hawaiian cowboys) herd cattle on rolling, fertile ranch lands. On the island's rugged east side is the lush, tropical Hawaii of travel posters.

In small towns like Paia and Hana you can see remnants of the past mingling with modern-day life. Ancient *heiau* (stone platforms once used as places of worship) line busy roadways. Old coral and brick missionary homes now house broadcasting networks. The antique smokestacks of sugar mills tower above communities where the children blend English, Hawaiian, Japanese, Chinese, Portuguese, Filipino, and more into one colorful language. Hawaii is a melting pot like no other. Visiting an eclectic mom-and-pop shop—such as Upcountry Makawao's Komoda Store and Bakery—can feel like stepping into another country, or back in time. The more you look here, the more you find.

WEST MAUI

Separated from the remainder of the island by steep *pali* (cliffs), West Maui has a reputation for attitude and action. Once upon a time this was the haunt of whalers, missionaries, and the kings and queens of Hawaii. Today the main drag, Front Street, is crowded with T-shirt and trinket shops, art galleries, and restaurants. Farther north is Kaanapali, Maui's first planned resort area. Its first hotel, the Sheraton, opened in 1963. Since then, massive resorts, luxury condos, and a shopping center have sprung up along the white-sand beaches, with championship golf courses across the road. A few miles farther up the coast is the ultimate in West Maui luxury, the resort area of Kapalua. In between, dozens of strip malls line both the *makai* (toward the sea) and *mauka* (toward the mountains) sides of the highway. There are gems here, too, like Napili Bay and its jaw-dropping crescent of sand.

LAHAINA

27 miles west of Kahului; 4 miles south of Kaanapali.

Lahaina is a bustling waterfront town packed with visitors from around the globe. Some may describe the area as tacky, with too many T-shirt vendors and not enough mom-and-pop shops, but this historic town houses some of Hawaii's best restaurants, boutiques, cafés, and galleries. **■TIP→ If you spend Friday afternoon exploring Front Street, hang around for Art Night, when the galleries stay open late and offer entertainment, including artists demonstrating their work.**

Sunset cruises and other excursions depart from Lahaina Harbor. At the southern end of town an important archaeological site—Mokuula—is currently being researched, excavated, and restored. This was once a spiritual and political center, as well as home to Maui's chiefs.

GETTING HERE AND AROUND

It's about a 45-minute drive from Kahului Airport to Lahaina (take Route 380 to Route 30), depending on the traffic on this heavily traveled route. Traffic can be slow around Lahaina, especially 4–6 pm. Shuttles and taxis are available from Kahului Airport. The Maui Bus Lahaina Islander route runs from Queen Kaahumanu Center in Kahului to the Wharf Cinema Center on Front Street, Lahaina's main thoroughfare.

TOURS

Fodor's Choice ★ **Maui Nei Native Expeditions.** Look past the souvenir shops and bustling eateries of West Maui, and you'll find a captivating history that isn't immediately apparent to most visitors. Maui Nei's knowledgeable guides lead a series of intimate tours that share a glimpse into Hawaiian culture and local history. The small group sizes ensure that you'll

Pailolo Channel
D.T. Fleming Beach
Slaughterhouse Beach
Kapalua Bay Beach
Honokohau
Honolua
Kapalua
Napili
Kahakuloa
West Maui Forest Reserve
Napili Beach
Kahana
WEST MAUI MOUNTAINS
340
30
Kahekili Hwy.
Honokowai
Kaanapali Beach
Hookipa Beach
Baldwin Beach
Hana Hwy.
Kaanapali
WEST MAUI
Kahului and Wailuku
see detail map
Kanaha Beach
Paia
Kahului Bay
Kahului Airport
NORTH
TO MOLOKAI
Puu Kukui 5,788 ft.
Lahaina
see detail map
Wailuku
Stream
32
Kahului
Baldwin Ave.
Iao Valley State Monument
Iao
Haleakala Hwy.
Kepaniwai Park & Heritage Gardens
Puunene Ave.
37
Haliimaile Rd.
Waikapu
311
CENTRAL MAUI
Launiupoko Beach Park
Honoapiilani Hwy.
TO LANAI
380
Omaopio Rd.
Honoapiilani Hwy.
Mokulele Hwy.
Auau Channel
Oluwalu Beach
MAUI
Maui Ocean Center
Kealia Pond National Wildlife Reserve
Ukumehame Beach Park
Maalaea
Maalaea Bay
N. Kihei Rd.
Kihei
Hawaiian Islands Humpback Whale National Marine Sanctuary
Piilani Hwy.
Kalepolepo Beach
Kamaole Beach Parks
S. Kihei Rd.
SOUTH SHORE
Mokapu Beach
Ulua Beach
Wailea
Keokea
Keawakapu
Wailea Beach
37
31
Kula Hwy.
Polo Beach
Kealaikahiki Channel
MauiWine
Molokini Crater
Makena
Ulupalakua Ranch
Alalakeiki Channel
Makena Beach State Park
La Pérouse Bay
KAHOOLAWE

Maui

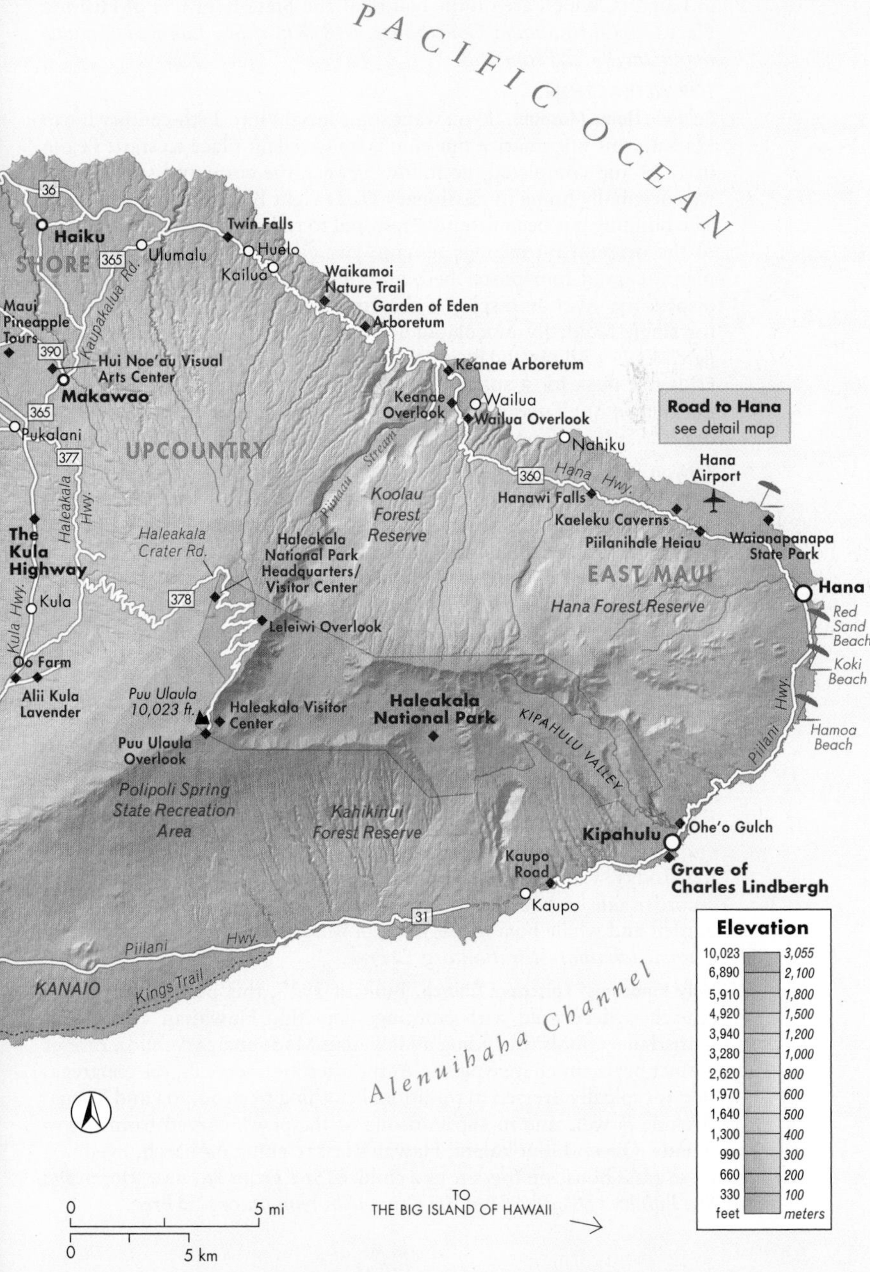

PACIFIC OCEAN
Haiku
SHORE
Ulumalu
Twin Falls
Huelo
Kailua
Waikamoi Nature Trail
Garden of Eden Arboretum
Maui Pineapple Tours
Kaupakalua Rd.
Hui Noe'au Visual Arts Center
Makawao
Keanae Arboretum
Keanae Overlook
Wailua
Wailua Overlook
Road to Hana see detail map
Pukalani
UPCOUNTRY
Nahiku
Hana Hwy.
Hana Airport
Koolau Forest Reserve
Hanawi Falls
Kaeleku Caverns
Piilanihale Heiau
Waianapanapa State Park
Haleakala Hwy.
The Kula Highway
Haleakala Crater Rd.
Haleakala National Park Headquarters/ Visitor Center
EAST MAUI
Hana
Hana Forest Reserve
Kula
Kula Hwy.
Leleiwi Overlook
Red Sand Beach
Koki Beach
Oo Farm
Alii Kula Lavender
Puu Ulaula 10,023 ft.
Haleakala Visitor Center
Haleakala National Park
KIPAHULU VALLEY
Puu Ulaula Overlook
Hamoa Beach
Piilani Hwy.
Polipoli Spring State Recreation Area
Kahikinui Forest Reserve
Ohe'o Gulch
Kipahulu
Grave of Charles Lindbergh
Kaupo Road
Kaupo
Piilani Hwy.
KANAIO
Kings Trail
Alenuihaha Channel
Elevation
10,023 3,055
6,890 2,100
5,910 1,800
4,920 1,500
3,940 1,200
3,280 1,000
2,620 800
1,970 600
1,640 500
1,300 400
990 300
660 200
330 100
feet meters
0 5 mi
0 5 km
TO THE BIG ISLAND OF HAWAII

enjoy personalized attention. Two-hour walking tours begin in Lahaina and Kaanapali, and a three-hour immersion program includes lessons in poi pounding, the Hawaiian art of printmaking, and more. Tour proceeds support the restoration of Mokuula island and Mokuhinia pond in Lahaina, which are on the National and State Registers of Historic Places. ✉ *Old Lahaina Courthouse, 648 Wharf St., Lahaina* 🌐 *www.mauinei.com* 🎫 *From $48.*

TOP ATTRACTIONS

Baldwin Home Museum. If you want some insight into 19th-century life in Hawaii, this informative museum is an excellent place to start. Begun in 1834 and completed the following year, the coral-and-stone house was originally home to missionary Dr. Dwight Baldwin and his family. The building has been carefully restored to reflect the period and many of the original furnishings remain: you can view the family's grand piano, carved four-poster bed, and most interestingly, Dr. Baldwin's dispensary. Also on display is the "thunderpot"—learn how the doctor single-handedly inoculated 10,000 Maui residents against smallpox. ■ **TIP→ Admission includes an orientation by the docent, or come Friday at dusk for a special candlelight tour every half hour.** ✉ *120 Dickenson St., Lahaina* ☎ *808/661–3262* 🌐 *www.lahainarestoration.org* 🎫 *$7, includes admission to Wo Hing Museum.*

Banyan Tree. Planted in 1873, this massive tree is the largest of its kind in the United States and provides a welcome retreat and playground for visitors and locals, who rest and play music under its awesome branches. Many Lahaina festivals and weekend arts and craft fairs center on the Banyan Tree. ■ **TIP→ The Banyan Tree is a popular and hard-to-miss meeting place if your party splits up for independent exploring.** It's also a terrific place to be when the sun sets—mynah birds settle in here for a screeching symphony, which is an event in itself. ✉ *Front St. between Hotel and Canal Sts., Lahaina* 🌐 *www.lahainarestoration.org.*

Hale Paahao (Old Prison). Lahaina's jailhouse is a reminder of rowdy whaling days. Its name literally means "stuck-in-irons house," referring to the wall shackles and ball-and-chain restraints. The compound was built in the 1850s by convict laborers out of blocks of coral that had been salvaged from the demolished waterfront fort. Most prisoners were sent here for desertion, drunkenness, or reckless horse riding. Today, a wax figure representing an imprisoned old sailor tells his recorded tale of woe. There are also interpretive signs for the botanical garden and whale boat in the yard. ✉ *Wainee and Prison Sts., Lahaina* 🌐 *www.lahainarestoration.org* 🎫 *Free.*

Holy Innocents' Episcopal Church. Built in 1927, this beautiful open-air church is decorated with paintings depicting Hawaiian versions of Christian symbols (including a Hawaiian Madonna and child), rare or extinct birds, and native plants. At the afternoon services, the congregation is typically dressed in traditional clothing from Samoa and Tonga. Anyone is welcome to slip into one of the pews, carved from native woods. Queen Liliuokalani, Hawaii's last reigning monarch, lived in a large grass house on this site as a child. ✉ *561 Front St., near Mokuhina St., Lahaina* ☎ *808/661–4202* 🌐 *www.holyimaui.org* 🎫 *Free.*

Once a whaling center, Lahaina Harbor bustles with tour boats, fishing vessels, and pleasure craft.

Fodor's Choice ★ **Martin Lawrence Galleries.** In business since 1975, Martin Lawrence displays the works of such world-renowned artists as Picasso, Erté, and Chagall in a bright and friendly gallery. Modern and pop-art enthusiasts will also find pieces by Keith Haring, Andy Warhol, and Japanese creative icon Takashi Murakami. ✉ *790 Front St., at Lahainaluna Rd., Lahaina* ☎ *808/661–1788* 🌐 *www.martinlawrence.com.*

Fodor's Choice ★ **Old Lahaina Courthouse.** The Lahaina Arts Society, Lahaina Vistor Center, and Lahaina Heritage Museum occupy this charming old government building in the center of town. Wander among the terrific displays and engage with an interactive exhibit about Lahaina's history, pump the knowledgeable visitor center staff for tips—be sure to ask for the walking-tour brochure covering historic Lahaina sites—and stop at the theater with a rotating array of films about everything from whales to canoes. Erected in 1859 and restored in 1999, the building has served as a customs and court house, governor's office, post office, vault and collector's office, and police court. On August 12, 1898, its postmaster witnessed the lowering of the Hawaiian flag when Hawaii became a U.S. territory. The flag now hangs above the stairway. ■ TIP→ **There's a public restroom in the building.** ✉ *648 Wharf St., Lahaina* ☎ *808/667–9193 for Lahaina Visitor Center, 808/661–3262 for Lahaina Heritage Museum* 🌐 *www.lahainarestoration.org* 🎟 *Free.*

Fodor's Choice ★ **Waiola Church and Wainee Cemetery.** Immortalized in James Michener's *Hawaii*, the original church from the early 1800s was destroyed once by fire and twice by fierce windstorms. Repositioned and rebuilt in 1954, the church was renamed Waiola ("water of life") and has been standing proudly ever since. The adjacent cemetery was the region's

Baldwin Home Museum 3
Banyan Tree 5
Hale Paahao (Old Prison) 6
Holy Innocents' Episcopal Church 7
Martin Lawrence Galleries 2
Old Lahaina Courthouse 4
Waiola Church and Wainee Cemetery 8
Wo Hing Museum 1

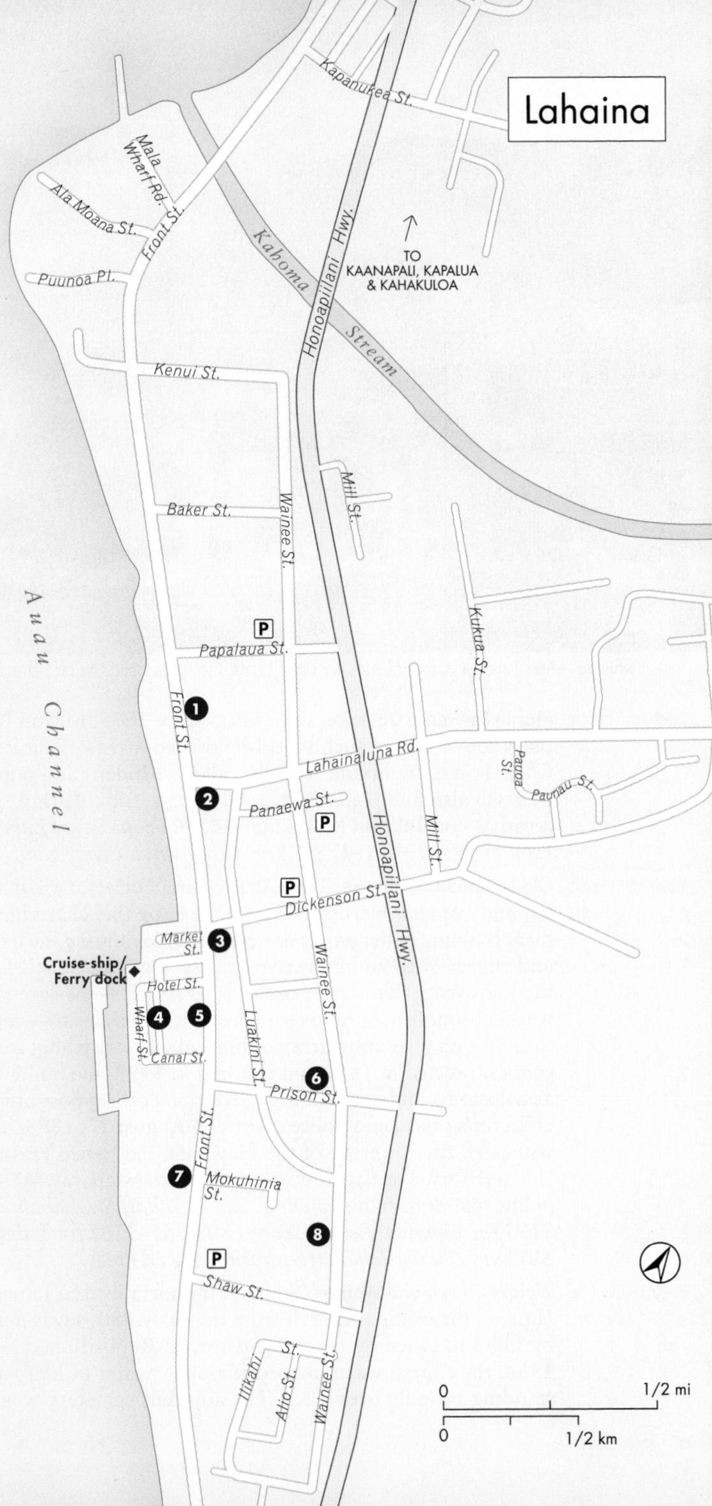

first Christian cemetery and is the final resting place of many of Hawaii's most important monarchs, including Kamehameha the Great's wife, Queen Keopuolani, who was baptized during her final illness. ✉ *535 Wainee St., Lahaina* ☎ *808/661–4349* 🌐 *www.waiola-church.org* 🎫 *Free.*

WALKING TOURS

Lahaina's side streets are best explored on foot. Both the Baldwin Home Museum and the Lahaina Visitor Center offer free, self-guided, walking-tour brochures with a map for $2 each. The historic trail map is easy to follow; it details three short but enjoyable loops of the town.

Fodor's Choice ★ **Wo Hing Museum.** Smack-dab in the center of Front Street, this eye-catching Chinese temple reflects the importance of early Chinese immigrants to Lahaina. Built by the Wo Hing Society in 1912, the museum contains beautiful artifacts, historic photo displays of Dr. Sun Yat-sen, and a Taoist altar. Don't miss the films playing in the rustic cookhouse next door—some of Thomas Edison's first films, shot in Hawaii circa 1898, show Hawaiian wranglers herding steer onto ships. Ask the docent for some star fruit from the tree outside, for an offering or for yourself. Note that the altar is open only during annual Chinese festivals. ■ TIP→ **If you're in town in late January or early February, this museum hosts a nice Chinese New Year festival.** ✉ *858 Front St., Lahaina* ☎ *808/661–5553* 🌐 *www.lahainarestoration.org* 🎫 *$7, includes admission to Baldwin Home.*

KAANAPALI AND NEARBY

4 miles north of Lahaina.

As you drive north from Lahaina, the first resort community you reach is Kaanapali, a cluster of high-rise hotels framing a world-class white-sand beach. This is part of West Maui's famous resort strip and is a perfect destination for families and romance seekers wanting to be in the center of the action. A little farther up the road lie the condo-filled beach towns of Honokowai, Kahana, and Napili, followed by Kapalua. Each boasts its own style and flavor, though most rely on a low-key beach vibe for people wanting upscale vacation rentals.

GETTING HERE AND AROUND

Shuttles and taxis are available from Kahului and West Maui airports. Resorts offer free shuttles between properties, and some hotels also provide complimentary shuttles into Lahaina. In the Maui Bus system the Napili Islander begins and ends at Whalers Village in Kaanapali and stops at most condos along the coastal road as far north as Napili Bay.

TOP ATTRACTIONS

Kaanapali. The theatrical look of Hawaii tourism—planned resort communities where luxury homes mix with high-rise hotels, fantasy swimming pools, and a theme-park landscape—began right here in the 1960s, when clever marketers built this sunny shoreline into a playground for the world's vacationers. Three miles of uninterrupted white-sand beach and placid water form the front yard of this artificial utopia, with its 40 tennis courts and two championship golf courses.

In ancient times, the area near Sheraton Maui was known for its bountiful fishing (especially lobster) and its seaside cliffs. The sleepy fishing village was washed away by the wave of Hawaii's new economy: tourism. Puu Kekaa (today incorrectly referred to as Black Rock) was a *lele*, a place in ancient Hawaii believed to be where souls leaped from into the afterlife. ✉ *Kaanapali.*

ISLAND HOPPING

If you have a week or more on Maui, consider taking a day or two for a trip to Molokai or Lanai. Tour operators such as Trilogy offer day-trip packages to Lanai that include snorkeling and a van tour. Ferries to both Islands have room for your golf clubs and mountain bike. (Avoid ferry travel on a blustery day.) If you prefer to travel to Molokai or Lanai by air and don't mind 4- to 12-seaters, you can take a small air taxi. Book with Pacific Wings (⇨ *see Air Travel in Travel Smart Hawaii*).

KAPALUA AND KAHAKULOA

Kapalua is 10 miles north of Kaanapali; 36 miles west of Kahului.

Upscale Kapalua is north of the Kaanapali resorts, past Napili, and is a hideaway for those with money who want to stay incognito. Farther along the Honoapiilani Highway is the remote village of Kahakuloa, a reminder of Old Hawaii.

GETTING HERE AND AROUND

Shuttles and taxis are available from Kahului and West Maui airports. The Ritz-Carlton, Kapalua, has a resort shuttle within the Kapalua Resort.

TOP ATTRACTIONS

Kahakuloa. The wild side of West Maui, this tiny village at the north end of Honoapiilani Highway is a relic of pre-jet-travel Maui. Remote villages similar to Kahakuloa were once tucked away in several valleys in this area. Many residents still grow taro and live in the old Hawaiian way. Driving this route is not for the faint of heart: the unimproved road weaves along coastal cliffs, and there are lots of blind curves; it's not wide enough for two cars to pass in places, so one of you (most likely you) will have to reverse on this nail-biter of a "highway." ⚠ **Watch out for stray cattle, roosters, and falling rocks.** True adventurers will find terrific snorkeling and swimming along this drive, as well as some good hiking trails, a labyrinth, and excellent banana bread. ✉ *Kahakuloa.*

Kapalua. Beautiful and secluded, Kapalua is West Maui's northernmost, most exclusive resort community. First developed in the late 1970s, the resort now includes the Ritz-Carlton, posh residential complexes, two golf courses, and the surrounding former pineapple fields. The area's distinctive shops and restaurants cater to dedicated golfers, celebrities who want to be left alone, and some of the world's richest folks. In addition to golf, recreational activities include hiking and snorkeling. Mists regularly envelop the landscape of tall Cook pines and rolling fairways in Kapalua, which is cooler and quieter than its southern neighbors. The beaches here, including Kapalua and D.T. Fleming, are among Maui's finest. ✉ *Kapalua.*

THE SOUTH SHORE

Blessed by more than its fair share of sun, the southern shore of Haleakala was an undeveloped wilderness until the 1970s, when the sun worshippers found it. Now restaurants, condos, and luxury resorts line the coast from the world-class aquarium at Maalaea Harbor through working-class Kihei to lovely Wailea, a resort community rivaling its counterpart, Kaanapali, on West Maui. Farther south, the road disappears and unspoiled wilderness still has its way.

Because the South Shore includes so many fine beach choices, a trip here—if you're staying elsewhere on the island—is an all-day excursion, especially if you include a visit to the aquarium. Get active in the morning with exploring and snorkeling, then shower in a beach park, dress up a little, and enjoy the cool luxury of the Wailea resorts. At sunset, settle in for dinner at one of the area's many fine restaurants.

MAALAEA

13 miles south of Kahului; 6 miles west of Kihei; 14 miles southeast of Lahaina.

Pronounced "Mah- *ah*-lye- *ah*," this spot is not much more than a few condos, an aquarium, and a wind-blasted harbor (where there are tour boats)—but that's more than enough for some visitors. Humpback whales seem to think Maalaea is tops for meeting mates, and green sea turtles treat it like their own personal spa, regularly seeking appointments with cleaner wrasses in the harbor. Surfers revere this spot for "freight trains," reportedly one of the world's fastest waves.

A small Shinto shrine stands at the shore here, dedicated to the fishing god Ebisu Sama. Across the street, a giant hook often swings heavy with the sea's bounty, proving the worth of the shrine. At the end of Hauoli Street (the town's sole road), a small community garden is sometimes privy to traditional Hawaiian ceremonies. That's all, there's not much else—but the few residents here like it that way.

GETTING HERE AND AROUND

To reach Maalaea from Kahului Airport, take Route 5 or 40 to Route 20. The town is also a transfer point for many Maui Bus routes.

TOP ATTRACTIONS

Maalaea Harbor. With so many good reasons to head out onto the water, this active little harbor is quite busy. Many snorkeling and whale-watching excursions depart from here. There was a plan to expand the facility, but surfers argued that would have destroyed their surf breaks. In fact, the surf here is world-renowned. The elusive spot to the left of the harbor, called "freight train," rarely breaks, but when it does, it's said to be the fastest anywhere. Shops, restaurants, and the Maui Ocean Center aquarium front the harbor. ✉ *101 Maalaea Boat Harbor Rd., off Honoapiilani Hwy., Maalaea.*

FAMILY
Fodor's Choice ★
Maui Ocean Center. You'll feel as though you're walking from the seashore down to the bottom of the reef at this aquarium, which focuses on creatures of the Pacific. Vibrant exhibits let you get close to turtles, rays, sharks, and the unusual creatures of the tide pools; allow two hours or so to explore it all. Opened in 2018, a new whale exhibit includes

interactive learning stations and a dome theater that uses 3-D technology to give viewers a whale's-eye-view. It's not an enormous facility, but it does provide an excellent (though pricey) introduction to the sea life that makes Hawaii special. The center is part of a complex of retail shops and restaurants overlooking the harbor. Enter from Honoapiilani Highway as it curves past Maalaea Harbor. ■TIP→ **The Ocean Center's gift shop is one of the best on Maui for artsy souvenirs and toys.** ✉ *192 Maalaea Rd., off Honoapiilani Hwy., Maalaea* ☎ *808/270–7000* 🌐 *www.mauioceancenter.com* 🎫 *$29.95.*

KIHEI

9 miles south of Kahului; 20 miles east of Lahaina.

Traffic lights and shopping malls may not fit your notion of paradise, but Kihei offers dependably warm sun, excellent beaches, and a front-row seat to marine life of all sorts. Besides all the sun and sand, the town's relatively inexpensive condos and excellent restaurants make this a home base for many Maui visitors.

County beach parks, such as Kamaole I, II, and III, have lawns, showers, and picnic tables. ■TIP→ **Remember: beach park or no beach park, the public has a right to the entire coastal strand but not to cross private property to get to it.**

GETTING HERE AND AROUND

Kihei is an easy 25-minute ride south of Kahului, easily accessed via the four-lane Maui Veteran's Highway, formerly Mokulele Highway (Route 311).

TOP ATTRACTIONS

FAMILY Fodor's Choice ★ **Hawaiian Islands Humpback Whale National Marine Sanctuary.** This nature center sits in prime humpback-viewing territory beside a restored ancient Hawaiian fishpond. Whether the whales are here or not, the education center is a great stop for youngsters curious to know more about underwater life, and for anyone eager to gain insight into the cultural connection between Hawaii and its whale residents. Interactive displays and informative naturalists explain it all, including the sanctuary that acts as a breeding ground for humpbacks. Throughout the year, the center hosts activities that include talks, labs, and volunteer opportunities. The sanctuary itself includes virtually all the waters surrounding the archipelago. ■TIP→ **Just outside the visitor center is the ancient Koieie fishpond; it is a popular place for locals to bring their children to wade in the water.** ✉ *726 S. Kihei Rd., Kihei* ☎ *808/879–2818, 800/831–4888* 🌐 *www.hawaiihumpbackwhale.noaa.gov* 🎫 *Free* 🕒 *Closed weekends.*

FAMILY **Kealia Pond National Wildlife Refuge.** Natural wetlands have become rare in the Islands, so the 700 acres of this reserve attract migratory birds, such as Hawaiian coots and long-legged Hawaiian stilts that casually dip their beaks into the shallow waters as traffic shuttles by; it's also home to other wildlife. The visitor center provides a good introduction, and interpretive signs on the half-mile elevated boardwalk, which stretches along the coast by North Kihei Road, explain the journey of the endangered hawksbill turtles and how they return to the sandy dunes year after year. The boardwalk includes ramps that lead to the adjacent beach so visitors can explore tidal pools. Note that there's no restroom at the boardwalk. ✉ *Mokulele Hwy., mile marker 6, Kihei* ✥ *The refuge's main entrance is on Mokulele Highway* ☎ *808/875–1582* 🌐 *www.fws.gov/kealiapond* 🎫 *Free* 🕑 *Visitor center closed weekends.*

WAILEA AND FARTHER SOUTH

15 miles south of Kahului, at the southern border of Kihei.

The South Shore's resort community, Wailea is slightly quieter and drier than its West Maui sister, Kaanapali. Many visitors cannot pick a favorite, so they stay at both. The luxury of the resorts (borderline excessive) and the simple grandeur of the coastal views make the otherwise stark landscape an outstanding destination. Take time to stroll the coastal beach path; a handful of perfect little beaches, all with public access, front the resorts.

The first two resorts were built here in the late 1970s. Soon a cluster of upscale properties sprang up, including the Four Seasons Resort Maui at Wailea and the Fairmont Kea Lani. Check out the Grand Wailea Resort's chapel, which tells a Hawaiian love story in stained glass.

GETTING HERE AND AROUND

From Kahului Airport, take Route 311 (Mokulele Highway) to Route 31 (Piilani Highway) until it ends in Wailea. Shuttles and taxis are available at the airport. If you're traveling by Maui Bus, the Kihei Islander route runs between The Shops at Wailea and Queen Kaahumanu Center in Kahului. There's a resort shuttle, and a paved shore path goes between the hotels.

CENTRAL MAUI

Kahului, where you most likely landed when you arrived on Maui, is the industrial and commercial center of the island. West of Kahului is Wailuku, the county seat since 1950 and the most charming town in Central Maui, with some good inexpensive restaurants. Outside these towns are attractions ranging from museums and historic sites to gardens.

You can combine sightseeing in Central Maui with some shopping at the Queen Kaahumanu Center, Maui Mall, and Maui Marketplace. This is one of the best areas on the island to stock up on groceries and supplies, thanks to major retailers including Walmart, Kmart, and Costco. Note that grocery prices are much higher than on the mainland.

KAHULUI

3 miles west of Kahului Airport; 9 miles north of Kihei; 31 miles east of Kaanapali; 51 miles west of Hana.

With the island's largest airport and commercial harbor, Kahului is Maui's commercial hub. But it also offers plenty of natural and cultural attractions. The town was developed in the early 1950s to meet the housing needs of the large sugarcane interests here, specifically those of Alexander & Baldwin. The company was tired of playing landlord to its many plantation workers and sold land to a developer who promised to create affordable housing. The scheme worked and "Dream City," the first planned city in Hawaii, was born.

GETTING HERE AND AROUND

From the airport, take Keolani Place to Route 36 (Hana Highway), which becomes Kaahumanu Avenue, Kahului's main drag. Run by Maui Bus, the Kahului Loop route traverses all of the town's major shopping centers; the fare is $2.

TOP ATTRACTIONS

Alexander & Baldwin Sugar Museum. Maui's largest landowner, A&B was one of the "Big Five" companies that spearheaded the planting, harvesting, and processing of sugarcane. At this museum, historic photos, artifacts, and documents explain the introduction of sugarcane to Hawaii. Exhibits reveal how plantations brought in laborers from other countries, forever changing the Islands' ethnic mix. Although sugarcane is no longer being grown on Maui, the crop was for many years the mainstay of the local economy. You can find the museum in a small, restored plantation manager's house across the street from the post office and the still-operating sugar refinery, where smoke billows up when cane is being processed. Their gift shop sells plantation-themed memorabilia, coffee, and a selection of history books. ✉ *3957 Hansen Rd., Puunene* ☎ *808/871–8058* 🌐 *www.sugarmuseum.com* 🎟 *$7.*

FAMILY **Maui Nui Botanical Gardens.** Hawaiian and Polynesian species are cultivated at this fascinating 7-acre garden, including Hawaiian bananas; local varieties of sweet potatoes and sugarcane; and native poppies, hibiscus, and *anapanapa,* a plant that makes a natural shampoo when rubbed between your hands. Reserve ahead for the weekly ethnobotany tours. Self-guided tour booklets and an audio tour wand is included with admission, and a docent tour is $10 (and must be arranged in advance). ✉ *150 Kanaloa Ave., Kahului* ☎ *808/249–2798* 🌐 *www.mnbg.org* 🎟 *$5* ⏲ *Closed Sun.*

WAILUKU

4 miles west of Kahului; 12 miles north of Kihei; 21 miles east of Lahaina.

Wailuku is peaceful now—although it wasn't always so. Its name means Water of Destruction, after the fateful battle in Iao Valley that pitted King Kamehameha the Great against Maui warriors. Wailuku was a politically important town until the sugar industry began to decline in the 1960s and tourism took hold. Businesses left the cradle of the West Maui Mountains and followed the new market (and tourists) to the shores. Wailuku houses the county government but has the feel of a town that's been asleep for several decades.

The shops and offices now inhabiting Market Street's plantation-style buildings serve as reminders of a bygone era, and continued attempts at "gentrification," at the very least, open the way for unique eateries, shops, and galleries. Drop by on the first Friday of the month for First Friday, when Market Street is closed to traffic and turns into a festival with live music, performances, food, and more.

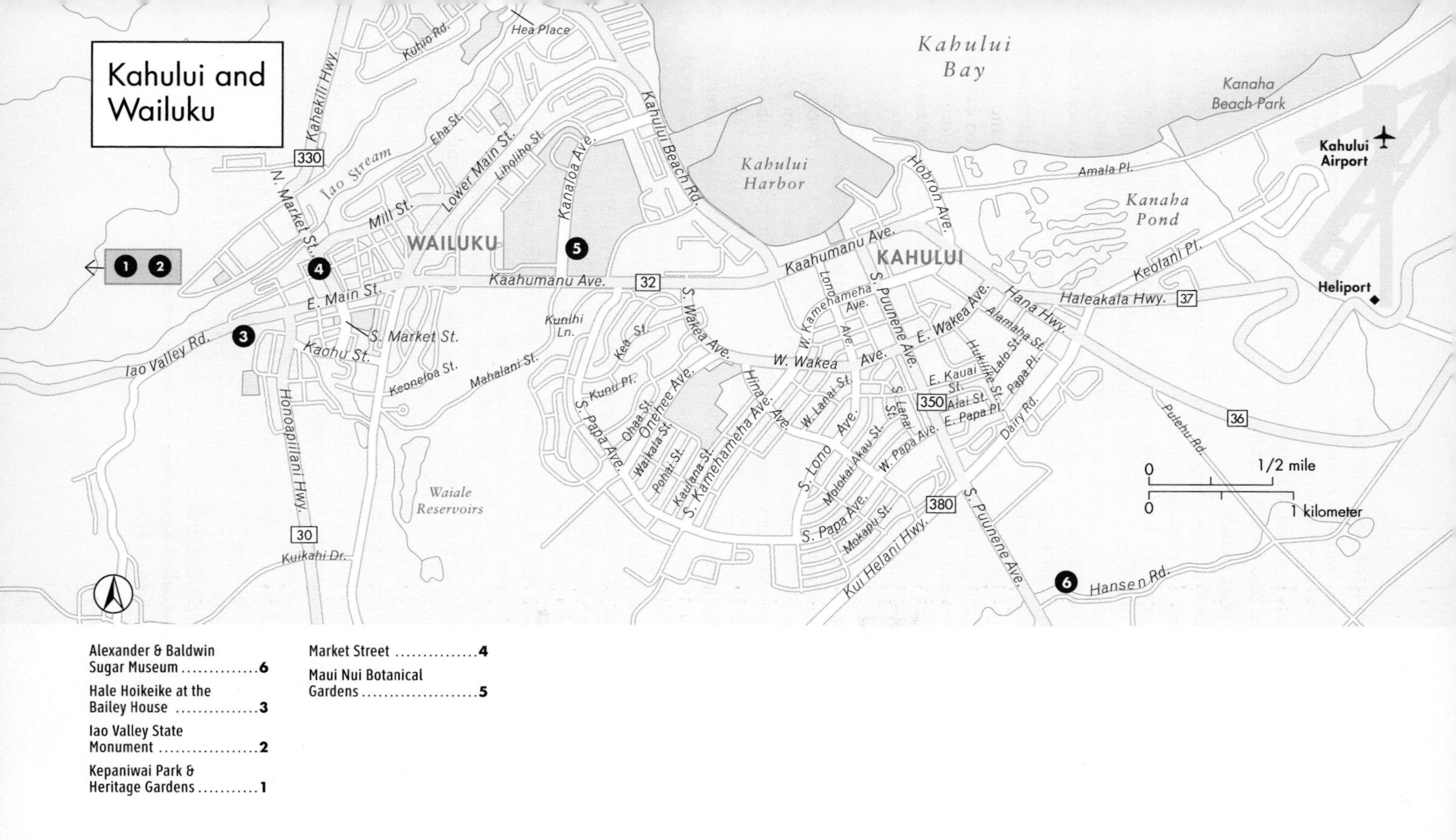
Kahului and Wailuku
Kahului Bay
Kanaha Beach Park
Kahului Airport
Heliport
Kahului Harbor
Kanaha Pond
WAILUKU
KAHULUI
Waiale Reservoirs
Iao Stream
Kahekili Hwy.
N. Market St.
Mill St.
Lower Main St.
Eha St.
Kuhio Rd.
Hea Place
Liholiho St.
Kanaloa Ave.
Kahului Beach Rd.
Kaahumanu Ave.
E. Main St.
S. Market St.
Kaohu St.
Iao Valley Rd.
Honoapiilani Hwy.
Kuikahi Dr.
Keoneloa St.
Mahalani St.
Kunihi Ln.
Kea St.
S. Kunu Pl.
S. Papa Ave.
Ohaa St.
Onehee Ave.
Waikala St.
Pohai St.
Kaulana St.
S. Kamehameha Ave.
S. Wakea Ave.
Hina Ave.
W. Wakea Ave.
W. Kamehameha Ave.
Lono Ave.
S. Puunene Ave.
W. Lanai St.
S. Lono Ave.
S. Lanai St.
Molokai Akau St.
W. Papa Ave.
Mokapu St.
Kui Helani Hwy.
E. Wakea Ave.
Hana Hwy.
Alamaha St.
Hukilike St.
Lalo St.
Papa Pl.
E. Kauai St.
Alai St.
E. Papa Pl.
Dairy Rd.
Hobron Ave.
Amala Pl.
Keolani Pl.
Haleakala Hwy.
Pulehu Rd.
Hansen Rd.
330
32
30
350
380
37
36
0
1/2 mile
0
1 kilometer

GETTING HERE AND AROUND

Heading to Wailuku from the airport, Hana Highway turns into Kaahumanu Avenue, the main thoroughfare between Kahului and Wailuku. Maui Bus system's Wailuku Loop stops at shopping centers, medical facilities, and government buildings; the fare is $2.

TOP ATTRACTIONS

Fodor's Choice ★ **Hale Hoikeike at the Bailey House.** This repository of the largest and best collection of Hawaiian artifacts on Maui includes objects from the sacred island of Kahoolawe. Erected in 1833 on the site of the compound of Kahekili (the last ruling chief of Maui), the building was occupied by the family of missionary teachers Edward and Caroline Bailey until 1888. Edward Bailey was something of a Renaissance man: not only a missionary, but also a surveyor, a naturalist, and an excellent artist. The museum contains missionary-period furniture and displays a number of Bailey's landscape paintings, which provide a snapshot of the island during his time. The grounds include gardens with native Hawaiian plants and a fine example of a traditional canoe. The gift shop is one of the best sources on Maui for items that are actually made in Hawaii. ✉ *2375A Main St., Wailuku* ☎ *808/244–3326* 🌐 *www.mauimuseum.org* 🎟 *$7* ⏲ *Closed Sun.*

Fodor's Choice ★ **Iao Valley State Monument.** When Mark Twain saw this park, he dubbed it the Yosemite of the Pacific. Yosemite it's not, but it is a lovely deep valley with the curious **Iao Needle,** a spire that rises more than 2,000 feet from the valley floor. You can walk from the parking lot across Iao Stream and explore the thick, junglelike topography. This park has some lovely short strolls on paved paths, where you can stop and meditate by the edge of a stream or marvel at the native plants. Locals come to jump from the rocks or bridge into the stream—this isn't recommended. Mist often rises if there has been a rain, which makes being here even more magical. Be aware that this area is prone to flash flooding; if it's been raining, stay out of the water. Parking is $5. ✉ *Western end of Rte. 32, Wailuku* 🌐 *www.hawaiistateparks.org* 🎟 *$5 per car.*

FAMILY **Kepaniwai Park & Heritage Gardens.** Picnic facilities dot the landscape of this county park, a memorial to Maui's cultural roots. Among the interesting displays are an early-Hawaiian *hale* (house), a New England–style saltbox, a Portuguese-style villa with gardens, and dwellings from such other cultures as China and the Philippines. Next door, the **Hawaii Nature Center** has excellent interactive exhibits and pathways for hikes that are easy enough for children.

The peacefulness here belies the history of the area. In 1790, King Kamehameha the Great from the Island of Hawaii waged a successful and bloody battle against Kahekili, the son of Maui's chief. An earlier battle at the site had pitted Kahekili himself against an older Hawaii Island chief, Kalaniopuu. Kahekili prevailed, but the carnage was so great that the nearby stream became known as Wailuku (Water of Destruction), and the place where fallen warriors choked the stream's flow was called Kepaniwai (Damming of the Waters). ✉ *870 Iao Valley Rd., Wailuku* 🎟 *Free.*

Market Street. An idiosyncratic assortment of shops makes Wailuku's Market Street a delightful place for a stroll. Brown-Kobayashi and the Bird of Paradise Unique Antiques are the best shops for interesting collectibles and furnishings. Wailuku Coffee Company holds works by local artists and occasionally offers live entertainment in the evening. On the first Friday evening of every month Market Street closes to traffic for Wailuku's First Friday celebration; the fun includes street vendors, live entertainment, and food. ✉ *Market St., Wailuku* 🌐 *www.mauifridays.com.*

HALEAKALA NATIONAL PARK

41 miles southeast of Wailuku; 28 miles southeast of Pukalani.

From the tropics to the moon! Two hours, 38 miles, 10,023 feet—those are the unlikely numbers involved in reaching Maui's highest point, the summit of the volcano Haleakala. Haleakala Crater is the centerpiece of the park, though it's not actually a crater; technically, it's an erosional valley, flushed out by water pouring from the summit through two enormous gaps. The mountain has terrific camping and hiking, including a trail that loops through the crater, but the chance to witness this unearthly landscape is reason enough for a visit. Another section of the park, Oheo Gulch in Kipahulu, can be reached only via the Road to Hana.

Exploring Haleakala Crater is one of the best hiking experiences on Maui. The volcanic terrain offers an impressive diversity of colors, textures, and shapes—almost as if the lava has been artfully sculpted. The barren landscape is home to many plants, insects, and birds that exist nowhere else on earth and have developed intriguing survival mechanisms, such as the sun-reflecting, hairy leaves of the silversword, which allow it to survive the intense climate.

Fodor's Choice ★ **Haleakala National Park.** Nowhere else on Earth can you drive from sea level to 10,023 feet in only 38 miles. And what's more shocking: in that short vertical ascent to the summit of the volcano Haleakala you'll journey from lush, tropical island landscape to the stark, moonlike basin of the volcano's enormous, otherworldly crater.

Established in 1916, Haleakala National Park covers an astonishing 33,222 acres, with the Haleakala Crater as its centerpiece. There's terrific hiking, including trails for one-hour, four-hour, eight-hour, and overnight hikes, one of which goes through the Waikamoi Cloud Forest on Monday and Thursday only, and requires reservations (call the park line no more than a week in advance). No other hikes require reservations. There is also on-site camping.

■ TIP→ Before you head up Haleakala, call for the latest weather conditions. Extreme gusty winds, heavy rain, and even snow in winter are not uncommon. Because of the high altitude, the mountaintop temperature is often as much as 30°F cooler than that at sea level, so bring a jacket.

There's a $25-per-car fee to enter the park, good for three days. Hold on to your receipt—it can also be used at Oheo Gulch in Kipahulu. Once inside the park, stop at the **Park Headquarters** to learn about the volcano's history, and pick up trail maps (and memorabilia, if you please) at the gift shop. Campers and hikers must check in here.

Those planning to view the sunrise from the summit must make reservations (www.recreation.gov) up to 60 days before your visit. This allows you to enter the summit area between 2 and 7 am. If you don't snag one of these coveted spots, consider visiting for sunset, which, on most days, offers equally stunning views.

■ TIP→ **The air is thin at 10,000 feet. Don't be surprised if you feel a little breathless while walking around the summit. Take it easy and drink lots of water. Anyone who has been scuba diving within the last 24 hours should not make the trip up Haleakala.** ✉ *Haleakala Crater Rd., Makawao* ☎ *808/572–4400, 866/944–5025 for weather conditions* 🌐 *www.nps.gov/hale* 🎫 *$25 per car.*

Haleakala Visitor Center. Standing at 9,740 feet, the visitor center has exhibits inside and a trail that leads to Pa Kaoao (aka White Hill)—a short, easy walk with even better views of the valley. ✉ *Haleakala Hwy., Makawao* ☎ *808/572–4459* 🌐 *www.nps.gov/hale.*

Leleiwi Overlook. Located at about the 8,800-foot level, the Leleiwi Overlook offers you your first awe-inspiring view of the crater. The small hills in the basin are cinder cones (*puu* in Hawaiian). If you're here in the late afternoon, it's possible you'll see yourself reflected on the clouds and encircled by a rainbow—a phenomenon called the Brocken Specter. Don't wait long for this, because it's not a daily occurrence. ✉ *Off Haleakala Hwy., Makawao.*

Puu Ulaula Overlook. The highest point on Maui is this 10,023-foot summit, where a glass-enclosed lookout provides a 360-degree view. The building is open 24 hours a day and has the best sunrise view. *The Maui News* posts the hour of sunrise, which falls between 5:45 and 7 am, depending on the time of year. Bring blankets or hotel towels to stay warm on the cold and windy summit. On a clear day you can see the islands of Molokai, Lanai, Kahoolawe, and the Big Island; on a *really* clear day you can even spot Oahu glimmering in the distance. ✉ *Makawao.*

UPCOUNTRY

The west-facing upper slope of Haleakala is considered "Upcountry" by locals and is a hidden gem by most accounts. Although this region is responsible for most of Maui's produce—lettuce, tomatoes, strawberries, sweet Maui onions, and more—it is also home to innovators, renegades, artists, and some of Maui's most interesting communities. It may not be the Maui of postcards, but some say this is the real Maui and is well worth at least a day or two of exploring.

Upcountry is also fertile ranch land; cowboys still work the fields of the historic 18,000-acre Ulupalakua Ranch and the 30,000-acre Haleakala Ranch. ■ TIP→ **Take an agricultural tour and learn more about the island's bounty. Lavender and wine are among the offerings.** Up here cactus thickets mingle with purple jacaranda, wild hibiscus, and towering eucalyptus trees. Keep an eye out for *pueo,* Hawaii's native owl, which hunts these fields during daylight hours.

A drive to Upcountry Maui from Wailea (South Shore) or Kaanapali (West Maui) can be an all-day outing if you take the time to visit Maui's Winery and the tiny but entertaining town of Makawao. You may want to cut these side trips short and combine your Upcountry tour with a visit to Haleakala National Park (⇨ *see Haleakala National Park feature*)—it's a Maui must-see/do. If you leave early enough to catch the sunrise from the summit of Haleakala, you should have plenty of time to explore the mountain, have lunch in Kula or at Ulupalakua Ranch, and end your day with dinner in Makawao.

THE KULA HIGHWAY

15 miles east of Kahului; 44 miles east of Kaanapali; 28 miles east of Wailea.

Kula: most Mauians say it with a hint of a sigh. Why? It's just that much closer to heaven. On the broad shoulder of Haleakala, this is blessed country. From the Kula Highway most of Central Maui is visible—from the lava-scarred plains of Kanaio to the cruise ship–lighted waters of Kahului Harbor. Beyond the central valley's sugarcane fields, the plunging profile of the West Maui Mountains can be seen in its entirety, wreathed in ethereal mist. If this sounds too dramatic a description, you haven't been here yet. These views, coveted by many, continue to drive real-estate prices further skyward. Luckily, you can still have them for free—just pull over on the roadside and inhale the beauty. Explore it for yourself on some of the area's agricultural tours.

GETTING HERE AND AROUND

From Kahului, take Route 37 (Haleakala Highway), which runs into Route 377 (Kula Highway). Upper and Lower Kula highways are both numbered 377, but join each other at two points.

TOP ATTRACTIONS

Alii Kula Lavender. Make time for tea and a scone at this lavender farm with a falcon's view: it's *the* relaxing remedy for those suffering from too much sun, shopping, or golf. Knowledgeable guides lead tours through winding paths of therapeutic lavender varieties, protea, and succulents. The gift shop is stocked with many locally made lavender products, such as honey, moisturizing lotions, and scone mixes. Make a reservation in advance for the tours. ✉ *1100 Waipoli Rd., Kula* ☎ *808/878–3004* 🌐 *www.aklmaui.com* 🎟 *$3, walking tours $12–$25 (reservations recommended).*

Fodor's Choice ★ **MauiWine.** Tour Maui's only winery and its historic grounds, the former Rose Ranch, for a chance to learn about its history—which includes visits by royal monarchs, sugar production, and cattle ranching—and to sample its coveted wines. The King's Cottage was built in the late 1800s for frequent visits of King Kalakaua, but today, tastings are held there daily. A more intimate tasting is held in the Old Jail building, and sometimes include unreleased wines or special bottlings. The winery's top seller, naturally, is the pineapple wine, Maui Blanc. The old Ranch Store across the road may look like a museum, but in fact it's an excellent pit stop—the elk burgers are fantastic. ✉ *Ulupalakua Vineyards, 14815 Piilani Hwy., Kula* ☎ *808/878–6058* 🌐 *www.mauiwine.com* 🎫 *Free.*

Fodor's Choice ★ **Oo Farm.** About a mile from Alii Kula Lavender are 8 acres of organic salad greens, herbs, vegetables, coffee, cocoa, fruits, and berries—all of it headed directly to restaurants in Lahaina. Oo Farm is owned and operated by the restaurateurs responsible for some of Maui's finest dining establishments, and more than 300 pounds of its produce end up on diners' plates every week. Reserve a space for the breakfast or the midday tours that include an informational walk around the pastoral grounds and an alfresco meal prepared by an on-site chef. Cap off the experience with house-grown, -roasted, and -brewed coffee. Reservations are necessary. ✉ *651 Waipoli Rd., Kula* ☎ *808/667–4341 for reservations only* 🌐 *www.oofarm.com* 🎫 *Lunch tours from $58* ⏲ *Closed weekends.*

MAKAWAO

10 miles east of Kahului; 10 miles southeast of Paia.

At the intersection of Baldwin and Makawao avenues, this once-tiny town has managed to hang on to its country charm (and eccentricity) as it has grown in popularity. Its good selection of specialized shops makes Makawao a fun place to spend some time.

The district was originally settled by Portuguese and Japanese immigrants who came to Maui to work the sugar plantations and then moved Upcountry to establish small farms, ranches, and stores. Descendants now work the neighboring Haleakala and Ulupalakua ranches. Every July 4 weekend the paniolo set comes out in force for the Makawao Rodeo.

The crossroads of town—lined with shops and down-home eateries—reflects a growing population of people who came here just because they liked it. For those seeking greenery rather than beachside accommodations, there are secluded bed-and-breakfasts around the town.

GETTING HERE AND AROUND

To get to Makawao by car, take Route 37 (Haleakala Highway) to Pukalani, then turn left on Makawao Avenue. You can also take Route 36 (Hana Highway) to Paia and make a right onto Baldwin Avenue. Either way takes you to the heart of Makawao.

TOP ATTRACTIONS

Fodor's Choice ★ **Hui No'eau Visual Arts Center.** The grande dame of Maui's visual arts scene, "the Hui" hosts exhibits that are always satisfying. Located just outside Makawao, the center's main building is an elegant two-story Mediterranean-style villa designed in 1917 by the defining Hawaii architect of the era, C.W. Dickey. Explore the grounds, sample locally made products, and learn about exceptional plant species during a one-hour tour held Monday and Wednesday at 10 am; it costs $12. A self-guided tour booklet is available for $6. ✉ *2841 Baldwin Ave., Makawao* ☎ *808/572–6560* 🌐 *www.huinoeau.com* 🎫 *Free.*

Maui Pineapple Tours. The quintessence of sun-blessed tropical flavor, pineapple exudes Hawaiian happiness. It just so happens Maui boasts the only tour of a working pineapple plantation in the United States. You'll join a worker on a stroll through the sunny fields of the

Continued on page 201

HALEAKALA NATIONAL PARK

From the Tropics to the Moon! Two hours, 38 miles, 10,023 feet—those are the unlikely numbers involved in reaching Maui's highest point, the summit of the volcano Haleakala. Nowhere else on earth can you drive from sea level (Kahului) to 10,023 feet (the summit) in only 38 miles. And what's more shocking—in that short vertical ascent, you'll journey from lush, tropical-island landscape to the stark, moonlike basin of the volcano's enormous, otherworldly crater.

Established in 1916, Haleakala National Park covers an astonishing 33,222 acres. Haleakala "Crater" is the centerpiece of the park though it's not actually a crater. Technically, it's an erosional valley, flushed out by water pouring from the summit through two enormous gaps. The mountain has terrific camping and hiking, including a trail that loops through the crater, but the chance to witness this unearthly landscape is reason enough for a visit.

THE CLIMB TO THE SUMMIT

To reach Haleakala National Park and the mountain's breathtaking summit, take Route 36 east of Kahului to the Haleakala Highway (Route 37). Head east, up the mountain to the unlikely intersection of Haleakala Highway and Haleakala Highway. If you continue straight the road's name changes to Kula Highway (still Route 37). Instead, turn left onto Haleakala Highway—this is now Route 377. After about 6 miles, make a left onto

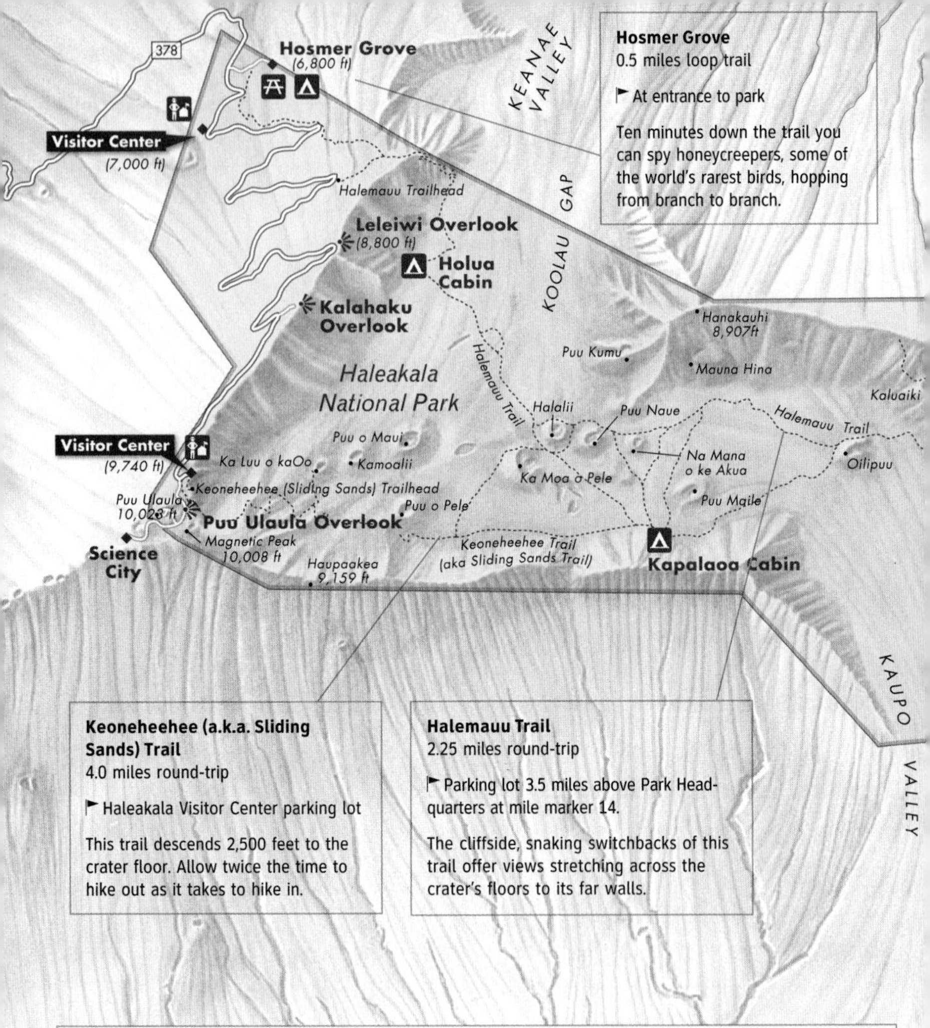

Hosmer Grove
0.5 miles loop trail

⚑ At entrance to park

Ten minutes down the trail you can spy honeycreepers, some of the world's rarest birds, hopping from branch to branch.

Keoneheehee (a.k.a. Sliding Sands) Trail
4.0 miles round-trip

⚑ Haleakala Visitor Center parking lot

This trail descends 2,500 feet to the crater floor. Allow twice the time to hike out as it takes to hike in.

Halemauu Trail
2.25 miles round-trip

⚑ Parking lot 3.5 miles above Park Headquarters at mile marker 14.

The cliffside, snaking switchbacks of this trail offer views stretching across the crater's floors to its far walls.

Crater Road (Route 378). After several long switchbacks (look out for downhill bikers!) you'll come to the park entrance.

■ TIP→ Before you head up Haleakala, call for the latest park weather conditions (☎ 866/944–5025). Extreme gusty winds, heavy rain, and even snow in winter are not uncommon. Because of the high altitude, the mountaintop temperature is often as much as 30 degrees cooler than that at sea level. Be sure to bring a jacket. Also make sure you have a full tank of gas. No service stations exist beyond Kula.

There's a car fee to enter the park; but it's good for three days and can be used at Oheo Gulch (Kipahulu), so save your receipt.

6,800 feet, Hosmer Grove. Just as you enter the park, Hosmer Grove has campsites and interpretive trails. Park rangers maintain a changing schedule of talks and hikes both here and at the top of the mountain. Call the park for current schedules.

7,000 feet, Park Headquarters/ Visitor Center. Not far from Hosmer Grove, the Park Headquarters/Visitor Center has trail maps and displays about the volcano's origins and eruption history. Hikers and campers

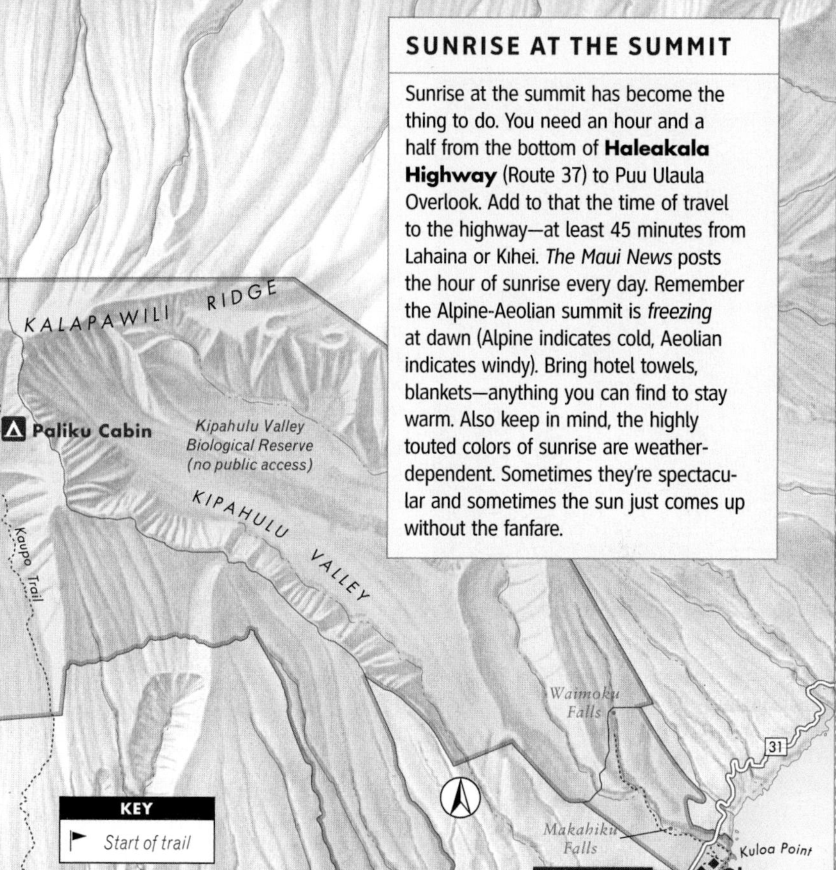

SUNRISE AT THE SUMMIT

Sunrise at the summit has become the thing to do. You need an hour and a half from the bottom of **Haleakala Highway** (Route 37) to Puu Ulaula Overlook. Add to that the time of travel to the highway—at least 45 minutes from Lahaina or Kihei. *The Maui News* posts the hour of sunrise every day. Remember the Alpine-Aeolian summit is *freezing* at dawn (Alpine indicates cold, Aeolian indicates windy). Bring hotel towels, blankets—anything you can find to stay warm. Also keep in mind, the highly touted colors of sunrise are weather-dependent. Sometimes they're spectacular and sometimes the sun just comes up without the fanfare.

should check-in here before heading up the mountain. Maps, posters, and other memorabilia are available at the gift shop.

8,800 feet, Leleiwi Overlook. Continuing up the mountain, you come to Leleiwi Overlook. A short walk to the end of the parking lot reveals your first awe-inspiring view of the crater. The small hills in the basin are volcanic cinder cones (called *puu* in Hawaiian), each with a small crater at its top, and each the site of a former eruption.

If you're here in the late afternoon, it's possible you'll experience a phenomenon called the Brocken Specter. Named after a similar occurrence in East Germany's Harz Mountains, the "specter" allows you to see yourself reflected on the clouds and encircled by a rainbow. Don't wait all day for this because it's not a daily occurrence.

9,000 feet, Kalahaku Overlook. The next stopping point is Kalahaku Overlook. The view here offers a different perspective of the crater, and at this elevation the famous silversword plant grows amid the cinders. This odd, endangered beauty grows only here and at the same elevation on the

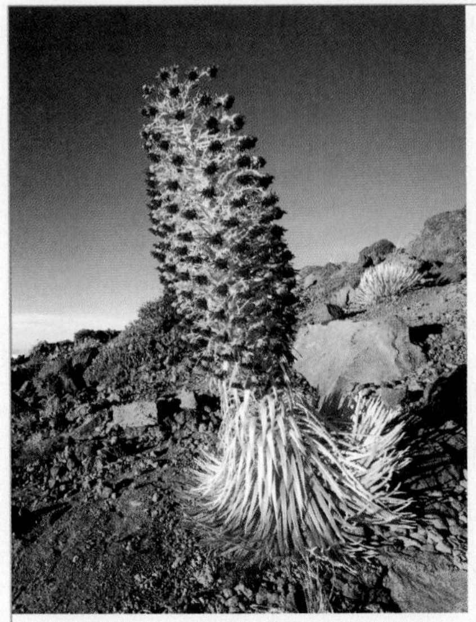

Big Island's two peaks. It begins life as a silver, spiny-leaf rosette and is the sole home of a variety of native insects (it's the only shelter around). The silversword reaches maturity between 7 and 17 years, when it sends forth a 3- to 8-foot-tall stalk with several hundred tiny sunflowers. It blooms once, then dies.

9,740 feet, HaleakalaVisitor Center. Another mile up is the Haleakala Visitor Center, open daily from sunrise to 3 pm except Christmas and New Year's. There are exhibits inside, and a trail from here leads to White Hill—a short easy walk that will give you an even better view of the valley.

10,023 feet, Puu Ulaula Overlook. The highest point on Maui is the Puu Ulaula Overlook, at the 10,023-foot summit. Here you find a glass-enclosed lookout with a 360-degree view. The building is open 24 hours a day, and this is where visitors gather for the best sunrise view. Dawn begins between 5:45 and 7, depending on the time of year. On a clear day you can see the islands of Molokai, Lanai, Kahoolawe, and Hawaii (the Big Island). On a *really* clear day you can even spot Oahu glimmering in the distance.

■ TIP→ The air is very thin at 10,000 feet. Don't be surprised if you feel a little breathless while walking around the summit. Take it easy and drink lots of water. Anyone who has been scuba diving within the last 24 hours should not make the trip up Haleakala.

On a small hill nearby, you can see **Science City**, an off-limits research and communications center straight out of an espionage thriller. The University of Hawaii maintains an observatory here, and the Department of Defense tracks satellites.

HIKING AND CAMPING

Exploring **Haleakala Crater** is one of the best hiking experiences on Maui. The volcanic terrain offers an impressive diversity of colors, textures, and shapes—almost as if the lava has been artfully sculpted. The barren landscape is home to many plants, insects, and birds that exist nowhere else on earth and have developed intriguing survival mechanisms, such as the sun-reflecting, hairy leaves of the silversword, which allow it to survive the intense climate.

Stop at park headquarters to register and pick up trail maps on your way into the park.

1-Hour Hike. Just as you enter Haleakala National Park, **Hosmer Grove** offers a short 10-minute hike and an hour-long, ½-mile loop trail that will give you insight into Hawaii's fragile ecology. Anyone can go on these hikes, whereas a longer trail through the Waikamoi Cloud Forest is accessible only with park ranger–guided hikes. Call park headquarters for the schedule. Facilities here include six campsites (no permit needed,

available on a first-come, first-served basis), pit toilets, drinking water, and cooking shelters.

4-Hour Hikes. Two half-day hikes involve descending into the crater and returning the way you came. The first, **Halemauu Trail** (trailhead is between mile markers 14 and 15), is 2.25 miles round-trip. The cliffside, snaking switchbacks of this trail offer views stretching across the crater's puu-speckled floor to its far walls. On clear days you can peer through the Koolau Gap to Hana. Native flowers and shrubs grow along the trail, which is typically misty and cool (though still exposed to the sun). When you reach the gate at the bottom, head back up.

The other hike, which is 5 miles round-trip, descends down **Keoneheehee (a.k.a. Sliding Sands) Trail** (trailhead is at the Haleakala Visitor Center) into an alien landscape of reddish black cinders, lava bombs, and silverswords. It's easy to imagine life before humans in the solitude and silence of this place. Turn back when you hit the crater floor.

■TIP→ Bring water, sunscreen, and a reliable jacket. These are demanding hikes. Take it slowly to acclimate, and allow additional time for the uphill return trip.

8-Hour Hike. The recommended way to explore the crater in a single, but full day is to go in two cars and ferry yourselves back and forth between the head of **Halemauu Trail** and the summit. This way, you can hike from the summit down **Keoneheehee Trail**, cross the crater's floor, investigate the **Bottomless Pit** and **Pele's Paint Pot**, then climb out on the **switchback trail (Halemauu)**. When you emerge, the shelter of your waiting car will be very welcome (this is an 11.2-mile hike). If you don't have two cars, hitching a ride from Halemauu back to the summit should be relatively safe and easy.

■ TIP→ Take a backpack with lunch, water, sunscreen, and a reliable jacket for the beginning and end of the 8-hour hike. This is a demanding trip, but you will never regret or forget it.

Overnight Hike. Staying overnight in one of Haleakala's three cabins or two wilderness campgrounds is an experience like no other. You'll feel like the only person on earth when you wake up inside this enchanted, strange landscape. The cabins, each tucked in a different corner of the crater's floor, are equipped with 12 bunk beds, wood-burning stoves, fake logs, and kitchen gear.

Holua cabin is the shortest hike, less than 4 hours (3.7 miles) from Halemauu Trail. **Kapalaoa** is about 5 hours (5.5 miles) down Keoneheehee Trail. The most cherished cabin is **Paliku,** an eight-hour (9.3-mile) hike starting from either trail. It's nestled against the cliffs above Kaupo Gap. Cabin reservations can be made up to 90 days in advance. Tent campsites at Holua and Paliku are free and easy to reserve on a first-come, first-served basis.

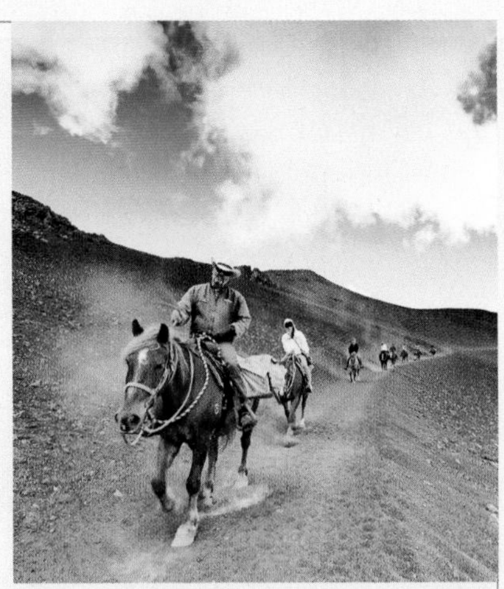

■ TIP→ **Toilets and nonpotable water are available—bring iodine tablets to purify the water. Open fires are not allowed and packing out your trash is mandatory.**

For more information on hiking or camping, contact the National Park Service (✉ Box 369, Makawao 96768 ☎ 808/572–4459 🌐 www.nps.gov/hale).

OPTIONS FOR EXPLORING

If you're short on time you can drive to the summit, take a peek inside, and drive back down. But the "House of the Sun" is really worth a day, whether you explore by foot, horseback, or helicopter.

BIKING

At this writing, all guided bike tours inside park boundaries were suspended indefinitely. However, the tours continue but now start outside the boundary of the park. These can provide a speedy, satisfying downhill trip. The park is still open to individual bikes for a fee. There are no bike paths, however—just the same road that is used by vehicular traffic. Whether you're on your own or with a tour, be careful!

HELICOPTER TOURS

Viewing Haleakala from above can be a mind-altering experience, if you don't mind dropping $225+ per person for a few blissful moments above the crater. Most tours buzz Haleakala, where airspace is regulated, then head over to Hana in search of waterfalls.

HORSEBACK RIDING

Several companies offer half-day, full-day, and even overnight rides into the crater. On one half-day ride you descend into the crater on Keoneheehee Trail and have lunch before you head back.

Hali'imaile Pineapple Plantation and hear all about the especially sweet Maui Gold pineapples (and sample its various stages of maturity along the way). The best part? Everyone gets a free pineapple at the end! **TIP→ Maui Pineapple Tours has recently partnered with Hali'maile Distilling Company, inviting guest after the plantation tour to visit the distillery and taste such island treats as Pau Maui Vodka, the world's only pineapple vodka.** ✉ *875 Haliimaile Rd., Haliimaile* ☎ *808/665–5491* 🌐 *www.mauipineappletour.com* 🎫 *From $65.*

THE NORTH SHORE

Blasted by winter swells and wind, Maui's North Shore draws water-sports thrill seekers from around the world. But there's much more to this area of Maui than coastline. Inland, a lush, waterfall-fed Garden of Eden beckons. In forested pockets, wealthy hermits have carved out a little piece of paradise for themselves.

North Shore action centers on the colorful town of Paia and the wind-surfing mecca of Hookipa Beach. It's a far cry from the more developed resort areas of West Maui and the South Shore. Paia is also a starting point for one of the most popular excursions in Maui, the Road to Hana. Waterfalls, phenomenal views of the coast and the ocean, and lush rain forest are all part of the spectacular 55-mile drive into East Maui.

PAIA

Fodor's Choice ★

9 miles east of Kahului; 4 miles west of Haiku.

At the intersection of Hana Highway and Baldwin Avenue, Paia has eclectic boutiques that supply everything from high fashion to hemp-oil candles. Some of Maui's best shops for surf trunks, Brazilian bikinis, and other beachwear are here. Restaurants provide excellent people-watching opportunities and an array of dining and takeout options, from flatbread to fresh fish. The abundance is helpful because Paia is the last place to snack before the pilgrimage to Hana and the first stop for the famished on the return trip.

This little town on Maui's North Shore was once a sugarcane enclave, with a mill, plantation camps, and shops. The old sugar mill finally closed, but the town continues to thrive. In the 1970s Paia became a hippie town, as dropouts headed for Maui to open boutiques, galleries, and unusual eateries. In the 1980s windsurfers—many of them European—discovered nearby Hookipa Beach and brought an international flavor to Paia. Today this historic town is hip and happening.

GETTING HERE AND AROUND

Route 36 (Hana Highway) runs directly though Paia; 4 miles east of town, follow the sign to Haiku, a short detour off the highway. You can take the Maui Bus from the airport and Queen Kaahumanu Shopping Center in Kahului to Paia and on to Haiku.

HAIKU

13 miles east of Kahului; 4 miles east of Paia.

At one time this area centered on a couple of enormous pineapple canneries. Both have been transformed into rustic warehouse malls. Because of the post office next door, Old Haiku Cannery earned the title of town center. Here you can try eateries offering everything from plate lunches to vegetarian dishes to juicy burgers and fantastic sushi. Follow windy Haiku Road to Pauwela Cannery, the other defunct factory-turned-hangout. This jungle hillside is a maze of flower-decked roads that seem to double back on themselves.

GETTING HERE AND AROUND

Haiku is a short detour off Hana Highway (Route 36) just past Hookipa Beach Park on the way to Hana. Haiku Road turns into Kokomo Road at the post office.

ROAD TO HANA

The Road to Hana is a 55-mile journey into the unspoiled heart of Maui. Tracing a centuries-old path, the road begins as a well-paved highway in Kahului and ends in the tiny rustic town of Hana on the island's rain-gouged windward side, spilling into a backcountry rarely visited by humans. Many travelers venture beyond Hana to **Ohe'o Gulch** in East Maui, where one can cool off in basalt-lined pools and waterfalls.

This drive is a Hawaii pilgrimage for those eager to experience what glossy magazines consider the "real" Hawaii. To most, the lure of Hana is its timelessness, and paired with the spectacular drive (which brings to life the old adage: the journey *is* the destination), this is one of Hawaii's best experiences. The Road to Hana is undoubtedly one of the most beautiful drives on the planet.

The challenging part of the road takes only an hour and a half, but the drive begs to be taken at a leisurely pace. You'll want to slow the passage of time to take in foliage-hugged ribbons of road and roadside banana-bread stands, to swim beneath a waterfall, and to inhale the lush Maui tropics in all its glory. You'll also want to stop often and let the driver enjoy the view, too.

HUELO, KAILUA, AND NEARBY

10 miles east of Haiku.

As the Road to Hana begins its journey eastward, the slopes get steeper and the Pacific Ocean pops into view. The first waterfall you see, Twin Falls, is around mile marker 2, and farther up the road is the Koolau Forest Reserve. Embedded in the forest are two townships, Huelo and Kailua, both of which are great places to pull over and take in the dramatic landscape.

GETTING HERE AND AROUND

Just after Haiku, the mile markers on the Hana Highway change back to 0. The towns of Huelo and Kailua are at mile markers 5 and 6. To reach the townships, follow the signs toward the ocean side of the road.

TOP ATTRACTIONS

The following sites are arranged geographically by mile marker en route to Hana.

Twin Falls. Keep an eye out for the Twin Falls Farm Stand just after mile marker 2 on the Hana Highway. Stop here and treat yourself to some fresh sugarcane juice. If you're feeling adventurous, follow the path

TIPS ON DRIVING THE ROAD TO HANA

If you're prone to motion sickness be aware that the Road to Hana has a fair share of twists and turns. Drive with your window down to allow in the fresh air—tinged with the aroma of guava and ginger.

With short stops, the drive from Paia to Hana should take you between two and three hours one-way. Lunching in Hana, hiking, and swimming can easily turn the round-trip into a full-day outing, especially if you continue past Hana to the Oheo Gulch and Kipahulu. If you go that far, you might consider continuing around the "back side" for the return trip. The scenery is completely different, and you'll end up in beautiful Upcountry Maui.

Because there's so much scenery to take in—including abundant waterfalls and beaches—we recommend staying overnight in Hana. It's worth taking time to enjoy the full experience without being in a hurry. Try to plan your trip for a day that promises fair sunny weather—although the drive can be even more beautiful when it's raining, the roads become more hazardous.

During high season (January–March and summer), the Road to Hana tends to develop trains of cars, with everyone in a line of six or more driving as slowly as the first car. The solution: leave early (dawn) and return late (dusk). If you find yourself playing the role of locomotive, pull over and let the other drivers pass. You can also let someone else take the turns for you—several companies offer van tours.

BASIC ROAD TIPS

■ Common courtesy in Hawaii dictates that slower drivers should pull over for faster drivers. Please don't try to zoom through this winding road.

■ When approaching one-lane bridges, it is local custom for about five cars to go in one direction at a time. If you happen to be the sixth car, stop before entering the bridge and let drivers traveling in the other direction pass.

■ Instead of stopping in the middle of the road or on a bridge to snap photos, park at a turnoff and carefully walk back to the waterfall to take your photos.

■ Although rain makes the drive more beautiful, with gushing waterfalls and rainbows, it also makes the roads slick. Drive slowly and cautiously on wet roads.

■ Just after Haiku the mile markers start at zero again.

beyond the stand to the paradisiacal waterfalls known as Twin Falls. Although it's still private property, the "no trespassing" signs have been replaced by colorfully painted arrows pointing toward the easily accessible falls. Several deep, emerald pools sparkle beneath waterfalls and offer excellent swimming and photo opportunities. In recent years, this natural attraction has become a tourist hot spot. Although the attention is well deserved, those who wish to avoid crowds may want to keep driving. ⊠ *Hana Hwy., past mile marker 2, Haiku-Pauwela.*

Huelo. When you see the colorful mailboxes on the *makai* (toward the ocean) side of the road around mile marker 5 on the Hana Highway, follow the windy road to the rural area of Huelo—a funky community that includes a mix of off-the-grid inhabitants and vacation rentals. The town features two picturesque churches, one of which is Kaulanapueo Church, constructed in 1853 out of coral blocks. If you linger awhile, you may meet local residents and learn about a rural lifestyle you might not have expected to find on the Islands. The same can be said for nearby Kailua (mile marker 6). ■ TIP→ **When you're back up on Hana Highway, pull into the Huelo Lookout Fruit Stand for yummy smoothies and killer views of the Pacific below.** ✉ *Hana Hwy., near mile marker 5, Huelo.*

Waikamoi Nature Trail. Slightly after the town of Huelo, the Hana Highway enters the Koolau Forest Reserve. Vines wrap around street signs, and waterfalls are so abundant that you don't know which direction to look. A good start is between mile markers 9 and 10, where the Waikamoi Nature Trail sign beckons you to stretch your car-weary limbs. A short (if muddy) trail leads through tall eucalyptus trees to a coastal vantage point with a picnic table. Signage reminds visitors: "Quiet, Trees at Work" and "Bamboo Picking Permit Required." *Awapuhi,* or Hawaiian shampoo ginger, sends up fragrant shoots along the trail. ■ TIP→ **The area has picnic tables and a restroom.** ✉ *Hana Hwy., between mile markers 9 and 10.*

KEANAE, WAILUA, AND NEARBY

13 miles east of Kailua.

Officially, Keanae is the halfway point to Hana, but for many, this is where the drive offers the most rewarding vistas. The greenery seems to envelop the skinny road, forcing drivers to slow to a crawl as they "ooh" and "aah" at the landscape. Keanae itself isn't much of a stunner—save the banana-bread shack at the bottom of the road—but the scenery as your car winds through these tropics makes the white-knuckle parts of the drive worth it. Around the village of Wailua, one of the most fiercely native Hawaiian regions on the island, there seem to be waterfalls at every turn.

TOP ATTRACTIONS

The following sites are arranged geographically by mile marker en route to Hana.

Garden of Eden Arboretum. Just beyond mile marker 10 on the Hana Highway, the Garden of Eden Arboretum offers interpretive trails through 26 acres of manicured gardens. Anyone with a green thumb will appreciate the care and attention given to the more than 500 varieties of tropical plants—many of them native. Trails lead to the lovely Puohokamoa Falls and provide a glimpse into the botanical wonders that thrive in this lush region. ✉ *10600 Hana Hwy., Haiku-Pauwela* ☎ *808/572–9899* 🌐 *www.mauigardenofeden.com* 🎫 *$15.*

Keanae Arboretum. Here you can add to your botanical education or enjoy a challenging hike into the forest. Signs help you learn the names of the many plants and trees now considered native to Hawaii. The meandering Piinaau Stream adds a graceful touch to the arboretum and provides a swimming pond. You can take a fairly rigorous hike from the arboretum if you can find the trail at one side of the large taro patch. Be careful not to lose the trail once you're on it. A

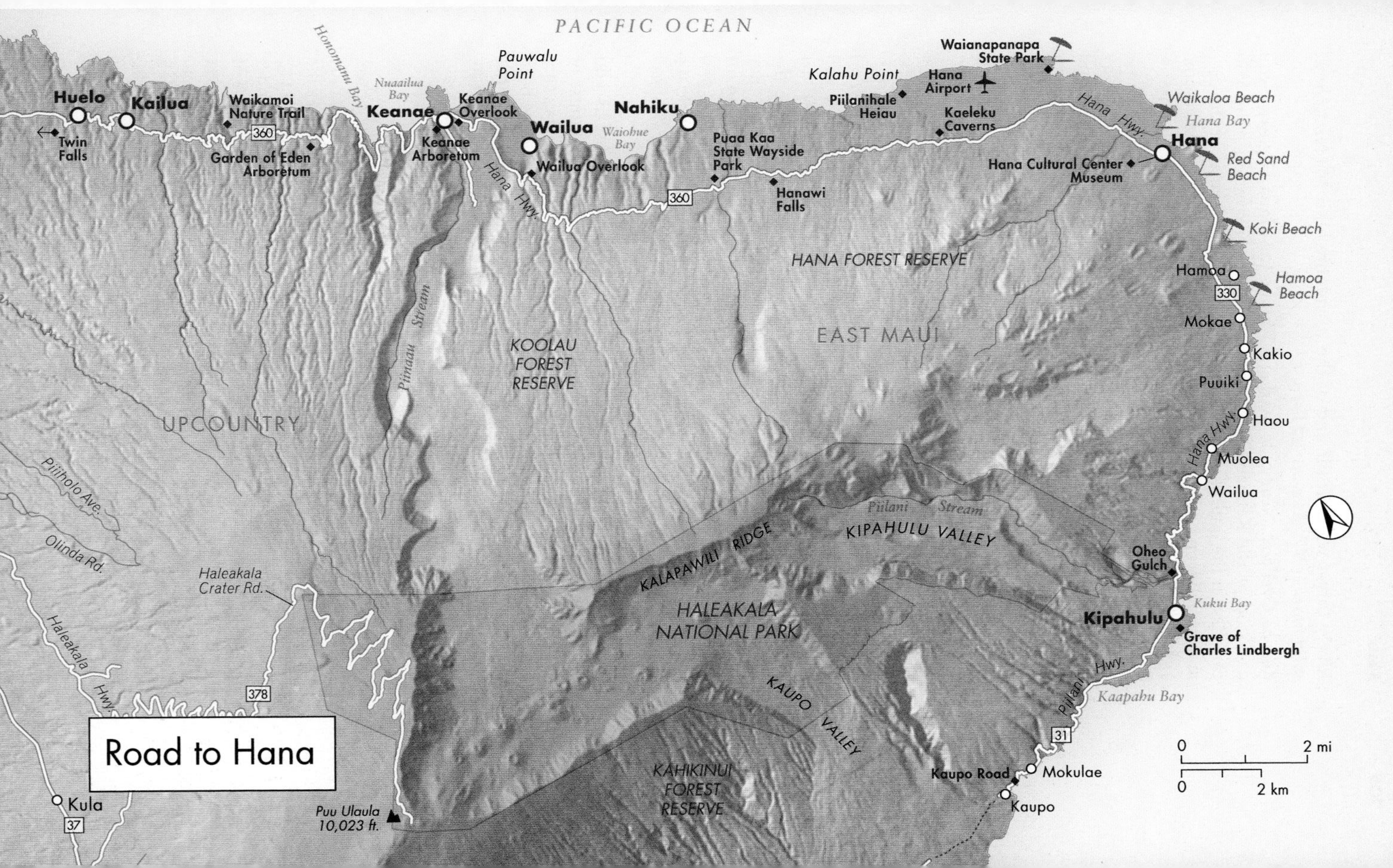
Road to Hana
PACIFIC OCEAN
Huelo
Kailua
Twin Falls
Waikamoi Nature Trail
360
Garden of Eden Arboretum
Honomanu Bay
Nuaailua Bay
Keanae
Keanae Overlook
Keanae Arboretum
Pauwalu Point
Wailua
Wailua Overlook
Hana Hwy.
Waiohue Bay
Nahiku
Puaa Kaa State Wayside Park
Hanawi Falls
Kalahu Point
Piilanihale Heiau
Hana Airport
Kaeleku Caverns
Waianapanapa State Park
Waikaloa Beach
Hana Bay
Hana
Hana Cultural Center Museum
Red Sand Beach
Koki Beach
Hamoa
330
Hamoa Beach
Mokae
Kakio
Puuiki
Haou
Muolea
Wailua
HANA FOREST RESERVE
EAST MAUI
KOOLAU FOREST RESERVE
Piinaau Stream
UPCOUNTRY
Piiholo Ave.
Olinda Rd.
Haleakala Crater Rd.
378
Haleakala Hwy.
Kula
37
Puu Ulaula 10,023 ft.
Piilani Stream
KIPAHULU VALLEY
KALAPAWILI RIDGE
HALEAKALA NATIONAL PARK
KAUPO VALLEY
KAHIKINUI FOREST RESERVE
Oheo Gulch
Kukui Bay
Kipahulu
Grave of Charles Lindbergh
Piilani Hwy.
Kaapahu Bay
31
Kaupo Road
Mokulae
Kaupo
0
2 mi
0
2 km

lovely forest waits at the end of the 25-minute hike. ✉ *Hana Hwy., mile marker 17, Keanae* 🎟 *Free.*

Keanae Overlook. Near mile marker 17 along the Hana Highway, you can stop at the Keanae Overlook. From this observation point you can take in the quiltlike effect the taro patches create against the dramatic backdrop of the ocean. In the other direction there are awesome views of Haleakala through the foliage. This is a great spot for photos. ✉ *Hana Hwy., near mile marker 17, Keanae.*

Wailua Overlook. From the parking lot on the side of the Hana Highway near mile marker 21, you can see Wailua Canyon in one direction and Wailua Village in the other. Photos are spectacular in the morning light of the verdant expanse below. Also from your perch, you can see Wailua Village's landmark 1860 church, which was allegedly constructed of coral that washed up onto the shore during a storm. ✉ *Hana Hwy., near mile marker 21, Wailua (Maui County).*

Puaa Kaa State Wayside Park. Many believe the stretch of landscape between mile markers 19 and 25 of the Hana Highway contain the most picturesque waterfalls on Maui. While there are stunning waterfalls in all directions, perhaps the loveliest is about a half mile beyond mile marker 22. The series of waterfalls gushing into a pool below will have you snapping screen savers. To get here, park at the turnoff just over the bridge and then carefully walk west across the bridge to the waterfalls. There are hiking trails that snake up the mountain, but they are muddy and slightly dangerous. **■ TIP→ Usually in the parking lot by the waterfalls, a couple of flatbed trucks are loaded with crafts and fruit breads for sale. Look around for Dave's banana-bread truck; it's some of the best on the island.** ✉ *Hana Hwy., Wailua (Maui County)* ✣ *½ mile past mile marker 22.*

Hanawi Falls. At mile marker 24 of the Hana Highway, just as you approach the bridge, look toward the mountains to catch a glimpse of Hanawi Falls. This lush spring-fed stream travels 9 miles to the ocean, and the waterfalls are real crowd-pleasers, even when rains have been light. The best views are from the bridge. ⚠ **It is not safe to hike to the falls, and you must cross private property to get there. We strongly advise against this.** ✉ *Hana Hwy., near mile marker 24, Keanae.*

HANA AND NEARBY

15 miles east of Keanae.

Even though the "town" is little more than a gas station, a post office, and a general store, the relaxed pace of life that Hana residents enjoy will likely have you in its grasp. Hana is one of the few places where the slow pulse of the island is still strong. The town centers on its lovely circular bay, dominated on the right-hand shore by a *puu* (volcanic cinder cone) called Kauiki. A short trail here leads to a cave, the birthplace of Queen Kaahumanu. Two miles beyond town, another puu presides over a loop road that passes Hana's two best beaches—Koki and Hamoa. The hill is called Ka Iwi O Pele (Pele's Bone). Offshore here, at tiny Alau Island, the demigod Maui supposedly fished up the Hawaiian Islands.

TROPICAL DELIGHTS

The drive to Hana wouldn't be as enchanting without a stop or two at one of the countless fruit and flower (and banana bread) stands by the highway. Every so often a thatch hut tempts passersby with apple bananas (a smaller, firmer variety), *lilikoi* (passion fruit), avocados, or star fruit just plucked from the tree. Leave a few dollars in the can for the folks who live off the land. Huge bouquets of tropical flowers are available for a handful of change, and some farms will ship.

One standout is **Keanae Landing Fruit Stand,** in the blink-and-you'll-miss-it community of Keanae. This legendary banana-bread shop is just past the coral-and-lava-rock church. Aunty Sandy's sweet loaves lure locals and tourists alike, but be sure to arrive early, because once the stand runs out, you'll have to scurry back up the main road to the **Halfway to Hana Fruit Stand** to find a tasty replacement.

Although sugar was once the mainstay of Hana's economy, the last plantation shut down in the 1940s. In 1946 rancher Paul Fagan built the Hotel Hana-Maui (now the Travassa Hana) and stocked the surrounding pastureland with cattle. Now it's the ranch and its hotel that put food on most tables. It's pleasant to stroll around this beautifully rustic property. In the evening, while local musicians play in the lobby bar, their friends jump up to dance hula. The cross you can see on the hill above the hotel was put there in memory of Fagan.

TOP ATTRACTIONS

The following sites are listed geographically by mile marker en route to Hana.

Hana Cultural Center Museum. If you're determined to spend some time and money in Hana after the long drive along the Hana Highway, head to the Hana Cultural Center Museum in the center of town. Besides operating a well-stocked gift shop, it displays artifacts, quilts, a replica of an authentic *kauhale* (an ancient Hawaiian living complex, with thatch huts and food gardens), as well as other Hawaiiana. The knowledgeable staff can explain it all to you. ✉ *4974 Uakea Rd., Hana* ☎ *808/248–8622* 🌐 *www.hanaculturalcenter.org* 🎫 *$3* 🕒 *Closed weekends.*

Kaeleku Caverns. If you're interested in spelunking, take the time to explore Kaeleku Caverns (aka Hana Lava Tube), just after mile marker 31 on the Hana Highway. The site is a mile down Ulaino Road. The friendly folks at the cave give a brief orientation and promptly send nature enthusiasts into Maui's largest lava tube, accented by colorful underworld formations. You can take a self-guided, 30- to 40-minute tour daily 10:30–4 for $11.95 per person. LED flashlights are provided. ✉ *Ulaino Rd., off Hana Hwy., Hana* ☎ *808/248–7308* 🌐 *www.mauicave.com* 🎫 *$11.95.*

Piilanihale Heiau. This temple was built for a great 16th-century Maui king named Piilani and his heirs. Hawaiian families continue to maintain and protect this sacred site as they have for centuries, and they have not been eager to turn it into a tourist attraction. However, there is now a brochure, so you can tour the property yourself, including the 122-acre **Kahanu Garden,** a federally funded research center focusing on the ethnobotany of the Pacific. ✉ *650 Ulaino Rd., Hana* ✣ *To get here, turn left onto Ulaino Rd. at Hana Hwy. mile marker 31; the road turns to gravel; continue 1½ miles* ☎ *808/248–8912* 🌐 *www.ntbg.org* 🎟 *$10* ⏲ *Closed Sun.*

Fodor's Choice ★ **Waianapanapa State Park.** Home to one of Maui's few black-sand beaches and freshwater caves for adventurous swimmers to explore, this park is right on the ocean. It's a lovely spot to picnic, hike, or swim. To the left you'll find the volcanic sand beach, picnic tables, and cave pools; to the right is an ancient trail that snakes along the ocean past blowholes, sea arches, and archaeological sites. The tide pools here turn red several times a year. Scientists say it's explained by the arrival of small shrimp, but legend claims the color represents the blood of Popoalaea, said to have been murdered in one of the caves by her husband, Chief Kakae. In either case, the dramatic landscape is bound to leave a lasting impression. ■ TIP→ **With a permit, you can stay in a state-run cabin for a steal. It's wise to book a year in advance as these spots book up quickly.** ✉ *Hana Hwy., near mile marker 32, Hana* ☎ *808/984–8109* 🌐 *www.hawaiistateparks.org* 🎟 *Free.*

EAST MAUI

East Maui defies definition. Part hideaway for renegades, part escape for celebrities, this funky stretch of Maui surprises at every turn. You might find a smoothie shop that powers your afternoon bike ride, or a hidden restaurant–artist gathering off a backcountry road serving organic cuisine that could have been dropped in from San Francisco. Farms are abundant, and the dramatic beauty seems to get better the farther you get from Hana. This route leads through stark ocean vistas rounding the back side of Haleakala and into Upcountry. If you plan to meander this way, be sure to check the weather and road conditions.

KIPAHULU AND NEARBY

11 miles east of Hana.

Most know Kipahulu as the resting place of Charles Lindbergh. Kipahulu devotes its energy to staying under the radar. There is not much for tourists, save an organic farm, a couple of cafés, and astounding natural landscapes. Maui's wildest wilderness might not beg for your tourist dollars, but it is a tantalizing place to escape just about everything.

GETTING HERE AND AROUND

To access Kipahulu from Hana, continue on Hana Highway, also known as 330, for 11 miles southeast. You can also reach the area from Upcountry's Highway 37, which turns into Highway 31, though this route can take up to two hours and is a bit rough on your rental car.

TOP ATTRACTIONS

Fodor's Choice ★ **Oheo Gulch.** One branch of Haleakala National Park runs down the mountain from the crater and reaches the sea here, 10 miles past Hana at mile marker 42 on the Hana Highway, where a basalt-lined stream cascades from one pool to the next. Some tour guides still incorrectly

The black sand of small Waianapanapa State Park on the Road to Hana is made up of volcanic pebbles. You can swim here or hike a memorable coastal path past sea arches and blowholes.

call this area Seven Sacred Pools, but in truth there are more than seven, and they've never been considered sacred. ⚠ **While you may be tempted to take a dip, know that the pools are often closed because of landslides and flash flooding. If you see a closure notice, take it seriously, as people have died here.** The place gets crowded, as most people who drive the Hana Highway make this their last stop. It's best to get here early to soak up the solace of these waterfalls. If you enjoy hiking, go up the stream on the 2-mile hike to **Waimoku Falls.** The trail crosses a spectacular gorge, then turns into a boardwalk that takes you through an amazing bamboo forest. You can pitch a tent in the grassy campground down by the sea. **■TIP→ The $25 entrance fee per car is good for three days and includes entry to Haleakala Volcano.** ✉ *Piilani Hwy., 10 miles south of Hana, Hana.*

Grave of Charles Lindbergh. Many people travel the mile past Oheo Gulch to see the grave of Charles Lindbergh. The world-renowned aviator chose to be buried here because he and his wife, writer Anne Morrow Lindbergh, spent a lot of time living in the area in a home they'd built. He was buried here in 1974, next to Palapala Hoomau Congregational Church. The simple one-room church sits on a bluff over the sea, with the small graveyard on the ocean side. Since this is a churchyard, be considerate and leave everything exactly as you found it. Next to the churchyard on the ocean side is a small county park, a good place for a peaceful picnic. ✉ *Palapala Hoomau Congregational Church, Piilani Hwy., Kipahulu.*

Kaupo Road. Also called Piilani Highway, this road winds through what locals say is one of the last parts of real Maui. It goes all the way around Haleakala's back side through Ulupalakua Ranch and into Kula. The desertlike area, with its grand vistas, is unlike anything else on the island. This road has a reputation for being treacherous, and while narrow sections and steep cliffs can be intimidating for some drivers, recent road improvements have made this a much smoother ride. ⚠ **Some car-rental agencies call the area off-limits for their passenger cars, and won't come to your rescue if you need emergency assistance. However four-wheel drive isn't necessary.** The small communities around East Maui cling tenuously to the old ways—please be respectful of that if you do pass this way. Between Kipahulu and Kula may be a mere 38 miles, but the twisty road makes the drive take up to two hours. If you must drive this road at night, keep an eye out for free-range cattle crossing your path. **■ TIP→ Fill up on gas and food, as the only stop out here is Kaupo Store, which hawks a few pricey necessities.**

BEACHES

Updated by Christie Leon

Of all the beaches on the Hawaiian Islands, Maui's are some of the most diverse. You can find the pristine, palm-lined shores you've always dreamed of, with clear and inviting waters the color of green sea glass, and you can also discover rich black-sand beaches, craggy cliffs with surging whitecaps, and year-round sunsets that quiet the soul. As on the other islands, all of Maui's beaches are public—but that doesn't mean it's not possible to find a secluded cove where you can truly get away from the world.

The island's leeward shores (West Maui and the South Shore) have the calmest, sunniest beaches. Hit the beach early, when the aquamarine waters are calm as bathwater. In summer, afternoon winds can be a sandblasting force and can chase away even the most dedicated sunbathers. From November through May, these beaches are also great spots to watch the humpback whales that spend winter and early spring in Maui's waters.

Windward shores (the North Shore and East Maui) are for the more adventurous. Beaches face the open ocean rather than other islands, and tend to be rockier and more prone to powerful swells. This is particularly true in winter, when the North Shore becomes a playground for big-wave riders and windsurfers. Don't let this keep you away, however; some of the island's best beaches are those slivers of volcanic sand found on the windward shore.

In terms of beach gear, Maui is the land of plenty when it comes to stores stocked full of body boards and beach mats. Look for Longs Drugs/CVS Drugs (in Kihei, Kahului, Lahaina, Pukalani, and Wailuku) or the ABC Stores (in Kaanapali, Lahaina, Kihei, and elsewhere) for sunscreen, shades, towels, umbrellas, and more. If you want better deals, stop by Target, Walmart, or Costco (membership required) located close to Kahului Airport. Equipment rentals are available at shops and resorts, surf and dive shops, and many condos come equipped with beach chairs, coolers, and water toys.

WEST MAUI

The beaches in West Maui are legendary for their glittering aquamarine waters backed by long stretches of golden sand. Reef fronts much of the western shore, making the underwater panorama something to behold. A few tips: parking can be challenging in resort areas; look for the blue "Shoreline Access" signs to find limited parking and a public path to the beach; and watch out for *kiawe* thorns when you park off-road, because they can puncture tires—and feet.

There are a dozen roadside beaches to choose from on Route 30, of which we like these best.

LAHAINA

FAMILY **Launiupoko Beach Park.** This is the beach park of all beach parks: both a surf break and a beach, it offers a little something for everyone with its inviting stretch of lawn, soft white sand, and gentle waves. The shoreline reef creates a protected wading pool, perfect for small children. Outside the reef, beginner surfers will find good longboard rides. From the long sliver of beach (good for walking), you can enjoy superb views of neighbor islands, and, land side, of deep valleys cutting through the West Maui Mountains. Because of its endless sunshine and serenity—not to mention such amenities as picnic tables and grills—Launiupoko draws a crowd on the weekends, but there's space for everyone (and overflow parking across the street). **Amenities:** parking (no fee); showers; toilets. **Best for:** sunset; surfing; swimming; walking. ✉ *Rte. 30, Lahaina* ⊕ *At mile marker 18.*

Olowalu. More an offshore snorkel and stand-up paddling spot than a beach, Olowalu is also a great place to watch for turtles and whales in season. The beach is literally a pullover from the road, which can make for some unwelcome noise if you're looking for quiet. The entrance can be rocky (reef shoes help), but if you've got your snorkel gear it's a 200-yard swim to an extensive and diverse reef. Shoreline visibility can vary depending on the swell and time of day; late morning is best. Except for during a south swell, the waters are usually calm. A half mile north of mile marker 14 you can find the rocky surf break, also called Olowalu. Snorkeling here is along pathways that wind among coral heads. Note: this is a local hangout and can be unfriendly at times. **Amenities:** none. **Best for:** snorkeling; stand-up paddling. ✉ *Rte. 30, Olowalu* ⊕ *Look for mile marker 14, south of Olowalu General Store.*

KAANAPALI AND NEARBY

Kaanapali Beach. If you're looking for quiet and seclusion, this is not the beach for you. But if you want lots of action, spread out your towel here. Stretching from the northernmost end of the Sheraton Maui Resort & Spa to the Hyatt Regency Maui Resort & Spa at its southern tip, Kaanapali Beach is lined with resorts, condominiums, restaurants, and shops. The center section in front of Whalers Village, also called Dig Me Beach, is one of Maui's best people-watching spots: windsurfers, stand-up paddleboarders, and folks in catamarans head out from here, while others take in the scenery. A concrete pathway weaves along the length of this 3-mile-long beach, leading from one astounding resort to the next.

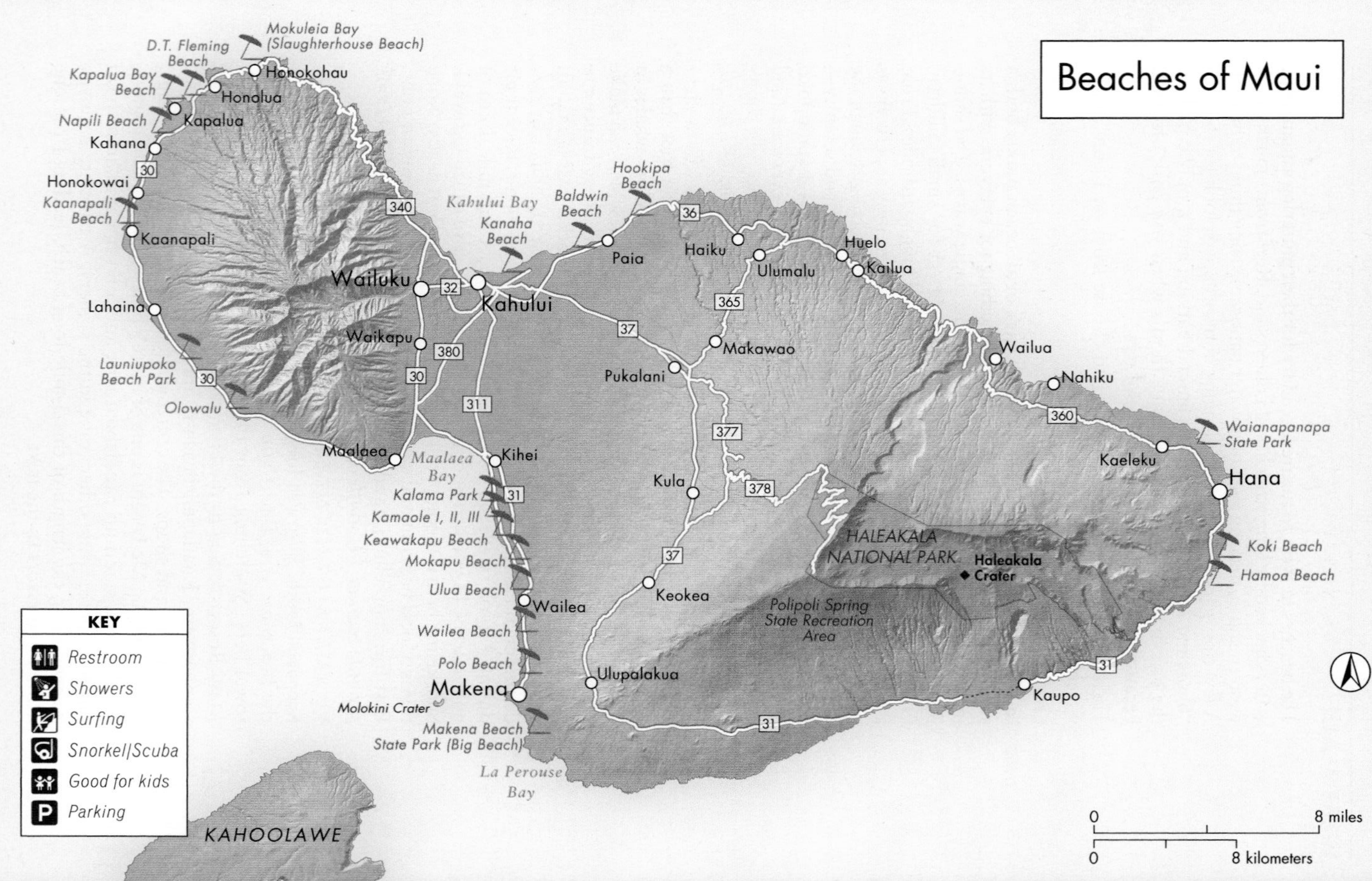
Beaches of Maui
Mokuleia Bay
(Slaughterhouse Beach)
D.T. Fleming
Beach
Kapalua Bay
Beach
Napili Beach
Honokohau
Honolua
Kapalua
Kahana
Honokowai
Kaanapali
Beach
Kaanapali
Lahaina
Launiupoko
Beach Park
Olowalu
Wailuku
Waikapu
Maalaea
Kahului
Kahului Bay
Kanaha
Beach
Baldwin
Beach
Hookipa
Beach
Paia
Haiku
Ulumalu
Huelo
Kailua
Makawao
Pukalani
Kula
Keokea
Ulupalakua
Wailua
Nahiku
Kaeleku
Waianapanapa
State Park
Hana
Koki Beach
Hamoa Beach
Kaupo
HALEAKALA
NATIONAL PARK
Haleakala
Crater
Polipoli Spring
State Recreation
Area
Kihei
Maalaea
Bay
Kalama Park
Kamaole I, II, III
Keawakapu Beach
Mokapu Beach
Ulua Beach
Wailea
Wailea Beach
Polo Beach
Makena
Molokini Crater
Makena Beach
State Park (Big Beach)
La Perouse
Bay
KAHOOLAWE
340
32
380
30
311
31
37
36
365
377
378
360
KEY
Restroom
Showers
Surfing
Snorkel/Scuba
Good for kids
Parking
0
8 miles
0
8 kilometers

The drop-off from Kaanapali's soft sugary sand is steep, but waves hit the shore with barely a rippling slap. The northern section, known as Puukekaa, was, in ancient Hawaii, a *leina a ke akua,* or jumping-off place for spirits. It's easy to get into the water from the beach to enjoy the prime snorkeling among the lava-rock outcroppings. ■ TIP→ **Strong rip currents are often present near Puukekaa; always snorkel with a companion.** Throughout the resort, blue "Shoreline Access" signs point the way to a few free-parking stalls and public rights-of-way to the beach. Kaanapali Resort public beach parking can be found between the Hyatt and the Marriott, between the Marriott and the Kaanapali Alii, next to Whalers Village, and at the Sheraton. You can park for a fee at most of the large hotels and at Whalers Village. The merchants in the shopping village will validate your parking ticket if you make a purchase. **Amenities:** parking (no fee); showers; toilets. **Best for:** snorkeling; sunset; swimming; walking. ☒ *Honoapiilani Hwy., Kaanapali* ✣ *Follow any of the 3 Kaanapali exits.*

FREE BEACH ACCESS

All of the island's beaches are free and open to the public—even those that grace the backyards of fancy hotels. Some of the prettiest beaches are often hidden by buildings; look for the blue "Shoreline Access" signs that indicate public rights-of-way through condominiums, resorts, and other private properties.

3

FAMILY Fodor's Choice ★ **Napili Beach.** Surrounded by sleepy condos, this round bay is a turtle-filled pool lined with a sparkling white crescent of sand. Sunbathers love this beach, which is also a terrific sunset spot. The shore break is steep but gentle, so it's great for body boarding and bodysurfing. It's easy to keep an eye on kids here as the entire bay is visible from everywhere. The beach is right outside the Napili Kai Beach Resort, a popular local-style resort for honeymooners and families, only a few miles south of Kapalua. **Amenities:** showers; toilets. **Best for:** sunset; surfing; swimming. ☒ *5900 Lower Honoapiilani Hwy., Napili* ✣ *Look for Napili Pl. or Hui Dr.*

KAPALUA AND KAHAKULOA

D.T. Fleming Beach. Because the current can be quite strong, this charming, mile-long sandy cove is better for sunbathing than for swimming or water sports. Still, it's one of the island's most popular beaches. It's a perfect spot to watch the spectacular Maui sunsets, and there are picnic tables and grills. Part of the beach runs along the front of the Ritz-Carlton, Kapalua—a good place to grab a cocktail and enjoy the view. **Amenities:** lifeguards; parking (no fee); showers; toilets. **Best for:** sunset; walking. ☒ *Rte. 30, Kapalua* ✣ *About 1 mile north of Kapalua.*

Fodor's Choice ★ **Kapalua Bay Beach.** Over the years Kapalua has been recognized as one of the world's best beaches, and for good reason: it fronts a pristine bay that is good for snorkeling, swimming, and general lazing. Just north of Napili Bay, this lovely sheltered shore often remains calm late into the afternoon, although currents may be strong offshore. Snorkeling is easy here, and there are lots of colorful reef fish. This popular area is bordered by the Kapalua Resort, so don't expect to have the beach to

Sheltered Kapalua Bay Beach is ideal for snorkeling and swimming.

yourself. Walk through the tunnel from the parking lot at the end of Kapalua Place to get here. **Amenities:** parking (no fee); showers; toilets. **Best for:** snorkeling; sunset; swimming. ✉ *Rte. 30, Kapalua* ✣ *Turn onto Kapalua Pl.*

Mokuleia Bay (Slaughterhouse Beach). The island's northernmost beach is part of the Honolua-Mokuleia Marine Life Conservation District. "Slaughterhouse" is the surfers' nickname for what is officially Mokuleia. Weather permitting, this is a great place for bodysurfing and sunbathing. Concrete steps and a green railing help you get down the cliff to the sand. The next bay over, Honolua, has no beach but offers one of the best surf breaks in Hawaii. Competitions are often held there; telltale signs are cars pulled off the road and parked in the old pineapple field. **Amenities:** none. **Best for:** sunset; surfing. ✉ *Rte. 30, Kapalua* ✣ *At mile marker 32.*

SOUTH SHORE

Sandy beach fronts nearly the entire southern coastline of Maui. The farther south, the better the beaches get. Kihei has excellent beach parks in town, with white sand, plenty of amenities, and paved parking lots. Good snorkeling can be found along the beaches' rocky borders. As good as Kihei is, Wailea is better. The beaches are cleaner, and the views more impressive. You can take a mile-long walk on a shore path from Ulua to near Polo Beach. Look for blue "Shoreline Access" signs for parking along the main thoroughfare, Wailea Alanui Drive. **■ TIP→ Break-ins have been reported at many parking lots, so don't**

leave valuables in the car. As you head to Makena, the terrain gets wilder; bring lunch, water, and sunscreen.

KIHEI

FAMILY **Kalama Park.** Stocked with grills and picnic pavilions, this 36-acre beach park with plenty of shade is great for families and sports lovers. With its extensive lawns and sports fields, the park welcomes volleyball, basketball, baseball, and tennis players, and even has a playground, skateboard park, and a roller hockey rink. The beach itself is all but nonexistent, but swimming is fair—though you must brave the rocky steps down to the water. If you aren't completely comfortable with this entrance, stick to the burgers and bocce ball. **Amenities:** parking (no fee); showers; toilets. **Best for:** partiers. ✉ *1900 S. Kihei Road, Kihei* ⊕ *Across from Kihei Kalama Village.*

FAMILY **Kamaole I, II, and III.** Three steps from South Kihei Road are three golden stretches of sand separated by outcroppings of dark, jagged lava rocks. You can walk the length of all three beaches if you're willing to get your feet wet. The northernmost of the trio, Kamaole I (across from the ABC Store—important to know if you forget your sunscreen) offers perfect swimming and an active volleyball court. There's also a great lawn, where you can spread out at the south end of the beach. Kamaole II is nearly identical except for the lawn, but there is no parking lot. The last beach, the one with all the people on it, is 10-acre Kamaole III, perfect for throwing a disk or throwing down a blanket. This is a great family beach, complete with a playground, barbecue grills, kite flying, and, frequently, rented inflatable castles—a must at birthday parties for cool kids. All three beach parks offer wheelchair ramps to the beach; Kamaole I is the only beach on Maui with a beach access chair.

Locally—and quite disrespectfully, according to Native Hawaiians—known as "Kam" I, II, and III, all three beaches have great swimming and lifeguards. In the morning the water can be as still as a lap pool. Kamaole III offers terrific breaks for beginning bodysurfers. **Amenities:** lifeguards; parking (no fee); showers; toilets. **Best for:** sunsets, surfing; swimming; walking. ✉ *S. Kiniihei Rd., between Alli Ke Alanui and Hale Kamaole Condominiums, Kihei* ☎ *808/270–6136 for beach wheelchair availability.*

Keawakapu Beach. Everyone loves Keawakapu, with its long stretch of golden sand, near-perfect swimming, and views of Puu Olai cinder cone. It's great fun to walk or jog this beach south into Wailea, as it's lined with over-the-top residences. It's best here in the morning—the winds pick up in the afternoon (beware of sandstorms). Keawakapu has three entrances: one is at the Mana Kai Maui resort (look for the blue "Shoreline Access" sign); the second is directly across from the parking lot on Kilohana Street (the entrance is unmarked); and the third is at the dead end of Kihei Road. Toilets are portable. **Amenities:** parking (no fee); showers; toilets. **Best for:** sunset; swimming; walking. ✉ *S. Kihei Rd., near Kilohana St., Kihei.*

WAILEA

Fodor's Choice ★ **Makena Beach State Park (Big Beach).** Locals successfully fought to turn Makena—one of Hawaii's most breathtaking beaches—into a state park. This stretch of deep golden sand abutting sparkling aquamarine water is 3,000 feet long and 100 feet wide. It's often mistakenly referred to as Big Beach, but natives prefer its Hawaiian name, Oneloa. Makena is never crowded, no matter how many cars cram into the lots. The water is fine for swimming, but use caution. **TIP→ The shore drop-off is steep, and swells can get deceptively big.** Despite the infamous "Makena cloud," a blanket that rolls in during the early afternoon and obscures the sun, it seldom rains here. For a dramatic view of the beach, climb Puu Olai, the steep cinder cone near the first entrance you pass if you're driving south. Continue over the cinder cone's side to discover "Little Beach"—clothing-optional by popular practice, although this is technically illegal. On Sunday, free spirits of all kinds crowd Little Beach's tiny shoreline for a drumming circle and bonfire. Little Beach has the island's best bodysurfing (no pun intended). Skim boarders catch air at Makena's third entrance, which is a little tricky to find (it's just a dirt path with street parking). **Amenities:** lifeguards; parking (no fee); toilets. **Best for:** surfing; swimming; walking. ✉ *Makena* ✣ *Off Wailea Alanui Dr.* 🌐 *www.hawaiistateparks.org.*

FAMILY **Mokapu and Ulua.** Look for a little road and public parking lot near the Wailea Beach Marriott Resort & Spa if you are heading to Mokapu and Ulua beaches. Although there are no lifeguards, families love this place. Reef formations create tons of tide pools for kids to explore, and the beaches are protected from major swells. Snorkeling is excellent at Ulua, the beach to the left of the entrance. Mokapu, to the right, tends to be less crowded. **Amenities:** parking (no fee); showers; toilets. **Best for:** snorkeling; swimming. ✉ *Halealii Pl., Wailea* ✣ *Before Shops of Wailea.*

Polo Beach. Small and secluded, this crescent fronts the Fairmont Kea Lani. Swimming and snorkeling are great here, and it's a good place to whale watch. As at Wailea Beach, private umbrellas and chaise lounges occupy the choicest real estate, but there's plenty of room for you and your towel. There's a nice grass picnic area, although it's a considerable distance from the beach. The pathway connecting the two beaches is a great spot to jog or to take in awesome views of nearby Molokini and Kahoolawe. Rare native plants grow along the ocean, or *makai,* side of the path—the honey-sweet-smelling one is *naio,* or false sandalwood. **Amenities:** parking (no fee); showers; toilets. **Best for:** snorkeling; swimming. ✉ *Kaukahi St., Wailea* ✣ *South of Fairmont Kea Lani entrance.*

Wailea Beach. A road near the Grand Wailea Resort takes you to Wailea Beach, a wide sandy stretch with snorkeling and swimming. If you're not a guest at the Grand Wailea or Four Seasons, the cluster of private umbrellas and chaise longues can be a little annoying, but the calm unclouded waters and soft white sand more than make up for this. From the parking lot, walk to the right to get to the main beach; to the left is another, smaller section that fronts the Four Seasons. There are picnic tables and grills away from the beach. **Amenities:** parking (no fee); showers; toilets. **Best for:** snorkeling; swimming. ✉ *Wailea Alanui Dr., Wailea* ✣ *South of Grand Wailea Resort entrance.*

MAUI'S TOP BEACHES

The leeward shores of West and South Maui have calm beaches and some great snorkeling, but experienced surfers and windsurfers gravitate to the windward (North Shore and East Maui) beaches that face the open ocean. Here are some of our favorites.

BEST FOR FAMILIES

Baldwin Beach, the North Shore. The long, shallow, calm end closest to Kahului is safe even for toddlers—with adult supervision, of course.

Kamaole III, the South Shore. Sand, gentle surf, a playground, a volleyball net, and barbecues all add up to great family fun.

Napili Beach, West Maui. Kids will love the turtles that snack on the *limu* (seaweed) growing on the lava rocks. This sometimes crowded crescent-shape beach offers sunbathing, snorkeling, swimming, bodysurfing, and startling sunsets.

BEST OFFSHORE SNORKELING

Olowalu, West Maui. The water remains shallow far offshore, and there's plenty to see.

Ulua, the South Shore. It's beautiful and the kids can enjoy the tide pools while the adults experience the excellent snorkeling.

BEST SURFING

Honolua Bay, West Maui. One bay over from Slaughterhouse (Mokuleia) Beach north of Kapalua you can find one of the best surf breaks in Hawaii.

BEST SUNSETS

Kapalua Bay, West Maui. The ambience here is as stunning as the sunset.

Keawakapu, the South Shore. Most active beachgoers enjoy this gorgeous spot before midafternoon, when the wind picks up, so it's never crowded at sunset.

BEST FOR SEEING AND BEING SEEN

Kaanapali Beach, West Maui. Backed by resorts, condos, and restaurants, this is not the beach for solitude. But the sand is soft, the waters are gentle, and the action varies from good snorkeling at Black Rock (Kekaa) to people-watching in front of Whalers Village—not for nothing is this section called "Dig Me Beach."

Wailea Beach, the South Shore. At this beach fronting the ultraluxurious Four Seasons and Grand Wailea resorts, you never know who might be hiding in that private cabana.

BEST SETTING

Makena (Oneloa), South Shore. Don't forget the camera for this beauty, a state park away from the Wailea resort area. Finding this long, wide stretch of golden sand and translucent offshore water is worth the effort. The icing on the cake is that this long beach is never crowded. Use caution for swimming, because the steep onshore break can get big.

Waianapanapa State Park, East Maui. This rustic black-sand beach will capture your heart—it's framed by lava cliffs and backed by bright-green beach *naupaka* bushes. Ocean currents can be strong, so enjoy the views and cool off in one of two freshwater pools. Get an early start, because your day's destination is just shy of Hana.

3

NORTH SHORE

Many of the people you see jaywalking in Paia sold everything they owned to come to Maui and live a beach bum's life. Beach culture abounds on the North Shore. But these folks aren't sunbathers; they're big-wave riders, windsurfers, or kiteboarders, and the North Shore is their challenging sports arena. Beaches here face the open ocean and tend to be rougher and windier than beaches elsewhere on Maui—but don't let that scare you off. On calm days the reef-speckled waters are truly beautiful and offer a quieter and less commercial beachgoing experience than the leeward shore. Be sure to leave your car in a paved parking area so that it doesn't get stuck in soft sand.

PAIA AND KAHULUI

FAMILY **Baldwin Beach.** A local favorite, this big stretch of comfortable golden sand is a good place to stretch out, jog, or swim, although the waves can sometimes be choppy and the undertow strong. Don't be alarmed by those big brown blobs floating beneath the surface; they're just pieces of seaweed awash in the surf. You can find shade along the beach beneath the ironwood trees, or in the large pavilion, regularly used for local parties and community events. There are picnic tables, grills, and a large playing field as well.

The long, shallow pool at the Kahului end of the beach is known as Baby Beach. Separated from the surf by a flat reef wall, this is where ocean-loving families bring their kids (and sometimes puppies) to practice a few laps. Take a relaxing stroll along the water's edge from one end of Baldwin Beach to Baby Beach and enjoy the scenery. The view of the West Maui Mountains is hauntingly beautiful. **Amenities:** lifeguard; parking (no fee); showers; toilets. **Best for:** swimming; walking. ⊠ *Hana Hwy., Paia* ✣ *About 1 mile west of Baldwin Ave.*

Fodor's Choice ★ **Hookipa Beach.** To see some of the world's finest windsurfers, hit this beach along the Hana Highway. It's also one of Maui's hottest surfing spots, with waves that can reach 20 feet. Hookipa is not a good swimming beach, nor the place to learn windsurfing, but it's great for hanging out and watching the pros. There are picnic tables and grills. Bust out your telephoto lens at the cliffside lookout to capture the aerial acrobatics of board sailors and kiteboarders. **Amenities:** lifeguard; parking (no fee); showers; toilets. **Best for:** surfing; windsurfing. ⊠ *Hana Hwy, Paia* ✣ *At mile marker 9, about 2 miles east of Paia.*

Kanaha Beach. Windsurfers, kiteboarders, joggers, and picnicking families like this long, golden strip of sand bordered by a wide grassy area with lots of shade that is within walking distance of Kahului Airport. The winds pick up in the early afternoon, making for the best kiteboarding and windsurfing conditions—if you know what you're doing, that is. The best spot for watching kiteboarders is at the far left end of the beach. **Amenities:** lifeguard; parking (no fee); showers; toilets. **Best for:** kiteboarding; walking; windsurfing. ⊠ *Amala Pl., Kahului* ✣ *From Kaahumanu Ave., turn makai onto Hobron St., then right onto Amala Pl. Drive just over a mile through an industrial area and take any of 3 entrances into Kanaha.*

ROAD TO HANA

East Maui's and Hana's beaches will literally stop you in your tracks—they're that beautiful. Black sand stands out against pewter skies and lush tropical foliage, creating picture-perfect scenes that seem too breathtaking to be real. Rough conditions often preclude swimming, but that doesn't mean you can't explore the shoreline.

3

HANA AND EAST MAUI

Hamoa Beach. Why did James Michener describe this stretch of salt-and-pepper sand as the most "South Pacific" beach he'd come across, even though it's in the North Pacific? Maybe it was the perfect half-moon shape, speckled with the shade of palm trees. Perhaps he was intrigued by the jutting black coastline, often outlined by rain showers out at sea, or the pervasive lack of hurry he felt here. Whatever it was, many still feel the lure. The beach can be crowded, yet it is nonetheless relaxing. Early mornings and late afternoons are best for swimming. At times the churning surf might intimidate swimmers, but the bodysurfing can be great. Hamoa is half a mile past Koki Beach on Haneoo Loop Road, 2 miles south of Hana town. **Amenities:** toilets. **Best for:** surfing; swimming. ✉ *Haneoo Loop Rd., Hana.*

Koki Beach. You can tell from the trucks parked alongside the road that this is a favorite local surf spot. ■ **TIP→ Watch conditions before swimming or bodysurfing, as rip currents can be mean.** Look for awesome views of the rugged coastline and a sea arch on the left end. *Iwa,* or white-throated frigate birds, dart like pterodactyls over the offshore Alau Islet. **Amenities:** none. **Best for:** surfing. ✉ *Haneoo Loop Rd., Hana* ✥ *About 2 miles south of Hana town.*

Fodor's Choice ★ **Waianapanapa State Park.** This black volcanic-pebble beach fringed with green beach vines and palms will remain in your memory long after your visit. Swimming here is both relaxing and invigorating. Strong currents bump smooth stones up against your ankles, while seabirds flit above a black, jagged sea arch, and fingers of white foam rush onto the beach. There are picnic tables and grills. At the edge of the parking lot, a sign tells you the sad story of a doomed Hawaiian princess. Stairs lead through a tunnel of interlocking Polynesian *hau* (a native tree) branches to an icy cave pool—the secret hiding place of the ancient princess (you can swim in this pool, but beware of mosquitoes). In the other direction a dramatic 3-mile coastal path continues past sea arches, blowholes, cultural sites, and even a ramshackle fishermen's shelter, all the way to Hana town. **Amenities:** parking (no fee); showers; toilets. **Best for:** swimming; walking. ✉ *Hana Hwy., Hana* ✥ *Near mile marker 32* ☎ *808/984–8109* 🌐 *www.hawaiistateparks.org.*

WHERE TO EAT

Updated by Kyle Ellison

For a place the size of Maui, there's a lot going on when it comes to the dining scene, from ethnic holes-in-the-wall to stunningly appointed hotel dining rooms, and from seafood trucks to oceanfront fish houses with panoramic views. Much of the food is excellent, but some of it is overpriced and touristy. If you're coming from a "food destination" city, you may have to adjust your expectations.

Follow the locavore trend, and at casual and fine-dining restaurants choose menu items made with products that are abundant on the island, like local fish, beef, venison, onions, avocados, cabbage, broccoli, asparagus, hydroponic tomatoes, myriad herbs, salad greens, *kalo* (taro), bananas, papaya, guava, *lilikoi* (passion fruit), coconut, mangoes, strawberries, and Maui pineapple. You can also look for treats grown on neighboring islands, such as mushrooms, purple sweet potatoes, and watermelon.

"Local food," a specific and official cuisine designated as such in the 1920s, is an amalgam of foods brought by the ethnic groups that have come here since the mid-1800s and also blended with the foods native Hawaiians have enjoyed for centuries. Dishes to try include *lomilomi* salmon, *laulau, poi,* Portuguese bean soup, *kalbi* ribs, chicken *katsu,* chow fun, hamburger steak, and macaroni salad. For a food adventure, take a drive into Central Maui and have lunch or dinner at one of the "local" spots recommended here. Or get even more adventurous and take a drive around Wailuku or Kahului and find your own hidden gem—there are plenty out there.

WEST MAUI

Beautiful West Maui encompasses the area from tiny Olowalu, with its famous mom-and-pop Olowalu General Store, full of local-style *bentos* (box lunches), all the way north to the ritzy Kapalua Resort, with its glitzy annual wine-and-food festival. In between are Lahaina, the historic former capital of Hawaii, with its myriad restaurants on and off Front Street, and the resort area of Kaanapali. Have some fun checking out restaurants in the nooks and crannies of Kahana, Honokowai, and Napili, north of Kaanapali. All over the west side you'll find a rainbow of cuisines in just about every price category.

OLOWALU

$ AMERICAN

Leoda's Kitchen and Pie Shop. Slow down as you drive through the little roadside village of Olowalu, about 15 minutes before Lahaina town if you're coming from the airport, so you don't miss this adorable farmhouse-chic restaurant and pie shop, where everything is prepared with care. All the breads are homemade and excellent, and most ingredients are sourced locally; try the signature ahi Benedict for breakfast, a sandwich or a burger with Kula onions for lunch, or comfort food from the rotating menu of nightly dinner specials. **Known for:** locally sourced ingredients; homemade pies—the banana cream is out of this world; freshly baked bread. *Average main: $12* ✉ *820 Olowalu Village Rd., Olowalu* ☎ *808/662–3600* 🌐 *www.leodas.com.*

LAHAINA

$ HAWAIIAN **Aloha Mixed Plate.** Freshly remodeled but still true to its roots, this longtime Lahaina oceanfront classic is run by the same group of wonderful folks who bring you Old Lahaina Luau. This is the place to try a "plate lunch"—a protein served in Asian-style preparation, along with two scoops of rice and macaroni salad—and also features Hawaiian favorites like laulau, saimin, kalua pork, shoyu chicken, and poi from the restaurant's own farm. **Known for:** Hawaiian cuisine; oceanfront setting; alii or kalua pig plate. *Average main: $11 1285 Front St., Lahaina 808/661–3322 www.alohamixedplate.com.*

$$$$ MEXICAN FUSION **Frida's Mexican Beach House.** No matter the cuisine, serial restaurateur Mark Ellman always delivers, as he does yet again with his third oceanfront eatery along Front Street. The oceanfront setting is reason enough to dine here, but the food—specializing in Latin-inspired dishes—attracts diners all on its own and 40 varieties of tequila dominate the bar. **Known for:** grilled Spanish octopus; oceanfront setting; selection of tequila and mezcal. *Average main: $37 1287 Front St., Lahaina 808/661–1278 www.fridasmaui.com.*

$$$$ FRENCH Fodor's Choice ★ **Gerard's.** Classically trained French chef Gerard Reversade, who started as an apprentice in acclaimed Paris restaurants when he was just 14, has for more than three decades remained true to his Gascony roots. He cooks *his* way, utilizing island ingredients in such dishes as escargots *forestière* (with garlic and mushrooms), chilled cucumber soup, and the ahi tartare with taro chips; the wine list is first-class, and the dessert list is extensive. **Known for:** fine French cuisine; impeccable service; world-class wine list. *Average main: $45 The Plantation Inn, 174 Lahainaluna Rd., Lahaina 808/661–8939 www.gerards-maui.com No lunch.*

$$$$ ECLECTIC **Honu Seafood & Pizza.** This oceanfront fish house and pizza restaurant is the work of celebrity chef, Mark Ellman, and it's right next door to his popular Mala Ocean Tavern. Much of the seafood comes from New England and the Pacific Northwest, and the pizzas are cooked in a wood-fired brick oven (is there any other way?). **Known for:** unparalleled ocean views with sea turtle sightings; fantastic selection of craft beers and cocktails; gluten-free options. *Average main: $36 1295 Front St., Lahaina 808/667–9390 www.honumaui.com.*

$$$$ AMERICAN **Lahaina Grill.** At the top of many "best restaurants" lists, this expensive upscale bistro is about as fashionably chic as it gets on Maui, and the interior is as pretty as the patrons. The Cake Walk (servings of Kona lobster crab cake, sweet Louisiana rock-shrimp cake, and seared ahi cake), bufala salad with locally grown tomatoes, and Kona-coffee-roasted rack of lamb are a few of the classics customers demand; the full menu—including dessert—is available at the bar. **Known for:** romantic ambience; downtown location; veal chops and seared lion paw scallops. *Average main: $48 127 Lahainaluna Rd., Lahaina 808/667–5117 www.lahainagrill.com No lunch.*

$$$$ ITALIAN **Longhi's.** A Lahaina landmark, Longhi's has been serving pasta and other Italian fare to throngs of visitors since 1976 in their two spacious, open-air dining levels. Classic dishes include the prawns Venice, filet Longhi style, and the signature lobster Longhi for two and there's a

gigantic, award-winning wine list. **Known for:** valet parking; exceptional seafood and homeade breakfast pastries; elegant Front Street setting. *Average main: $40 ✉ 888 Front St., Lahaina ☎ 808/667–2288 🌐 www.longhis.com.*

$$$$ MODERN HAWAIIAN Fodor's Choice ★ **Mala Ocean Tavern.** Chef-owner Mark Ellman has been revolutionizing Maui's food scene since the 1980s, and the menu at this oceanfront—the lanai juts out over the water—standout reflects Mark's and his wife Judy's world travels, with dishes influenced by the Middle East, the Mediterranean, Italy, Bali, and Thailand. There's a focus on ingredients that promote local sustainability, and as you might expect, the cocktails and wine list are great, too. **Known for:** seared ahi bruschetta; whole wok-fried fish; oceanfront setting. *Average main: $38 ✉ 1307 Front St., Lahaina ☎ 808/667–9394 🌐 www.malaoceantavern.com.*

$$$$ MODERN HAWAIIAN **Pacific'O.** Sophisticated outdoor dining on the beach (yes, truly *on* the beach) and creative Island cuisine using local, fresh-caught fish and greens and veggies grown in the restaurant's own Upcountry O'o Farm (and, quite possibly, picked that very morning)—this is the Maui dining experience you've been dreaming about. Start with the award-winning appetizer of prawn-and-basil wontons, move on to any of the fantastic fresh fish dishes, and for dessert, finish with the banana pineapple *lumpia* served hot with homemade ice cream. **Known for:** beachfront dining; in-house produce; exceptional wine list. *Average main: $38 ✉ 505 Front St., Lahaina ☎ 808/667–4341 🌐 www.pacificomaui.com.*

$$ ITALIAN **Sale Pepe.** Aromas from a wood-fired oven lure you into this cozy Italian restaurant set just off of Front Street, and the wine list tempts you to stay awhile. Quality is paramount here—the flour, mozzarella, San Marzano tomatoes, and olive oil are imported directly from Italy—and chef-owner Michele Bari (also from Italy) honed his skills at the prestigious Scuola Italiana Pizzaioli (International School of Pizza) in Venice. **Known for:** attached wine bar, A Fianco; salumi and house-made focaccia; brick-oven pizzas. *Average main: $22 ✉ 878 Front St., Units 7 and 8, Lahaina ☎ 808/667–7667 🌐 www.salepepemaui.com.*

$ ASIAN Fodor's Choice ★ **Star Noodle.** This local favorite—despite its industrial park location—is one of Maui's most popular restaurants. A communal table in the center of the room (there are smaller tables around the perimeter) sets the scene for menu-musts like the Ahi Avo, shrimp tempura, and noodle dishes like the Lahaina fried soup that's served with fat chow fun, pork, and bean sprouts. **Known for:** steamed pork buns; shared, small-plate dining; house-made noodles. *Average main: $13 ✉ 286 Kupuohi St., Lahaina ☎ 808/667–5400 🌐 www.starnoodle.com.*

KAANAPALI

$ AMERICAN **CJ's Deli & Diner.** Chef Christian Jorgensen left fancy hotel kitchens behind to open a casual place serving simple, delicious food—mango-glazed ribs, burgers, and classic Reuben sandwich—at reasonable prices including a vegan menu and kombucha on tap. If you're staying in a condo, the Chefs to Go service is a great alternative to picking up fast food (run-of-the-mill and usually lousy) as everything is prepped and comes with easy cooking instructions. **Known for:** filling, affordable food; mochiko chicken plate (a traditional Hawaiian fried chicken dish);

casual atmosphere with Wi-Fi. $ *Average main: $12* ✉ *Fairway Shops, 2580 Kekaa Dr., Kaanapali* ☎ *808/667–0968* 🌐 *www.cjsmaui.com.*

$$$ MODERN HAWAIIAN FAMILY ✕ **Hula Grill.** A bustling, family-oriented spot on Kaanapali Beach, this restaurant designed to look like a sprawling '30s beach house serves large dinner portions with an emphasis on fresh local fish. But if you're just in the mood for an umbrella-adorned cocktail and some tasty, more casual fare, head to the popular Barefoot Bar, where you can wiggle your toes in the sand. **Known for:** macadamia nut-crusted fresh catch; location along Kaanapali boardwalk; classic cocktails and lively bar scene. $ *Average main: $29* ✉ *Whalers Village shopping center, 2435 Kaanapali Pkwy., Kaanapali* ☎ *808/667–6636* 🌐 *www.hulagrillkaanapali.com.*

$$$$ ASIAN ✕ **Japengo.** Located inside the Hyatt Regency, this spot offers stunning ocean views and a gorgeous glassed-in sushi bar. The views aside, it's the food that makes Japengo worth a visit, as the award-winning sashimi-style hamachi and watermelon is delicious, the fresh local fish is well prepared—as are the sushi and hand rolls—and the desserts are amazing. **Known for:** live Hawaiian and acoustic entertainment; dishes offered in half-portions at half-price; ocean views from the bar; the flaming piña colada crème. $ *Average main: $38* ✉ *Hyatt Regency Maui Resort & Spa, 200 Nohea Kai Dr., Kaanapali* ☎ *808/667–4909* 🌐 *www.japengomaui.com* ⏲ *No lunch.*

$$$$ ITALIAN ✕ **Pulehu, an Italian Grill.** This restaurant proves that good food doesn't need to be complicated, using many local Maui products to do what the Italians do best: craft simple, delicious food that lets the ingredients shine. Must-haves include the panfried gnocchi Genovese, risotto-crusted fresh catch, and the deconstructed tiramisu. **Known for:** lobster risotto; porcini-dusted lamb chops; excellent selection of Italian wines. $ *Average main: $36* ✉ *The Westin Kaanapali Ocean Resort Villas, 6 Kai Ala Dr., Kaanapali* ☎ *808/667–3254* 🌐 *www.pulehurestaurant-maui.com* ⏲ *Closed Tues. and Wed. No lunch.*

$$$$ MODERN HAWAIIAN Fodor's Choice ★ ✕ **Roy's Kaanapali.** Roy Yamaguchi is a James Beard Award–winning chef and the granddaddy of East-meets-West cuisine. His eponymous Maui restaurant, located next to the golf course clubhouse near Kaanapali's main entrance, features signature dishes like fire-grilled, Szechuan-spiced baby back ribs, Roy's original blackened ahi, and hibachi-style grilled salmon, as well as an exceptionally user-friendly wine list. **Known for:** classic Hawaiian regional cuisine; golf course setting; hot chocolate soufflé. $ *Average main: $42* ✉ *2990 Kaanapali Pkwy., Kaanapali* ☎ *808/669–6999* 🌐 *www.royshawaii.com.*

$$$$ STEAKHOUSE ✕ **Son'z Steakhouse.** To enter the steak house, you descend a grand staircase into an amber-lighted dining room with soaring ceilings and a massive artificial lagoon complete with swans, ducks, waterfalls, and tropical gardens. Chef Geno Sarmiento's classic menu features favorites like the bone-in rib eye and Tomahawk steaks, and lighter appetites like the must-try black and blue ahi starter; the wine selection is one of Kaanapali's best. **Known for:** 100% USDA-certified-prime steaks; popular bar and happy hour; private, lagoon-front setting. $ *Average main: $40* ✉ *Hyatt Regency Maui, 200 Nohea Kai Dr., Kaanapali* ☎ *808/667–4506* 🌐 *www.sonzsteakhouse.com* ⏲ *No lunch.*

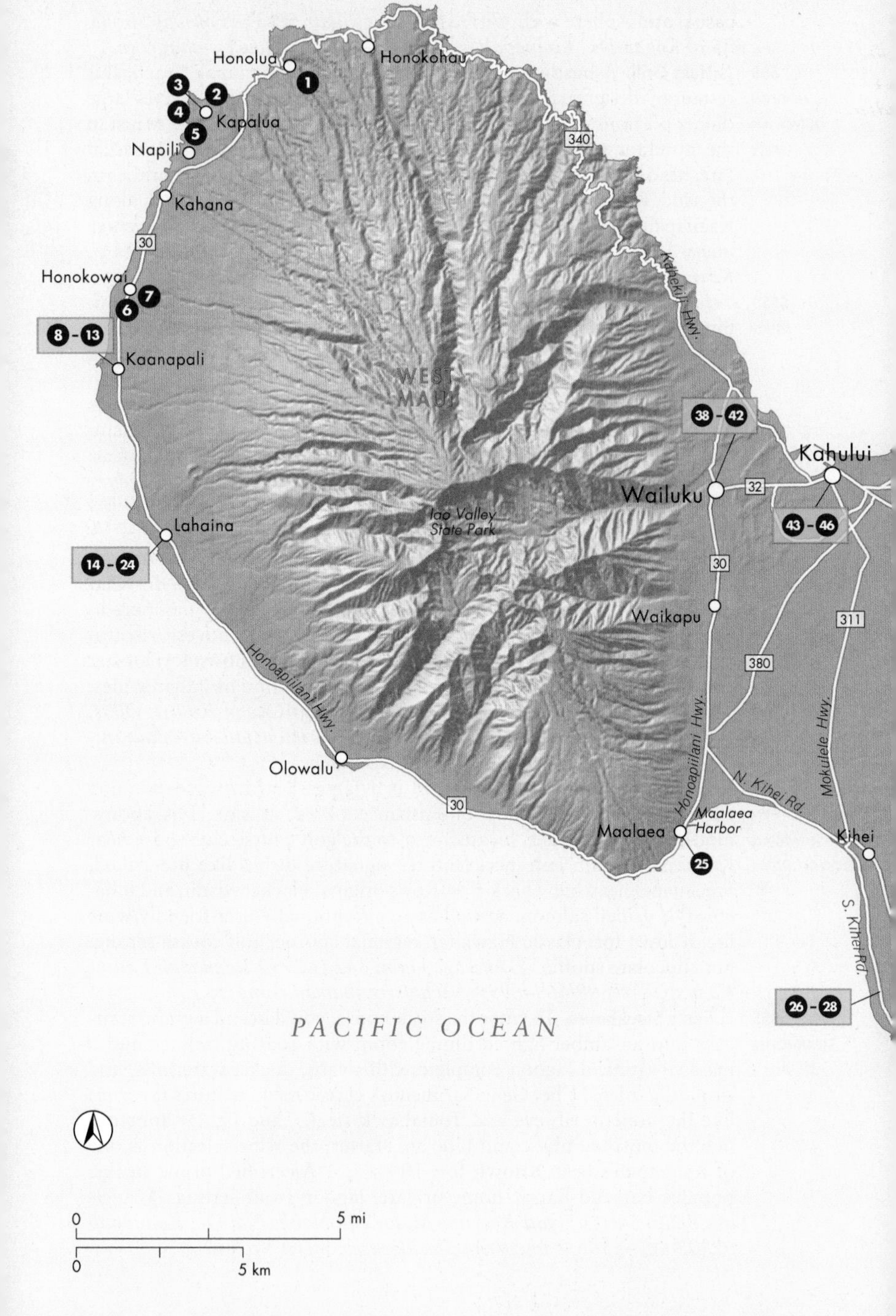

Honolua
Honokohau
Kapalua
Napili
Kahana
Honokowai
Kaanapali
Lahaina
Olowalu
Maalaea
Maalaea Harbor
Waikapu
Wailuku
Kahului
Kihei
WEST MAUI
Iao Valley State Park
Kahekili Hwy.
Honoapiilani Hwy.
Honoapiilani Hwy.
N. Kihei Rd.
Mokulele Hwy.
S. Kihei Rd.
340
30
30
30
30
32
311
380
1
2
3
4
5
6
7
8 - 13
14 - 24
25
26 - 28
38 - 42
43 - 46
PACIFIC OCEAN

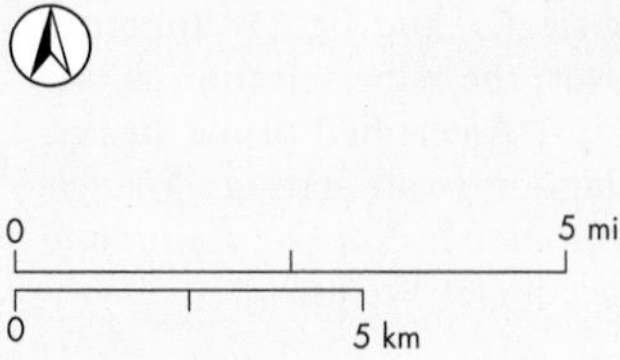

0
5 mi
0
5 km

Where to Eat on Maui

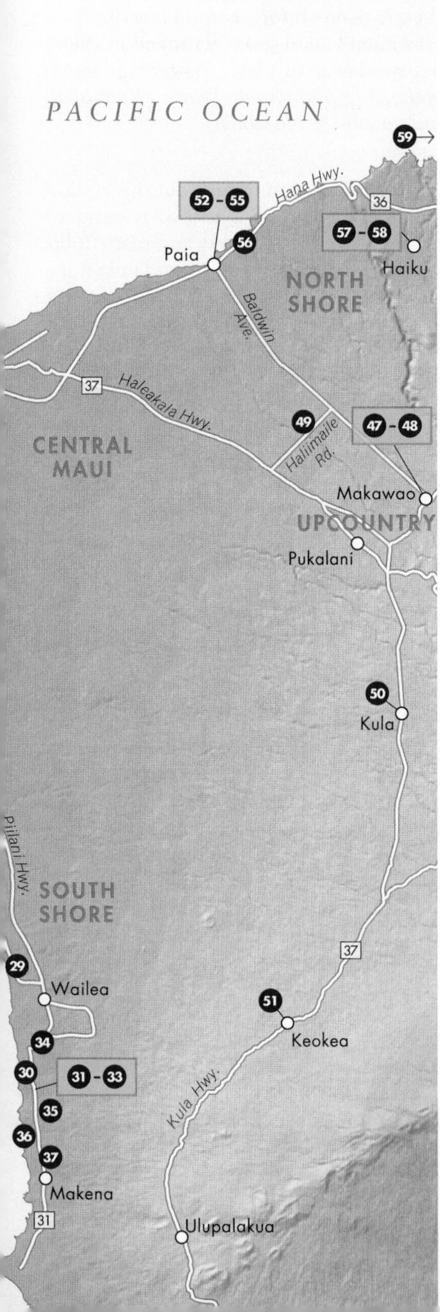

West Maui

Restaurant	No.
Aloha Mixed Plate	15
CJ's Deli & Diner	8
Frida's Mexican Beach House	22
The Gazebo Restaurant	5
Gerard's	17
Honu Seafood & Pizza	16
Hula Grill	9
Japengo	13
Lahaina Grill	20
Leoda's Kitchen and Pie Shop	24
Longhi's	18
Mala Ocean Tavern	14
Merriman's Kapalua	4
Pacific'O	19
Pineapple Grill	2
Pizza Paradiso	7
Plantation House Restaurant	1
Pulehu, an Italian Grill	6
Roy's Kaanapali	11
Sale Pepe	23
Sansei Seafood Restaurant & Sushi Bar	3
Son'z Steakhouse	10
Star Noodle	21
Tiki Terrace	12

The South Shore

Restaurant	No.
Ferraro's Bar e Ristorante	33
Humuhumunukunukuapuaa	36
Ka'ana Kitchen	31
Kihei Caffe	26
Monkeypod Kitchen	34
Morimoto Maui	32
Pita Paradise Mediterranean Bistro	35
Sarento's on the Beach	29
Seascape Maalaea Restaurant	25
South Shore Tiki Lounge	28
Spago	37
Thailand Cuisine	27
Tommy Bahama	30

Central Maui

Restaurant	No.
Aria's	41
A Saigon Cafe	42
Ba-Le Sandwiches & Plate Lunch	39
Da Kitchen	46
Marco's Grill & Deli	44
The Mill House	43
Poi by the Pound	45
Sam Sato's	38
Tokyo Tei	40

Upcountry

Restaurant	No.
Casanova Italian Restaurant & Deli	47
Grandma's Maui Coffee	51
Haliimaile General Store	49
Kula Bistro	50
Polli's Mexican Restaurant	48

North Shore

Restaurant	No.
Café des Amis	52
Cafe Mambo	55
Colleen's at the Cannery	57
Flatbread Company	53
Mama's Fish House	56
Nuka	58
Paia Fishmarket Restaurant	54

Road to Hana

Restaurant	No.
Hana Fresh Market	59

$$ MODERN HAWAIIAN **Tiki Terrace.** Executive chef Tom Muromoto is a local boy who loves to cook modern, upscale Hawaiian food, and he augments the various fresh fish dishes on his menu with items influenced by Hawaii's ethnic mix. This casual, open-air restaurant is the only place on Maui—maybe in Hawaii—where you can have a native Hawaiian combination plate that is as healthful as it is authentic. **Known for:** seafood lawalu (food wrapped in green ti leaves); Hawaiian laulau (pork wrapped in leaves that's cooked until tender); native Hawaiian plate. *Average main: $26 Kaanapali Beach Hotel, 2525 Kaanapali Pkwy., Kaanapali 808/667–0124 www.kbhmaui.com No lunch.*

KAPALUA AND NEARBY

$ DINER **The Gazebo Restaurant.** Breakfast is the reason to seek out this restaurant located poolside at the Napili Shores Resort. The food is standard diner fare, but the portions are big, the prices are low, and many folks think the pancakes—with either pineapple, bananas, macadamia nuts, or white chocolate chips— are the best in West Maui. **Known for:** ocean views with breakfast; create-your-own pancakes; enormous omelets. *Average main: $12 Napili Shores Maui, 5315 Lower Honoapiilani Hwy., Napili 808/669–5621 No dinner.*

$$$$ MODERN HAWAIIAN Fodor's Choice ★ **Merriman's Kapalua.** Perched above the postcard-perfect Kapalua Bay, this is the place to impress your date, as Chef Peter Merriman highlights the Islands' bounty by using fresh seafood and ingredients from local farms. With so many tempting creations—macadamia nut–crusted mahi or the Kahua Ranch rack of lamb—consider the duo option, which features two smaller-size entrées on one plate; gluten-free diners will be impressed with the selection as well. **Known for:** panoramic ocean views; exceptional wine list; fire pit on the outdoor lanai. *Average main: $44 One Bay Club Pl., Kapalua 808/669–6400 No lunch.*

$$$$ MODERN HAWAIIAN **Pineapple Grill.** High on the hill overlooking the Kapalua golf course, this casual restaurant offers ocean, mountain, and resort views. Menu options range from the Reuben sandwich with homemade bread at lunch to ahi poke tostadas or seafood risotto at dinner; there's an extensive wine list and selection of craft beers. **Known for:** lunch and drinks after a round of golf; pineapple upside-down cake served in a caramel rum sauce; chimichi-crusted ahi. *Average main: $38 200 Kapalua Dr., Kapalua 808/669–9600 www.pineapplegrillmaui.com.*

$ ITALIAN **Pizza Paradiso.** When it opened in 1995 this was an over-the-counter pizza place, but it's evolved over the years into a local favorite, serving Italian, Mediterranean, and Middle Eastern comfort food as well as pizza. The pies are so popular because of the top ingredients—100% pure Italian olive oil and Maui produce whenever possible. **Known for:** chicken Parmesan; gelato; pizzas with local Maui produce. *Average main: $14 Honokowai Marketplace, 3350 Lower Honoapiilani Rd., Honokowai 808/667–2929 www.pizzaparadiso.com.*

$$$$ MODERN HAWAIIAN **Plantation House Restaurant.** It's a bit of a drive, but when you get there you'll find a beautiful and comfortable restaurant with expansive views of the ocean below and the majestic mountains above. Chef JoJo Vasquez, who is known for local sourcing of as many ingredients as possible, calls his cuisine Hawaiian eclectic. **Known for:** views of Molokai from right at your table; overlooking the Plantation Golf

Course; macadamia nut–crusted Hawaiian fish. 💲 *Average main: $40* ✉ *Plantation Course Clubhouse, 2000 Plantation Club Dr., Kapalua* ☎ *808/669–6299* 🌐 *www.theplantationhouse.com.*

$$ ASIAN Fodor's Choice ★ **Sansei Seafood Restaurant & Sushi Bar.** One of the most wildly popular restaurants in Hawaii with locations on three islands, Sansei takes sushi, sashimi, and contemporary Japanese food to a new level—if you're a fish or shellfish lover, this is the place for you. There are great deals on sushi and small plates for early birds and night owls. **Known for:** award-winning Shrimp Dynamite (tempura shrimp with a garlic masago aioli); panko-crusted ahi sashimi; late-night sushi specials. 💲 *Average main: $26* ✉ *600 Office Rd., Kapalua* ☎ *808/669–6286* 🌐 *sanseihawaii.com* ⏲ *No lunch.*

3

SOUTH SHORE

South Maui's dining scene begins at Maalaea Harbor and wends its way through the beach towns of Kihei and Wailea. There are plenty of casual, relatively inexpensive eateries along the way—until you reach Wailea, where most of the dining is pricey. Some of it, fortunately, is worth it.

Feel like getting food delivered instead of eating out? **Hopper Maui** offers South Maui delivery with selections from over a dozen restaurants, and the food is brought right to your door. ☎ *808/214–6171* 🌐 *www.hoppermaui.com.*

KIHEI AND MAALAEA

$ AMERICAN Fodor's Choice ★ **Kihei Caffe.** This unassuming popular spot across the street from Kalama Beach Park has a breakfast menu that runs the gamut from healthy yogurt-filled papaya to the local classic *loco moco*—two eggs, ground beef patty, rice, and brown gravy—and everything in between. And the best thing about it is that the breakfast menu is served all day long. **Known for:** breakfast burrito; enormous portions; pork fried rice with eggs. 💲 *Average main: $9* ✉ *1945 S. Kihei Rd., Kihei* ☎ *808/879–2230* 🌐 *www.kiheicaffe.com* ⏲ *No dinner.*

$$$$ ITALIAN **Sarento's on the Beach.** This upscale Italian restaurant's setting right on spectacular Keawakapu Beach, with views of Molokini and Kahoolawe, is irresistible. The brunch menu lasts until 3 pm, and dinner has a decidedly Italian bent, with dishes like spaghetti with Kobe meatballs and veal osso buco. **Known for:** oceanfront setting; rack of lamb Placourakis; veal milanese. 💲 *Average main: $38* ✉ *2980 S. Kihei Rd., Kihei* ☎ *808/875–7555* 🌐 *www.sarentosonthebeach.com.*

$$$ SEAFOOD FAMILY **Seascape Maalaea Restaurant.** Maui Ocean Center's signature restaurant is a great choice for seafood (aquarium admission is not required to dine here) and offers harbor and ocean views from its open-air perch. The restaurant promotes heart-healthy cuisine, using sustainable seafood and trans fat–free items, and is now open for dinner three nights per week. **Known for:** crab cakes with wild-caught blue crab; island fish tacos; full kids' menu. 💲 *Average main: $28* ✉ *Maui Ocean Center, 192 Maalaea Rd., Maalaea* ☎ *808/270–7068* 🌐 *www.mauioceancenter.com* ⏲ *No dinner Mon.–Thurs.*

$ AMERICAN ✕ **South Shore Tiki Lounge.** Consistently voted "Best Bar" (and "Best Pizza") by locals, this tiki bar—tucked into Kihei Kalama Village—serves burgers, sandwiches, and delicious specialty pizzas that are crafted from scratch with sauces made from fresh roma tomatoes and Maui herbs. **Known for:** kitchen is open until 10 pm; all-day happy hour; late-night dancing under the gaze of the lounge's namesake tiki. *Average main: $15* ✉ *Kihei Kalama Village, 1913-J S. Kihei Rd., Kihei* ☎ *808/874–6444* 🌐 *www.southshoretikilounge.com.*

$ THAI ✕ **Thailand Cuisine.** Sure it's set in a shopping mall, but the care and expense that has gone into the interior—glittering Buddhist shrines, elaborate hardwood facades, fancy napkin folds, and matching blue china—also applies to the cuisine. Start with the coconut-ginger chicken soup, then continue with flavorful pad Thai and curries before finishing off this authentic meal with fried bananas and ice cream. **Known for:** crispy fried chicken; family dinners for two or four; tom yum seafood soup. *Average main: $15* ✉ *Kukui Mall, 1819 S. Kihei Rd., Kihei* ☎ *808/875–0839* 🌐 *www.thailandcuisinemaui.net* ⊙ *No lunch Sun.*

WAILEA AND SOUTH SHORE (MAKENA)

$$$$ ITALIAN ✕ **Ferraro's Bar e Ristorante.** Overlooking the ocean from a bluff above Wailea Beach, this outdoor Italian restaurant at Four Seasons Resort Maui at Wailea is beautiful both day and night. For lunch, indulge in a lobster sandwich or one of a variety of stone-baked pizzas, and at dinner, try the Italian-inspired salads and a house-made pasta. **Known for:** romantic ambience; excellent selection of Italian wines; classical music in the moonlight. *Average main: $42* ✉ *Four Seasons Resort Maui at Wailea, 3900 Wailea Alanui Dr., Wailea* ☎ *808/874–8000* 🌐 *www.fourseasons.com/maui.*

$$$$ MODERN HAWAIIAN ✕ **Humuhumunukunukuapuaa.** This Polynesian-style thatch-roof, open-air restaurant "floats" atop a saltwater lagoon, which gives it an exotic romantic feel that's suited for special occasions. Obviously, fresh fish dominates the menu here, but there's also Tomahawk Ribeye steaks and flavorful racks of lamb. **Known for:** ulu risotto; sunset views; humu chocolate garden dessert. *Average main: $45* ✉ *Grand Wailea, 3850 Wailea Alanui Dr., Wailea* ☎ *808/875–1234* 🌐 *www.grandwailea.com* ⊙ *No lunch.*

$$$$ MODERN HAWAIIAN Fodor's Choice ★ ✕ **Ka'ana Kitchen.** This signature restaurant at the island's most stylish luxury resort, Andaz Maui at Wailea, has it all: ingredients sourced within the Islands, marvelous wine list, stellar service, and spectacular views from every table. The whole space has been masterfully designed—there are dining seats available at the cocktail bar and at strategic locations around the gorgeous exhibition kitchen "counters"—and guests are encouraged to walk around to see what the cadre of cooks are up to and ask questions. **Known for:** breakfast buffet; home-inspired layout; plantation flavors with a modern twist. *Average main: $40* ✉ *Andaz Maui at Wailea, 3550 Wailea Alanui Dr., Wailea* ☎ *808/573–1234* 🌐 *www.maui.andaz.hyatt.com* ⊙ *No lunch.*

$$ ECLECTIC ✕ **Monkeypod Kitchen.** The wooden surfboards hanging above the bar and surf videos playing in the background set a decidedly chill vibe at this buzzing restaurant, the creation of local celebrity-chef Peter Merriman. He offers a menu that highlights local bounty, with such standout

dishes as poke tacos, pumpkin ravioli, and a wood-fired, Bourgeois pizza that's topped with lobster, wild mushrooms, and garlic white sauce. **Known for:** craft cocktails like the Monkeypod mai tai; seared ahi melt; late-night happy hour until 11 pm. $ *Average main: $25* ✉ *10 Wailea Ike Dr., Wailea* ☎ *808/891–2322* 🌐 *www.monkeypodkitchen.com/wailea.*

$$$$ MODERN ASIAN Fodor's Choice ★

Morimoto Maui. "Iron Chef" Masaharu Morimoto's eponymous restaurant, located at the Andaz Maui resort, has some of Maui's most creative presentations and arguably, some of its best food. Outdoor tables, a bustling dining room, and a sushi bar all make it a lively choice, but the food is ultimately the reason to go, where you can feast on slices of tuna pizza, or go all-in with an omakase dinner that includes seven or 10 different courses. **Known for:** pork gyoza with bacon foam; bagna cauda, served with a hot oil bath; Waialua chocolate doughnuts, served with sake caramel. $ *Average main: $43* ✉ *Andaz Maui at Wailea, 3550 Wailea Alanui Dr., Wailea* ☎ *808/243–4766* 🌐 *www.morimotomaui.com.*

$$ MEDITERRANEAN Fodor's Choice ★

Pita Paradise Mediterranean Bistro. This restaurant's owner is a fisherman himself, so you know the fish here is the freshest available. Lunch features affordable and delicious sandwiches and burgers, but in the evening the space is transformed into an Italian-Greek bistro with entrées like chicken fettuccine and moussaka; save room for the award-winning baklava ice-cream cake. **Known for:** Mediterranean chicken pita; baklava ice-cream cake with Roselani ice cream; lamb gnocchi, made in-house. $ *Average main: $20* ✉ *Wailea Gateway Center, 34 Wailea Ike Dr., A-108, Wailea* ☎ *808/879–7177* 🌐 *www.pitaparadisehawaii.com.*

$$$$ MODERN HAWAIIAN

Spago. It's a marriage made in Hawaii heaven: the California cuisine of celebrity-chef Wolfgang Puck combined with Maui flavors and served lobby-level and oceanfront at the luxurious Four Seasons Resort. Try the spicy ahi poke in sesame-miso cones to start and then see what the chefs-in-residence can do with some of Maui's fantastic local fish. **Known for:** exceptional wine list; pan-roasted opakapaka with lobster-crusted potatoes; wild lilikoi crème brûlée. $ *Average main: $46* ✉ *Four Seasons Resort Maui at Wailea, 3900 Wailea Alanui Dr., Wailea* ☎ *808/879–2999* 🌐 *www.wolfgangpuck.com* ⏲ *No lunch.*

$$$ MODERN AMERICAN Fodor's Choice ★

Tommy Bahama. It's more "Island-style" than Hawaii—and yes, it's a chain—but the food is consistently great, the service is filled with aloha, and the ambience is Island refined. Try the ahi poke or the Kalua pork sandwich, and the crab bisque is worthy of a cross-island drive—as are the desserts. **Known for:** miso-glazed King Salmon; wagyu beef burger; festive bar scene. $ *Average main: $35* ✉ *The Shops at Wailea, 3750 Wailea Alanui Dr., Wailea* ☎ *808/875–9983* 🌐 *www.tommybahama.com.*

CENTRAL MAUI

Central Maui is where the locals live, and the area where you can find just about every ethnic cuisine in the Islands. Savory saimin shops and small joints dishing up *loco moco*—hamburger patties set on top of two scoops of rice with rich brown gravy—are plentiful. Be sure to check out Wailuku: drive along Lower Main Street, and take a chance on any of the numerous mom-and-pop eateries—it's truly a culinary adventure. If you walk along historic Market Street, you can shop for antiques between bites.

Kahului offers more variety, because it's in the main traffic corridor and near the big-box stores; on a few menus you can even find potatoes instead of rice. If you want to eat like a local and, more importantly, at local prices, don't miss Central Maui.

KAHULUI

$ ECLECTIC FAMILY Fodor's Choice ★

Da Kitchen. This extremely popular purveyor of all food "local" is bright, shiny, comfortable, and just minutes from Kahului airport. Try the signature mahimahi tempura, loco moco, Hawaiian plate, chicken katsu, and daily mixed bentos; and rest assured that everything on the menu is delicious and portions are gigantic.There's an "express" location in Kihei, but we recommend the happy, always-crowded Kahului location. **Known for:** fried spam musubi; enormous plate lunches; Polynesian paralysis moco with fish tempura, kalua pork, two eggs, onion, mushrooms, and gravy—all served over fried rice. *Average main: $16 425 Koloa St., Kahului 808/871–7782 www.dakitchen.com Closed Sun.*

$$ ITALIAN

Marco's Grill & Deli. One of the go-to places for airport comers and goers, this popular Italian restaurant also draws a steady crowd of local residents, mostly for "business" lunches. Meatballs, sausages, and sauces are all made in-house, there's a long list of sandwiches that are available all day, and the affordable salads are big enough to share; substitutions or special requests are not recommended. **Known for:** gluten-free options; chicken Parmesan; proximity to Kahului airport. *Average main: $18 444 Hana Hwy., Kahului 808/877–4446.*

$ HAWAIIAN

Poi by the Pound. If you're looking for authentic Hawaiian food, this local favorite near Kahului airport is the best place to find it. The luau leaf is grown here on Maui and you can pick up the taro-based snack, *kulolo,* as well as staples like laulau, lomi salmon, poke, squid luau, and poi; this is distinctly different from "local food" of the typical mixed-plate variety, which usually draws from a mixed heritage background and technically isn't Hawaiian. **Known for:** huge portions of Hawaiian food; proximity to Kahului airport; Hawaiian plate with laulau, kaulua pork, chicken long rice, lomi salmon, poke, poi, and mac salad. *Average main: $16 430 Kele St., Kahului 808/283–9381 www.poibythepound.com.*

WAILUKU

$$ ASIAN FUSION

Aria's. Dinner and lunch items are affordable and delicious at this Asian bistro, but Sunday breakfast is equally tempting. At lunch, try the flavor-packed *char siu bao* (barbecue-pork-filled bun) sliders and the gigantic crab club sandwich, and favorite dinner options include the Asian-braised pork belly and the vegetarian putanesca. **Known for:** location in Wailuku's Old Town; upscale dining at affordable prices; braised chocolate chipotle lamb shank. *Average main: $19* *2062 W. Vineyard St., Wailuku* *808/242–2742* *ariasmaui.com* *No dinner Sun.–Wed.*

$$ VIETNAMESE **A Saigon Cafe.** Locals have been flocking to this off-the-beaten path gem for years, lured in by the reliably delicious Vietnamese cuisine served family-style at decent prices. It's tucked behind a nondescript overpass—and only recently did they put a sign on its building—but you can't go wrong with the green papaya salad, rice in a clay pot, and the make-your-own Vietnamese burritos. **Known for:** funky, out-of-the-way location; authentic Com Tay Cam (rice in a clay pot); known locally as "Jennifer's". *Average main: $19* *1792 Main St., Wailuku* *808/243–9560* *www.asaigoncafe.com.*

$ VIETNAMESE Fodor's Choice ★ **Ba-Le Sandwiches & Plate Lunch.** It began as a French-Vietnamese bakery on Oahu and has branched into popular small restaurants sprinkled throughout the Islands. Some are kiosks in malls; others are standalones with some picnic tables out front, as is the case at this location The Vietnamese *pho* (the famous soups laden with seafood or rare beef, fresh basil, bean sprouts, and lime) share menu space with local-style saimin and plates of barbecue or spicy chicken, beef, pork, or local fish served with jasmine rice. **Known for:** affordable Vietnamese cuisine; banh mi; opakapaka with garlic shrimp. *Average main: $10* *1824 Oihana St., Wailuku* *808/249–8833* *www.balemaui.com.*

$$$ ECLECTIC **The Mill House.** The food is so fresh at this Waikapu standout that while seated at your mountain view table you can see the fields where the food was grown. The innovative creative cuisine is dependent upon the seasons, but some of the staples include chicken bao, gnocchi, pork belly, and ceviche; on select nights, they also offer a multicourse, award-winning Chef's Table. **Known for:** tapas-style small-plate dining; innovative flavors and farm-to-table freshness; eclectic menu that changes daily. *Average main: $27* *1670 Honoapiilani Hwy., Waikapu* *808/270–0333* *www.millhousemaui.com* *No breakfast.*

$ HAWAIIAN Fodor's Choice ★ **Sam Sato's.** Every island has its noodle shrine, and this is Maui's. Dry mein, saimin, chow fun—they all come in different-size portions and with add-ins to satisfy every noodle craving; try a teriyaki beef stick or two while you wait for your bowl. **Known for:** manju (a traditional Japanese pastry filled with bean paste); turnovers (pineapple, coconut, apple, or peach); affordable local hideout. *Average main: $8* *The Millyard, 1750 Wili Pa Loop, Wailuku* *808/244–7124* *No credit cards* *Closed Sun. No dinner.*

$ JAPANESE Fodor's Choice ★ **Tokyo Tei.** Tucked in the back corner of a covered parking garage, Tokyo Tei is worth seeking out for wonderful local-style Japanese food; at lunch you can rub elbows with bankers and construction workers, and at dinner, three generations might be celebrating *tutu's* (grandma's) birthday at the next table. Enjoy the freshest sashimi, feather-light yet crispy shrimp and vegetable tempura, and local-style bentos and plate lunches. **Known for:** bona fide local institution that's been around for more than eight decades; misoyaki-glazed fish; unlikeliest of locations for great food. *Average main: $12* *1063 Lower Main St., Wailuku* *808/242–9630* *www.tokyoteimaui.com* *No lunch Sun. Closed Mon.–Sat. 1:30–5 pm.*

UPCOUNTRY

Take the drive up the slopes of magnificent Mt. Haleakala and you can find an abundance of restaurants catering to both locals and visitors. Haliimaile General Store is a landmark in the middle of rolling pineapple fields (Maui Gold Pineapple Company is still growing pineapple in this area), and in the *paniolo* (cowboy) town of Makawao you can sidle up to everything from an Italian restaurant to a farm-to-table standout. Upcountry also encompasses cool Kula, with a few mom-and-pops. Many visitors opt to check out nearby farm tours between meals.

$$$ ITALIAN **Casanova Italian Restaurant & Deli.** An authentic Italian dinner house and nightclub—the place turns positively raucous (in a good way) on Wednesday, Friday, and Saturday nights—this place is smack in the middle of Maui's paniolo town of Makawao. The brick wood-burning oven, imported from Italy, has been turning out perfect pies and steaming-hot focaccia for more than 20 years; you can pair a pie with a salad (they're all big enough to share) and a couple of glasses of wine without breaking the bank. **Known for:** fabulous deli for breakfast, cappuccino, croissants, and people-watching; linguine pescatore; $5 wine carafes from 5 to 6 pm. *Average main: $28 1188 Makawao Ave., Makawao 808/572–0220 www.casanovamaui.com.*

$ AMERICAN **Grandma's Maui Coffee.** If you're taking a drive through gorgeous Upcountry, this is a great place to stop for a truly homegrown cup of coffee and a snack. The baked goods are fabulous, and the variety of menu items for breakfast and lunch is vast. **Known for:** Keokea omelet; coffee roasted on-site; idyllic country location. *Average main: $12 9232 Kula Hwy., Keokea 808/878–2140 www.grandmascoffee.com.*

$$$$ MODERN HAWAIIAN **Haliimaile General Store.** Chef-restaurateur Beverly Gannon's first restaurant remains a culinary destination after more than a quarter century, serving classic dishes like Bev's "Famous" Crab Pizza and Asian duck, brie, and grape quesadilla; there are daily and nightly specials as well. The big, rambling former plantation store has two dining rooms: sit in the front to be seen and heard; head on back for some quiet and privacy. **Known for:** Bev Gannon's classic recipes; exquisite dining and specialty cocktails in an unlikely location; paniolo ribs served with a housemade citrus barbecue sauce. *Average main: $38 900 Haliimaile Rd., Haliimaile Take the exit on the left halfway up Haleakala Hwy. 808/572–2666 www.hgsmaui.com.*

$$ ITALIAN **Kula Bistro.** Dishing up home-style comfort food with an Italian accent, this out-of-the-way eatery is worth the drive to scenic Kula, no matter when you arrive. Start the day with their crab cake Benedict, grab any one of their outstanding panini around lunchtime, or come for dinner, when a dizzying array of choices await, including favorites such as vodka pomodoro with seafood, vegetable lasagna, and filet mignon. **Known for:** BYOB; family and group friendly; enormous chicken Parmesan that's big enough for two. *Average main: $25 4566 Lower Kula Rd., Kula 808/871–2960 www.kulabistro.com No breakfast Mon.*

$ MEXICAN Fodor's Choice ★ **Polli's Mexican Restaurant.** A Makawao staple since 1981, Polli's is set in the town's only intersection. The margaritas are legendary, and the enormous fajitas, burritos, and enchiladas ensure you'll never leave hungry; there are vegetarian options too. **Known for:** mango margaritas; seafood enchilada with black beans; surf videos on the television and a group of regulars at the bar. *Average main: $16* *1202 Makawao Ave., Makawao* *808/572–7808* *www.pollis-mexicanrestaurant.com.*

NORTH SHORE

The North Shore sets the dramatic stage for Maui's most famous—and most expensive—restaurant, Mama's Fish House in Kuau. The area also encompasses the great food town of Paia and the up-and-coming restaurant town of Haiku. Be sure to bring your bathing suit for a dip in the ocean at one of the nearby beaches.

HAIKU

$$ AMERICAN Fodor's Choice ★ **Colleen's at the Cannery.** You'd never guess what's inside by the nondescript exterior and the location in an old pineapple cannery–cum–strip mall, but this is one of Maui's most overlooked and underrated restaurants. Popular with locals for breakfast and lunch, dinner's when the candles come out and it's time for martinis and fresh fish; you'll feel like you're at a hip urban eatery. **Known for:** excellent food featuring Upcountry's best produce; specialty artisan pizzas and enormous salads; eggs Benedict and Bloody Marys. *Average main: $20* *Haiku Cannery Marketplace, 810 Haiku Rd., Haiku-Pauwela* *808/575–9211* *www.colleensinhaiku.com.*

$$ ASIAN FUSION **Nuka.** This off-the-beaten-path izakaya-style Japanese eatery is worth the trek to sleepy Haiku. Diners flock here for the eclectic menu that includes everything from specialty French fries and fusion sushi rolls to fresh sashimi and some of the best tempura around—all based on what's fresh from local farmers and fishermen. **Known for:** so popular it's hard to get a table; homemade green tea and black sesame ice cream; exceptional sushi and sashimi. *Average main: $18* *780 Haiku Rd., Haiku-Pauwela* *808/575–2939* *www.nukamaui.com* *Closed daily 1:30–4:30 pm. No lunch on weekends.*

KUAU

$$$$ SEAFOOD **Mama's Fish House.** Set in an intimate location on the beach, Mama's has been *the* Maui destination for special occasions for almost four decades. A path of gecko-shape stones leads to an ever-changing fantasyland of Hawaiian kitsch, where savvy servers can explain the various fish types and preparations, and you'd be wise to heed their recommendation; the fish is so fresh that the daily menu lists who caught it that morning. **Known for:** Polynesian Black Pearl dessert; exceptionally fresh fish; ambience and romance. *Average main: $50* *799 Poho Pl.* *808/579–8488* *www.mamasfishhouse.com.*

PAIA

$ ECLECTIC **Café des Amis.** The menu at this budget-friendly café is a little neurotic—in a good way—featuring Mediterranean and Indian dishes, but the food is fresh and tasty. Expect flavors and preparations not easily obtainable at other Island eateries, with a nice selection of sweet and savory crepes, Indian wraps, and salads and cocktails, wine, and beer to compliment. **Known for:** delicious, good-value food like the chicken, avocado, and mozzarella crepe; butternut squash and garbanzo bean curry served with complimentary chutney; excellent people-watching. *Average main: $16 42 Baldwin Ave., Paia 808/579–6323 www.cdamaui.com.*

$ ECLECTIC **Cafe Mambo.** Paia is one of Maui's most interesting food towns, and this colorful, airy, and brightly painted hangout is right in the thick of things. The menu features everything from burgers and fish to Mediterranean tastes, and aside from the great, well-priced food, the people-watching is fascinating. **Known for:** kalua duck quesadilla; slow-cooked lamb in Moroccan spices; locally inspired tapas. *Average main: $15 30 Baldwin Ave., Paia 808/579–8021 www.cafemambomaui.com.*

$$ PIZZA FAMILY **Flatbread Company.** This Vermont-based company marched right in to Paia in 2007 and instantly became a popular restaurant and a valued addition to the community as it gives back to local nonprofits. The bustling restaurant uses organic, local, sustainable products, including 100% organically grown wheat for the made-fresh-daily dough, and it's a good spot to take the kids; there's a no-reservations policy, but there's "call-ahead seating," so you can put your name on the wait list before you arrive. **Known for:** Mopsy kalua pork pizza served with kiawe-smoked free-range pork shoulder and homemade organic mango barbecue sauce; jam-packed Tuesday benefit nights; wood-fired, clay-oven pizzas and the small but lively bar. *Average main: $22 89 Hana Hwy., Paia 808/579–8989 www.flatbreadcompany.com.*

$ SEAFOOD Fodor's Choice ★ **Paia Fishmarket Restaurant.** If you're okay with communal picnic tables, or taking your meal to a nearby beach, this place in funky Paia town serves, arguably, the best fresh fish for the best prices on this side of the island. Four preparations are offered and, on any given day, there are at least four to six fresh fishes from which to choose; there are burgers, chicken, and pasta for the non–fish fans. **Known for:** delectable side dishes; grilled opah; local fish and local beer at low, local prices. *Average main: $15 100 Hana Hwy., Paia 808/579–8030 www.paiafishmarket.com.*

ROAD TO HANA

HANA

$ AMERICAN Fodor's Choice ★ **Hana Fresh Market.** Directly in front of (and associated with) Hana Health, you'll find rows of tables laden with delicious and organic fresh salads and entrées worthy of any chic farm-to-table restaurant. Fresh fish plates, poke bowls, panini, and wraps are just a few of the always-changing choices, and best of all, the produce comes from the restaurant's own farm, directly behind the health center. **Known for:** freshly made salads and hot panini; fish kebabs; locally grown coffee and fresh fruit smoothies. $ *Average main: $10* ✉ *4590 Hana Hwy., Hana* ✥ *Located between mile markers 34 and 35* ☎ *808/248–7515* 🌐 *www.hanafresh.org* ⏲ *No breakfast or dinner.*

WHERE TO STAY

Updated by Christie Leon

Maui's accommodations run the gamut from rural bed-and-breakfasts to opulent megaresorts, and in between there's something for every vacation style and budget. The large resorts, hotels, and condominiums for which Maui is noted are on the sunny, leeward, southern, and western shores. They bustle with activity and are near plenty of restaurants, shopping, golf, and water sports. Those seeking a different experience can try the inns, B&Bs, and rentals in the small towns and quieter areas along the North Shore and Upcountry on the verdant slopes of Haleakala.

If the latest and greatest is your style, be prepared to spend a small fortune. Properties like the Ritz-Carlton, Kapalua; the Four Seasons Resort Maui at Wailea; the sparkling Andaz Maui at Wailea; and condo complexes such as the luxe Wailea Beach Villas may set you back at least $600 a night.

Although there aren't many of them, small B&Bs are charming. They tend to be in residential or rural neighborhoods around the island, sometimes beyond the resort areas of West Maui and the South Shore. The B&Bs offer both a personalized experience and a window into authentic local life. The rates tend to be the lowest available on Maui, sometimes less than $200 per night.

Apartment and condo rentals are ideal for families, groups of friends, and those traveling on modest budgets. Not only are the nightly rates lower than hotel rooms, but eating in—all have kitchens of some description—is substantially less expensive than dining out. There are literally hundreds of these units all over the island, ranging in size from studios to luxurious four-bedroom properties with multiple baths. The vast majority are found along the sunny coasts, from Makena to Kihei on the South Shore and Lahaina up to Kapalua in West Maui.

Rates depend on the size of the unit and its proximity to the beach, as well as the amenities and services offered. For about $250 a night, you can get a lovely one-bedroom apartment without many frills or flourishes, close to but probably not on the beach. Many rentals have minimum stays (usually three to five nights).

Most of Maui's resorts—several are megaresorts—have opulent gardens, fantasy swimming pools, championship golf courses, and full-service fitness centers and spas. Expect to spend at least $350 a night at the less posh resort hotels; they are all in the Wailea resort area on the South Shore and Kaanapali in West Maui. At all lodgings, ask about discounts and deals (free nights with longer stays, for example), which have proliferated. Unfortunately, most resorts now charge both parking and resort fees.

CONDOS AND RENTALS

The recent boom in high-end condo developments in Wailea, North Kaanapali, and Kapalua means you no longer have to compromise on luxury to get the comfort and convenience of a condo rental. For those seeking more budget-friendly options, condos in West Maui in Napili, Honokowai, or Kahana, and on the South Shore in Kihei remain a smart choice. Many are oceanfront and offer the amenities of a hotel without the cost. Be sure to ask about minimum stays. Besides the condos listed here, Maui has condos rented through central agents. They may represent an entire resort property, most of the units at one property, or even individually owned units. The companies listed here have a long history of excellent service to Maui visitors.

AA Oceanfront Rentals and Sales. As the name suggests, the specialty is "oceanfront." With rental units in more than 25 condominium complexes on the South Shore from the northernmost reaches of Kihei all the way to Wailea, there's something for everyone at rates that run $90–$450 a night. ✉ *1279 S. Kihei Rd., #107, Kihei* ☎ *808/879–7288, 800/488–6004* 🌐 *www.aaoceanfront.com.*

Bello Maui Vacations. These real-estate experts have a full range of vacation rentals in 20 South Shore condominium complexes. They also have gorgeous houses for rent. Condos start at around $100 per night (most are $200 or less); houses will run you up to $1,700 a night. ✉ *95 E. Lipoa, #201, Kihei* ☎ *808/879–3328, 800/541–3060* 🌐 *www.bellomaui.com.*

Chase 'n Rainbows. Family-owned and -operated, this is the largest property management company in West Maui, with the largest selection of rentals, from studios to three bedrooms. Rentals are everywhere from Lahaina town to Kapalua. Rates run about $100–$1,500 per night. The company has been in business since 1980, and is good at what it does. ✉ *118 Kupuohi St., Suite C6, Lahaina* ☎ *808/667–7088, 877/611–6022* 🌐 *www.westmauicondos.com.*

Destination Residences Hawaii. If it's the South Shore luxury of Wailea and Makena you seek, look no further. This company has hundreds of condominiums and villas ranging in size from studios to five bedrooms, and in price from $189 per night for a studio at Wailea Grand Champions Villas, to more than $4,000 (yes, per night) for the splashy Wailea Beach Villas. The company offers excellent personalized service (including a $155 restaurant/spa credit and a Tesla shuttle service—all included in the price) and is known for particularly fine housekeeping services. Check-in for all properties is at the company's well-appointed office in Wailea Gateway. ✉ *34 Wailea Gateway Pl., Suite A102, Wailea* ☎ *808/891–6200, 800/367–5246* 🌐 *www.destinationresidenceshawaii.com.*

Maalaea Bay Realty and Rentals. A little strip of condominiums within the isthmus that links Central and West Maui, Maalaea is often overlooked, but it shouldn't be. This company has more than 100 one- and two-bedroom units at $100–$300 per night. The wind is usually strong here, but there's a nice beach, a harbor, and some good shopping and decent restaurants. ✉ *280 Hauoli St., Maalaea* ☎ *808/244–5627, 800/367–6084* 🌐 *www.maalaeabay.com.*

Maui Condo & Home Vacations. This Maui-based agency manages more than 200 condos. Most units are near the beach or golf courses, and are located in Kihei, Wailea, and West Maui. Studios to three-bedroom units run $100–$450 per night. ✉ *1819 S. Kihei Rd., Suite D103, Kihei* ☎ *800/451–5008* 🌐 *www.mauicondo.com.*

Private Paradise Villas. For exceptional accommodations and service, this company has it all. It books huge, luxurious condominium villas and private beach houses, and provides customized services with attention to the smallest details. Rates start at $750 per night for a villa up to $16,500 per night for a home. ✉ *310 Ohukai Rd., Suite 304, Kihei* ☎ *888/875–2818* 🌐 *www.tropicalvillavacations.com.*

3

WEST MAUI

LAHAINA

Lahaina doesn't have a huge range of accommodations, but it does make a great headquarters for active families or those who want to avoid spending a bundle on resorts. One major advantage is the proximity of restaurants, shops, and activities—everything is within walking distance. It's a business district, however, and won't provide the same peace and quiet as resorts or secluded vacation rentals. Still, Lahaina has a nostalgic charm, especially early in the morning before the streets have filled with visitors and vendors.

$$$$ B&B/INN Fodor's Choice ★ **Hooilo House.** A luxurious intimate getaway without resort facilities, this stunning, 2-acre B&B in the foothills of the West Maui Mountains, just south of Lahaina town, exemplifies quiet perfection. **Pros:** friendly, on-site hosts (Amy and Dan Martin); beautiful furnishings; gazebo for weddings and special events. **Cons:** not good for families with younger children; three-night minimum; far from shops and restaurants. $ *Rooms from: $369* ✉ *138 Awaiku St., Lahaina* ☎ *808/667–6669* 🌐 *www.hooilohouse.com* *6 rooms* *Free breakfast.*

$ B&B/INN **Lahaina Inn.** An antique jewel in the heart of town, this two-story timbered building will transport romantics back to the turn of the 20th century. **Pros:** easy walking distance to shops, restaurants, and attractions; lovely antique style; the price is right. **Cons:** rooms are small, bathrooms particularly so; some street noise; two stories, no elevator. $ *Rooms from: $119* ✉ *127 Lahainaluna Rd., Lahaina* ☎ *808/661–0577, 800/222–5642* 🌐 *www.lahainainn.com* *12 units* *No meals.*

$$ RENTAL **Lahaina Shores Beach Resort.** You really can't get any closer to the beach than this seven-story rental property that offers panoramic ocean and mountain views and fully equipped kitchens. **Pros:** right on the beach; historical sites, attractions, and activities are a short walk away; no additional costs and no resort fee. **Cons:** older property; no posh, resort-type amenities; no restaurant on-site. $ *Rooms from: $250* ✉ *475 Front St., Lahaina* ☎ *808/661–4835, 866/934–9176* 🌐 *www.lahainashores.com* *199 rooms* *No meals.*

KAANAPALI

With its long stretch of beach lined with luxury resorts, shops, and restaurants, Kaanapali is a playground. Expect top-class service here, and everything you could want a few steps from your room, including

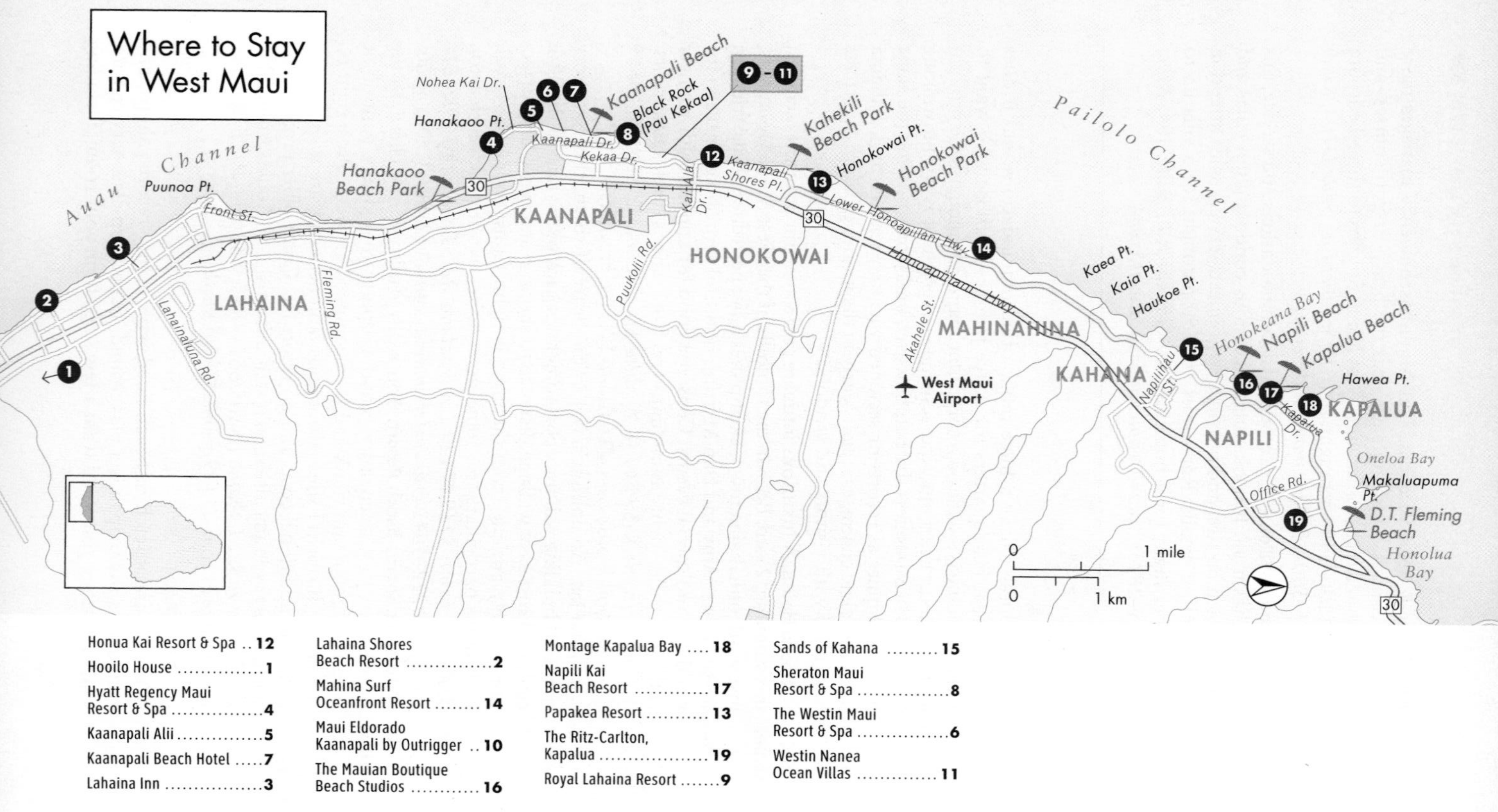

Honua Kai Resort & Spa .. 12
Hooilo House ... 1
Hyatt Regency Maui Resort & Spa ... 4
Kaanapali Alii ... 5
Kaanapali Beach Hotel ... 7
Lahaina Inn ... 3
Lahaina Shores Beach Resort ... 2
Mahina Surf Oceanfront Resort ... 14
Maui Eldorado Kaanapali by Outrigger .. 10
The Mauian Boutique Beach Studios ... 16
Montage Kapalua Bay ... 18
Napili Kai Beach Resort ... 17
Papakea Resort ... 13
The Ritz-Carlton, Kapalua ... 19
Royal Lahaina Resort ... 9
Sands of Kahana ... 15
Sheraton Maui Resort & Spa ... 8
The Westin Maui Resort & Spa ... 6
Westin Nanea Ocean Villas ... 11

WHERE TO STAY IN MAUI

	Local Vibe	Pros	Cons
West Maui	Popular and busy, West Maui includes the picturesque, touristy town of Lahaina and the upscale resort areas of Kaanapali and Kapalua.	A wide variety of shops, water sports, and historic sites provide plenty to do. To relax, there are great beaches and brilliant sunsets.	Traffic is usually congested; parking is hard to find; beaches can be crowded.
South Shore	The protected South Shore of Maui offers diverse experiences and accommodations, from comfortable condos to luxurious resorts—and golf, golf, golf.	Many beautiful beaches; sunny weather; great snorkeling.	Numerous strip malls; crowded with condos; there can be lots of traffic.
Upcountry	Country and chic come together in farms, ranches, and trendy towns on the cool, green slopes of Haleakala.	Cooler weather at higher elevations; panoramic views of nearby islands; distinctive shops, boutiques, galleries, and restaurants.	Fewer restaurants; no nightlife; can be very dark at night and difficult to drive for those unfamiliar with roads and conditions.
North Shore	A hub for surfing, windsurfing, and kiteboarding. When the surf's not up, the focus is on shopping: Paia is full of galleries, shops, and hip eateries.	Wind and waves are terrific for water sports; colorful small towns to explore without the intrusion of big resorts.	Weather inland may not be as sunny as other parts of the island, and coastal areas can be windy; little nightlife; most stores in Paia close early, around 6 pm.
Road to Hana and East Maui	Remote and rural, laid-back and tropical Hana and East Maui are special places to unwind.	Natural experience; rugged coastline and lush tropical scenery; lots of waterfalls.	Accessed by a long and winding road; no nightlife; wetter weather; few places to eat or shop.

the calm waters of sun-kissed Kaanapali Beach. Wandering along the beach path between resorts is a recreational activity unto itself. Weather is dependably warm, and for that reason as well as all the others, Kaanapali is a popular—at times, downright crowded—destination.

$$$$ RESORT FAMILY **Hyatt Regency Maui Resort & Spa.** Splashing waterfalls, swim-through grottoes, a lagoonlike swimming pool, and a 150-foot waterslide "wow" guests of all ages at this bustling Kaanapali resort; the grounds are the big deal as rooms are modest presentations of plantation style, with a little sitting area and lanai. **Pros:** nightly Drums of the Pacific luau and the must-see rooftop Astronomy Tour of the Stars; contemporary restaurant and bar; water wonderland will thrill families. **Cons:** can be difficult to find a space in self-parking; popular resort might not offer the most peaceful escape; daily resort and parking fees. *Rooms from: $559* ✉ *200 Nohea Kai Dr., Kaanapali* ☎ *808/661–1234* 🌐 *www.maui.regency.hyatt.com* *806 rooms* *No meals.*

$$$$ RENTAL **Kaanapali Alii.** Amenities like daily maid service, an activities desk, a small store with complimentary DVDs for guests to borrow, and a 24-hour front-desk service—and no pesky resort fees—make this a winning choice for families and those wanting to play house on Maui's most stunning shores. **Pros:** large comfortable units on the beach; quiet compared to other hotels in the resort; free parking. **Cons:** parking can be crowded during high season; no on-site restaurant; small pools can get crowded. *Rooms from: $585* *50 Nohea Kai Dr., Kaanapali* *808/667–1400, 877/713–2844* *www.kaanapalialii.com* *264 units* *No meals.*

$$ HOTEL Fodor's Choice ★ **Kaanapali Beach Hotel.** This charming beachfront hotel is full of aloha—locals say it's one of the few resorts on the island where you can get a true Hawaiian experience as the entire staff takes part in the hotel's Pookela program, which teaches guests about the history, traditions, and values of Hawaiian culture. **Pros:** no resort fee; friendly staff; weekly Legends of Kaanapali luau. **Cons:** the property is older than neighboring modern resorts; fewer amenities than other places along this beach; daily parking fee. *Rooms from: $223* *2525 Kaanapali Pkwy., Kaanapali* *808/661–0011, 800/262–8450* *www.kbhmaui.com* *432 rooms* *No meals.*

$ RENTAL Fodor's Choice ★ **Maui Eldorado Kaanapali by Outrigger.** The Kaanapali Golf Course's fairways wrap around this fine, well-priced, two-story condo complex that boasts spacious studios, one- and two-bedroom units with fully equipped kitchens, and access to a stocked beach cabana on a semi-private beach. **Pros:** privileges at the Kaanapali Golf Courses; Wi-Fi in all units; friendly staff. **Cons:** not right on beach; some distance from attractions of the Kaanapali Resort; no housekeeping but check-out cleaning fee. *Rooms from: $150* *2661 Kekaa Dr., Kaanapali* *808/661–0021* *www.mauieldorado.com* *204 units* *No meals.*

$$ RESORT **Royal Lahaina Resort.** Built in 1962, this grand property on the uncrowded, sandy shore in North Kaanapali has hosted millionaires and Hollywood stars, and today it pleases families and budget seekers as well as luxury travelers with a variety of lodging styles. **Pros:** on-site luau nightly; variety of lodgings and rates; tennis ranch with 11 courts and a pro shop. **Cons:** older property; daily self-parking fee; evening luau noise can be loud. *Rooms from: $220* *2780 Kekaa Dr., Kaanapali* *808/661–3611, 800/447–6925* *www.royallahaina.com* *447 units* *No meals.*

$$$$ RESORT **Sheraton Maui Resort & Spa.** Set among dense gardens on Kaanapali's best stretch of beach, the Sheraton offers a quieter, more low-key atmosphere than its neighboring resorts and sits next to and on top of the 80-foot-high Puu Kekaa, scene of a nightly torch-lighting and cliff-diving ritual. **Pros:** free shuttle to Lahaina and shopping malls; great snorkeling right off the beach; thrice weekly Maui Nei luau. **Cons:** extensive property can mean a long walk from your room to the lobby, restaurants, and beach; daily resort and parking fees; beach subject to seasonal erosion. *Rooms from: $659* *2605 Kaanapali Pkwy., Kaanapali* *808/661–0031, 866/500–8313* *www.sheraton-maui.com* *508 units* *No meals.*

$$$$ RESORT FAMILY **The Westin Maui Resort & Spa.** The cascading waterfall in the lobby of this hotel gives way to an aquatic playground with five heated swimming pools, abundant waterfalls, lagoons complete with pink flamingos and swans, and a premier location right on famed Kaanapali Beach. **Pros:** free shuttle to Lahaina town; activity programs for all ages; one adults-only pool. **Cons:** daily resort and parking fees; a lot going on; crowded pool and common areas. *Rooms from: $669* ✉ *2365 Kaanapali Pkwy., Kaanapali* ☎ *808/667–2525, 866/716–8112* 🌐 *www.westinmaui.com* *759 rooms* *No meals.*

KAPALUA AND NEARBY

The neighborhoods north of Kaanapali—Honokowai, Mahinahina, Kahana, Napili, and finally, Kapalua—blend almost seamlessly into one another along Lower Honoapiilani Highway. Each has a few shops and restaurants and a secluded bay or two to call its own. Many visitors have found a second home here, at one of the condominiums nestled between beach-access roads and groves of mango trees. You won't get the stellar service of a resort (except at Kapalua), but you'll be among the locals here, in a relatively quiet part of the island. Be prepared for a long commute, though, if you're planning to do much exploring elsewhere on the island. Kapalua is the area farthest north, but well worth all the driving to stay at the elegant Ritz-Carlton, which is surrounded by misty greenery and overlooks beautiful D.T. Fleming Beach.

$$ RENTAL FAMILY **Papakea Resort.** All studios and one- and two-bedroom units at this casual, oceanfront condominium complex face the ocean and, because the units are spread out among 11 low-rise buildings on about 13 acres of land, there is built-in privacy and easy parking. **Pros:** units have large rooms; lovely garden landscaping; complimentary activities include yoga, putting greens, lei making, and tennis lessons. **Cons:** no beach in front of property; pool can get crowded; busy, family-oriented property. *Rooms from: $225* ✉ *3543 Lower Honoapiilani Hwy., Honokowai* ☎ *808/669–4848, 866/774–2924* 🌐 *www.astonatpapakea.com* *364 units* *No meals.*

$$$$ RENTAL FAMILY **Honua Kai Resort & Spa.** Two high-rise towers contain these individually owned, eco-friendly (and family-friendly) units combining the conveniences of a condo with the full service of a hotel. **Pros:** large spacious rooms with full kitchens; upscale appliances and furnishings; beautiful, well-maintained grounds. **Cons:** can be windy here; housekeeping is every other day; beach is small and rocky so not good for swimming. *Rooms from: $514* ✉ *130 Kai Malina Pkwy., Honokowai* ☎ *808/662–2800, 855/718–5789* 🌐 *www.honuakai.com* *628 units* *No meals.*

$ RENTAL **Mahina Surf Oceanfront Resort.** Of the many condo complexes lining the ocean-side stretch of Honoapiilani Highway, this one offers friendly service, a saline oceanfront pool, and affordable units—some with million-dollar views. **Pros:** oceanfront barbecues; resident turtles hang out on the rocks below; no hidden fees. **Cons:** rocky shoreline rather than a beach; no housekeeping, cleaning fee at checkout; minimum three-night stay. *Rooms from: $180* ✉ *4057 Lower Honoapiilani Hwy.* ☎ *808/669–6068, 800/367–6086* 🌐 *www.mahinasurf.com* *56 units* *No meals.*

$$ RENTAL

The Mauian Boutique Beach Studios. If you're looking for a low-key place with a friendly staff, this small, delightful beachfront property on Napili Bay may be for you. **Pros:** reasonable rates; located on one of Maui's top swimming and snorkeling beaches; free parking and no resort fees. **Cons:** units are small; some may find the motel-like design reduces privacy; few amenities. *Rooms from: $229 5441 Lower Honoapiilani Hwy., Napili 808/669–6205 www.mauian.com 44 rooms Free breakfast.*

$$$$ RESORT FAMILY Fodor's Choice ★

Montage Kapalua Bay. The newest luxury resort in tony Kapalua caters to well-heeled travelers who want the comfort and privacy of a condo unit combined with resort-style service and amenities—-think elegantly furnished one to four-bedroom units with gourmet kitchens, in-unit washers/dryers, and the largest lanai to be found. **Pros:** Kapalua Bay offers prime snorkeling; there are great kids clubs for children and teens; large rooms are well appointed. **Cons:** pricey daily parking and resort fees; large property means lots of walking; far distance to other Maui attractions. *Rooms from: $725 1 Bay Dr., Kapalua 808/662–6600 www.montagehotels.com/kapaluabay 56 units No meals.*

$$$ RESORT FAMILY Fodor's Choice ★

Napili Kai Beach Resort. Spread across 10 beautiful acres along one of the best beaches on Maui, the family-friendly Napili Kai with its "old Hawaii" feel draws a loyal following to its island-style rooms that open onto private lanai. **Pros:** kids' hula performances and weekly Hawaiian slack-key guitar concert; fantastic swimming and sunning beach; no resort fees. **Cons:** not as modern as other resorts in West Maui; beach subject to periodic erosion; A/C installation underway, be sure to ask. *Rooms from: $335 5900 Lower Honoapiilani Hwy., Napili 808/669–6271, 800/367–5030 www.napilikai.com 163 units No meals.*

$$$$ RESORT Fodor's Choice ★

The Ritz-Carlton, Kapalua. This notable hillside property features luxurious service and upscale accommodations along with an enhanced Hawaiian sense of place. **Pros:** Kapalua offers a spa, golf, walking trails, and many other activities; AAA 4-Diamond Banyan Tree restaurant will please locavores; many cultural and recreational programs. **Cons:** can be windy on the grounds and at the pool; far from major attractions such as Haleakala; daily parking and resort fees. *Rooms from: $549 1 Ritz-Carlton Dr., Kapalua 808/669–6200, 800/262–8440 www.ritzcarlton.com/kapalua 463 units No meals.*

$$$ RENTAL

Sands of Kahana. Meandering gardens, spacious rooms, and an on-site restaurant distinguish this large condominium complex—units on the upper floors benefit from the height, with unrivalled ocean views stretching away from private lanai. **Pros:** restaurant on the premises; amenities include a fitness center, tennis courts, and sand volleyball court; one-, two-, and three-bedroom units available. **Cons:** this is primarily a time-share property so you may be approached about buying a unit; street-facing units can get a bit noisy; property a bit dated. *Rooms from: $319 4299 Lower Honoapiilani Hwy., Kahana 808/669–0400 property phone, 800/332–1137 for vacation rentals (Sullivan Properties) www.mauiresorts.com 196 units No meals.*

$$$$ RESORT FAMILY **Westin Nanea Ocean Villas.** It's rare to find a resort that so thoroughly incorporates authentic Hawaiian cultural symbols and traditions into its design, but this deluxe beachfront property in North Kaanapali, opened in 2017, carries this commitment into its native landscaping and Puuhonua O Nanea cultural center that hosts artifacts, displays, activities, and talks. **Pros:** "zero-entry" family pool with sandy bottom and water slide; great location for snorkeling and water sports; free shuttle to Lahaina town and other Westin resorts. **Cons:** may be pitched to join time-share club; outside main Kaanapali resort; limited dining options. *Rooms from: $939* ⊠ *45 Kai Malina Pkwy., Kahana* ☎ *808/662–6300* *www.westinnanea.com* *939 units* *No meals.*

3

SOUTH SHORE

KIHEI

The South Shore comprises two main communities: resort-filled Wailea and down-to-earth Kihei. In general, the farther south you go, the fancier the accommodations get. **TIP→ North Kihei tends to have great prices, but it also has some windy beaches scattered with seaweed. (This isn't a problem if you don't mind driving to another beach.)** As you travel down South Kihei Road, you can find condos both fronting and across the street from inviting beach parks and close to shops and restaurants. Once you hit Wailea, the opulence quotient takes a giant leap; this is the land of perfectly groomed resorts. Wailea and West Maui's Kaanapali continuously compete over which is more exclusive and which has better weather. In our opinion, it's a draw.

$$$$ RENTAL FAMILY **Aston Maui Hill.** Take in sweeping views of the ocean and Haleakala from the large lanai of the one- to three-bedroom units on this sprawling, well-maintained property just outside the swanky Wailea Resort. **Pros:** great option for large groups needing multiple units; no resort or parking fees; spacious layout makes property seem less crowded. **Cons:** decor may seem dated; units are not handicapped-accessible; stairs and walking distances may be challenging to guests with mobility issues. *Rooms from: $354* ⊠ *2881 South Kihei Rd., Kihei* ☎ *808/879–6321, 855/945–4044* *www.mauilea.com* *140 units* *No meals.*

$$$ RENTAL **Hale Hui Kai.** This modest three-story condo complex of mostly two-bedroom units is just steps away from the beach. **Pros:** far enough from the noise and tumult of "central" Kihei; a hidden gem for bargain hunters; free parking. **Cons:** nondescript 1970s architecture; some of the units are dated; no daily housekeeping. *Rooms from: $310* ⊠ *2994 S. Kihei Rd., Kihei* ☎ *808/879–1219, 800/809–6284* *www.halehuikaimaui.com* *40 units* *No meals.*

$$ RENTAL FAMILY **Kamaole Sands.** This South Kihei property is a good choice for active families, with its swimming pool, tennis courts, and an ideal family beach (Kamaole III) just across the street. **Pros:** in the seemingly endless strip of Kihei condos, this stands out for its pleasant grounds and well-cared-for units; unlike many low-rise condos, this one has elevators; free assigned parking. **Cons:** the complex of buildings may seem a bit too "citylike"; lack of diversity among the building facades; older property.

$ Rooms from: $249 ✉ 2695 S. Kihei Rd., Kihei ☎ 808/874–8700, 877/367–1912 ⊕ www.castleresorts.com ⇨ 400 units ¶ No meals.

$ RENTAL Fodor's Choice ★ **Luana Kai Resort.** If you don't need everything to be totally modern, consider setting up house at this great value condominium-by-the-sea. **Pros:** meticulously landscaped grounds; excellent management team; free parking. **Cons:** no elevators; no maid service; not all units have air conditioning. *$ Rooms from: $149 ✉ 940 S. Kihei Rd., Kihei ☎ 808/879–1268, 800/669–1127 ⊕ www.luanakai.com ⇨ 113 units ¶ No meals.*

$$$ RENTAL FAMILY **Mana Kai Maui.** You simply cannot get any closer to gorgeous Keawakapu Beach than this unsung hero of South Shore hotels, offering both renovated hotel rooms and condos that may be older than its competitors but are well priced and have marvelous ocean views, especially during the winter humpback whale season; one- and two-bedroom condos have private lanai and kitchens. **Pros:** arguably the best beach on the South Shore; good for families; free assigned parking. **Cons:** older property; interior design might not appeal to discerning travelers; four-night minimum. *$ Rooms from: $312 ✉ 2960 S. Kihei Rd., Kihei ☎ 808/879–1561, 800/525–2025 ⊕ www.manakaimaui.com ⇨ 98 units ¶ No meals.*

$$ RENTAL **Kohea Kai Resort Maui.** Located in the quieter north end of Kihei, this relaxed, adults-only property has 26 units—15 with full kitchens—that range from standard rooms to three-bedroom, two-bath "penthouses." Formerly the Maui Sunseeker Resort, the property has been refreshed since new ownership took over in 2016, and there's a rooftop deck and various outdoor "rooms" in the well-maintained tropical garden. **Pros:** no resort or parking fees; no minimum stay; a hearty complimentary breakfast buffet. **Cons:** small pool; located next to busy South Kihei Road; most rooms lack views. *$ Rooms from: $239 ✉ 551 S. Kihei Rd., Kihei ☎ 808/879–1261 ⊕ www.koheakai.com ⇨ 26 units ¶ Free Breakfast.*

WAILEA

Warm, serene, and luxurious, Wailea properties offer less "action" than West Maui resorts. The properties here tend to focus on ambience, thoughtful details, and natural scenery. Nightlife is pretty much nil, save for a few swanky bars. However, you have your choice of sandy beaches with good snorkeling. Farther south, Makena is a little less developed. Expect everything—even bottled water—to double in price when you cross the line from Kihei to Wailea.

$$$$ RESORT Fodor's Choice ★ **Andaz Maui at Wailea Resort.** Sophisticated travelers and romance-seeking couples will swoon at the sleek luxury of this eco-friendly, beachfront resort. **Pros:** outstanding service and dining; a one-of-a-kind resort on Maui; free shuttle service around Wailea. **Cons:** rooms are on the small side; guests with kids can find better amenities elsewhere; slick design style might feel cold to some. *$ Rooms from: $609 ✉ 3550 Wailea Alanui Dr., Wailea ☎ 808/573–1234 ⊕ www.andazmaui.com ⇨ 301 units ¶ No meals.*

$$$$ RESORT FAMILY **Fairmont Kea Lani Maui.** Gleaming white spires and tiled archways are the hallmark of this stunning resort that's particularly good for families. **Pros:** all rooms are suites; 22,000-square-foot water complex; located on near-private Polo Beach. **Cons:** noisy families at play may be a turnoff for some; daily resort and parking fees; lounge chairs in

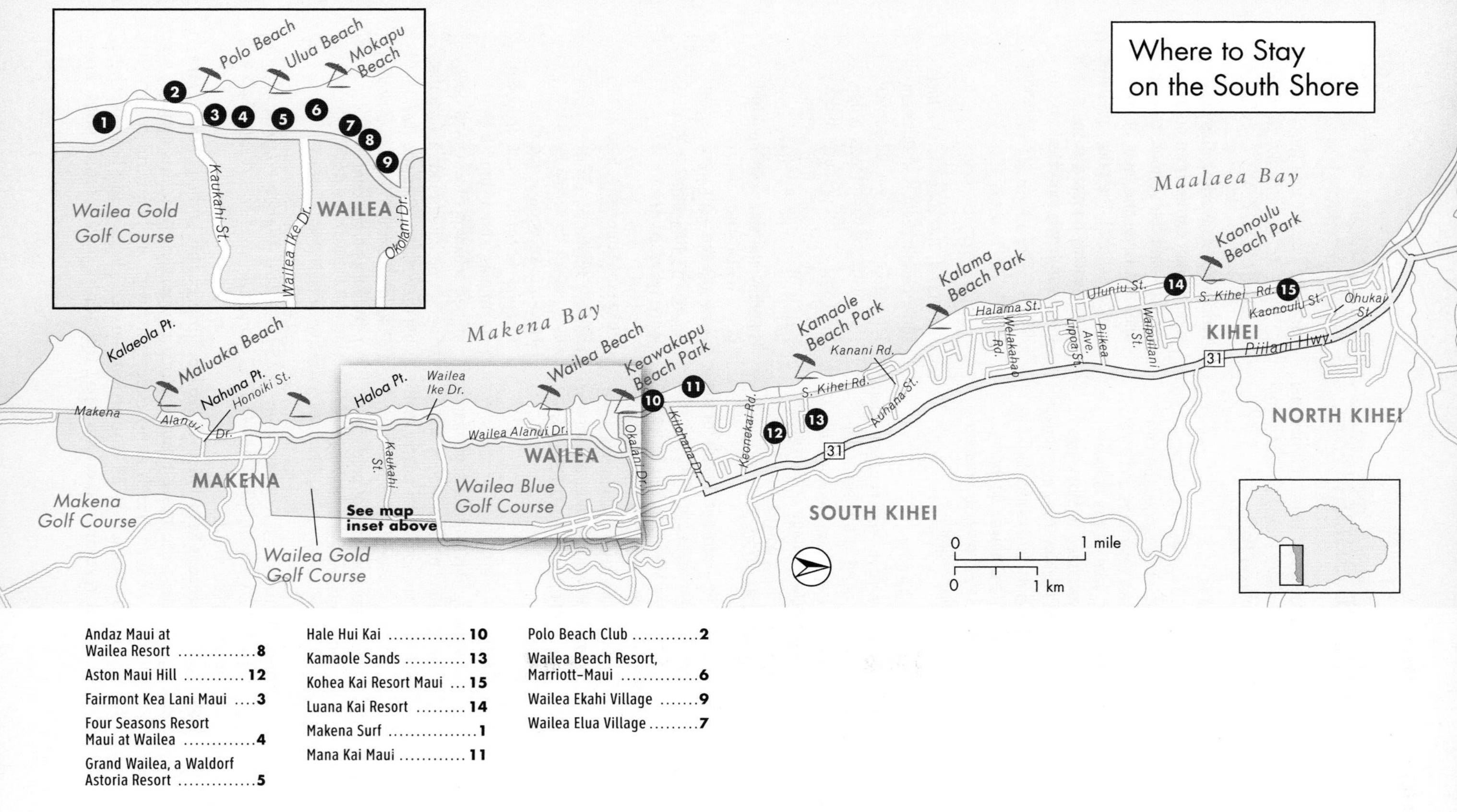
Where to Stay on the South Shore
Polo Beach
Ulua Beach
Mokapu Beach
Kaukahi St.
Wailea Ike Dr.
Okolani Dr.
WAILEA
Wailea Gold Golf Course
Maalaea Bay
Kaonoulu Beach Park
Kalama Beach Park
Kamaole Beach Park
Keawakapu Beach Park
Wailea Beach
Makena Bay
Maluaka Beach
Kalaeola Pt.
Nahuna Pt.
Honoiki St.
Haloa Pt.
Wailea Ike Dr.
Makena Alanui Dr.
Wailea Alanui Dr.
Okalani Dr.
Kilohana Dr.
Keonekai Rd.
S. Kihei Rd.
Kanani Rd.
Auhana St.
Welakahao Rd.
Halama St.
Lipoa St.
Piikea Ave.
Waipuilani St.
Uluniu St.
Kaonoulu St.
Ohukai St.
Piilani Hwy.
31
KIHEI
NORTH KIHEI
SOUTH KIHEI
MAKENA
Makena Golf Course
Wailea Blue Golf Course
Wailea Gold Golf Course
See map inset above
0
1 mile
1 km
Andaz Maui at Wailea Resort 8
Aston Maui Hill 12
Fairmont Kea Lani Maui 3
Four Seasons Resort Maui at Wailea 4
Grand Wailea, a Waldorf Astoria Resort 5
Hale Hui Kai 10
Kamaole Sands 13
Kohea Kai Resort Maui ... 15
Luana Kai Resort 14
Makena Surf 1
Mana Kai Maui 11
Polo Beach Club 2
Wailea Beach Resort, Marriott–Maui 6
Wailea Ekahi Village 9
Wailea Elua Village 7

FOOD SHOPPING FOR RENTERS

Condo renters in search of food and takeout meals should try these great places around Maui.

WEST MAUI

Foodland Farms. This large supermarket combines the best of gourmet selections and local products, with all the familiar staples you need to stock your vacation kitchen. They also make a mean *poke* (seafood salad). ✉ *Lahaina Gateway Shopping Center, 345 Keawe St., Lahaina* ☎ *808/662–7088.*

SOUTH SHORE

Safeway. Find everything you could possibly need at this supermarket, the largest on Maui, located in the Piilani Village Shopping Center. ✉ *277 Piikea Ave., Kihei* ☎ *808/891–9120.*

Times Supermarket. Watch for the parking lot barbecue on Wednesday and Friday, when chicken, teriyaki beef, steak, and shrimp are served plate lunch–style outside this supermarket. Hawaiian plates are served up on Thursday. ✉ *1310 S. Kihei Rd., Kihei.*

CENTRAL MAUI

Safeway. This 24-hour supermarket has a deli, a prepared-foods and seafood section, and a bakery that are all fantastic. There's a good wine selection, tons of produce, and a flower shop where you can treat yourself to a fresh lei. ✉ *170 E. Kaahumanu Ave., Kahului* ☎ *808/877–3377.*

Whole Foods Market. This busy supermarket carries local organic produce, and the seafood, bakery, beer and wine, and meat offerings are exceptional. The pricey prepared foods—including pizza, sushi, a salad bar, Asian bowls, and Mexican fare—attract crowds. ✉ *70 E. Kaahumanu Ave., Kahului.*

UPCOUNTRY

Foodland. This member of a local supermarket chain is at Pukalani Terrace Center; it is a full-service store with prepared foods, a deli, fresh sushi, local produce, and a good seafood section in addition to the usual fare. On Friday and Saturday, the store sets up a grill in the parking to barbecue tender steak and teriyaki beef. Open 24 hours. ✉ *55 Pukalani St., Pukalani* ☎ *808/572–0674.*

Pukalani Superette. Stop at this family-owned store on your way up or down Haleakala for fresh Maui-grown produce and meat, flowers, chocolate *haupia* (coconut) cream pies, and a surprisingly refined selection of wine and beer. The hot prepared foods are another big draw. ✉ *15 Makawao Ave., Pukalani* ☎ *808/572–7616* 🌐 *www.pukalanisuperette.com.*

high demand. $ *Rooms from: $759* ✉ *4100 Wailea Alanui, Wailea* ☎ *808/875–4100, 800/798–4552* 🌐 *www.fairmont.com/kealani* *450 units* 🍴 *No meals.*

$$$$ RESORT Fodor's Choice ★ **Four Seasons Resort Maui at Wailea.** "Impeccably stylish" and "extravagant" describe most Four Seasons properties, and this elegant one fronting Wailea Beach is no exception, with its beautiful courtyards and luxuries such as 24-hour room service, twice-daily housekeeping, excellent restaurants, on-site spa, and adults-only serenity pool. **Pros:**

no resort fee; complimentary kids' club, snorkeling, outrigger canoe rides, tennis; great shopping and local crafts and artwork market. **Cons:** adults-only pool chairs fill up fast; a bit ostentatious for some; when fully booked facilities can seem crowded. $ *Rooms from: $689* ✉ *3900 Wailea Alanui Dr., Wailea* ☎ *808/874–8000, 800/332–3442* 🌐 *www.fourseasons.com/maui* *383 rooms* *No meals.*

$$$$ RESORT FAMILY **Grand Wailea, a Waldorf Astoria Resort.** "Grand" is no exaggeration for this opulent, sunny 40-acre resort—either astounding or over the top, depending on your point of view—that's wildly entertaining due to its elaborate water features such as a "canyon riverpool" with enclosed "lava tube," slides, caves, a Tarzan swing, and a water elevator. **Pros:** set on beautiful Wailea Beach; Camp Grande has a game room and movie theater for kids; many shops. **Cons:** daily resort and parking fees; sometimes too much is just too much; limited poolside chairs. $ *Rooms from: $369* ✉ *3850 Wailea Alanui Dr., Wailea* ☎ *808/875–1234, 800/888–6100* 🌐 *www.grandwailea.com* *776 units* *No meals.*

$$$$ RENTAL **Makena Surf.** For travelers who've done all there is to do on Maui and just want simple but luxurious relaxation at a condo that spills onto a private beach, this is the spot. **Pros:** away from it all, yet still close enough to "civilization"; great snorkeling right off the beach; laundry facilities in every unit. **Cons:** too secluded and "locked-up" for some; split-level units may be difficult for guests with mobility issues; check-in is at a different location (*34 Wailea Gateway Plaza*). $ *Rooms from: $779* ✉ *4820 Makena Alanui, Makena* ☎ *808/891–6200, 800/367–5246* 🌐 *www.destinationresidenceshawaii.com* *103 units* *No meals.*

$$$$ RENTAL **Polo Beach Club.** Lording over a hidden section of Polo Beach, this wonderful, older eight-story rental property's charm somehow manages to stay under the radar. **Pros:** herb garden you can pick from; beautiful beach fronting the building; superb management. **Cons:** some may feel isolated; split-level units potentially challenging for those with impaired mobility; check-in is at a different location (*34 Wailea Gateway Plaza*). $ *Rooms from: $795* ✉ *4400 Makena Rd., Makena* ☎ *808/891–6249, 800/367–5246* 🌐 *www.destinationresidencesmaui.com* *71 units* *No meals.*

$$$$ RESORT FAMILY Fodor's Choice ★ **Wailea Beach Resort, Marriott-Maui.** The Marriott, which sits closer to the crashing surf than most resorts, promises not only dramatic views but luxurious amenities and spacious accommodations. **Pros:** hosts the only Starbucks in Wailea; short walk to Shops of Wailea; Te Au Moana Luau four nights a week. **Cons:** rocky shore that is not quite beachfront; there can be a lot of foot traffic on coastal beach walk; $35 daily resort fee and $30 daily self-parking fee (valet $35). $ *Rooms from: $795* ✉ *3700 Wailea Alanui, Wailea* ☎ *808/879–1922, 800/292–4532* 🌐 *www.waileamarriott.com* *547 units* *No meals.*

$$$$ RESORT **Wailea Ekahi Village.** Overlooking Keawakapu Beach, this family-friendly vacation resort features studios and one- and two-bedroom suites in low-rise buildings that span 34 acres of tropical gardens and won't cost your child's entire college fund. **Pros:** convenient access to a great beach; en-suite kitchen and laundry facilities; daily housekeeping. **Cons:** the large complex can be tricky to find your way around;

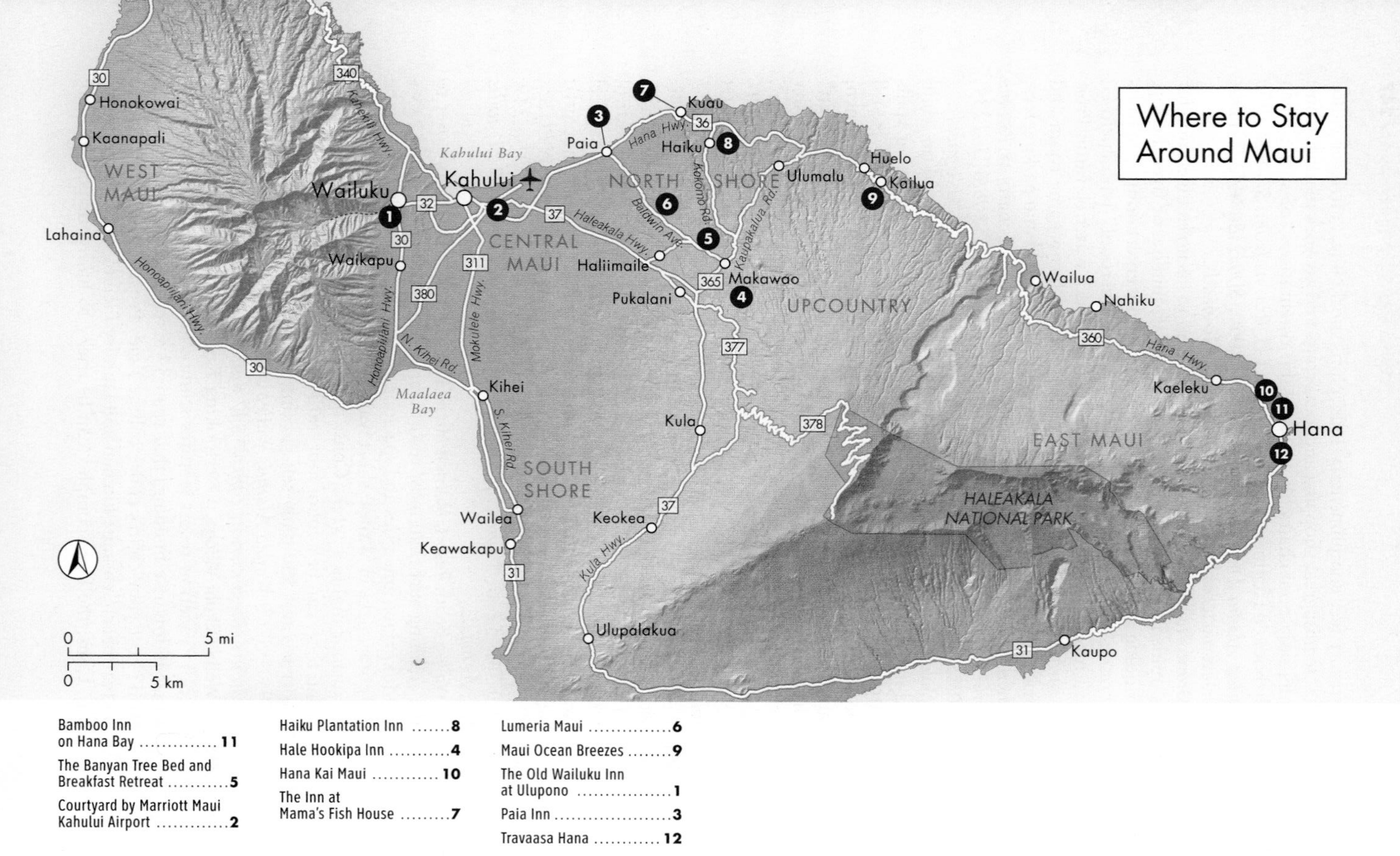

Bamboo Inn on Hana Bay 11
The Banyan Tree Bed and Breakfast Retreat 5
Courtyard by Marriott Maui Kahului Airport 2
Haiku Plantation Inn 8
Hale Hookipa Inn 4
Hana Kai Maui 10
The Inn at Mama's Fish House 7
Lumeria Maui 6
Maui Ocean Breezes 9
The Old Wailuku Inn at Ulupono 1
Paia Inn 3
Travaasa Hana 12

check-in is at a different location (*34 Wailea Gateway Plaza*); decor in individually owned units may differ. *Rooms from: $408* *3300 Wailea Alanui, Wailea* *808/891–6200, 800/357–5246* *www.destinationresidenceshawaii.com* *289 units* *No meals.*

$$$$ RESORT **Wailea Elua Village.** Located on Ulua Beach, one of the Island's most beloved snorkeling spots, these upscale one-, two-, and three-bedroom condo suites have spectacular views and 24 acres of manicured lawns and gardens. **Pros:** easy access to the designer boutiques and upscale restaurants at the Shops at Wailea; daily housekeeping; $155 Wailea restaurant/spa credit. **Cons:** large complex; hard to find your way around; check-in is at a different location (*34 Wailea Gateway Plaza*). *Rooms from: $609* *3600 Wailea Alanui, Wailea* *808/891–6200, 800/367–5246* *www.destinationresidenceshawaii.com* *152 suites* *No meals.*

3

CENTRAL MAUI

Kahului and Wailuku, the commercial, residential, and government centers that make up Central Maui, are not known for their lavish accommodations, but there are options that meet some travelers' needs perfectly.

$$$ HOTEL **Courtyard by Marriott Maui Kahului Airport.** At the entrance to Kahului Airport, this hotel offers many amenities for business travelers as well as tourists. **Pros:** great for business and pleasure; central location; conference and banquet rooms available. **Cons:** not on the beach; airport and city noise; daily parking fee. *Rooms from: $289* *532 Keolani Pl., Kahului* *808/871–1800, 877/852–1880* *www.marriott.com* *138 rooms* *No meals.*

$$ B&B/INN Fodor's Choice ★ **The Old Wailuku Inn at Ulupono.** Built in 1924 and listed on the State of Hawaii Register of Historic Places, this home with knowledgeable innkeepers offers the charm of old Hawaii, including authentic decor and architecture. **Pros:** walking distance to civic center, restaurants, historic Wailuku town; lovely garden setting; immaculately maintained. **Cons:** closest beach is a 15-minute drive away; you may hear traffic noise at certain times; parking can be tight. *Rooms from: $185* *2199 Kahookele St., Wailuku* *808/244–5897, 800/305–4899* *www.mauiinn.com* *10 rooms* *Free breakfast.*

UPCOUNTRY

Upcountry accommodations (those in Kula, Makawao, and Haliimaile) are generally on country properties and are privately owned vacation rentals. Situated at a high elevation, these lodgings offer splendid views of the island, temperate weather, and a "getting away from it all" feeling—which is actually the case, as most shops and restaurants are a fair drive away, and beaches even farther. You'll definitely need a car here.

$ B&B/INN FAMILY Fodor's Choice ★ **The Banyan Tree Bed and Breakfast Retreat.** If a taste of rural Hawaii life in plantation days coupled with quiet time and privacy is what you crave, you can find it at this 2-acre property awash in tropical foliage, banyan trees, and the 50-foot, saltwater pool and in-ground spa that afford views of Maui's northern coast and Molokai. **Pros:** one cottage and the pool are outfitted for travelers with disabilities; free on-site parking; you can walk to quaint Makawao town for dining and shopping. **Cons:** cottages have pretty basic furniture and few amenities; some daytime traffic noise; not all units have air-conditioning. *Rooms from: $175 ✉ 3265 Baldwin Ave., Makawao ☎ 808/572–9021 www.bed-breakfast-maui.com 7 cottage suites Free breakfast.*

$ B&B/INN **Hale Hookipa Inn.** A handsome 1924 Craftsman-style house in the heart of Makawao town is on both the Hawaii and the National Historic Registers, and provides a great base for excursions to Haleakala, Hana, or North Shore beaches. **Pros:** genteel rural setting; price includes buffet breakfast with organic fruit from the garden; charming architecture and decor. **Cons:** a 20-minute drive to the nearest beach; this is not the sun, sand, and surf surroundings of travel posters; no food allowed in rooms. *Rooms from: $140 ✉ 32 Pakani Pl., Makawao ☎ 808/281-2074 www.maui-bed-and-breakfast.com 4 units Free breakfast.*

$$$ B&B/INN **Lumeria Maui.** Peace, tranquility, and a healthful experience are what you will find at this beautifully restored historic property—among the sprawling 6 acres there is a forest with hammocks, a meditation lawn, a yoga pavilion, saltwater pool, fire pits, and an outdoor yoga area. **Pros:** 1,700-square-foot Yoga Shala accommodates larger yoga classes, workshops, concerts, and meetings; a unique Maui retreat; room rate includes unlimited classes. **Cons:** most bathrooms have showers only; no beaches, restaurants, or shops in walking distance; no air-conditioning. *Rooms from: $329 ✉ 1813 Baldwin Ave., Makawao ☎ 808/579–8877, 855/579–8877 www.lumeriamaui.com 24 rooms Free breakfast.*

NORTH SHORE

You won't find any large resorts or condominium complexes along the North Shore, yet there's a variety of accommodations from the surf town of Paia, through tiny Kuau, and along the rain-forested Hana Highway through Haiku. Some are oceanfront but not necessarily beachfront (with sand); instead, look for tropical gardens overflowing with ginger, bananas, papayas, and nightly bug symphonies. Some have breathtaking views or the type of solitude that seeps in, easing your tension before you know it. You may encounter brief powerful downpours, but that's what makes this part of Maui green and lush. You'll need a car to enjoy staying on the North Shore.

HAIKU

$ B&B/INN **Haiku Plantation Inn.** Water lilies and a shade tree bedecked in orchids greet you at this forested bend in the road, where a gracious estate, built in 1870 for the plantation-company doctor, continues the healing tradition with its wellness programs. **Pros:** quiet setting; close to restaurants, gas station, and bus stop; opportunities to experience authentic Hawaiian culture. **Cons:** no resort amenities; 15-minute drive to closest beach; no A/C. *Rooms from: $170 ✉ 555 Haiku Rd., Haiku-Pauwela ☎ 808/575–7500 www.haikuleana.net 4 rooms Free breakfast.*

KUAU

$$$ RENTAL FAMILY Fodor's Choice ★ **The Inn at Mama's Fish House.** Nestled in gardens adjacent to one of Maui's most popular dining spots (Mama's Fish House) and fronting a small beach known as Ku'au Cove, these well-maintained studios, suites, and one- and two-bedroom cottages have a retro-Hawaiian style with rattan furnishings and local artwork. **Pros:** daily maid service; free parking and Wi-Fi; next to Hookipa Beach and Paia town shops and restaurants. **Cons:** Mama's Fish House restaurant can get crowded during the evening (it's more mellow during the day); limited swimming at beach; not a full-service hotel with concierge. *Rooms from: $275 ✉ 799 Poho Pl. ☎ 808/579–9764, 800/860–4852 www.innatmamas.com 12 units No meals.*

$ RENTAL **Maui Ocean Breezes.** The cool ocean breeze rolls through these pretty, eco-friendly rentals, making this a perfect spot to relax and enjoy the gorgeous scenery along the ocean side of the famed Road to Hana. **Pros:** quiet, private atmosphere; located in an upscale, rural subdivision with large lots; expansive lawn with ocean views. **Cons:** isolated from stores, beaches, activities, and public transportation, making a rental car a must; five-night minimum preferred; no A/C. *Rooms from: $180 ✉ 240 N. Holokai Rd., Haiku-Pauwela ☎ 808/218–1186 www.mauivacationhideaway.com 4 units No meals.*

PAIA

$$$ B&B/INN **Paia Inn.** Located in the former plantation town of Paia, along Hana Highway, this chic inn with Southeast Asian influences is surprisingly quiet and includes oceanfront accommodations. **Pros:** unique and varied shops and dining just steps away in funky beach town; situated in heart of North Shore water-sports scene; well-maintained property. **Cons:** some of the rooms are very small; limited on- and off-site parking; lots of street action. *Rooms from: $299 ✉ 93 Hana Hwy., Paia ☎ 808/579-6000, 800/721–4000 www.paiainn.com 10 units No meals.*

ROAD TO HANA

$$ B&B/INN **Bamboo Inn on Hana Bay.** A thatched-roof gate opens to the courtyard of this informal Balinese-inspired guest house with a sweeping view of Hana Bay. The ground-floor studio has a private outdoor shower and the other two units have private whirlpool hot tubs on their second-floors decks—all have kitchenettes. **Pros:** fall asleep to the sound of waves lapping at the rocky coast; close to town center; light breakfast included. **Cons:** limited mobile service, Wi-Fi available only in courtyard; no air-conditioning; no nightlife in this early-to-bed, early-to-rise town. *Rooms from: $210 ✉ 4869 Uakea Rd., Hana ☎ 808/248–7718 www.bambooinn.com 3 rooms Free Breakfast.*

$$ RENTAL Fodor's Choice ★ **Hana Kai Maui.** Perfectly situated on Hana Bay, this two-story "condotel" has an excellent reputation for cleanliness and visitor hospitality—and the ocean views are stunning. **Pros:** a 10-minute walk to Hana Bay; one-night rentals are accepted; daily housekeeping. **Cons:** no nightlife or excitement in Hana town; no elevator; no air conditioning or

TV. $ *Rooms from: $220* ✉ *4865 Uakea Rd., Hana* ☎ *808/248–8426, 800/346–2772* 🌐 *www.hanakaimaui.com* ⇋ *17 units* 🍴 *No meals.*

$$$$ RESORT **Travaasa Hana.** A destination in itself, this secluded and quietly luxurious property still delivers the tropical Hawaii of your dreams; for additional peace and privacy, splurge with a stay in the Ocean Bungalows set on sprawling lawns overlooking the rugged coastline. **Pros:** no resort or parking fees; no-tipping policy for everything except dining; a truly unique property in a special place. **Cons:** mobile service is spotty; it's oceanfront but doesn't have a sandy beach (however, free shuttle to Hamoa Beach); don't expect any nightlife in Hana. $ *Rooms from: $525* ✉ *5031 Hana Hwy., Hana* ☎ *808/248–8211, 888/820–1043* 🌐 *www.travaasa.com/hana* ⇋ *76 units* 🍴 *No meals.*

NIGHTLIFE AND PERFORMING ARTS

Updated by Lehia Apana

Looking for wild island nightlife? This island has little of Waikiki's after-hours decadence, and the club scene can be quirky, depending on the season and the day of the week. But Maui will surprise you with a big-name concert or world-class DJ, and local block parties are always entertaining. Outdoor music festivals are usually held at the Maui Arts & Cultural Center, or even a randomly scouted performance space in Hana.

Block parties in each town happen on Friday, with Wailuku leading the pack. Main streets are blocked for local bands, food vendors, and street performers, and it's a family-friendly affair. Lahaina, Paia, and Kihei are your best bets for action. Lahaina tries to uphold its reputation as a party town, and succeeds every Halloween when thousands of masqueraders converge for a Mardi Gras–style party on Front Street. Kihei has more club venues for live music but can attract something of a rough-and-tumble crowd in parts. On the right night, the towns stir with activity, and if you don't like one scene, there's always next door.

Outside Lahaina and Kihei, you might be able to hit an "on" night in Paia (North Shore) or Makawao (Upcountry). Charley's in Paia is the go-to venue for mainland and international DJs looking to play an intimate set. But generally these towns are on the mellow side.

NIGHTLIFE

Your best bet when it comes to bars on Maui? If you walk by and it sounds like it's happening, go in. If you want to scope out your options in advance, check the free *Maui Time Weekly,* available at most stores and restaurants, to find out who's playing where. The resorts and their bars and restaurants often have a good scene, too. The *Maui News* also publishes an entertainment schedule in its Thursday edition of the "Maui Scene." With an open mind (and a little luck), you can usually find some fun.

WEST MAUI

Alaloa Lounge. When ambience weighs heavy on the priority list, this spot at the Ritz-Carlton, Kapalua, might just be the ticket. Nightly performances range from jazz to island rhythms, and the menu includes

Performers in colorful costumes help make luau appealing to all ages.

a fantastic island-style po' boy served with Hawaiian sweet bread. Step onto the lanai for that plumeria-tinged Hawaiian air and gaze at the deep blue of the Pacific. ✉ *The Ritz-Carlton, Kapalua, 1 Ritz-Carlton Dr., Kapalua* ☎ *808/669–6200* 🌐 *www.ritzcarlton.com.*

Cheeseburger in Paradise. A chain joint on Front Street, this place is known for—what else?—big beefy cheeseburgers, not to mention a great turkey burger. It's a casual place to start your evening, as they have live music (usually classic or contemporary rock) until 11 pm. The second-floor balcony gives you a bird's-eye view of Lahaina's Front Street action. ✉ *811 Front St., Lahaina* ☎ *808/661–4855* 🌐 *www.cheeseburgernation.com.*

Cool Cat Café. You could easily miss this casual 1950s-style diner while strolling through Lahaina. Tucked in the second floor of the Wharf Cinema Center, its semi-outdoor area plays host to rockin' local music nightly until 10 pm. The entertainment lineup covers jazz, contemporary Hawaiian, and traditional island rhythms. It doesn't hurt that the kitchen dishes out specialty burgers, fish that's fresh from the harbor, and delicious homemade sauces from the owner's family recipes. ✉ *658 Front St., Lahaina* ☎ *808/667–0908* 🌐 *www.coolcatcafe.com.*

THE SOUTH SHORE

Fodor's Choice ★ **Vibe Bar and Nightclub.** A South Maui favorite, Vibe is a lively hangout for house music and Top 40 favorites, with DJs turning up the volume nightly. It's the size of a living room, but mixology is given more consideration here than at other venues. ✉ *1913 S. Kihei Rd., Kihei* ☎ *808/891–1011* 🌐 *www.ambrosiamaui.com.*

Fodor's Choice ★ **Lobby Lounge at the Four Seasons Resort Maui.** This lofty resort's lobby lounge is perfect when you want live Hawaiian music, a bit of hula, and freshly prepared sushi all in one sitting. If you're not in the mood for a ceremonious sit-down meal but still crave something out of the ordinary, the place is perfect for a quick bite. The artisanal cocktails are well done and highlight locally distilled spirits. Gorgeous orange ceilings, stark-white stone columns, and modern wicker furnishing pull off the understated look quite well. The fiery sunset over Lanai isn't too shabby either. ✉ *Four Seasons Resort Maui at Wailea, 3900 Wailea Alanui Dr., Wailea* ☎ *808/874–8000* 🌐 *www.fourseasons.com.*

South Shore Tiki Lounge. Good eats are paired with cool tunes in this breezy tropical tavern. Local acts and DJs are featured from 4 to 6 pm most evenings, and DJs get the dance floor shaking at 10 pm. Happy hour specials run from 11 to 6. This is the bar where locals hang out, so if you'd like to mix with the local scene, this is the spot. ✉ *Kihei Kalama Village, 1913-J S. Kihei Rd., Kihei* ☎ *808/874–6444* 🌐 *www.southshoretikilounge.com.*

UPCOUNTRY AND THE NORTH SHORE

Casanova Italian Restaurant & Deli. Casanova sometimes brings big acts and electronic dance music DJs from the mainland. Most Friday and Saturday nights attract a hip local scene with live bands and eclectic DJs spinning house, funk, and world music. Wednesday is Ladies Night (i.e. ladies get in free), which can be on the smarmy side, but hey, vacation is a no-judgment zone. For everyone else, there's a $10 cover. ✉ *1188 Makawao Ave., Makawao* ☎ *808/572–0220* 🌐 *www.casanovamaui.com.*

Fodor's Choice ★ **Charley's Restaurant & Saloon.** The closest thing to country Maui has to offer, Charley's is a down-home dive bar in the heart of Paia. It hosts reggae, house, Latin soul, and jazz nights, as well as one-off events with sought-after DJs. Live bands are featured throughout the week. And, despite its robust nightly offerings—or because of them?—Charley's is also known for its great breakfasts. ✉ *142 Hana Hwy., Paia* ☎ *808/579–8085* 🌐 *www.charleysmaui.com.*

Stopwatch Bar & Grill. This friendly dive bar hosts karaoke nights on Thursday and Saturday, and books favorite local bands on Friday for a $4 admission. ✉ *1127 Makawao Ave., Makawao* ☎ *808/572–1380.*

PERFORMING ARTS

Before 10 pm there's a lot to offer by way of luau shows, dinner cruises, and tiki-lighted cocktail hours. Aside from that, you should at least be able to find some down-home DJ-spinning or the strum of acoustic guitars at your nearest watering hole or restaurant.

DINNER CRUISES AND SHOWS

There's no better place to see the sun set on the Pacific than from one of Maui's many boat tours. You can find a tour to fit your mood, as the options range from a quiet, sit-down dinner to a festive, beer-swigging booze cruise. Note, however, that many cocktail cruises have put a cap on the number of free drinks offered with open bars, instead including a limited number of drinks per ticket.

Tours leave from Maalaea or Lahaina harbors. Be sure to arrive at least 15 minutes early (count in the time it will take to park). The dinner cruises typically feature music and are generally packed, which is great if you're feeling social but you might have to fight for a good seat. You can usually get a much better meal at one of the local restaurants, and then opt for a different type of tour. Most nondinner cruises offer *pupu* (appetizers) and sometimes a chocolate-and-champagne toast.

3

Winds are consistent in summer but variable in winter—sometimes making for a rocky ride. If you're worried about seasickness, you might consider a catamaran, which is much more stable than a monohull. Keep in mind that the boat crews are experienced in dealing with such matters. A Dramamine before the trip should keep you in tip-top shape, but if you feel seasick, you should sit in the shade, place a cold rag or ice on the back of your neck, and *breathe* as you look at the horizon.

George Kahumoku Jr.'s Slack Key Show: Masters of Hawaiian Music. Grammy-winning musician George Kahumoku Jr. hosts this program on Wednesday, which features a rotating lineup of the Islands' finest slack-key artists as well as other traditional forms of Hawaiian music. The setup at Aloha Pavilion is humble, but you'll enjoy these beloved musicians in an intimate setting. ✉ *Napili Kai Beach Resort, 5900 Lower Honoapiilani Rd., Lahaina* ☎ *808/669–3858* 🌐 *www.slackkeyshow.com* 🎟 *$38 in advance, $45 at the door.*

FAMILY Fodor's Choice ★ ***Hula Girl.*** This custom catamaran is one of the slickest and best-equipped boats on the island, complete with a VIP lounge by the captain's fly bridge. The initial cost doesn't include the cooked-to-order meals, but guests can choose from a relatively extensive menu that includes filet mignon, daily fish specials, and crème brûlée. If you're willing to splurge a little for live music, an onboard chef, and upscale service, this is your best bet. From mid-December to early April the cruise focuses on whale-watching. Check-in is in front of Leilani's restaurant at Whalers Village. ✉ *2435 Kaanapali Pkwy., Kaanapali* ☎ *808/665–0344, 808/667–5980* 🌐 *www.sailingmaui.com* 🎟 *$80.*

Pride of Maui. A 65-foot catamaran built specifically for Maui's waters, the *Pride of Maui* has a spacious cabin for live entertainment, a dance floor, and a large upper deck for unobstructed sightseeing. Evening cruises include top-shelf cocktails and an impressive spread cooked onboard, including baby back ribs, Maui onion tartlets, and honey-glazed chicken, plus seasonal desserts. ✉ *Maalaea Harbor, 101 Maalaea Boat Harbor Rd., Maalaea* ☎ *844/896–4786* 🌐 *www.prideofmaui.com* 🎟 *$69.*

Teralani Sailing Charters. These catamarans are modern, spotless, and laid out nicely for dining and lounging. They head back shortly after sunset, which means there's plenty of light to savor dinner and the view. During whale-watching season, the best seats are the corner booths by the stern of the boat. Catered by local fave Pizza Paradiso, the meal outdoes most dinner-cruise spreads, with ratatouille, chipotle-citrus rotisserie chicken, grilled fish, and potato gratin with sun-dried tomatoes. The trip departs from Kaanapali Beach in front of Leilani's at Whalers Village. ✉ *2435 Kaanapali Pkwy., Kaanapali* ☎ *808/661–7245* 🌐 *www.teralani.net* 🎟 *$96.*

LUAU

A trip to Hawaii isn't complete without a good luau. With the beat of drums and the sway of hula, a luau gives you a snippet of Hawaiian culture left over from a long-standing tradition. Early Hawaiians celebrated many occasions with a luau—weddings, births, battles, and more. The feasts originally brought people together as an offering to the gods, and to practice *hookipa,* the act of welcoming guests. The word *luau* itself refers to the taro root, a staple of the Hawaiian diet, which, when pounded, makes a gray, puddinglike substance called *poi.* You'll find poi at all the best feasts, along with platters of salty fish, fresh fruit, and *kalua* pork (baked underground).

Locals still hold luau to mark milestones or as informal, family-style gatherings. For tourists, luau are a major attraction and, for that reason, have become big business. Keep in mind—some are watered-down tourist traps just trying to make a buck; others offer a night you'll never forget. As the saying goes, you get what you pay for. ■ **TIP→ Many of the best luau book up weeks or months in advance, so reserve early. Plan your luau night early on in your trip to help you get into the Hawaiian spirit.**

FAMILY **Drums of the Pacific Luau.** By Kaanapali Beach, this luau shines in every category—convenient parking, well-made food, smooth-flowing buffet lines, and a nicely paced program that touches on Hawaiian, Samoan, Tahitian, Fijian, Tongan, and Maori cultures. Some guests get tickled by the onstage audience hula tutorial. The finale features three fire-knife dancers. You'll feast on delicious Hawaiian delicacies like *huli huli* chicken (grilled chicken marinated in a pineapple/soy sauce mixture), *lomilomi* salmon (tossed in a salad with tomatoes and Maui onions), and Pacific ahi *poke* (pickled raw tuna, tossed with herbs and seasonings). The dessert spread consists of chocolate, pineapple, and coconut indulgences. An open bar offers beer, wine, and standard tropical mixes. ✉ *Hyatt Regency Maui, 200 Nohea Kai Dr., Kaanapali* ☎ *808/667–4727* 🌐 *www.drumsofthepacificmaui.com* 🎫 *$119–$153.*

Fodor's Choice ★ **Feast at Lele.** This place redefines the luau by crossing it with Islands-style fine dining in an intimate beach setting. Each course of this succulent sit-down meal is prepared by the award-winning Pacific'O restaurant, and coincides with the island cultures—Hawaiian, Samoan, Aotearoan, Tahitian—featured onstage. Wine, spirits, and cocktail options are copious and go beyond the usual tropical concoctions. Lahaina's gorgeous sunset serves as the backdrop to the show, which forgoes gimmicks and pageantry for an authentic expression of Polynesian chants and dances. Lele, by the way, is a more traditional name for Lahaina. ✉ *505 Front St., Lahaina* ☎ *808/667–5353* 🌐 *www.feastatlele.com* 🎫 *$125* ✍ *Reservations essential.*

The Feast at Mokapu. Held on the grounds of the posh Andaz, it's no surprise that this oceanfront luau is elevated to luxurious heights. A live band sets the soundtrack for an evening of storytelling, traditional and modern dance from across Polynesia, and an energetic fire-knife dance. The onstage performance is matched by eye-catching culinary creations delivered directly to your table and served family style. Indeed, standard luau fare goes gourmet with a multicourse dinner that blends traditional foods with modern flare. Preshow cultural activities, an open bar, and a complimentary printed photo are additional perks. ✉ *Andaz Maui at Wailea Resort, 3550 Wailea Alanui Dr., Wailea* ☎ *808/573–1234* 🌐 *www.feastatmokapu.com* 🎟 *$200.*

FAMILY **Grand Luau at Honuaula.** This show captivates with a playful interpretation of Hawaiian mythology and folklore. Indulge in pre-luau fun with Hawaiian games, lei making, and photo ops with the cast, then witness the unearthing of the kalua pig from the underground oven. Traditional dances share a vision of the first Polynesian voyage to the island, and there are also dancers on stilts, an iridescent aerialist suspended by silk, and many elaborate costumes. As a finale, a champion fire-knife dancer brings the house down with a spectacular display. ✉ *Grand Wailea Resort & Spa, 3850 Wailea Alanui Dr., Wailea* ☎ *808/875–7710* 🌐 *www.honuaula-luau.com* 🎟 *$120–$140.*

3

FAMILY Fodor's Choice ★ **Old Lahaina Luau.** Considered the best luau on Maui, it's certainly the most traditional. Before the show starts, immerse yourself in Hawaiian culture through interactive stations, and witness a traditional *imu* (underground oven) being unearthed. Sitting either at a table or on a *lauhala* (mat made of leaves), you can dine on Hawaiian cuisine such as pork *laulau* (wrapped with taro sprouts in *ti* leaves), ahi poke (raw ahi salad), lomilomi salmon (traditional Hawaiian diced side dish), and haupia. At sunset, the historical journey touches on the arrival of the Polynesians, the influence of missionaries and, later, the advent of tourism. Talented performers will charm you with beautiful music, powerful chanting, and a variety of hula styles, from *kahiko,* the ancient way of communicating with the gods, to *auana,* the modern hula. You won't see fire dancers here, as they aren't considered traditional. ■ TIP→ **This luau sells out regularly, so make reservations before your trip to Maui.** ✉ *1251 Front St., near Lahaina Cannery Mall, Lahaina* ☎ *808/667–1998* 🌐 *www.oldlahainaluau.com* 🎟 *$125* ✍ *Reservations essential.*

Te Au Moana. Te Au Moana means "ocean tide," which is all you need to know about the simply breathtaking backdrop for this South Maui luau at Wailea Beach Resort–Marriott, Maui. The tasty buffet serves a plethora of local staples and desserts like haupia, macadamia-nut brownies, and key lime squares. Longtime local entertainment company Tihati Productions seamlessly intertwines ancient Hawaiian stories and contemporary songs with traditional hula and Polynesian dances, concluding with a jaw-dropping solo fire-knife dance. ✉ *Wailea Beach Resort—Marriott, Maui, 3700 Wailea Alanui Dr., Wailea* ☎ *808/827–2740* 🌐 *www.teaumoana.com* 🎟 *$118* ✍ *Reservations essential.*

THEATER

For live theater, check local papers for events and show times.

FAMILY Fodor's Choice ★ ***Ulalena* at Maui Theatre.** One of Maui's hottest tickets, *Ulalena* is a musical extravaganza that has received accolades from audiences and Hawaiian culture experts. The powerful ensemble of singers, dancers, and musicians (more than 100 instruments played live) use creative stage wizardry to give an enchanting portrayal of island history and mythology. Native rhythms from authentic and rare instruments are blended with heart-wrenching chants and aerialist precision, making the 75-minute production seem like a whirlwind. Beer and wine are for sale at the concession stand. **TIP→ Call for details about dinner-theater packages in conjunction with local restaurants.** ✉ *Maui Theatre, 878 Front St., Lahaina* ☎ *808/856–7900* 🌐 *www.mauitheatre.com* 🎫 *$70–$115* ✍ *Reservations essential.*

Warren & Annabelle's. This is a hearty comedy with amazing sleight of hand. Magician Warren Gibson entices guests into his swank nightclub with a gleaming mahogany bar, a grand piano, and a resident ghost named Annabelle who tickles the ivories. Servers efficiently ply you with appetizers (coconut shrimp, crab cakes), desserts (chocolate pots de crème, assorted pies and cheesecakes, crème brûlée), and cocktails, while obliging a few impromptu song requests. Then, guests are ushered into a small theater where magic hilariously ensues. Because this is a nightclub act, no one under 21 is allowed. ✉ *The Outlets of Maui, 900 Front St., Lahaina* ☎ *808/667–6244* 🌐 *www.warrenandannabelles.com* 🎫 *$69–$115* ✍ *Reservations essential.*

SHOPS AND SPAS

Updated by Lehia Apana

We hope you've saved room in your suitcase. With our shopping guide, you can find the top shops for everything "Maui-grown," from *lilikoi* (passion fruit) jams and fresh pineapples to koa wood bowls and swimwear. Style hunters can get their fill of bohemian-resort chic in Paia, luxury brands in Wailea, and *paniolo* (cowboy) threads in Upcountry's quiet Makawao town. And before packing up your plunder, conjure up some Zen by soaking in Maui's natural resources at one of the island's top spas.

If you're seeking authentic Hawaiian artistry, check out the handcrafted instruments at Mele Ukulele and Maui Divers' jewelry designs. Splurge on an heirloom Niihau shell lei found in art galleries around the island or score pretty *puka* charms from the Maui Swap Meet in Kahului. Maxed out on your luggage weight? No problem. There's Hello Makana (🌐 *www.hellomakana.com*), a subscription service that curates food and gift items from high-quality local artisans and ships to your doorstep. Although the cost of basic goods might be higher on the Islands, keep in mind that the state has a much lower sales tax (4%) than the mainland.

Specialty food products—pineapples, coconuts, or Maui onions—and "Made in Maui" jams and jellies make great, less expensive souvenirs. Cook Kwee's Maui Cookies have gained a following, as have Kitch'n Cook'd The Original Maui Potato Chip Company. Coffee sellers now offer Maui-grown and roasted beans alongside the better-known Kona varieties. Remember that fresh fruit must be inspected by the U.S. Department of Agriculture before it can leave the state, so it's safest to buy a box that has already passed inspection.

Business hours for individual shops on the island are usually 9–5, seven days a week. Shops on Front Street and in shopping centers tend to stay open later (until 9 or 10 on weekends).

To unwind on your trip, you can rejuvenate in a yoga class and then enter one of the island's world-class spas. Many treatments use ingredients indigenous to Hawaii, like *kukui* nut and coconut. With coveted beauty lines like Eminence or Epicuren sharing the shelves with locally made Ala Lani Bath and Body, you're bound to find a spa product or two to bring home.

Traditional Swedish massage and European facials anchor most spa menus on the island, though you can also find shiatsu, ayurveda, aromatherapy, and other body treatments drawn from cultures across the globe. It can be fun to try some more local treatments or ingredients, though. *Lomilomi,* traditional Hawaiian massage involving powerful strokes down the length of the body, is a regional specialty passed down through generations. Many treatments incorporate local plants and flowers. *Awapuhi,* or Hawaiian ginger, and *noni,* a pungent-smelling fruit, are regularly used for their therapeutic benefits. *Limu,* or seaweed, and even coffee are employed in rousing salt scrubs and soaks.

3

WEST MAUI

BOOKSTORES

Fodor's Choice ★ **Maui Friends of the Library.** Behind the Wharf Cinema Center, this non-profit bookstore is run by volunteers who are happy to let you spend a few minutes (or hours) browsing shelves filled with mystery, sci-fi, fiction, military history, and "oddball" volumes. There's a nice section reserved for new Hawaiiana books. If you've finished with your vacation reading, donate it to benefit the island's public libraries. There are also locations at Queen Kaahumanu Center and behind the former Puunene School in Kahului. ✉ *658 Front St., Lahaina* ☎ *808/667–2696* 🌐 *www.mfol.org* ⏲ *Closed Sun.*

CLOTHING

Honolua Surf Company. If you're in the market for colorful print shirts and sundresses, check out this surf shop. It's popular with young women and men for surf trunks, casual clothing, and accessories. There are two locations on Front Street, plus branches in Lahaina Cannery Mall, the Shops at Wailea, Kihei, and Paia. ✉ *845 Front St., Lahaina* ☎ *808/661–8848* 🌐 *www.honoluasurf.com.*

FOOD

Take Home Maui. The folks at this colorful grocery and deli in West Maui will supply, pack, and deliver produce to your hotel. They can even ship pineapples, papayas, and sweet Maui onions straight from the farm to your door (U.S. mainland only). ✉ *121 Dickenson St., Lahaina* ☎ *808/661–6185* 🌐 *www.takehomemaui.com.*

GALLERIES

Fodor's Choice ★ **Lahaina Printsellers Ltd.** Available here are Hawaii's largest selection of original antique maps and prints of Hawaii and the Pacific. You can also buy museum-quality reproductions, plus paintings and photographs, many from local artists. Visit their production gallery at 1013 Limahana Place in Lahaina for an even greater selection. ✉ *764 Front St., Lahaina* ☎ *808/667–5815* 🌐 *www.printsellers.com.*

Lik Lahaina. Fine art photographer Peter Lik is known all over the world. It's easy to understand why when you see his exquisite and hyper-real pictures of vast Maui landscapes displayed in this Lahaina gallery. ✉ *712 Front St., Lahaina* ☎ *808/661–6623* 🌐 *www.lik.com/galleries/lahaina.html.*

Village Galleries Maui. This gallery houses the landscape paintings of popular local artists Betty Hay Freeland, George Allan, Joseph Fletcher, Pamela Andelin, Fred KenKnight, and Macario Pascual. There's a second location at the Ritz-Carlton, Kapalua. ✉ *120 Dickenson St., Lahaina* ☎ *808/661–4402* 🌐 *www.villagegalleriesmaui.com.*

HOME FURNISHINGS

Hale Zen. If you're shopping for gifts in West Maui, don't miss this store packed with beautiful island-inspired pieces for the home. Most of the teak furniture and home accessories are imported from Bali, but local purveyors supply the inventory of clothing, jewelry, beauty products, kitchenware, and food. ✉ *180 Dickenson St., Suite 111, Lahaina* ☎ *808/661–4802* 🌐 *www.halezen.com.*

JEWELRY

Maui Divers Jewelry. This company has been crafting pearls, coral, and traditional gemstones into jewelry for more than 55 years. There are branches at Whalers Village in Kaapanali, inside Hilo Hattie in Lahaina, and at the Kahului Airport. ✉ *658 Wharf St., Lahaina* ☎ *808/662–8666* 🌐 *www.mauidivers.com.*

SHOPPING CENTERS

FAMILY **Lahaina Cannery Mall.** This mall, housed inside an old pineapple cannery, hosts free events year-round like the Keiki Hula Festival and an annual ice-sculpting competition. Free ukulele lessons are available on Tuesday afternoon, and there are free hula shows throughout the week. Recommended stops include Na Hoku, purveyor of striking Hawaiian heirloom-quality jewelry and pearls, and Banana Wind, which carries ocean-inspired home decor. Whether you're searching for surf and skate threads or tropical resort wear, Crazy Shirts, Hawaiian Island Creations, Serendipity, and other retailers give you ample selections. The building underwent a massive renovation project in early 2018 to retain the center's historic character. ✉ *1221 Honoapiilani Hwy., Lahaina* ☎ *808/661–5304* 🌐 *www.lahainacannerymall.com.*

Fodor's Choice ★ **Whalers Village.** Chic Whalers Village has a whaling museum and wonderful oceanfront restaurants and shops. Upscale haunts include Louis Vuitton, Barron & Leeds, and Kate Spade New York, and beautyphiles can get their fix at Sephora. Elegant home accessories at Martin and MacArthur and Totally Hawaiian Gift Gallery are perfect Hawaii-made souvenirs, while the many great surf and swimwear shops will prepare you for a day at the beach. The outdoor mall also offers free weekly entertainment, lei-making classes, and hula lessons; check their website for a complete schedule. ✉ *2435 Kaanapali Pkwy., Kaanapali* ☎ *808/661–4567* 🌐 *www.whalersvillage.com.*

THE SOUTH SHORE

CLOTHING

Cruise. Sundresses, swimwear, sandals, bright beach towels, and stylish resort wear fill this upscale resort boutique. There is a second location in Whalers Village. ✉ *Grand Wailea Resort, 3850 Wailea Alanui Dr., Wailea* ☎ *808/874–3998.*

Tommy Bahama. Ranging from solid colors to full-on floral prints, you'll find classic island-inspired men's shirts, plus a wide range of styles that epitomizes resort wear. And just to prove you're on vacation, grab a post-shopping drink or dessert at the restaurant attached to the shop. ✉ *The Shops at Wailea, 3750 Wailea Alanui Dr., Wailea* ☎ *808/879–7828* 🌐 *www.tommybahama.com.*

3

FOOD

Fodor's Choice ★ **Tutu's Pantry.** In the middle of Kihei Kalama Village is this humble nook with an abundant supply of coffees, teas, cookies, jams, and other specialty-food items made on Maui. You're encouraged to ask for samples. ✉ *1941 S. Kihei Rd., Kihei* ☎ *808/874–6400* 🌐 *www.tutuspantry.com.*

SHOPPING CENTERS

Azeka Place Shopping Center. Spread across two phases on either side of South Kihei Road, this no-frills shopping center is in the heart of Kihei. The mall is comprised of more than 50 stores, including a scuba shop for rentals and dive bookings, a gas station, several great takeout and dine-in restaurants, a coffee shop, and a post office. Ample free parking makes this an easy stop to fulfill your basic needs. ✉ *1279 and 1280 S. Kihei Rd., Kihei* ☎ *808/879–5000.*

Kihei Kalama Village. Encompassing more than 40 specialty shops and restaurants, this area known as "the Triangle" attracts visitors and locals alike. In addition to the brick-and-mortar establishments, there are shaded outdoor stalls selling everything from printed and hand-painted T-shirts and sundresses to jewelry, pottery, wood carvings, fruit, and gaudily painted coconut husks—some, but not all, made by local craftspeople. ✉ *1941 S. Kihei Rd., Kihei* ☎ *808/879–6610.*

The Shops at Wailea. Stylish, upscale, and close to most of the resorts, this mall brings high fashion to Wailea. Luxury boutiques such as Gucci, Cos Bar, and Tiffany & Co. are represented, as are less expensive chains like Gap, Lululemon, and Tommy Bahama. The Market at the Shops, held every second and fourth Wednesday of the month, features local farmers, specialty food purveyors, and discounts from merchants. There are wonderful galleries, including Kii Gallery, where you can find glass art, prints, and Tahitian pearl jewelry. Island Gourmet Markets offers everything from grocery essentials to locally made food products, plus a wide selection of takeaway food options. ✉ *3750 Wailea Alanui Dr., Wailea* ☎ *808/891–6770* 🌐 *www.shopsatwailea.com.*

Wailea Gateway Center. Although lunch at chef Peter Merriman's Monkeypod is reason enough to venture to Wailea Gateway Center, you might also be enticed by the artisanal confections from Sweet Paradise Chocolate, fine foods at Market by Capische, and all things lovely and lacy at Panties in Paradise. ✉ *34 Wailea Gateway Pl., Wailea* 🌐 *www.wailea-gateway.com.*

CENTRAL MAUI

ARTS AND CRAFTS

Fodor's Choice ★ **Mele Ukulele.** For a professional-quality, authentic ukulele, skip the souvenir shops. Mele's handcrafted beauties are made of koa or mahogany and strung and finished by the store's owner, Michael Rock. There is a second location in the Shops at Wailea. ✉ *1750 Kaahumanu Ave., Wailuku* ☎ *808/244–3938* 🌐 *www.meleukulele.com.*

Fodor's Choice ★ **Native Intelligence.** This store in the heart of Wailuku champions cultural traditions and craftsmanship. It has curated Hawaiian and Polynesian works of art that include traditional wear, jewelry, weaponry, photography, books, music, and even surfboards. ✉ *1980 Main St., Wailuku* ☎ *808/249–2421* 🌐 *www.native-intel.com* ⏲ *Closed Sun.*

CLOTHING

Ha Wahine. At this clothing store, statement Polynesian prints are redefined in vibrantly colored blouses, *pareos* (beach wraps), dresses, and aloha shirts. All clothing is designed and made locally, as is most of the jewelry. ✉ *53 N. Market St., Wailuku* ☎ *808/344–1642* ⏲ *Closed Sat. and Sun.*

Fodor's Choice ★ **Hi-Tech.** Stop here immediately after deplaning to stock up on surf trunks, windsurfing gear, bikinis, or sundresses. You can also rent a surfboard or sign up for windsurfing or kiteboarding lessons while you're at it. You'll find additional branches in Kihei and Paia. ✉ *425 Koloa St., Kahului* ☎ *808/877–2111* 🌐 *www.surfmaui.com.*

FLEA MARKETS

Maui Swap Meet. Crafts, souvenirs that range from authentic to generic, fruit, shells, and aloha attire make this flea market in a college parking lot the island's biggest bargain. Maui's food trucks and freshly cracked coconuts are an added draw. ✉ *Off Kahului Beach Rd., Kahului* ☎ *808/244–3100* 🌐 *www.mauiexposition.com* 🎟 *50¢.*

FOOD

Maui Coffee Roasters. The best stop on Maui for Kona and Island coffees is this café and roasting house near Kahului Airport. Salespeople give good advice and will ship items, and you even get a free cup of joe in a signature to-go cup when you buy a pound of coffee. ✉ *444 Hana Hwy., Kahului* ☎ *808/877–2877* 🌐 *www.mauicoffeeroasters.com.*

SHOPPING CENTERS

Maui Marketplace. On the busy stretch of Dairy Road, this behemoth mall near Kahului Airport couldn't be more conveniently located. The 20-acre complex houses several outlet stores and big retailers, such as Pier One Imports, Sports Authority, and Old Navy. Sample local and ethnic cuisines at the Kau Kau Corner food court. ✉ *270 Dairy Rd., Kahului* ☎ *808/873–0400* 🌐 *www.mauimarketplacehi.com.*

Puunene Shopping Center. This relatively new strip mall near the Kahului Airport is anchored by Target (which includes a Starbucks inside). Other retailers include Maui Tacos, Starbucks, and the popular farm-to-table takeout joint Fork & Salad. ✉ *Corner of Maui Veterans Hwy. and Hookele St., Kahului.*

Queen Kaahumanu Center. Maui's largest shopping center has more than 100 stores and restaurants, a movie theater, and a food court. The mall's interesting rooftop, composed of a series of manta ray–like umbrella shades, is easily spotted. Stop at Camellia Seeds for what locals call "crack seed," a snack made from dried fruits, or swing by 180 Boardshop for Hawaii-based streetwear like 808 All Day or In4mation. For surf-inspired gear, stop by Local Motion and Shapers. Other stops include mall standards such as Macy's, Pacific Sunwear, and American Eagle Outfitters. Beyond retail therapy, the mall also hosts a creative lineup of events throughout the month, including a farmers' market, live music, and car shows. ✉ *275 W. Kaahumanu Ave., Kahului* ☎ *808/877–3369* 🌐 *www.queenkaahumanucenter.com.*

UPCOUNTRY, THE NORTH SHORE, AND HANA

CLOTHING

Designing Wahine Emporium. At this Upcountry haven for Hawaiian merchandise and Balinese imports, you can find endless gift options like authentic aloha shirts, jams and jellies, children's clothes and books, bath and beauty products, and home decor crafted from wood. ✉ *3640 Baldwin Ave., Makawao* ☎ *808/573–0990.*

Pink By Nature. Owner Desiree Martinez knows what the modern bohemian wants to wear. She keeps her rustic store stocked with local jewelry and feminine pieces from Indah, Bella Dahl, and Novella Royale. Versatile plaid shirts from Rails are popular, as are their selections of Samudra bags and Lovely Bird hats. An equally stylish men's and home branch is located a few shops down. ✉ *3663 Baldwin Ave., Makawao* ☎ *808/572–9576* 🌐 *www.pinkbynaturemaui.com.*

FOOD

Fodor's Choice ★ **Mana Foods.** At this bustling health food store you can stock up on local fish and grass-fed beef for your barbecue. You'll find the best selection of organic produce on the island, as well as a great bakery and deli. The healthy and beauty room has a dizzying selection of products that promise to keep you glowing. ✉ *49 Baldwin Ave., Paia* ☎ *808/579–8078* 🌐 *www.manafoodsmaui.com.*

Paia Gelato. Fresh gelato made with locally sourced ingredients is the draw here. Try the lilikoi quark cheese flavor and thank us later. You'll also find jams, jellies, and dressings from Jeff Gomes, coffees from Maui Coffee Roasters, and treats from Maui Sweet Cakes. ✉ *99C Hana Hwy., Paia* ☎ *808/579–9201* 🌐 *www.paiagelato.com.*

GALLERIES

Fodor's Choice ★ **Hana Coast Gallery.** One of the most well-curated galleries on the island, this 3,000-square-foot facility has handcrafted koa furniture, marble sculptures, photography, and jewelry on consignment from local artists. ✉ *Travaasa Hana, 5031 Hana Hwy., Hana* ☎ *808/248–8636, 800/637–0188* 🌐 *www.hanacoast.com.*

Fodor's Choice ★ **Maui Crafts Guild.** The island's only artist cooperative, Maui Crafts Guild is crammed with treasures. Resident artists produce lead-glazed pottery, basketry, glass and feather art, photography, ceramics, and pressed-flower art. The prices are surprisingly low. ✉ *120 Hana Hwy., Paia* ☎ *808/579–9697* 🌐 *www.mauicraftsguild.com.*

Maui Hands. This gallery shows work by hundreds of local artists: exquisite woodwork, lovely ceramics, authentic Niihau shell lei, wave metal etchings by Richard DiGiacomo, and whimsical clay figures by Steven Lee Smeltzer. There are locations in Lahaina, Makawao, and at the Hyatt Regency Maui in Kaanapali. ✉ *84 Hana Hwy., Paia* ☎ *808/579–9245* 🌐 *www.mauihands.com.*

Viewpoints Gallery. This friendly gallery is co-owned by local artists and offers eclectic paintings, sculptures, photography, ceramics, and glass, along with locally made jewelry and quilts. Located along a cozy courtyard, its free monthly exhibits feature artists from various disciplines. ✉ *3620 Baldwin Ave., Makawao* ☎ *808/572–5979* 🌐 *www.viewpointsgallerymaui.com.*

MAUI'S BEST OMIYAGE

Omiyage is the Japanese term for food souvenirs.

- Lavender-salt seasoning from **Alii Kula Lavender**
- Maui Gold Pineapple from **Take Home Maui**
- Peaberry beans from **Maui Coffee Company**
- Nicky Beans from **Maui Coffee Roasters**
- Jeff's Jams and Jellies from **Paia Gelato**
- Hot Sauces from **Adoboloco**
- Hawaiian spice blends from **Volcano Spice Co. Store**

JEWELRY

Maui Master Jewelers. The shop's exterior is as rustic as all the old buildings of Makawao and belies the elegance of the handcrafted jewelry displayed within. The store has added a diamond collection to its designs. ✉ *3655 Baldwin Ave., Makawao* ☎ *808/573–5400* 🌐 *www.mauimasterjewelers.com.*

SWIMWEAR

Fodor's Choice ★ **Maui Girl.** This is *the* place on Maui for swimwear, cover-ups, beach hats, and sandals. Maui Girl designs its own suits, which have been spotted in *Sports Illustrated* fashion shoots, and imports tinier versions from Brazil as well. Tops and bottoms can be purchased separately, increasing your chances of finding the perfect fit. You can also find Tori Praver Swimwear designs here. ✉ *12 Baldwin Ave., Paia* ☎ *808/579–9266* 🌐 *www.maui-girl.com.*

SPAS

WEST MAUI

Fodor's Choice ★ **Spa Montage, Kapalua Bay.** This spa's nondescript entrance opens onto an airy, modern beach house with panoramic island and ocean views. With amenities including a café and juice bar, movement studio, gym, a coed infinity pool, and outdoor hydrotherapy circuits, you can easily spend a day meandering about the spa's expansive layout without feeling cooped up. The spa menu includes therapies that incorporate local ingredients harvested from nearby Mauna Kahalawai (West Maui's mountain) and calming ingredients from the sea. ✉ *1 Bay Dr., Kapalua* ☎ *808/665-8282* 🌐 *www.spamontagekapalua.com* ☞ *$215 for 60-min massage; 10% discount on 3 or more treatments.*

Waihua Spa, The Ritz-Carlton, Kapalua. At this gorgeous 17,500-square-foot spa, you enter a blissful maze where floor-to-ceiling riverbed stones lead to serene treatment rooms, couples' *hales* (cabanas), and a rain forest–like grotto with a Jacuzzi, dry cedar sauna, and eucalyptus steam rooms. Hang out in the coed waiting area, where sliding-glass doors open to a whirlpool overlooking a taro-patch garden. Exfoliate any rough spots with an alaea salt (Hawaiian red sea salt) scrub, then wash off in a private outdoor shower garden before indulging in a lomilomi massage. High-end beauty treatments include advanced oxygen technology to tighten and nourish mature skin. The boutique has a highly coveted collection of organic, local, and high-end beauty products, fitness wear, and Maui-made Nina Kuna jewelry and natural skin-care lines. ✉ *The Ritz-Carlton, Kapalua, 1 Ritz-Carlton Dr., Kapalua* ☎ *808/669–6200, 800/262–8440* 🌐 *www.ritzcarlton.com* ☞ *$190 for 50-min massage, $350 spa packages.*

3

SOUTH SHORE

Awili Spa and Salon, Andaz Maui at Wailea Resort. At Awili Spa and Salon's apothecary or blending bar (*awili* means "to mix"), consultants assist in creating your personalized oils made from local ingredients. Set aside an extra hour to fully indulge in the blending bar, or opt for ready-made concoctions. The cool, soothing interior of this spa is an extension of the minimalist, monochromatic style of the Andaz Maui at Wailea Resort. Relaxation lounges are stocked with thoughtful amenities like tea, coconut shortbread cookies, and house-made granola. ✉ *Andaz Maui at Wailea Resort, 3550 Wailea Alanui Dr., Wailea* ☎ *808/573–1234* 🌐 *maui.andaz.hyatt.com* ☞ *$185 for 60-min massage.*

Fodor's Choice ★ **The Spa at Four Seasons Resort Maui.** Thoughtful gestures like fresh flowers beneath the massage table, organic ginger tea in the relaxation room, and your choice of music ease your mind and muscles before the treatment even begins. Shop for sustainable and organic beauty products like ISUN and Ola Hawaii from the Big Island, or book an appointment at the Ajne blending bar to customize a scent according to your body chemistry. For the ultimate indulgence, reserve one of the seaside open-air *hale hau* (traditional thatch-roof houses). Taking wellness to heart, the spa partnered with a clinical nutritionist, Dr. Mark Emerson, who gives a complimentary consultation and then designs a "Wellness Your Way" program befitting the guest's health needs. Offerings include noninvasive laser body shaping treatments, indoor or outdoor fitness activities, and a nourishing menu created by the hotel's culinary team. ✉ *Four Seasons Resort Maui at Wailea, 3900 Wailea Alanui Dr., Wailea* ☎ *808/874–8000* 🌐 *www.fourseasons.com/maui* ☞ *$189 for 50-min massage.*

Fodor's Choice ★ **Willow Stream Spa, Fairmont Kea Lani.** This spa makes meticulous use of Hawaii's natural elements to replenish your Zen. Give a full hour to enjoy the fascinating amenities, two if you plan to work out. At the mud bar, small bowls of volcanic ash eucalyptus clay or white lavender and taro clay can be applied to the body before you head to the steam room. From there, rinse off in a high-tech shower that combines color, sound, and hydrotherapy to mimic different types of Hawaiian rain. A heated stone bench awaits to deepen the relaxation before the treatment. The spa has advanced technology like a wave massage table to simulate floating or LED light and microcurrent electric pulse to tighten the skin. ✉ *4100 Wailea Alanui, Wailea* ☎ *808/875–2229* 🌐 *www.willowstreamspamaui.com* ☞ *$189 for 60-min Stress Relaxation massage, $369 spa package.*

ROAD TO HANA

The Spa at Travaasa Hana. A bamboo gate opens into an outdoor sanctuary with a lava-rock basking pool and hot tub. At first glimpse, this spa seems to have been organically grown, not built. Ferns still wet from Hana's frequent downpours nourish the spirit as you rest with a cup of Hawaiian herbal tea, take an invigorating dip in the cold plunge pool, or have a therapist stretch your limbs as you soak in the warm waters of the aquatic therapy pool. Luxurious skin-care treatments feature organic products from Epicuren and Honua Skincare, and body treatments incorporate organic Maui-made Ala Lani Bath and Body products. ✉ *Travaasa Hana, 5031 Hana Hwy., Hana* ☎ *808/270–5290* 🌐 *www.travaasa.com/hana* ☞ *$175 for 60-min massage, $250 spa package; prices reflect gratuity.*

WATER SPORTS AND TOURS

Updated by Lehia Apana

Getting into (or onto) the water may well be the highlight of your Maui trip. The Valley Isle is an aquatic wonderland where you can learn to surf, stand-up paddle, or scuba dive. Vibrant snorkel sites can be explored right off the shore, or easily accessed aboard a kayak, motorized raft, or power catamaran. From November through April (peak season January–March), whale-watching adventures are a top draw as humpbacks escaping Alaska's frigid winter arrive in Maui's warm protected waters to frolic, mate, and birth.

Along Maui's leeward coastline, from Kaanapali on the West Shore all the way down to Waiala Cove on the South Shore, you can discover great spots for snorkeling and swimming, some more crowded than others. On a good day, you might encounter dozens of green sea turtles at an underwater cleaning station, a pod of dolphins riding by the catamaran's bow, and an abundance of colorful fish hovering by bright cauliflower coral reefs.

When your preferred sport calls for calm glassy waters, get an early start when visibility is best; plus the trade winds begin to roll through the valleys in the late morning and pick up speed in the afternoon. For those thrill seekers who flock to Hawaii for the wind, it's best to head out to the North Shore's Hookipa, where consistent winds keep kiteboarders flying and windsurfers jibing; or Peahi (aka Jaws) where surfers seasonally get towed in to glide on 30- to 60-foot waves.

Treat the ocean with respect, and for your safety choose activities that suit your skill level and health condition. If in doubt, skip the rental and pay for a lesson so that you can have proper instructions in navigating swells and wind, and someone with you in case you get in a bind. The ocean might be beautiful, but it can be unpredictable.

Surf can be enjoyed all year, and avid surfers live for the winter swells when the north and west coasts get really "lit up." Whale season on Maui is nothing short of majestic at its peak, late January–mid-March. You can spot them from the shore, or get up close from a motorized raft or catamaran.

BODY BOARDING AND BODYSURFING

Bodysurfing and "sponging" (as body boarding is called by the regulars; "boogie boarding" is another variation) are great ways to catch some waves without having to master surfing—and there's no balance or coordination required. A body board (or "sponge") is softer than a hard fiberglass surfboard, which means you can ride safely in the rough-and-tumble surf zone. If you get tossed around—which is half the fun—you don't have a heavy surfboard nearby to bang your head on but you do have something to hang onto. Serious spongers invest in a single short-clipped fin to help propel them into the wave.

BEST SPOTS

In West Maui, **D.T. Fleming Beach** offers great surf almost daily along with some nice amenities: ample parking, restrooms, a shower, grills, picnic tables, and a daily lifeguard. Caution is advised, especially during winter months, when the current and undertow can get rough.

Between Kihei and Wailea on the South Shore, **Kamaole III** is a good spot for bodysurfing and body boarding. It has a sandy floor, with 1- to 3-foot waves breaking not too far out. It's often crowded late in the day, especially on weekends when local kids are out of school. Don't let that chase you away; the waves are wide enough for everyone.

If you don't mind public nudity (officially illegal but practiced nonetheless), Puu Olai **(aka Little Beach)** on the South Shore is the best break on the island for body boarding and bodysurfing. The shape of the sandy shoreline creates waves that break a long way out and tumble into shore. Because it's sandy, you only risk stubbing a toe on the few submerged rocks. Don't try body boarding at neighboring Oneloa **(aka Big Beach)**—waves will slap you onto the steep shore. To get to Little Beach, take the first entrance to Makena State Beach Park; climb the rock wall at the north end of the beach.

On the North Shore, **Paia Bay** has waves suitable for spongers and body surfers. The beach is just before Paia town, beyond the large community building and grass field.

EQUIPMENT

Most condos and hotels have body boards available to guests—some in better condition than others (beat-up boards work just as well for beginners). You can also pick up a body board from any discount shop, such as Target or Longs Drugs (now owned by CVS), for upward of $30.

Auntie Snorkel. You can rent decent body boards here for $6.25 a day or $18.75 a week. ✉ *2439 S. Kihei Rd., Kihei* ☎ *808/879–6263* 🌐 *www.auntiesnorkel.com.*

West Maui Sports and Fishing Supply. This old country store has been around since 1987 and has some of the best prices on the west side. Surfboards go for $15 a day or $70 a week. Snorkel and fishing gear, beach chairs, and umbrellas are also available. ✉ *843 Wainee St., Lahaina* ☎ *808/661–6252* 🌐 *www.westmauisports.com.*

DEEP-SEA FISHING

If fishing is your sport, Maui is your island. In these waters you'll find ahi, *aku* (skipjack tuna), barracuda, bonefish, *kawakawa* (bonito), mahimahi, Pacific blue marlin, ono, and *ulua* (jack crevalle). You can fish year-round and you don't need a license.

Plenty of fishing boats run out of Lahaina and Maalaea harbors. If you charter a private boat, expect to spend in the neighborhood of $700 to $1,000 for a thrilling half day in the swivel seat. You can share a boat for much less if you don't mind close quarters with a stranger who may get seasick, drunk, or worse: lucky! Before you sign up, you should know that some boats keep the catch. Most will, however, fillet a nice piece for you to take home. And if you catch a real beauty, you might even be able to have it professionally mounted. ■ TIP→ **Because boats fill up fast during busy seasons, make reservations before coming to Maui.**

You're expected to bring your own lunch and beverages in unbreakable containers. (Shop the night before; it's hard to find snacks at 6 am.) Boats supply coolers, ice, and bait. A 7% tax is added to the cost of a trip, and a 10%–20% tip for the crew is suggested.

BOATS AND CHARTERS

***Finest Kind* Sportfishing.** An 1,118-pound blue marlin was reeled in by the crew aboard *Finest Kind,* a lovely 37-foot Merritt kept so clean you'd never guess the action it's seen. Captain Dave has been around these waters for about 40 years, long enough to befriend other expert fishers. This family-run company operates three boats and specializes in skilled trolling. Shared charters start at $150 for four hours and go up to $220 for a full day. Private trips run $800–$1,300. No bananas on board, please; the captain thinks they're bad luck for fishing. ✉ *Lahaina Harbor, Slip 7, Lahaina* ☎ *877/688–0999* 🌐 *www.finestkindsportfishing.com.*

Die Hard Sportfishing. Captain Fuzzy Alboro runs a highly recommended operation on the 33-foot *Die Hard*. Check-in is at 1:45 am, returning around noon. He takes a minimum of four and a maximum of six people. The cost is from $220 for a shared boat to $1,500 for a private charter. ✉ *Lahaina Harbor, Slip 10, Lahaina* ☎ *808/344–5051* 🌐 *www.diehardsportfishing.com.*

KAYAKING

Kayaking is a fantastic and eco-friendly way to experience Maui's coast up close. Floating aboard a "plastic Popsicle stick" is easier than you might think, and allows you to cruise out to vibrant, living coral reefs and waters where dolphins and even whales roam. Kayaking can be a leisurely paddle or a challenge of heroic proportions, depending on your ability, the location, and the weather. ■ TIP→ **Although you can rent kayaks independently, we recommend hiring a guide.**

An apparently calm surface can hide extremely strong ocean currents. Most guides are naturalists who will steer you away from surging surf, lead you to pristine reefs, and point out camouflaged fish, like the stalking hawkfish. Not having to schlep your gear on top of your rental car is a bonus. A half-day tour runs around $75.

If you decide to strike out on your own, tour companies will rent kayaks for the day with paddles, life vests, and roof racks, and many will meet you near your chosen location. Ask for a map of good entries and plan to avoid paddling back to shore against the wind (schedule extra time for the return trip regardless). Read weather conditions, bring binoculars, and take a careful look from the bay before heading in. For beginners, get there early in the day before the trade wind kicks in, and try sticking close to the shore. When you're ready to snorkel, secure your belongings in a dry pack on board and drag your kayak by its bowline behind you. (This isn't as hard as it sounds.)

BEST SPOTS

Makena Landing is an excellent starting point for a South Shore adventure. Enter from the paved parking lot or the small sandy beach a little south. The shoreline is lined with million-dollar mansions. The bay itself is virtually empty, but the right edge is flanked with brilliant coral heads and juvenile turtles. If you round the point on the right, you come across Five Caves, a system of enticing underwater arches. In the morning you may see dolphins, and the arches are havens for lobsters, eels, and spectacularly hued butterfly fish.

In West Maui, past the steep cliffs on the Honoapiilani Highway, there's a long stretch of inviting coastline that includes **Ukumehame Beach.** This is a good spot for beginners; entry is easy, and there's much to see in every direction. Pay attention if trade winds pick up from the late morning onward; paddling against them can be challenging. If you want to snorkel, the best visibility is farther out at Olowalu Beach. Watch for sharp kiawe thorns buried in the sand on the way into the water. Water shoes are recommended.

EQUIPMENT AND TOURS

Kelii's Kayak Tours. One of the highest-rated kayak outfitters on the island, Kelii's offers kayaking trips and combo adventures where you can also surf, snorkel, or hike to a waterfall. Leading groups of up to eight people, the guides show what makes each reef unique. Trips are available on the island's north, south, and west shores. ✉ *1993 S. Kihei Rd., Suite 12, Kihei* ☎ *808/874–7652*, 🌐 *www.keliiskayak.com.*

Fodor's Choice ★ **South Pacific Kayaks.** These guys pioneered recreational kayaking on Maui, so they know their stuff. Guides are friendly, informative, and eager to help you get the most out of your experience; we're talking true, fun-loving, kayak geeks who will maneuver away from crowds when exploring prime snorkel spots. South Pacific stands out as adventurous *and* environmentally responsible, plus their gear and equipment are well maintained. They offer a variety of trips leaving from both West Maui and South Shore locations. ✉ *95 Halekuai St., Kihei* ☎ *808/875–4848,* 🌐 *www.southpacifickayaks.com* 🎫 *From $74.*

PARASAILING

Parasailing is an easy exhilarating way to earn your wings: just strap on a harness attached to a parachute, and a powerboat pulls you up and over the ocean from a launching dock or a boat's platform. **■ TIP→ Parasailing is limited to West Maui, and "thrill craft"—including parasails—are prohibited in Maui waters during humpback-whale calving season, December 15–May 15.**

LESSONS AND TOURS

West Maui Parasail. Soar at 800 feet above the ocean for a bird's-eye view of Lahaina, or be daring at 1,200 feet for smoother rides and even better views. The captain will be glad to let you experience a "toe dip" or "freefall" if you request it. Hour-long trips departing from Lahaina Harbor and Kaanapali Beach include 8- to 10-minute flights and run from $85 for the 800-foot ride to $95 for the 1,200-foot ride. Observers pay $40 each. **■ TIP→ No parasailing during whale season.** ✉ *Lahaina Harbor, Slip 15, Lahaina* ☎ *808/661–4060* 🌐 *www.westmauiparasail.com.*

RAFTING

The high-speed, inflatable rafts you find on Maui are nothing like the raft that Huck Finn used to drift down the Mississippi. While passengers grip straps, these rafts fly, skimming and bouncing across the sea. Because they're so maneuverable, they go where the big boats can't—secret coves, sea caves, and remote beaches. Two-hour trips run around $50, half-day trips upward of $100. **■ TIP→ Although safe, these trips are not for the faint of heart. If you have back or neck problems or are pregnant, you should reconsider this activity.**

TOURS

Blue Water Rafting. One of the few ways to get to the stunning Kanaio Coast (the roadless southern coastline beyond Ahihi-Kinau), this rafting tour begins conveniently at the Kihei boat ramp on the South Shore. Dolphins, turtles, and other marine life are the highlight of this adventure, along with majestic sea caves, lava arches, and views of Haleakala. The Molokini stop is usually timed between the bigger catamarans, so you can enjoy the crater without the usual massive crowd. If conditions permit, you'll be able to snorkel the back wall, which has much more marine life than the inside. ✉ *Kihei Boat Ramp, S. Kihei Rd., Kihei* ☎ *808/879–7238* 🌐 *www.bluewaterrafting.com* 🎫 *From $60.*

Ocean Riders. Start the day with a spectacular view of the sun rising above the West Maui Mountains, then cross the Auau Channel to Lanai's Kaiolohia (commonly referred to as Shipwreck Beach). After a short swim at a secluded beach, this tour circles Lanai, allowing you to view the island's 70 miles of remote coast. The "back side" of Lanai is one of Hawaii's unsung marvels, and you can expect to stop at three protected coves for snorkeling. You might chance upon sea turtles, monk seals, and a friendly reef shark, as well as rare varieties of angelfish and butterfly fish. Guides are knowledgeable and slow down long enough for you to marvel at sacred burial caves and interesting rock formations. Sit toward the back bench if you are sensitive to motion sickness. Tours include snorkel gear, a fruit breakfast, and a satisfying deli lunch. ✉ *Mala Wharf, Front St., Lahaina* ☎ *808/661–3586* 🌐 *www.mauioceanriders.com* 🎫 *From $139.*

3

Fodor's Choice ★ **Redline Rafting.** This company's raft tours begin with a trip to Molokini Crater for some snorkeling. If weather permits, the raft explores the crater's back wall, too. There's a quick stop at La Perouse Bay to spot dolphins, and then it's off to Makena for more underwater fun and a deli lunch. The rafts provide great seating, comfort, and shade. Whale-watching excursions are $45, and snorkel trips are $135. ✉ *Kihei Boat Ramp, 2800 S. Kihei Rd., Kihei* ☎ *808/201–7450* 🌐 *www.redlinerafting.com.*

SAILING

With the islands of Molokai, Lanai, Kahoolawe, and Molokini a stone's throw away, Maui waters offer visually arresting backdrops for sailing adventures. Sailing conditions can be fickle, so some operations throw in snorkeling or whale-watching, and others offer sunset cruises. Winds are consistent in summer but variable in winter, and afternoons are generally windier throughout the year. Prices range from around $40 for two-hour trips to $80 for half-day excursions. ■ TIP→ **You won't be sheltered from the elements on the trim racing boats, so be sure to bring a hat that won't blow away, a light jacket, sunglasses, and sunscreen.**

BOATS AND CHARTERS

Paragon Sailing Charters. If you want to snorkel and sail, this is your boat. Many snorkel cruises claim to sail but actually motor most of the way—Paragon is an exception. Both Paragon vessels (one catamaran in Lahaina, the other in Maalaea) are shipshape, and crews are accommodating and friendly. Its mooring in Molokini Crater is particularly good, and tours will often stay after the masses have left. The Lanai trip includes a picnic lunch at Manele Bay, snorkeling, and a quick afternoon blue-water swim. Extras on the trips to Lanai include mai tais, sodas, dessert, and champagne. Hot and cold appetizers come with the sunset sail, which departs from Lahaina Harbor every Monday through Saturday. Sunset sail starts at $75, snorkel at $125. ✉ *Maalaea Harbor, Maalaea* ☎ *808/419-3422,* 🌐 *www.sailmaui.com.*

Fodor's Choice ★ **Trilogy Excursions.** With more than four decades of experience and some good karma from their reef-cleaning campaigns, Trilogy has a great reputation in the community. It's one of only two companies that sail, rather than motor, to Molokini Crater. A two-hour sail starts at $60. The sunset trip includes appetizers, beer, wine, champagne, margaritas, and mai tais. Tours depart from Lahaina Harbor; Maalaea Harbor; and, in West Maui, in front of the Kaanapali Beach Hotel. ✉ *Lahaina Harbor, 675 Wharf St., Lahaina* ☎ *808/874–5649, 888/225–6284* 🌐 *www.sailtrilogy.com.*

SCUBA DIVING

Maui has been rated one of the top 10 dive spots in the United States. It's common to see huge sea turtles, eagle rays, and small reef sharks, not to mention many varieties of angelfish, parrotfish, eels, and octopuses. Most of the species are unique to this area, making it unlike other popular dive destinations. In addition, the terrain itself is different from other dive spots. Here you can find ancient and intricate lava flows full of nooks where marine life hide and breed. Although the water tends to be a bit rougher—not to mention colder—divers are given a great thrill during humpback-whale season, when you can actually hear whales singing underwater. Be sure to check conditions before you head out.

Some of the finest diving spots in all of Hawaii lie along the Valley Isle's western and southwestern shores. Dives are best in the morning, when visibility can hold a steady 100 feet. If you're a certified diver, you can rent gear at any Maui dive shop simply by showing your PADI or NAUI card. Unless you're familiar with the area, however, it's probably best to hook up with a dive shop for an underwater tour. Tours include tanks and weights and start around $130. Wet suits and buoyancy compensators are rented separately, for an additional $15–$30. Shops also offer introductory dives ($100–$160) for those who aren't certified. ■ **TIP→ Before signing on with any outfitter, it's a good idea to ask a few pointed questions about your guide's experience, the weather outlook, and the condition of the equipment.**

BEST SPOTS

Honolua Bay, a marine preserve in West Maui, is alive with many varieties of coral and tame tropical fish, including large ulua, kahala, barracuda, and manta rays. With depths of 20–50 feet, this is a popular summer dive spot, good for all levels. ■ **TIP→ High surf often prohibits winter dives.**

On the South Shore, one of the most popular dive spots is **Makena Landing** (also called Nahuna Point, Five Graves, or Five Caves). You can revel in underwater delights—caves, ledges, coral heads, and an outer reef home to a large green–sea turtle colony called Turtle Town. ■ **TIP→ Entry is rocky lava, so be careful where you step. This area is for more experienced divers.**

Three miles offshore from Wailea on the South Shore, **Molokini Crater** is world-renowned for its deep, crystal clear, fish-filled waters. A crescent-shape islet formed by the eroding top of a volcano, the crater is a marine preserve ranging 10–80 feet deep. The numerous tame fish and brilliant coral within the crater make it a popular introductory dive site. On calm days, the back side of Molokini Crater (called Back Wall) can be a dramatic sight for advanced divers, with visibility of up to 150 feet. The enormous drop-off into the Alalakeiki Channel offers awesome seascapes, black coral, and chance sightings of larger fish and sharks.

Some of the southern coast's best diving is at **Ahihi Bay,** part of the Ahihi-Kinau Natural Area Reserve. The area frequently closes due to shark sightings; call ahead before visiting. The area is best known for its "Fishbowl," a small cove right beside the road, next to a hexagonal house. Here you can find excellent underwater scenery, with many types of fish and coral. ■ **TIP→ Be careful of the rocky-bottom entry (wear reef shoes if you have them)**. The Fishbowl can get crowded, especially in high season. If you want to steer clear of the crowds, look for a second entry ½ mile farther down the road—a gravel parking lot at the surf spot called Dumps. Entry into the bay here is trickier, as the coastline is all lava.

Formed from the last lava flow two centuries ago, **La Perouse Bay** brings you the best variety of fish—more than any other site. The lava rock provides a protective habitat, and all four types of Hawaii's angelfish can be found here. To dive the spot called Pinnacles, enter anywhere along the shore, just past the private entrance to the beach. Wear your reef shoes, as entry is sharp. To the right, you'll be in the Ahihi-Kinau Natural Area Reserve; to the left, you're outside. Look for the white sandy bottom with massive coral heads. Pinnacles is for experienced divers only.

EQUIPMENT, LESSONS, AND TOURS

Fodor's Choice ★ **Ed Robinson's Diving Adventures.** Ed Robinson wrote the book, literally, on Molokini. Because he knows so much, he includes a "Biology 101" talk with every dive. An expert marine photographer, he leads dives to South Maui and the back side of Molokini Crater. There's a discount if you book multiple dives. Prices start at $129.95, plus $20 for the gear. ✉ *165 Halekuai St., Kihei* ☎ *808/879–3584* 🌐 *www.mauiscuba.com.*

Extended Horizons. This eco-friendly dive boat stands apart by being the only commercial vessel on Maui to run on 100% locally made biodiesel. Its popular Lanai charter has divers swimming through dramatic archways and lava structures, while other trips venture along West Maui. Shore and night dives are also available. Tours are run by enthusiastic and professional guides who are keen at not only identifying underwater creatures, but also interpreting their behavior. ✉ *Mala Wharf, Lahaina* ☎ *808/667–0611* 🌐 *www.extendedhorizons.com* 🎫 *From $119.*

Maui Dive Shop. With three locations islandwide, Maui Dive Shop offers scuba charters, diving instruction, and equipment rental. Excursions go to Molokini, Shipwreck Beach, and Cathedrals on Lanai. Intro dives are done offshore. Night dives, scooter dives, and customized trips are available, as are full SSI and PADI certificate programs. ✉ *1455 S. Kihei Rd., Kihei* ☎ *808/879–3388, 800/542–3483* 🌐 *www.mauidiveshop.com.*

Mike Severns Diving. This company has been around for nearly four decades and takes groups of up to 12 certified divers with two dive masters to both popular and off-the-beaten-path dive sites. Boat trips leave from Kihei Boat Ramp, and go wherever conditions are best: the Molokini Marine Life Conservation District, Molokini Crater's Back Wall, Makena, or beyond La Perouse Bay. ✉ *Kihei Boat Ramp, S. Kihei Rd., Kihei* ☎ *808/879–6596* 🌐 *www.mikesevernsdiving.com* 🎫 *Dives from $139; charters from $1,670.*

SNORKELING

Fodor's Choice ★ There are two ways to approach snorkeling—by land or by sea. At around 7 am daily, a parade of boats heads out to Lanai or to Molokini Crater, that ancient cone of volcanic cinder off the coast of Wailea. Boat trips offer some advantages—deeper water, seasonal whale-watching, crew assistance, lunch, and gear. But much of Maui's best snorkeling is found just steps from the road. Nearly the entire leeward coastline from Kapalua south to Ahihi-Kinau offers opportunities to ogle fish and turtles. If you're patient and sharp-eyed, you may glimpse eels, octopuses, lobsters, eagle rays, and even a rare shark or monk seal. ■ TIP→ **Visibility is best in the morning, before the trade winds pick up.**

BEST SPOTS

Snorkel sites here are listed from north to south, starting at the northwest corner of the island.

Just north of Kapalua, the **Honolua Bay Marine Life Conservation District** has a superb reef for snorkeling. ■ TIP→ **Bring a fish key with you, as you're sure to see many species of triggerfish, filefish, and wrasses.** The coral formations on the right side of the bay are particularly dramatic, with pink, aqua, and orange varieties. On a lucky day, you might even be snorkeling with a pod of dolphins nearby. Take care entering the water; there's no beach, and the rocks and concrete ramp can be slippery. The northeast corner of this windward bay periodically gets hammered by big waves in winter. Avoid the bay then, as well as after heavy rains.

Minutes south of Honolua Bay, dependable **Kapalua Bay** beckons. As beautiful above the water as it is below, Kapalua is exceptionally calm, even when other spots get testy. Needle and butterfly fish dart just past the sandy beach, which is why it's sometimes crowded. ■ TIP→ **The sand can be particularly hot here—watch your toes!**

Black Rock, in front of the Sheraton Maui Resort & Spa at the northernmost tip of **Kaanapali Beach,** is great for snorkelers of any skill level. The entry couldn't be easier—dump your towel on the sand and in you go. Beginners can stick close to shore and still see lots of action. Advanced snorkelers can swim to the tip of Black Rock to see larger fish and eagle rays. One of the underwater residents here is a turtle whose hefty size earned him the name Volkswagen. He sits very still, so you have to look closely. Equipment can be rented on-site. Parking, in a small lot adjoining the hotel, is the only hassle.

Along Honoapiilani Highway there are several favorite snorkel sites, including the area just out from the cemetery at **Hanakaoo Beach Park.**

Snorkelers can see adorable green sea turtles around Maui.

At depths of 5 and 10 feet, you can see a variety of corals, especially as you head south toward Wahikuli Wayside Park.

South of Olowalu General Store, the shallow coral reef at **Olowalu** is good for a quick underwater tour, but if you're willing to venture out about 50 yards, you'll have easy access to an expansive coral reef with abundant turtles and fish—no boat required. Swim offshore toward the pole sticking out of the reef. Except for during a south swell, this area is calm, and good for families with small children. Boats sometimes stop here (they refer to this site as Coral Gardens) when conditions in Honolua Bay are not ideal. During low tide, be extra cautious when hovering above the razor-sharp coral.

Excellent snorkeling is found down the coastline between Kihei and Makena on the South Shore. **■ TIP→ The best spots are along the rocky fringes of Wailea's beaches—Mokapu, Ulua, Wailea, and Polo—off Wailea Alanui Drive.** Find one of the public parking lots sandwiched between Wailea's luxury resorts (look for a blue sign reading "Shoreline Access" with an arrow pointing to the lot), and enjoy the sandy entries, calm waters with relatively good visibility and variety of fish. Of the four beaches, Ulua has the best reef. You may listen to snapping shrimp and parrotfish nibbling on coral.

In South Maui, the end of the paved section of Makena Road is where you'll find the **Ahihi-Kinau Natural Area Reserve.** Despite its lava-scorched landscape, the area is very popular, especially with sharks, causing the area to be closed quite frequently. Call ahead to make sure it's open. It's difficult terrain and the area does sometimes get crowded, but it's worth a visit to experience some of the reserve's outstanding treasures, such as the sheltered cove known as the Fish Bowl. ■TIP→ **Be sure to bring water: this is a hot and unforgiving wilderness.**

Between Maui and neighboring Kahoolawe you'll find the world-famous **Molokini Crater.** Its crescent-shape rim acts as a protective cove from the wind and provides a sanctuary for birds and colorful marine life. Most snorkeling tour operators offer a Molokini trip, and it's not unusual for your charter to share this dormant volcano with five or six other boats. The journey to this sunken crater takes more than 90 minutes from Lahaina, an hour from Maalaea, and less than half an hour from the South Shore.

EQUIPMENT

Most hotels and vacation rentals offer free use of snorkel gear. Beachside stands fronting the major resort areas rent equipment by the hour or day. If you're squeamish about using someone else's gear (or need a prescription lens), pick up your own at any discount shop. Costco and Longs Drugs have better prices than ABC stores; dive shops have superior equipment.

■TIP→ **Don't shy away from asking for instructions; a snug fit makes all the difference in the world. A mask fits if it sticks to your face when you inhale deeply through your nose. Fins should cover your entire foot (unlike diving fins, which strap around your heel).**

Maui Dive Shop. You can rent pro gear (including optical masks, body boards, and wet suits) from three locations islandwide. Pump these guys for weather info before heading out; they'll know better than last night's news forecaster, and they'll give you the real deal on conditions. ✉ *1455 S. Kihei Rd., Kihei* ☎ *808/879–3388* 🌐 *www.mauidiveshop.com.*

Snorkel Bob's. Here you can rent fins, masks, and snorkels, and Snorkel Bob's will throw in a carrying bag, map, and snorkel tips for as little as $9 per week. Avoid the circle masks and go for the split-level ($30 per week) or premium snorkel package ($38 per week); it's worth the extra money. There are six Snorkel Bob's locations on Maui, including Kihei, Napili, Wailea, and Lahaina. ✉ *5425 C Lower Honoapiilani Hwy., Napili* ☎ *808/669–9603* 🌐 *www.snorkelbob.com.*

SNORKELING TOURS

The same boats that offer whale-watching, sailing, and diving also offer snorkeling excursions. Trips usually include visits to two locales, lunch, gear, instruction, and possible whale or dolphin sightings. Some captains troll for fish along the way.

Molokini Crater, a crescent about 3 miles offshore from Wailea, is the most popular snorkel cruise destination. You can spend half a day floating above the fish-filled crater for about $80. Some say it's not as good as it's made out to be, and that it's too crowded, but others consider it to be one of the best spots in Hawaii. Visibility is generally outstanding and fish are incredibly tame. Your second stop will be somewhere along the leeward coast, either Turtle Town near Makena or Coral Gardens toward Lahaina. ■TIP→ **On blustery mornings, there's a good chance the waters will be too rough to moor in Molokini Crater, and you'll end up snorkeling somewhere off the shore, where you could have driven for free.**

Continued on page 282

SNORKELING IN HAWAII

Molokini Crater

The waters surrounding the Hawaiian Islands are filled with life—from giant manta rays cruising off the Big Island's Kona Coast to humpback whales giving birth in the waters around Maui. Dip your head beneath the surface to experience a spectacularly colorful world: pairs of milletseed butterflyfish dart back and forth, redlipped parrotfish snack on coral algae, and spotted eagle rays flap past like silent spaceships. Sea turtles bask at the surface while tiny wrasses give them the equivalent of a shave and a haircut. The water quality is typically outstanding; many sites afford 30-foot-plus visibility. On snorkel cruises, you can often stare from the boat rail right down to the bottom.

Certainly few destinations are as accommodating to every level of snorkeler as Hawaii. Beginners can tromp in from sandy beaches while more advanced divers descend to shipwrecks, reefs, craters, and sea arches just offshore. Because of Hawaii's extreme isolation, the island chain has fewer fish species than Fiji or the Caribbean—but many of the fish that live here exist nowhere else. The Hawaiian waters are home to the highest percentage of endemic fish in the world.

The key to enjoying the underwater world is slowing down. Look carefully. Listen. You might hear the strange crackling sound of shrimp tunneling through coral, or you may hear whales singing to one another during winter. A shy octopus may drift along the ocean's floor beneath you. If you're hooked, pick up a waterproof fishkey from Long's Drugs. You can brag later that you've looked the Hawaiian turkeyfish in the eye.

Picasso Triggerfish	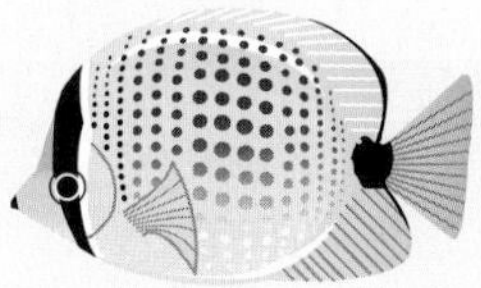 Milletseed Butterflyfish*	 Yellow Tang
 Moorish Idol	 Hawaiian Whitespotted Toby*	 Saddleback Wrasse*
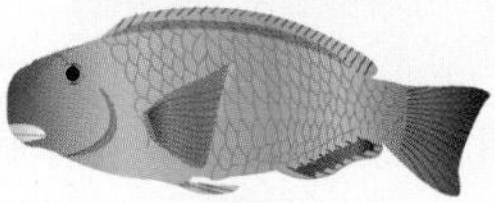 Redlip Parrotfish	 Hawaiian Turkeyfish*	 Zebra Moray Eel
 Stocky Hawkfish	 Green Sea Turtle (Honu)	 Spotted Eagle Ray

*endemic to Hawaii

POLYNESIA'S FIRST CELESTIAL NAVIGATORS: HONU

Honu is the Hawaiian name for two native sea turtles, the hawksbill and the green sea turtle. Little is known about these dinosaur-age marine reptiles, though snorkelers regularly see them foraging for *limu* (seaweed) and the occasional jellyfish in Hawaiian waters. Most female honu nest in the uninhabited Northwestern Hawaiian Islands, but a few sociable ladies nest on Maui and Big Island beaches. Scientists suspect that they navigate the seas via magnetism—sensing the earth's poles. Amazingly, they will journey up to 800 miles to nest—it's believed that they return to their own birth sites. After about 60 days of incubation, nestlings emerge from the sand at night and find their way back to the sea by the light of the stars.

SNORKELING

Many of Hawaii's reefs are accessible from shore.

The basics: Sure, you can take a deep breath, hold your nose, squint your eyes, and stick your face in the water in an attempt to view submerged habitats . . . but why not protect your eyes, retain your ability to breathe, and keep your hands free to paddle about when exploring underwater? That's what snorkeling is all about.

Equipment needed: A mask, snorkel (the tube attached to the mask), and fins. In deeper waters (any depth over your head), life jackets are advised.

Steps to success: If you've never snorkeled before, it's natural to feel a bit awkward at first, so don't sweat it. Breathing through a mask and tube, and wearing a pair of fins take getting used to. Like any activity, you build confidence and comfort through practice.

If you're new to snorkeling, begin by submerging your face in shallow water or a swimming pool and breathing calmly through the snorkel while gazing through the mask.

Next you need to learn how to clear water out of your mask and snorkel, an essential skill since splashes can send water into tube openings and masks can leak. Some snorkels have built-in drainage valves, but if a tube clogs, you can force water up and out by exhaling through your mouth. Clearing a mask is similar: lift your head from water while pulling forward on mask to drain. Some masks have built-in purge valves, but those without can be cleared underwater by pressing the top to the forehead and blowing out your nose (charming, isn't it?), allowing air to bubble into the mask, pushing water out the bottom. If it sounds hard, it really isn't. Just try it a few times and you'll soon feel like a pro.

Now your goal is to get friendly with

fins—you want them to be snug but not too tight—and learn how to propel yourself with them. Fins won't help you float, but they will give you a leg up, so to speak, on smoothly moving through the water or treading water (even when upright) with less effort.

Flutter stroking is the most efficient underwater kick, and the farther your foot bends forward the more leg power you'll be able to transfer to the water and the farther you'll travel with each stroke. Flutter kicking movements involve alternately separating the legs and then drawing them back together. When your legs separate, the leg surface encounters drag from the water, slowing you down. When your legs are drawn back together, they produce a force pushing you forward. If your kick creates more forward force than it causes drag, you'll move ahead.

Submerge your fins to avoid fatigue rather than having them flailing above the water when you kick, and keep your arms at your side to reduce drag. You are in the water—stretched out, face down, and snorkeling happily away—but that doesn't mean you can't hold your breath and go deeper in the water for a closer look at some fish or whatever catches your attention. Just remember that when you do this, your snorkel will be submerged, too, so you won't be breathing (you'll be holding your breath). You can dive head-first, but going feet-first is easier and less scary for most folks, taking less momentum. Before full immersion, take several long, deep breaths to clear carbon dioxide from your lungs.

If your legs tire, flip onto your back and tread water with inverted fin motions while resting. If your mask fogs, wash condensation from lens and clear water from mask.

TIPS FOR SAFE SNORKELING

- Snorkel with a buddy and stay together.
- Plan your entry and exit points prior to getting in the water.
- Swim into the current on entering and then ride the current back to your exit point.
- Carry your flippers into the water and then put them on, as it's difficult to walk in them, and rocks may be slippery.
- Make sure your mask fits properly and is not too loose.
- Pop your head above the water periodically to ensure you aren't drifting too far out, or too close to rocks.
- Think of the water as someone else's home—don't take anything that doesn't belong to you, or leave any trash behind.
- Don't touch any sea creatures; they may sting.
- Wear a T-shirt over your swimsuit to help protect you from being fried by the sun.
- When in doubt, don't go without a snorkeling professional; try a guided tour.
- Don't go in if the ocean seems rough.

Green sea turtle (Honu)

If you've tried snorkeling and are tentatively thinking about scuba, you may want to try "snuba," a cross between the two. With snuba, you dive 20 feet below the surface, only you're attached to an air hose from the boat. Many boats now offer snuba (for an extra fee of $45–$65) as well as snorkeling.

Snorkel cruises vary—some serve mai tais and steaks whereas others offer beer and cold cuts. You might prefer a large ferryboat to a smaller sailboat, or vice versa. Be sure you know where to go to board your vessel; getting lost in the harbor at 6 am is a lousy start. ■ **TIP→ Bring sunscreen, an underwater camera (they're double the price on board), a towel, and a cover-up for the windy return trip.** Even tropical waters get chilly after hours of swimming, so consider wearing a rash guard. Wet suits can usually be rented for a fee.

Alii Nui Maui. On this 65-foot luxury catamaran, you can come as you are (with a bathing suit, of course); towels, sunblock, and all your gear are provided. Because the owners also operate Maui Dive Shop, snorkel and dive equipment are top-of-the-line. Wet-suit tops are available to use for sun protection or to keep extra warm in the water. The boat, which holds a maximum of 60 people, is nicely appointed. A morning snorkel sail (there's a diving option, too) heads to Turtle Town or Molokini Crater and includes a continental breakfast, lunch, and post-snorkel alcoholic drinks. The three-, five-, or six-hour snorkel trip offers transportation from your hotel. Videography and huka (similar to snuba) are available for a fee. ✉ *Maalaea Harbor, Slip 56, Maalaea* ☎ *800/542–3483, 808/875–0333* 🌐 *www.aliinuimaui.com* 🎟 *From $99.*

FAMILY **Maui Classic Charters.** Hop aboard the *Four Winds II,* a 55-foot, glass-bottom catamaran (great fun for kids), for one of the most dependable snorkel trips around. You'll spend more time than other charter boats at Molokini Crater and enjoy turtle-watching on the way home. The trip includes optional snuba ($59 extra), continental breakfast, barbecue lunch, beer, wine, and soda. With its reasonable price, the trip can be popular and crowded. The crew works hard to keep everyone happy, but if the trip is fully booked, you will be cruising with more than 100 new friends. For a more intimate experience, opt for the *Maui Magic,* Maalaea's fastest PowerCat, which holds fewer people than some of the larger vessels. ✉ *Maalaea Harbor, Slips 55 and 80, Maalaea* ☎ *808/879–8188, 800/736–5740* 🌐 *www.mauiclassiccharters.com* 🎟 *From $44.*

Teralani Sailing Charters. Choose between a standard snorkel trip with a deli lunch or a top-of-the-line excursion that's an hour longer and includes two snorkel sites and a barbecue-style lunch. The company's cats could hold well over 100 people, but 49 is the maximum per trip. The boats are kept in pristine condition. Freshwater showers are available, as is an open bar after the second snorkel stop. A friendly crew provides all your gear, a flotation device, and a quick course in snorkeling. During whale season, only the premier trip is available. Boarding is right off Kaanapali Beach fronting Whalers Village. ✉ *Kaanapali Beach, Kaanapali* ☎ *808/661–7245* 🌐 *www.teralani.net* 🎟 *From $115.*

Fodor's Choice ★ **Trilogy Excursions.** Many people consider a trip with Trilogy Excursions to be a highlight of their vacation. Maui's longest-running operation has comprehensive offerings, with seven beautiful 50- to 64-foot sailing vessels at three departure sites. All excursions are staffed by energetic crews who will keep you well fed and entertained with local stories and corny jokes. A full-day catamaran cruise to Lanai includes a continental breakfast and barbecue lunch, a guided tour of the island, a "Snorkeling 101" class, and time to snorkel in the waters of Lanai's Hulopoe Marine Preserve (Trilogy Excursions has exclusive commercial access). The company also offers Molokini Crater and Olowalu snorkel cruises that are top-notch. Tours depart from Lahaina Harbor; Maalaea Harbor; and, in West Maui, in front of the Kaanapali Beach Hotel. ✉ *Kaanapali* ☎ *808/874–5649, 888/225–6284* 🌐 *www.sailtrilogy.com* 🎫 *From $125.*

STAND-UP PADDLING

Also called stand-up paddle surfing or paddleboarding, stand-up paddling is the "comeback kid" of surf sports; you stand on a longboard and paddle out with a canoe oar. While stand-up paddling requires even more balance and coordination than regular surfing, it is still accessible to just about every skill level. Most surf schools now offer stand-up paddle lessons. Advanced paddlers can amp up the adrenaline with a downwind coastal run that spans almost 10 miles from North Shore's Maliko Gulch to Kahului Harbor, sometimes reaching speeds up to 30 mph.

The fun thing about stand-up paddling is that you can enjoy it whether the surf is good or the water is flat. However, as with all water sports, it's important to read the environment and be attentive. Look at the sky and assess the wind by how fast the clouds are moving. Note where the whitecaps are going and always point the nose of your board perpendicular to the wave. ■ TIP→ **Because of the size and speed of a longboard, stand-up paddling can be dangerous, so lessons are highly recommended, especially if you intend to surf.**

LESSONS

Maui Surfer Girls. Owner and bona fide water woman Dustin Tester has been surfing since she was seven and has been a multisport athlete ever since. Class sizes are limited to three guests per instructor to ensure highly personalized lessons. Board, paddle, rash guard, and booties are included. Locations vary, depending on wind conditions, but you'll most likely go to beginner-friendly Ukumehame Beach (Thousand Peaks) at mile marker 12. Rates begin at $110 per person for a group lesson, or $200 for a private lesson. ✉ *Lahaina* ☎ *808/201–6109* 🌐 *www.mauisurfergirls.com.*

Stand-Up Paddle Surf School. Maui's first school devoted solely to stand-up paddling was founded by the legendary Maria Souza, the first woman to surf the treacherous waves of Peahi (nicknamed "Jaws") on Maui's North Shore. Although most surf schools offer stand-up paddling, Maria's classes are in a league of their own. They include a proper warm-up with a hula-hoop and balance ball and a cool-down with yoga. A private session is $199. Locations vary depending on conditions. ✉ *Kihei* ☎ *808/579–9231* 🌐 *www.standuppaddlesurfschool.com.*

SURFING

Maui's coastline has surf for every level of waterman or -woman. Waves on leeward-facing shores (West and South Maui) tend to break in gentle sets all summer long. Surf instructors in Kihei and Lahaina can rent you boards, give you onshore instruction, and then lead you out through the channel, where it's safe to enter the surf. They'll shout encouragement while you paddle like mad for the thrill of standing on water—most will give you a helpful shove. These areas are great for beginners; the only danger is whacking a stranger with your board or stubbing your toe against the reef.

The North Shore is another story. Winter waves pound the windward coast, attracting water champions from every corner of the world. Adrenaline addicts are towed in by Jet Ski to a legendary, deep-sea break called Jaws. Waves here periodically tower upward of 40 feet. The only spot for viewing this phenomenon (which happens just a few times a year) is on private property. So, if you hear the surfers next to you crowing about Jaws "going off," cozy up and get them to take you with them.

Whatever your skill, there's a board, a break, and even a surf guru to accommodate you. A two-hour lesson is a good intro to surf culture.

You can get the wave report each day by checking page 2 of the *Maui News,* logging on to the Glenn James weather site (🌐 *www.hawaiiweathertoday.com*), or by calling ☎ *808/871–5054* (for the weather forecast) or ☎ *808/877–3611* (for the surf report).

BEST SPOTS

On the South Shore, beginners can hang ten at Kihei's **Cove Park,** a sometimes crowded but reliable 1- to 2-foot break. Boards can easily be rented across the street, or in neighboring Kalama Park's parking lot. The only bummer is having to balance the 9-plus-foot board on your head while crossing busy South Kihei Road.

For advanced wave riders, **Hookipa Beach Park** on the North Shore boasts several well-loved breaks, including "Pavilions," "Lanes," "the Point," and "Middles." Surfers have priority until 11 am, when windsurfers move in on the action. **■ TIP→ Competition is stiff here. If you don't know what you're doing, consider watching.**

Long- or shortboarders in West Maui can paddle out at **Launiupoko State Wayside.** The east end of the park has an easy break, good for beginners.

Also called Thousand Peaks, **Ukumehame** is one of the better beginner spots in West Maui. You'll soon see how the spot got its name—the waves here break again and again in wide and consistent rows, giving lots of room for beginning and intermediate surfers.

Good surf spots in West Maui include "Grandma's" at **Papalaua Park,** just after the *pali* (cliff) where waves are so easy a grandma could ride 'em; **Puamana Beach Park** for a mellow longboard day; and **Lahaina Harbor,** which offers an excellent inside wave for beginners (called Breakwall), as well as the more advanced outside (a great lift if there's a big south swell).

EQUIPMENT AND LESSONS

Surf camps are becoming increasingly popular, especially with women. One- or two-week camps offer a terrific way to build muscle and self-esteem simultaneously.

Big Kahuna Adventures. Rent soft-top longboards here for $20 for two hours, or $30 for the day. Weekly rates are $125. The shop also offers surf lessons starting at $65, and rents kayaks, stand-up paddleboards, plus snorkel and beach gear. The company is across from Cove Park. ✉ *1913-C S. Kihei Rd., Kihei* ☎ *808/875–6395* 🌐 *www.bigkahunaadventures.com.*

3

Goofy Foot. Surfing "goofy foot" means putting your right foot forward. They might be goofy, but we like the right-footed gurus here. This shop is just plain cool and only steps away from "Breakwall," a great beginner's spot in Lahaina. A two-hour class with five or fewer students is $70, and you're guaranteed to be standing by the end or it's free. A private two-hour lesson is $160. ✉ *505 Front St., Suite 123, Lahaina* ☎ *808/244–9283* 🌐 *www.goofyfootsurfschool.com.*

Fodor's Choice ★ **Hi-Tech Surf Sports.** Hi-Tech has some of the best boards, advice, and attitude around. It rents even its best surfboards—choose from longboards, shortboards, and hybrids—starting at $25 per day. There's another shop in Paia, and a third location in Kihei across the street from Cove Park, a popular surf spot for beginners. ✉ *425 Koloa St., Kahului* ☎ *808/877–2111* 🌐 *www.surfmaui.com.*

Maui Surfer Girls. Maui Surfer Girls started in 2001 with surf camps for teen girls, but quickly branched out to offer surfing lessons year-round. Located away from the crowds, Maui Surfer Girls specializes in private lessons and small groups, and their ratio of four students per instructor is the smallest in the industry. The highly popular summer camps are still run for teen girls, and are now open to women as well. ✉ *Lahaina* ☎ *808/201–6109* 🌐 *www.mauisurfergirls.com.*

FAMILY Fodor's Choice ★ **Maui Surf Clinics.** Instructors here will get even the shakiest novice riding with the school's beginner program. A two-hour group lesson (up to five students) is $85. Private lessons with the patient and meticulous instructors are $170 for two hours. The company provides boards, rash guards, and water shoes, all in impeccable condition—and it's tops in the customer-service department. ✉ *505 Front St., Suite 201, Lahaina* ☎ *808/244–7873* 🌐 *www.mauisurfclinics.com.*

WHALE-WATCHING

From December into May whale-watching becomes one of the most popular activities on Maui. During the season *all* outfitters offer whale-watching in addition to their regular activities, and most do an excellent job. Boats leave the wharves at Lahaina and Maalaea in search of humpbacks, allowing you to enjoy the awe-inspiring size of these creatures in closer proximity. From November through May, the Pacific Whale Foundation sponsors the Maui Whale Festival, a variety of whale-related events for locals and visitors; check the calendar at 🌐 *www.mauiwhalefestival.org.*

As it's almost impossible *not* to see whales in winter on Maui, you'll want to prioritize: is adventure or comfort your aim? If close encounters with the giants of the deep are your desire, pick a smaller boat that promises sightings. Those who think "green" usually prefer the smaller, quieter vessels that produce the least amount of negative impact to the whales' natural environment. For those wanting to sip mai tais as whales cruise by, stick with a sunset cruise ($40 and up) on a boat with an open bar and *pupu* (Hawaiian tapas). ■ **TIP→ Afternoon trips are generally rougher because the wind picks up, but some say this is when the most surface action occurs.**

Every captain aims to please during whale season, getting as close as legally possible (100 yards). Crew members know when a whale is about to dive (after several waves of its heart-shape tail) but can rarely predict breaches (when the whale hurls itself up and almost entirely out of the water). Prime viewing space (on the upper and lower decks, around the railings) is limited, so boats can feel crowded even when half full. If you don't want to squeeze in beside strangers, opt for a smaller boat with fewer bookings. Don't forget to bring sunscreen, sunglasses, a light long-sleeve cover-up, and a hat you can secure. Winter weather is less predictable and at times can be extreme, especially as the wind picks up. Arrive early to find parking.

BEST SPOTS

The northern end of **Keawakapu Beach** on the South Shore seems to be a whale magnet. Situate yourself on the sand or at the nearby restaurant and watch mamas and calves. From mid-December to mid-April, the Pacific Whale Foundation has naturalists at Ulua Beach and at the scenic viewpoint at **Papawai Point Lookout.** Like the commuting traffic, whales can be spotted along the pali of West Maui's Honoapiilani Highway all day long. Make sure to park safely before craning your neck out to see them.

BOATS AND CHARTERS

Maui Adventure Cruises. Whale-watching from this company's raft puts you right above the water surface and on the same level as the whales. You'll forgo the cocktail in your hand but you won't have to deal with crowds, even if the vessel is at max capacity with 36 people. The whales can get up close if they like, and when they do it's absolutely spectacular. These rafts can move with greater speed than a catamaran, so you don't spend much time motoring between whales or pods. Refreshments are included. Prices are $49 for adults and $39 for kids 5–12 years old (children younger than 5 are not admitted). ✉ *Lahaina Harbor, Slip 11, Lahaina* ☎ *808/661–5550* 🌐 *www.mauiadventurecruises.com.*

FAMILY **Pacific Whale Foundation.** With a fleet of 10 boats, this nonprofit organization pioneered whale-watching back in 1979. The crew (including a certified marine biologist) offers insights into whale behavior and suggests ways for you to help save marine life worldwide. One of the best things about these trips is the underwater hydrophone that allows you to listen to the whales sing. Trips meet at the organization's store, which sells whale-theme and local souvenirs. You'll share the boat with about 100 people in stadium-style seating. If you prefer a smaller crowd, book their eco-friendly raft cruises instead. ✉ *Maui Harbor Shops, 300 Maalaea Rd., Suite 211, Maalaea* ☎ *808/427–2460* 🌐 *www.pacificwhale.org.*

WINDSURFING

3

Windsurfing, invented in the 1950s, found its true home at Hookipa on Maui's North Shore in 1980. Seemingly overnight, windsurfing pros from around the world flooded the area. Equipment evolved, amazing film footage was captured, and a new sport was born.

If you're new to the action, you can get lessons from the experts islandwide. For a beginner, the best thing about windsurfing is that (unlike surfing) you don't have to paddle. Instead, you have to hold on like heck to a flapping sail as it whisks you into the wind. Needless to say, you're going to need a little coordination and balance to pull this off. Instructors start you out on a beach at Kanaha, where the big boys go. Lessons range from two-hour introductory classes to five-day advanced "flight school."

BEST SPOTS

After **Hookipa Bay** was discovered by windsurfers four decades ago, this windy North Shore beach 10 miles east of Kahului gained an international reputation. The spot is blessed with optimal wave-sailing wind and sea conditions, and offers the ultimate aerial experience.

In summer, the windsurfing crowd heads to **Kalepolepo Beach** on the South Shore. Trade winds build in strength, and by afternoon a swarm of dragonfly-sails can be seen skimming the whitecaps, with Mauna Kahalawai (often called the West Maui Mountains) as a backdrop.

A great site for speed, **Kanaha Beach Park** is dedicated to beginners in the morning hours, before the waves and wind really get roaring. After 11 am, the professionals choose from their quiver of sails the size and shape best suited for the day's demands. This beach tends to have smaller waves and forceful winds—sometimes sending sailors flying at 40 knots. If you aren't ready to go pro, this is a great place for a picnic while you watch from the beach. To get here, use any of the three entrances on Amala Place, which runs along the shore just north of Kahului Airport.

EQUIPMENT AND LESSONS

Action Sports Maui. The quirky, friendly professionals here will meet you at Kanaha Beach Park on the North Shore, outfit you with your sail and board, and guide you through your first "jibe," or turn. They promise your learning time for windsurfing will be cut in half. Lessons begin at 9 am every day except Sunday and cost $89 for a 2½-hour class. Three- and five-day courses cost $279 and $469, respectively. ✉ *96 Amala Pl., Kahului* ☎ *808/283–7913* 🌐 *www.actionsportsmaui.com.*

Fodor's Choice ★ **Hawaiian Sailboarding Techniques.** Considered one of Maui's finest windsurfing schools, Hawaiian Sailboarding Techniques brings you quality instruction by skilled sailors. Founded by Alan Cadiz, an accomplished World Cup Pro, the school sets high standards for a safe, quality windsurfing experience. Intro classes start at $99 for 2½ hours, gear included. The company is inside Hi-Tech Surf Sports, which offers

Humpback whale calves are plentiful in winter; this one is breaching off West Maui.

excellent equipment rentals. ✉ *Hi-Tech Surf Sports, 425 Koloa St., Kahului* ☎ *808/871–5423* 🌐 *www.hstwindsurfing.com.*

GOLF, HIKING, AND OUTDOOR ACTIVITIES

Updated by Christie Leon

We know how tempting it is to spend your entire vacation on the beach (many days we're tempted as well), but if you do, you'll miss out on the "other side of Maui": the eerie, moonlike surface of Haleakala Crater, the lush rain forests of East Maui, and the geological wonder that is Iao Valley State Monument, to name just a few. Even playing a round of golf on one of the world-class courses provides breathtaking vistas, reminding you just why you chose to come to Maui in the first place.

Maui's exceptional climate affords year-round opportunities for outdoor adventures, whether it's exploring cascading waterfalls on a day hike, riding horseback through verdant valleys, soaring across vast gulches on a zipline, or taking an exhilarating bicycle ride down Haleakala. When you take time to get off the beaten path, you'll discover just why Maui *no ka oi* (is the best). But make sure not to overbook yourself—one or two activities per day is plenty. You're on vacation, remember.

CLOSE UP

The Humpback's Winter Home

The humpback whales' attraction to Maui is legendary, and seeing them December–May is a highlight for many visitors. More than half the Pacific's humpback population winters in Hawaii, especially in the waters around the Valley Isle, where mothers can be seen just a few hundred feet offshore, training their young calves in the fine points of whale etiquette. Watching from shore, it's easy to catch sight of whales spouting, or even breaching—when they leap almost entirely out of the sea, slapping back onto the water with a huge splash.

At one time there were thousands of the huge mammals, but a history of overhunting and marine pollution reduced the world population to about 1,500. In 1966 humpbacks were put on the endangered-species list. Hunting or harassing whales is illegal in the waters of most nations, and in the United States boats and airplanes are restricted from getting too close. The jury is still out, however, on the effects of military sonar testing on the marine mammals.

Marine biologists believe the humpbacks (much like humans) keep returning to Hawaii because of its warmth. Having fattened themselves in subarctic waters all summer, the whales migrate south in the winter to breed, and a rebounding population of thousands cruise Maui waters. Winter is calving time, and the young whales probably couldn't survive in the frigid Alaskan waters. No one has ever seen a whale give birth here, but experts know that calving is their main winter activity, because the 1- and 2-ton youngsters suddenly appear while the whales are in residence.

The first sighting of a humpback whale spout each season is exciting for locals on Maui. A collective sigh of relief can be heard: "Ah, they've returned." In the not-so-far distance, flukes and flippers can be seen rising above the ocean's surface. It's hard not to anthropomorphize the tail waving; it looks like such an amiable gesture. Each fluke is uniquely patterned, like a human's fingerprint, and is used to identify the giants as they travel halfway around the globe and back.

AERIAL TOURS

Helicopter flight-seeing excursions can take you over the West Maui Mountains, Haleakala Crater, or the island of Molokai. This is a beautiful, thrilling way to see the island, and the *only* way to see some of its most dramatic areas and waterfalls. Tour prices usually include a digital video of your trip so you can relive the experience at home. Prices run from about $210 for a half-hour flight to more than $350 for a 75-minute tour with an ocean or cliffside landing. Discounts may be available online or, if you're willing to chance it, by calling at the last minute.

Tour operators come under sharp scrutiny for passenger safety and equipment maintenance. Don't be shy; ask about a company's safety record, flight paths, age of equipment, and level of operator experience. Generally, though, if it's still in business, it's doing something right.

Air Maui Helicopters. Priding itself on a perfect safety record, Air Maui provides 45- to 75-minute flights covering the waterfalls of the West Maui Mountains, Haleakala Crater, Hana, and the spectacular sea cliffs of Molokai. Prices range from $220 for West Maui/Molokai or Hana/Haleakala tour to $353 for a 75-minute tour with ocean or cliffside landings. Discounts are available online. Charter flights are also available. ✉ *1 Kahului Airport Rd. , Hangar 110, Kahului* ☎ *877/238–4942, 808/877–7005* 🌐 *www.airmaui.com.*

Sunshine Helicopters. Take a tour of Maui in Sunshine's FXStar or WhisperStar aircraft. Prices start at $260 for 45 minutes, with discounts available online. First-class seating is available for an additional fee. Sunshine also offers tours that combine helicopter flights with either a horseback ride or submarine adventure. Charter flights can be arranged. A pilot-narrated digital record of your actual flight is available for purchase. ✉ *Kahului Airport Rd. , Hangar 107, Kahului* ☎ *808/270–3999, 866/501–7738* 🌐 *www.sunshinehelicopters.com.*

BIKING

Long distances and mountainous terrain keep biking from being a practical mode of travel on Maui. Still, painted bike lanes enable cyclists to travel all the way from Makena to Kapalua, and you'll see hardy souls battling the trade winds under the hot Maui sun.

Several companies offer guided bike tours down Haleakala. This activity is a great way to enjoy an easy, gravity-induced bike ride, but isn't for those not confident on a bike. The ride is inherently dangerous due to the slope, sharp turns, and the fact that you're riding down an actual road with cars on it. That said, the guided bike companies take every safety precaution. A few companies offer unguided (or, as they like to say, "self-guided") tours where they provide you with the bike and transportation to the mountain and then you're free to descend at your own pace. Most companies offer discounts for Internet bookings.

Haleakala National Park no longer allows commercial downhill bicycle rides within the park's boundaries. As a result, tour amenities and routes differ by company. Ask about sunrise viewing from the Haleakala summit (be prepared to leave *very* early in the morning), if this is an important feature for you. Some lower-price tours begin at the 6,500-foot elevation just outside the national park boundaries, where you will be unable to view the sunrise over the crater. Weather conditions on Haleakala vary greatly, so a visible sunrise can never be guaranteed. Sunrise is downright cold at the summit, so be sure to dress in layers and wear closed-toe shoes.

Each company has age and weight restrictions, and pregnant women are discouraged from participating, although they are generally welcome in the escort van. Reconsider this activity if you have difficulty with high altitudes, have recently been scuba diving, or are taking medications that may cause drowsiness.

BEST SPOTS

Thompson Road. Street bikers will want to head out to scenic Thompson Road. It's quiet, gently curvy, and flanked by gorgeous views on both sides. Because it's at a higher elevation, the air temperature is cooler and the wind lighter. The coast back down toward Kahului on the Kula Highway is worth the ride up. ✉ *Kula Hwy., off Rte. 37, Keokea.*

EQUIPMENT AND TOURS

Fodor's Choice ★ **Bike It Maui.** Small and family-owned, this company offers predawn and early morning guided tours that take riders from the 6,500-foot elevation of Haleakala down 22 miles of stunning scenery to Makawao town. The price of $140 includes transfers from your hotel. Riders must be at least 12 and weigh no more than 260 pounds. ✉ *Kula* ☎ *808/878–3364,* 🌐 *www.bikeitmaui.com.*

Fodor's Choice ★ **Cruiser Phil's Volcano Riders.** In the downhill bicycle industry since 1983, "Cruiser" Phil Feliciano offers a New Dawn Sunrise Experience ($163) and morning tours ($147) that include hotel transfers, coffee and snacks, and a guided 26-mile ride down the mountain. Participants should be between 13 and 65, at least 5 feet tall, weigh less than 250 pounds, and have ridden a bicycle in the past year. Feliciano also offers structured independent bike tours ($109) and van-only tours ($96). Discounts are available for online bookings. ✉ *58-A Amala Pl., Kahului* ☎ *808/893–2332, 877/764–2453* 🌐 *www.cruiserphil.com.*

Haleakala Bike Company. If you're thinking about a Haleakala bike trip, consider Haleakala Bike Company. Meet at the Old Haiku Cannery and take the van shuttle to the summit. Along the way you can learn about the history of the island, the volcano, and other Hawaiiana. Food is not included, but there are several spots along the way down to stop, rest, and eat. The simple, mostly downhill route takes you right back to the cannery where you started. HBC also offers bike sales, rentals, and services, as well as van tours. Tour prices run $85–$160, with discounts available for online bookings. ✉ *810 Haiku Rd., Suite 120, Haiku-Pauwela* ☎ *808/575–9575, 888/922–2453* 🌐 *www.bikemaui.com.*

Island Biker. Maui's premier bike shop for rentals, sales, and service offers standard front-shock bikes, road bikes, and full-suspension mountain bikes. Daily rental rates run $60–$75, and weekly rates are $210–$250. The price includes a helmet, pump, water bottle, cages, tire-repair kit, and spare tube. Car racks are $5 per day (free with weekly rentals). The staff can suggest routes appropriate for mountain or road biking. ✉ *415 Dairy Rd., Kahului* ☎ *808/877–7744* 🌐 *www.islandbikermaui.com.*

Krank Cycles. Krank Cycles is located in Upcountry Maui, close to the Makawao Forest Reserve. They offer full-day and weekly rentals of high-end road and mountain bikes. Owner Moose will provide you with maps and trail reports, in addition to your rental bike. ✉ *1120 Makawao Ave., Makawao* ☎ *808/572–2299* 🌐 *www.krankmaui.com.*

West Maui Cycles. Serving the island's west side, West Maui Cycles offers cruisers for $15 per day, hybrids for $35 per day, and performance road bikes for $45–$130 per day. Per day rates are discounted for longer-term rentals. Sales and service are available. ✉ *1087 Limahana Pl., No. 6, Lahaina* ☎ *808/661–9005* 🌐 *www.westmauicycles.com.*

GOLF

Fodor's Choice ★ Maui's natural beauty and surroundings offer some of the most jaw-dropping vistas imaginable on a golf course; add a variety of challenging, well-designed courses and it's easy to explain the island's popularity with golfers. Holes run across small bays, past craggy lava outcrops, and up into cool forested mountains. Most courses have mesmerizing ocean views, some close enough to feel the salt in the air. Although many of the courses are affiliated with resorts (and therefore a little pricier), the general-public courses are no less impressive. Playing on Lanai is another option.

Greens Fees: Golf can be costly on Maui. Greens fees listed here are the highest course rates per round on weekdays and weekends for U.S. residents. (Some courses charge non-U.S. residents higher prices.) Rental clubs may or may not be included with the greens fee. Discounts are often available for resort guests, for twilight tee times, and for those who book online.

■ TIP→ Resort courses, in particular, offer more than the usual three sets of tees, so bite off as much or as little challenge as you like. Tee it up from the tips and you can end up playing a few 600-yard par 5s and see a few 250-yard forced carries.

Fodor's Choice ★ **The Dunes at Maui Lani.** Robin Nelson is at his minimalist best here, creating a bit of British links in the middle of the Pacific. Holes run through ancient, lightly wooded sand dunes, 5 miles inland from Kahului Harbor. Thanks to the natural humps and slopes of the dunes, Nelson had to move very little dirt and created a natural beauty. During the design phase he visited Ireland, and not so coincidentally the par-3 3rd looks a lot like the Dell at Lahinch: a white dune on the right sloping down into a deep bunker and partially obscuring the right side of the green—just one of several blind to semiblind shots here. ✉ *1333 Maui Lani Pkwy., Kahului* ☎ *808/873–0422* 🌐 *www.dunesatmauilani.com* *$95* *18 holes, 6841 yards, par 72.*

Kaanapali Golf Courses. The Royal Kaanapali (North) Course (1962) is one of three in Hawaii designed by Robert Trent Jones Sr., the godfather of modern golf architecture. The greens average a whopping 10,000 square feet, necessary because of the often-severe undulation. The par-4 18th hole (into the prevailing trade breezes, with out-of-bounds on the left and a lake on the right) is notoriously tough. Designed by Arthur Jack Snyder, the Kaanapali Kai (South) Course (1976) shares similar seaside-into-the-hills terrain, but is rated a couple of strokes easier, mostly because putts are less treacherous. ✉ *2290 Kaanapali Pkwy., Lahaina* ☎ *808/661–3691, 866/454–4653* 🌐 *www.kaanapali-golfcourses.com* *Royal Kaanapali (North) Course $255, Kaanapali Kai (South) Course $205* *Royal Kaanapali (North) Course: 18 holes, 6700 yards, par 71; Kaanapali Kai (South) Course: 18 holes, 6400 yards, par 70.*

Fodor's Choice ★ **Kapalua Golf.** Perhaps Hawaii's best-known golf resort and the crown jewel of golf on Maui, Kapalua hosts the PGA Tour's first event each January: the Sentry Tournament of Champions at the **Plantation Course**. On this famed course, Ben Crenshaw and Bill Coore (1991) tried to incorporate traditional shot values in a nontraditional site, taking into account slope, gravity, and the prevailing trade winds. The par-5 18th hole, for instance, plays 663 yards from the back tees (600 yards from the resort tees). The hole drops 170 feet in elevation, narrowing as it goes to a partially guarded green, and plays downwind and down-grain. Despite the longer-than-usual distance, the slope is great enough and the wind at your back usually brisk enough to reach the green with two well-struck shots—a truly unbelievable finish to a course that will challenge, frustrate, and reward the patient golfer.

The **Bay Course** (Arnold Palmer and Francis Duane, 1975) is the more traditional of Kapalua's courses, with gentle rolling fairways and generous greens. The most memorable hole is the par-3 5th hole, with a tee shot that must carry over a turquoise inlet of Oneloa Bay. Each of the courses has a separate clubhouse. ✉ *2000 Plantation Club Dr., Kapalua* ☎ *808/669–8044, 877/527–2582* 🌐 *www.golfatkapalua.com* 🎫 *Bay Course $229, Plantation Course $329* ⛳ *Bay Course: 18 holes, 6600 yards, par 72. Plantation Course: 18 holes, 7411 yards, par 73.*

Kapalua Golf Academy. Along with 23 acres of practice turf, an 18-hole putting course, and 3-hole walking course, the Kapalua Golf Academy offers individual lessons, corporate clinics, golf schools, daily clinics, and custom off-site instruction. ✉ *1000 Office Rd., Kapalua* ☎ *808/665–5455, 877/527–2582* 🌐 *www.golfatkapalua.com.*

Pukalani Country Club. At 1,110 feet above sea level, Pukalani (Bob Baldock, 1980) provides one of the finest vistas in all Hawaii. Holes run up, down, and across the slopes of Haleakala. The trade winds tend to come up in the late morning and afternoon. This, combined with frequent elevation change, makes club selection a test. The fairways tend to be wide, but greens are undulating and quick. ✉ *360 Pukalani St., Pukalani* ☎ *808/572–1314* 🌐 *www.pukalanigolf.com* 🎫 *$89* ⛳ *18 holes, 6962 yards, par 72.*

Wailea Blue Course. Wailea's original course, the Blue Course (1971), nicknamed "The Grand Lady of Wailea," is operated from a separate clubhouse from the Gold and Emerald courses, its newer siblings. Here, judging elevation change is key. Fairways and greens tend to be wider and more forgiving than on the newer courses, and they run through colorful flora that includes hibiscus, wiliwili, bougainvillea, and plumeria. ✉ *100 Wailea Ike Dr., Wailea* ☎ *808/875–7450, 888/328–6284* 🌐 *www.waileagolf.com* 🎫 *$190* ⛳ *18 holes, 6765 yards, par 71.*

Fodor's Choice ★ **Wailea Golf Club.** Wailea is the only Hawaii resort to offer three different courses: Gold, Emerald, and Blue—the latter at a different location with a separate pro shop. Designed by Robert Trent Jones Jr. (Gold and Emerald) and Arthur Jack Snyder (Blue), these courses share similar terrain, carved into the leeward slopes of Haleakala. Although the ocean does not come into play, its beauty is visible on almost every hole. ■ TIP→ **Remember, putts break dramatically toward the ocean.**

Jones refers to the **Gold Course** at Wailea (1994) as the "masculine" course. It's all trees and lava, and regarded as the hardest of the three courses. The trick here is to note even subtle changes in elevation. The par-3 8th, for example, plays from an elevated tee across a lava

DID YOU KNOW?
Lush vegetation and stunning views of the crystalline ocean make golfing on Maui a memorable experience.

TIPS FOR GOLFING ON MAUI

Golf is golf and Hawaii is part of the United States, but island golf nevertheless has its own quirks. Here are a few tips to make your golf experience in the Islands more pleasant.

- Sunscreen: Buy it, apply it (we're talking a minimum of 30 SPF). The subtropical rays of the sun are intense, even in December. Good advice is to apply sunscreen, at a minimum, on the 1st and 10th tees.

- Stay hydrated. Spending four-plus hours in the sun and heat means you'll perspire away considerable fluids and energy.

- All resort courses and many daily-fee courses provide rental clubs. In many cases, they're the latest lines from top manufacturers. This is true both for men and women, as well as for left-handers, which means you don't have to schlep clubs across the Pacific.

- Pro shops at most courses are well stocked with balls, tees, and other accoutrements, so even if you bring your own bag, it needn't weigh a ton.

- Come spikeless—few Hawaii courses still permit metal spikes. Also, most of the resort courses require a collared shirt.

- Maui is notorious for its trade winds. Consider playing early or at twilight if you want to avoid the breezes, and remember that although they will frustrate you at times and make club selection difficult, you may well see some of your longest drives ever.

- In theory you can play golf in Hawaii 365 days a year, but there's a reason the Hawaiian Islands are so green: an umbrella and light jacket can come in handy.

- Unless you play a muni or certain daily-fee courses, plan on taking a cart. Riding carts are mandatory at most courses and are included in the greens fee.

ravine to a large, well-bunkered green framed by palm trees, the blue sea, and tiny Molokini. The course demands strategy and careful club selection. The **Emerald Course** (1994) is the "feminine" layout with lots of flowers and bunkering away from greens. Although this may seem to render the bunker benign, the opposite is true. A bunker well in front of a green disguises the distance to the hole. Likewise, the Emerald's extensive flower beds are dangerous distractions because of their beauty. The Gold and Emerald courses share a clubhouse, practice facility, and 19th hole. ✉ *100 Wailea Golf Club Dr., Wailea* ☎ *808/875–7450, 888/328–6284* 🌐 *www.waileagolf.com* *Gold Course $250, Emerald Course $250* *Gold Course: 18 holes, 7078 yards, par 72; Emerald Course: 18 holes, 6825 yards, par 72.*

HANG GLIDING AND PARAGLIDING

If you've always wanted to know what it feels like to fly, hang gliding or paragliding might be your perfect Maui adventure. You'll get open-air, bird's-eye views of the Valley Isle that you'll likely never forget. And you don't need to be a daredevil to participate.

LESSONS AND TOURS

Hanggliding Maui. Armin Engert will take you on an instructional powered hang-gliding trip out of Hana Airport in East Maui. With more than 13,000 hours in the air and a perfect safety record, Armin flies you over Maui's most beautiful coast. A 30-minute flight lesson costs $190, a 45-minute lesson costs $250, and a 60-minute lesson is $310. Snapshots of your flight from a wing-mounted camera cost an additional $40, and a 34-minute DVD of the flight from a wing-mounted camera is available for $80. Reservations are required. ✉ *Hana Airport, Alalele Pl., off Hana Hwy., Hana* ☎ *808/264-3287* 🌐 *www.hangglidingmaui.com.*

Proflyght Paragliding. This is the only paragliding outfit on Maui to offer solo, tandem, and instruction at Polipoli Spring State Recreation Area. The leeward slope of Haleakala lends itself to paragliding with breathtaking scenery and air currents that increase during the day. Polipoli creates tremendous thermals that allow you to peacefully descend 3,000 feet to land. Tandem instruction prices run $115–$225. Solo paragliding certification is also available. ✉ *1100 Waipoli Rd., Kula* ☎ *808/874–5433* 🌐 *www.paraglidemaui.com.*

HIKING

Hikes on Maui include treks along coastal seashore, verdant rain forest, and alpine desert. Orchids, hibiscus, ginger, heliconia, and anthuriums grow wild on many trails, and exotic fruits like mountain apple, *lilikoi* (passion fruit), and strawberry guava provide refreshing snacks for hikers. Much of what you see in lower-altitude forests is alien, brought to Hawaii at one time or another by someone hoping to improve on nature. Plants like strawberry guava may be tasty, but they grow over native plants and have become problematic weeds.

The best hikes get you out of the imported landscaping and into the truly exotic wilderness. Hawaii possesses some of the world's rarest plants, insects, and birds. Pocket field guides are available at most grocery or drug stores and can really illuminate your walk. If you watch the right branches quietly, you can spot the same honeycreepers or happy-face spiders scientists have spent their lives studying.

BEST SPOTS

HALEAKALA NATIONAL PARK

Fodor's Choice ★ **Haleakala Crater.** Undoubtedly the best hiking on the island is at Haleakala Crater. If you're in shape, do a day hike descending from the summit along **Keoneheehee Trail** (aka Sliding Sands Trail) to the crater floor. You might also consider spending several days here amid the cinder cones, lava flows, and all that loud silence. Entering the crater is like landing on a different planet. In the early 1960s, NASA actually brought moon-suited astronauts here to practice what it would be like to "walk on the moon." Tent camping and cabins are available with permits. On the 30 miles of trails you can traverse black sand and wild lava formations, follow the trail of blooming *ahinahina* (silverswords), and take in tremendous views of big sky and burned-red cliffs.

The best time to go into the crater is in the summer months, when the conditions are generally more predictable. Be sure to bring layered clothing—and plenty of warm clothes if you're staying overnight. It may be scorching hot during the day, but it gets mighty chilly after dark. Bring your own drinking water, as potable water is available only at the two visitor centers. Overnight visitors must get a permit at park headquarters before entering the crater. *Moderate to difficult.* ✉ *Haleakala Crater Rd., Makawao* ☎ *808/572–4400* 🌐 *www.nps.gov/hale* 🎫 *$25 park entrance fee per vehicle (good for 3 days).*

OHEO GULCH

A branch of Haleakala National Park, Oheo Gulch is famous for its pools (the area is sometimes called the Seven Sacred Pools). Truth is, there are more than seven pools and there's nothing sacred about them. A former owner of the Travaasa Hotel Hana started calling the area Seven Sacred Pools to attract the masses to sleepy old Hana. His plan worked and the name stuck, much to the chagrin of many Mauians.

The best time to visit the pools is in the morning, before the crowds and tour buses arrive. Start your day with a vigorous hike. Oheo has some fantastic trails to choose from, including our favorite, the Pipiwai Trail. When you're done, nothing could be better than going to the pools, lounging on the rocks, and cooling off in the freshwater reserves. (Keep in mind, however, that the park periodically closes the pools to swimming when the potential for flash flooding exists.)

You can find Oheo Gulch on Route 31, 10 miles past Hana town. To visit, you must pay the $25-per-car National Park fee, which is valid for three days and can be used at Haleakala's summit as well. For information about scheduled orientations and cultural demonstrations, be sure to visit Haleakala National Park's Kipahulu Visitor Center, 10 miles past Hana. Note that there is no drinking water here.

Fodor's Choice ★ **Pipiwai Trail.** This 2-mile trek upstream leads to the 400-foot Waimoku Falls, pounding down in all its power and glory. Following signs from the parking lot, head across the road and uphill into the forest. The trail borders a sensational gorge and passes onto a boardwalk through a mystifying forest of giant bamboo. This stomp through muddy and rocky terrain takes around three hours to fully enjoy. Although this trail is never truly crowded, it's best done early in the morning before the tours arrive. Be sure to bring mosquito repellent. *Moderate.* ✉ *Hana Hwy., Hana* ✣ *Near mile marker 42* 🌐 *www.nps.gov/hale* 🎫 *$25 park entrance fee per vehicle (good for 3 days).*

IAO VALLEY STATE MONUMENT

Fodor's Choice ★ **Iao Needle Lookout Trail & Ethnobotanical Loop.** Anyone (including grandparents) can handle this short walk from the parking lot at Iao Valley State Monument. On your choice of two paved walkways, you can cross the Iao Stream and explore the junglelike area. Ascend the stairs

Silverswords start as spiny-leaf rosettes, then grow stalks for 7–17 years; after they bloom once, they die.

up to the Iao Needle for spectacular views of Central Maui. Be sure to stop at the lovely Kepaniwai Heritage Gardens, which commemorate the cultural contributions of various immigrant groups. *Easy.* ✉ *Trailhead: Iao Valley State Monument parking lot, Rte. 32, Wailuku* 🌐 *www.dlnr.hawaii.gov/dsp/parks/maui/iao-valley-state-monument* 🎟 *$5 parking per car.*

THE SOUTH SHORE AND WEST MAUI

Hoapili Trail (King's Trail). A challenging hike through eye-popping scenery in southwestern Maui is this 5½-mile coastal trail beyond the Ahihi-Kinau Natural Area Reserve. Named after a bygone king, it follows the shoreline, threading through the remains of ancient villages. King Hoapili created an islandwide road, and this wide path of stacked lava rocks is a marvel to look at and walk on. (It's not the easiest surface for the ankles and feet, so wear sturdy shoes.) This is brutal territory with little shade and no facilities, and extra water is a must. To get here, follow Makena Road to La Perouse Bay. The trail can be a challenge to find—walk south along the ocean through the *kiawe* trees, where you'll encounter numerous wild goats (don't worry—they're gentle), and past a scenic little bay. The trail begins just around the corner to the left. *Difficult.* ✉ *Trailhead: La Perouse Bay, Makena Rd., Makena.*

Kapalua Resort. The resort offers free access to miles of hiking trails as a self-guided experience. Trail information and maps are available at the Kapalua Village Center. The Village Walking Trails offer a network of exercise opportunities on former golf cart paths, including the 3.6-mile Lake Loop, which features sweeping views and a secluded lake populated with quacking ducks. The Coastal Trail provides views of the ocean and wildlife as it crosses the golden sand dunes of Oneloa Bay and past Ironwood Beach and the Ritz-Carlton, Kapalua, to its terminus at D.T. Fleming Beach Park. Sightings of green sea turtles, dolphins, and humpback whales (in season) are likely, along with nesting seabirds called *uaua kani*. Guided 1½ mile hikes on the coastal trail that include tide pool exploration are available for $99 through the Jean-Michel Cousteau Ambassadors of the Environment program at the Ritz-Carlton, Kapalua. ✉ *2000 Village Rd., corner of Office Rd., Kapalua* ☎ *808/665–4386 Kapalua Village Center concierge, 808/665-7292 Jean-Michel Cousteau Ambassadors of the Environment* 🌐 *www.kapalua.com.*

3

GOING WITH A GUIDE

Fodor's Choice ★ **Friends of Haleakala National Park.** This nonprofit offers overnight trips into the volcanic crater. The purpose of your trip, the service work itself, isn't too much—mostly native planting, removing invasive plants, and light cabin maintenance. But participants are asked to check the website to learn more about the trip and certify readiness for service work. A knowledgeable guide accompanies each trip, taking you to places you'd otherwise miss and teaching you about the native flora and fauna. ☎ *808/876–1673* 🌐 *www.fhnp.org.*

Fodor's Choice ★ **Hike Maui.** Started in 1983, the area's oldest hiking company remains extremely well regarded for waterfall, rain-forest, and crater hikes led by enthusiastic, highly trained guides who weave botany, geology, ethnobotany, culture, and history into the outdoor experience. Prices run $95–$259 for excursions lasting 3–11 hours (discounts for booking online). Hike Maui supplies day packs, rain gear, mosquito repellent, first-aid supplies, bottled water, snacks, lunch for the longer trips, and transportation to and from the site. Hotel transfers are available for most hikes (extra fee may apply). ✉ *Kahului* ☎ *808/879–5270, 866/324–6284* 🌐 *www.hikemaui.com.*

Sierra Club. One great avenue into the island's untrammeled wilderness is Maui's chapter of the Sierra Club. Join one of the club's hikes into pristine forests, along ancient coastal paths, to historic sites, and to Haleakala Crater. Some outings require volunteer service, but most are just for fun. Bring your own food and water, rain gear, sunscreen, sturdy shoes, and a suggested donation of $5 for hikers over age 14 ($3 for Sierra Club members). This is a true bargain. 🌐 *www.mauisierraclub.org.*

HORSEBACK RIDING

GOING WITH A GUIDE

Mendes Ranch. Family-owned and run, Mendes operates out of the beautiful ranch land of Kahakuloa on the windward slopes of the West Maui Mountains. Morning and afternoon trail rides lasting 1½ hours ($110) are available. Cowboys take you cantering up rolling pastures into the lush rain forest, and then you'll descend all the way down to the ocean for a photo op with a dramatic backdrop. Don't expect a Hawaiian cultural experience here—it's all about the horses and the ride. ✉ *3530 Kahekili Hwy., Wailuku* ☎ *808/244–7320 for office, 800/871–5222 for reservations* 🌐 *www.mendesranch.com.*

ZIP-LINE TOURS

Fodor's Choice ★ **Flyin' Hawaiian Zipline.** These guys have the longest line in the state (a staggering 3,600 feet), as well as the most unique course layout. You build confidence on the first line, then board a four-wheel-drive vehicle that takes you 1,500 feet above the town of Waikapu to seven more lines that carry you over 11 ridges and nine valleys. The total distance covered is more than 2½ miles, and the views are astonishing. The price ($185) includes water and snacks. You must be able to hike over steep, sometimes slippery terrain while carrying a 10-pound metal trolley. ✉ *Waikapu* ☎ *808/463–5786* 🌐 *www.flyinhawaiianzipline.com.*

Fodor's Choice ★ **Piiholo Ranch Zipline.** Four- to seven-line zipline courses are on this gorgeous 900-acre family ranch, with prices starting at $140. Access to the fifth and longest line is via a four-wheel-drive vehicle to the top of Piiholo Hill, where you are treated to stunning bicoastal views. Guides do a good job of weaving Hawaiian culture into the adventure. You must be able to climb three steep suspension bridges while hefting a 12-pound trolley over your shoulder. For those who fear heights, cheaper rates are available to follow along on foot. For the ultimate adventure, try the Zipline/Waterfall Hike ($238), for which the company has partnered with Hike Maui, the oldest land company in Hawaii. Piiholo offers significant discounts for online bookings. ✉ *Piiholo Rd., Makawao* ☎ *800/374–7050* 🌐 *www.piiholozipline.com.*

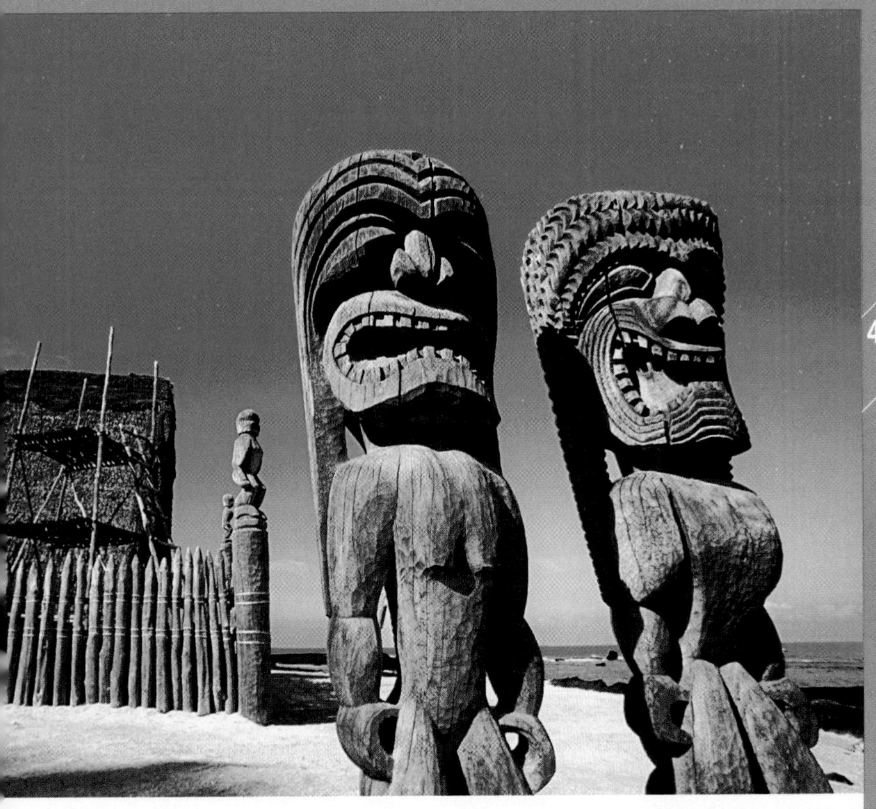

THE BIG ISLAND

WELCOME TO THE BIG ISLAND

TOP REASONS TO GO

★ **Hawaii Volcanoes National Park:** Catch the lava fireworks at night and explore newly made land, lava tubes, steam vents, and giant craters.

★ **Waipio Valley:** Experience a real-life secret garden, the remote spot known as the Valley of the Kings.

★ **Kealakekua Bay:** Watch spinner dolphins near the Captain Cook Monument, then go snorkeling over the fabulous coral reefs.

★ **The heavens:** Stargaze through high-tech telescopes on snow-topped Maunakea.

★ **Hidden beaches:** Discover one of the Kohala Coast's lesser-known gems.

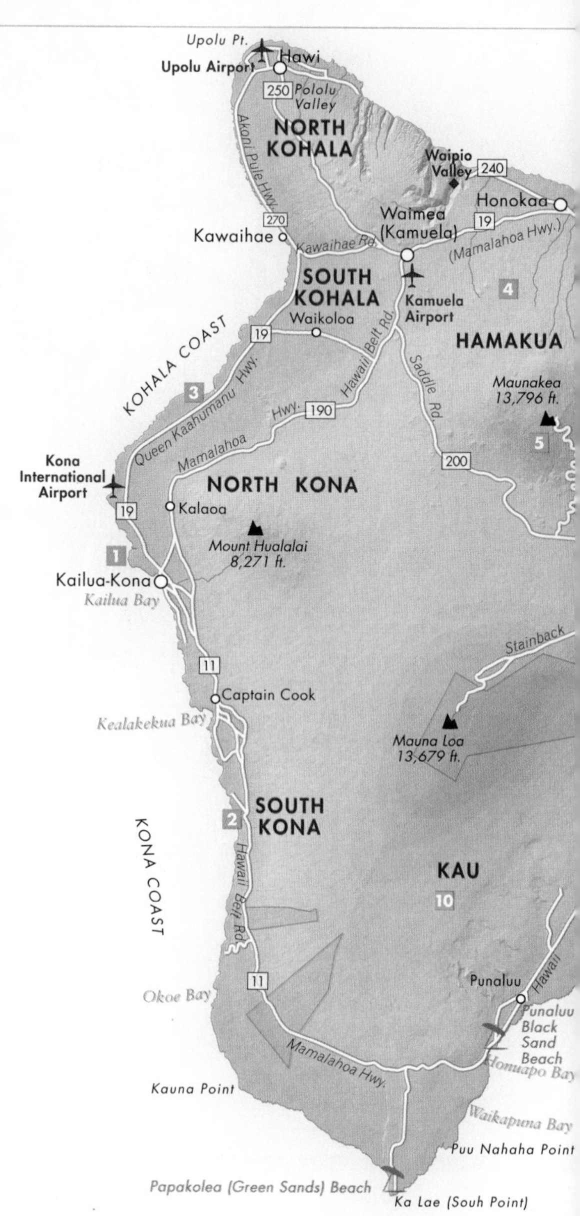

1 Kailua-Kona. This seaside town is packed with restaurants and shops.

2 The Kona Coast. This area stretches a bit north of Kailua-Kona. South Kona is the place to taste samples of world-famous Kona Coffee.

3 The Kohala Coast. The sparkling coast is home to all those long, white-sand beaches.

4 Waimea. Ranches sprawl across the cool, upland hills of the area.

5 Maunakea. Climb (or drive) this 13,796-foot mountain to check out the world's best stargazing.

6 The Hamakua Coast. Waterfalls, dramatic cliffs, and Waipio Valley are just a few of the treats here.

7 Hilo. Known as the City of Rainbows for all its rain, Hilo is what many consider the "real" Hawaii.

8 Puna. This is where the most recent lava flows are happening.

9 Hawaii Volcanoes National Park and vicinity. The land around the park is continually expanding, thanks to Kilauea Volcano.

10 Kau and Ka Lae (South Point). Round the southernmost part of the island for two of the Big Island's most unusual beaches.

GREAT ITINERARIES

Yes, the Big Island is big, and yes, there's a lot to see. If you're short on time, consider flying into one airport and out from the other. That will give you the opportunity to see both sides of the island without ever having to backtrack. If you'd prefer to spend your last few days near the beach, go from east to west; if hiking through rain forests and showering in waterfalls sounds like a better way to wrap up the trip, move from west to east. Or, head straight for Hawaii Volcanoes National Park and briefly visit Hilo before traveling the Hamakua Coast route and making your new base in Kailua-Kona.

Hike Volcanoes

Devote a full day (at least) to exploring Hawaii Volcanoes National Park. Head out on the Kilauea Iki trail—a moderately challenging, 4-mile loop near Thurston Lava Tube—by late morning. Leave the park to grab lunch at a nearby restaurant in Volcano Village, or plan ahead and pack your own picnic. Later, stroll past the steam vents and sulfur banks, and then hit the Jaggar Museum, which offers great views of the glow of Halemaumau Crater at night.

Black and Green Sand

Check out some of the unusual beaches you'll find only on the Big Island. Start with a hike into Green Sands Beach near South Point and plan to spend some time marveling at the surreal beauty of this spot. When you've had your fill, hop back in the car and head south about half an hour to Punaluu Black Sand Beach, the favorite nesting place of endangered Hawaiian turtles. Although the surf is often too rough here to swim, get out the camera because there are typically at least three or four turtles napping on the beach at any given moment.

Majestic Waterfalls and Valley of the Kings

Take a day to enjoy the splendors of the Hamakua Coast—almost any gorge you see on the road may indicate a waterfall waiting to surprise you. For a sure bet, head to beautiful Waipio Valley. Book a horseback, hiking, or four-wheel-drive tour, or walk on in yourself (just keep in mind that it's an arduous hike back up—a 25% grade for a little over a mile).

Once in the valley, take your first right to get to the black-sand beach. Pause for a moment to reflect here—the ancient Hawaiians believed this was where souls crossed over to the afterlife. Whether you buy that or not, you will admit there's something unmistakably mystical about this place.

Waterfalls abound in the valley, depending on the amount of recent rainfall. Hike left until you reach the end of the beach; the spot is gorgeous and worthy of a million photos.

Sun and Stars

Spend the day lounging on a Kohala Coast beach (Hapuna, Kaunaoa—also known as Maunakea—or Kua Bay), then catch a one-of-a-kind island sunset that evening from Maunakea's summit. For the safest, most comfortable experience, book a turnkey summit tour. Or stop in at the Onizuka Center for International Astronomy, a visitor center located at about 9,000 feet. If you have a 4WD (check with your rental car company for permission), you can join their free summit tour at 1 pm on weekends, and return to the center to use the free telescopes for evening stargazing. Helpful U.H. Hilo astronomy students will guide you.

Updated by Kristina Anderson

Nicknamed "The Big Island," Hawaii Island is a microcosm of Hawaii the state. From long white-sand beaches and crystal-clear bays to rain forests, waterfalls, valleys, exotic flowers, and birds, all things quintessentially Hawaii are well represented here.

An assortment of happy surprises also distinguishes the Big Island from the rest of Hawaii—an active volcano (Kilauea) oozing red lava and creating new earth every day, the clearest place in the world to view stars in the night sky (Maunakea), and some seriously good coffee from the famous Kona district, and also from neighboring Kau.

Home to eight of the world's 13 sub-climate zones, this is the land of fire (thanks to active Kilauea volcano) and ice (compliments of not-so-active Maunakea, topped with snow and expensive telescopes). At just under a million years old, Hawaii is the youngest of the main Hawaiian Islands. Three of its five volcanoes are considered active: Mauna Loa, Hualalai, and Kilauea. The Southeast Rift Zone of Kilauea has been spewing lava regularly since January 3, 1983; another eruption began at Kilauea's summit caldera in March 2008, the first since 1982. Back in 1984, Mauna Loa's eruptions crept almost to Hilo, and it could fire up again any minute—or not for years. Hualalai last erupted in 1801, and geologists say it will definitely do so again within 100 years. Maunakea is currently considered dormant but may very well erupt again. Kohala, which last erupted some 120,000 years ago, is inactive, but on volatile Hawaii Island, you can never be sure.

AGRICULTURE

In the 19th- and mid-20th centuries, sugar was the main agricultural and economic staple of all the Islands, but especially the Big Island. The drive along the Hamakua Coast, from Hilo or Waimea, illustrates diverse agricultural developments on the island. Sugarcane stalks have been replaced by orchards of macadamia-nut trees, eucalyptus, and specialty crops from lettuce to strawberries. Macadamia-nut orchards on the Big Island supply 90% of the state's yield, while coffee continues to be big business, dominating the mountains above Kealakekua Bay. Orchids keep farmers from Honokaa to Pahoa afloat, and small organic farms produce meat, fruits, vegetables, and even goat cheese for high-end resort restaurants.

HISTORY

Hawaii's history is deeply rooted in its namesake island, which was home to the first Polynesian settlements and has the state's best-preserved *heiau* (temples) and *puuhonua* (refuges). Kamehameha, the greatest king in Hawaiian history and the man credited with uniting the Islands, was born here, raised in Waipio Valley, and died peacefully in Kailua-Kona. The other man who most affected Hawaiian history, Captain James Cook, spent the bulk of his time in the Islands here, docked in Kealakekua Bay. (He landed first on Kauai, but had little contact with the residents there.) Thus it was here that Western influence was first felt, and from here that it spread to the rest of Hawaii.

BIG ISLAND PLANNER

GETTING HERE AND AROUND

AIR TRAVEL

Flying time to the Big Island is about 10 hours from New York, 8 hours from Chicago, 5 hours from Los Angeles, and 15 hours from London, not including layovers. Some of the major airline carriers serving Hawaii fly direct to the Big Island, allowing you to bypass connecting flights out of Honolulu and Maui. If you're a more spontaneous traveler, island-hopping flights depart daily every 20 to 30 minutes or so.

Those flying to the Big Island regularly land at one of two fields. Ellison Onizuka Kona International Airport at Keahole, on the west side, serves Kailua-Kona, Keauhou, the Kohala Coast, North Kohala, Waimea, and points south. There are Visitor Information Program (VIP) booths located by all baggage-claim areas to assist travelers. Additionally, the airport offers news and lei stands, Laniakea By Centerplate, and a small gift and sundries shop. A modernization project launched in 2017 aims to join the two terminals (now separate) so that baggage and passenger screening can be streamlined and retail options enhanced.

Serving Kona are Air Canada, Alaska Airlines, American Airlines, Delta Airlines, Hawaiian Airlines, Japan Airlines, Mokulele, United Airlines, Virgin Atlantic, and Westjet. Hawaiian, Mokulele, and United fly into Hilo. Airlines schedule flights seasonally, meaning the number of daily flights—and sometimes the carriers themselves—vary according to demand.

CAR TRAVEL

It's essential to rent a car when visiting the Big Island. As the name suggests, it's a very big island, and it takes a while to get from point A to point B.

Fortunately, when you circle the island by car, you are treated to miles and miles of wondrous vistas of every possible description. In addition to using standard compass directions such as north and south, Hawaii residents often refer to places as being either *mauka* (toward the mountains) or *makai* (toward the ocean).

It's difficult to get lost along the main roads of the Big Island. Although their names may challenge the visitor's tongue, most roads are well marked; in rural areas look for mile marker numbers. Free publications containing basic road maps are given out at car rental agencies, but if you are doing a lot of driving, invest about $4 in the standard Big Island map available at local retailers. GPS is often unreliable.

For those who want to travel from the west side to the east side, or vice versa, the newly rerouted and repaved Saddle Road, now known as the Daniel K. Inouye Highway, is a nice shortcut across the middle of the island. This is especially convenient if you are staying on the Kohala side of the island and wish to visit the east side. Hazardous conditions such as fog are common.

Turning right on a red light is legal, except where noted. Hawaii has a strict seat-belt law that applies to both drivers and passengers. The fine for not wearing a seat belt is $102. Mobile phone use is strictly limited to talking on a hands-free mobile device, and only for those over 18. Many police officers drive their own cars while on duty, strapping the warning lights to the roof. Because of the color, locals call them "blue lights."

ISLAND DRIVING TIMES Before you embark on your day trip, it's a good idea to know how long it will take you to get to your destination. Some areas, like downtown Kailua-Kona and Waimea, can become congested at certain times of day. For those traveling to South Kona, the county has opened a long-awaited bypass road between Keauhou and Kealakekua, which has alleviated congestion considerably during rush hour. In general, you can expect the following average driving times:

DRIVING TIMES	
Kailua-Kona to Kealakekua Bay	14 miles/25 mins
Kailua-Kona to Kohala Coast	32 miles/40 mins
Kailua-Kona to Waimea	40 miles/1 hr
Kailua-Kona to Hamakua Coast	53 miles/1 hr 40 mins
Kailua-Kona to Hilo	75 miles/2½ hrs
Kohala Coast to Waimea	16 miles/20 mins
Kohala Coast to Hamakua Coast	29 miles/55 mins
Hilo to Volcano	30 miles/40 mins

HOTELS

Consider spending part of your vacation at a resort and part of it at a small inn or bed-and-breakfast. The big resorts sit squarely on some of the best beaches on the Big Island, and they have a lot to offer—spas, golf, and five-star restaurants for starters. The B&Bs provide a more intimate experience in settings as diverse as an upcountry ranch, a rainforest tree house, or a Victorian mansion perched on a dramatic sea cliff. Several romantic B&Bs nestle in the lush, misty forests surrounding

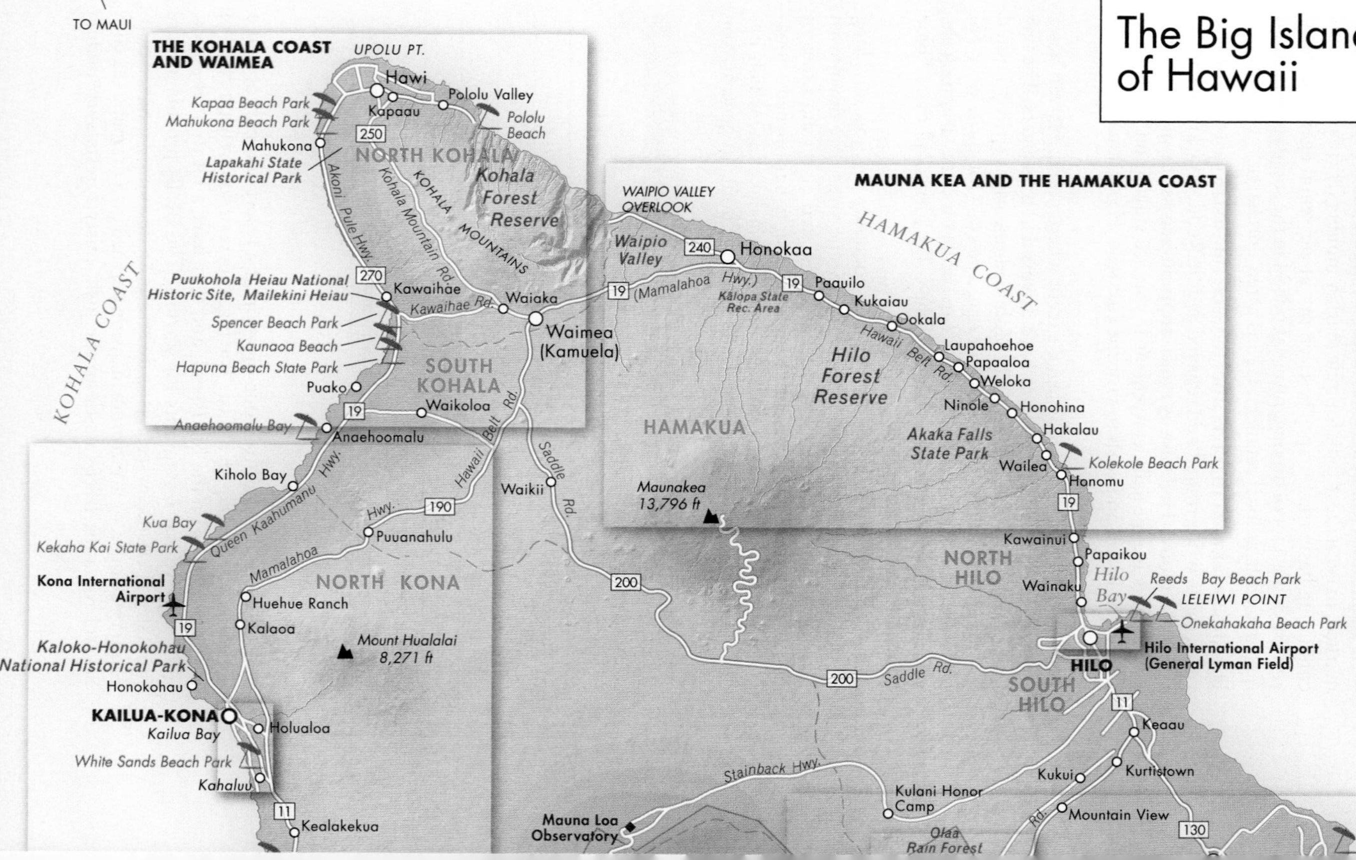

The Big Island of Hawaii
TO MAUI
THE KOHALA COAST AND WAIMEA
UPOLU PT.
Hawi
Kapaau
Pololu Valley
Pololu Beach
Kapaa Beach Park
Mahukona Beach Park
Mahukona
250
NORTH KOHALA
Lapakahi State Historical Park
Akoni Pule Hwy.
Kohala Mountain Rd.
KOHALA MOUNTAINS
Kohala Forest Reserve
270
Puukohola Heiau National Historic Site, Mailekini Heiau
Kawaihae
Kawaihae Rd.
Waiaka
Waimea (Kamuela)
Spencer Beach Park
Kaunaoa Beach
Hapuna Beach State Park
SOUTH KOHALA
Puako
19
Waikoloa
Anaehoomalu Bay
Anaehoomalu
KOHALA COAST
MAUNA KEA AND THE HAMAKUA COAST
WAIPIO VALLEY OVERLOOK
HAMAKUA COAST
Waipio Valley
240
Honokaa
19
(Mamalahoa Hwy.)
Kalopa State Rec. Area
Paauilo
Kukaiau
Ookala
Hawaii Belt Rd.
Laupahoehoe
Papaaloa
Weloka
Ninole
Honohina
Hilo Forest Reserve
HAMAKUA
Akaka Falls State Park
Hakalau
Kolekole Beach Park
Wailea
Honomu
Maunakea 13,796 ft
Kawainui
Papaikou
NORTH HILO
Hilo Bay
Reeds Bay Beach Park
LELEIWI POINT
Wainaku
Onekahakaha Beach Park
Hilo International Airport (General Lyman Field)
HILO
SOUTH HILO
Saddle Rd.
200
Waikii
Kiholo Bay
Queen Kaahumanu Hwy.
Hawaii Belt Rd.
190
Kua Bay
Kekaha Kai State Park
Puuanahulu
Mamalahoa Hwy.
NORTH KONA
Kona International Airport
Huehue Ranch
Kalaoa
Mount Hualalai 8,271 ft
Kaloko-Honokohau National Historical Park
Honokohau
KAILUA-KONA
Holualoa
Kailua Bay
White Sands Beach Park
Kahaluu
11
Kealakekua
Stainback Hwy.
Kulani Honor Camp
Mauna Loa Observatory
Olaa Rain Forest
Keaau
Kukui
Kurtistown
Mountain View
Rd.
130
Kapoho Tide Pools

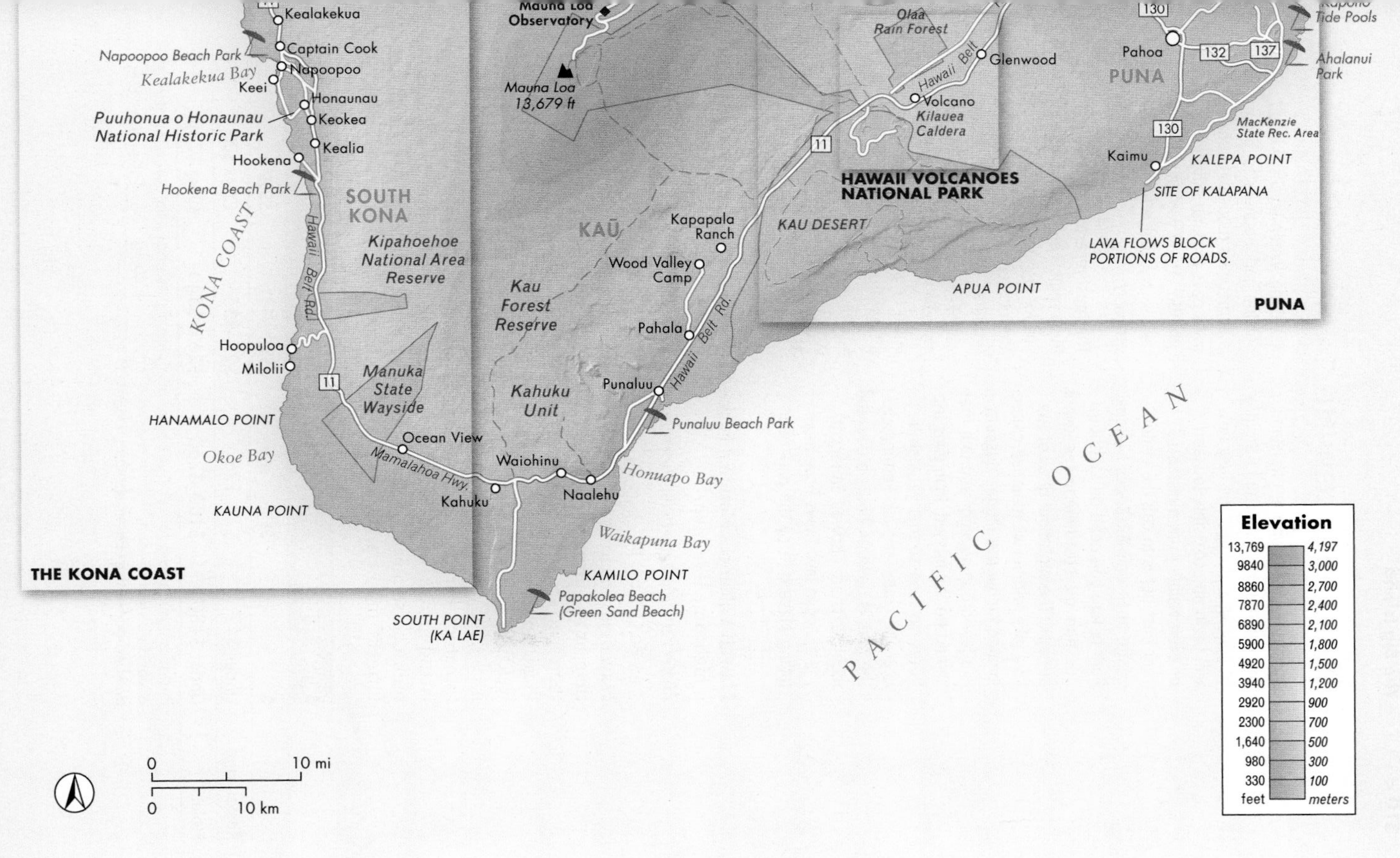
THE KONA COAST
Kealakekua
Captain Cook
Napoopoo Beach Park
Napoopoo
Kealakekua Bay
Keei
Honaunau
Puuhonua o Honaunau National Historic Park
Keokea
Kealia
Hookena
Hookena Beach Park
SOUTH KONA
KONA COAST
Hawaii Belt Rd.
Kipahoehoe National Area Reserve
Hoopuloa
Milolii
Manuka State Wayside
11
HANAMALO POINT
Okoe Bay
Ocean View
Mamalahoa Hwy.
Kahuku
KAUNA POINT
Mauna Loa Observatory
Mauna Loa 13,679 ft
KAŪ
Kau Forest Reserve
Kahuku Unit
Waiohinu
Naalehu
SOUTH POINT (KA LAE)
Papakolea Beach (Green Sand Beach)
KAMILO POINT
Waikapuna Bay
Honuapo Bay
Punaluu
Punaluu Beach Park
Pahala
Wood Valley Camp
Kapapala Ranch
Olaa Rain Forest
Hawaii Belt
Glenwood
Volcano
Kilauea Caldera
HAWAII VOLCANOES NATIONAL PARK
KAU DESERT
APUA POINT
PUNA
Pahoa
130
132
137
Ahalanui Park
Tide Pools
MacKenzie State Rec. Area
Kaimu
KALEPA POINT
SITE OF KALAPANA
LAVA FLOWS BLOCK PORTIONS OF ROADS.
PACIFIC OCEAN
Elevation
13,769 4,197
9840 3,000
8860 2,700
7870 2,400
6890 2,100
5900 1,800
4920 1,500
3940 1,200
2920 900
2300 700
1,640 500
980 300
330 100
feet meters
0 10 mi
0 10 km

WILL I SEE FLOWING LAVA?

Lava often flows on the Big Island, but you may not know until the day of your visit whether the lava flow will be in an accessible location, or even visible from a distance. Your best bet is to call the visitor center at Hawaii Volcanoes National Park before you head out. Without question, the best time to see lava is at night. The nighttime glow of the lava lake within Halemaumau crater, located below the Jaggar Museum, is a jaw-dropping sight and one that should not be missed. Plan your trip to the volcano so that you can be near the crater at dusk. Fortunately, the park is open 24 hours a day, and night visits are allowed. In recent years, active lava flows have been taking place outside the park near Kalapana. When lava is flowing outside park boundaries, hiking is sometimes regulated because trails pass through private land. Pay attention to all warning signs, and take safety advice from park rangers seriously.

The most recent lava flows in the Puna region are still too dangerous for visitors, and most efforts are focused on helping the area's residents. At some point visitors will likely be allowed to visit; when it's safe, local outfitters will once again begin trips. ■ TIP→ **Bring a flashlight, water, and sturdy shoes, and be prepared for some rough going over the lava fields at night.**

Hawaii Volcanoes National Park—very convenient (and romantic) after a nighttime lava hike.

Hotel reviews have been shortened. For full information, visit Fodors.com.

RESTAURANTS

Hawaii is a melting pot of cultures, and nowhere is this more apparent than in its cuisine. From luau and "plate lunches" to sushi and steak, there's no shortage of interesting flavors and presentations. The "grow local, buy local" movement is in full force on the Big Island. This is a welcome shift from years past, in which many foods were imported, and it's a happy trend for visitors, who get to taste juicy, flavorful Waimea tomatoes, handmade Hamakua goat cheese, locally raised beef, or even island-grown wine. Whether you're looking for a quick snack or a multicourse meal, you can find the best that the island has to offer at farmers' markets, restaurants, and cafés.

WHAT IT COSTS

	$	$$	$$$	$$$$
Restaurants	Under $17	$17–$26	$27–$35	Over $35
Hotels	Under $180	$180–$260	$261–$340	Over $340

Restaurant prices are for a main course at dinner. Hotel prices are for two people in a standard double room in high season. Condo price categories reflect studio and one-bedroom rates. Prices do not include 13.42% tax.

VISITOR INFORMATION

Contacts Island of Hawaii Visitors Bureau. ✉ *68-1330 Mauna Lani Dr., Ste. 109A* 🌐 *www.gohawaii.com.*

EXPLORING

Updated by Kristina Anderson

The first secret to enjoying the Big Island: Rent a car. The second: Plan well and stay more than three days or return again and again to really explore this fascinating place. With 266 miles of coastline comprised of white coral, black lava, and a dusting of green-olivine beaches, interspersed with lava cliffs, emerald gorges, and crashing waterfalls, the Big Island just about has it all. Depending on the number of days you have available, consider dividing your time between the Hilo and Kona sides of the island in order to take in the attractions of each district.

4

KAILUA-KONA

Kailua-Kona is about 7 miles south of the Kona airport.

A fun and quaint seaside town, Kailua-Kona has the souvenir shops and open-air restaurants you'd expect in a small tourist hub, plus a surprising number of historic sites. Quite a few nice oceanfront restaurants here offer far more affordable fare than those at the resorts on the Kohala Coast and in Waimea.

Except for the rare deluge, the sun shines year-round. Mornings offer cooler weather, smaller crowds, and more birds singing in the banyan trees; you'll see tourists and locals out running on Alii Drive, the town's main drag, by about 5 am every day. Afternoons sometimes bring clouds and light rain, but evenings often clear up for cool drinks, brilliant sunsets, gentle trade winds, and lazy hours spent gazing out over the ocean. Though there are better beaches north of town on the Kohala Coast, Kailua-Kona is home to a few gems, including a fantastic snorkeling beach (Kahaluu) and a tranquil bay perfect for kids (Kamakahonu Beach, in front of the Courtyard King Kamehameha's Kona Beach Hotel).

Scattered among the shops, restaurants, and condo complexes of Alii Drive are Ahuena Heiau, a temple complex restored by King Kamehameha the Great and the spot where he spent his last days (he died here in 1819); the last royal palace in the United States (Hulihee Palace); and a battleground dotted with the graves of ancient Hawaiians who fought for their way of life and lost. It was also here in Kailua-Kona that Kamehameha's successor, King Liholiho, broke and officially abolished the ancient *kapu* (roughly translated as "forbidden," it was the name for the strict code of conduct that islanders were compelled to follow) system by publicly sitting and eating with women. The following year, on April 4, 1820, the first Christian missionaries came ashore here, changing life in the Islands forever.

Hulihee Palace 3
Kailua Pier 2
Kamakahonu and Ahuena Heiau ... 1
Mokuaikaua Church 4

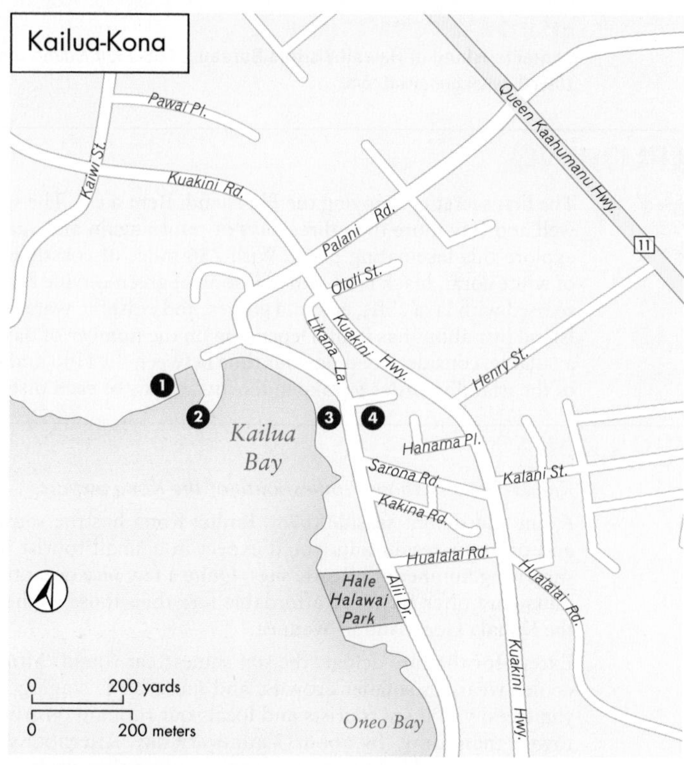

GETTING HERE AND AROUND

The town closest to Kona International Airport (it's about 7 miles away), Kailua-Kona is a convenient home base from which to explore the island.

Half a day is plenty of time to explore Kailua-Kona, as most of the town's sights are located in or near the downtown area. Still, if you add in a beach trip (Kahaluu Beach has some of the best and easiest snorkeling on the island), it's tempting to while away the day here. Another option for making a day of it is to tack on a short trip up a small hill to the charming, artsy village of Holualoa or to the coffee farms in the mountains just above Kealakekua Bay.

The easiest place to park your car is at Courtyard King Kamehameha's Kona Beach Hotel, but you'll have to pay a daily parking fee. Some free parking is also available: When you enter Kailua via Palani Road (Highway 190), turn left onto Kuakini Highway, drive for a half block, and turn right into the small marked parking lot. Walk *makai* (toward the ocean) on Likana Lane a half block to Alii Drive, and you'll be in the heart of Kailua-Kona.

TOURS

Kona Historical Society. The society sells a 24-page booklet, which has a map and more than 40 historic photos, so you can take a self-guided walking tour to learn more about the village's fascinating past. ✉ *81-6551 Mamalahoa Hwy., Kealakekua* ☎ *808/323–3222* 🌐 *www.konahistorical.org.*

TOP ATTRACTIONS

Fodor's Choice ★ **Hulihee Palace.** A lovely two-story oceanfront home surrounded by jewel-green grass and elegant coco palms and fronted by an elaborate wrought-iron gate, Hulihee Palace is one of only three royal palaces in America (the other two are in Honolulu). The royal residence was built by Governor John Adams Kuakini in 1838, a year after he completed Mokuaikaua Church. During the 1880s, it served as King David Kalakaua's summer palace. Built of lava rock and coral lime mortar, it features vintage koa furniture, weaving, portraits, tapa cloth, feather work, and Hawaiian quilts. The palace is on the National Register of Historic Places and is operated by the Daughters of Hawaii, a nonprofit organization dedicated to preserving the culture and royal heritage of the Islands. ✉ *75-5718 Alii Dr., Kailua-Kona* ☎ *808/329–1877* 🌐 *www.daughtersofhawaii.org* 🎫 *$8 self-guided tour, $10 guided.*

Kailua Pier. Though most fishing boats use Honokohau Harbor, this pier dating from 1918 is still a hub of ocean activity. Outrigger canoe teams practice and race, shuttles transport cruise ship passengers to and from town, and tour boats depart from these docks daily. Along the seawall, children and old-timers cast their lines. For youngsters, a bamboo pole and hook are easy to come by, and plenty of locals are willing to give pointers. September brings the world's largest long-distance canoe race, while in October, 1,700 elite athletes leave from the pier to swim 2.4 miles as part of the famous Ironman World Championship triathlon. ✉ *Alii Dr., across from King Kamehameha's Kona Beach Hotel, Kailua-Kona.*

Fodor's Choice ★ **Kamakahonu and Ahuena Heiau.** In the early 1800s, King Kamehameha the Great built a royal compound at Kamakahonu, the bay fronting what is now the Courtyard King Kamehameha's Kona Beach Hotel. Kamakahonu means "eye of the turtle," and it was named for a prominent turtle-shaped rock there, covered in cement when the hotel was built. It was a 4-acre homestead, complete with several houses and religious sites. In 1813, the king rebuilt Ahuena Heiau, a stunning temple dedicated to Lono, the Hawaiian god of peace and prosperity. It was also used as a seat of government. Today the compound is on the National Register of Historic Places and is a National Historic Landmark. One of the most revered and historically significant in all of Hawaii, the site sustained some damage in the 2011 tsunami and has been repaired. (Rather spookily, the tsunami waters caused widespread damage at the hotel but did not impact its rare Hawaiian artifacts or the paintings by famed Hawaiian artist Herb Kane.) ✉ *75-5660 Palani Rd., Kailua-Kona.*

4

Fodor's Choice ★ **Mokuaikaua Church.** Site of the first Christian church in the Hawaiian Islands, this solid lava-rock structure, built in 1836, is mortared with burned lime, coral, and kukui oil and topped by an impressive steeple. The ceiling and interior were crafted of timbers harvested from a forest on Hualalai and held together with wooden pegs, not nails. Inside, behind a panel of gleaming koa wood, rests a model of the brig *Thaddeus* as well as a koa wood table crafted by Henry Boshard, pastor for 43 years. The gift shop is open most mornings, and a talk is given by the church historian Sundays at noon. You may also encounter Aloha Greeters within the sanctuary, who love to share the history of Mokuaikaua with visitors. The church still holds services and hosts community events, so please be respectful when entering the building. ✉ *75-5713 Alii Dr., Kailua-Kona* ☎ *808/329–0655* 🌐 *www.mokuaikaua.org* 🎟 *Free.*

THE KONA COAST

South of Kailua-Kona, Highway 11 hugs splendid coastlines and rural towns, leaving busy streets behind. The winding, upcountry road takes you straight to the heart of coffee country, where fertile plantations and jaw-dropping views offer a taste of what Hawaii was like before the resorts took over. Much of the farmland is in leasehold status, which explains why this part of the Big Island has remained rather untouched by development. Tour one of the coffee farms to find out what the big deal is about Kona coffee, and enjoy a free sample while you're at it.

A 20-minute drive off the highway from Captain Cook leads to beautiful Kealakekua Bay, where Captain James Cook arrived in 1778, dying here not long after. Hawaiian spinner dolphins frolic in the bay, now a Marine Life Conservation District, nestled alongside immensely high green cliffs that jut dramatically out to sea. Snorkeling is superb here, so you may want to bring your gear and spend an hour or so exploring the coral reefs. This is also a nice kayaking spot; the bay is normally extremely calm. ■ TIP→ **One of the best ways to spend a morning is to kayak in the pristine waters of Kealakekua Bay, paddling over to see the spot where Cook died. Guided tours are your best bet, and you'll likely see plenty of dolphins along the way.**

North of Kona International Airport, along Highway 19, brightly colored bougainvillea stand out in relief against miles of jet-black lava fields stretching from the mountain to the sea. Sometimes visitors liken it to landing on the moon when they first see it. True, the dry barren landscape may not be what you'd expect to find on a tropical island, but it's a good reminder of the island's evolving volcanic nature.

SOUTH KONA AND KEALAKEKUA BAY

Kealakekua Bay is 14 miles south of Kailua-Kona.

Between its coffee plantations, artsy havens, and Kealakekua Bay—one of the most beautiful spots on the Big Island—South Kona has plenty of activities to occupy a day. Bring a swimsuit and snorkel gear, and hit Kealakekua Bay first thing in the morning. You'll beat the crowds, have a better chance of a dolphin sighting, and see more fish. After a

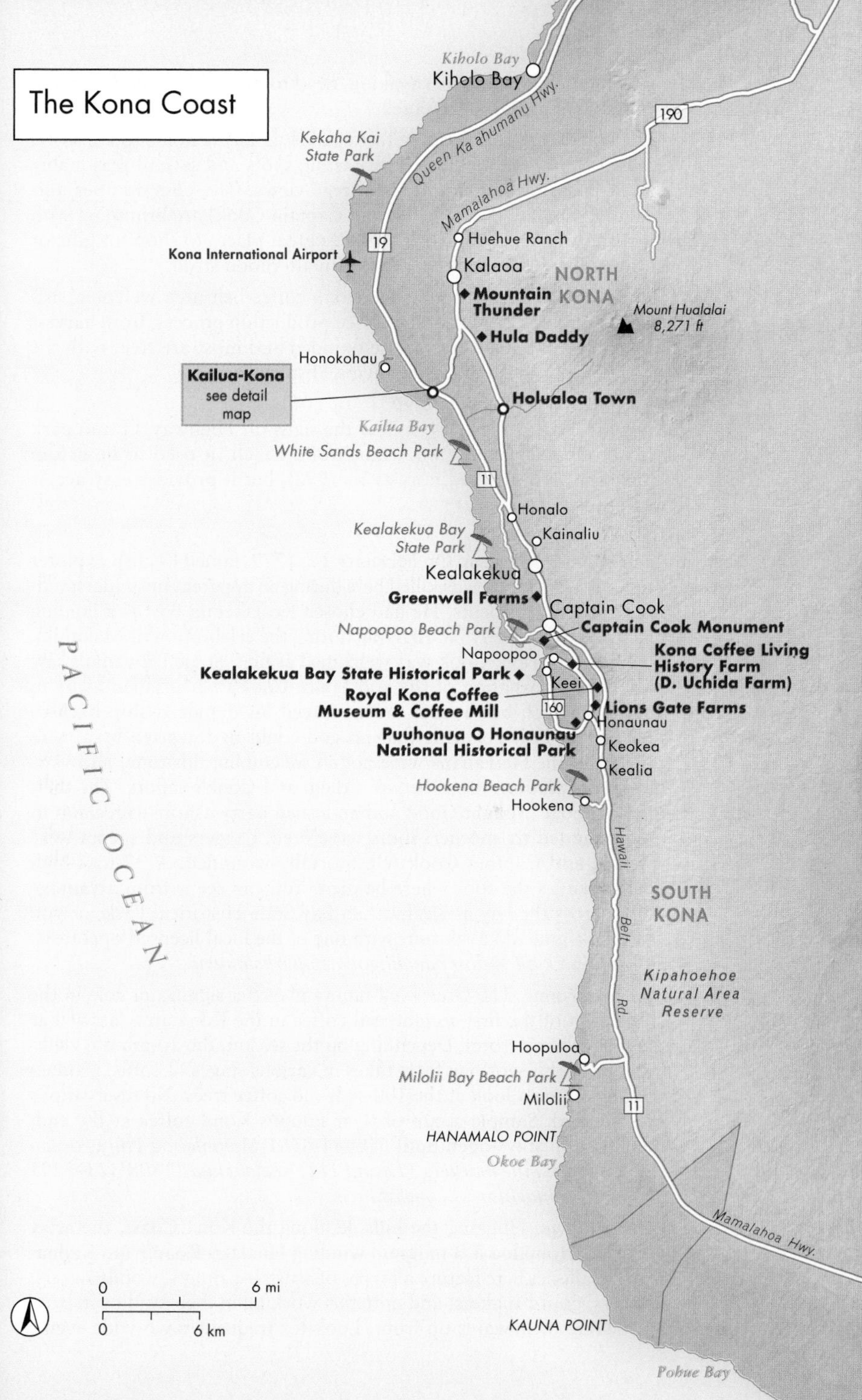

The Kona Coast
Kiholo Bay
Kiholo Bay
Queen Ka ahumanu Hwy.
190
Kekaha Kai
State Park
Mamalahoa Hwy.
19
Huehue Ranch
Kona International Airport
Kalaoa
NORTH
KONA
Mountain
Thunder
Mount Hualalai
8,271 ft
Hula Daddy
Honokohau
Kailua-Kona
see detail
map
Holualoa Town
Kailua Bay
White Sands Beach Park
11
Honalo
Kealakekua Bay
State Park
Kainaliu
Kealakekua
Greenwell Farms
Captain Cook
Napoopoo Beach Park
Captain Cook Monument
Napoopoo
Kona Coffee Living
History Farm
(D. Uchida Farm)
Kealakekua Bay State Historical Park
Keei
Royal Kona Coffee
Museum & Coffee Mill
160
Lions Gate Farms
Honaunau
Puuhonua O Honaunau
National Historical Park
Keokea
Kealia
PACIFIC OCEAN
Hookena Beach Park
Hookena
Hawaii
Belt
Rd.
SOUTH
KONA
Kipahoehoe
Natural Area
Reserve
Hoopuloa
Milolii Bay Beach Park
Milolii
11
HANAMALO POINT
Okoe Bay
Mamalahoa Hwy.
0
6 mi
0
6 km
KAUNA POINT
Pohue Bay

morning of swimming or kayaking, head to one of the homey cafés in nearby Captain Cook to refuel.

The meandering road leading to Kealakekua Bay is home to a historic painted church, as well as coffee-tasting spots and several reasonably priced bed-and-breakfasts with great views. The communities surrounding the bay (Kealakekua and Captain Cook) are brimming with local and transplanted artists. They're great places to shop for gifts or antiques, have some coffee, or take an afternoon stroll.

Several coffee farms around the Kona coffee-belt area welcome visitors to watch all or part of the coffee-production process, from harvest to packaging. Some tours are self-guided and most are free, with the exception of the Kona Coffee Living History Farm.

GETTING HERE AND AROUND

To get to Kealakekua Bay, follow the signs off Highway 11 and park at Napoopoo Beach. It's not much of a beach (it used to be before Hurricane Iniki washed it away in 1992), but it provides easy access into the water.

TOP ATTRACTIONS

Fodor's Choice ★ **Captain Cook Monument.** On February 14, 1779, famed English explorer Captain James Cook was killed here during an apparent misunderstanding with local residents. He had chosen Kealakekua Bay as a landing place in November 1778. Arriving during the celebration of Makahiki, the harvest season, Cook was welcomed at first. Some Hawaiians saw him as an incarnation of the god Lono. Cook's party sailed away in February 1779, but a freak storm forced his damaged ship back to Kealakekua Bay. Believing that no god could be thwarted by a mere rainstorm, the Hawaiians were not so welcoming this time, and various confrontations arose between them and Cook's sailors. The theft of a longboat brought Cook and an armed party ashore to reclaim it. One thing led to another: shots were fired, daggers and spears were thrown, and Captain Cook fell, mortally wounded. A 27-foot-high obelisk marks the spot where he died. You can see it from a vantage point across the bay at Kealakekua Bay State Historical Park, or you can take a guided kayak tour with one of the local licensed operators. ✉ *Captain Cook* 🌐 *dlnr.hawaii.gov/dsp/parks/hawaii.*

FAMILY **Greenwell Farms.** The Greenwell family played a significant role in the cultivation of the first commercial coffee in the Kona area (as well as the first grocery store). Depending on the season, the 20-minute walking tour of this working farm takes in various stages of coffee production, including a look at the 100-year-old coffee trees. No reservations are required. Sample a cup of their famous Kona coffee at the end; the gift shop stays open until 5. ✉ *81-6581 Mamalahoa Hwy., ocean side, between mile markers 112 and 111, Kealakekua* ☎ *808/323–2295* 🌐 *www.greenwellfarms.com* 🎫 *Free.*

Holualoa Town. Hugging the hillside along the Kona Coast, the artsy village of Holualoa is 3 miles up winding Hualalai Road from Kailua-Kona. Galleries here feature all types of artists—painters, woodworkers, jewelers, gourd-makers, and potters—working in their studios in back and selling their wares up front. Look for frequent town-wide events such as art strolls and block parties. Then relax with a cup of coffee in one of the many cafés or stores. Formerly the exclusive domain of coffee plantations, Holualoa still boasts quite a few coffee farms offering free tours and inviting cups of Kona. ✉ *Holualoa* 🌐 *www.holualoahawaii.com.*

Hula Daddy. On a walking tour of this working coffee farm (by advance reservation only), visitors can witness the workings of a small plantation, pick and pulp their own coffee beans, watch a roasting demonstration, and have a tasting. The gift shop carries whole beans and logo swag including bags, T-shirts and mugs. ✉ *74-4944 Mamalahoa Hwy., Holualoa* ☎ *808/327–9744, 888/553–2339* 🌐 *www.huladaddy.com* 🎫 *From $10* ⏲ *Closed Sun.*

Fodor's Choice ★ **Kealakekua Bay State Historical Park.** This underwater marine reserve is one of the most beautiful spots in the state. Dramatic cliffs surround super-deep, crystal-clear, turquoise water chock-full of stunning coral pinnacles and tropical fish. The protected dolphins that frequent the sanctuary should not be disturbed, as they use the bay to escape predators and sleep. There's very little sand at west-facing **Napoopoo Beach,** but this is a nice easy place to enter the water and swim, as it's well protected from currents. There are no lifeguards; at times, you may feel tiny jellyfish stings. Stay at least 300 feet from the shoreline along the cliffs, which have become unstable during recent earthquakes. ✉ *Beach Rd., off Government Rd. from Puuhonua Rd. (Hwy. 160), Captain Cook* 🌐 *dlnr.hawaii.gov/dsp/parks/hawaii* ☞ *Bathrooms, limited parking, pavilion, shower.*

Kona Coffee Living History Farm (D. Uchida Farm). On the National Register of Historic Places, this perfectly preserved farm was completely restored by the Kona Historical Society. It includes a 1913 farmhouse surrounded by coffee trees, a Japanese bathhouse, *kuriba* (coffee-processing mill), and *hoshidana* (traditional drying platform). Caretakers still grow, harvest, roast, and sell the coffee exactly as they did more than 100 years ago. The H.N. Greenwell Store Museum is located on the same property. ✉ *82-6199 Mamalahoa Hwy., mile marker 110, Captain Cook* ☎ *808/323–2006* 🌐 *www.konahistorical.org* 🎫 *$15* ⏲ *Closed weekends.*

Lions Gate Farms. For a century, three generations have grown coffee on this pretty farm with spectacular ocean views in the heart of Honaunau. The coffee is processed in a mill that dates to 1942. Tours given by the friendly proprietors proudly show visitors how coffee and macadamia nuts are cultivated and harvested. The farm also sells packaged coffee, nuts, and jams and jellies from this year's harvest and are passionate about producing only the best estate-grown Kona coffee. ✉ *Hwy. 11, Mile Marker 105, Honaunau* ☎ *808/989–4883* 🌐 *www.coffeeofkona.com* 🎫 *Free.*

Mountain Thunder. This organic coffee producer offers hourly "bean-to-cup" tours, including a tasting and access to the processing plant, which shows dry milling, sizing, coloring, sorting, and roasting. Private VIP tours ($) let you be roast master for a day. Hawaiian teas, handmade chocolate, and macadamia nuts grown on-site are also available.

You may also take a self-guided tour. Remember that afternoon rains are common at this elevation so bring an umbrella and sturdy shoes. ✉ *73-1944 Hao St., Kailua-Kona* ☎ *808/443–7593* 🌐 *www.mountainthunder.com* 🎫 *Free.*

Fodor's Choice ★ **Puuhonua O Honaunau National Historical Park** (*Place of Refuge*). This 420-acre National Historical Park houses the best preserved *puuhonua* (place of refuge) in the state. Providing a safe haven for noncombatants, *kapu* (taboo) breakers, defeated warriors, and others, the *puuhonua* (place of refuge) offered protection and redemption for anyone who could reach its boundaries, by land or sea. The oceanfront, 960-foot stone wall still stands and is one of the park's most prominent features. A number of ceremonial temples, including the restored **Hale o Keawe Heiau** (circa 1700), have served as royal burial chambers. An aura of ancient sacredness and serenity still imbues the place. ✉ *Rte. 160, Honaunau* ✣ *About 20 miles south of Kailua-Kona* ☎ *808/328–2288* 🌐 *www.nps.gov/puho* 🎫 *$5 per vehicle.*

Royal Kona Coffee Museum & Coffee Mill. Take an easy, self-guided tour by following the descriptive plaques located around the coffee mill. Then stop off at the small museum to see coffee-making relics, peruse the gift shop, and watch an informational film. Visitors are also invited to enjoy the beautiful views as well as stroll through a real lava tube on the property. ✉ *83-5427 Mamalahoa Hwy., next to the tree house, Captain Cook* ☎ *808/328–2511* 🌐 *www.royalkonacoffee.com* 🎫 *Free.*

NORTH KONA

The North Kona district is characterized by vast lava fields, dotted with turnoff points to some of the most beautiful beaches in the world. Most of the lava flows here originate from the last eruptions of Hualalai, in 1800 and 1801, although some flows by the resorts hail from Mauna Loa. The stark black lavascapes contrast spectacularly with luminous azure waters framed by coco palms and white-sand beaches. Some of the turnoffs will take you to state parks with parking lots and bathrooms, while others are simply a park-on-the-highway-and-hike-in adventure.

GETTING HERE AND AROUND

Head north from Kona International Airport and follow Highway 19 along the coast. Take caution driving at night between the airport and where resorts begin on the Kohala Coast; it's extremely dark and there are few road signs or traffic lights on this two-lane road, and wild donkeys may appear on the roadway without warning.

THE KOHALA COAST

The Kohala Coast is about 32 miles north of Kailua-Kona.

If you had only a weekend to spend on the Big Island, this is probably where you'd want to be. The Kohala Coast is a mix of the island's best beaches and swankiest hotels, yet is not far from ancient valleys and temples, waterfalls, and funky artist enclaves.

The resorts on the Kohala Coast lay claim to some of the island's finest restaurants, golf courses, and destination spas. But the real attraction here is the island's glorious beaches. On a clear day, you can see Maui, and during the winter months, numerous glistening humpback whales cleave the waters just offshore.

Rounding the northern tip of the island, the arid coast shifts rather suddenly to green villages and hillsides, leading to lush Pololu Valley in North Kohala, as the hot sunshine along the coast gives way to cooler temperatures.

As you drive north, you'll find the quaint sugar-plantation-towns-turned-artsy-villages of Hawi and Kapaau. New galleries are interspersed with charming reminders of old Hawaii—wooden boardwalks, quaint local storefronts, ice cream shops, delicious neighborhood restaurants, friendly locals, and a delightfully slow pace. There's great shopping for everything from antiques and designer beachwear to authentic Hawaiian crafts.

GETTING HERE AND AROUND

Two days is sufficient time for experiencing each unique side of Kohala—one day for the resort perks: the beach, the spa, the golf, the restaurants; one day for hiking and admiring the waterfalls and valleys of North Kohala, coupled with a wander around Hawi and Kapaau.

Diving and snorkeling are primo along the Kohala Coast, so bring or rent equipment. If you're staying at one of the resorts, they will usually have any equipment you could possibly want. If you're feeling adventurous, get your hands on a four-wheel-drive vehicle and head to one of the unmarked beaches along the Kohala Coast—you may end up with a beach to yourself.

The best way to explore the valleys of North Kohala is with a hiking tour. Look for one that includes lunch and a dip in one of the area's waterfall pools. There are a number of casual lunch options in Hawi and Kapaau (sandwiches, sushi, seafood, local-style "plate lunch"), and a few good dinner spots.

VISITOR INFORMATION

Contacts North Kohala Welcome Center. ✉ *55-3393 Akoni Pule Hwy., Hawi* ✥ *Just past the "Welcome to Kohala" sign* ☎ *808/889–5523* 🌐 *www.northkohala.org.*

TOP ATTRACTIONS

Ackerman Gift Gallery. In Kapaau, browse through this longtime gallery's collections of local art, including glass, woodworks, bowls, fine art photography, and paintings. There's also a small café and gift shop a couple of doors away. ✉ *54-3897 Akoni Pule Hwy., Hwy. 270, Kapaau* ☎ *808/889–5138* 🌐 *www.ackermangalleries.com.*

Hawi and Kapaau. Near the birthplace of King Kamehameha, these North Kohala towns thrived during the plantation days, once bustling with hotels, saloons, and theaters—even a railroad. They took a hit when "Big Sugar" left the island, but both towns are blossoming once again, thanks to strong local communities, tourism, athletic events, and an influx of artists keen on honoring the towns' past. They are full of lovingly restored vintage buildings housing fun and funky shops, galleries, and eateries, and worth a stop or a break for a quick bite. Hawi is

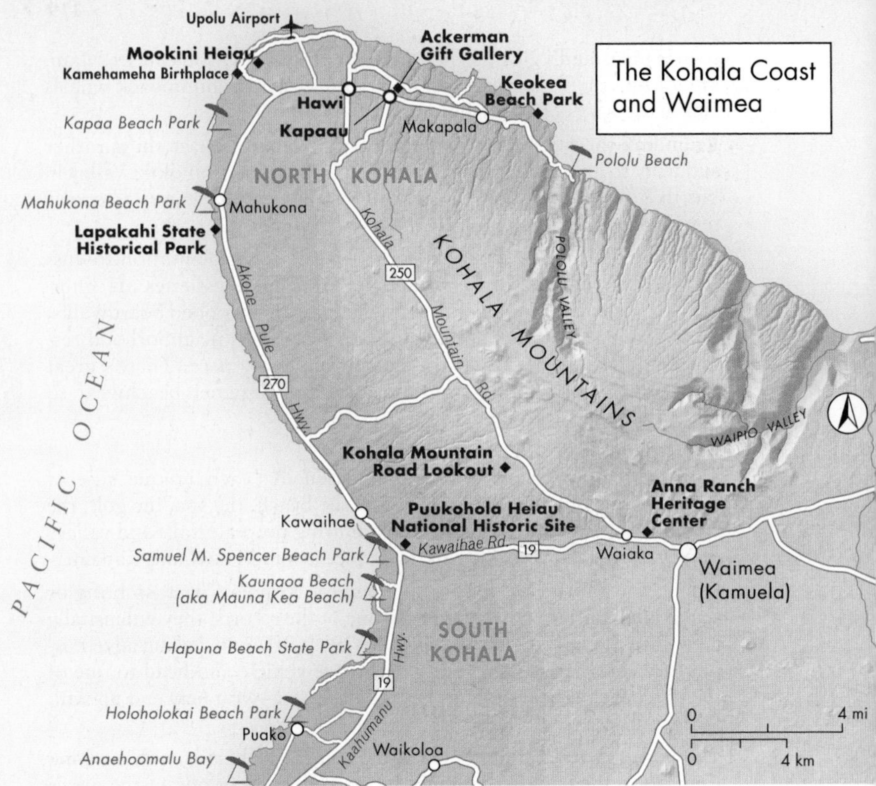

internationally known as the turnaround point for the cycling portion of the Ironman event. ✉ *Along Hwy. 270.*

Keokea Beach Park. A newly renovated pavilion (damaged in the 2006 quake) welcomes visitors to this 7-acre beach park fronting the rugged shore in North Kohala. It's a popular local spot for picnics, fishing, and surfing. ⚠ **Enjoy the scenery, but don't try to swim here—the water is very rough, and be careful on the hairpin curve going down.** ✉ *Hwy. 270, on the way to Pololu Valley near mile marker 27, Kapaau.*

Kohala Mountain Road Lookout. The road between North Kohala and Waimea is one of the most scenic drives in Hawaii, passing Parker Ranch, open pastures, rolling hills, and tree-lined mountains. There are a few places to pull over and take in the view; the lookout at mile marker 8 provides a splendid vista of the Kohala Coast and Kawaihae Harbor far below. On clear days, you can see well beyond the resorts to Maui, while other times an eerie mist drifts over the view. ✉ *Kohala Mountain Rd. (Hwy. 250), Waimea (Hawaii County).*

Lapakahi State Historical Park. A self-guided, 1-mile walking tour leads through the ruins of the once-prosperous fishing village Koaie, which dates as far back as the 15th century. Displays illustrate early Hawaiian fishing and farming techniques, salt gathering, games, and legends. Because the shoreline near the state park is an officially designated

Marine Life Conservation District (and part of the site itself is considered sacred), swimming, swim gear, and sunscreen are not allowed in the water. Portable restrooms are available but not drinking water. ⚠ **Use caution: the water is often rough here.** ✉ *Hwy. 270, mile marker 14 between Kawaihae and Mahukona, Waimea (Hawaii County)* ☎ *808/327–4958* 🌐 *www.hawaiistateparks.org* 🎫 *Free.*

Mookini Heiau. This isolated National Historic Landmark within Kohala Historical Sites State Monument is so impressive in size and atmosphere that it's guaranteed to give you what locals call "chicken skin" (goose bumps). Dating as early as AD 480, the parallelogram structure is a stunning example of a *luakini* heiau, used for ritualized human sacrifice to the Hawaiian war god Ku. The place feels haunted, more so if you are the only visitor and the skies are dark and foreboding. Visit with utmost care and respect. Nearby is Kapakai Royal Housing Complex, the birthplace of Kamehameha the Great. Although now under the care of the National Park Service, the site is still watched over by family descendents. ⚠ **Don't drive out here if it's been raining; even with a four-wheel drive, you could easily get stuck.** ✉ *Coral Reef Pl./Upolu Point Rd., , off Upolu Airport Rd. and Hwy. 270 (Akoni Pule Hwy.), Hawi* ✥ *Turn at sign for Upolu Airport, near Hawi, and hike or drive 1½ miles southwest* ☎ *808/961–9540* 🌐 *www.nps.gov* ⏲ *Closed Wed.*

Fodor's Choice ★ **Puukohola Heiau National Historic Site.** Quite simply, this is one of the most historic and commanding sites in all of Hawaii. It was here in 1810, on top of Puukohala (Hill of the Whale), that Kamehameha the Great built the war heiau that would serve to unify the Hawaiian Islands, ending 500 years of almost continually warring chiefdoms. The oceanfront, fortresslike site is foreboding and impressive. A paved ½-mile, looped trail runs from the visitor center to the main temple sites. An even older temple, dedicated to the shark gods, lies submerged just offshore, where sharks can be spotted swimming, usually first thing in the morning. A new museum displays ancient Hawaiian weapons, including clubs, spears, a replica of a bronze cannon that warriors dragged into battle on a Hawaiian sled, and three original paintings by artist Herb Kane. Rangers are available to answer questions, or you can take a free audio tour on your own smartphone. Plan about an hour to see everything. ✉ *62-3601 Kawaihae Rd., Kawaihae* ☎ *808/882–7218* 🌐 *www.nps.gov/puhe/index.htm* 🎫 *Free.*

WAIMEA

Waimea is 40 miles northeast of Kailua-Kona and 10 miles east of the Kohala Coast.

Thirty minutes over the mountain from Kohala, Waimea offers a completely different experience than the rest of the island. Rolling green hills, large open pastures, light rain, cool evening breezes and morning mists, along with abundant cattle, horses, and regular rodeos are just a few of the surprises you'll stumble upon here in *paniolo* (Hawaiian for "cowboy") country.

Waimea is also where some of the island's top Hawaii regional-cuisine chefs practice their art using local ingredients, which makes it an ideal place to find yourself at dinnertime. In keeping with the recent restaurant trend toward featuring local farm-to-table ingredients, a handful of Waimea farms and ranches supply most of the restaurants on the island, and many sell to the public as well. With its galleries, coffee shops, brewpubs, restaurants, beautiful countryside, and *paniolo* (cowboy) culture, Waimea is well worth a stop if you're heading to Hilo or Maunakea. ■ **TIP→ And the short highway, or mountain road, that connects Waimea to North Kohala (Highway 250) affords some of our favorite Big Island views.**

GETTING HERE AND AROUND

You can see most of what Waimea has to offer in one day, but if you're heading up to Maunakea for stargazing—which you should—it could easily be stretched to two. If you stay in Waimea overnight (there are many bed-and-breakfast options), spend the afternoon browsing through town or touring some of the area's ranches and historic sites. Then indulge in a gourmet dinner before heading up the Daniel K. Inouye Highway, also known as the Saddle Road, for world-renowned stargazing on Maunakea.

A word to the wise—there are no services or gas stations on Saddle Road, the only way to reach the summit of Maunakea. Fill up on gas and bring water, snacks, and warm clothes with you (there are plenty of gas stations, cafés, and shops in Waimea).

TOP ATTRACTIONS

Fodor's Choice ★ **Anna Ranch Heritage Center.** This stunning heritage property, on the National and State Registers of Historic Places, belonged to the "first lady" of Hawaii ranching, Anna Lindsey Perry-Fiske. Here is a rare opportunity to see a fully restored cattle ranch compound and learn about the life of this fascinating woman, who butchered cattle by day and threw lavish parties by night. Wander the picturesque grounds and gardens on a self-guided walk, watch a master saddle maker and an ironsmith in action, and take a guided tour (by appointment only) of the historic house, where Anna's furniture, gowns, and elaborate *pau* (parade riding) costumes are on display. The knowledgeable staff shares anecdotes about Anna's amazing life. (Some staff and visitors have even reported strange goings-on in the main house, suggesting that Anna herself may still be "around.") ✉ *65-1480 Kawaihae Rd., Waimea (Hawaii County)* ☎ *808/885–4426* 🌐 *www.annaranch.org* 🎫 *Grounds and Discovery Trail free; historic home tours $10* ⏲ *Closed Sat.–Mon.*

MAUNAKEA

Fodor's Choice ★ *Maunakea's summit is 18 miles southeast of Waimea and 34 miles northwest of Hilo.*

Maunakea ("white mountain") offers the antithesis of the typical tropical island experience. Freezing temperatures and arctic conditions are common at the summit, and snow can fall year-round. You can even snowboard or ski up here. Seriously. But just because you can doesn't mean you'll want to. You should be in very good shape and a close-to-expert boarder or skier to get down the slopes near the summit and

DID YOU KNOW?

Coffee beans are actually the seeds of these cherry-like fruit, appropriately named coffee cherries. Be sure to sample some Kona brew while you're in the area.

then up again in the thin air with no lifts. During the winter months, lack of snow is usually not a problem.

But winter sports are the least of the reasons that most people visit this starkly beautiful mountain. From its base below the ocean's surface to its summit, Maunakea is the tallest island mountain on the planet. It's also home to little Lake Waiau, one of the highest natural lakes in the world, though lately, the word "pond" is closer to the truth.

Maunakea's summit—at 13,796 feet—is the best place in the world for viewing the night sky. For this reason, the summit is home to the largest and most productive astronomical observatories in the world—and $1 billion (with a "B") worth of equipment. Research teams from 11 different countries operate 13 telescopes on Maunakea, several of which are record holders: the world's largest optical–infrared telescopes (the dual Keck telescopes), the world's largest dedicated infrared telescope (UKIRT), and the largest submillimeter telescope (the JCMT). A still-larger 30-meter telescope (TMT) had been cleared for construction and was slated to open its record-breaking eye to the heavens until it got delayed by some Native Hawaiian protests. It's since been cleared again for construction.

Maunakea is tall, but there are higher mountains in the world, so what makes this spot so superb for astronomy? It has more to do with atmosphere than with elevation. A tropical-inversion-cloud layer below the summit keeps moisture from the ocean and other atmospheric pollutants down at the lower elevations. As a result, the air around the Maunakea summit is extremely dry, which helps in the measurement of infrared and submillimeter radiation from stars, planets, and the like. There are also rarely clouds up here; the annual number of clear nights here blows every other place out of the water. And, because the mountain is far away from any interfering artificial lights (not a total coincidence—in addition to the fact that the nearest town is nearly 30 miles away, there's an official ordinance limiting certain kinds of streetlights on the island), skies are dark for the astronomers' research. To quote the staff at the observatory, astronomers here are able to "observe the faintest galaxies that lie at the very edge of the observable universe."

Teams from various universities around the world gather on an 18-month waiting list to get the chance to use the telescopes on Maunakea. They have made major astronomical discoveries, including several about the nature of black holes, the discovery of new satellites around Jupiter and Saturn, new Trojans (asteroids that orbit, similar to moons) around Neptune, new moons and rings around Uranus, and new moons around Pluto. Their studies of galaxies are changing the way scientists think about time and the evolution of the universe.

What does all this mean for you? A visit to Maunakea is a chance to see more stars than you've likely ever seen before, and an opportunity to learn more about mind-boggling scientific discoveries in the very spot where these discoveries are being made. For you space geeks, a trip to Maunakea may just be the highlight of your trip.

If you're in Hilo, be sure to visit the Imiola Astronomy Center, which is near the University of Hawaii at Hilo. It offers presentations and planetarium films about the mountain and the science being conducted there, as well as exhibits describing the deep knowledge of the heavens possessed by the ancient Hawaiians.

GETTING HERE AND AROUND

The summit of Maunakea isn't terribly far, but the drive takes about 90 minutes from Hilo and an hour from Waimea thanks to the steep road. Between the ride there, sunset on the summit, and stargazing, allot at least five hours for a Maunakea visit.

To reach the summit, you must take Saddle Road (Highway 200, now known as the Daniel K. Inouye Highway), which has been rerouted and repaved and is now a beautiful shortcut across the middle of the island. At mile marker 28, John A. Burns Way, the access road to the visitor center (9,200 feet), is fine, but the road from there to the summit is a lot more precarious because it's unpaved washboard and very steep. Only four-wheel-drive vehicles with low range should attempt this journey. Two-wheel-drive cars are unsafe, especially in winter conditions. Unsuitable cars may experience engine failure as a result of the low oxygen levels. Legislation is pending regarding a total ban of anything but four-wheel-drive vehicles on the summit. And if you're driving back down in the dark, slow and cautious is the name of the game. ⚠ **Most rental car companies will not permit you to drive to the summit of Maunakea. Driving there without permission will void your contract and leave you responsible for damages. This happens more often than you'd think.**

Also remember that Maunakea's extreme altitude can cause altitude sickness, leading to disorientation, headaches, and light-headedness. Keeping hydrated is crucial. Scuba divers must wait at least 24 hours before traveling to the summit. Children under 16, pregnant women, and those with heart, respiratory, or weight problems should not go higher than the visitor center. While you can park at the visitor center and hike to the summit if you are in good shape, the trip takes approximately seven hours one way, and no camping is allowed. That means you must leave in the pre-dawn hours to be back before dark; a permit is also required for this hike.

The last potential obstacle: it's cold—as in freezing—usually with significant wind chill, ice, and snow. Winds have been clocked at well over 100 miles per hour. Most summit tour operators provide down parkas and ski gloves.

TOURS

Companies that provide organized tours of Maunakea and its summit are headquartered in both Hilo and Kailua-Kona.

Arnott's Lodge & Hiking Adventures. This outfitter takes you to the summit for sunset and then stops along the way down the mountain, where guides give visual lectures (dependent on clear skies) using lasers. They focus on major celestial objects and Polynesian navigational stars. The excursion departs from Hilo and includes parkas and hot beverages. Pickup is available from Hilo hotels. If you drive yourself and park at Puu Huluhulu, across Maunakea Access Road, the cost is lower. The price is even lower if you stay at their traveler's lodge, which offers a variety of rooms, and even tent camping. ✉ *98 Apapane Rd., Hilo* ☎ *808/339–0921* 🌐 *www.arnottslodge.com* 🎫 *From $150.*

Fodor's Choice ★ **Hawaii Forest & Trail.** The ultra-comfortable, highly educational Summit & Stars tour packs a lot of fun into a few hours. Guides are knowledgeable about astronomy and Hawaii's geologic and cultural history, and the small group size (max of 14) encourages camaraderie. Included in the tour are dinner at an old ranching station, catered by a favorite local restaurant; sunset on the summit; and a fantastic private star show mid-mountain. The company's powerful 11-inch Celestron Schmidt-Cassegrain telescope reveals lots of interesting celestial objects, including seasonal stars, galaxies, and nebula. The moon alone, if present, will knock your socks off. Everything from water bottles, parkas, and gloves to hot chocolate and brownies is included. Their new Maunakea sunrise tour begins in the wee hours before the sun comes up and includes a hike among the endangered silverswords as well as breakfast at the visitor center. And of course, the main event—a spectacular sunrise on the summit. The company also offers a daytime version of the summit tour. ✉ *73-5598 Olowalu St., Kailua-Kona* ☎ *808/331–8505, 800/464–1993* 🌐 *www.hawaii-forest.com* 🎫 *From $220.*

Mauna Kea Summit Adventures. As the first company to specialize in tours to the mountain, Mauna Kea Summit Adventures is a small outfit that focuses on stars. Cushy vans with panoramic windows journey first to the visitor center, where participants enjoy a hearty lasagna dinner on the lanai and acclimatize for 45 minutes before donning hooded arctic-style parkas and ski gloves for the sunset trip to the 14,000-foot summit. With the help of knowledgeable guides, stargazing through a powerful Celestron telescope happens mid-mountain, where the elevation is more comfortable and skies are just as clear. The tour includes dinner, hot cocoa and biscotti, west-side pickup and runs 364 days a year, weather permitting. ■ TIP→ **Book at least one month prior, as these tours sell out fast.** ✉ *Kailua-Kona* ☎ *808/322–2366, 888/322–2366* 🌐 *www.maunakea.com* 🎫 *From $216.*

TOP ATTRACTIONS

Head to the summit before dusk so you can witness the stunning sunset and emerging star show. Only the astronomers are allowed to use the telescopes and other equipment, but the scenery is available to all. After the sun sinks, head down to the visitor center to warm up and stargaze, or do your stargazing first and then head up here. If you were blown away by the number of stars crowding the sky over the visitor center, this vantage point will leave you speechless.

If you haven't rented a four-wheel-drive vehicle from Harper's—the only rental company that allows their vehicles on the summit—don't want to deal with driving to the summit, or don't want to wait in line to use the handful of telescopes at the visitor center, the best thing to do is book a commercial tour. Operators provide transportation to and from the summit along with expert guides; some also provide parkas, gloves, telescopes, dinner, hot beverages, and snacks.

Fodor's Choice ★ **Onizuka Center for International Astronomy Visitor Information Station.** At 9,200 feet, this excellent amateur observation site has a handful of telescopes and a knowledgeable staff. You can enjoy stargazing sessions from 6 to 10 pm on Tuesday, Wednesday, Friday, and Saturday, or just stop here to acclimate yourself to the altitude if you're heading for the summit. Fortunately, it's a pleasure to do so. Sip hot chocolate and peruse exhibits on ancient Hawaiian celestial navigation, about the mountain's significance as a quarry for the best basalt in the Hawaiian Islands and as a revered spiritual destination, on modern astronomy, and about ongoing projects at the summit. Nights are clear 90% of the year, so the chances are good of seeing some amazing sights in the sky. Parking is limited and the staff may turn you away if the lot fills up. **■ TIP→ Keep in mind that most summit telescope facilities are not open to the public, so your best bet for actual stargazing is at the visitor center.** ✉ *Mauna Kea* ☎ *808/961–2180, 808/935–6268 Current road conditions* 🌐 *www.ifa.hawaii.edu/info/vis* 🎫 *Free, donations welcome.*

4

THE HAMAKUA COAST

The Hamakua Coast is about 25 miles east of Waimea.

The spectacular waterfalls, mysterious jungles, emerald fields, and stunning ocean vistas along Highway 19 northwest of Hilo are collectively referred to as the Hilo–Hamakua Heritage Coast. Brown signs featuring a sugarcane tassel reflect the area's history: thousands of former acres of sugarcane are now idle, with little industry to support the area since "King Sugar" left the island in the early 1990s.

This is a great place to wander off the main road and see "real" Hawaii—untouched valleys, overgrown banyan trees, tiny coastal villages, and little plantation towns Papaikou, Laupahoehoe, and Paauilo among them. Some small communities are still hanging on quite nicely, well after the demise of the big sugar plantations that first engendered them. They have homey cafés, gift shops, galleries, and a way of life from a time gone by.

The dramatic Akaka Falls is only one of hundreds of waterfalls here, many of which tumble into refreshing swimming holes, so bring your swimsuit when you explore this area. The pristine Waipio Valley was once a favorite getaway spot for Hawaiian royalty. The isolated valley floor has maintained the ways of old Hawaii, with taro patches, wild horses, and a handful of houses. The view from the lookout is breathtaking.

GETTING HERE AND AROUND

Though Highway 19 is the fastest route through the area, any turnoff along this coast could lead to an incredible view, so take your time and go exploring up and down the side roads. If you're driving from Kailua-Kona, rather than around the northern tip of the island, cut across on the Mamalahoa Highway (Highway 190) to Waimea, and then catch Highway 19 to the coast. It takes a little longer but is worth it.

Signs mark various sites of historical interest, as well as scenic views along the 40-mile stretch of coastline. Keep an eye out for them and try to stop at the sights mentioned—you won't be disappointed.

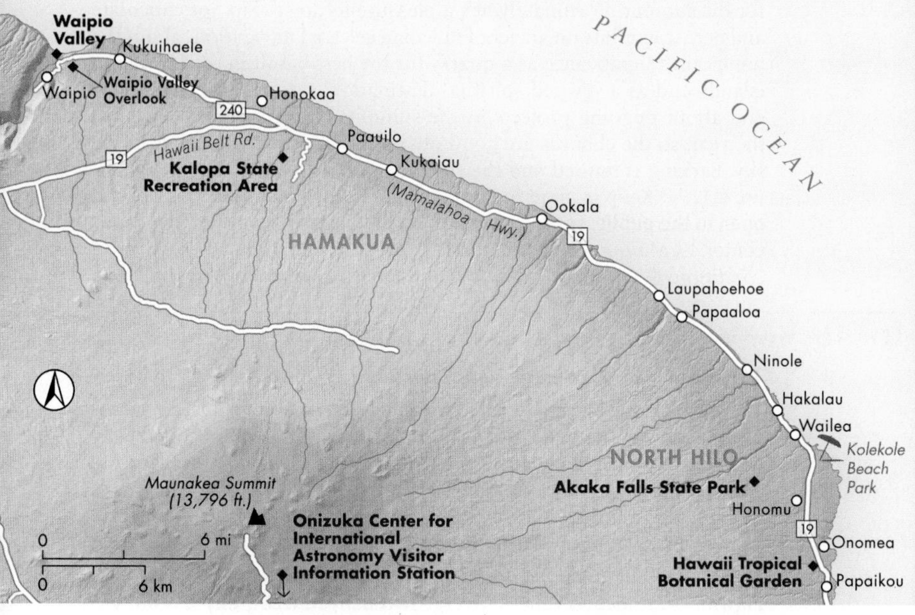

TIP→ The "Heritage Drive," a 4-mile loop just off the main highway, is well worth the detour.

Once back on Highway 19, you'll pass the road to Honokaa, which leads to the end of the road bordering Waipio Valley.

If you've stopped to explore the quiet little villages with wooden boardwalks and dogs dozing in backyards, or if you've spent several hours in Waipio Valley, night will undoubtedly be falling. Don't worry: the trip to Hilo via Highway 19 takes only about an hour, or you can go in the other direction to stop for dinner in Waimea before heading to the Kohala Coast (another 25 to 45 minutes). Although you shouldn't have any trouble exploring the Hamakua Coast in a day, a handful of romantic bed-and-breakfasts are available if you want to spend more time.

GUIDED TOURS

A guided tour is one of the best ways to see Waipio Valley. You can walk down and up the steep narrow road yourself, but you won't see as much. And as locals say, it's 15 minutes to walk down, but about 45 minutes to walk back up. The cost for a tour depends on both the company and the transport mode.

Waipio Naalapa Stables. Friendly horses and friendly guides take guests on tours of the valley floor. The 2½-hour tours run Monday through Saturday (the valley rests on Sunday) with check-in times of 9 am and

12:30 pm. Riders meet at Waipio Valley Artworks, near the lookout, where they are transported to the valley floor in a four-wheel-drive van. ✉ *48-5416 Kukuihale Rd., Waipio Valley Artworks Bldg., Honokaa* ☎ *808/775–0419* 🌐 *www.naalapastables.com* 🎫 *From $90.*

Waipio on Horseback. This outfit offers guided, 2½-hour horseback-riding tours on the Waipio Valley floor. Riders experience lush tropical foliage, flowering trees, a scenic beach, tranquil streams, and 3,000-foot-tall cliff walls. Paniolo guides share the history, culture, and mythology of this magical valley and also give you a sneak peek of a traditional family farm. ✉ *Hwy. 240, mile marker 7.5, northwest of Honokaa* ☎ *808/775–7291, 877/775–7291* 🌐 *www.waipioonhorseback.com* 🎫 *From $105.*

Waipio Valley Shuttle. Not up for hiking in and out of the valley on foot? These informative, 1½- to 2-hour, four-wheel-drive tours do the driving for you, exploring the valley with lots of stops and run Monday through Saturday. The windows on the van are removed, allowing guests to snap unobstructed photos. You have the option to stay at the beach for two to four hours and come back up with the next tour. ✉ *48-5416 Kukuihaele Rd., Honokaa* ☎ *808/775–7121* 🌐 *www.waipiovalleyshuttle.com* 🎫 *From $59.*

Waipio Valley Wagon Tours. Mule-drawn wagon tours take visitors through the valley Monday through Saturday at 10:30, 12:30, and 2:30; the excursion lasts 1½ hours. Narration by friendly guides offers history and cultural background. Reservations are highly recommended. The pickup spot is at the Last Chance Store, 8 miles outside Honokaa. ✉ *48-5300 Kuikuihaele Rd., Honokaa* ☎ *808/775–9518* 🌐 *www.waipiovalleywagontours.com* 🎫 *$62.50.*

TOP ATTRACTIONS

Fodor's Choice ★ **Akaka Falls State Park.** A paved, 10-minute loop trail (approximately ½ mile) takes you to the best spots to see the spectacular cascades of Akaka. The majestic upper Akaka Falls drops more than 442 feet, tumbling far below into a pool drained by Kolekole Stream amid a profusion of fragrant white, yellow, and red torch ginger and other tropical foliage. Another 400-foot falls is on the lower end of the trail. Restroom facilities are available but no drinking water. ⚠ **A series of steps along parts of the trail may prove challenging for some visitors.** ✉ *Off Hwy. 19, 4 miles inland, near Honomu* ☎ *808/974–6200* 🎫 *$5 per vehicle (nonresidents); $1 for nonresident walk-ins.*

Hawaii Tropical Botanical Garden. Eight miles north of Hilo, stunning coastline views appear around each curve of the 4-mile scenic jungle drive that accesses this privately owned nature preserve next to Onomea Bay. Paved pathways in the 17-acre botanical garden lead past ponds, waterfalls, and more than 2,000 species of plants and flowers, including palms, bromeliads, ginger, heliconia, orchids, and ornamentals. The garden is well worth a stop, and your entry fee helps the nonprofit preserve plants, seeds, and rain forests for future generations. ✉ *27-717 Old Mamalahoa Hwy., Papaikou* ☎ *808/964–5233* 🌐 *www.hawaiigarden.com* 🎫 *$15.*

FAMILY **Kalopa State Recreation Area.** North of the old plantation town of Paauilo, at a cool elevation of 2,000 feet, lies this sweet 100-acre state park. There's a lush forested area with picnic tables and restrooms, and an easy ¾-mile loop trail with additional paths in the adjacent forest reserve. Small signs identify some of the plants, including the gothic-looking native ohia. Three campground areas with full-service kitchen as well as four cabins can be reserved online. ✉ *44-3375 Kalopa Mauka Rd., Honokaa* ✣ *12 miles north of Laupahoehoe and 3 miles inland off Hwy. 19* ☎ *808/775–8852* 🎫 *Free.*

Fodor's Choice ★ **Waipio Valley.** Bounded by 2,000-foot cliffs, the "Valley of the Kings" was once a favorite retreat of Hawaiian royalty. Waterfalls drop 1,200 feet from the Kohala Mountains to the valley floor, and the sheer cliff faces make access difficult. The lush valley is breathtaking in every way and from every vantage. Though almost completely off the grid today, Waipio was once a center of Hawaiian life; somewhere between 4,000 and 20,000 people made it their home between the 13th and 17th centuries. In addition, it is a highly historical and culturally signifcant site as it housed *heiau* (temples) and *puuhonua* (places of refuge) in addition to royal residences. King Kamehameha the Great launched a great naval battle from here, which marked the start of his unification (some would say conquest) and reign of the Hawaiian Islands. To preserve this pristine part of the island, commercial-transportation permits are limited—only a few outfitters offer organized valley floor trips.

A paved road leads down from the **Waipio Valley Overlook,** but no car-rental companies on the island allow their cars to be driven down. The distance is actually less than a mile from the lookout point—just keep in mind the climb back gains 1,000 feet in elevation and is highly strenuous, so bring water and a walking stick. Area landowners do not look kindly on public trespassing to access Hiilawe Falls at the back of the valley, so stick to the front by the beach. Hike all the way to the end of the beach for a glorious vantage. Swimming, surfing, and picnics are all popular activities here, conditions permitting. You can also take the King's Trail from the end of the beach to access another waterfall not far down the trail. (Waterfalls can come and go depending on the level of recent rains.) If you do visit here, respect this area, as it is considered highly sacred to Hawaiians and is still home to several hundred full-time residents who cultivate taro on family farms. ✉ *Hwy. 240, 8 miles northwest of Honokaa* ⏲ *Closed Sun.*

HILO

Hilo is 55 miles southeast of Waimea, 95 miles northeast of Kailua-Kona, and just north of the Hilo Airport.

In comparison to Kailua-Kona, Hilo is often deemed "the old Hawaii." With significantly fewer visitors than residents, more historic buildings, and a much stronger identity as a long-established community, this quaint, traditional town does seem more authentic and local. It stretches from the banks of the Wailuku River to Hilo Bay, where a few hotels line stately Banyan Drive. The vintage buildings that make up Hilo's downtown have been spruced up as part of a revitalization effort.

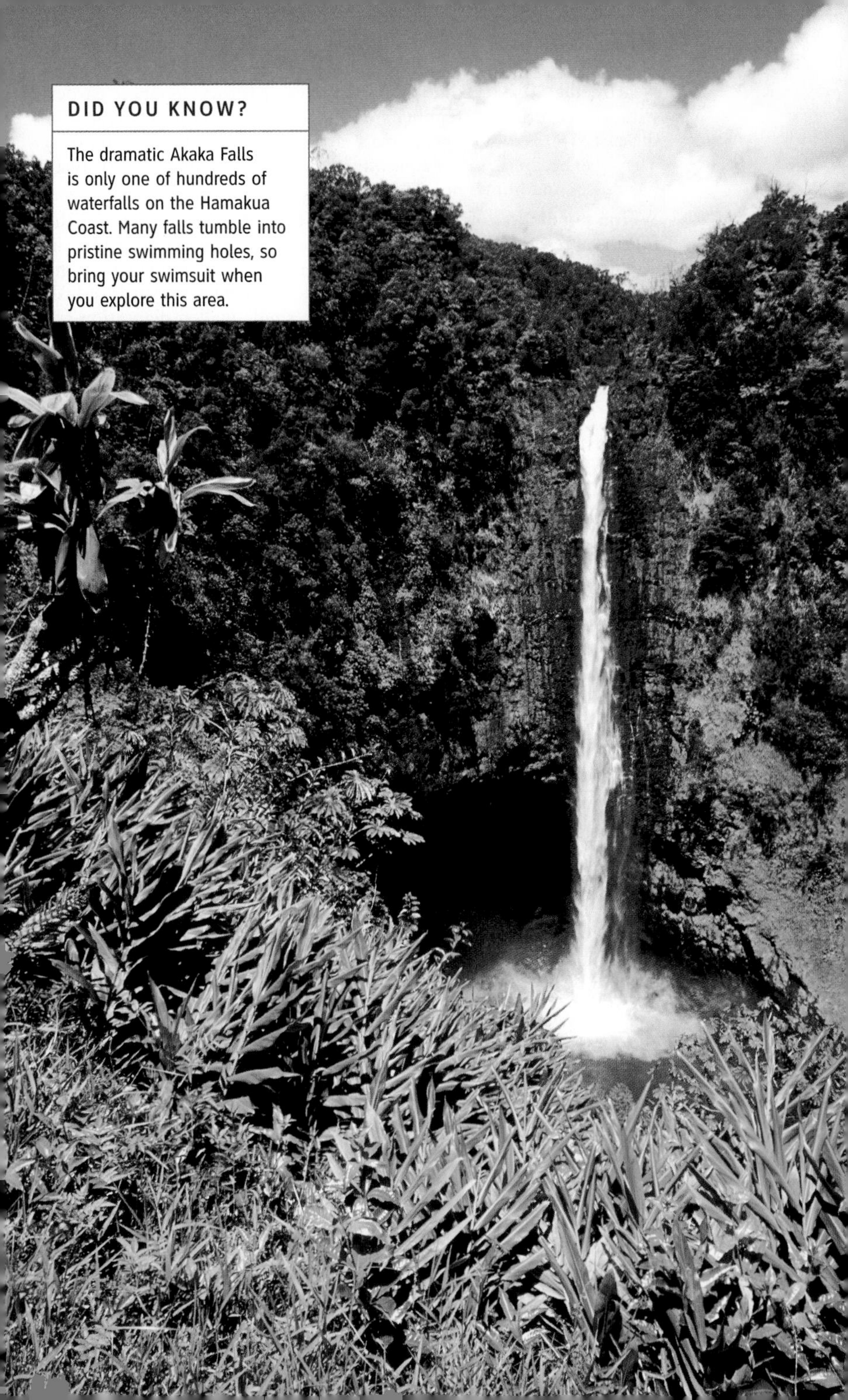

DID YOU KNOW?

The dramatic Akaka Falls is only one of hundreds of waterfalls on the Hamakua Coast. Many falls tumble into pristine swimming holes, so bring your swimsuit when you explore this area.

Nearby, the 30-acre Liliuokalani Gardens, a formal Japanese garden with arched bridges, stepping stones and waterways, were created in the early 1900s to honor the area's Japanese sugar-plantation laborers. They also became a safety zone after a devastating tsunami swept away businesses and homes on May 22, 1960, killing 61 people.

With a population of almost 50,000 in the entire district, Hilo is the fourth-largest city in the state and home to the University of Hawaii at Hilo. Although it is the center of government and commerce for the island, Hilo is clearly a residential town. Mansions with yards of lush tropical foliage share streets with older, single-walled plantation-era houses with rusty corrugated roofs. It's a friendly community, populated primarily by descendants of the contract laborers—Japanese, Chinese, Filipino, Puerto Rican, and Portuguese—brought in to work the sugarcane fields during the 1800s.

One of the main reasons visitors have tended to steer clear of the east side of the island is its weather. With an average rainfall of 130 inches per year, it's easy to see why Hilo's yards are so green and its buildings so weatherworn. Outside of town, the Hilo District boasts scenic beach valleys, rain forests and waterfalls, a terrain unlike the hot and dry white-sand beaches of the Kohala Coast. But when the sun does shine—usually part of nearly every day—the town sparkles, and, during winter, the snow glistens on Maunakea, 25 miles in the distance. Best of all is when the mists fall and the sun shines at the same time, leaving behind the colorful arches that earn Hilo its nickname: the City of Rainbows.

The Merrie Monarch Hula Festival takes place in Hilo every year during the second week of April, and dancers and admirers flock to the city from all over the world. If you're planning a stay in Hilo during this time, be sure to book your room and car rentals well in advance.

GETTING HERE AND AROUND

Hilo is a great base for exploring the eastern and southern parts of the island; just be sure to bring an umbrella for—sporadic and sometimes torrential—showers. If you're just passing through town or making a day trip, make the first right turn into the town off Highway 19 (it comes up fast) and grab a parking spot in the lot on your left or on any of the surrounding streets. Downtown Hilo is best experienced on foot.

There are plenty of gas stations and restaurants in the area. Hilo is a good spot to load up on food and supplies—just south of downtown there are several large budget retailers. If you're here on Wednesday or Sunday, be sure to stop by the expansive Hilo Farmers' Market to peruse stalls and stalls of produce, flowers, baked goods, coffee, honey, and more.

TOP ATTRACTIONS

Boiling Pots. Four separate streams fall into a series of circular pools here, forming the Peepee Falls. The resulting turbulent action—best seen after a good rain—has earned this scenic stretch of the Wailuku River the nickname Boiling Pots. There's no swimming allowed at Peepee Falls or anywhere in the Wailuku River, due to extremely dangerous currents and undertows. The falls are 3 miles northwest of Hilo off Waianuenue Avenue; keep to the right when the road splits and look for the sign.

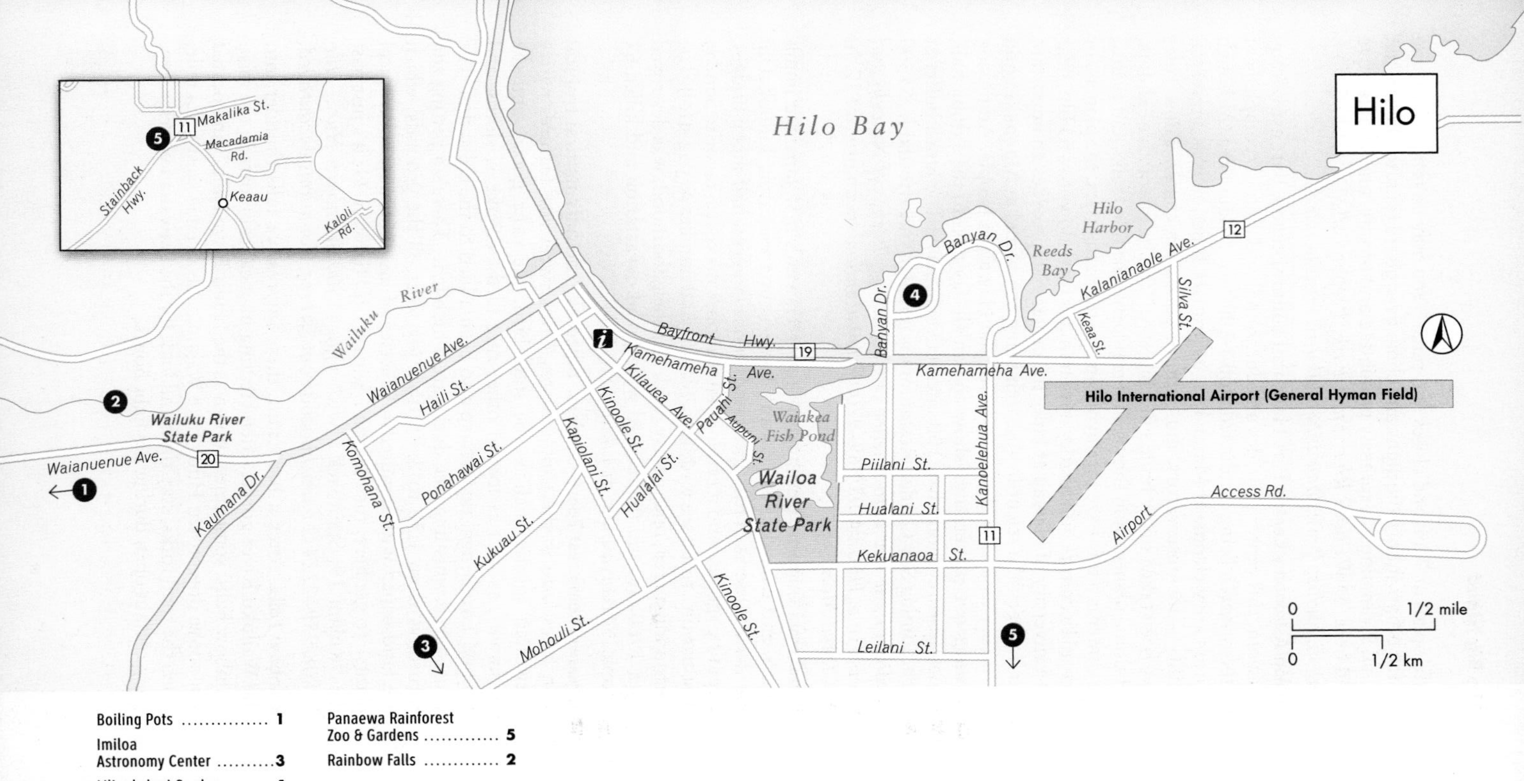

Hilo
Hilo Bay
Hilo Harbor
Reeds Bay
Hilo International Airport (General Hyman Field)
Kalanianaole Ave.
12
Silva St.
Keaa St.
Banyan Dr.
Kamehameha Ave.
Bayfront Hwy.
19
Kanoelehua Ave.
11
Access Rd.
Airport
Piilani St.
Hualani St.
Kekuanaoa St.
Leilani St.
Waiakea Fish Pond
Wailoa River State Park
Pauahi St.
Aupuni St.
Kilauea Ave.
Kinoole St.
Hualalai St.
Kapiolani St.
Mohouli St.
Kukuau St.
Ponahawai St.
Haili St.
Komohana St.
Waianuenue Ave.
Wailuku River
Wailuku River State Park
20
Kaumana Dr.
Makalika St.
Macadamia Rd.
Stainback Hwy.
Keaau
Kaloli Rd.
0
1/2 mile
0
1/2 km
Boiling Pots 1
Imiloa Astronomy Center 3
Liliuokalani Gardens 4
Panaewa Rainforest Zoo & Gardens 5
Rainbow Falls 2

Gate opens at 7 am and closes at 6 pm. ⚠ **You may be tempted, as you watch others ignore the signs and climb over guard rails, to jump in, but resist. Swimming is expressly prohibited and unsafe, and people have died here.** ✉ *Wailuku River State Park, Peepee Falls Dr., Hilo* 🌐 *dlnr.hawaii.gov/dsp/parks/hawaii/wailuku-river-state-park/.*

Fodor's Choice ★ **Imiloa Astronomy Center.** Part Hawaiian cultural center, part astronomy museum, this center provides an educational and cultural complement to the research being conducted atop 14,000-foot Maunakea. Although visitors are welcome at Maunakea, its primary function is as a research facility—not observatory, museum, or education center. Those roles have been taken on by Imiloa in a big way. With its interactive exhibits, full-dome planetarium shows, and regularly scheduled talks and events, the center is a must-see for anyone interested in the stars, the planets, or Hawaiian culture and history. Five minutes from downtown Hilo, near the University of Hawaii at Hilo, the center also provides an important link between the scientific research being conducted at Maunakea and its history as a sacred mountain for the Hawaiian people. Admission includes one planetarium show and an all-day pass to the exhibit hall, which features more than 100 interactive displays. The lunch buffet at the adjoining Sky Garden Restaurant is popular and affordable. ✉ *600 Imiloa Pl., at UH Hilo Science & Technology Park, off Nowelo and Komohana, Hilo* ☎ *808/969–9700* 🌐 *www.imiloahawaii.org* 🎟 *$17.50* ⏲ *Closed Mon.*

Liliuokalani Gardens. Designed to honor Hawaii's first Japanese immigrants and named after Hawaii's last reigning monarch, Liliuokalani Gardens' 30 acres of fish-filled ponds, stone lanterns, half-moon bridges, elegant pagodas, and a ceremonial teahouse make it a favorite Sunday destination. You'll see weddings, picnics, and families as you stroll. The surrounding area, once a busy residential neighborhood, was destroyed by a 1960 tsunami that caused widespread devastation and killed 61 people. ✉ *Banyan Dr., at Lihiwai St., Hilo* 🎟 *Free.*

FAMILY Fodor's Choice ★ **Panaewa Rainforest Zoo & Gardens.** Billed as "the only natural tropical rain forest zoo in the United States," this sweet zoo features native Hawaiian species such as the state bird, the nene goose, and the *io* (hawk), as well as lots of other rare birds, monkeys, sloths, and lemurs. Two Bengal tigers have also been added to the collection. The white-faced whistling tree ducks are a highlight. There's a petting zoo Saturdays from 1:30 to 2:30. It's a joy to stroll the grounds, which are landscaped with hundreds of species of lush and unusual tropical plants. To get here, turn left on Mamaki off Highway 11; it's just past the "Kulani 19, Stainback Hwy." sign. ✉ *800 Stainback Hwy., Hilo* ☎ *808/959–7224* 🌐 *www.hilozoo.com* 🎟 *Free, donations encouraged.*

Rainbow Falls. After a hard rain, these impressive falls thunder into the Wailuku River gorge, often creating magical rainbows in the mist. Rainbow Falls, sometimes known as the "Hilo Town Falls," are located just above downtown Hilo. Take Waianuenue Avenue west for a mile; when the road forks, stay right and look for the Hawaiian warrior sign. They remain open during daylight hours.

At another point inside the park along the Wailuku River, four separate streams fall into a series of circular pools, forming the Peepee Falls. The resulting turbulent action—best seen after a good rain—has earned this scenic stretch of the river the nickname Boiling Pots. There's no swimming allowed at Peepee Falls or anywhere in the Wailuku River, due to extremely dangerous currents and undertows. The falls are 3 miles northwest of Hilo off Waianuenue Avenue; keep to the right when the road splits and look for the sign. The gate opens at 7 am and closes at 6 pm. ⚠ **You may be tempted, as you watch others ignore signs and climb over guard rails, to jump in, but resist. More than a few people have died here.** ✉ *Wailuku River State Park, Rainbow Dr., Hilo* 🌐 *dlnr.hawaii.gov/dsp/parks/hawaii.*

PUNA

Puna is about 6 miles south of Hilo.

The Puna District is wild in every sense of the word. The jagged black coastline is changing all the time; the trees are growing out of control, forming canopies over the few paved roads; the land is dirt cheap and there seem to be few building codes; and the people—well, there's something about living in an area that could be destroyed by lava at any moment (as Kalapana was in 1990, or Kapoho in 1960, or parts of Pahoa Town in 2014, or Vacationland in 2018) that makes the norms of modern society seem silly. Vets, surfers, hippies, yoga teachers, and other free spirits abound. And also a few ruffians. So it is that Puna has its well-deserved reputation as an "outlaw" region of the Big Island.

That said, it's well worth a detour, especially if you're near this part of the island anyway. Volcanically heated springs and tide pools burst with interesting sea life, and some mighty fine people-watching opportunities exist in Pahoa, a funky little town that the "Punatics" call home.

This is also farm country for both legal and illicit crops. Local farmers grow everything from orchids and anthuriums to papayas, bananas, and macadamia nuts. Several of the island's larger, rural, residential subdivisions are nestled between Keaau and Pahoa, including Hawaiian Paradise Park, Orchidland Estates, Hawaiian Acres, and Hawaiian Beaches.

When dusk falls here, the air fills with the high-pitched symphony of thousands of coqui frogs. Though they look cute on the signs and seem harmless, the invasive frogs are pests both to local crops and to locals tired of their shrieking, all-night calls.

GETTING HERE AND AROUND

The sprawling Puna District includes part of the Volcano area and stretches northeast down to the coast. If you're staying in Hilo for the night, driving around wild lower Puna is a great way to spend a morning.

The roads connecting Pahoa to Kapoho and the Kalapana coast form a loop that's about 25 miles long; driving times are from two to three hours, depending on the number of stops you make and the length of time at each stop. There are restaurants, stores, and gas stations in Pahoa, but services elsewhere in the region are spotty. Long stretches

Puna
KURTISTOWN
11
130
MOUNTAIN VIEW
Kahakai Blvd.
Kapoho
Kapoho Tide Pools
132
137
Pahoa Town
Hawaii Belt Hwy
Pahoa Pohoiki Rd.
Isaac Hale
VOLCANO VILLAGE
PUNA
KILAUEA CALDERA
Crater Rim Dr.
Hawaii Volcanoes National Park
Kehena Beach
Kehena
EAST RIFT ZONE
Kaimu
SOUTHWEST RIFT ZONE
Hilina Pali Rd.
Chain of Craters Rd.
1983–Present Lava Flow
KAU DESERT
HILINA PALI
Road closed due to lava
PACIFIC OCEAN
0
4 mi
0
4 km

of the road may be completely isolated at any given point; this can be a little scary at night but beautiful and tranquil during the day.

Compared to big-city living, it's pretty tame, but there is a bit of a "locals-only" vibe in parts of Puna, and some areas suffer crime and drug problems. Don't wander around alone at night or get lost on backcountry roads. Further, the most recent eruptions of Kilauea have some isolated parts of this region, and some areas will be inaccessible for the long-term.

HAWAII VOLCANOES NATIONAL PARK AND VICINITY

Fodor's Choice ★ *Hawaii Volcanoes National Park is about 22 miles southwest from the start of the Puna district, and about 27 miles southwest of Hilo.*

Few visitors realize that in addition to "the volcano" (Kilauea)—that mountain oozing new layers of lava onto its flanks—there's also Volcano, the village. Conveniently located next to Hawaii Volcanoes National Park, Volcano Village is a charming little hamlet in the woods that offers dozens of excellent inns and bed-and-breakfasts, a great diner, and a handful of things to see and do that don't include the village's namesake.

For years, writers, artists, and meditative types have been coming to the volcano to seek inspiration, and many of them have settled in and around the village. Artist studios (open to the public by appointment) are scattered in the forest, laden with ferns and mists.

Do plan to visit the Halemaumau summit crater at night. It's fun to start with a sunset cocktail at the Volcano House, where you can sit by a large picture window and watch the glow of the crater fill the room. Then after dark (stay for dinner if you wish), head over to the Jaggar Museum, where you can stand at the crater's edge and see the live eruption in all its glory, as park rangers and docents give impromptu talks.

Much of the national park's most popular areas (including the visitor center, Volcano House, the Jaggar Museum, and Kilauea Military Camp) were closed after the most recent Kilauea eruption in May 2018. That situation is likely to change, but it's difficult to predict when the park will be able to reopen as eruptions can last weeks or months. The Kahuku Unit, however, is fully open.

GETTING HERE AND AROUND

There is a handful of dining options, a couple of stores, and gas stations available in Volcano Village, so most of your needs should be covered. If you can't find what you're looking for, Hilo is about a 35-minute drive away, and the Keaau grocery store and fast-food joints are 25 minutes away.

Many visitors choose to stay the night in Volcano to see the dramatic glow at the summit caldera, which has been filling and dropping repeatedly in recent years. (If you do stay, bring a fleece or sweater, as temperatures drop at night and mornings are usually cool and misty.) Currently, there are two active eruption sites: one at the summit caldera (Halemaumau, sometimes known by locals as the lava lake) and the other from the Puu oo vent in the southeast rift zone. Chain of Craters

"I learned that the best viewing area was at the end of the Pahoa Kalapana Road past the Keauohana Forest Reserve."—NickiGgert, Fodors.com photo contest participant

Road intersects with Crater Rim Drive and is open for the full 19 miles to the ocean.

Speed limits in this area are very reduced for a reason. Not only is the region seismically active, the park wishes to maintain protection for the endangered Hawaiian nene goose and for the safety of all visitors.

Parts of the national park were closed in mid-2018 due to ongoing erruptions of Kilauea. Check with the park before planning any trips here.

TOP ATTRACTIONS

Fodor's Choice ★ **Hawaii Volcanoes National Park.** Kilauea Volcano has been spewing lava rather dramatically since its current eruption began in 1983, and it shows no signs of abating. Hawaii Volcanoes National Park encompasses two of the volcanoes (Kilauea and Mauna Loa) that helped form the Big Island nearly half a million years ago. If you do nothing else on the Big Island, make an effort to see the live active volcano. Many people spend a few nights in the Volcano area just to witness the lava flow glowing against the night sky.

Begin your visit at the visitor center, where you'll find a store selling maps, books, and DVDs; information on trails, ranger-led talks and walks, and special events; and current weather, road, and lava-viewing conditions. Free volcano-related film showings, lectures, and other presentations are regularly scheduled. Rangers lead daily walks at 10:30 am and 1:30 pm into different areas; check with the visitor center for details as times and destinations depend on weather conditions and eruptions. Over 60 companies hold permits to lead hikes at HVNP.

One of the busiest attractions in the park is the Jaggar Museum of volcanology, which displays historical scientific instruments, as well as equipment and protective clothing that has actually been used by scientists here (and which has sometimes gotten too close to the lava), and even working seismographs. At the museum's lookout, you might even spot the rare endangered nene (Hawaii's state bird).

Visitors with limited time may want to just take Crater Rim Drive, which has both scenic viewpoints and short trails into the lava fields. About five miles of Crater Rim Drive (after Jaggar Museum and intersecting with Chain of Craters Road) has been closed since 2008 due to hazardous volcanic gases and particulates being ejected from Halemaumau Crater. If you have a bit more time, you can see the far side of the park on the 19-mile Chain of Craters Road.

Even if lava-viewing conditions aren't ideal, you can hike and camp amid wide expanses of *aa* (rough) and *pahoehoe* (smooth) lava, a fascinating experience.

Weather conditions fluctuate daily, sometimes hourly. It can be rainy, foggy, and chilly even during the summer; the temperature usually is 14° cooler at the 4,000-foot-high summit of Kilauea than at sea level. Expect hot, dry, and windy coastal conditions at the end of Chain of Craters Road. Bring rain gear, and wear layered clothing, sturdy shoes, sunglasses, a hat, and sunscreen. Also bring snacks and water if you plan to hike or stay a while.

"Vog" (volcanic smog) can cause headaches; breathing difficulties; lethargy; irritations of the skin, eyes, nose, and throat; and other health problems. Pregnant women, young children, and people with asthma and heart conditions are most susceptible, and should avoid areas such as Halemaumau Crater, where fumes can be thick. Wear long pants and boots or closed-toe shoes with good tread for hikes on lava. Stay on marked trails and step carefully. Lava is composed of 50% silica (glass) and can cause serious injury if you fall. Remember that these are active volcanoes, and eruptions can cause parts of the park to close at any time. ⚠ **Check the park's website or call ahead for last-minute updates before your visit.** ✉ *Hwy. 11, Volcano* ☎ *808/985–6000* 🌐 *www.nps.gov/havo* 🎫 *$25 per car for 7 days, $12 for pedestrians and bicyclists.*

KAU AND KA LAE

Ka Lae (South Point) is 50 miles south of Kailua-Kona.

Perhaps the most desolate region of the island, Kau is nevertheless home to some spectacular sights. Mark Twain wrote some of his finest prose here, where macadamia-nut farms, remote green-sand beaches, and tiny communities offer rugged, largely undiscovered beauty. The drive from Kailua-Kona to windswept Ka Lae (South Point) winds away from the ocean through a surreal moonscape of lava plains and patches of scrub forest. Coming from Volcano, as you near South Point, the barren lavascape gives way to lush vistas from the ocean to the hills.

At the end of the 12-mile, two-lane road to Ka Lae, you can park and hike about an hour to Papakolea Beach (Green Sands Beach). Back on

Continued on page 346

HAWAII VOLCANOES NATIONAL PARK

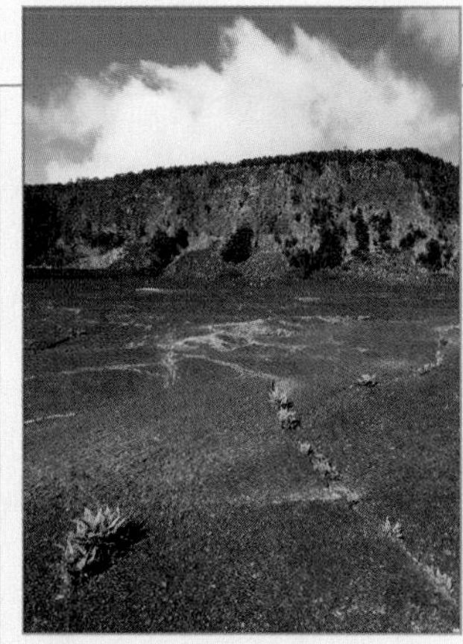

Exploring the surface of the world's most active volcano—from the moonscape craters at the summit to the red-hot lava flows on the coast to the kipuka, pockets of vegetation miraculously left untouched—is the ultimate ecotour and one of Hawaii's must-dos.

The park sprawls over 520 square miles and encompasses Kilauea and Mauna Loa, two of the five volcanoes that formed the Big Island nearly half a million years ago. Kilauea, youngest and most rambunctious of the Hawaiian volcanoes, erupted at its summit from the 19th century through 1982. Since then, the top of the volcano had been more or less quiet, frequently shrouded in mist; an eruption in the Halemaumau Crater in 2008 ended this period of relative inactivity.

Kilauea's eastern side sprang to life on January 3, 1983, shooting molten lava four stories high. This eruption has been ongoing, and lava flows are generally steady and slow, appearing and disappearing from view. Over 500 acres have been added to Hawaii's eastern coast since the activity began, and scientists say this eruptive phase is not likely to end anytime soon.

If you're lucky, you'll be able to catch creation at its most elemental—when molten lava meets the ocean, cools, and solidifies into brand-new stretches of coastline. Even if lava-viewing conditions aren't ideal, you can hike 150 miles of trails and camp amid wide expanses of *aa* (rough) and *pahoehoe* (smooth) lava. There's nothing quite like it.

✉ 1 Crater Rim DG,
National Park, HI 96718

☎ 808/985-6000

🌐 www.nps.gov/havo

$25 per vehicle; $12 for pedestrians and bicyclists. Ask about passes. Admission is good for seven consecutive days.

The park is open daily, 24 hours.
Kilauea Visitor Center: 9 am–5 pm.
Thomas A. Jaggar Museum: 10–8.
Volcano Art Center Gallery: 9–5.

(top) Kilauea Iki Trail
(left) Fuming rim of Puu Oo, source of the current eruption

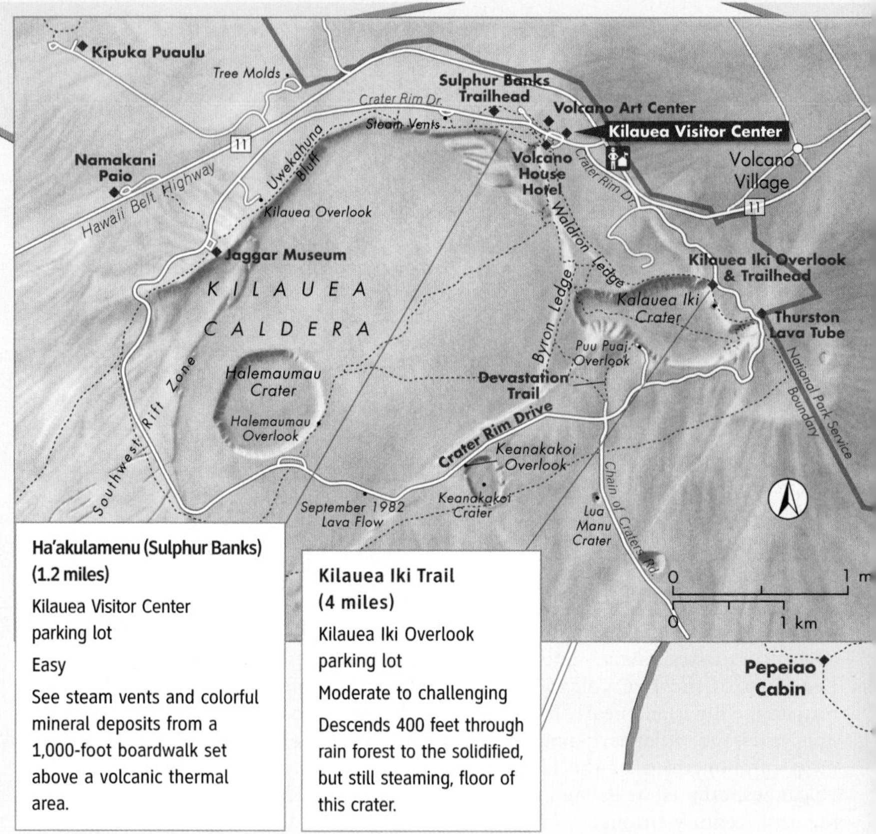

Ha'akulamenu (Sulphur Banks) (1.2 miles)

Kilauea Visitor Center parking lot

Easy

See steam vents and colorful mineral deposits from a 1,000-foot boardwalk set above a volcanic thermal area.

Kilauea Iki Trail (4 miles)

Kilauea Iki Overlook parking lot

Moderate to challenging

Descends 400 feet through rain forest to the solidified, but still steaming, floor of this crater.

SEEING THE SUMMIT

The best way to explore the summit of Kilauea is to cruise along Crater Rim Drive to Kilauea Overlook. From Kilauea Overlook you can see all of Kilauea Caldera and Halemaumau Crater, an awesome depression in Kilauea Caldera measuring 3,000 feet across and nearly 300 feet deep. It's a huge and breathtaking view with pluming steam vents. At this writing, lava flows in the Southwest Rift Zone have closed parts of the 11-mile loop road indefinitely, including Halemaumau Overlook.

Near Kilauea Overlook is the Thomas A. Jaggar Museum, which offers similar views, plus geologic displays, video presentations of volcanic eruptions, and exhibits of seismographs once used by volcanologists at the adjacent Hawaiian Volcano Observatory (not open to the public).

Other Highlights along Crater Rim Drive include sulfur and steam vents, a walk-through lava tube, and deep fissures, fractures, and gullies along Kilauea's flanks. Kilauea Iki Crater, on the way down to Chain of Crater's Road, is smaller, but just as fascinating when seen from Puu Pai Overlook.

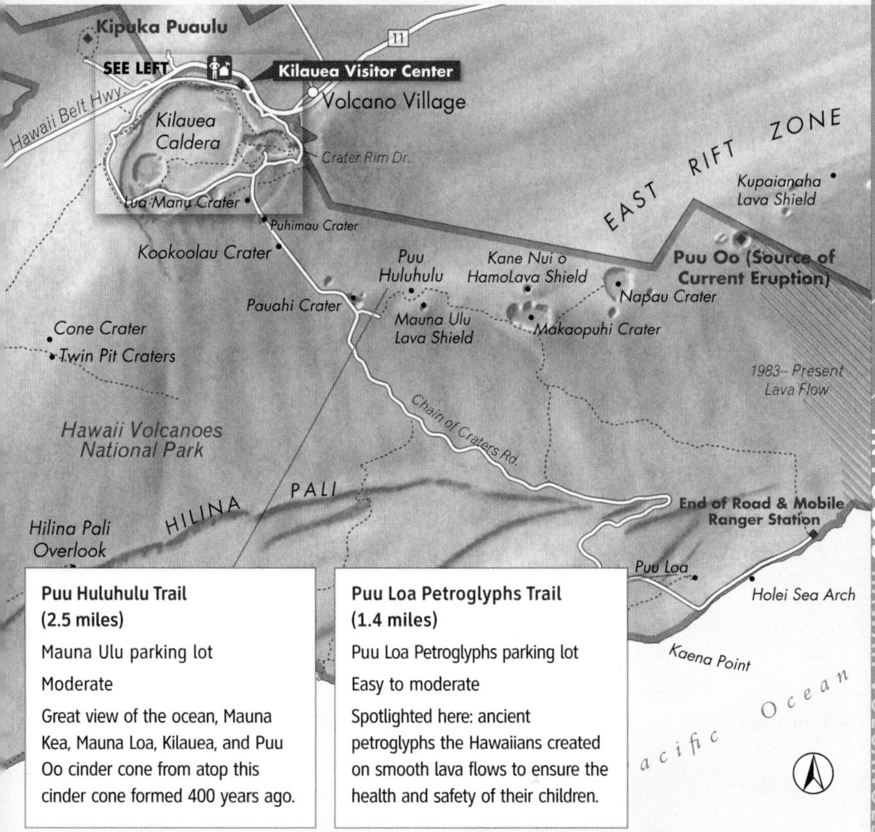

Puu Huluhulu Trail (2.5 miles)

Mauna Ulu parking lot

Moderate

Great view of the ocean, Mauna Kea, Mauna Loa, Kilauea, and Puu Oo cinder cone from atop this cinder cone formed 400 years ago.

Puu Loa Petroglyphs Trail (1.4 miles)

Puu Loa Petroglyphs parking lot

Easy to moderate

Spotlighted here: ancient petroglyphs the Hawaiians created on smooth lava flows to ensure the health and safety of their children.

SEEING LAVA

Before you head out to find flowing lava, pinpoint the safe viewing spots at the Visitor Center. One of the best places usually is at the end of 18-mile Chain of Craters Road. Magnificent plumes of steam rise where the rivers of liquid fire meet the sea.

There are three guarantees about lava flows in HVNP. First: They constantly change. Second: Because of that, you can't predict when and where you'll be able to see them. Third: New land formed when lava meets the sea is highly unstable and can collapse at any time. Never go into areas that have been closed.

■ TIP→ The view of brilliant red-orange lava flowing from Kilauea's east rift zone is most dramatic at night.

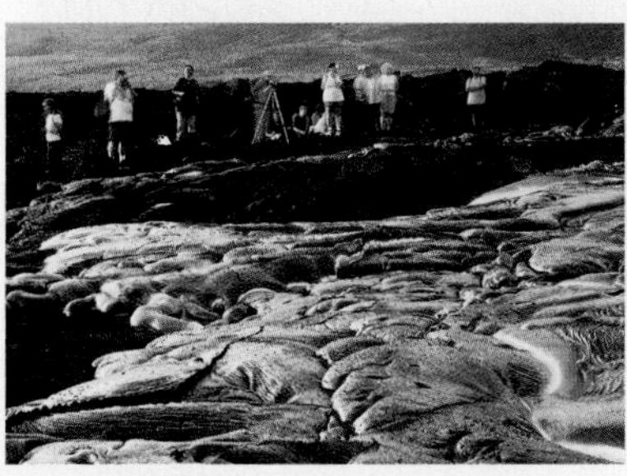

People watching lava flow at HVNP

PLANNING YOUR TRIP TO HVNP

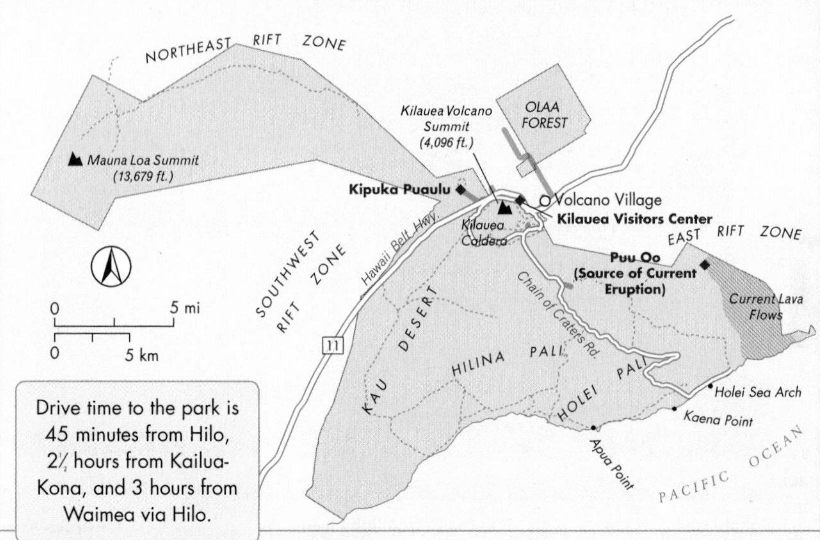

Drive time to the park is 45 minutes from Hilo, 2½ hours from Kailua-Kona, and 3 hours from Waimea via Hilo.

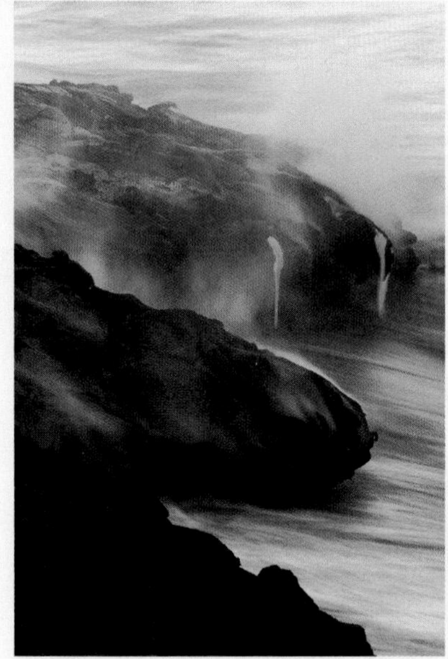

Lava entering the ocean

WHERE TO START

Begin your visit at the Visitor Center, where you'll find maps, books, and DVDs; information on trails, ranger-led walks, and special events; and current weather, road, and lava-viewing conditions. Free volcano-related film showings, lectures, and other presentations are regularly scheduled.

WEATHER

Weather conditions fluctuate daily, sometimes hourly. It can be rainy and chilly even during the summer; the temperature usually is 14° cooler at the 4,000-foot-high summit of Kilauea than at sea level.

Expect hot, dry, and windy coastal conditions at the end of Chain of Craters Road. Bring rain gear, and wear layered clothing, sturdy shoes, sunglasses, a hat, and sunscreen.

Halemaumau Crater, Kilauea

FOOD

It's a good idea to bring your own favorite snacks and beverages; stock up on provisions in Volcano Village, 1½ miles away or at the store in Kilauea Military Camp.

PARK PROGRAMS

Rangers lead daily walks at 10:30 and 1:30 into different areas; check with the Visitor Center for details as times and destinations depend on weather conditions and eruptions.

Over 60 companies hold permits to lead hikes at HVNP. Good choices are Hawaii Forest & Trail (www.hawaii-forest.com), Hawaiian Walkways (www.hawaiianwalkways.com), and Native Guide Hawaii (www.nativeguidehawaii.com).

CAUTION

"Vog" (volcanic smog) can cause headaches; breathing difficulties; lethargy; irritations of the skin, eyes, nose, and throat; and other health problems. Pregnant women, young children, and people with asthma and heart conditions are most susceptible, and should avoid areas such as Halemaumau Crater where fumes are thick.

Wear long pants and boots or closed-toe shoes with good tread for hikes on lava. Stay on marked trails and step carefully. Lava is composed of 50% silica (glass) and can cause serious injury if you fall.

Carry at least 2 quarts of water on hikes. Temperatures near lava flows can rise above 100°F, and dehydration, heat exhaustion, and sunstroke are common consequences of extended exposure to intense sunlight and high temperatures.

Remember that these are active volcanoes, and eruptions can cause parts of the park to close at any time. Check the park's website or call ahead for last-minute updates before your visit.

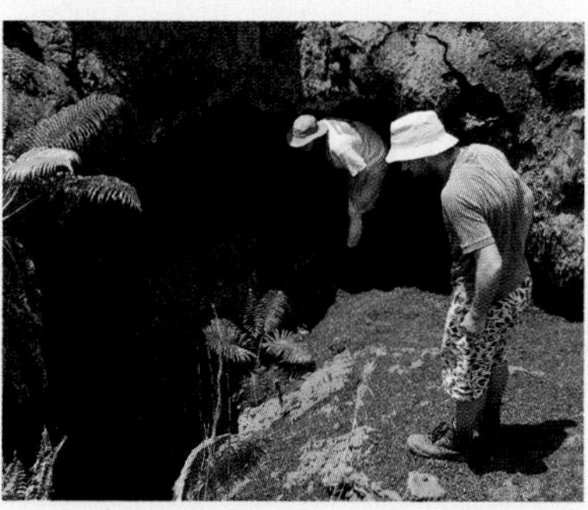

Volcanologists inspecting a vent in the East Rift Zone

the highway, the coast passes verdant cattle pastures and sheer cliffs and the village of Naalehu on the way to the black-sand beach of Punaluu, a common nesting place of the Hawaiian green sea turtle.

GETTING HERE AND AROUND

Kau and Ka Lae are destinations usually combined with a quick trip to the volcano from Kona. This is probably cramming too much into one day, however. Visiting the volcano fills up at least a day (two is better), and the sights of this southern end of the island are worth more than a cursory glance.

Instead, make Green Sands Beach or Punaluu a full beach day, and see some of the other sights on the way there or back. Bring sturdy shoes, water, and a sun hat if Green Sands Beach is your choice (reaching the beach requires a hike). You can pay some enterprising locals $5 a head to give you a ride in their pickups to the beach. And be careful in the surf here. Don't go in unless you're used to ocean waves. There are no lifeguards at this remote beach. It's decidedly calmer and you can sometimes snorkel at Punaluu, but use caution at these and all Hawaii beaches.

The drive from Kailua-Kona to Ka Lae is a long one (roughly 2½ hours); from Volcano it's approximately 45 minutes. You can fill up on gas and groceries in Ocean View, or you can eat, fuel up, and get picnic fixings in Naalehu. Weather tends to be warm, dry, and windy.

TOP ATTRACTIONS

Hawaii Volcanoes National Park: Kahuku Unit. Located off Highway 11 at mile marker 70.5, the Kahuku section of the park takes visitors over many trails through ancient lava flows and native forests. Endangered plants and animals are on display in this beautiful but isolated region of Hawaii Volcanoes National Park, encompassing more than 116,000 acres of protected parklands. Guided hikes with knowledgeable rangers are a regularly scheduled highlight. ✉ *Hwy 11, Mile Marker 70.5, Kau* 🌐 *www.nps.gov/havo/planyourvisit/kahuku-hikes.htm* ⏲ *Closed Mon.–Thurs.*

Ka Lae (South Point). It's thought that the first Polynesians came ashore at this southernmost point of land in the United States, also a National Historic Landmark. Old canoe-mooring holes, visible today, were carved through the rocks, possibly by settlers from Tahiti as early as AD 750. To get here, drive 12 miles on the turnoff road, past rows of giant electricity-producing windmills powered by the nearly constant winds sweeping across this coastal plain. Bear left when the road forks, and park in the lot at the end. Walk past the boat hoists toward the little lighthouse. South Point is just past the lighthouse at the southernmost cliff. You may see brave locals jumping off the cliffs and then climbing up rusty old ladders, but swimming here is not recommended. Don't leave anything of value in your car. It's isolated and without services. ✉ *South Point Rd., off Mamalahoa Hwy. near mile marker 70, Naalehu* 🎫 *Free.*

FAMILY **Manuka State Wayside.** This lowland forest preserve spreads across several relatively recent lava flows. A semi-rugged trail follows a 2-mile loop past a pit crater, winding around interesting trees such as *hau* and *kukui*. It's a nice spot to get out of the car and stretch your legs—you can wander through the well-maintained arboretum, snap a few photos of the eerie forest, and let the kids scramble around trees so large they can't get their arms around them. The pathways can get muddy and rough, so bring appropriate shoes if you plan to hike. Large populations of the Hawaiian hoary bat inhabit the area, which, in totality, encompasses 25,000 of forest reserve. Restrooms, picnic areas, and camping sites (by permit) are available. ✉ *Hwy. 11, , north of mile marker 81* ☎ *808/974–6200* 🌐 *dlnr.hawaii.gov/dsp/parks/hawaii* 🎫 *Free.*

Pahala. About 16 miles east of Naalehu, beyond Punaluu Beach Park, Highway 11 passes directly by this little town. You'll miss it if you blink. Pahala, once a booming sugar plantation company town, is sleepy today but still inhabited by retired cane workers and their descendants. Behind it, along a wide, paved cane road, is Wood Valley, once a prosperous community, now just a peaceful road heavily scented by eucalyptus trees, coffee blossoms, and night-blooming jasmine and often laden in mist. ✉ *Pahala.*

4

Wood Valley Temple (*Nechung Temple*). Behind the remote town of Pahala, this serene and beautiful Tibetan Buddhist temple, established in 1973, has hosted more than 50 well-known lamas, including the Dalai Lama on two occasions. Known as Nechung Dorje Drayang Ling, or "Immutable Island of Melodious Sound," this peaceful place welcomes all creeds. You can visit and meditate, leave an offering, walk the lush gardens shared by strutting peacocks, browse the gift shop, or stay in the temple's guesthouse, available for peaceful, nondenominational retreats taught by masters. ✉ *Pahala* ☎ *808/928–8539* 🌐 *www.nechung.org* 🎫 *$5.*

BEACHES

Updated by Kristina Anderson

Don't believe anyone who tells you that the Big Island lacks beaches. It's just one of the myths about Hawaii's largest island that has no basis in fact. It's not so much that the Big Island has fewer beaches than the other islands, just that there's more island, so getting to the beaches can be slightly less convenient.

That said, there are plenty of those perfect white-sand stretches you think of when you hear "Hawaii," and the added bonus of black- and green-sand beaches, thanks to the relative young age of the island and its active volcanoes. New beaches appear and disappear regularly, created and destroyed by volcanic activity. In 1989, a black-sand beach, Kamoamoa, formed when molten lava shattered as it hit cold ocean waters; it was enjoyed for a few years before it was closed by new lava flows in 1992. It's part of the ongoing process of the volcano's creation-and-change dynamic.

Hawaii's largest coral reef systems lie off the Kohala Coast. Waves have battered them over millennia to create abundant white-sand beaches on the northwest side of the island. Black-, mixed-, and green-sand beaches lie in the southern regions and along the coast nearest the volcano. On the eastern side of the island, beaches tend to be of the rocky-coast–surging-surf variety, but there are still a few worth visiting, and this is where the Hawaii shoreline is at its most picturesque.

KAILUA-KONA

There are a few good sandy beaches in and near town. However, the coastline is generally rugged black lava rock, so don't expect long stretches of white sand. The beaches in Kailua-Kona get lots of use by local residents, and visitors enjoy them, too. Excellent opportunities for snorkeling, scuba diving, swimming, kayaking, and other water sports are easy to find.

Kahaluu Beach Park. This shallow and easily accessible salt-and-pepper beach is one of the Big Island's most popular swimming and snorkeling sites, thanks to the fringing reef that helps keep the waters calm, visibility high, and reef life—especially turtles and colorful fish—plentiful. Because it is so protected, it's great for first-time snorkelers, but outside the reef, very strong rip currents can run, so caution is advised. Never hand-feed the unusually tame reef fish here; it upsets the balance of the reef. You will see a lot of *honu*—the endangered green sea turtles. Resist the urge to get too close to them; they are protected from harassment by federal and state law. ■TIP→ **Experienced surfers find good waves beyond the reef, and scuba divers like the shore dives—shallow ones inside the breakwater, deeper ones outside.** Snorkel equipment and boards are available for rent nearby, and surf schools operate here. Kahaluu was a favorite of the Hawaiian royal family, especially King Kalakaua. **Amenities:** food and drink; lifeguards; parking (no fee); showers; toilets. **Best for:** snorkeling; swimming; surfing. ✉ *78-6720 Alii Dr., Kailua-Kona* ✥ *5½ miles south of Kailua-Kona, across from Beach Villas* ☎ *808/961–8311.*

FAMILY **Kamakahonu Beach.** This is where King Kamehameha spent his final days—the restored Ahuena Heiau sits on a platform across from the sand. Fronting the Courtyard King Kamehameha's Kona Beach Hotel and adjacent to Kailua Pier, this scenic crescent of white sand is one of the few beaches in downtown Kailua-Kona. The water here is almost always calm and the beach clean, making this a perfect spot for kids. For adults, it's a great place for a swim, some stand-up paddleboarding (SUP), watching outrigger teams practice, or enjoying a lazy beach day. It can get crowded on weekends. Snorkeling can be good north of the beach, and snorkeling, SUP, and kayaking equipment can be rented nearby. ■TIP→ **A little family of sea turtles likes to hang out next to the seawall, so keep an eye out.** There's lots of grass and shade, and free parking in county lots is a short stroll away. **Amenities:** food and drink; showers; toilets; water sports. **Best for:** snorkeling; swimming. ✉ *75-5660 Palani Rd., at Alii Dr., Kailua-Kona.*

THE KONA COAST

This ruggedly beautiful coastline harbors a couple of scenic beaches that take you off the beaten track. Napoopoo and Hookena offer great swimming, snorkeling, diving, and kayaking.

Fodor's Choice ★ **Kealakekua Bay State Historical Park.** When Hurricane Iniki slammed into Hawaii in 1992, this park lost all of its sand, which is slowly returning decades later. The shoreline is rocky but don't let that deter you. The

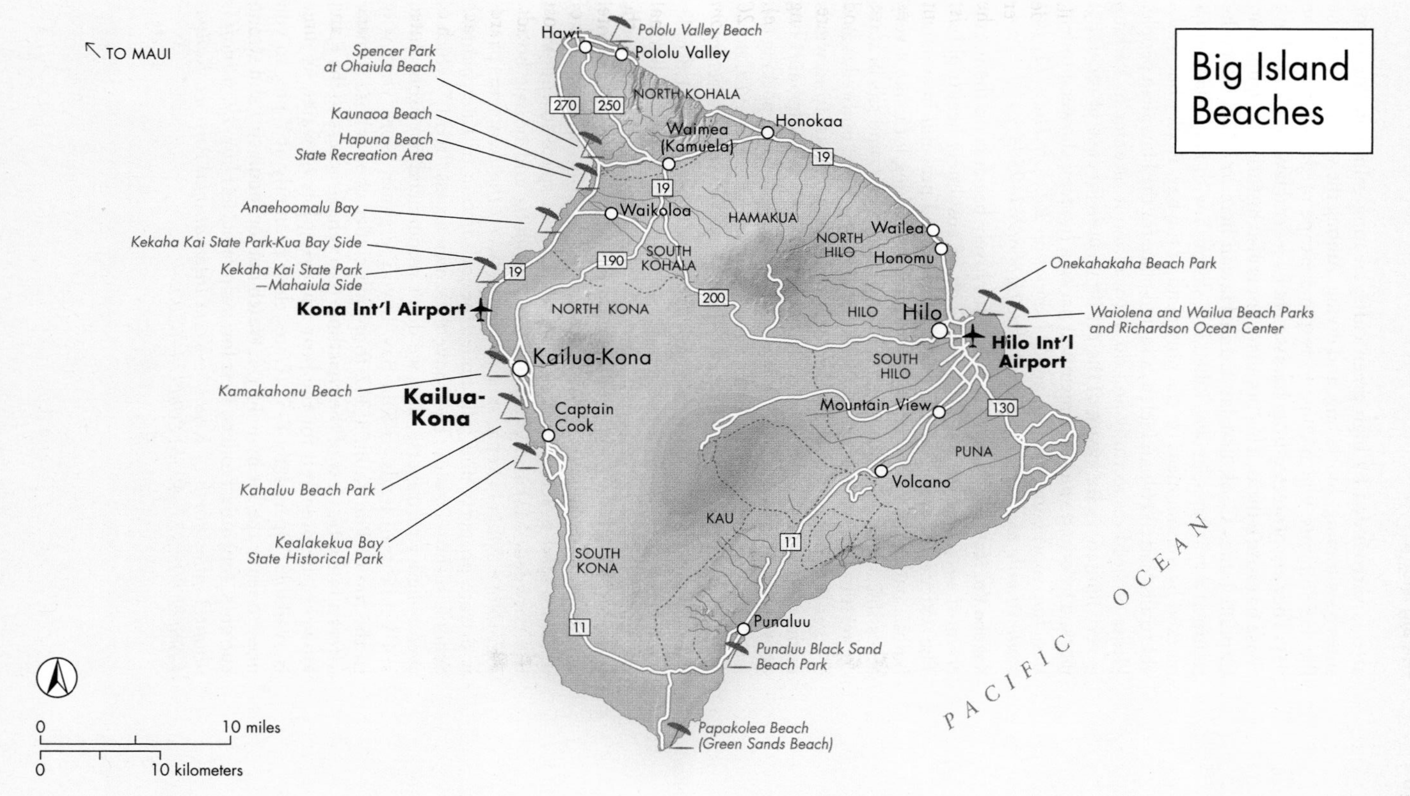
Big Island Beaches
TO MAUI
Pololu Valley Beach
Hawi
Pololu Valley
Spencer Park at Ohaiula Beach
NORTH KOHALA
270
250
Kaunaoa Beach
Hapuna Beach State Recreation Area
Honokaa
Waimea (Kamuela)
19
Anaehoomalu Bay
Waikoloa
HAMAKUA
Kekaha Kai State Park-Kua Bay Side
Kekaha Kai State Park —Mahaiula Side
190
SOUTH KOHALA
NORTH HILO
Wailea
Honomu
Onekahakaha Beach Park
200
Kona Int'l Airport
NORTH KONA
HILO
Hilo
Waiolena and Wailua Beach Parks and Richardson Ocean Center
Hilo Int'l Airport
Kailua-Kona
SOUTH HILO
Kamakahonu Beach
Kailua-Kona
Captain Cook
Mountain View
130
PUNA
Volcano
Kahaluu Beach Park
KAU
Kealakekua Bay State Historical Park
11
SOUTH KONA
PACIFIC OCEAN
Punaluu
Punaluu Black Sand Beach Park
0
10 miles
0
10 kilometers
Papakolea Beach (Green Sands Beach)

area is surrounded by high green cliffs, creating calm conditions for superb swimming, snorkeling, and diving. Among the variety of marine life are dolphins, which come to rest and escape predators during the day. They are protected from harassment by federal law, so please don't chase or disturb them. This popular spot is also historically significant. Captain James Cook first landed in Hawaii here in 1778. When he returned a year later, he was killed in a skirmish with Hawaiians, now marked by a monument on the north end of the bay. Rocky but walkable trails lead to Hikiau Heiau, a sacred place for the Hawaiian people. Please proceed respectfully and do not walk on it or enter it. Parking is very limited. ⚠ **Be aware of the off-limits area (in case of rockfalls) marked by orange buoys.** **Amenities:** parking (no fee); showers; toilets. **Best for:** snorkeling; swimming. ✉ *Napoopoo Rd., off Hwy. 11, just south of mile marker 111, Kealakekua* ☎ *808/961–9544.*

Kekaha Kai State Park—Kua Bay Side. This lovely beach is on the northernmost stretch of the park's coastline on an absolutely beautiful bay. The water is crystal clear, deep aquamarine, and peaceful in summer, but the park's paved entrance, amenities, and parking lot make it very accessible and, as a result, often crowded. Fine white sand sits in stark contrast to old black lava flows with little shade—bring umbrellas as it can get hot. Rocky shores on either side protect the beach from winds in the afternoon. Gates open daily from 8 to 7. ⚠ **In winter, surf can get very rough and often the sand washes away.** **Amenities:** parking (no fee); showers; toilets. **Best for:** surfing; swimming. ✉ *Hwy. 19, north of mile marker 88, Kailua-Kona* ✥ *Across from Veterans Cemetery.*

Fodor's Choice ★ **Kekaha Kai State Park—Mahaiula Side.** It's slowgoing down a 1.8-mile, bumpy but paved road off Highway 19 to this beach park, but it's worth it. This state park encompasses three beaches (from south to north, Mahaiula, Makalawena, and Kua Bay, which has its own entrance). Mahaiula and Makalawena are beautiful, wide expanses of white-sand beach with dunes; there's a lot of space so you won't feel crowded. Makalawena has great swimming and boogie boarding. (Note: Makalawena, sandwiched between the two state parks, is private property and falls under the jurisdiction of Kamehameha Schools Bishop Estates. They have their own access "road," which is even rougher to traverse, and we don't recommend it!) From there, a 4½-mile trail leads to Kua Bay. If you're game, work your way to the top of Puu Kuili, a 342-foot-high cinder cone whose summit offers a fantastic view of the coastline. (No vehicle access to the Puu.) However, be prepared for the heat and bring lots of water, as none is available. Open daily 8–7. (Gates close promptly at 7 pm, so you need to leave the lot by 6:30.) ⚠ **Watch out for rough surf and strong currents.** **Amenities:** toilets. **Best for:** swimming. ✉ *Hwy. 19, turnoff is about 2 miles north of Keahole–Kona International Airport, Kailua-Kona* ☎ *808/327–4958, 808/974–6200.*

Kua Bay is protected from wind by the rocky shores that surround it.

THE KOHALA COAST

Most of the Big Island's white sandy beaches are found on the Kohala Coast, which is also called the "Gold Coast" and is, understandably, home to the majority of the island's world-class resorts. Hawaii's beaches are public property and the resorts are required to provide public access, so don't be frightened off by a guard shack and a fancy sign. Most resorts do have public parking, although it's limited. Resort beaches aside, there are some real hidden gems, accessible only by boat, four-wheel drive, or a 15- to 20-minute hike. It's well worth the effort to get to at least one of these. ■ **TIP→ The west side of the island tends to be calmer, but the surf still gets rough in winter.**

FAMILY Fodor's Choice ★ **Anaehoomalu Bay** (*A-Bay*). Also known as "A-Bay," this expansive stretch of white sand, classically fringed with coco palms, fronts the Waikoloa Beach Marriott and is a perfect spot for swimming, windsurfing, snorkeling, and diving. Unlike some Kohala Coast beaches near hotel properties, this one is very accessible to the public and offers plenty of free parking. The bay is well protected, so even when surf is rough or trades are blasting, it's fairly calm here. (Mornings are calmest.) Snorkel gear, kayaks, and boogie boards are available for rent at the north end. Behind the beach are two ancient Hawaiian fishponds, **Kuualii** and **Kahapapa,** that once served ancient Hawaiian royalty. A walking trail follows the coastline to the Hilton Waikoloa Village next door, passing by tide pools, ponds, and a turtle sanctuary where sea turtles can often be spotted sunbathing on the sand. Footwear is recommended for the trail. **Amenities:** food and drink; parking (no fee); showers; toilets; water sports. **Best for:** snorkeling; swimming; sunsets;

Calm Kailua Bay is an excellent spot for outrigger paddling, snorkeling, and swimming.

walking. ✉ *69-275 Waikoloa Beach Dr., Waikoloa* ✣ *Just south of Waikoloa Beach Marriott; turn left at Kings' Shops.*

FAMILY Fodor's Choice ★ **Hapuna Beach State Recreation Area.** One of Hawaii's finest beaches, Hapuna is a ½-mile-long stretch of white perfection. The turquoise water is calm in summer with just enough rolling waves to make body-surfing and body boarding fun. Watch for the undertow; in winter it can be rough. There is excellent snorkeling around the jagged rocks that border the beach on either side, but high surf brings strong currents. Known for awesome sunsets, this is one of the best places on the island to see the "green flash" as the sun dips below a clear horizon. The north end of the beach fronts the Hapuna Beach Prince Hotel, which rents water-sports equipment and has a food concession with shaded picnic tables. There is ample parking, although the lot can fill up by midday and the beach can get crowded on holidays. Lifeguards, on duty during peak hours, cover only the state park section, not areas north of the rocky cliff that juts out near the middle of the beach. Renovations have temporarily closed off portions of the parking lot. **Amenities:** food and drink; lifeguards; parking (fee); showers; toilets; water sports. **Best for:** sunset; surfing; swimming; walking. ✉ *Hwy. 19, near Mile Marker 69, Waimea (Hawaii County)* ✣ *Just south of the Hapuna Beach Prince Hotel* ☎ *808/961–9544* 🎫 *$5 per vehicle.*

FAMILY Fodor's Choice ★ **Kaunaoa Beach** (*Maunakea Beach*). Hands down one of the most beautiful beaches on the island, if not the whole state, Kaunaoa features a long crescent of pure white sand framed by coco palms. The beach, which fronts the Mauna Kea Beach Hotel, slopes very gradually, and there's great snorkeling along the rocks. Classic Hawaii postcard views abound, especially in winter, when snow tops Maunakea to the east. When conditions permit, waves are good for body- and board surfing also. Currents can be strong in winter, so be careful. Get a cocktail at the beach cabana and enjoy the sunset. ■ TIP→ **Public parking is limited to a few spaces, so arrive before 10 am or after 4 pm. If the lot is full, head to nearby Hapuna Beach, where there's a huge parking lot ($5 per vehicle). Try this spot again another day—it's worth it!** **Amenities:** parking (no fee); showers; toilets; water sports. **Best for:** sunset; swimming; walking. ✉ *62-100 Mauna Kea Beach Dr., entry through gate to Mauna Kea Beach Hotel, Waimea (Hawaii County).*

Pololu Valley Beach. On the North Kohala peninsula, this is one of the Big Island's most scenic black-sand beaches. After about 8 miles of lush, winding road past Hawi Town, Highway 270 ends at the overlook of Pololu Valley. Snap a few photos of the stunning view, then take the 15-minute hike down (twice as long back up) to the beach. The trail is steep and rocky; it can also be muddy and slippery, so watch your step. The beach itself is a wide expanse of fine grey sand with piles of round boulders, surrounded by sheer green cliffs and backed by high dunes and ironwood trees. A gurgling stream leads from the beach to the back of the valley. ⚠ **This is not a safe swimming beach even though locals do swim, body board, and surf here. Dangerous rip currents and usually rough surf pose a real hazard.** Because this is a remote, isolated area far from emergency help, extreme caution is advised. **Amenities:** none. **Best for:** solitude. ✉ *Hwy. 270, end of road, Kapaau.*

FAMILY **Spencer Park at Ohaiula Beach.** This white-sand beach is popular with local families because of its reef-protected waters. ■ TIP→ **It's probably the safest beach in West Hawaii for young children.** It's also safe for swimming year-round, which makes it a reliable spot for a lazy day at the beach. There is a little shade, plus a volleyball court and pavilion, and the soft sand is perfect for sand castles. It does tend to get crowded with families and campers on weekends, but the beach is generally clean. Although you won't see a lot of fish if you're snorkeling here, in winter you can usually catch sight of a breaching whale or two. The beach park lies just below Puukohola Heiau National Historic Park, site of the historic war temple built by King Kamehameha the Great in 1810 after uniting the Islands. **Amenities:** lifeguards (weekends and holidays only); parking (no fee); showers; toilets. **Best for:** sunsets; swimming. ✉ *Hwy. 270, Kawaihae* ✣ *Toward Kawaihae Harbor, just after road forks from Hwy. 19* ☎ *808/961–8311.*

HILO

Hilo isn't exactly known for tropical white-sand beaches, but there are a few nice ones in the area that offer good swimming and snorkeling opportunities, and some are surrounded by lush rain forest.

FAMILY **Onekahakaha Beach Park.** Shallow, rock-wall-enclosed tide pools and an adjacent grassy picnic area make this park a favorite among Hilo families with small children. The protected pools are great places to look for Hawaiian marine life like sea urchins and anemones. There isn't much white sand, but access to the water is easy. The water is usually rough beyond the line of large boulders protecting the inner tide pools, so be careful if the surf is high. This beach gets crowded on weekends. **Amenities:** lifeguards (weekends, holidays, and summer only); parking (no fee); showers; toilets. **Best for:** swimming. ✉ *Onekahakaha Rd. and Kalanianaole Ave., via Kanoelehua St., Hilo ✥ 3 miles east of Hilo ☎ 808/961–8311.*

FAMILY **Waiolena and Wailua Beach Parks and Richardson Ocean Center.** Just east of Hilo, almost at the end of the road, three adjacent parks make up one beautiful spot with a series of bays, protected inlets, lagoons, and pretty parks. This is one of the best snorkeling sites on this side of the island, as rocky outcrops provide shelter for schools of reef fish, sea turtles, and dolphins. Resist the urge to get too close to turtles or disturb them; they are protected from harassment by federal and state law. Local kids use the small black-sand pocket beach for body boarding. The shaded grassy areas are great for picnics. Be warned, this place is very crowded on weekends. **Amenities:** lifeguards (weekends, holidays, and summer only); parking (no fee); showers; toilets. **Best for:** snorkeling; walking. ✉ *2349 Kalanianaole Ave., 4 miles east of Hilo, Hilo ☎ 808/961–8311.*

KAU

You shouldn't expect to find sparkling white-sand beaches on the rugged and rocky coasts of Kau, and you won't. What you will find is something a bit rarer and well worth the visit: black- and green-sand beaches. And there's the chance to see the endangered hawksbill or Hawaiian green sea turtles close up.

Papakolea Beach (*Green Sands Beach*). Tired of the same old gold-, white-, or black-sand beach? Then how about a green-sand beach? You'll need good hiking shoes or sneakers to get to this olive-green crescent, one of the most unusual beaches on the island. It lies at the base of Puu O Mahana, at Mahana Bay, where a cinder cone formed during an early eruption of Mauna Loa. The greenish tint is caused by an accumulation of olivine crystals that form in volcanic eruptions. The dry, barren landscape is totally surreal but stunning, as aquamarine waters lap on green sand against reddish cliffs. The surf is often rough, and swimming is hazardous due to strong currents, so caution is advised. Drive down to Ka Lae (South Point); at the end of the 12-mile paved road, take the road to the left and park at the end. Don't pay anyone for parking, but you may encounter some enterprising folks willing to take you to the beach in the back of their truck for a small fee. Of course, lock your car and don't leave valuables inside. To reach the beach, follow the 2¼-mile coastal trail, which ends in a steep and dangerous descent down the cliffside on an unimproved trail. The hike takes about two hours each way and it can get hot and windy, so bring lots of drinking water. Four-wheel-drive vehicles are no longer permitted on the trail. **Amenities:** none. **Best for:** solitude; walking. ✉ *Hwy. 11, Naalehu ✥ 2½ miles northeast of South Point.*

Fodor's Choice ★ **Punaluu Black Sand Beach Park.** A must-do on a south–southeast–bound trip to the volcano, this easily accessible black-sand beach is backed by low dunes, brackish ponds, and tall coco palms. The shoreline is jagged, reefed, and rocky. Most days, large groups of sea turtles nap on the sand—a stunning sight. Resist the urge to get too close or disturb them; they're protected by federal and state law, and fines for harassment can be hefty. Removing black sand is also prohibited. ⚠ **Extremely strong rip currents prevail, so only experienced ocean swimmers should consider getting in the water here.** Popular with locals and tour buses alike, this beach park can get very busy, especially on weekends (the north parking lot is usually quieter). Shade from palm trees provides an escape from the sun, and at the northern end of the beach, near the boat ramp, lie the ruins of Kaneeleele Heiau, an old Hawaiian temple. The area was a sugar port until the 1946 tsunami destroyed the buildings. Developers tried to bring a huge resort experience here in the early 1990s, but that has mostly failed. (You'll drive by a few abandoned resort buildings on your way to the beach.) **■ TIP→ Bring your camera and a picnic lunch.** **Amenities:** parking (no fee); showers; toilets. **Best for:** walking. ✉ *Hwy. 11, between mile markers 55 and 56, Naalehu* ✣ *27 miles south of Hawaii Volcanoes National Park* ☎ *808/961–8311.*

WHERE TO EAT

Updated by Karen Anderson

Between star chefs and myriad local farms, the Big Island restaurant scene is becoming a destination for foodies. Food writers are praising the chefs of the Big Island for their ability to turn the local bounty into inventive blends inspired by the island's cultural heritage.

Resorts along the Kohala Coast have long invested in culinary programs offering memorable dining experiences that include inventive entrées, spot-on wine pairings, and customized chef's table options. But great food on the Big Island doesn't begin and end with the resorts. A handful of chefs have retired from the fast-paced hotel world and opened their own small bistros in upcountry Waimea, or other places off the beaten track. Unique and wonderful restaurants have cropped up in Hawi, Kainaliu, and Holualoa, and on the east side of the island in Hilo.

In addition to restaurants, festivals devoted to island products draw hundreds of attendees to learn about everything from breadfruit and mango to avocado, chocolate, and coffee. Agritourism has turned into a fruitful venture for farmers as farm tours afford the opportunity to meet with and learn from a variety of local producer. Some tours conclude with a meal of items sourced from the same farms. From goat farms churning creamy, savory goat cheese to Waimea farms planting row after row of bright tomatoes to high-tech aquaculture operations at NELHA (Natural Energy Lab of Hawaii Authority), visitors can see exactly where their next meal comes from.

KAILUA-KONA

$ AMERICAN Fodor's Choice ★

✕ **Bongo Ben's Island Café.** At the entry of this super-casual, oceanfront diner, menus printed on the giant bongos tell the story. Offering great deals on a plethora of breakfast, lunch, and dinner items, the open-air restaurant bakes its own breads, cinnamon rolls, desserts, pizza crust, and hamburger buns on-site. **Known for:** oceanfront views of Kailua

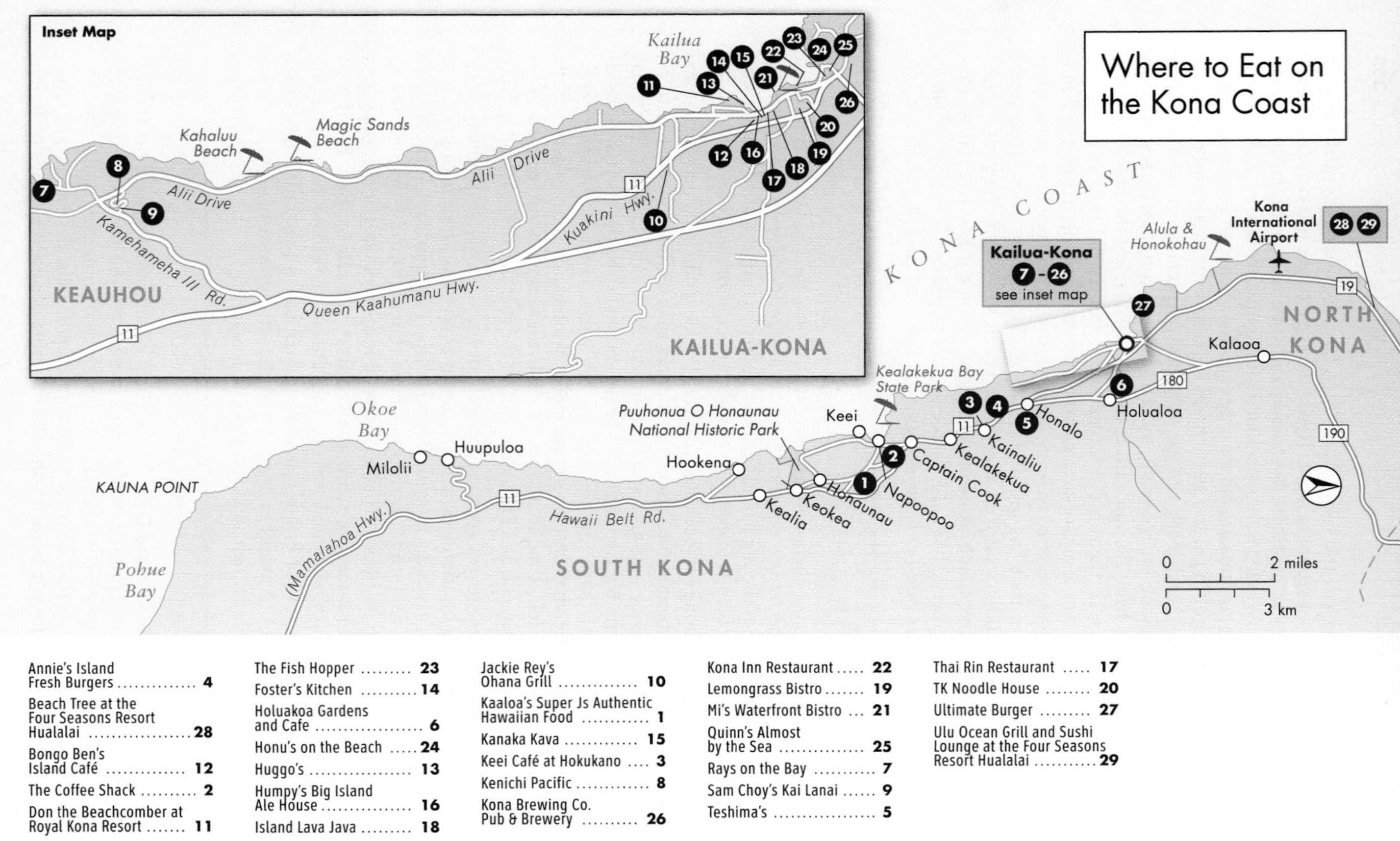

- Annie's Island Fresh Burgers 4
- Beach Tree at the Four Seasons Resort Hualalai 28
- Bongo Ben's Island Café 12
- The Coffee Shack 2
- Don the Beachcomber at Royal Kona Resort 11
- The Fish Hopper 23
- Foster's Kitchen 14
- Holuakoa Gardens and Cafe 6
- Honu's on the Beach 24
- Huggo's 13
- Humpy's Big Island Ale House 16
- Island Lava Java 18
- Jackie Rey's Ohana Grill 10
- Kaaloa's Super Js Authentic Hawaiian Food 1
- Kanaka Kava 15
- Keei Café at Hokukano 3
- Kenichi Pacific 8
- Kona Brewing Co. Pub & Brewery 26
- Kona Inn Restaurant 22
- Lemongrass Bistro 19
- Mi's Waterfront Bistro ... 21
- Quinn's Almost by the Sea 25
- Rays on the Bay 7
- Sam Choy's Kai Lanai 9
- Teshima's 5
- Thai Rin Restaurant 17
- TK Noodle House 20
- Ultimate Burger 27
- Ulu Ocean Grill and Sushi Lounge at the Four Seasons Resort Hualalai 29

Bay; prime rib night and other weekly specials; discounts on morning and happy hour cocktails. $ *Average main: $15* ✉ *75-5819 Alii Dr., Kailua-Kona* ☎ *808/329–9203* 🌐 *www.bongobens.com.*

$$ HAWAIIAN ✕ **Don the Beachcomber at Royal Kona Resort.** The "original home of the mai tai," Don the Beachcomber features a retro, tiki-bar setting with the absolute best view of Kailua Bay in town. Service can be slow, but the coconut prawns are worth the wait, as is the New York steak paired with bacon-wrapped shrimp. **Known for:** slow-roasted prime rib; dining on the water's edge; Don's Mai Tai Bar serves menu items and 10 types of mai tais. $ *Average main: $20* ✉ *Royal Kona Resort, 75-5852 Alii Dr., Kailua-Kona* ☎ *808/329–3111* 🌐 *www.royalkona.com/Dining.cfm* ⊙ *No lunch in main restaurant. No dinner in main restaurant Sun.–Wed.*

4

$$ SEAFOOD FAMILY ✕ **The Fish Hopper.** With a bayside view in the heart of Historic Kailua Village, the open-air Hawaii location of the popular Monterey, California, restaurant has an expansive menu for breakfast, lunch, and dinner. Inventive fresh-fish specials as well as simple fish-and-chips and clam chowder are what the original is known for. **Known for:** award-winning clam chowder; tropical oceanfront venue; signature Volcano flaming cocktail. $ *Average main: $24* ✉ *75-5683 Alii Dr., Kailua-Kona* ☎ *808/326–2002* 🌐 *www.fishhopper.com/kona.*

$$ AMERICAN Fodor's Choice ★ ✕ **Foster's Kitchen.** Ocean breezes flow through this open-air, bay-front restaurant on Alii Drive. Cajun and island influences can be found on the quality menu, where almost all dishes are made to order and feature non-GMO, hormone-free, or USDA certified organic ingredients. **Known for:** scratch-made food and cocktails; steak house pasta; two happy hours daily. $ *Average main: $23* ✉ *75-5805 Alii Dr., Kailua-Kona* ☎ *808/326–1600* 🌐 *www.fosterskitchen.com.*

$$ HAWAIIAN ✕ **Holuakoa Gardens and Cafe.** This respected slow-food restaurant in Holualoa Village features fine dining in a lush, open-air setting beneath the shade of an old monkeypod tree. The proprietors, top chefs from the Bay Area, strive to use all local and organic ingredients for such dinner entrées as handcrafted house gnocchi or Mediterranean seafood stew. **Known for:** farm-to-table cuisine; adjacent coffeehouse lounge; biodynamic and organic wines. $ *Average main: $25* ✉ *76-5900 Old Government Rd., Holualoa* ☎ *808/322–2233* 🌐 *www.holuakoacafe.com* ⊙ *No dinner Sun.*

$$$ HAWAIIAN ✕ **Honu's on the Beach.** Featuring al fresco dining near the sand, this is one of the few truly beachfront restaurants in Historic Kailua Village. Part of Courtyard by Marriott King Kamehameha's Kona Beach Hotel, the venue offers prime views of Kailua Pier and the historic grounds of Kamakahonu Bay. **Known for:** views of sacred temple; magical beachside setting; tiki torches at night. $ *Average main: $28* ✉ *Courtyard King Kamehameha's Kona Beach Hotel, 75-5660 Palani Rd., Kailua-Kona* ☎ *808/329–2911* 🌐 *www.konabeachhotel.com/dining.htm* ⊙ *No lunch.*

$$$$ HAWAIIAN ✕ **Huggo's.** This is one of the few restaurants in town with prices and atmosphere comparable to the splurge restaurants at the Kohala Coast resorts. Dinner offerings sometimes fall short, considering the prices, but the *pupus* (appetizers) and small plates are usually a good bet. **Known for:** dining at the water's edge; landmark Kona restaurant; nightlife hot

spot. $ *Average main: $36* ✉ *75-5828 Kahakai Rd., off Alii Dr., Kailua-Kona* ☎ *808/329–1493* 🌐 *www.huggos.com* ⏲ *No lunch.*

$ AMERICAN

Humpy's Big Island Alehouse. This place is usually packed for a reason: the more than 36 craft brews on tap, plus an upstairs and downstairs bar with plenty of outdoor seating. Take in the oceanfront view while chowing down on stone-baked pizza, fresh salads, fish-and-chips, fish tacos, burgers, stone-baked subs, and lots of appetizers. **Known for:** largest selection of craft beer on the island; great crab cakes; monkeypod cocktail bars. $ *Average main: $15* ✉ *Coconut Grove MarketPlace, 75-5815 Alii Dr., Kailua-Kona* ☎ *808/324-2337* 🌐 *humpyskona.com.*

$$ AMERICAN

Island Lava Java. Located just steps away from its previous landmark location, Island Lava Java is no longer just a colorful coffeeshop with sidewalk seating. With a cocktail bar upstairs and downstairs, the transformed restaurant has upped its food game, too, increasing the prices to boot. **Known for:** large portions using mostly local organic ingredients; new bar with extensive cocktail menu; 100% Kona coffee. $ *Average main: $20* ✉ *Coconut Grove MarketPlace, 75-5801 Alii Dr., Kailua-Kona* ☎ *808/327–2161* 🌐 *www.islandlavajava.com.*

$$ AMERICAN FAMILY Fodor's Choice ★

Jackie Rey's Ohana Grill. This brightly decorated, open-air restaurant is a favorite lunch and dinner destination of visitors and residents, thanks to generous portions and a nice variety of chef's specials, steaks, and seafood dishes. Meals pair well with selections from Jackie Rey's well-rounded wine list. **Known for:** strong local following; great value lunch menu with ribs and fish-and-chips; friendly servers and upbeat atmosphere. $ *Average main: $23* ✉ *Pottery Terrace, 75-5995 Kuakini Hwy., Kailua-Kona* ☎ *808/327–0209* 🌐 *www.jackiereys.com* ⏲ *No lunch weekends.*

$ HAWAIIAN

Kanaka Kava. This is a popular local hangout, and not just because the kava makes you mellow. The Hawaiian proprietors also serve traditional Hawaiian food, including fresh poke, bowls of pulled kalua pork, and healthy organic greens, available in fairly large portions for less than you'll pay elsewhere. **Known for:** kava served in coconut cups; authentic Hawaiian food; Hawaiian specialties like fresh fish and laulau; colorful clientele. $ *Average main: $12* ✉ *Coconut Grove Marketplace, 75-5803 Alii Dr., Space B6, Kailua-Kona* ☎ *808/327–1660* 🌐 *www.kanakakava.com.*

$$ JAPANESE Fodor's Choice ★

Kenichi Pacific. With black-lacquer tables and lipstick-red banquettes, Kenichi offers a more sophisticated dining atmosphere than what's normally found in Kona. This is where residents go when they feel like splurging on top-notch sushi, steak, and Asian-fusion cuisine. **Known for:** upscale dining at much less than resort prices; happy hour discounts on sushi; cheaper lounge menu of small plates. $ *Average main: $25* ✉ *Keauhou Shopping Center, 78-6831 Alii Dr., D-125, Kailua-Kona* ☎ *808/322–6400* 🌐 *www.kenichirestaurants.com* ⏲ *No lunch.*

$ AMERICAN FAMILY Fodor's Choice ★

Kona Brewing Co. Pub & Brewery. This ultrapopular destination with an outdoor patio offers an excellent and varied menu, including famous brews, pulled-pork quesadillas, gourmet pizzas, and a killer spinach salad with Gorgonzola cheese, macadamia nuts, and strawberries. The most affordable option for lunch or dinner is the veggie slice and salad —the garden salad is generous and the slice is moist and loaded with toppings. **Known for:** Longboard Lager and other famous brews made on-site; good pizza; money-saving beer sampler. *Average main: $12 74-5612 Pawai Pl., off Kaiwi St. at end of Pawai Pl., Kailua-Kona 808/329–2739 www.konabrewingco.com.*

$$ AMERICAN **Kona Inn Restaurant.** This vintage open-air restaurant at the historic Kona Inn Shopping Village offers a beautiful oceanfront setting on Kailua Bay. It's a great place to have a mai tai and some appetizers while watching the sunset, or to enjoy a calamari sandwich, clam chowder, or salad at lunch. **Known for:** sunset-watching spot; nice bar and lounge at all times; inconsistent food at dinner. *Average main: $20 Kona Inn Shopping Village, 75-5744 Alii Dr., Kailua-Kona 808/329–4455 www.windandsearestaurants.com.*

4

$$ ASIAN **Lemongrass Bistro.** This well-kept secret occupies a small stylish venue across from the Kailua-Kona public library. The Asian-fusion menu—everything is made to order—includes Thai, Vietnamese, Japanese, Laotian, and Filipino dishes. **Known for:** braised oxtail; $10 lunch special; close to village shops. *Average main: $20 75-5742 Kuakini Hwy., Suite 103, Kailua-Kona 808/331–2708.*

$ AMERICAN FAMILY Fodor's Choice ★ **Quinn's Almost by the Sea.** With the bar in the front and the dining patio in the back, Quinn's may seem like a bit of a dive at first glance, but this venerable restaurant serves up the best darn cheeseburger and fries in town. Appropriate for families, the restaurant stays busy for lunch and dinner, while the bar attracts a cast of colorful regulars. **Known for:** strong cocktails; comfort food like meatballs; open late (until 11 pm). *Average main: $15 75-5655 Palani Rd., Kailua-Kona 808/329–3822 www.quinnsalmostbythesea.com.*

$$ SOUTH PACIFIC Fodor's Choice ★ **Rays on the Bay.** The Sheraton Kona's signature restaurant overlooks Keauhou Bay, offering nighttime views of native manta rays that appear nightly beneath the balcony. The stellar dinner menu includes fresh-catch seafood, island-raised beef, and farm-fresh salads, plus tantalizing appetizers like kampachi sashimi, pork potstickers and poke. **Known for:** spectacular bay-front location; late-night dining; spotlights attract manta rays below the restaurant after dark. *Average main: $25 Sheraton Kona Resort & Spa, 78-128 Ehukai St., Keauhou 808/930–4949 www.sheratonkona.com/dining/rays-on-the-bay-kona No lunch.*

$$ HAWAIIAN FAMILY **Sam Choy's Kai Lanai.** Perched above a shopping center with a coastline view, celebrity chef Sam Choy's namesake restaurant includes a bar that looks like a charter-fishing boat and granite-topped tables with ocean views from every seat. Open for breakfast, lunch, and dinner daily, the restaurant has reasonably priced entrées, highlighted by Sam's trio of fish served with shiitake-mushroom cream sauce. **Known for:** limited parking for such a popular place; family-friendly with a kid's menu; happy hour at the Short Bait Bar. *Average main: $22 Keauhou Shopping Center, 78-6831 Alii Dr., Suite 1000, Kailua-Kona 808/333–3434 www.samchoyskailanai.com.*

$$ THAI **Thai Rin Restaurant.** This dependable oceanfront restaurant near Island Lava Java on Alii Drive offers an excellent selection of Thai food at decent prices. Everything is cooked to order, and the menu is brimming with choices, including five curries, a green-papaya salad, and deep-fried fish. **Known for:** great views with both indoor and outdoor seating;

appetizer platters for sharing; convenient to village shops. [$] *Average main: $18* ✉ *75-5799 Alii Dr., Kailua-Kona* ☎ *808/329–2929* 🌐 *www.aliisunsetplaza.com.*

$ ASIAN FUSION ✕ **TK Noodle House.** Former resort chef TK Keosavang serves up inventive Asian-fusion cuisine with the emphasis on noodles. Generous portions are beautifully plated, like the crispy pork belly sauté with Chinese greens and garlic sauce. **Known for:** ample parking; noodle soups and salads; shabu shabu. [$] *Average main: $12* ✉ *75 Hanama Pl., Kailua-Kona* ✦ *Near Big Island Grill* ☎ *808/327–0070* 🌐 *www.cheftk.com.*

$ DINER FAMILY Fodor's Choice ★ ✕ **Ultimate Burger.** Located in the Office Max shopping complex in Kailua-Kona, this excellent burger joint may look like a chain, but it's an independent, locally owned and operated eatery that serves 100% organic, grass-fed Big Island beef on buns locally made. Be sure to order a side of seasoned Big Daddy fries served with house-made aioli dipping sauce. **Known for:** organic, hormone-free ingredients; supporting local farmers and ranchers; excellent French fries. [$] *Average main: $8* ✉ *Kona Commons Shopping Center, 74-5450 Makala Blvd., Kailua-Kona* ☎ *808/329–2326* 🌐 *www.ultimateburger.net.*

THE KONA COAST

SOUTH KONA

$ MODERN AMERICAN FAMILY ✕ **Annie's Island Fresh Burgers.** At this upcountry burger restaurant in Kona, the burgers are made of succulent, 100% island-raised beef, while the hand-cut garlic-basil French fries are a highlight. Leather couches, hardwood floors, artwork, and live palm trees growing through the floor up through the roof create a casual yet well-appointed feel. **Known for:** local, grass-fed beef burgers; stylish interior; lilikoi (passion fruit) spritzer with rum. [$] *Average main: $13* ✉ *Mango Court, 79-7460 Hawaii Belt Rd., #105, Kainaliu* ☎ *808/324–6000* 🌐 *www.anniesislandfreshburgers.com.*

$ AMERICAN ✕ **The Coffee Shack.** Visitors enjoy stopping here for breakfast or lunch after a morning of snorkeling at Kealakekua Bay, and for good reason: the views of the Honaunau coast from this roadside restaurant are stunning. Breads are all homemade, and you get to choose your favorite when ordering a generously sized sandwich brimming with Black Forest ham and the like. **Known for:** scenic views of South Kona coastline; house-baked bread; its own brand of Kona coffee. [$] *Average main: $12* ✉ *83-5799 Mamalahoa Hwy., Captain Cook* ☎ *808/328–9555* 🌐 *www.coffeeshack.com* ⏲ *No dinner.*

$ HAWAIIAN Fodor's Choice ★ ✕ **Kaaloa's Super Js Authentic Hawaiian Food.** It figures that the best laulau in West Hawaii can be found at a roadside hole-in-the-wall rather than at an expensive resort luau. In fact, this humble family-run eatery was featured on the Food Network's *The Best Thing I Ever Ate*. **Known for:** authentic Hawaiian food; friendly and welcoming proprietors; plate lunches with chicken or pork laulau. [$] *Average main: $9* ✉ *83-5409 Mamalahoa Hwy., between mile markers 106 and 107, Honaunau* ☎ *808/328–9566* ⏲ *Closed Sun.*

$$ ECLECTIC

✕ **Keei Café at Hokukano.** This nicely appointed restaurant, perched above the highway just 15 minutes south of Kailua-Kona, serves delicious dinners with Brazilian, Asian, and European flavors highlighting fresh ingredients from local farmers. Favorites are the Brazilian seafood chowder or peanut-miso salad, followed by pasta primavera smothered with a basil-pesto sauce. **Known for:** most upscale restaurant in South Kona; live music; cash only. *Average main: $20* ✉ *79-7511 Mamalahoa Hwy., Kealakekua* ✣ *½ mile south of Kainaliu* ☎ *808/322–9992* 🌐 *www.keeicafe.net* ▭ *No credit cards* ⏲ *Closed Sun. and Mon. No lunch.*

$$ ITALIAN

✕ **Mi's Waterfront Bistro.** Overlooking Kailua Bay at its new location in Waterfront Row, this steady presence in the Kona dining scene offers a reliable, consistent menu. The restaurant's husband-and-wife owners prepare homemade pastas and focaccia daily and also offer some delicious pasta specials. **Known for:** waterfront views; consistent menu; good desserts. *Average main: $18* ✉ *75-5770 Alii Drive, Kailua-Kona* ☎ *808/323–3880* 🌐 *www.miswaterfront.com.*

$ JAPANESE FAMILY

✕ **Teshima's.** Teshima's doesn't look like much, either inside or out, but it's been a *kamaaina* (local) favorite since 1929 for a reason. Locals gather at this small landmark restaurant 15 minutes south of Kailua-Kona whenever they're in the mood for fresh sashimi, puffy shrimp tempura, or *hekka* (beef and vegetables cooked in an iron pot) at a reasonable price. **Known for:** excellent tempura combos; long-standing family-owned establishment; local flavor. *Average main: $15* ✉ *79-7251 Mamalahoa Hwy., Honalo* ☎ *808/322–9140* 🌐 *www.teshimarestaurant.com.*

NORTH KONA

$$$ MODERN ITALIAN FAMILY Fodor's Choice ★

✕ **Beach Tree at the Four Seasons Resort Hualalai.** This beautifully designed venue provides a relaxed and elegant setting for alfresco dining near the sand, with its boardwalk-style deck, outdoor seating under the trellis, and enormous vaulted ceiling. The menu features brick-oven pizzas, grilled fresh catch of the day, pasta, risotto, seafood entrées, steak, and an array of farm-fresh salads. **Known for:** special Ohana Table four-course dinner; 60 wines by the glass; elegant resort atmosphere. *Average main: $35* ✉ *Four Seasons Resort Hualalai, 72-100 Kaupulehu Dr., Kailua-Kona* ☎ *808/325–8000* 🌐 *www.fourseasons.com/hualalai.*

$$$$ MODERN HAWAIIAN Fodor's Choice ★

✕ **Ulu Ocean Grill and Sushi Lounge at the Four Seasons Resort Hualalai.** Casual elegance takes center stage at the resort's flagship oceanfront restaurant, one of the most upscale restaurants on the Big Island. Breakfast can be à la carte or buffet, but nighttime is when the magic happens, starting with an impressive wine program that includes boutique wines and world-class imports. **Known for:** sushi lounge; sources ingredients from 160 local purveyors; oceanfront dining. *Average main: $45* ✉ *Four Seasons Resort Hualalai, 72-100 Kaupulehu Dr., Kailua-Kona* ☎ *808/325–8000* 🌐 *www.uluoceangrill.com* ⏲ *No lunch.*

THE KOHALA COAST

$$ ASIAN

Bamboo Restaurant & Gallery. This popular restaurant in the heart of Hawi provides a historical setting in which to enjoy a menu brimming with Hawaiian country flair. Most of the creative entrées feature fresh island fish prepared several ways. **Known for:** Pacific Rim menu; colorful plantation-style interiors; weekend entertainment. *Average main: $25 55-3415 Akoni Pule Hwy. (Hwy. 270), Hawi 808/889–5555 www.bamboorestaurant.info Closed Mon. No dinner Sun.*

$$$$ MODERN HAWAIIAN Fodor's Choice ★

Brown's Beach House at the Fairmont Orchid Hawaii. Sitting right on the resort's sandy bay, Brown's Beach House offers beautiful sunset dining and innovative cuisine. Attention to detail is evident in the sophisticated menu, which may include crab-crusted Kona kampachi, roasted duck breast, or Kona Coffee-crusted venison. **Known for:** equally good for seafood and non-seafood entrees; tiki torches beneath starry skies; dietary accommodations. *Average main: $40 Fairmont Orchid Hawaii, 1 N. Kaniku Dr. 808/885–2000 www.fairmont.com/orchid-hawaii No lunch.*

$$$$ ECLECTIC Fodor's Choice ★

CanoeHouse at the Mauna Lani Bay Hotel & Bungalows. One of the most romantic settings on the Kohala Coast, this landmark restaurant on the oceanfront showcases traditional Hawaiian flavors, artful presentations, and locally grown or raised products. The progressive menu spotlights grass-fed beef, lamb, fresh fish caught locally, shellfish, island-fresh greens, local goat cheese, and farm-to-table ingredients. **Known for:** memorable sunsets with tiki torches; good choice of wines by the glass; elaborate tasting menu at the Captain's table. *Average main: $42 Mauna Lani Bay Hotel & Bungalows, 68-1400 Mauna Lani Dr. 808/885–6622 www.maunalani.com No lunch.*

$$ MODERN HAWAIIAN

Hau Tree at the Mauna Kea Beach Hotel. Though it sits on a patio by the pool, this beachside restaurant and beach bar is not just for pupus and cocktails. The island-infused dinner menu features excellent entrées such as the grass-fed Kulana beef tenderloin brochettes, plus plentiful seafood dishes and greens from local farms. **Known for:** famous Fredrico cocktail; great sunset views; Saturday clambake. *Average main: $18 Mauna Kea Beach Hotel, 62-100 Mauna Kea Beach Dr., Kawaihae Between Puako and Kawaihae 808/882–5707 www.maunakeabeachhotel.com.*

$$ SEAFOOD

Kawaihae Seafood Bar & Grill. Upstairs in a historical building, this seafood bar has been a hot spot for years, serving up a dynamite and well-priced bar menu with tasty pupus, and an always-expanding dinner menu that includes at least four fresh-fish specials daily. There's fare for landlubbers, too, including boneless braised short ribs, rib-eye steak, specialty pizza, and lots of salad options. **Known for:** affordable prices; kitchen open late; two nightly happy hours. *Average main: $19 61-3642 Kawaihae Harbor, Hwy. 270, Kawaihae 808/880–9393 www.seafoodbargrill.com.*

$$$$ MODERN HAWAIIAN

KPC (Kamuela Provision Company) at the Hilton Waikoloa Village. The breezy lanai has the most spectacular view of the leeward coast of any restaurant on the Big Island. It's the perfect accompaniment to the elegant yet down-to-earth Hawaii Regional Cuisine and specialty cocktails, like the Island Passion mango martini. **Known for:** tapas menu;

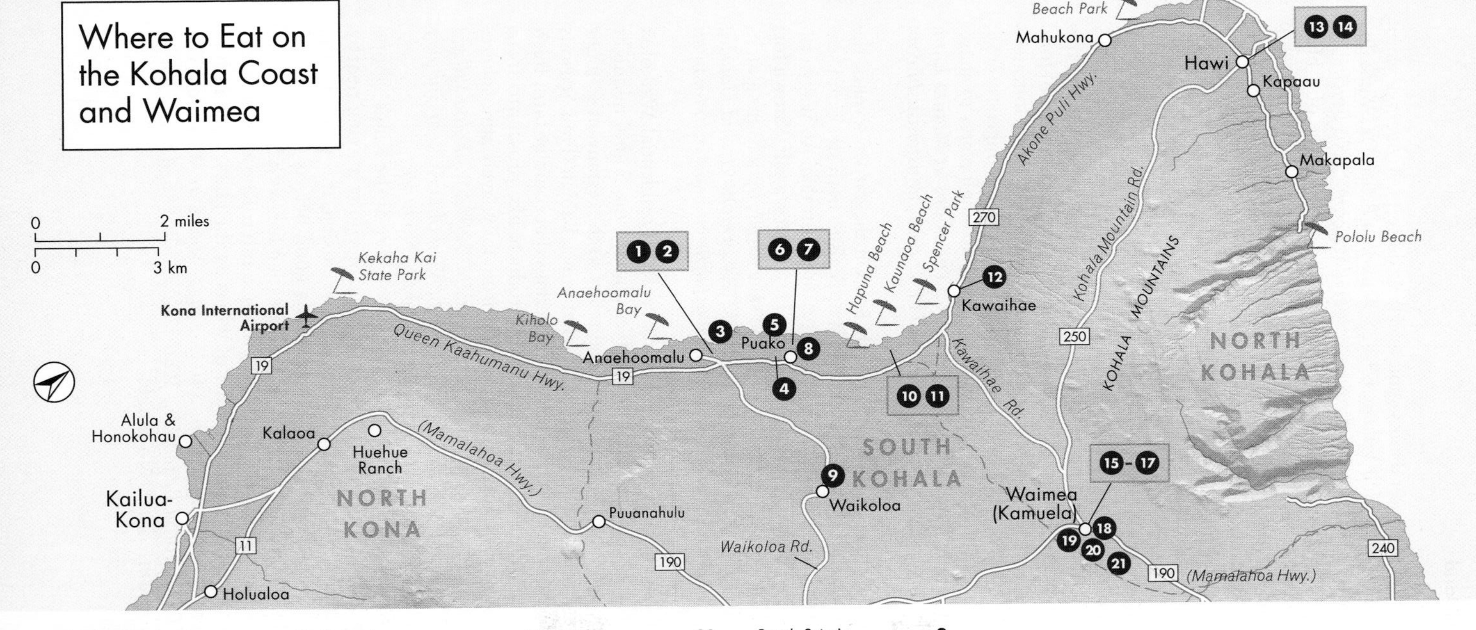

Bamboo Restaurant & Gallery 13
Big Island Brewhaus 15
Brown's Beach House at the Fairmont Orchid Hawaii 7
CanoeHouse at the Mauna Lani Bay Hotel & Bungalows 5
The Fish and the Hog Market Cafe 21
Hau Tree at the Mauna Kea Beach Hotel 11
Kawaihae Seafood Bar & Grill 12
KPC (Kamuela Provision Company) at the Hilton Waikoloa Village 3
Lilikoi Café 20
Manta at the Mauna Kea Beach Hotel 10
Merriman's 16
Monstera 8
Noodle Club 18
Norio's Japanese Steakhouse and Sushi Bar 6
Pueo's Osteria 9
Red Water Cafe 17
Roy's Waikoloa Bar & Grill .. 1
Sansei Seafood Restaurant & Sushi Bar 2
Sushi Rock 14
Tommy Bahama Tropical Café 4
Village Burger 19

the island's best sunset drinks spot; excellent desserts. *Average main: $36 ✉ Hilton Waikoloa Village, 69-425 Waikoloa Beach Dr., Waikoloa ☎ 808/886–1234 ⊕ www.hiltonwaikoloavillage.com ⊙ No lunch.*

$$$$ MODERN HAWAIIAN Fodor's Choice ★

Manta at the Mauna Kea Beach Hotel. Perched on the edge of a bluff overlooking the sparkling waters of Kaunaoa Beach, the resort's flagship restaurant is a compelling spot for a romantic meal at sunset, especially at one of the outside tables. The culinary team's take on Hawaii regional cuisine highlights locally sourced, sustainable fish, chicken, and beef. **Known for:** beachfront balcony dining; exhibition kitchen; Sunday brunch. *Average main: $40 ✉ Mauna Kea Beach Hotel, 62-100 Mauna Kea Beach Dr., Kawaihae ☎ 808/882–5707 ⊕ www.maunakeabeachhotel.com ⊙ No lunch.*

$$ JAPANESE FAMILY

Monstera. It may not be beachfront with a view of the sunset, but this eatery is worth a visit for its sophisticated *izakaya* (Japanese pub) food with a touch of local inspiration. Executive Chef Anthony Gonzales's dinner menu includes Norio's Original 69 Roll with Dungeness crab. **Known for:** sushi bar; sizable noodle dishes and small plates to share; late-night dining. *Average main: $20 ✉ The Shops at Mauna Lani, 68-1330 Mauna Lani Dr. ☎ 808/887–2711 ⊕ www.monsterasushi.com ⊙ No lunch.*

$$$$ JAPANESE

Norio's Japanese Steakhouse and Sushi Bar. On the garden level of the Fairmont Orchid, this classy restaurant appeals to both steak and seafood lovers. The star attraction is the signature Australian A6 Wagyu rib eye, seasoned with five different kinds of Hawaiian sea salt. **Known for:** sushi bar and lounge; extensive wine and sake roster; options for gluten- and soy-free diners. *Average main: $42 ✉ Fairmont Orchid Hawaii, 1 N. Kaniku Dr. ☎ 808/885–2000 ⊕ www.fairmont.com/orchid-hawaii ⊙ Closed Tues.–Wed. No lunch.*

$$ ITALIAN

Pueo's Osteria. Hidden in a shopping center in residential Waikoloa Village, this late-night destination serves dinner from 5 until midnight (*pueo* means "owl" in Hawaiian, and refers to the restaurant's "night owl" concept). Renowned executive chef James Babian (Four Seasons Hualalai, Fairmont Orchid) serves up offerings that combine farm-fresh ingredients with fine imported Italian products like prosciutto from Parma. **Known for:** premium ingredients from Italy; lively atmosphere; Tuscan-inspired dining room. *Average main: $20 ✉ Waikoloa Village Highlands Center, 68-1845 Waikoloa Rd., Waikoloa ✣ Near Subway ☎ 808/339–7566 ⊕ www.pueososteria.com ⊙ No lunch.*

$$$$ MODERN HAWAIIAN FAMILY

Roy's Waikoloa Bar & Grill. Overlooking the lake at the Kings' Shops is, granted, not an oceanfront setting, but if you're staying nearby and are looking for reliable, albeit pricey, cuisine, this place fits the bill. The three-course, prix fixe meal is a good bet, as is blackened ahi, and the macadamia nut–crusted Hawaiian fish with Kona lobster cream sauce is a melt-in-your-mouth encounter. **Known for:** great appetizers to share; extensive list of wines by the glass; outstanding kid's menu. *Average main: $40 ✉ Kings' Shops at Waikoloa Village, 250 Waikoloa Beach Dr., Waikoloa ☎ 808/886–4321 ⊕ www.roysrestaurant.com ⊙ No lunch.*

$$ JAPANESE FAMILY ✕ **Sansei Seafood Restaurant & Sushi Bar.** Creative sushi and contemporary Asian cuisine take center stage at this entertaining restaurant at Queens' MarketPlace. The lauded menu includes shrimp dynamite in a creamy garlic masago aioli and unagi glaze, and panko-crusted ahi sashimi sushi roll. **Known for:** early-bird 50% discount Sun. and Mon.; private dining room; karaoke on the weekends. *Average main: $20 ✉ Queens' MarketPlace, 201 Waikoloa Beach Dr., Ste. 801, Waikoloa ☎ 808/886–6286 www.sanseihawaii.com No lunch.*

$$ JAPANESE Fodor's Choice ★ ✕ **Sushi Rock.** Located in historic Hawi Town, Sushi Rock isn't big on size—its narrow dining room is brightly painted and casually decorated with Hawaiian and Japanese knickknacks—but discerning locals and *akamai* (in-the-know) visitors come here for some of the island's best sushi. The restaurant prides itself on using local ingredients like grass-fed beef tenderloin, goat cheese, macadamia nuts, and mango in the Islands-inspired sushi rolls. **Known for:** well-priced trios; cone sushi; extensive salad menu. *Average main: $23 ✉ 55-3435 Akoni Pule Hwy., Hawi ☎ 808/889–5900 sushirockrestaurant.net.*

$$$ MODERN HAWAIIAN FAMILY ✕ **Tommy Bahama Tropical Café.** This breezy, open-air restaurant, located upstairs at the Shops at Mauna Lani, offers an excellent roster of appetizers, including seared-scallop sliders and coconut-crusted crab cakes. The chef here has freedom to cook up his own daily specials, and the seared ahi is a standout. **Known for:** reliable cuisine and relaxed vibe; popular cocktail bar and lounge; house-baked breads and specialty butters. *Average main: $34 ✉ The Shops at Mauna Lani, 68-1330 Mauna Lani Dr., No. 102 ☎ 808/881–8686 www.tommybahama.com.*

WAIMEA

$ AMERICAN ✕ **Big Island Brewhaus.** Owner Tom Kerns is a veteran brewer who's now churning out premium ales, lagers, and specialty beers from his on-site brewery in Waimea. With a focus on fresh ingredients, the brewpub's menu includes burgers, poke, fish tacos, burritos, rellenos, and quesadillas fresh to order. **Known for:** pioneering local brewmaster; outdoor lanai seating; reliable pub menu. *Average main: $11 ✉ 64-1066A Mamalahoa Hwy., Waimea (Hawaii County) ☎ 808/887–1717 www.bigislandbrewhaus.com.*

$ ECLECTIC ✕ **The Fish and the Hog Market Cafe.** This casual little restaurant along the highway serves up generous sandwiches, salads, and melt-in-your-mouth barbecue items, including kiawe-smoked meat like pulled pork, ribs, pork ribs, and brisket. Additional options range from pupu platters and gumbo to salads made with produce grown in Waimea. **Known for:** roadhouse vibe; slow-food creds; fresh seafood caught by the owners. *Average main: $15 ✉ 64-957 Mamalahoa Hwy. (Hwy. 11), Waimea (Hawaii County) ☎ 808/885–6268.*

$ EUROPEAN FAMILY ✕ **Lilikoi Café.** This gem of a café is tucked away in the back of the Parker Ranch Center. Locals love that it's hard to find because they want to keep its delicious breakfast crepes, freshly made soups, and croissants Waimea's little secret. **Known for:** handpainted murals; large variety of salads; creative sandwiches and hot lunch entrees. *Average main: $9*

✉ *Parker Ranch Center, 67-1185 Mamalahoa Hwy. (Hwy. 11), Waimea (Hawaii County)* ☎ *808/887–1400* ⏲ *Closed Sun. No dinner.*

$$$$ MODERN HAWAIIAN ✕ **Merriman's.** Located in upcountry Waimea, this signature restaurant of Peter Merriman, one of the pioneers of Hawaii Regional Cuisine, is the home of the original wok-charred ahi: it's seared on the outside and sashimi on the inside. If you prefer meat, try the Kahua Ranch braised lamb, raised locally to the restaurant's specifications, or the prime bone-in New York steak, grilled to order. **Known for:** great lunch specials; extensive wine list; chocolate oblivion torte. $ *Average main: $45* ✉ *Opelo Plaza, 65-1227 Opelo Rd., Waimea (Hawaii County)* ☎ *808/885–6822* 🌐 *www.merrimanshawaii.com.*

$ JAPANESE FUSION FAMILY ✕ **Noodle Club.** Star Wars toys and action figures line the shelves of Noodle Club, a fun destination with serious food in Parker Ranch Center. Veteran resort chef Edwin Goto simmers his broths for up to 36 hours to create the noodle or saimin dishes such as the savory Bowl of Seoul, or the All Things Pork Ramen. **Known for:** homemade pork, beef, and vegetable broths; bao buns with Hamakua Alii mushrooms; delicous desserts. $ *Average main: $14* ✉ *Parker Ranch Center, 67-1185 Mamalahoa Hwy A106, Waimea (Hawaii County)* ☎ *808/885–8825* 🌐 *www.noodleclubwaimea.com* ⏲ *Closed Mon.*

$$$ ECLECTIC FAMILY ✕ **Red Water Cafe.** Chef David Abraham serves Hawaiian café food with a twist and a side of aloha. The specialty is multicultural cuisine, like a Thai Caesar salad with crispy calamari croutons that is big enough to share. **Known for:** entrées served in half or full portions; sushi bar; good kids' menu. $ *Average main: $30* ✉ *65-1299 Kawaihae Rd., Waimea (Hawaii County)* ☎ *808/885–9299* 🌐 *www.redwater-cafe.com* ⏲ *No lunch.*

$ AMERICAN FAMILY ✕ **Village Burger.** This little eatery brings a whole new meaning to gourmet hamburgers. Locally raised, grass-fed, hormone-free beef is ground fresh, hand-shaped daily on-site, and grilled to perfection right before your eyes. **Known for:** great local brioche buns; lots of toppings for burgers; locally made ice cream. $ *Average main: $10* ✉ *Parker Ranch Center, 67-1185 Mamalahoa Hwy., Waimea (Hawaii County)* ☎ *808/885–7319* 🌐 *www.villageburgerwaimea.com.*

HILO

$ DINER FAMILY Fodor's Choice ★ ✕ **Bears' Coffee.** This favorite, cozy breakfast spot, a fixture downtown since the late 1980s, is much loved for its fresh-fruit waffles and tasty morning coffee. For lunch the little diner serves up huge deli sandwiches and decent entrée-size salads, plus specials like hearty meat loaf, roasted chicken, and pot roast. **Known for:** reliable breakfasts; local landmark; friendly atmosphere. $ *Average main: $10* ✉ *106 Keawe St., Hilo* ☎ *808/935–0708* ⏲ *No dinner.*

$ HAWAIIAN FAMILY ✕ **Café 100.** Established in 1948, this family-owned restaurant is famous for its tasty loco moco, prepared in more than three dozen ways, and its low-priced breakfast and lunch specials. (You can stuff yourself for $5 if you order right.) The word "restaurant," or even "café," is used loosely here—you order at a window and eat on one of the outdoor benches provided—but you come here for the food, prices, and authentic, old-Hilo experience. **Known for:** local flavor; Super Loco

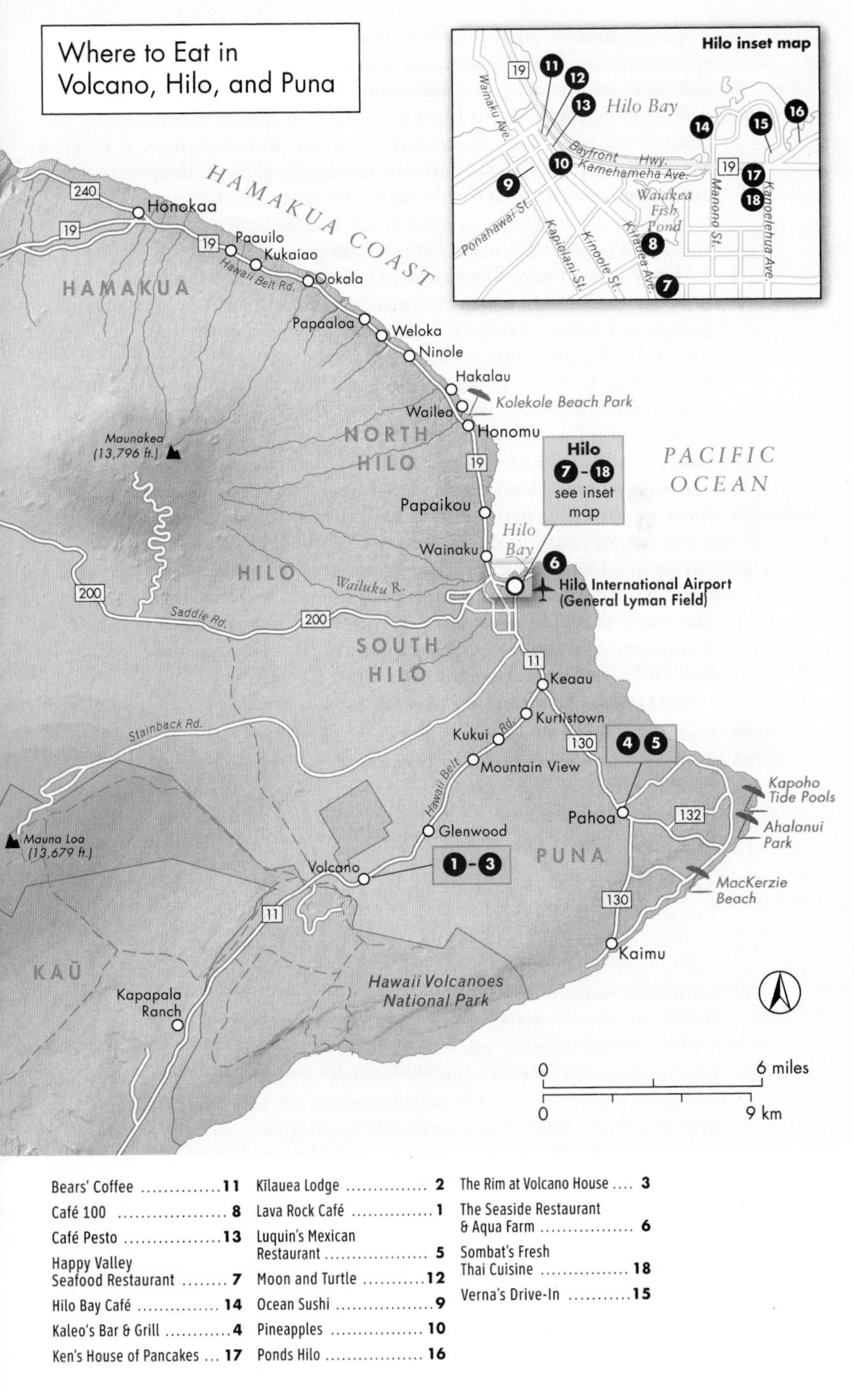
Where to Eat in Volcano, Hilo, and Puna
Hilo inset map
Hilo Bay
Wainaku Ave.
Bayfront Hwy.
Kamehameha Ave.
Waiakea Fish Pond
Ponahawai St.
Kapiolani St.
Kinoole St.
Kilauea Ave.
Manono St.
Kanoelehua Ave.
HAMAKUA COAST
HAMAKUA
Honokaa
Paauilo
Kukaiao
Hawaii Belt Rd.
Ookala
Papaaloa
Weloka
Ninole
Hakalau
Kolekole Beach Park
Wailea
Honomu
NORTH HILO
Maunakea (13,796 ft.)
Hilo 7-18 see inset map
PACIFIC OCEAN
Papaikou
Hilo Bay
Wainaku
HILO
Wailuku R.
Hilo International Airport (General Lyman Field)
Saddle Rd.
SOUTH HILO
Keaau
Kurtistown
Kukui Rd.
Stainback Rd.
Mountain View
Hawaii Belt
Kapoho Tide Pools
Pahoa
Ahalanui Park
Glenwood
Mauna Loa (13,679 ft.)
Volcano
PUNA
MacKerzie Beach
Kaimu
KAŪ
Kapapala Ranch
Hawaii Volcanoes National Park
0 6 miles
0 9 km
Bears' Coffee 11
Café 100 8
Café Pesto 13
Happy Valley Seafood Restaurant 7
Hilo Bay Café 14
Kaleo's Bar & Grill 4
Ken's House of Pancakes ... 17
Kīlauea Lodge 2
Lava Rock Café 1
Luquin's Mexican Restaurant 5
Moon and Turtle 12
Ocean Sushi 9
Pineapples 10
Ponds Hilo 16
The Rim at Volcano House 3
The Seaside Restaurant & Aqua Farm 6
Sombat's Fresh Thai Cuisine 18
Verna's Drive-In 15

Moco; generous portions. [$] *Average main: $6* ✉ *969 Kilauea Ave., Hilo* ☎ *808/935–8683* 🌐 *www.cafe100.com* ⏲ *Closed Sun.*

$$ ITALIAN **Café Pesto.** Located in a beautiful and historical venue, Café Pesto offers exotic pizzas (with fresh Hamakua mushrooms, artichokes, and rosemary Gorgonzola sauce, for example). You can make a meal of the Asian-inspired pastas and risottos, fresh seafood, delicious salads, and appetizers. **Known for:** historic interiors; wood-fired pizza; happy hour from 2 pm. [$] *Average main: $20* ✉ *308 Kamehameha Ave., Hilo* ☎ *808/969–6640* 🌐 *www.cafepesto.com.*

$ CHINESE **Happy Valley Seafood Restaurant.** Don't let the name fool you. Though Hilo's best Chinese restaurant does specialize in seafood (the salt-and-pepper prawns are fantastic), it also offers a wide range of other Cantonese treats, including a sizzling lamb platter, salt-and-pepper pork, Mongolian lamb, and vegetarian specialties like garlic eggplant and crispy green beans. **Known for:** authentic Cantonese Chinese food; easy parking; good soups. [$] *Average main: $12* ✉ *1263 Kilauea Ave., Suite 320, Hilo* ☎ *808/933–1083.*

$$ AMERICAN Fodor's Choice ★ **Hilo Bay Café.** This popular upscale restaurant overlooks Hilo Bay from its towering perch on the waterfront; the sophisticated second-floor dining room looks like it's straight out of Manhattan. A sushi bar complements the excellent selection of fresh fish, pork, beef, vegan options; premium wines and sake are featured. **Known for:** excellent bayside views; Blue Bay burger with shoestring fries; most upscale restaurant in Hilo. [$] *Average main: $20* ✉ *123 Lihiwai St., Hilo* ☎ *808/935–4939* 🌐 *www.hilobaycafe.com* ⏲ *Closed Sun.*

$ DINER FAMILY Fodor's Choice ★ **Ken's House of Pancakes.** For years, this 24-hour diner on Banyan Drive between the airport and the hotels has been a gathering place for Hilo residents and visitors. Breakfast is the main attraction: Ken's serves 11 types of pancakes, plus all kinds of fruit waffles (banana, peach) and popular omelets, like Da Bradda, teeming with meats. **Known for:** local landmark with old-fashioned vibe; extensive menu; weekly special nights like Sunday spaghetti and Tuesday tacos. [$] *Average main: $10* ✉ *1730 Kamehameha Ave., Hilo* ☎ *808/935–8711* 🌐 *www.kenshouseofpancakes.com.*

$$$ INTERNATIONAL **Moon and Turtle.** This sophisticated intimate restaurant in a bayfront building offers a classy selection of international fare with the focus on locally sourced meats, produce, and seafood. The menu changes daily—mushroom pappardelle and smoky sashimi are highlights, along with seafood chowder, spicy Kajiki Tartare and crispy moi whole-fried Pacific Threadfin. **Known for:** ever-changing international menu; lychee martinis; high prices for Hilo. [$] *Average main: $25* ✉ *51 Kalakaua St., Hilo* ☎ *808/961–0599* ⏲ *Closed Sun. and Mon.*

$ JAPANESE FAMILY **Ocean Sushi.** What this restaurant lacks in ambience it certainly makes up for in quality and value. We're talking about light and crispy tempura; tender, moist teriyaki chicken; and about 25 specialty sushi rolls, all at unbeatable prices. **Known for:** family restaurant; reasonable prices; good kid's menu. [$] *Average main: $12* ✉ *235 Keawe St., Hilo* ☎ *808/961–6625* ⏲ *Closed Sun.*

$ AMERICAN FAMILY **Pineapples.** If you expect that a restaurant named Pineapples would serve tropical libations in hollowed-out pineapples, you'd be exactly correct. Always packed, this open-air bistro looks like a tourist trap, but there is a fine-dining component to the menu, which includes fresh catch, kalbi ribs, teriyaki flank steak, burgers, wraps, and sandwiches. **Known for:** surprisingly inventive island cuisine; great pineapple salsa; delicous tropical drinks. *Average main: $14 332 Keawe St, Hilo 808/238-5324 www.pineappleshilo.com Closed Mon.*

$$ HAWAIIAN FAMILY **Ponds Hilo.** Perched on the waterfront overlooking a scenic and serene pond, this restaurant has the look and feel of an old-fashioned, harbor-side steak house and bar. The menu features a good range of burgers and salads, steak and seafood—but the fish-and-chips are the star attraction. **Known for:** scenic location; difficult parking; popular Sunday brunch. *Average main: $20 135 Kalanianaole Ave., Hilo 808/934–7663 www.pondshilo.com.*

4

$$ SEAFOOD FAMILY **The Seaside Restaurant & Aqua Farm.** The Nakagawa family has been running this eatery since the early 1920s. The latest son to manage it has transformed both the menu and the decor, and that, paired with the setting (on a 30-acre natural, brackish fishpond) makes this one of the most interesting places to eat in Hilo. **Known for:** authentic local experience; ocean and pond views at sunset; mullet from their aqua farm. *Average main: $23 1790 Kalanianaole Ave., Hilo 808/935–8825 www.seasiderestauranthilo.com Closed Mon. No lunch.*

$ THAI Fodor's Choice ★ **Sombat's Fresh Thai Cuisine.** There's a reason why locals flock to this hideaway for the best Thai cuisine in Hilo. Fresh local ingredients highlight proprietor Sombat Saenguthai's menu (many of the herbs come from her own garden) to create authentic and tasty Thai treats like coconut curries, fresh basil rolls, eggplant stir-fry, and green papaya salad. **Known for:** special seasonings; friendly service; excellent pad Thai. *Average main: $13 Waiakea Kai Plaza, 88 Kanoelehue Ave., Hilo Close to Ken's Pancakes 808/969–9336 www.sombats.com Closed Sun. No lunch.*

$ HAWAIIAN **Verna's Drive-In.** Verna's is tried and true among locals, who come for the juicy homemade burgers and filling plate lunches. The price is right with a burger combo that includes fries and a drink. **Known for:** local grindz; plate lunches; superlow prices. *Average main: $6 1765 Kamehameha Ave., Hilo 808/935–2776.*

PUNA

$$ AMERICAN **Kaleo's Bar and Grill.** Pahoa Town isn't necessarily known for gourmet dining choices, but that's all changed with the arrival of Kaleo's. Hawaiian-inspired fare blends the gamut of island ethnic influences with such choices as kalua pork won tons, tempura ahi rolls, grilled burgers, and banana spring rolls. **Known for:** sophisticated menu; nightly entertainment; full bar. *Average main: $20 15-2969 Pahoa Village Road, Pahoa 808/965–5600 www.kaleoshawaii.com.*

$ MEXICAN **Luquin's Mexican Restaurant.** Long an island favorite for tasty, albeit greasy, Mexican grub, this landmark is making a comeback in the funky town of Pahoa after a tragic fire burned the original restaurant to the ground in 2017. Breakfast is popular and includes delicious huevos rancheros. **Known for:** longtime Pahoa restaurant; affordable fare; community gathering spot. 💲 *Average main: $9* ✉ *15-2942 Pahoa Village Rd., Pahoa* ☎ *808/965–9990* 🌐 *www.luquins.com.*

HAWAII VOLCANOES NATIONAL PARK AND VICINITY

VOLCANO

$$$ EUROPEAN ✕ **Kilauea Lodge.** The roaring fire, koa-wood tables, and intimate lighting are in keeping with this cozy lodge in the heart of Volcano Village. The dinner menu changes daily and features such entrées as venison, duck à l'orange with an apricot-mustard glaze, and lamb provençal garnished with papaya-apple-mint sauce. **Known for:** landmark location; fine dining with prices to match; popular Sunday brunch. 💲 *Average main: $30* ✉ *19-3948 Old Volcano Rd., Volcano* ☎ *808/967–7366* 🌐 *www.kilauealodge.com.*

$ DINER FAMILY ✕ **Lava Rock Café.** This is an affordable place to grab a sandwich or a coffee and check your email (Wi-Fi is free with purchase of a meal) before heading to Hawaii Volcanoes National Park. The homey, sit-down diner caters to families, serving up heaping plates of pancakes and French toast for breakfast. **Known for:** roadhouse atmosphere; family-friendly atmosphere; diner-style comfort food. 💲 *Average main: $10* ✉ *19-3972 Old Volcano Hwy., Volcano* ✢ *Next to Kilauea General Store* ☎ *808/967–8526* ⏲ *No dinner Sun. and Mon.*

$$ HAWAIIAN FAMILY ✕ **The Rim at Volcano House.** This fine-dining restaurant overlooks the rim of Kilauea caldera and its fiery glow. Featuring two bars, a lounge, and live entertainment, it highlights island-inspired cuisine and incorporates locally sourced produce and other ingredients. **Known for:** views of Halemaumau Crater; hot-buttered rum; well-priced Taste of Hawaii lunch special. 💲 *Average main: $25* ✉ *Volcano House Hotel, Crater Rim Dr., Volcano* ☎ *808/756–9625* 🌐 *www.hawaiivolcanohouse.com.*

WHERE TO STAY

Updated by Karen Anderson

Even among locals, there is an ongoing debate about which side of the Big Island is "better," so don't worry if you're having a tough time deciding where to stay. Our recommendation? Do both. Each side offers a different range of accommodations, restaurants, and activities.

Consider staying at one of the upscale resorts along the Kohala Coast or in a condo in Kailua-Kona for half of your trip. Then, shift gears and check into a romantic bed-and-breakfast on the Hamakua Coast, South Kona, Hilo, or near the volcano. If you've got children in tow, opt for a vacation home or a stay at one of the island's many family-friendly hotels. On the west side, explore the island's most pristine beaches or try some of the fine-dining restaurants; on the east side, hike through rain forests, witness majestic waterfalls, or go for a plate lunch.

Some locals like to say that the east is "more Hawaiian," but we argue that King Kamehameha himself made Kailua-Kona his final home during his sunset years. Another reason to try a bit of both: your budget. You can justify splurging on a stay at a Kohala Coast resort for a few nights because you'll spend the rest of your time paying one-third that rate at a cozy cottage in Volcano or a vacation rental on Alii Drive. And although food at the resorts is very expensive, you don't have to eat every meal there. Condos and vacation homes can be ideal for a family trip or for a group of friends looking to save money and live like *kamaainas* (local residents) for a week or two. Many of the homes also have private pools and hot tubs, lanai, ocean views, and more—you can go as budget or as high-end as you like.

If you choose a bed-and-breakfast, inn, or an out-of-the-way hotel, explain your expectations fully to the proprietor and ask plenty of questions before booking. Be clear about your travel and location needs. Some places require stays of two or three days.

CONDOS AND VACATION RENTALS

Renting a condo or vacation house gives you much more living space than the average hotel, plus the chance to meet more people (neighbors are usually friendly), lower nightly rates, and the option of cooking or barbecuing rather than eating out. When booking, remember that most properties are individually owned, with rates and amenities that differ substantially depending on the place. Some properties are handled by rental agents or agencies, while many are handled directly through the owner. The following is a list of our favorite booking agencies for various lodging types throughout the island. Be sure to call and ask questions before booking.

Contacts **Abbey Vacation Rentals.** ☎ *886/456–4252* 🌐 *www.konarentals.com.* **Big Island Villas.** ☎ *808/936–3870, 808/443–6991* 🌐 *www.bigislandvillas.com.* **CJ Kimberly Realtors.** ☎ *808/329–7000* 🌐 *www.cjkimberly.com.* **Hawaiian Beach Rentals.** ☎ *844/261–0464* 🌐 *www.hawaiianbeachrentals.com.* **Hawaii Vacation Rentals.** ☎ *808/882–7000* 🌐 *www.vacationbigisland.com.* **Keauhou Property Management.** ☎ *808/326–7053* 🌐 *www.konacondo.net.* **Kolea Vacations.** ☎ *888/565–3244* 🌐 *www.koleavacations.com.* **Kona Coast Vacations.** ☎ *808/329–2140* 🌐 *www.konacoastvacations.com.* **Kona Hawaii Vacation Rentals.** ☎ *808/329–3333* 🌐 *www.konahawaii.com.* **Knutson and Associates.** ☎ *808/329–1010* 🌐 *www.konahawaiirentals.com.* **South Kohala Management.** ☎ *808/883–8500* 🌐 *www.southkohala.com.*

KAILUA-KONA

The bustling historic village full of restaurants, shops, and entertainment also offers tons of lodging options. In addition to a half-dozen hotels, oceanfront Alii Drive is lined with condos and vacation homes. All the conveniences are here, and there are several grocery stores and big-box retailers nearby for those who need to stock up on supplies. Kailua-Kona has a handful of beaches—Magic Sands, Kahaluu, and Kamakahonu (at the pier) among them. The downside to staying here is that you'll have to drive 30 to 45 minutes up the road to the Kohala Coast to visit Hawaii's signature, long, white-sand beaches. However, you'll also pay about half what you would at any of the major resorts, not to mention that Kailua-Kona offers a bit more local charm.

WHERE TO STAY ON THE BIG ISLAND

	Local Vibe	Pros	Cons
Kailua-Kona	A bustling little village; Alii Drive brims with hotels and condo complexes.	Plenty to do, day and night; everything within easy walking distance of most hotels; many grocery stores in the area.	More traffic than anywhere else on the island; limited number of beaches; traffic noise on Alii Drive.
South Kona and Kau	Popular Kealakekua Bay has plenty of B&Bs and vacation rentals; with a few more farther south in Kau.	Kealakekua Bay is popular for kayaking and snorkeling and has some good restaurants; Captain Cook and Kainaliu have coffee farms.	Vog (volcano fog) from Kilauea often settles here; few sandy beaches; Kau is quite remote.
The Kohala Coast	Home to most of the Big Island's major resorts. Blue sunny skies prevail here, along with the island's best beaches.	Beautiful beaches; high-end shopping and dining; lots of activities for adults and children.	Pricey; long driving distances to Volcano, Hilo, and Kailua-Kona.
Waimea	Though it seems a world away, Waimea is only about a 15- to 20-minute drive from the Kohala Coast.	Beautiful scenery, *paniolo* (cowboy) culture; home to some exceptional local restaurants.	Can be cool and rainy year-round; nearest beaches are a 20-minute drive away.
The Hamakua Coast	A nice spot for those seeking peace, tranquility, and an alternative to the tropical-beach-vacation experience.	Close to Waipio Valley; foodie and farm tours in the area; good spot for honeymooners.	Beaches are an hour's drive away; convenience shopping is limited.
Hilo	Hilo is the wet and lush, eastern side of the Big Island. It's less touristy than the west side but retains much local charm.	Proximity to waterfalls, rain-forest hikes, museums, and botanical gardens; good B&B options.	The best white-sand beaches are on the other side of the island; noise from coqui frogs can be distracting at night.
Puna	Puna doesn't attract as many visitors as other regions, so you'll find good deals on rentals and B&Bs here.	A few black-sand beaches; off the beaten path and fairly wild; hot ponds; lava has flowed into the sea here in years past.	Few dining and entertainment options; no resorts or resort amenities; noisy coqui frogs at night.
Hawaii Volcanoes National Park and Vicinity	There are any number of enchanting B&B inns in fern-shrouded Volcano Village, near the park.	Good location for nighttime lava-watching; great for hiking, nature tours, and bike riding; close to Hilo and Puna.	Just a few dining options; not much nightlife; can be cold and wet.

$ RENTAL **Casa de Emdeko.** A large and pretty complex on the *makai* (oceanfront) side of Alii Drive, Casa de Emdeko offers a few more amenities than most condo complexes, including a florist, hair salon, and an on-site convenience store that makes sandwiches. **Pros:** oceanfront fresh- and saltwater pools; hidden from the street; very private. **Cons:** quality and

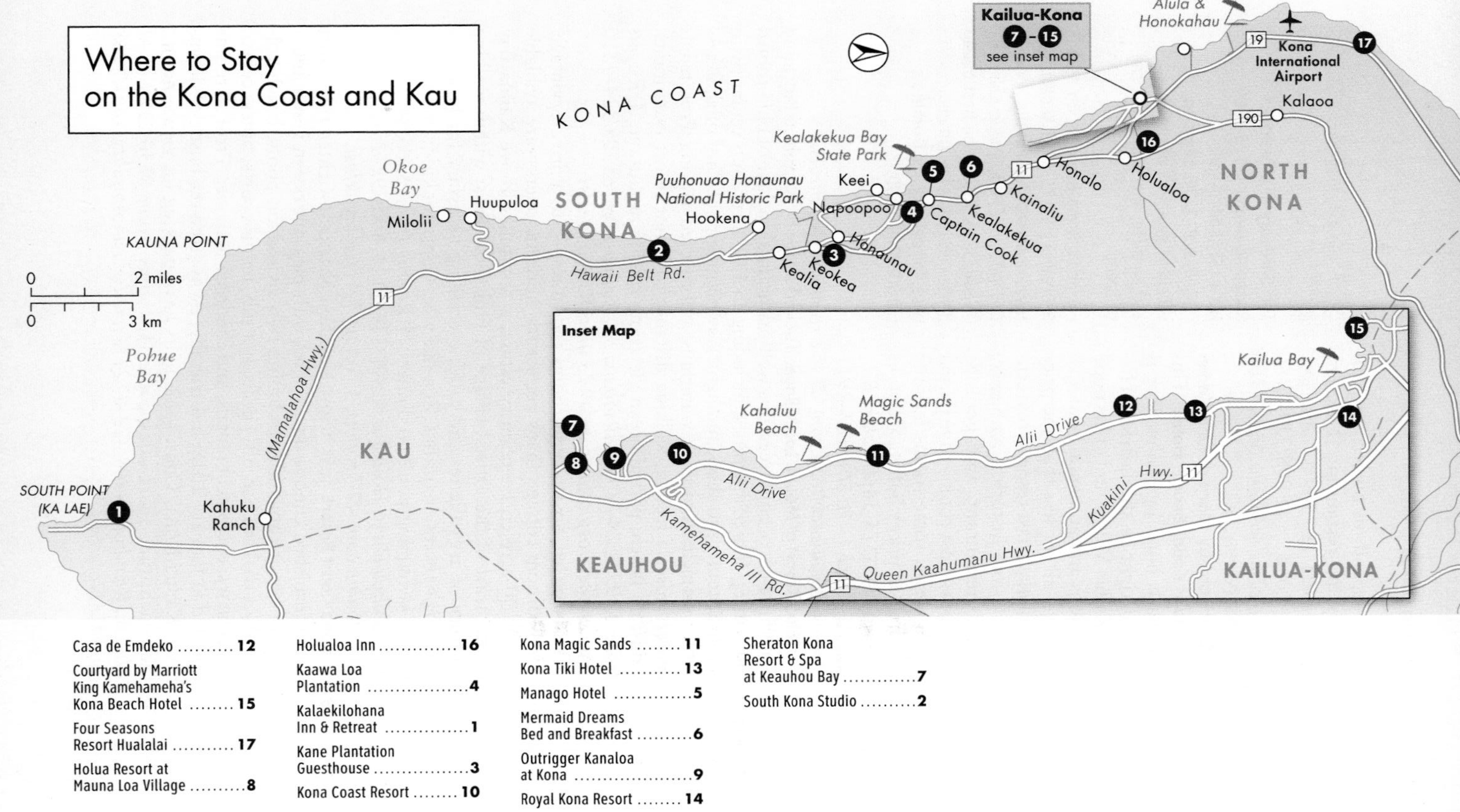

Casa de Emdeko **12**
Courtyard by Marriott King Kamehameha's Kona Beach Hotel **15**
Four Seasons Resort Hualalai **17**
Holua Resort at Mauna Loa Village **8**
Holualoa Inn **16**
Kaawa Loa Plantation **4**
Kalaekilohana Inn & Retreat **1**
Kane Plantation Guesthouse **3**
Kona Coast Resort **10**
Kona Magic Sands **11**
Kona Tiki Hotel **13**
Manago Hotel **5**
Mermaid Dreams Bed and Breakfast **6**
Outrigger Kanaloa at Kona **9**
Royal Kona Resort **14**
Sheraton Kona Resort & Spa at Keauhou Bay **7**
South Kona Studio **2**

prices depend on owner; not kid-friendly; no restaurant. $ *Rooms from: $125 ✉ 75-6082 Alii Dr., Kailua-Kona ☎ 808/329–2160 🌐 www.casadeemdeko.org ⇨ 106 units 🍴 No meals.*

$$$ HOTEL FAMILY **Courtyard by Marriott King Kamehameha's Kona Beach Hotel.** This landmark hotel by Kailua Pier is located right in the heart of Historic Kailua Village and offers good vibrations and authentic local hospitality—all for less than the price of a Kohala Coast resort. **Pros:** central location; historical ambience; on-site restaurant and poolside bar. **Cons:** most rooms have partial ocean views; some rooms face the parking lot; pricey buffet. $ *Rooms from: $339 ✉ 75-5660 Palani Rd., Kailua-Kona ☎ 808/329–2911 🌐 www.konabeachhotel.com ⇨ 452 rooms 🍴 No meals.*

KONA CONDO COMFORTS

The **Safeway** at Crossroads Shopping Center (✉ *75-1000 Henry St., Kailua-Kona* ☎ *808/329–2207*) offers an excellent inventory of groceries and produce, although prices can be steep.

For pizza, **Kona Brewing Co. Pub & Brewery** (✉ *75-5629 Kuakini Hwy., accessed through the Kona Old Industrial Park, Kailua-Kona* ☎ *808/329–2739*) is the best bet, if you can pick it up. Otherwise, for delivery, try **Domino's** (☎ *808/329–9500*).

$$ RESORT Fodor's Choice ★ **Holua Resort at Mauna Loa Village.** Tucked away by Keauhou Bay amid a plethora of coconut trees, this well-maintained enclave of blue-roofed villas offers lots of amenities, including an 11-court tennis center (with a center court, pro shop, and lights), swimming pools, hot tubs, fitness center, manicured gardens, waterfalls, and covered parking. **Pros:** tennis center; upscale feeling; walking distance to major resort restaurants. **Cons:** no beach; partial ocean views; no on-site restaurant. $ *Rooms from: $199 ✉ 78-7190 Kaleiopapa St., Kailua-Kona ☎ 808/324–1550 🌐 www.shellhospitality.com ⇨ 73 units 🍴 No meals.*

$$$$ B&B/INN Fodor's Choice ★ **Holualoa Inn.** Six spacious rooms and suites—plus a private, vintage, one-bedroom cottage that's perfect for honeymooners—are available at this 30-acre coffee-country estate, a few miles above Kailua Bay in the heart of the artists' village of Holualoa. **Pros:** within walking distance of art galleries and cafés; everything necessary for hosting a wedding or event; luxurious, Zen-like vibe. **Cons:** not kid-friendly; non-heated swimming pool; no dinners. $ *Rooms from: $365 ✉ 76-5932 Mamalahoa Hwy., Holualoa ☎ 808/324–1121, 800/392–1812 🌐 www.holualoainn.com ⇨ 7 rooms, 1 cottage 🍴 Free breakfast.*

$$ RENTAL FAMILY **Kona Coast Resort.** Just below Keauhou Shopping Center, this resort offers furnished condos on 21 acres with pleasant ocean views and a host of on-site amenities including two swimming pools, beach volleyball, a cocktail bar, BBQ grills, hot tub, tennis courts, fitness center, hula classes, equipment rentals, and children's activities. **Pros:** all rooms updated in January 2018; kid-friendly; away from the bustle of downtown Kailua-Kona. **Cons:** some units have parking lot views; not on the beach; time-share salespeople. $ *Rooms from: $230 ✉ 78-6842 Alii Dr., Keauhou ☎ 808/324–1721 🌐 www.shellhospitality.com ⇨ 268 units 🍴 No meals.*

$ RENTAL **Kona Magic Sands.** Cradled between a lovely grass park and Magic Sands Beach Park, this condo complex is great for swimmers, surfers, and sunbathers. **Pros:** next door to popular beach; affordable; oceanfront view from all units. **Cons:** studios only; some units are dated; no restaurant. *Rooms from: $150 77-6452 Alii Dr., Kailua-Kona 808/329–9393, 800/622–5348 www.konamagicsands.org 15 units No meals.*

$ HOTEL **Kona Tiki Hotel.** This three-story walk-up budget hotel about a mile south of downtown Kailua Village, with modest, pleasantly decorated rooms—all of which have lanai right next to the ocean—is simply the best deal in town. **Pros:** friendly staff; oceanfront lanai and pool; free parking. **Cons:** only one studio has a kitchen (others have fridges only); no TV in rooms; parking can be a challenge. *Rooms from: $119 75-5968 Alii Dr., Kailua-Kona 808/329–1425 www.konatikihotel.com 16 rooms Free breakfast.*

$$$ RENTAL **Outrigger Kanaloa at Kona.** The 18-acre grounds provide a peaceful and verdant background for this low-rise condominium complex bordering the Keauhou-Kona Country Club and within a five-minute drive of the nearest beaches (Kahaluu and Magic Sands). **Pros:** within walking distance of Keauhou Bay; three pools with hot tubs; shopping center and restaurants nearby. **Cons:** no restaurant on property; mandatory cleaning fee at check-in; A/C available only by paying a daily fee. *Rooms from: $280 78-261 Manukai St., Kailua-Kona 808/322–9625, 808/322–7222, 800/688–7444 www.outrigger.com 63 units No meals.*

$ RESORT FAMILY **Royal Kona Resort.** This is a great option if you're on a budget—the location is central; the bar, lounge, pool, and restaurant are right on the water; and the rooms feature contemporary Hawaiian decor with Polynesian accents. **Pros:** convenient location; waterfront pool; low prices. **Cons:** can be crowded; parking is tight; in-room Internet is extra. *Rooms from: $149 75-5852 Alii Dr., Kailua-Kona 808/329–3111, 800/222–5642 www.royalkona.com 430 rooms No meals.*

$$ RESORT FAMILY **Sheraton Kona Resort & Spa at Keauhou Bay.** What this big concrete structure lacks in intimacy, it makes up for with its beautifully manicured grounds, historical sense of place, stylish interiors, and stunning location on Keauhou Bay. Many rooms have great views of the bay and feel like they're right on the water, and each is decorated in a modern Polynesian style. **Pros:** cool pool; manta rays on view nightly; resort style at lower price. **Cons:** no beach; long walk from parking area; Wi-Fi can be spotty. *Rooms from: $240 78-128 Ehukai St., Keauhou 808/930–4900 www.sheratonkona.com 509 rooms No meals.*

THE KONA COAST

There are no resorts in this area, but there are plenty of fantastic B&Bs and vacation rental homes at Kealakekua Bay and in the hills above. The towns of Captain Cook and Kainaliu offer excellent dining and shopping options, and there are several coffee farms open for tours. You can get to the volcano in about 90 minutes, and you're also close to several less well-known but wonderful beaches, including Hookena and Honomolino. Kailua-Kona is a 30-minute drive from Captain Cook, while the great, sandy beaches of the Kohala Coast are an hour or more away.

SOUTH KONA

$ B&B/INN **Kaawa Loa Plantation.** Proprietors Mike Martinage and Greg Nunn operate a grand B&B on a 5-acre coffee farm above Kealakekua Bay. The home features a 2,000-square-foot wraparound veranda with excellent views of the bay and the entire Honaunau coast. **Pros:** gracious and friendly hosts; excellent breakfast; Hawaiian steam room. **Cons:** not within walking distance of bay; some rooms share a bath; 20 minutes from downtown. *Rooms from: $154 ✉ 82-5990 Napoopoo Rd., Captain Cook ☎ 808/323–2686 🌐 www.kaawaloaplantation.com 4 rooms, 1 cottage Free breakfast.*

$$ B&B/INN Fodor's Choice ★ **Kane Plantation Guesthouse.** The former home of late legendary artist Herb Kane, this luxury boutique guesthouse occupies a 16-acre avocado farm overlooking the South Kona coastline. **Pros:** sauna, hot tub, massage therapy room; upscale amenities; beautiful artwork. **Cons:** not on the beach; off the beaten track; 25 minutes to downtown. *Rooms from: $260 ✉ 84-1120 Telephone Exchange Rd., off Hwy. 11, Honaunau ↔ ¼ mile past mile marker 105, south of Captain Cook ☎ 808/328–2416 🌐 www.kaneplantationhawaii.com 3 suites Free breakfast.*

$ HOTEL **Manago Hotel.** This historical hotel is a good option if you want to escape the touristy thing but still be close to the water and attractions like Kealakekua Bay and Puuhonua O Honaunau National Historical Park. **Pros:** local color; rock-bottom prices; terrific on-site restaurant. **Cons:** not the best sound insulation between rooms; cheapest rooms share a community bath; some rooms have highway noise. *Rooms from: $72 ✉ 81-6155 Mamalahoa Hwy., Captain Cook ☎ 808/323–2642 🌐 www.managohotel.com 64 rooms, 42 with bath No meals.*

$$ B&B/INN **Mermaid Dreams Bed and Breakfast.** "Aloha" is the operative word at this mermaid-themed B&B a 10-minute drive from Kealakekua Bay. A self-proclaimed mermaid herself, hostess/proprietor Heather Reynolds takes guests on morning mermaid swims in the bay, where they can learn to swim while wearing a tail (she even has mermaid tails for rent if you need one). **Pros:** gracious hosts; beautifully landscaped grounds; fireside lounge outside for evening cocktails. **Cons:** not on the beach; no children under age 13; two-night minimum stay. *Rooms from: $177 ✉ 81-1031 Keopuka Mauka Rd., Kealakekua ☎ 808/649–9911 🌐 www.mermaiddreamsbedandbreakfast.com 5 rooms Free breakfast.*

$ RENTAL **South Kona Studio.** This little studio is a great find for travelers on a budget: not only does it offer a kitchenette and private barbecue area, but it's just up the hill from a secluded beach with great snorkeling. **Pros:** budget friendly; cozy interior; ocean views. **Cons:** rural location; two guests max; steep hill to beach. *Rooms from: $120 ✉ Kaohe Rd. and Hwy. 11, Captain Cook ☎ 808/938–1172 🌐 southkonastudio.com 1 room No meals.*

NORTH KONA

$$$$ RESORT FAMILY Fodor'sChoice ★ **Four Seasons Resort Hualalai.** Beautiful views everywhere, polished wood floors, custom furnishings and linens in warm earth and cool white tones, and Hawaiian fine artwork make this resort a peaceful retreat. **Pros:** beautiful location; gourmet restaurants; renowned service. **Cons:** not the best beach among the resorts; quite pricey; 20-minute drive to Kailua-Kona. *Rooms from: $889 ✉ 72-100 Kaupulehu Dr., Kailua-Kona ☎ 808/325–8000, 888/340–5662 ⊕ www.fourseasons.com/hualalai ⇨ 243 rooms No meals.*

THE KOHALA COAST

The Kohala Coast is home to most all of the Big Island's megaresorts. Dotting the coastline, manicured lawns and golf courses, luxurious hotels, and white-sand beaches break up the long expanse of black lava rock along Queen Kaahumanu Highway. Many visitors to the Big Island check in here and rarely leave the area. If you're looking to be pampered and lounge on the beach or by the pool all day with an umbrella drink in hand, this is where you need to be. You can still see the rest of the island since most of the hiking and adventure-tour companies offer pick-ups at the Kohala Coast resorts, and many of the hotels have connections to car-rental agencies (though the number of cars is limited, and you will need to book ahead). Housing developments in Waikoloa and the Kawaihae area have vacation homes for rent, primarily through local property management companies. However, some owners prefer to handle rentals themselves, through websites like ⊕ *www.vrbo.com* and ⊕ *airbnb.com*. Nothing in this area will be far from beaches, restaurants, airport, and good weather, but double-check that the home is located on the coast and not in North Kohala (which is beautiful but a bit of a drive to the beach). Be sure to ask about parking, pools, and cleaning deposits.

KOHALA CONDO COMFORTS

If you require anything not provided by the management, both the **Kings' Shops** (✉ *250 Waikoloa Beach Dr., Waikoloa* ☎ *808/886–8811*) and the **Queens' MarketPlace** (✉ *201 Waikoloa Beach Dr., Waikoloa* ☎ *808/886–8822*) in the Waikoloa Beach Resort are good places to go. There is a small general store with liquor department and several nice restaurants at the Kings' Shops. Across the street, Queens' MarketPlace also has a food court and sit-down restaurants, as well as a gourmet market where you can get pizza baked to order.

$$ RENTAL FAMILY **Aston Shores at Waikoloa.** Villas with terra-cotta–tile roofs are set amid landscaped lagoons and waterfalls at the edge of the championship Waikoloa Village Golf Course. **Pros:** good prices for the area; great location; kid-friendly. **Cons:** no restaurants; daily resort fee; older decor in some rooms. *Rooms from: $189 ✉ 69-1035 Keana Pl., Waikoloa ☎ 808/886–5001, 800/922–7866 ⊕ www.astonhotels.com ⇨ 120 rooms No meals.*

$$$$ RESORT FAMILY Fodor's Choice ★ **Fairmont Orchid Hawaii.** This first-rate resort overflows with tropical gardens, cascading waterfalls, sandy beach cove, beautiful wings with "open sesame" doors, a meandering pool, and renovated rooms with all the amenities. **Pros:** oceanfront location; excellent pool; aloha hospitality. **Cons:** top resort features come at a high price; 40-minute drive to Kailua-Kona; not the best beach among Kohala Coast resorts. *Rooms from: $499 ✉ 1 N. Kaniku Dr. ☎ 808/885–2000, 800/845–9905 🌐 www.fairmont.com 540 rooms No meals.*

$$$ B&B/INN **Hawaii Island Retreat at Ahu Pohaku Hoomaluhia.** Here, above the sea cliffs in North Kohala's Hawi, sustainability meets luxury without sacrificing comfort: the resort generates its own solar and wind-turbine power, harnesses its own water, and grows much of its own food. **Pros:** stunning location; ancient Hawaiian spiritual sites; eco-friendly. **Cons:** somewhat isolated and not within walking distance of restaurants; yurts don't have in-unit showers; some luxury details are lacking. *Rooms from: $298 ✉ 250 Maluhia Rd., off Hwy. 270 in Hawi, Kapaau ☎ 808/889–6336 🌐 www.hawaiiislandretreat.com 20 rooms Free breakfast.*

$$ RESORT FAMILY **Hilton Waikoloa Village.** Dolphins swim in the lagoon; pint-size guests zoom down the 175-foot waterslide; a bride poses on the grand staircase; a fire-bearing runner lights the torches along the seaside path at sunset—these are some of the typical scenes at this 62-acre megaresort. **Pros:** family-friendly; lots of restaurant and activity options, including 2 golf courses; close to retail shopping. **Cons:** gigantic and crowded; lots of kids; restaurants are pricey. *Rooms from: $301 ✉ 69-425 Waikoloa Beach Dr., Waikoloa ☎ 808/886–1234, 800/445–8667 🌐 www.hiltonwaikoloavillage.com 1,241 rooms No meals.*

$$$ RENTAL FAMILY Fodor's Choice ★ **Kolea at Waikoloa Beach Resort.** These modern, impeccably furnished condos appeal to the high-end visitor typically associated with the Mauna Lani Bay Hotel & Bungalows, with far more amenities than the average condo complex, including both an infinity pool and a sand-bottom children's pool at its oceanside Beach Club; a fitness center; and a hot tub. **Pros:** high design; close to beach and activities; resort amenities of nearby Hilton. **Cons:** pricey; no on-property restaurants; limited view from some units. *Rooms from: $375 ✉ Waikoloa Beach Resort, 69-1000 Kolea Kai Circle, Waikoloa ☎ 808/987–4519 🌐 www.kolea.com 53 units No meals.*

$$$$ RENTAL FAMILY Fodor's Choice ★ **Lava Lava Beach Club Cottages.** Spend the day swimming at the beach just steps away from your private lanai and fall asleep to the sound of the ocean at these four artfully decorated one-room cottages, located right on the sandy beach at Anaehoomalu Bay. It's a short stroll to the adjacent Lava Lava Beach Club bar/restaurant, which serves lunch and dinner daily. **Pros:** on the beach; fully air-conditioned; free Wi-Fi. **Cons:** beach is public, so there will be people on it in front of cottage; quite expensive; often booked. *Rooms from: $500 ✉ 69-1081 Kuualii Pl., Waikoloa ☎ 808/769–5282 🌐 www.lavalavabeachclub.com 4 cottages No meals.*

$$$$ RESORT **Mauna Kea Beach Hotel.** The grande dame of the Kohala Coast has long been regarded as one of the state's premier vacation resort hotels, and it borders one of the island's finest white-sand beaches, Kaunaoa.

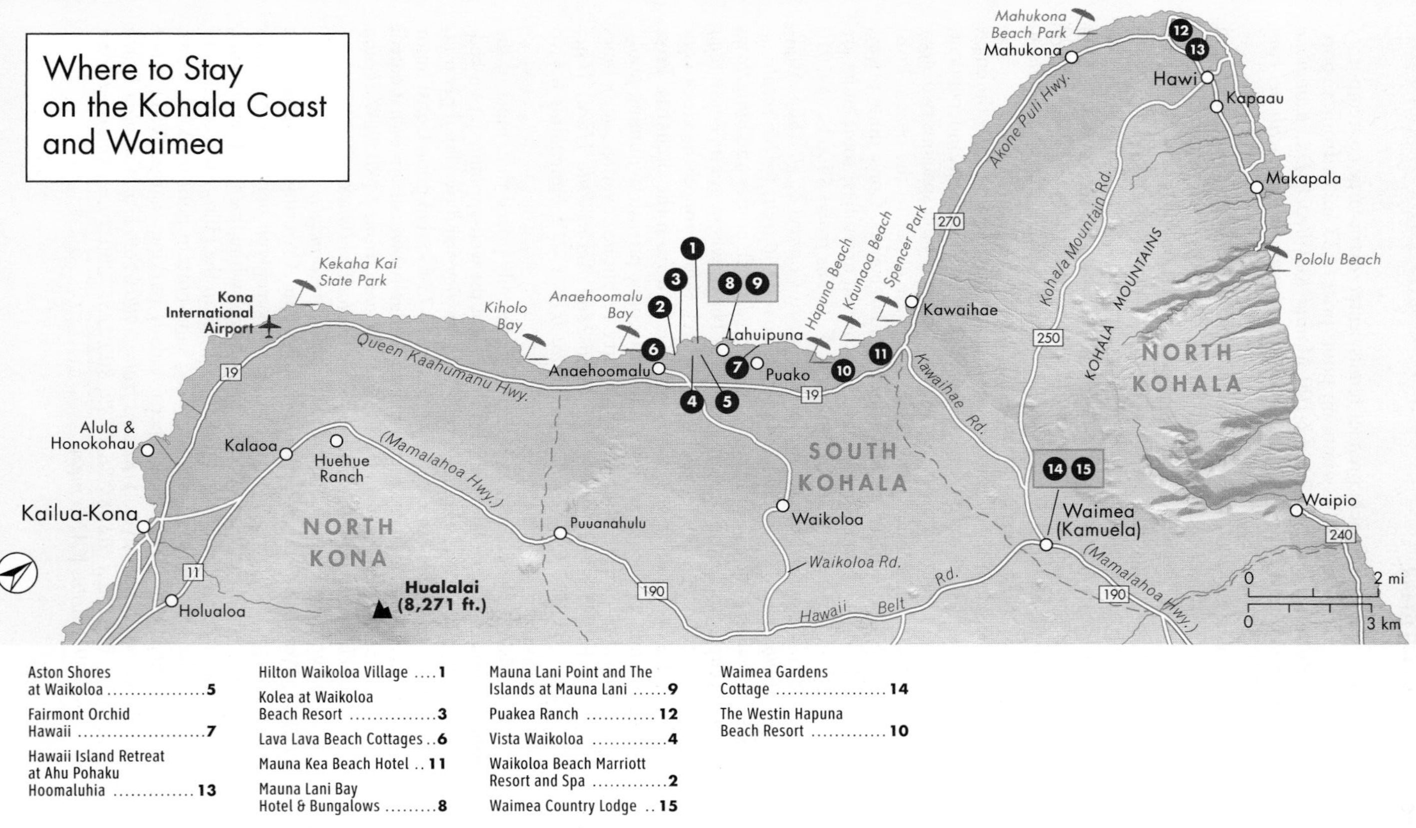

Aston Shores at Waikoloa 5
Fairmont Orchid Hawaii 7
Hawaii Island Retreat at Ahu Pohaku Hoomaluhia 13
Hilton Waikoloa Village 1
Kolea at Waikoloa Beach Resort 3
Lava Lava Beach Cottages ..6
Mauna Kea Beach Hotel ..11
Mauna Lani Bay Hotel & Bungalows 8
Mauna Lani Point and The Islands at Mauna Lani 9
Puakea Ranch 12
Vista Waikoloa 4
Waikoloa Beach Marriott Resort and Spa 2
Waimea Country Lodge ..15
Waimea Gardens Cottage 14
The Westin Hapuna Beach Resort 10

Pros: beautiful beach; premier tennis center; extra-large contemporary rooms. **Cons:** small swimming pool; pricey; 27 miles from airport. *Rooms from: $625 62-100 Mauna Kea Beach Dr., Kawaihae 808/882–7222, 866/977–4589 www.maunakeabeachhotel.com 252 rooms No meals.*

$$$$ RESORT FAMILY Fodor's Choice ★ **Mauna Lani Bay Hotel & Bungalows.** Popular with honeymooners and anniversary couples for decades, this elegant Kohala Coast classic is still one of the most beautiful resorts on the island, highlighted by a breathtaking, open-air lobby with cathedral-like ceilings, Zen-like koi ponds, and illuminated sheets of cascading water. **Pros:** beautiful design; award-winning spa; many cultural programs. **Cons:** no luau; on-going renovations; 26 miles from airport. *Rooms from: $429 68-1400 Mauna Lani Dr. 808/885–6622, 800/367–2323 www.maunalani.com 336 rooms, 5 bungalows No meals.*

$$$$ RENTAL **Mauna Lani Point and the Islands at Mauna Lani.** Surrounded by the emerald greens of a world-class oceanside golf course, private, independent, luxury condominiums at Islands at Mauna Lani offer spacious two-story suites, while Mauna Lani Point's villas are closer to the beach. **Pros:** friendly front desk; stellar views; extra-large units. **Cons:** quite pricey; individually owned units vary in decor and amenities; some units are a distance from the BBQ/pool area. *Rooms from: $400 68-1050 Mauna Lani Point Dr., Waimea (Hawaii County) 808/885–5022, 800/642–6284 www.classicresorts.com 66 units No meals.*

$$$ RENTAL FAMILY Fodor's Choice ★ **Puakea Ranch.** Four beautifully restored ranch houses and bungalows occupy this historic country estate in Hawi, where guests enjoy their own private swimming pools, horseback riding, round-the-clock concierge availability, and plenty of fresh fruit from the orchards. **Pros:** charmingly decorated; beautiful bathrooms; private swimming pools. **Cons:** 15 minutes to the beach; spotty cellphone coverage; sometimes windy. *Rooms from: $289 56-2864 Akoni Pule Hwy., Hawi 808/315–0805 www.puakearanch.com 4 bungalows No meals.*

$ RENTAL FAMILY **Vista Waikoloa.** Older and more reasonably priced than most of the condo complexes along the Kohala Coast, the well-appointed, two-bedroom, two-bath Vista condos have ocean views and two lanai per unit. **Pros:** reasonably priced; very large units; 75-foot lap pool. **Cons:** hit or miss on decor because each unit is individually owned; somewhat dated; some units don't allow children. *Rooms from: $180 Waikoloa Beach Resort, 69-1010 Keana Pl., Waikoloa 808/886–3594 www.waikoloabeachresort.com 122 units No meals.*

$$$$ RESORT FAMILY **Waikoloa Beach Marriott Resort and Spa.** Covering 15 acres with ancient fishponds, historic trails, and petroglyph fields, the Marriott has rooms with sleek modern beds, bright white linens, Hawaiian art, and private lanai. **Pros:** more low-key than the Hilton Waikoloa; sunset luau Wednesday and Saturday; sand-bottom pool for kids. **Cons:** some rooms lack views; expensive daily parking charge; Wi-Fi is not free (and expensive). *Rooms from: $400 69-275 Waikoloa Beach Dr., Waikoloa 808/886–6789, 800/228–9290 www.marriott.com 297 rooms No meals.*

$$ RESORT FAMILY **The Westin Hapuna Beach Resort.** More reasonably priced than its neighbor resorts and with direct access to the Big Island's largest sandy beach, this massive hotel has enormous columns and a terraced, open-air lobby with rotunda ceiling, curved staircases, and skylights. **Pros:** extra-large rooms, all ocean-facing; direct access to one of island's best beaches; resort has 18-hole championship golf course. **Cons:** fitness center a five-minute walk from the hotel; expensive daily resort fee; 27 miles from airport. *Rooms from: $425* *62-100 Kaunaoa Dr.* *808/880–1111, 866/774–6236* *wwwhapunabeachresort.com* *349 rooms* *No meals.*

WAIMEA

Though it seems a world away, Waimea is only about a 15- to 20-minute drive from the Kohala Coast resorts, which places it considerably closer to the island's best beaches than Kailua-Kona. Yet few visitors think to book lodging in this pleasant upcountry ranching community, where you can enjoy cool mornings and evenings after a day spent basking in the sun. To the delight of residents and visitors, there are some very good restaurants. Sightseeing is easy from here, too: Maunakea is a short drive away, and Hilo and Kailua-Kona are about an hour away. There aren't as many condos and hotels here, but there are some surprisingly good B&B and cottage options—as well as some great deals, especially considering their vantage point. Many have spectacular views of Maunakea, the ocean, and the beautiful green hills of Waimea.

$ HOTEL **Waimea Country Lodge.** In the heart of cowboy country, this modest ranch house–style lodge offers views of the green, rolling slopes of Maunakea. **Pros:** affordable; kitchenettes in some rooms; free coffee in morning. **Cons:** not near the beach; no pool; no breakfast. *Rooms from: $116* *65-1210 Lindsey Rd., Waimea (Hawaii County)* *808/885–4100, 800/367–5004* *www.waimeacountrylodge.com* *21 rooms* *No meals.*

$ RENTAL **Waimea Gardens Cottage.** Surprisingly luxe yet cozy and quaint, the three charming country cottages and one suite at this historical Hawaiian homestead are surrounded by flowering private gardens and a backyard stream. **Pros:** charming self-contained units; manicured gardens; cascading stream. **Cons:** requires 50% deposit within two weeks of booking and payment in full six weeks prior to arrival; cash only; three-night minimum stay. *Rooms from: $170* *Waimea (Hawaii County)* *Located off Kawaihae Rd., 2 miles from Waimea town* *808/885–8550* *www.waimeagardens.com* *No credit cards* *4 units* *Free breakfast* *Physical address given out only after a confirmed reservation.*

THE HAMAKUA COAST

A stretch of coastline between Waimea and Hilo is an ideal spot for those seeking peace, tranquility, and beautiful views, which makes it a favorite with honeymooners avoiding the big resorts. Several über-romantic B&Bs dot the coast, each with its own personality and views. As with Hilo, the beaches are an hour's drive away or more, so most visitors spend a few nights here and a few closer to the beaches on the west side. A handful of vacation homes provide an extra level of privacy for couples, groups, or families. Honokaa Town is a charming area with a couple of restaurants, banks, and convenience stores.

$$ B&B/INN **The Palms Cliff House Inn.** This handsome Victorian-style mansion, 15 minutes north of downtown Hilo and a few minutes from Akaka Falls, is perched on the sea cliffs 100 feet above the crashing surf of the tropical coast. **Pros:** stunning views; terrific breakfast; all rooms have private outdoor entrances. **Cons:** no pool; remote location means you have to drive 13 miles to Hilo for dinner; 50% booking deposit required. *Rooms from: $299 28-3514 Mamalahoa Hwy., Honomu 866/963–6076, 808/963–6076 www.palmscliffhouse.com 8 rooms Free breakfast.*

HILO

Hilo is the wettest part of the Big Island, full of waterfalls and rainforest hikes, a very different alternative to the warm, dry, white-sand beaches of the Kohala Coast. Locals have taken a greater interest in Hilo, signs showing in new restaurants, restored buildings, and a handful of clean and pleasant parks. Hilo has a few decent hotels, but no high-end resorts. Hilo's fantastic B&Bs have taken over lovely historical homes and serve breakfast comprising ingredients from backyard gardens. The volcano is only a 30-minute drive, as are the sights of the Puna region. There are also a number of nice beaches and surf spots, though nothing in the class of South Kohala.

$ B&B/INN **The Bay House.** Overlooking Hilo Bay and just steps away from the Singing Bridge near Hilo's historical downtown area, this small, quiet B&B is vibrantly decorated, with Hawaiian-quilted beds and private lanai in each of the three rooms. **Pros:** every room has its own oceanfront lanai; cliffside hot tub; Hilo Bay views. **Cons:** only two people per room; occasional street noise; no twin beds. *Rooms from: $175 42 Pukihae St., Hilo 888/235–8195, 808/961–6311 www.bayhousehawaii.com 3 rooms Free breakfast.*

$ HOTEL FAMILY **Dolphin Bay Hotel.** Units in this circa-1950s motor lodge are modest but charming, as well as clean and inexpensive; a glowing lava flow sign marks the office and bespeaks owner John Alexander's passion for the volcano. **Pros:** great value; full kitchens in all units; helpful and pleasant staff. **Cons:** no pool; no phones in the rooms; dated decor. *Rooms from: $109 333 Iliahi St., Hilo 808/935–1466 www.dolphinbayhotel.com 24 rooms No meals.*

$ HOTEL FAMILY **Grand Naniloa Hotel–A Doubletree by Hilton.** Hilo isn't known for its fancy resort hotels, but the recently renovated Grand Naniloa Hotel attempts to remedy that situation in grand fashion. **Pros:** within walking distance of botanical park and Coconut Island; rental kayaks, bikes, and SUPs; free golf at adjacent 9-hole course and driving range. **Cons:** some rooms don't have ocean views; limited parking spaces; small swimming pool. *Rooms from: $149 93 Banyan Dr., Hilo 808/969–3333 www.grandnaniloahilo.com 388 rooms No meals.*

$ B&B/INN **Hale Kai Bed & Breakfast.** On a bluff above Honolii surf beach, this modern 5,400-square-foot home is 2 miles from downtown Hilo and features four rooms—each with patio, deluxe bedding, and grand ocean views within earshot of the surf. **Pros:** delicious hot breakfast; panoramic views of Hilo Bay; smoke-free property. **Cons:** no kids under 13; just outside walking distance to downtown Hilo; occasional coqui frog noise. *Rooms from: $170* *111 Honolii Pl., Hilo* *808/935–6330* *www.halekaihawaii.com* *4 rooms* *Free breakfast.*

$ HOTEL FAMILY **Hilo Hawaiian Hotel.** This landmark hotel has large bayfront rooms offering spectacular views of Maunakea and Coconut Island on Hilo Bay. Street-side rooms overlook the golf course, and the hotel is within walking distance to the botanical park. **Pros:** Hilo Bay views; private lanai in most rooms; free parking. **Cons:** pricey breakfast buffet; older hotel; lacks amenities. *Rooms from: $169* *71 Banyan Dr., Hilo* *808/935–9361, 800/367–5004 from mainland, 800/272–5275 inter-island* *www.castleresorts.com* *286 rooms* *No meals.*

$ HOTEL **Hilo Seaside Hotel.** Ten minutes from the airport, this local-flavor destination is a friendly, laid-back, and otherwise peaceful place, with tropical rooms that have private lanai. **Pros:** private lanai; friendly staff; budget friendly with frequent specials. **Cons:** not walking distance to historic bayfront; hotel is a little dated; no restaurant. *Rooms from: $119* *126 Banyan Way, Hilo* *808/935–0821, 800/560–5557* *www.hiloseasidehotel.com* *133 rooms* *No meals.*

PUNA

Puna is a world apart—wild jungles, volcanically heated hot springs, and not a resort for miles around. There are, however, a handful of well-priced vacation homes and B&Bs. It's not your typical vacation spot: there are a few black-sand beaches (some of them clothing-optional), few dining or entertainment options, and quite a few, er, interesting locals. That said, for those who want to have a unique experience, get away from everything, witness molten lava flowing into the ocean (depending on activity), and don't mind the sound of the chirping coqui frogs at night, this is the place to do it. The volcano and Hilo are both within easy driving distance. Ongoing eruptions of Kilauea have made some parts of Puna inaccessible and closed roads.

$ RENTAL **Your Hawaiian Retreat.** A collection of three little rentals deep in the heart of Puna and well off the beaten path comprise this exotic destination on an organic farm. **Pros:** sustainable; breakfast items stocked for Mango and Avocado House; Ohana House good for groups. **Cons:** remote; not on the beach; three-night minimum stay. *Rooms from: $100* *13-809 Kamaili Rd., Pahoa* *6 miles south of Pahoa* *808/965–7088* *www.yourhawaiianretreat.org* *3 units* *No meals.*

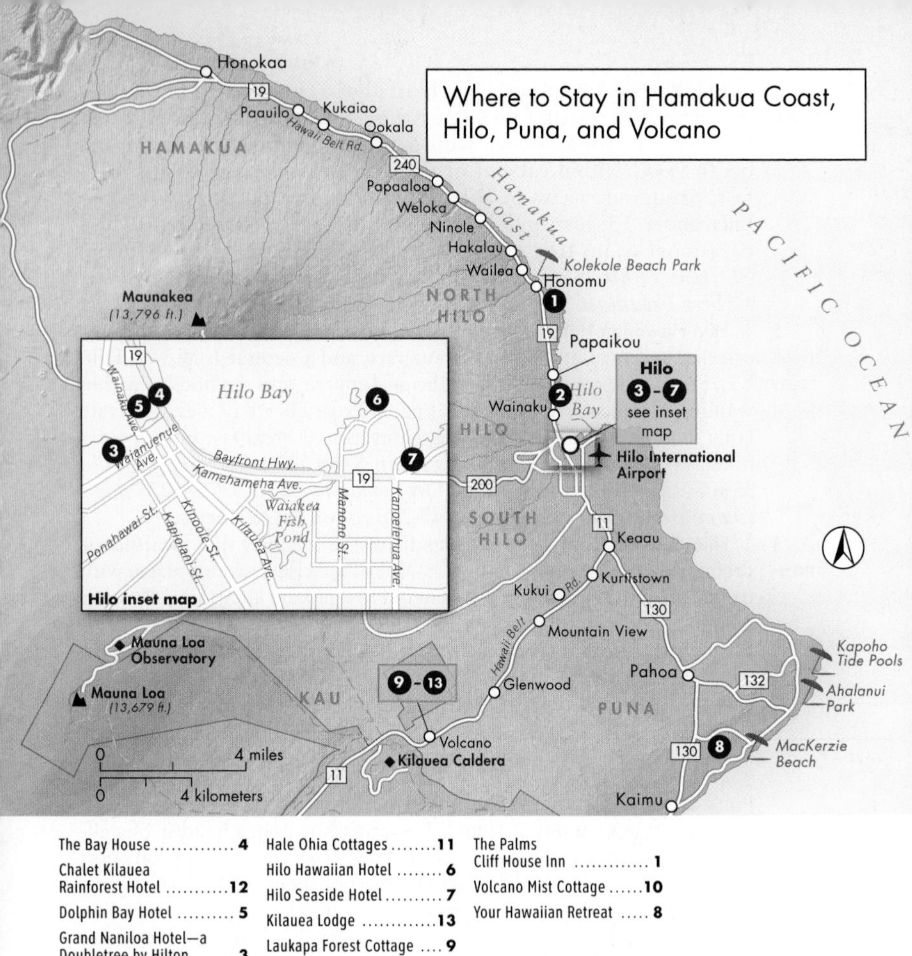

The Bay House **4**

Chalet Kilauea Rainforest Hotel **12**

Dolphin Bay Hotel **5**

Grand Naniloa Hotel—a Doubletree by Hilton **3**

Hale Kai Bed & Breakfast ... **2**

Hale Ohia Cottages **11**

Hilo Hawaiian Hotel **6**

Hilo Seaside Hotel **7**

Kilauea Lodge **13**

Laukapa Forest Cottage **9**

The Palms Cliff House Inn **1**

Volcano Mist Cottage **10**

Your Hawaiian Retreat **8**

HAWAII VOLCANOES NATIONAL PARK AND VICINITY

If you are going to visit Hawaii Volcanoes National Park—and you should—spend one night in Volcano Village. This allows you to see the glow of Halemaumau Crater at night—if there's activity, that is—without worrying about driving an hour or more back to your condo, hotel, or B&B. There are plenty of places to stay in the area, and many are both charming and reasonable. Volcano Village has just enough dining and shopping options to satisfy you for a day or two, and you're also close to Hilo, the Puna region, and Punaluu Black Sand Beach, should you decide to make Volcano your home base for longer.

$ RENTAL FAMILY **Hale Ohia Cottages.** A stately and comfortable Queen Anne–style mansion, Hale Ohia was built in the 1930s as a summer home for a wealthy Scotsman (the property is listed on the State Historic Register). **Pros:** unique architecture; free Wi-Fi and parking; privacy. **Cons:** no TVs; simple breakfast offerings; 30 minutes from downtown Hilo via car. *Rooms from: $149 ✉ 11-3968 Hale Ohia Rd., Volcano ☎ 808/967–7986, 800/455–3803 ⊕ www.haleohia.com 15 rooms Free breakfast.*

$ HOTEL FAMILY **Chalet Kilauea Rainforest Hotel.** This quirky, yet upscale accommodation features four artistically distinctive rooms that unveil beautiful views of the rain forest from a great location five minutes from Hawaii Volcanoes National Park. **Pros:** unique decor; friendly front desk; hot tub. **Cons:** space heaters; not close to the beach; can get cold at night. *Rooms from: $165 ✉ 19-4178 Wright Rd., Volcano ☎ 808/967–7786, 800/937–7786 ⊕ www.volcano-hawaii.com 4 rooms No meals.*

$$ HOTEL Fodor's Choice ★ **Kilauea Lodge.** A mile from the entrance of Hawaii Volcanoes National Park, this lodge was initially built as a YMCA camp in the 1930s; now it is a pleasant inn, tastefully furnished with European antiques, photographs, and authentic Hawaiian quilts. **Pros:** great restaurant; close to volcano; fireplaces. **Cons:** no TV or phone in lodge rooms; 45 minutes to downtown Hilo; few shopping options nearby. *Rooms from: $199 ✉ 19-3948 Old Volcano Rd., 1 mile northeast of national park, Volcano ☎ 808/967–7366 ⊕ www.kilauealodge.com 12 rooms, 4 cottages Free breakfast.*

$$$ RENTAL **Volcano Mist Cottage.** Both rustic and Zen, this magical cottage in the rain forest features cathedral ceilings, spruce walls, cork flooring, and amenities not usually found at Volcano vacation rentals, like bathrobes, a Bose home theater system, and Trek mountain bikes. **Pros:** private; outdoor Jacuzzi tub; upscale amenities. **Cons:** not large enough for families; 45 minutes from downtown Hilo; limited shopping options nearby. *Rooms from: $300 ✉ 11-3932 9th St., Volcano ☎ 808/895–8359 ⊕ www.volcanomistcottage.com 1 cottage Some meals.*

$ RENTAL Fodor's Choice ★ **Laukapa Forest Cottage.** Outfitted in cedar with beautiful architectural accents, this upscale accommodation in Volcano Village offers a romantic retreat perfect for couples, with no details spared to create a comfortable hideaway. **Pros:** unique architecture; well-equipped kitchen; upscale amenities including bags of Hawaii-grown coffee. **Cons:** no nightlife nearby; two-night minimum; limited shopping nearby. *Rooms from: $150 ✉ Volcano ☎ 808/967–7990, 877/967–7990 ⊕ www.volcano-places.com 1 No meals ☞ Physical address given only upon a confirmed reservation.*

KAU

Far from the West Hawaii resorts, Kau is a good place for those looking to get away from it all. You won't find a lot in terms of amenities, but there are several nice options including vacation rental cottages, B&B inns, and a condo resort complex with golf course. The main visitor attraction is the beautiful Punaluu Black Sand Beach, home of the endangered hawksbill turtle.

$$$$ B&B/INN **Kalaekilohana Inn and Retreat.** You wouldn't really expect to find a top-notch B&B in Kau, but just up the road from South Point, this grand residence offers large private suites with locally harvested hardwood floors, private lanai with ocean and mountain views, and big, comfy beds with high-thread-count sheets and fluffy down comforters. **Pros:** luxurious beds; beautiful decor reminscent of Old Hawaii; delicious breakfast. **Cons:** not for children under 12; no pool; very limited nearby shopping. *Rooms from: $369 ✉ 94-2152 South Point Rd., Naalehu ☎ 808/939–8052 🌐 www.kau-hawaii.com 4 rooms 🍴 Free breakfast.*

NIGHTLIFE AND PERFORMING ARTS

Updated by Kristina Anderson

If you're the sort of person who doesn't come alive until after dark, you might be a little lonely on the Big Island. Blame it on the sleepy plantation heritage. People did their cane raising in the morning, thus very limited late-night fun.

Still, there are a few lively bars on the island, a handful of great local playhouses, half a dozen or so movie houses (including those that play foreign and independent films), and plenty of musical entertainment to keep you happy.

Also, many resorts have bars and late-night activities and events, and keep pools and gyms open late so there's something to do after dinner.

And let's not forget the luau. These fantastic dance and musical performances are combined with some of the best local food on the island and are plenty of fun for the whole family.

NIGHTLIFE

KAILUA-KONA

BARS

Gertrude's Jazz Bar. You know you're in the right place when you climb the stairs to this little gem and notice that the steps are painted like piano keys. With a location in the heart of town, including a perfect view of Kailua Bay, this open-air club features an incredible variety of music (jazz, Latin, country, classical) and special events such as dance lessons, art nights, and themed dress-up parties. There's a small cover charge, but that helps pay the musicians a living wage. *✉ 75-5699 Alii Dr., Kailua-Kona ☎ 808/327–5299 🌐 gertrudesjazzbar.com.*

Humpy's Big Island Alehouse. Beer lovers appreciate the 36 craft brews on tap at this oceanfront restaurant, with dining downstairs and another bar upstairs that features live music and dancing. It's always busy with young local revelers. Humpy's food can be hit or miss, but it's great for late-hour grill items. Happy-hour specials are available weekdays 3 to 6, and the bar stays open until 2 am. ✉ *75-5815 Alii Dr., Kailua-Kona* ☎ *808/324–2337* 🌐 *www.humpyskona.com.*

Fodor's Choice ★ **Kona Brewing Co. Pub & Brewery.** The only genuine brewpub in Kona, this spot is beloved by locals and visitors alike. Good pizzas and salads, excellent locally brewed beer (go for the sampler and try four of them), and an outdoor patio with live music on Sunday night means this place can get crowded, especially on weekends. The location isn't at all scenic, but that's not the draw of the brewpub. The main entrance is at the end of Pawai Street, in the Old Industrial area. ✉ *75-5629 Kuakini Hwy., Kailua-Kona* ☎ *808/334–2739* 🌐 *www.konabrewingco.com.*

BEST SUNSET MAI TAIS

Huggo's on the Rocks (Kailua-Kona). Table dining in the sand, plus live music Friday and Saturday.

Kona Inn (Kailua-Kona). Wide, unobstructed view of the Kailua-Kona coastline.

Rays on the Bay at the Sheraton Kona Resort (Kailua-Kona). Fantastic sunset views from plush lounge chairs, followed by spotlighted glimpses of nearby manta rays.

Waioli Lounge in the Hilo Hawaiian Hotel (Hilo). A nice view of Coconut Island, live music Friday and Saturday nights.

Korner Pocket. A favored haunt of the South Kona crowd, Korner Pocket is tucked in the back of a strip mall. But don't let that deter you. It has fantastic affordable food, pool tables, and live music and dancing on the weekend with no cover. ✉ *81-970 Haleki'i St., Kealakekua* ☎ *808/322–2994.*

CLUBS

Huggo's on the Rocks. Jazz, Island, and classic-rock bands perform here nightly, and outside you may see people dancing in the sand. The food can miss, but the location, on the waterfront by the Royal Kona Resort, doesn't get better. Happy hour is 3 to 6. ✉ *75-5828 Kahakai Rd., at Alii Dr., Kailua-Kona* ☎ *808/329–1493* 🌐 *www.huggosontherocks.com.*

Laverne's Sports Bar. On weekends, live concerts are on tap. Sometimes Hawaiian and Island Music headliners perform here, like recording artist Anuhea and Rebel Souljahz. After 10, DJs spin on the ocean-breeze-cooled dance floor. ✉ *Coconut Grove Marketplace, 75-5819 Alii Dr., Kailua-Kona* ☎ *808/331–2633* 🌐 *www.laverneskona.com.*

THE KOHALA COAST

BARS

Luana Lounge. This wood-paneled lounge in the Fairmont Orchid has a large terrace and an impressive view. The bartenders are skilled, service is impeccable. The crowd is subdued, so it's a nice place for an early evening cocktail or after-dinner liqueur. There's live music at sunset until 9 pm. ✉ *Fairmont Orchid, 1 N. Kaniku Dr., Waimea (Hawaii County)* ☎ *808/885–2000* 🌐 *www.fairmont.com/orchid.*

4

HILO

BARS

Cronies Bar & Grill. A sports bar by night and hamburger joint by day, Cronies is a local favorite. When the lights go down, the bar gets packed. ✉ *11 Waianuenue Ave., Hilo* ☎ *808/935–5158* 🌐 *www.crofnieshawaii.com*.

PERFORMING ARTS

LUAU AND POLYNESIAN REVUES

KAILUA-KONA

Haleo Luau at the Sheraton Kona Resort & Spa at Keauhou Bay. On the graceful grounds of the Sheraton Kona Resort & Spa at Keauhou Bay, this popular luau (Monday and Friday evenings) takes you on a journey of song and dance, celebrating the historic Keauhou region, birthplace of King Kamehameha III. Before the show, you can participate in workshops on topics ranging from coconut-frond weaving to poi ball techniques. The excellent buffet is a feast of local favorites, including kalua pig, poi, ahi poke, chicken long rice, fish, and mango chutney. Generous mai tai refills are a plus, and a highlight is the dramatic fire-knife dance finale. ✉ *Sheraton Kona Resort & Spa at Keauhou Bay, 78-128 Ehukai St., Kailua-Kona* ☎ *808/930–4900* 🌐 *www.sheratonkona.com* 🎟 *$125*.

Island Breeze Luau. With traditional dancing showcasing the interconnected Polynesian roots of Hawaii, Samoa, Tahiti, and New Zealand, the "We Are *Ohana* (family)" luau is not a hokey tourist-trap event. These performers take their art seriously. The historic oceanfront location at King Kamehameha's former royal compound near Ahuena Heiau adds to the authenticity, and the bounty of food includes kalua pig cooked in an underground *imu* (oven). Validated parking at the hotel. ✉ *75-5660 Palani Rd., Kailua-Kona* ☎ *866/482–9775* 🌐 *www.islandbreezeluau.com* 🎟 *$101.77*.

KOHALA COAST

Hawaii Loa Luau. This gorgeous show is slickly produced and well choreographed, incorporating both traditional and contemporary music and dance, along with an array of beautiful costumes. It tells the tale of Hawaiiloa, the great navigator from Tahiti and of the celestial object— *Hokulea* , "Star of Gladness"—that guided him to the islands later named Hawaii. Presented under the stars at the Fairmont Orchid Hawaii on Saturdays, the meal offers several stations with a variety of Hawaiian and Hawaii regional dishes, and there's a full bar for mai tais and other tropical libations. ✉ *Fairmont Orchid Hawaii, 1 N. Kaniku Dr., Waimea (Hawaii County)* ☎ *808/885–2000, 808/326–4969* 🌐 *www.gatheringofthekings.com* 🎟 *$115*.

FAMILY **Legends of Hawaii Luau at Hilton Waikoloa Village.** Presented outdoors at the Kamehameha Court, this show is aptly subtitled, "Our Big Island Story." A delicious buffet offers Big Island–grown luau choices as well as more familiar fare and an open tropical bar. Pay a small fee and upgrade to Alii seating for a front-row vantage and your own buffet station. A children's station has kid favorites. Delicious desserts such as haupia cream puffs and Kona-coffee cheesecake top it all off. ✉ *Hilton*

Waikoloa Village, 69-425 Waikoloa Beach Dr., Waikoloa ☎ *808/886–1234* 🌐 *www.hiltonwaikoloavillage.com/resort-experiences/legends-of-hawaii-luau* 🎟 *$135.*

Mauna Kea Beach Hotel Clambake. The weekly clambake near the sand at Hau Tree beach restaurant features an extensive menu with oysters on the half shell, Manila clams, Dungeness crab legs, mussels, sashimi, and "all-you-can-eat" Keahole lobster. There's even prime rib and a dessert station. Live Hawaiian music is often accompanied by a graceful hula dancer. ✉ *Mauna Kea Beach Hotel, 62-100 Mauna Kea Beach Dr., Waimea (Hawaii County)* ☎ *808/882–5707* 🌐 *maunakeabeachhotel.com* 🎟 *$122.*

Waikoloa Beach Marriott Resort & Spa Sunset Luau. Overlooking the white sands of Anaehoomalu Bay, this Polynesian luau includes a spectacular Samoan fire dance performance as well as cultural music and dances from various Pacific Island cultures. Traditional dishes are served alongside more familiar Western fare, and there's also an open bar. ✉ *Waikoloa Beach Marriott Resort & Spa, 69-275 Waikoloa Beach Dr., Waikoloa* ☎ *808/886–8111* 🌐 *www.waikoloabeachresort.com* 🎟 *$106.25.*

FESTIVALS

There is a festival dedicated to just about everything on the Big Island. Some of them are small community affairs, but a handful of film, food, and music festivals provide quality entertainment for visitors and locals alike. The following are our favorites.

King Kamehameha Day Celebration Parade. Each June on the Saturday following King Kamehameha Day, at least 100 regal riders on horseback parade through historic Kailua Village, showing off the colorful flora and aloha spirit of Hawaii. The traditional royal pau riders include a queen and princesses representing the major Hawaiian Islands. A cultural festival with live music always follows. ✉ *Historic Kailua Village, Alii Dr., Kailua-Kona* ☎ *808/322–9944* 🌐 *www.konaparade.org.*

Kona Brewers Festival. At this lively annual celebration in early March by Kailua Pier, 70 types of ales and lagers by Hawaii and mainland craft brewers are showcased, along with culinary contributions by Hawaii Island chefs. There's also live "Blues & Brews" music, an art auction, a home brewers competition, fashion shows, a fun run, and a golf tournament. The multiday event is a community fundraiser and local favorite, but you must be 21 to attend. ■ TIP→ **Get tickets early online as this event always sells out.** ✉ *Courtyard King Kamehameha's Kona Beach Hotel, 75-5660 Palani Rd., Kailua-Kona* ☎ *808/331–3033* 🌐 *www.konabrewersfestival.com.*

Kona Coffee Cultural Festival. Held over 10 days in early November, on the Kona side, the longest-running food festival in Hawaii celebrates world-renowned Kona coffee. The highly anticipated festival includes coffee contests, serious cupping competitions, a lecture series, label contests, farm tours, and a colorful community parade featuring the newly crowned Miss Kona Coffee. During the Holualoa Village Coffee and Art Stroll, you can meet artists and sample estate coffees. ✉ *Kailua-Kona* ☎ *808/323–2006* 🌐 *www.konacoffeefest.com.*

Catch a Big Island sunset while hiking on mountaintops covered with lava fields.

Fodor's Choice ★ **Merrie Monarch Festival.** The mother of all Hawaii festivals, the world-class Merrie Monarch celebrates all things hula for one fantastic week every April in Hilo with competitions, activities, parades, and more. The esteemed event honors the legacy of King David Kalakaua, the man responsible for reviving fading Hawaiian cultural traditions including hula. The three-day hula competition is staged at the Edith Kanakaole Multi-Purpose Stadium during the first week following Easter Sunday. Hula *halau* (studios) worldwide come to perform both *kahiko* (ancient) and *auana* (modern) dance styles, both solo and in groups. **TIP→ You should reserve accommodations and rental cars up to a year in advance. Ticket requests must be mailed and postmarked after December 26 of the preceding year.** ✉ *Edith Kanakaole Multi-Purpose Stadium, 350 Kalanikoa St., Hilo* ☎ *808/935–9168* 🌐 *www.merriemonarch.com.*

THEATER

Kahilu Theatre. This intimate theater regularly hosts internationally acclaimed performers and renowned Hawaiian artists such as Jake Shimabukuro, Kealii Reichel, and the Brothers Cazimero. They share the calendar with regional and national modern-dance troupes, community theater and dance groups, ukulele festivals, and classical music performances. Even Barishnikov danced here. Tremendous community support revived the theater after it closed due to financial hardship in 2012. ✉ *Parker Ranch Center, 67-1185 Mamalahoa Hwy., Waimea (Hawaii County)* ☎ *808/885–6868* 🌐 *kahilutheatre.org.*

SHOPS AND SPAS

Updated by Karen Anderson

Residents like to complain that there isn't a lot of great shopping on the Big Island, but unless you're searching for winter coats, you can find plenty to deplete your pocketbook.

Dozens of shops in Kailua-Kona offer a range of souvenirs from far-flung corners of the globe and plenty of local coffee and foodstuffs to take home to everyone you left behind. Housewares and artworks made from local materials (lauhala, coconut, koa, and milo wood) fill the shelves of small boutiques and galleries throughout the island. Upscale shops in the resorts along the Kohala Coast carry high-end clothing and accessories, as do a few boutiques scattered around the island. Galleries and gift shops, many showcasing the work of local artists, fill historical buildings in Waimea, Kainaliu, Holualoa, and Hawi. Hotel shops generally offer the most attractive and original resort wear, but, as with everything else at resorts, the prices run higher than elsewhere on the island.

High prices are entirely too common at the island's resort spas, but a handful of unique experiences are worth every penny. Beyond the resorts, the Big Island is also home to independent massage therapists and day spas that offer similar treatments for lower prices, albeit usually in a slightly less luxurious atmosphere. In addition to the obvious relaxation benefits of any spa trip, the Big Island's spas have done a fantastic job incorporating local traditions and ingredients into their menus. Massage artists work with coconut or *kukui* (candlenut) oil, hot-stone massages are conducted with volcanic stones, and ancient healing techniques such as *lomilomi*—a massage technique with firm, constant movement—are staples at every island spa.

KAILUA-KONA

SHOPPING CENTERS

Coconut Grove Marketplace. This meandering oceanfront marketplace includes gift shops, cafés, restaurants (Outback Steakhouse, Humpy's Big Island Alehouse, Bongo Ben's, Lava Java, Foster's Kitchen, Fumi's Kitchen), sports bars, sushi, boutiques, a frozen-yogurt shop, Jack's Diving Locker, and several art galleries. At night, locals gather to watch outdoor sand volleyball games held in the courtyard or grab a beer and enjoy live music. This place is always hopping, and it has the biggest free parking lot in downtown Kailua-Kona. ✉ *75-5795–75-5825 Alii Dr., Kailua-Kona.*

Crossroads Shopping Center. This in-town shopping center includes a Safeway with an excellent deli section for on-the-go snacks, as well as a Walmart, where visitors can find affordable Hawaiian souvenirs, including discounted Kona coffee and macadamia nuts. For a quick meal, there's a Denny's, a Subway, and a Domino's, as well as a small sushi restaurant. Crystal Hair & Salon offers affordable hair and nail services, and accepts walk-ins. ✉ *75-1000 Henry St., Kailua-Kona* ☎ *808/329–4822.*

Kaloko Light Industrial Park. This large retail complex near the airport includes Costco, the best place to stock up on food if you're staying at a vacation rental. Kona Wine Market and the Spoon Shop feature gourmet finds, and Mrs. Barry's Kona Cookies sells beautifully packaged, delicious "souvenirs." ✉ *Off Hwy. 19 and Hina Lani St. , near Kona airport, Kailua-Kona.*

Keauhou Shopping Center. About 5 miles south of Kailua Village, this neighborhood shopping center includes KTA Superstore, Longs Drugs, Kona Stories bookstore, and a multiplex movie theater. Kenichi Pacific, an upscale sushi restaurant, and Peaberry & Galette, a café that serves excellent crepes, are favorite eateries joined by Bianelli's Pizza and Sam Choy's Kai Lanai, which is perched above the center. You can also grab a quick bite at Los Habaneros, Subway, or L&L Hawaiian Barbecue. ✉ *78-6831 Alii Dr., Kailua-Kona* ☎ *808/322–3000* 🌐 *www.keauhoushoppingcenter.com.*

Kona Commons. This downtown center features a Ross Dress for Less (for suitcases, shoes, swimsuits, and aloha wear), or Hawaiian Island Creations (for a great selection of surf gear, clothing, and accessories). Food and drink options include fast-food standbys like Dairy Queen, Subway, and Panda Express; as well as Ultimate Burger for local beef and delicious homemade fries, and Genki Sushi, where the goods are delivered via conveyer belt. ■ TIP→ **Target has fresh-flower leis for a fraction of the cost that local florists charge.** ✉ *75-5450 Makala Blvd., Kailua-Kona* 🌐 *www.konacommons.com.*

Kona Inn Shopping Village. Originally a hotel, the Kona Inn was built in 1928 to woo a new wave of wealthy travelers. As newer condos and resorts opened along the Kona and Kohala coasts, it was transformed into a low-rise, outdoor shopping village with dozens of clothing boutiques, art galleries, gift shops, and island-style eateries. Broad lawns with coconut trees on the ocean side provide a lovely setting for an afternoon picnic. The open-air Kona Inn Restaurant is a local favorite for sunset mai tais. ✉ *75-5744 Alii Dr., Kailua-Kona.*

ARTS AND CRAFTS

Fodor's Choice ★ **Hula Lamps of Hawaii.** Located near Costco in the Kaloko Light Industrial complex, this one-of-a-kind shop features the bronze creations of artist Charles Moore. Inspired by the vintage hula-girl lamps of the 1930s, Moore creates art pieces sought by visitors and residents alike. Mix and match with an array of hand-painted lamp shades. ✉ *73-5613 Olowalu St., Suite 2, Kailua-Kona* ✣ *Near Costco on upper road* ☎ *808/326–9583* 🌐 *www.hulalamps.com* ⏲ *Closed Sat.–Sun.*

Just Ukes. As the name suggests, this place is all about ukeleles—from music books to T-shirts to accessories like cases and bags. The independently owned shop carries a variety of ukuleles ranging from low-priced starter instruments to high-end models made of koa and mango. ✉ *Kona Inn Shopping Village, 75-5744 Alii Dr., Kailua-Kona* ☎ *808/769–5101* 🌐 *justukes.com.*

CLOTHING AND SHOES

Mermaids Swimwear. Local residents know that Mermaids is the best place in Kona to buy fashion-forward ladies' swimwear, sandals, hats, and other stylish beach accessories. The owner's husband, Tony, is a famous surfboard maker whose World Core surf shop is just around the corner. ✉ *Kona Inn Shopping Village, 75-5744 Alii Dr., Kailua-Kona* ☎ *808/329–6677.*

FOOD AND WINE

Fodor's Choice ★ **Keauhou Store.** This historical roadside store has been transformed into a combination convenience store, bakeshop, lunch stop, gift shop, and museum. When Kurt and Thea Brown purchased the property in 2010, they discovered a treasure trove of untouched inventory dating to the 1920s. These artifacts are on display, along with such gift items as koa bowls, cool retro T-shirts, and Kona coffee grown on-site. Stop by for fresh produce, beverages, spirits, ice cream, Thea's yummy fresh-baked cookies, or a burger or sandwich enjoyed on the outdoor lanai overlooking the coffee trees. ✉ *78-7010 Mamalahoa Hwy., Holualoa* ☎ *808/322–5203* 🌐 *www.keauhoustore.com* ⏲ *Closed Sun.*

Kona Wine Market. Near Costco, this longtime local wineshop carries both local and imported varietals (with more than 600 high-end wines), specialty liquors, 150 craft beers, gourmet foods, and even cigars. As a bonus, the market delivers wine and gift baskets to hotels and homes. ✉ *73-5613 Olowalu St., Kailua-Kona* ☎ *808/329–9400* 🌐 *www.konawinemarket.com.*

Mrs. Barry's Kona Cookies. For 30 years, Mrs. Barry and her family have been serving yummy home-baked cookies, including macadamia nut, white chocolate–macadamia nut, oatmeal raisin, and coffee crunch. Packaged in beautiful gift boxes or bags, the cookies make excellent gifts for family back home. Stop by on your way to Costco or the airport and pick up a bag or two or three. Ah heck, just ask Mrs. Barry to ship your stash instead. ✉ *73-5563 Maiau St., Kailua-Kona* ✣ *Below Costco in the New Industrial.* ☎ *808/329–6055* 🌐 *www.konacookies.com.*

Fodor's Choice ★ **The Spoon Shop.** Williams-Sonoma has nothing on this excellent gourmet kitchenware store that brims with every manner of accoutrement for the avid cook. There's a great selection of gourmet seasonings, olive oils, dressings, and condiments, and, if you're planning a party or reception during your stay in paradise, the Spoon Shop has items for every occasion. Cooking classes with guest chefs take place weekly in the store's high-end demo kitchen. ✉ *73-4976 Kamanu St. , #105, Kailua-Kona* ✣ *Near Home Depot in New Industrial area* ☎ *808/887–7666* 🌐 *www.thespoonshopkona.com* ⏲ *Closed Sun.*

Fodor's Choice ★ **Westside Wines.** Tucked away in a small downtown Kona retail center below Longs, this nifty gourmet wine and spirits shop offers restaurant-quality "wine list" wines at affordable prices. It's also the place to find large-format craft beers, French Champagne, single-malt Scotches, organic vodka, small-batch bourbon, rye whiskey, fresh bread, and artisan cheese from around the world. George Clooney's Casamigos tequila is the store's house tequila. A certified wine specialist, proprietor Alex Thropp was one of the state's top wholesale wine reps for decades. Wine tastings take place Friday and Saturday afternoons from 3 to 6. ✉ *75-5660 Kopiko St. #4, Kailua-Kona* ✣ *Below Longs Drugs in Lanihau Center* ☎ *808/329–1777.*

MARKETS

Alii Gardens Marketplace. This mellow, parklike market, open Tuesday through Sunday 10 to 5, features outdoor stalls offering tropical flowers, produce, soaps, kettle corn, coffee, coconut postcards, cookies, jewelry, koa wood, clothing, antiques and collectibles, handmade leis, silk flowers, and kitschy crafts. The homemade barbecue is a real hit. A food kiosk also serves shave ice, fish tacos, coconut water, fresh-fruit smoothies, and hamburgers. You can also book spearfishing excursions here. Free parking and Wi-Fi are available. ✉ *75-6129 Alii Dr., Kailua-Kona* ✣ *1½ miles south of Kona Inn Shopping Village* 🌐 *alii-gardens-marketplace.business.site* ⏲ *Closed Sun.*

Keauhou Farmers Market. Held once a week in the parking lot at Keauhou Shopping Center, this cheerful market is the place to go on Saturday morning for live music, local produce (much of it organic), goat cheese, honey, island-raised meat, flowers, macadamia nuts, fresh-baked pastries, Kona coffee, and plenty of local color. ✉ *Keauhou Shopping Center, 78-6831 Alii Dr., Kailua-Kona* 🌐 *www.keauhou-farmersmarket.com.*

Kona Inn Farmers' Market. An awesome florist creates custom arrangements while you wait at this touristy farmers' market near the ocean. There are more than 40 vendors with lots of crafts for sale as well as some of the best prices on fresh produce and orchids in Kona. The market is held in a parking lot at the corner of Hualalai Road and Alii Drive, Wednesday to Sunday 7 to 4. ✉ *75-7544 Alii Dr., Kailua-Kona.*

THE KOHALA COAST

SHOPPING CENTERS

Kawaihae Harbor Shopping Center. This almost-oceanfront shopping plaza houses the exquisite Harbor Gallery, which represents more than 200 Big Island artists. Stroll inside before or after your meal at the acclaimed Café Pesto, Kohala Burger and Taco, or Kawaihae Kitchen. Try the Big Island–made ice cream and shave ice (the best in North Hawaii) at local favorite Anuenue. Also here are Mountain Gold Jewelers and Kohala Divers. ✉ *61-3665 Akoni Pule Hwy. 270, Kawaihae.*

Kings' Shops at Waikoloa Beach Resort. Stores here include Martin & MacArthur, featuring koa furniture and accessories, and Tori Richard, which offers upscale resort wear, as well as a small Macy's and high-end chains Coach, Tiffany, L'Occitane, and Michael Kors. Gourmet offerings include Roy's Waikoloa Bar & Grill, A-Bay's Island Grill, Island Fish and Chips, and the Koa Table by Chef Ippy. Stock your hotel fridge with fresh local produce from the Kings' Shops Farmers Market, held Wednesday 8:30 to 2:30. ✉ *Waikoloa Beach Resort, 250 Waikoloa Beach Dr., Waikoloa* ☎ *808/339–7145* 🌐 *www.kingsshops.com.*

Queens' MarketPlace. The largest shopping complex on the Kohala Coast, Queens' MarketPlace houses fashionable clothing stores, jewelry boutiques, galleries, gift shops, and restaurants, including Sansei Seafood, Steakhouse and Sushi Bar; Daylight Mind; and Romano's Macaroni Grill. Island Gourmet Markets and Starbucks are also here, as is an affordable food court. Waikoloa Luxury Cinemas offers the ultimate movie experience and includes a restaurant called Bistro at the Cinemas. ✉ *Waikoloa Beach Resort, 201 Waikoloa Beach Dr., Waikoloa* ☎ *808/886–8822* 🌐 *www.queensmarketplace.net.*

The Shops at Mauna Lani. The best part about this complex is its roster of restaurants, which includes coffee, smoothies, and sandwich shops, Tommy Bahama Tropical Restaurant, Ruth's Chris Steakhouse, Under the Bodhi Tree café for gourmet vegetarian options, and Monstera for noodles and sushi. You can find tropical apparel at Jams World, high-end housewares at Oasis Lifestyle, and original art at a number of galleries. Kids love the "adventure ride" theater, boasting the only "4-D" screens in Hawaii. ✉ *68-1330 Mauna Lani Dr., Waimea (Hawaii County)* ☎ *808/885–9501* 🌐 *www.shopsatmaunalani.com.*

4

ARTS AND CRAFTS

Elements Jewelry & Fine Crafts. The beautiful little shop carries lots of original handmade jewelry made by local artists as well as carefully chosen gifts, including unusual ceramics, paintings, prints, glass items, baskets, fabrics, bags, and toys. ✉ *55-3413 Akoni Pule Hwy., next to Bamboo Restaurant, Hawi* ☎ *808/889–0760* 🌐 *www.elementsjewelryandcrafts.com.*

Hawaiian Quilt Collection. The Hawaiian quilt is a work of art that is prized and passed down through generations. At this store, you'll find everything from hand-quilted purses and bags to wall hangings and blankets. You can even get a take-home kit and sew your very own Hawaiian quilt. ✉ *Queens' MarketPlace, 69-201 Waikoloa Beach Dr., #305, Waikoloa* ☎ *808/886–0494* 🌐 *www.hawaiian-quilts.com.*

Island Pearls by Maui Divers. Among the fine jewelry at this boutique is a wide selection of high-end pearl jewelry, including Tahitian black pearls, South Sea white and golden pearls, and chocolate Tahitian pearls. Also here are freshwater pearls in the shell, black coral (the Hawaii state gemstone), and diamonds. Prices are high but so is the quality. ✉ *Queens' MarketPlace, 69-201 Waikoloa Beach Dr. , Space J11, Waikoloa* ☎ *808/886–4817* 🌐 *www.mauidivers.com.*

CLOTHING AND SHOES

As Hawi Turns. This landmark North Kohala shop, housed in the 1932 Toyama Building, brings sophisticated offerings in resort wear with items made of hand-painted silk in tropical designs by local artists. There are plentiful vintage treasures, jewelry, gifts, hats, bags, and toys, plus handmade ukuleles by local luthier David Gomes. ✉ *55-3412 Akoni Pule Hwy., Hawi* ☎ *808/889–5023.*

Blue Ginger. The Waikoloa branch of this fashion veteran offers really sweet matching aloha outfits for the entire family. There are also handbags, shoes, robes, jewelry, and lotions. ✉ *Queens' MarketPlace, 69-201 Waikoloa Beach Dr., Waikoloa* ☎ *808/886–0022* 🌐 *www.blueginger.com.*

GALLERIES

Ackerman Fine Art Gallery. This multiple-gallery/café is truly a family affair. Local artist Gary Ackerman's wife, Yesan, runs Ackerman Fine Art Gallery, featuring Gary's original oil paintings, fused glass art, and glass sculpture, plus works from other local artists. Down the street, Gary's daughter, Alyssa, and her husband, Ronnie, run Ackerman Gift Gallery, which showcases fine art, photography, and gifts, and their own King's View Cafe, located across from the historic King Kamehameha statue. ✉ *54-3878 Akoni Pule Hwy., Kapaau* ☎ *808/889–5138 Ackerman Fine Art Gallery* 🌐 *www.ackermangalleries.com.*

Harbor Gallery. Since 1990, this gallery has been enticing visitors with a vast collection of paintings and sculptures by more than 200 Big Island artists. There are also antique maps and prints, wooden bowls, paddles, koa furniture, jewelry, and glasswork. The shop hosts two annual wood shows. ✉ *Kawaihae Harbor Shopping Center, 61-3665 Akoni Pule Hwy., Kawaihae* ☎ *808/882–1510* 🌐 *www.harborgallery.biz.*

Rankin Gallery. Watercolorist and oil painter Patrick Louis Rankin showcases his own work at his shop in a restored plantation store next to the bright-green Chinese community and social hall, on the way to Pololu Valley. The building sits right at a curve in the road, in the Palawa *ahupuaa* (land division) past Kapaau. ✉ *53-4380 Akoni Pule Hwy., Kapaau* ☎ *808/889–6849* 🌐 *www.patricklouisrankin.net.*

WAIMEA

SHOPPING CENTERS

Parker Ranch Center. With a snazzy ranch-style motif, this shopping hub includes a supermarket, some great local eateries (Village Burger, Noodle Club, and Lilikoi Café), a coffee shop, natural foods store, galleries, and clothing boutiques. The Parker Ranch Store and Parker Ranch Visitors Center and Museum are also here. ✉ *67-1185 Mamalahoa Hwy., Waimea (Hawaii County)* 🌐 *www.parkerranchcenterads.com.*

Parker Square. Although the Gallery of Great Things is this center's star attraction, it's also worth looking in at the Waimea General Store; Sweet Wind, for books, chimes, and beads; and Sassafras, which sells locally crafted Hawaiian jewelry. Waimea Coffee Company satisfies with salads, sandwiches, and Kona coffee. ✉ *65-1279 Kawaihae Rd., Waimea (Hawaii County).*

ARTS AND CRAFTS

Fodor's Choice ★ **Gallery of Great Things.** You might lose yourself exploring the trove of fine art and collectibles in every price range at this gallery, which represents hundreds of local artists and has a low-key, unhurried atmosphere. The "things" include hand-stitched quilts, ceramic sculptures, vintage kimonos, original paintings, koa-wood bowls and furniture, etched glassware, Niihau shell lei, and feather art by local artist Beth McCormick. ✉ *Parker Square, 65-1279 Kawaihae Rd., Waimea (Hawaii County)* ☎ *808/885–7706* 🌐 *www.galleryofgreatthingshawaii.com.*

Wishard Gallery. A Big Island–born artist whose verdant landscapes and *paniolo* (cowboy)-themed paintings have become iconic throughout the Islands, Harry Wishard showcases his original oils at this Parker Ranch Center gallery, along with works by other renowned local artists like Kathy Long, Edward Kayton, and Lynn Capell. ✉ *Parker Ranch Center, 67-1185 Mamalahoa Hwy., D103, Waimea (Hawaii County)* ☎ *808/887–2278* 🌐 *www.wishardgallery.com.*

FOOD AND WINE

Fodor's Choice ★ **Kamuela Liquor Store.** From the outside it doesn't look like much, but this store sells the best selection of premium spirits, wines, and gourmet items on the island. Alvin, the owner, is a collector of fine wines, as evidenced by his multiple cellars. Wine-and-cheese tastings take place Friday afternoon from 3 to 6 and Saturday at noon—the store offers an extensive selection of artisanal cheeses from around the world. Favorites like duck mousse round out the inventory. ✉ *64-1010 Mamalahoa Hwy., Waimea (Hawaii County)* ☎ *808/885–4674.*

Fodor's Choice ★ **Waimea General Store.** Since 1970, this Waimea landmark at Parker Square has been a favorite of locals and visitors alike. Although specialty kitchenware takes center stage, the shop brims with local gourmet items, books, kimonos, and Hawaiian gifts and souvenirs. ✉ *Parker Square, 65-1279 Kawaihae Rd., Suite 112, Waimea (Hawaii County)* ☎ *808/885–4479* 🌐 *www.waimeageneralstore.com.*

THE HAMAKUA COAST

ARTS AND CRAFTS

Glass from the Past. Near Akaka Falls, this is a fun place to shop for a quirky gift or just to poke around. The store is chock-full of old Hawaiian bottles, antiques, vintage clothing, Japanese collectibles, and interesting ephemera. There's often even a "free" table out front to add to the discovery. ✉ *28-1672 Old Mamalahoa Hwy., Honomu* ☎ *808/963–6449.*

GALLERIES

Waipio Valley Artworks. In this quaint gallery in a vintage home, you can find finely crafted wooden bowls, koa furniture, paintings, and jewelry—all made by local artists. There's also a great little café where you can pick up a sandwich or ice cream before descending into Waipio Valley. ✉ *485416 Kukuihaele Rd., Kukuihaele* ☎ *808/775–0958* 🌐 *www.waipiovalleyartworks.com.*

Woodshop Gallery. Run by local artists Peter and Jeanette McLaren, this Honomu gallery showcases their woodwork and photography collections along with beautiful ceramics, photography, glass, and paintings from other Big Island artists. The McLarens also serve up plate lunches, shave ice, homemade ice cream, and espresso to hungry tourists in the adjoining café. The historical building still has a working soda fountain dating from 1935. ✉ *28-1690 Old Government Rd., Honomu* ✣ *2 miles from Akaka Falls, 13 miles north of Hilo* ☎ *808/963–6363* 🌐 *www.woodshopgallery.com.*

4

HILO

SHOPPING CENTERS

Prince Kuhio Plaza. The Big Island's most comprehensive mall has indoor shopping, entertainment (a multiplex), and dining, including KFC, Hot Dog on a Stick, Cinnabon, Genki Sushi, the island's only IHOP, and Maui Tacos. The kids might like the arcade (near the food court), while you enjoy the stores, anchored by Macy's and Sears. ✉ *111 E. Puainako St., Hilo* ☎ *808/959–3555* 🌐 *www.princekuhioplaza.com.*

ARTS AND CRAFTS

Most Irresistible Shop in Hilo. This place lives up to its name by stocking unique gifts from around the Pacific, be it pure Hawaiian ohia lehua honey, ka'u coffee, aloha wear, or tinkling wind chimes. ✉ *256 Kamehameha Ave., Hilo* ☎ *808/935–9644.*

BOOKS AND MAGAZINES

Fodor's Choice ★ **Basically Books.** Boasting a new location, this legendary shop stocks one of Hawaii's largest selections of maps, including topographical and relief maps, and Hilo's largest selection of Hawaiian music. Of course, it also has a wealth of books about Hawaii, including great choices for children. If you're in need of an umbrella on a rainy Hilo day, this bookstore has plenty of them. Open seven days a week. ✉ *1672 Kamehameha Ave., Hilo* ⊕ *Near Ken's House of Pancakes* ☎ *808/961–0144,* 🌐 *www.basicallybooks.com.*

CLOTHING AND SHOES

Sig Zane Designs. This acclaimed boutique sells distinctive island wearables with bold colors and motifs designed by the legendary Sig Zane, known for his artwork honoring native flora and fauna. All apparel is handcrafted in Hawaii, and is often worn by local celebrities and businesspeople. ✉ *122 Kamehameha Ave., Hilo* ☎ *808/935–7077* 🌐 *www.sigzane.com.*

FOOD

Fodor's Choice ★ **Big Island Candies.** A local legend in the cookie- and chocolate-making business, Big Island Candies is a must-see for connoisseurs of fine chocolates. The packaging is first-rate, which makes these world-class confections the ideal gift or souvenir. Enjoy a free cookie sample and a cup of Kona coffee as you watch through a window as sweets are being made. The store has a long list of interesting and tasty products, but it is best known for its chocolate-dipped shortbread cookies. ✉ *585 Hinano St., Hilo* ☎ *808/935–8890* 🌐 *www.bigislandcandies.com.*

Fodor's Choice ★ **Sugar Coast Candy.** Located on the bayfront in downtown Hilo, this beautifully decorated candy boutique, owned by interior decorator Carolyn Arashiro, is a blast from the past, featuring an amazing array of nostalgic candies, artisan chocolates, and wooden barrels overflowing with saltwater taffy and other delights. ✉ *274 Kamehameha Ave., Hilo* ☎ *808/935–6960.*

Two Ladies Kitchen. This hole-in-the-wall confections shop has made a name for itself thanks to its pillowy *mochi* (Japanese rice pounded into a sticky paste and molded into shapes). The proprietors are best known for their huge ripe strawberries wrapped in a white mochi covering, which won't last as long as a box of chocolates—most mochi items are good for only two or three days. To guarantee you get your fill, call and place your order ahead of time. ✉ *274 Kilauea Ave., Hilo* ☎ *808/961–4766* ⏲ *Closed Sun. and Mon.*

MARKETS

Fodor's Choice ★ **Hilo Farmers Market.** The 200 vendors here—stretching a couple of blocks at the bay front—sell a profusion of tropical flowers, locally grown produce, aromatic honey, tangy goat cheese, hot breakfast and lunch items, and fresh baked specialties at extraordinary prices. This colorful, open-air market—the largest and most popular on the island—opens for business Wednesday and Saturday from 6 am to 4 pm. A smaller version on the other days features more than 30 vendors. ✉ *Kamehameha Ave. and Mamo St., Hilo* ☎ *808/933–1000* 🌐 *www.hilofarmersmarket.com.*

SPAS

Most of the full-service spas on the Big Island are at the resorts. With the exception of the Four Seasons Spa at Hualalai, these spas are open to anyone. In fact, many of the hotels outsource spa management, and there is no price difference for guests and nonguests, although guests can receive in-room services.

KAILUA-KONA

Pau Hana Massage. This top-quality, upscale studio offers affordable massage at a convenient location in the heart of downtown Kailua-Kona. Longtime Kona *kamaainas,* this husband-and-wife team serves up authentic Hawaiian hospitality and pampering. ✉ *75-5741 Kuakini Hwy., Bldg. A, Kailua-Kona* ☎ *808/327–5664* 🌐 *www.pauhanamassage.com.*

The Spa at Hualalai. For the exclusive use of Four Seasons Resort guests and members, this spa features 28 massage treatment areas. Tropical breezes waft through 14 outdoor massage *hales* (huts), situated in beautiful garden settings. The therapists are top-notch, and a real effort is made to incorporate local traditions. Apothecary services allow you to customize your treatment with almost 40 ingredients like kukui nuts, Hawaiian salts, and coconut. Massage options range from traditional lomilomi to Thai. ✉ *Four Seasons Resort Hualalai, 72-100 Kaupulehu Dr., Kailua-Kona* ☎ *808/325–8000* 🌐 *www.fourseasons.com/hualalai/spa.*

THE KONA COAST

Mamalahoa Hot Tubs and Massage. Tucked into a residential neighborhood above Kealakekua, this is a welcome alternative to the large Kohala Coast resort spas. It feels like a secret hideaway aglow with tiki torches, and offers Hawaiian lomilomi and hot-stone massages at affordable prices. ■ **TIP→ Soaking tubs, enclosed in their own thatched gazebos with roof portholes for stargazing, are great for a couple's soak.** ✉ *81-1016 St. John's Rd., Kealakekua* ☎ *808/323–2288* 🌐 *www.mamalahoa-hottubs.com* ⏲ *Closed Sun.–Tues.*

THE KOHALA COAST

Hawaii Island Retreat Maluhia Spa. This remote and elegant sanctuary in North Kohala offers three artfully appointed indoor treatment rooms and two outdoor massage platforms that overlook the valley. The spa is first-rate, with handcrafted wooden lockers, rain-style showerheads, and a signature line of lotions and scrubs that's made locally. The owners also create their own scrubs and wraps from ingredients grown on the property. The Papaya Delight lives up to its name and features roasted ground papaya seeds mixed with goat yogurt and geranium. The slate of massages includes lomilomi, Thai, and deep tissue. ⊠ *250 Maluhia Rd., Kapaau* ☎ *808/889–6336* 🌐 *www.hawaiiislandretreat.com.*

Fodor's Choice ★ **Mauna Lani Spa.** This is a one-of-a-kind experience with a mix of traditional standbys (lomilomi massage, moisturizing facials) and innovative treatments influenced by ancient traditions and incorporating local products. Most treatments take place in outdoor thatched hales surrounded by lava rock. An exception is Watsu therapy, in which clients are cradled in the arms of a certified therapist in warm saltwater in a 1,000-square-foot grotto between two lava tubes. (It's great for people with disabilities who can't enjoy traditional massage.) Black volcanic clay applications are offered in a natural lava sauna. Aesthetic treatments incorporate high-end products from Epicuran and Emminence, so facials have lasting therapeutic effects. The spa also offers a full regimen of fitness and yoga classes. ⊠ *Mauna Lani Bay Hotel & Bungalows, 68-1365 Pauoa Rd., Waimea (Hawaii County)* ☎ *808/881–7922* 🌐 *www.maunalani.com.*

Fodor's Choice ★ **Spa Without Walls at the Fairmont Orchid Hawaii.** This ranks among the best massage facilities on the island, partially due to the superlative setting—private massage areas are situated amid the waterfalls, saltwater pools, and meandering gardens, as well as right on the beach. ■ TIP→ **The Fairmont Orchid is one of the few resorts on the island to offer beachside massage.** Splurge on the 110-minute Alii Experience, with hot coconut oil treatments, lomilomi, and hot-stone massage. Other great treatments include caviar facials, fragrant herbal wraps, and coffee-and-vanilla scrubs. Where else can you relax to the sounds of cascading waterfalls while watching tropical yellow tang swim beneath you through windows in the floor? ⊠ *Fairmont Orchid Hawaii, 1 N. Kaniku Dr., Waimea (Hawaii County)* ☎ *808/887–7540* 🌐 *www.fairmont.com/orchid-hawaii/spa/.*

HILO

Spa Vive. Occupying a circa-1897 house just above Hilo Town on the way to Rainbow Falls, this charming day spa and salon features 10 treatment rooms, a nail and hair salon, a hot tub, a dry sauna, and aesthetician services. Body scrubs and waxings are also available upon request. ⊠ *306 Lehua St., Hilo* ✣ *Drive up Waianuenue Ave., turn right at Keawe, and proceed across small bridge into a residential neighborhood* ☎ *808/930–3830* 🌐 *www.spavive.com.*

WATER SPORTS AND TOURS

Updated by Kristina Anderson

The ancient Hawaiians, who took much of their daily sustenance from the ocean, also enjoyed playing in the water. In fact, surfing was the sport of kings. Though it's easy to be lulled into whiling away the day baking in the sun on a white-, gold-, black-, or green-sand beach, getting into or onto the water is a highlight of most trips.

All of the Hawaiian Islands are surrounded by the Pacific Ocean, and blessed with a temperate latitude, making them some of the world's greatest natural playgrounds. But certain experiences are even better on the Big Island: nighttime diving trips to see manta rays; deep-sea fishing in Kona's fabled waters, where dozens of Pacific blue marlin of 1,000 pounds or more have been caught; and kayaking among the dolphins in Kealakekua Bay, to name a few.

From almost any point on the Big Island, the ocean is nearby. Whether it's body boarding and snorkeling or kayaking and surfing, there is a water sport for everyone. For most activities, you can rent gear and go it alone. Or book a group excursion with an experienced guide, who offers convenience and security, as well as special insights into Hawaiian marine life and culture. Want to try surfing? Contrary to what you may have heard, there *are* waves on the Big Island. You can take lessons that promise to have you standing the first day out.

The Kona and Kohala coasts of West Hawaii boast the largest number of ocean sports outfitters and tour operators. They operate from the small-boat harbors and piers in Kailua-Kona, Keauhou, Kawaihae, and at the Kohala Coast resorts. There are also several outfitters in the East Hawaii and Hilo areas.

As a general rule, the waves are gentler here than on the other Islands, but there are a few things to be aware of. First, don't turn your back on the ocean. It's unlikely, but if conditions are right, a wave could come along and push you face-first into the sand or drag you out to sea. Second, when the Big Island does experience high surf, dangerous conditions prevail and can change rapidly. Watch the ocean for a few minutes before going out. If it looks rough, don't chance it. Third, realize that ultimately you must keep yourself safe. We strongly encourage you to obey lifeguards and weather advisories, and heed the advice of outfitters from whom you rent equipment, and even from locals on shore. It could save your trip, or even your life.

BODY BOARDING AND BODYSURFING

According to the movies, in the Old West there was always friction between cattle ranchers and sheep ranchers. A somewhat similar situation exists between surfers and body boarders (and between surfers and stand-up paddleboarders). That's why they generally keep to their own separate areas. Often the body boarders, who lie on their stomachs on shorter boards, stay closer to shore and leave the outside breaks to the board surfers. Or the board surfers may stick to one side of the beach and the body boarders to the other. The truth is, body boarding (often called "boogie boarding," in homage to the first commercial

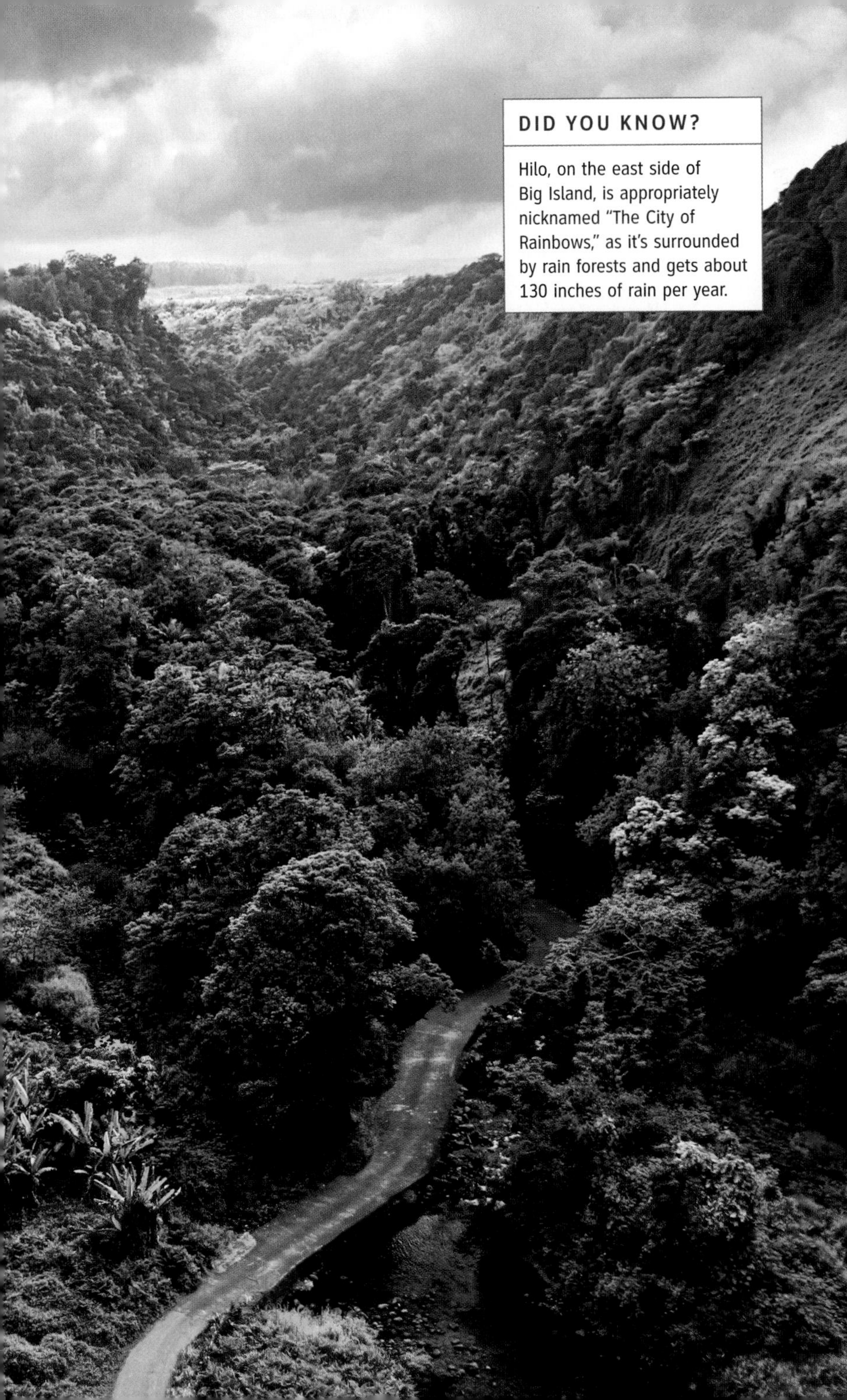

DID YOU KNOW?

Hilo, on the east side of Big Island, is appropriately nicknamed "The City of Rainbows," as it's surrounded by rain forests and gets about 130 inches of rain per year.

manufacturer of this slick, little, flexible-foam board) is a blast. Most surfers also sometimes carve waves on a body board, no matter how much of a purist they claim to be. ■ TIP→ **Novice body boarders should catch shore-break waves only. Ask lifeguards or locals for the best spots.** You'll need a pair of short fins to get out to the bigger waves offshore (not recommended for newbies). As for bodysurfing, just catch a wave and make like Superman going faster than a speeding bullet.

BEST SPOTS

Hapuna Beach State Recreation Area. Often considered one of the top 10 beaches in the world, Hapuna Beach State Recreation Area offers fine white sand, turquoise water, and easy rolling surf on most days, making it great for bodysurfing and body boarding at all levels. Ask the lifeguards—who only cover areas south of the rocky cliff that juts out near the middle of the beach—about conditions before heading into the water, especially in winter. Sometimes northwest swells create a dangerous undertow. ✉ *Hwy. 19, near mile marker 69, just south of Mauna Kea Hotel, Kohala Coast* 🌐 *dlnr.hawaii.gov/dsp/parks/hawaii/hapuna-beach-state-recreation-area.*

Honolii Cove. North of Hilo, this is the best body-boarding spot on the east side of the island. ✉ *Off Hwy. 19, near mile marker 4, Hilo.*

Magic Sands Beach Park (White Sands Beach). This white-sand, shore-break cove is great for beginning to intermediate bodysurfing and body boarding. Sometimes in winter, much of the sand here washes out to sea and forms a sandbar just offshore, creating fun wave conditions. Also known as White Sands, it's popular and can get crowded with locals, especially when school is out. Watch for nasty rip currents at high tide. ■ TIP→ **If you're not using fins, wear reef shoes for protection against sharp rocks.** ✉ *Alii Dr., just north of mile marker 4, Kailua-Kona.*

EQUIPMENT

Equipment-rental shacks are located at many beaches and boat harbors, along the highway, and at most resorts. Body-board rental rates are around $12–$15 per day and around $60 per week. Ask the vendor to throw in a pair of fins—some will for no extra charge.

Orchidland Surfboards & Surf Shop. This venerable shop—in business more than 40 years—carries a wide variety of surf and other water sports equipment for sale or rent. They stock professional custom surfboards, body boards, and surf apparel. Owner Stan Lawrence, famous for his "Drainpipe" legacy, was probably the last person to surf that famous break before lava flows claimed the Kalapana area (the rubber slippers he left on the beach burned up before he got out of the water). Old photos, surf posters, and memorabilia on the walls add to the nostalgia. Through the shop, he hosts surf contests here and on Oahu, and does the daily surf report for local radio stations. Located in the heart of historic downtown Hilo, this surf shop is as authentic as they get. ✉ *262 Kamehameha Ave., Hilo* ☎ *808/935–1533* 🌐 *www.orchidlandsurf.com* 🎟 *From $15 body board; $25 surfboard.*

Fodor's Choice ★ **Pacific Vibrations.** This family-owned surf shop—in business more than 35 years—holds the distinction of being the oldest, smallest surf shop in the world. Even at a compact 400 square feet, this place stocks tons of equipment, surf wear and gear, sunglasses, and GoPro cameras. You can rent a surfboard, stand-up paddleboard, or a body board, but you have to buy or bring your own fins. Located oceanfront in downtown Kailua Town, it is tucked away fronting a vintage cul de sac, and is worth a stop just for the cool Hawaii surf vibe. ✉ *75-5702 Likana La., #B, at Alii Dr., Kailua-Kona* ☎ *808/329–4140* 🎫 *$15/day, surfboard; $15/hr., paddleboard; $5/day, body board.*

DEEP-SEA FISHING

4

The Kona Coast has some of the world's most exciting "blue-water" fishing. Although July, August, and September are peak months, with the best fishing and a number of tournaments, charter fishing goes on year-round. You don't have to compete to experience the thrill of landing a Pacific blue marlin or other big-game fish. Some 60 charter boats, averaging 26 to 58 feet, are available for hire, all of them out of **Honokohau Harbor,** north of Kailua-Kona.

The Kona Coast is world-famous for the presence of large marlin, particularly the Pacific blue. In fact, it's also known as "Grander Alley" for the fish caught here that weigh more than 1,000 pounds. The largest blue marlin on record was caught in 1984 and weighed 1,649 pounds. In total, more than 60 Granders have been reeled in here by top sportfishing teams.

For an exclusive charter, prices generally range from $600 to $950 for a half-day trip (about four hours) and $800 to $1,600 for a full day at sea (about eight hours). For share charters, rates are about $100 to $140 per person for a half day and $200 for a full day. If fuel prices increase, expect charter costs to rise. Most boats are licensed to take up to six passengers, in addition to the crew. Tackle, bait, and ice are furnished, but you usually have to bring your own lunch. You won't be able to keep your catch, although if you ask, many captains will send you home with a few fillets.

Honokohau Harbor's Fuel Dock. Show up around 11 am and watch the weigh-in of the day's catch from the morning charters, or around 3:30 pm for the afternoon charters, especially during the summer tournament season. Weigh-ins are fun when the big ones come in, but these days, with most of the marlin being released, it's not a sure thing. **■TIP→ On Kona's Waterfront Row, look for the "Grander's Wall" of anglers with their 1,000-pound-plus prizes.** There's also a display at the Kona Inn. ✉ *Honokohau Harbor, Kealakehe Pkwy. at Hwy. 11, Kailua-Kona.*

BOATS AND CHARTERS

Bwana Sportfishing. Full-, half-, quarter-, three-quarter-day, and overnight charters are available on the 46-foot *Bwana.* The boat features the latest electronics, top-of-the-line equipment, and air-conditioned cabins. Captain Teddy comes from a fishing family; father Pete was a legend on Kona waters for decades. ✉ *Honokohau Harbor, Slip H-17, 74-381 Kealakehe Pkwy., just south of Kona airport, Kailua-Kona* ☎ *808/936–5168* 🎫 *From $1,250.*

Charter Locker. This experienced company offers half- and full-day charter fishing trips on 36- to 53-foot vessels. Featured boats include *Kona Blue, JR's Hooker, Strong Persuader,* and *Kila Kila*. Rates depend on the boat. ✉ *Honokohau Harbor #16, 74-381 Kealakehe Pkwy., just south of Kona airport, Kailua-Kona* ☎ *808/326–2553* 🌐 *www.charterlocker.com* 🎟 *From $395.*

Humdinger Sportfishing. This game-fisher guide has more than five decades of fishing experience in Kona waters, and the expert crew are marlin specialists. The 37-foot *Humdinger* has the latest in electronics and top-line rods and reels. Book online for discounts and specials. ✉ *Honokohau Harbor, Slip B-4, 74-381 Kealakehe Pkwy., Kailua-Kona* ☎ *808/425–9225, 800/926–2374, 808/425–9228 boat phone* 🌐 *www.humdingersportfishing.com* 🎟 *From $399.*

Jeff Rogers Charters. One of Kona's friendliest "old salts," Captain Jeff has been leading personalized big game and other fishing charters since 1982. Using a few tricks of the trade (including targeting the bottom), he's able to find the right fish in the right place, nearly without fail. You may ask him to fillet part of your catch. Holder of six world records and six state records, one of his marlins was even a grander (over 1,000 lbs.). He is also one of the few captains in Kona who will allow groups of guests to share a charter to save costs, so check online for the updated list of available shares. ☎ *808/895–1852* 🌐 *www.fishinkona.com* 🎟 *From $375.*

KAYAKING

The leeward (west coast) areas of the Big Island are protected for the most part from the northeast trade winds, making for ideal near-shore kayaking conditions. There are miles and miles of uncrowded Kona and Kohala coastline to explore, presenting close-up views of stark, raw, lava-rock shores and cliffs; lava-tube sea caves; pristine, secluded coves; and deserted beaches. There's even guided kayaking in a hand-built irrigation ditch dating from the early 1900s.

Ocean kayakers can get close to shore—where the commercial snorkel and dive cruise boats can't reach. This opens up all sorts of possibilities for adventure, such as near-shore snorkeling among the expansive coral reefs and lava rock formations that teem with colorful tropical fish and Hawaiian green sea turtles. You can pull ashore at a quiet cove for a picnic and a plunge into turquoise waters. With a good coastal map and some advice from the kayak vendor, you might paddle by ancient battlegrounds, burial sites, bathing ponds for Hawaiian royalty, or old villages.

Kayaking can be enjoyed via a guided tour or on a self-guided paddling excursion. Either way, the kayak outfitter can brief you on recommended routes, safety, and how to help preserve and protect Hawaii's ocean resources and coral reef system.

BEST SPOTS

Hilo Bay. This is a favorite kayak spot. The best place to put in is at **Reeds Bay Beach Park.** Parking is plentiful and free at the bayfront. Most afternoons you'll share the bay with local paddling clubs. Stay inside the breakwater unless the ocean is calm (or you're feeling unusually adventurous). Conditions range from extremely calm to quite choppy. ✉ *Banyan Way and Banyan Dr., 1 mile from downtown Hilo.*

Kailua Bay and Kamakahonu Beach. The small sandy beach that fronts the Courtyard King Kamehameha's Kona Beach Hotel is a nice place to rent or launch kayaks. You can unload in the cul-de-sac and park in nearby free or paid lots. The water here is especially calm, and the surroundings are historical and scenic. ✉ *Alii Dr., next to Kailua Pier, Kailua-Kona.*

Kealakekua Bay State Historical Park. The excellent snorkeling and likelihood of seeing dolphins (morning is best) make Kealakekua Bay one of the most popular kayaking spots on the Big Island. An ocean conservation district, the bay is usually calm and tranquil. (Use caution and common sense during surf advisories.) Tall coral pinnacles and clear visibility surrounding the monument also make for stupendous snorkeling. Regulations permit only a few operators to lead kayak tours in the park. ✉ *Napoopoo Rd. and Manini Bch. Rd., Captain Cook* 🌐 *dlnr.hawaii.gov/dsp/parks/hawaii.*

Oneo Bay. Right downtown, this is usually a placid place to kayak. It's fairly easy to get to. If you can't find parking along the road, there's a free lot across the street from the library and farmers' market. ✉ *Alii Dr., Kailua-Kona.*

EQUIPMENT, LESSONS, AND TOURS

There are several rental outfitters on Highway 11 between Kainaliu and Captain Cook, but only a few are specially permitted to lead kayak trips in Kealakekua Bay.

Aloha Kayak Co. This outfitter is one of the few permitted to guide tours to the stunningly beautiful Kealakekua Bay, leaving from Napoopoo, including about 1½ hours at the Captain Cook Monument. The 3½-hour morning and afternoon tours include snacks and drinks, while the 5-hour tour includes lunch. Local guides discuss the area's cultural, historical, and natural significance. You may see dolphins, but you must observe them from a distance only, as this is a protected marine reserve. Keauhou Bay tours are also available, including a two-hour evening manta ray tour. ✉ *79-7248 Mamalahoa Hwy., across from Teshima's Restaurant, Honalo* ☎ *808/322–2868* 🌐 *www.alohakayak.com* 🎫 *Tours from $99.*

Fodor's Choice ★ **Kona Boys.** On the highway above Kealakekua Bay, this full-service, environmentally conscious outfitter handles kayaks, body boards, surfboards, stand-up paddleboards, and snorkeling gear. Single-seat and double kayaks are offered. Surfing and stand-up paddleboarding lessons are available for private or group instruction. Tours such as their Morning Magic and Midday Meander include two half-day guided kayaking and snorkeling trips with gear, lunch, snacks, and beverages. Kona Boys also run a beach shack fronting the King Kamehameha's Kona Beach Hotel and are happy to give advice on the changing regulations regarding South Kona bay usage. ■ TIP→ **The Kailua-Kona location offers Hawaiian outrigger canoe rides, SUP lessons, and rentals of beach mats, chairs, and other gear.** ✉ *79-7539 Mamalahoa Hwy., Kealakekua* ☎ *808/328–1234, 808/329–2345* 🌐 *www.konaboys.com* 💵 *Tours from $189.*

Ocean Safari's Kayak Adventures. On the guided 3½-hour morning sea-cave tour that begins in Keauhou Bay, you can visit lava-tube sea caves along the coast, then swim ashore for a snack. The kayaks are already on the beach, so you won't have the hassle of transporting them. They also offer stand-up paddleboard lessons. ✉ *End of Kamehameha III Rd., Kailua-Kona* ✣ *Next to Sheraton Kona Resort & Spa at Keauhou Bay* ☎ *808/326–4699* 🌐 *www.oceansafariskayaks.com* 💵 *From $79.*

SAILING

For old salts and novice sailors alike, there's nothing like a cruise on the Kona or Kohala Coast. Calm waters, serene shores, and the superb scenery of Maunakea, Mauna Loa, and Hualalai, the Big Island's primary volcanic peaks, make for a great sailing adventure. You can drop a line over the side and try your luck at catching dinner, or grab some snorkel gear and explore when the boat drops anchor in one of the quiet coves and bays. A cruise may well be the most relaxing and adventurous part of a Big Island visit.

Honu Sail Charters. The fully equipped 32-foot cutter-rigged sloop *Honu* (Hawaiian for sea turtle) carries six passengers on full-day, half-day, and sunset sailing excursions along the scenic Kona Coast, which include time to snorkel in clear waters over coral reefs. This friendly outfitter allows passengers to get some hands-on sailing experience or just to kick back and relax. Prices include food, snorkel equipment, towels, etc. ✉ *Honokōhau Harbor, Kailua-Kona* ☎ *808/896–4668* 🌐 *www.sailkona.com* 💵 *Tours from $100.*

Kohala Sail & Sea. Based at the new Kawaihae South Small Boat Harbor, this company offers morning snorkeling, day sailing, and sunset cruises, and humpback whale-watching in season. Owned and operated by Captain Steve Turner, the crew aboard the 34-foot Riva focuses on sharing the wonders of the Kawaihae area, including the impressive Puukohola Heiau National Historic Site, the Puako reef, and views of Big Island volcanoes and even Maui's Haleakala. ✉ *Kawaihae Harbor South, Slip #8, 61-3527 Kawaihae Rd., Kawaihae* ☎ *808/895–1781* 🌐 *kohalasailandsea.com* 💵 *From $106.*

SCUBA DIVING

The Big Island's underwater world is the setting for a dramatic diving experience. With generally warm and calm waters, vibrant coral reefs and rock formations, and plunging underwater drop-offs, the Kona and Kohala coasts offer premier scuba diving. There are also some good dive locations in East Hawaii, not far from the Hilo area. Divers find much to occupy their time, including marine reserves teeming with tropical reef fish, Hawaiian green sea turtles, an occasional and critically endangered Hawaiian monk seal, and even some playful spinner dolphins. On special night dives to see manta rays, divers descend with bright underwater lights that attract plankton, which in turn attract these otherworldly creatures. The best spots to dive are all on the west coast.

BEST SPOTS

Garden Eel Cove. Accessible only by boat, this is a great place to see manta rays somersaulting overhead as they feast on a plankton supper. It's also home to hundreds of tiny garden eels darting out from their sandy homes. There's a steep drop-off and lots of marine life. ✉ *Rte. 19, near the Kona Airport, Kailua-Kona.*

Manta Village. Booking with a night-dive operator is required for the short boat ride to this area, one of Kona's best night-dive spots. If you're a diving or snorkeling fanatic, it's well worth it to experience manta rays drawn by the lights of the hotel. ■ TIP→ **If night swimming isn't your cup of tea, you can catch a glimpse of the majestic creatures from the Sheraton's viewing areas.** (No water access is allowed from the hotel's property.) ✉ *78-128 Ehukai St., off Sheraton Kona Resort & Spa at Keauhou Bay, Kailua-Kona.*

Pawai Bay Marine Perserve. Clear waters, abundant reef life, and interesting coral formations make protected Pawai Bay Marine Preserve ideal for diving. Explore sea caves, arches, and lava rock formations and dive into lava tubes. An easy, boat-only dive spot is ½ mile north of Old Airport. (No shoreline access to protected Pawai Bay is available due to its cultural and environmental significance.) ✉ *Kuakini Hwy., north of Old Kona Airport Park, Kailua-Kona.*

Puako. Just south of Hapuna Beach State Recreation Area, beautiful Puako offers easy entry to some fine reef diving. Deep chasms, sea caves, and rock arches abound with varied marine life. ✉ *Puako Rd., off Hwy. 19, Kailua-Kona.*

EQUIPMENT, LESSONS, AND TOURS

There are quite a few good dive shops along the Kona Coast. Most are happy to take on all customers, but a few focus on specific types of trips. Trip prices vary, depending on whether you're already certified and whether you're diving from a boat or from shore. Instruction with PADI, SDI, or TDI certification in three to five days costs $600 to $850. Most instructors rent dive equipment and snorkel gear, as well as underwater cameras. Most organize otherworldly manta ray dives at night and whale-watching cruises in season.

Big Island Divers. This company offers several levels of certification as well as numerous excursions, including night dives, two-tank charters, and in-season whale watching. ✉ *74-5467 Kaiwi St., Kailua-Kona* ☎ *808/329–6068* 🌐 *bigislanddivers.com* 💳 *From $135.*

Jack's Diving Locker. Good for novice and intermediate divers, Jack's has trained and certified tens of thousands of divers since 1981, with classrooms and a dive pool for instruction. Four boats that accommodate up to 18 divers and 6 snorkelers visit more than 80 established dive sites along the Kona coast, yielding sightings of turtles, manta rays, garden eels, and schools of barracuda. They even take you lava tube diving. Snorkelers can accompany their friends on the dive boats or take guided morning trips and manta night trips, and dolphin-watch and reef snorkels. Combined sunset/night manta ray dives are offered as well. ■ **TIP→ Kona's best deal for scuba newbies is Jack's two-part introductory dive from Kailua Pier.** ✉ *75-5813 Alii Dr., Kailua-Kona* ☎ *808/329–7585, 800/345–4807* 🌐 *www.jacksdivinglocker.com* 🎟 *Tours from $135.*

Nautilus Dive Center. Across from Hilo Bay, Nautilus Dive Center is the oldest and most experienced dive shop on the island. It offers a broad range of services for both beginners and experienced divers. Owner Bill De Rooy has been diving around the Big Island since 1982, has personally certified more than 2,000 divers, and can provide you with underwater maps and show you the best dive spots in Hilo. He also provides PADI instruction, one- and two-tank dives, and snorkeling tours. ✉ *382 Kamehameha Ave., Hilo* ☎ *808/935–6939* 🌐 *www.nautilusdivehilo.com* 🎟 *Certification from $400.*

SNORKELING

A favorite pastime on the Big Island, snorkeling is perhaps one of the easiest and most enjoyable water activities for visitors. By floating on the surface, peering through your mask, and breathing through your snorkel, you can see lava rock formations, sea arches, sea caves, and coral reefs teeming with colorful tropical fish. While the Kona and Kohala coasts boast more beaches, bays, and quiet coves to snorkel, the east side around Hilo and at Kapoho are also great places to get in the water.

BEST SPOTS

Kahaluu Beach Park. Since ancient times, the waters around Kahaluu Beach have provided traditional throw net–fishing grounds. With super-easy access, the bay offers good swimming and outstanding snorkeling, revealing turtles, angelfish, parrotfish, needlefish, puffer fish, and many types of tang. ■ **TIP→ Stay inside the breakwater and don't stray too far, as dangerous and unpredictable currents swirl outside the bay.** ✉ *Alii Dr., Kailua-Kona.*

Kapoho Tide Pools. Here you'll find the best snorkeling on the Hilo side. Fingers of lava from the 1960 flow that destroyed the town of Kapoho jut into the sea to form a network of tide pools. Conditions near the shore are excellent for beginners, while farther out is challenging enough for experienced snorkelers. ✉ *End of Kapoho-Kai Rd., off Hwy. 137, Hilo.*

Kealakekua Bay State Historical Park. This protected Marine Life Conservation District is hands-down one of the best snorkeling spots on the island, thanks to clear visibility, fabulous coral reefs, and generally calm waters. Pods of dolphins can be abundant, but they're protected under federal law and may not be disturbed or approached. Access to the area is restricted, but a few companies are permitted to escort tours to the bay. ■ **TIP→ Overland access is difficult, so opt for one of the guided**

The Kona Coast's relatively calm waters and colorful coral reefs are excellent for scuba diving.

snorkel cruises permitted to moor here. ✉ *Napoopoo, at end of Beach Rd. and Hwy. 160, Kailua-Kona.*

Magic Sands Beach Park. Also known as White Sands or Disappearing Sands Beach Park, this is a great place for beginning and intermediate snorkelers. In winter, it's also a prime spot to watch for whales. ✉ *Alii Dr., Kailua-Kona.*

Puako Tide Pools. There's a large shelf of extensive reef and tide pools at this sleepy beach town along the Kohala Coast, where you'll find fantastic snorkeling as long as conditions are calm. ✉ *South end of Puako Beach Rd., off Hwy. 11.*

EQUIPMENT, LESSONS, AND TOURS

FAMILY **Body Glove Cruises.** This operator is a good choice for families; kids love the waterslide and the high-dive platform. On the Snorkel & Dolphin Watch Adventure, the 65-foot catamaran sets off for uncrowded Red Hill in stunning South Kona from Kailua-Kona pier daily for a morning snorkel cruise that includes breakfast and a BBQ burger lunch, with vegetarian options. A three-hour historical dinner cruise to Kealakekua Bay is a great way to relax, watch the sunset, and learn about Kona's history. It includes a Hawaiian-style buffet, complimentary cocktail, and live music. (A lunch version is also available.) Seasonal whale-watch cruises and all dolphin snorkel cruises guarantee you will see the featured mammals or you can go again for free; the company implements a NOAA-approved Dolphin SMART policy on all of their cruises. Children under five are always free. ✉ *75-5629 Kuakini Hwy., Kailua-Kona* ☎ *808/326–7122, 800/551–8911* 🌐 *www.bodyglovehawaii.com* 🎫 *From $132.*

FAMILY Fodor's Choice ★ **Fair Wind Cruises.** In business since 1971, Fair Wind offers morning and afternoon snorkel trips into breathtaking Kealakekua Bay. Great for families with small kids, the custom-built, 60-foot catamaran has two 15-foot waterslides, freshwater showers, and a staircase descending directly into the water for easy access. Snorkel gear is included, along with flotation equipment and prescription masks. The 4½-hour cruise is known for its delicious meals; 3½-hour snack cruises are offered, too. For ages seven and older, the company also operates the *Hula Kai* snorkel cruise, a 55-foot luxury hydrofoil catamaran that takes guests to several remote South Kona locations. Their five-hour morning snorkel cruise includes a gourmet breakfast buffet and barbecue lunch. ✉ *Keauhou Bay, 78-7130 Kaleiopapa St., Kailua-Kona* ☎ *808/322–2788, 800/677–9461* 🌐 *www.fair-wind.com* 🎫 *Cruises from $145.*

Sea Quest. Careful stewardship of the Kona Coast and its sea life is a major priority for this company, which provides catamaran charters and other snorkeling excursions. Trips leave from Keauhou Bay and head to Captain Cook Monument and other points south. ☎ *808/329–7238* 🌐 *www.seaquesthawaii.com* 🎫 *From $78.*

STAND-UP PADDLING

Stand-up paddleboarding (or SUP for short), a sport with roots in the Hawaiian Islands, has grown popular worldwide in recent years. It's available for all skill levels and ages, and even novice stand-up paddleboarders can get up, stay up, and have a great time paddling around a protected bay or exploring the gorgeous coastline. All you need to get started is a large body of calm water, a board, and a paddle. The workout tests your core strength as well as your balance and offers an unusual vantage point from which to enjoy the beauty of island and ocean.

BEST SPOTS

Anaehoomalu Bay Beach (A-Bay). In this well-protected bay, even when surf is rough on the rest of the island, it's usually fairly calm here, though trades pick up heartily in the afternoon. Boards are available for rent at the north end, and the safe area for stand-up paddling is marked by buoys. ✉ *Off Waikoloa Beach Dr., south of Waikoloa Beach Marriott, Kohala Coast.*

Hilo Bay. At this favorite among locals, the best place to put in is at **Reeds Bay Beach Park.** Most afternoons you'll share the bay with local paddling clubs. Stay inside the breakwater unless the ocean is calm (or you're feeling unusually adventurous). Conditions range from extremely calm to quite choppy. ✉ *Banyan Way and Banyan Dr., 1 mile from downtown Hilo.*

Kailua Bay and Kamakahonu Beach. The small sandy beach that fronts the Courtyard King Kamehameha's Kona Beach Hotel is great for kids; the water here is especially calm and gentle. If you're more daring, you can easily paddle out of the bay and along the coast for some great exploring. ✉ *Alii Dr., next to Kailua Pier, Kailua-Kona.*

EQUIPMENT AND LESSONS

Fodor's Choice ★ **Hypr Nalu Hawaii.** SUP master Ian Foo is the king of the stand-up paddleboard in downtown Kailua-Kona. At his small oceanfront shop across from the pier, he stocks paddleboards and surfboards, all beautifully custom-made. They also offer OC1 lessons, rentals, active ocean gear, and apparel. He and his family are serious and enthusiastic about ocean sports and are awesome teachers. ✉ *75-5663A Palani Rd., Kailua-Kona* ☎ *808/960–4667* 🌐 *www.hyprnalu.com.*

Ocean Sports. This outfitter rents equipment, offers lessons, and has the perfect location for easy access to the bay. Ocean Sports also operates rental shacks at the Hilton Waikoloa Village, Whale Center Kawaihae, Queens' MarketPlace, and at Anaehoomalu Bay. They can also set you up with cruises, dives, and charters elsewhere on the island. ✉ *Waikoloa Beach Marriott, 69-275 Waikoloa Beach Dr., Waikoloa* ☎ *808/886–6666* 🌐 *www.hawaiioceansports.com* 🎫 *SUP rental $50/hr.*

4

SUBMARINE TOURS

FAMILY **Atlantis Submarines.** Want to stay dry while exploring the tropical undersea world? Climb aboard the 48-passenger *Atlantis X* submarine, anchored off Kailua Pier, across from Courtyard King Kamehameha's Kona Beach Hotel. A large glass dome in the bow and 13 viewing ports on each side allow clear views of the aquatic world more than 100 feet down. This is a great trip for kids and nonswimmers. ✉ *75-5669 Alii Dr., Kailua-Kona* ☎ *808/326–7939, 800/381–0237* 🌐 *www.atlantisadventures.com* 🎫 *$119.*

SURFING

The Big Island does not have the variety of great surfing spots found on Oahu or Maui, but it does have decent waves and a thriving surf culture. Local kids and avid surfers frequent a number of places up and down the Kona and Kohala coasts of West Hawaii; some have become famous surf champions. Expect high surf in winter and much calmer activity during summer. The surf scene is much more active on the Kona side.

EQUIPMENT AND LESSONS

Hawaii Lifeguard Surf Instructors. This family-owned, lifeguard-certified school helps novices become wave riders at Kahaluu Beach Park and offers lessons for more experienced riders at Kona's top surf spots. A two-hour introductory lesson has one instructor per two to four students. Private instruction is available as well. If the waves are on the smaller side, they convert to stand-up paddleboard lessons for the same prices as surfing. ✉ *75-5909 Alii Dr., Kailua-Kona* ☎ *808/324–0442, 808/936–7873* 🌐 *www.surflessonshawaii.com* 🎫 *From $75.*

Fodor's Choice ★ **Ocean Eco Tours Surf School.** Family-owned and -operated, Kona's oldest surf school emphasizes the basics and specializes in beginners. It's one of a handful of operators permitted to conduct business in Kaloko-Honokohau National Historical Park, which gets waves even when other spots on the west side are flat. All lessons are taught by certified instructors, and the school guarantees that you will surf. If you're hooked, sign up for a three-day package. There's an authentic soul surfer's vibe to this operation, and they are equally diehard about teaching you about the ocean and having you standing up riding waves on your first day. Group, private, and semiprivate lessons available. ✉ *King Kam Hotel, 75-5660 Palani Rd., Suite 304, Kailua-Kona* ☎ *808/324–7873* 🌐 *www.oceanecotours.com* 🎫 *From $95.*

Fodor's Choice ★ **Orchidland Surfboards & Surf Shop.** On Big Island radio stations, you're likely to hear the familiar voice of shop owner and local surf legend Stan Lawrence delivering the daily surf reports. Around since the 1970s, his shop, located in the heart of Hilo's historic district, is a veritable testament to Big Island surfing, with surf culture/Hawaiiana on the walls, along with vintage boards, old photos, and plenty of stories. The shop offers custom surfboards, body boards, and other gear for sale or rent along with the latest surf apparel. ✉ *262 Kamehameha Ave., Hilo* ☎ *808/935–1533* 🌐 *www.orchidlandsurf.com.*

WHALE-WATCHING

Each winter, some two-thirds of the North Pacific humpback whale population (about 4,000–5,000 animals) migrate over 3,500 miles from the icy Alaska waters to the warm Hawaiian ocean to mate and, the following year, give birth to and nurse their calves. Recent reports indicate that the whale population is on the upswing—a few years ago one even ventured into the mouth of Hilo Harbor, which marine biologists say is quite rare. Humpbacks are spotted here from early December through the end of April, but other species, like sperm, pilot, and beaked whales as well as spinner, spotted, and bottlenose dolphins, can be seen year-round. ■ **TIP→ If you take a morning cruise, you're more likely to see dolphins.** *In addition to the outfitters listed below, see Snorkeling for more outfitters that offer whale- and dolphin-watching cruises.*

TOURS

Captain Dan McSweeney's Whale Watch Learning Adventures. Captain Dan McSweeney, self-described whale researcher and conservationist, offers three-hour trips on his double-decker, 40-foot cruise boat. In addition to humpbacks (in winter), he'll try to show you dolphins and some of the six other whale species that live off the Kona Coast throughout the year. McSweeney guarantees you'll see whales or he'll take you out again for free. ✉ *Honokōhau Harbor, 74-381 Kealakehe Pkwy., Kailua-Kona* ☎ *808/322–0028, 888/942–5376* 🌐 *www.ilovewhales.com* 🎫 *$120.*

Hawaii Nautical. The only NOAA-designated "Dolphin SMART" operator in Hawaii, this company practices strict guidelines for viewing protected marine animals, including dolphins and whales. You can be assured that you'll enjoy a wonderful ocean tour, see plenty of animals, and not be a part of harming or impacting the animal's activities or habitats. ✉ *74-425 Kealakehe Parkway, Slip I-10, Kailua-Kona* ☎ *808/234-7245* 🌐 *www.hawaiinautical.com* 🎫 *From $79.*

A classic Anaehoomalu Beach Surf Shack

GOLF, HIKING, AND OUTDOOR ACTIVITIES

Updated by Kristina Anderson

You can explore by bike, helicopter, ATV, zip line, or horse, or you can put on your hiking boots and use your own horsepower. No matter how you get around, you'll be treated to breathtaking backdrops along the Big Island's 266-mile coastline and within its 4,028 square miles (and still growing!). Aerial tours take in the latest eruption activity and lava flows, as well as the island's gorgeous tropical valleys, gulches, and coastal plains. Trips into the backcountry wilderness explore the rain forest, private ranch lands, and coffee farms, while sleepy sugar-plantation villages offer a glimpse of Hawaii's bygone days.

Golfers will find acclaimed championship golf courses at the Kohala coast resorts—Mauna Kea Beach Hotel, Hapuna Beach Prince Hotel, Mauna Lani Bay Hotel & Bungalows, and Waikoloa Beach Resort, among others. And during the winter, if snow conditions allow, you can even go skiing on top of Maunakea (elevation: 13,796 feet). It's a skiing experience unlike any other.

AERIAL TOURS

There's nothing quite like the aerial view of a waterfall crashing down a couple of thousand feet into cascading pools, or watching lava flow to the ocean as exploding clouds of steam billow into the air. You can get this bird's-eye view from a helicopter or a fixed-wing small plane. All operators pay strict attention to safety. So how to get the best experience for your money? ■ **TIP→ Before you choose a company, be a savvy**

traveler and ask the right questions. What kind of aircraft do they fly? What is their safety record?

Big Island Air Tours. This small company, in business since the 1980s, offers fixed-wing tours of the island, including a circle island, Kilauea sunset tour, or Maui-Big Island tour. They also feature charter or cargo service between all the major islands except Kauai. This is a good alternative to the pricier helicopter tours. ☎ *808/329–4868* 🌐 *www.bigislandair.com* 🎫 *From $345.*

Blue Hawaiian Helicopters. Hawaii Island's premier flight is on the roomy, $3-million Eco-Star helicopter—so smooth and quiet you hardly realize you're taking off. No worries about what seat you get because there are great views from each. Pilots are also state of Hawaii–certified tour guides, so they are very knowledgeable and experienced but not overly chatty. In the breathtaking Waimanu Valley, the helicopter hovers amazingly close to 2,600-foot cliffs and cascading waterfalls. The two-hour Big Island Spectacular also takes in Kilauea Volcano lava flows as well as the valleys; you can even choose an optional waterfall landing as part of it. Most tours leave from Blue Hawaiian's Waikoloa heliport, but the 50-minute Circle of Fire tour departs from Hilo for the volcano's wonders. Tours on the company's A-Star helicopters are less expensive. ✉ *Waikoloa Heliport, Hwy. 19, Waikoloa* ☎ *808/961–5600* 🌐 *www.bluehawaiian.com* 🎫 *From $259.*

Fodor's Choice ★ **Paradise Helicopters.** This locally owned adventure tour company offers numerous helicopter tour options, many of which are completely unique. The "Doors-off Lava & Rainforests Adventure" shows guests Hilo's rain forests and Waianuenue (Rainbow Falls) before getting you so close to the lava flows that you can feel the heat, while the Sunset Experience allows you to experience glowing lava plus a Kona sunset over Puuhonua o Honaunau. Pilots, many of whom have military backgrounds, are fun and knowledgeable. ■ **TIP→ The only helicopter company in Hawaii certified by the Hawaii Ecotour Association, Paradise offers you the option to offset your tour's carbon footprint by having a tree planted in Hawaii for each ride you take.** ☎ *808/969–7392, 866/876–7422* 🌐 *www.paradisecopters.com* 🎫 *From $274.*

ATV TOURS

Fodor's Choice ★ **Waipio Ride the Rim.** A fabulous way to experience the extraordinary beauty atop lush Waipio Valley, the tour is led by fun and knowledgeable guides along private trails to the headwaters of the twin Hiilawe Falls, Hawaii's highest single-fall waterfall. You'll stop for a snack and swim in a ginger-laden grotto with a refreshing waterfall (disclaimer: it's freezing cold!) and travel to a series of lookouts; bring a bathing suit and be prepared to get wet and muddy. Beginners are welcome, but to drive your own ATV, you must be 16 or over. Adults who don't wish to drive may book the buggy. ✉ *Waipio Valley Artworks Bldg., 48-5416 Kukuihaele Rd., Kukuihaele* ☎ *808/775–1450, 877/775–1450* 🌐 *www.ridetherim.com* 🎫 *From $199.*

BIKING

The Big Island's biking trails and road routes range from easy to moderate coastal rides to rugged backcountry wilderness treks that challenge the most serious cyclists. You can soak up the island's storied scenic vistas and varied geography—from tropical rain forest to rolling ranch country, from high-country mountain meadows to dry lava deserts. It's dry, windy, and hot on Kona's and Kohala's coastal trails, mountainous through South Kona, and cool, wet, and muddy in the upcountry Waimea and Volcano areas, as well as in lower Puna. There are long distances between towns, few bike lanes, narrow single-lane highways, and scanty services in the Kau, Puna, South Kona, and Kohala Coast areas, so plan accordingly for your weather, water, food, and lodging needs before setting out. ■ TIP→ **Your best bet is to book with an outfitter who has all the details covered.**

4

EQUIPMENT AND TOURS

There are rental shops in Kailua-Kona and a couple in Waimea and Hilo. Many resorts rent bicycles that can be used around the properties. Most outfitters can provide a bicycle rack for your car, and all offer reduced rates for rentals longer than one day. All retailers offer excellent advice about where to go; they know the areas well.

BikeVolcano.com. This outfitter leads three- or five-hour bike rides through Hawaii Volcanoes National Park, mostly downhill, that take in fantastic sights, from rain forests to craters. Equipment, support van, and food are included; pickup locations in Hilo and Volcano (and Kona by request). The company also coordinates and leads rides to the active lava flows. ✉ *Hilo* ☎ *808/934–9199, 888/934–9199* 🌐 *www.bikevolcano.com* 💳 *From $115.*

Mid Pacific Wheels. The oldest bike shop on the Big Island, this community-oriented shop near the university carries a full line of bikes and accessories and rents mountain bikes for exploring the Hilo area. The friendly staff provides expert advice on where to go and what to see and do on a self-guided tour. They also carry a large selection of cycling accesssories, bikes, and repair parts. ✉ *1133C Manono St., Hilo* ☎ *808/935–6211* 🌐 *www.midpacificwheelsllc.com* 💳 *From $35.*

CAVING

Fodor's Choice ★ **Kula Kai Caverns.** Expert cave guides lead groups into the fantastic underworld of these caverns near South Point. The braided lava-tube system attracts scientists from around the world, who come to study and map them (more than 40 miles so far). Tours range from the "Lighted Trail" (in the lighted show cave, which is easy walking), to the "Two Hour," a deep-down-under spelunking adventure that often takes closer to three hours and allows you to see archaeological evidence of the ancient Hawaiians. Longer, customized tours are also available and programs are tailored to each group's interest and abilities; all gear is provided. Tours start at an Indiana Jones–style expedition tent, complete with a topographic map and divulge fascinating details about the caves' geologic and cultural history. Reservations are required. ✉ *Kula Kai Estates, Lauhala Dr. at Kona Kai Blvd.* ☎ *808/929–9725* 🌐 *www.kulakaicaverns.com* 💳 *From $20.*

GOLF

For golfers, the Big Island is a big deal—starting with the Mauna Kea Golf Course, which opened in 1964 and remains one of the state's top courses. Black lava and deep blue sea are the predominant themes on the island. In the roughly 40 miles from the Kona Country Club to the Mauna Kea resort, nine courses are carved into sunny seaside lava plains, with four more in the hills above. Indeed, most of the Big Island's best courses are concentrated along the Kohala Coast, statistically the sunniest spot in Hawaii. Vertically speaking, although the majority of courses are seaside or at least near sea level, three are located above 2,000 feet, another one at 4,200 feet. This is significant because in Hawaii temperatures drop 3°F for every 1,000 feet of elevation gained.

Green Fee: Green fees listed here are the highest course rates per round on weekdays for U.S. residents. Courses with varying weekend rates are noted in the individual listings. (Some courses charge non–U.S. residents higher prices.) **TIP→ Discounts are often available for resort guests and for those who book tee times online, as well as for those willing to play in the afternoon. Twilight rates are also usually offered.**

KAILUA-KONA

Big Island Country Club. Set 2,000 feet above sea level on the slopes of Hualalai, this course is out of the way but well worth the drive. In 1997, Pete and Perry Dye created a gem that plays through upland woodlands—more than 2,500 trees line the fairways. On the par-5 16th, a giant tree in the middle of the fairway must be avoided with the second shot. Five lakes and a meandering natural mountain stream bring water into play on nine holes. The most dramatic is the par-3 17th, where Dye created a knockoff of his infamous 17th at the TPC at Sawgrass. *71-1420 Hawaii Belt Rd., Kailua-Kona 808/325–5044 www.bigislandcountryclub.com $135 with cart, bottled water, range balls 18 holes, 7075 yards, par 72.*

THE KOHALA COAST

Hapuna Golf Course. Hapuna's challenging play and environmental sensitivity make it one of the island's most unusual courses. Designed by Arnold Palmer and Ed Seay, it is nestled into the natural contours of the land from the shoreline to about 700 feet above sea level. There are spectacular views of mountains and sea (Maui is often visible in the distance). Holes wind through kiawe scrub, beds of jagged lava, and tall fountain grasses. Hole 12 is favored for its beautiful views and challenging play. *62-100 Kanunaoa Dr., Waimea (Hawaii County) 808/880–3000 www.hapunabeachresort.com/golf $160, $100 after 1 pm 18 holes, 6875 yards, par 72.*

Fodor's Choice ★ **Mauna Kea Golf Course.** Originally opened in 1964, this golf course is one of the most revered in the state. It underwent a tee-to-green renovation by Rees Jones, son of the original architect, Robert Trent Jones Sr. Hybrid grasses were planted, the number of bunkers increased, and the overall yardage was expanded. The par-3 3rd is one of the world's most famous holes—and one of the most photographed. You play from a cliffside tee across a bay to a cliffside green. Getting across the ocean is just half the battle because the green is surrounded by seven bunkers, each one large and undulated. The course is a shot-maker's paradise and follows Jones's "easy bogey, tough par" philosophy. **TIP→ Since you're in Hawaii, try the new Golfboard, a surf-inspired alternative to a golf cart.** ✉ *62-100 Kaunaoe Dr., Waimea (Hawaii County)* ☎ *808/882–5400* 🌐 *www.maunakeagolf.com* 🎫 *$285, $195 after 1:30 pm, add Golfboard for $35* ⛳ *18 holes, 7250 yards, par 72.*

Fodor's Choice ★ **Mauna Lani Resort.** Black lava flows, lush green turf, white sand, and the Pacific's multihues of blue define the 36 holes at Mauna Lani. The South Course includes the par-3 15th across a turquoise bay, one of the most photographed holes in Hawaii. But it shares "signature hole" honors with the 7th, a long par 3, which plays downhill over convoluted patches of black lava, with the Pacific immediately to the left and a dune to the right. The North Course plays a couple of shots tougher. Its most distinctive hole is the 17th, a par 3 with the green set in a lava pit 50 feet deep. The shot from an elevated tee must carry a pillar of lava that rises from the pit and partially blocks a view of the green. ✉ *68-1310 Mauna Lani Dr., Waimea (Hawaii County)* ☎ *808/885–6655* 🌐 *www.maunalani.com* 🎫 *$235 before 1, $155 after 1* ⛳ *North Course: 18 holes, 6057 yards, par 72. South Course: 18 holes, 6025 yards, par 72.*

Fodor's Choice ★ **Waikoloa Beach Resort.** Robert Trent Jones Jr. built the Beach Course at Waikoloa (1981) on an old flow of crinkly *aa* lava, which he used to create holes that are as artful as they are challenging. The par-5 12th hole is one of Hawaii's most picturesque and plays through a chute of black lava to a seaside green. At the Kings' Course (1990), Tom Weiskopf and Jay Morrish built a links-esque track. It turns out lava's natural humps and declivities replicate the contours of seaside Scotland. But there are a few island twists—such as seven lakes. This is "option golf," as Weiskopf and Morrish provide different risk-reward tactics on each hole. **TIP→ Fees vary depending on the time of day, the cheapest being a midday tee-time.** ✉ *600 Waikoloa Beach Dr., Waikoloa* ☎ *808/886–7888* 🌐 *www.waikoloabeachgolf.com* 🎫 *From $125, including cart* ⛳ *Beach Course: 18 holes, 6566 yards, par 70; Kings' Course: 18 holes, 7074 yards, par 72.*

HAWAII VOLCANOES NATIONAL PARK & VICINITY

Volcano Golf & Country Club. Just outside Hawaii Volcanoes National Park—and barely a stone's throw from Halemaumau Crater—this is by far Hawaii's highest course. At 4,200-feet elevation, shots tend to fly a bit farther than at sea level, even in the often cool, misty air. Because of the elevation and climate, this Hawaii course features Bermuda and seashore Paspalum grass putting greens. The course is mostly flat, and holes play through stands of *ohia lehua* (flowering evergreen trees), and multitrunk hau trees. The uphill par-4 15th doglegs through a tangle of hau. ✉ *Pii Mauna Dr., off Hwy. 11, Hawaii Volcanoes National Park* ☎ *808/967–7331* 🌐 *www.volcanogolfshop.com* 🎫 *$61, including cart* ⛳ *18 holes, 6106 yards, par 72.*

The Kohala Coast along the east side of Big Island is known for its shimmering blue water, beaches, and sunshine.

HILO

Hilo Municipal Golf Course. Hilo Muni is proof that you don't need sand bunkers to create a challenging course. Trees and several meandering creeks are the danger here. The course, which offers views of Hilo Bay from most holes, has produced many of the island's top players over the years. Taking a divot reminds you that you're playing on a volcano—the soil is dark black crushed lava. ✉ *340 Haihai St., Hilo* ☎ *808/959–7711* 🌐 *www.hawaiicounty.gov/pr-golf* *$35 weekdays, $40 weekends* *18 holes, 6325 yards, par 71.*

HIKING

Ecologically diverse, Hawaii Island has four of the five major climate zones and 8 of 13 sub-climate zones—a lot of variation for one island—and you can experience them all on foot. Part of the King's Trail at Anaehoomalu winds through a field of lava rocks covered with ancient petroglyphs. Many other trails, historic and modern, crisscross the huge Hawaii Volcanoes National Park and other parts of the island. Plus, the serenity of remote beaches, such as Papakolea Beach (Green Sands Beach), is accessible only to hikers. Check the statewide trail system website at 🌐 *hawaiitrails.ehawaii.gov* for up-to-date information for hiking trails.

Department of Land and Natural Resources, State Parks Division. The division provides information on all the Big Island's state parks and jurisdictions. Check online for the latest information and advisories. ✉ *75 Aupuni St., Hilo* ☎ *808/961–9544* 🌐 *www.dlnr.hawaii.gov/dsp/parks/hawaii.*

BEST SPOTS

Hawaii Volcanoes National Park. Perhaps the Big Island's premier area for hikers, the park has more than 155 miles of trails providing close-up views of fern and rain forest environments, cinder cones, craters, steam vents, lava fields, rugged coastline, and current eruption activity. Day hikes range from easy to moderately difficult, and from one or two hours to a full day. For a bigger challenge, consider an overnight or multiday backcountry hike with a stay in a park cabin (available en route to the remote coast, in a lush forest, or atop frigid Mauna Loa). To do so, you must first obtain a permit at the backcountry office in the Visitor Emergency Operations Center. ■ TIP→ **Daily guided hikes are led by knowledgeable, friendly park rangers.** The bulletin boards outside Kilauea Visitor Center and inside Jaggar Museum have the day's schedule. Perhaps the Big Island's premier area for hikers, the park has 150 miles of trails providing close-up views. ✉ *Hwy. 11, 30 miles south of Hilo, Hawaii Volcanoes National Park* ☎ *808985–6000* 🌐 *www.nps.gov/havo/index.htm.*

4

Kekaha Kai State Park. A 1.8-mile unimproved road leads to Mahaiula Bay, a gorgeous little piece of paradise, while on the opposite end of the park is lovely Kua Bay. Connecting the two is the 4½-mile Ala Kahakai historic coastal trail. Midway between the two white-sand beaches, you can hike to the summit of Puu Kuili, a 342-foot-high cinder cone with an excellent view of the coastline. Mahaiula has picnic tables and vault toilets. It's dry and hot with no drinking water, so pack sunblock, hats, and extra water. Gates close at 7 pm sharp. ✉ *Trailhead on Hwy. 19, About 2 miles north of Kona airport, Kailua-Kona* 🌐 *dlnr.hawaii.gov/dsp/parks/hawaii.*

Muliwai Trail. On the western side of mystical Waipio Valley, this trail leads to the back of the valley, then switchbacks up through a series of gulches, and finally emerges at Waimanu Valley. Only very experienced hikers should attempt the very remote entire 18-mile trail, the hike of a lifetime. It can take two to three days of backpacking and camping, which requires camping permits from the Division of Forestry and Wildlife in Hilo. ✉ *Trailhead at end of Hwy. 240, Honokaa* ☎ *808/974–4221* 🌐 *hawaiitrails.ehawaii.gov.*

Onomea Bay Trail. This short but beautiful trail is packed with stunning views of the cliffs, bays, and gulches of the Hamakua Coast, on the east side of the island. The trail is just under a mile and fairly easy, with access down to the shore if you want to dip your feet in, although we don't recommend swimming in the rough waters. Unless you pay the $15 entry fee to the nearby botanical garden, entering its gates (even by accident) will send one of the guards running after you to nicely but firmly point you back to the trail. ✉ *Trailhead on Old Hawaiian Belt Rd., just before botanical garden.* 🌐 *hawaiitrails.ehawaii.gov.*

GOING WITH A GUIDE

Fodor's Choice ★ **Hawaii Forest & Trail.** Since 1993, this locally owned and operated outfit has built a reputation for outstanding nature tours and eco-adventures. Sustainability, cultural sensitivity, and forging island connections are company missions. They have access to thousands of acres of restricted or private lands and employ expert, certified guides who are entertaining and informative. Choose an Endangered Native Habitats bird-watching tour, or journey deep into the Hakalau Forest National Wildlife Refuge. Other tours include a Twilight Volcano Adventure excursion, Kohala waterfall trip, or the Kohala Canopy adventure. If you want to see it all in one day, you can't beat the circle-island Epic Island Volcano Journey, which visits spots off the beaten path—three national parks/historic sites combined with caving in a lava tube. Breakfast, lunch, and a farm-to-fork dinner prepared by a renowned chef are included. ✉ *73-5593 A Olowalau St., Kailua-Kona* ☎ *808/331–8505, 800/464–1993* 🌐 *www.hawaii-forest.com* 🎫 *From $69.*

KapohoKine Adventures. This friendly outfitter offers several hiking adventures in Hawaii Volcanoes National Park and surrounding areas, including a 12-hour tour that explores the region by day and sees the lava at night. The Kilauea Hike & Glow tour leads guests to an enormous, still-steaming crater and into areas of the park not normally visited by tour groups. The Evening Volcano Explorer takes you to what remains of the lava-inundated town of Kalapana, explores the park, and ends with dinner at the historic Volcano Winery. The Lava Expedition tour traverses the flow fields looking for lava breakouts while the Secrets of Puna takes you along the rugged coast where you experience a region that's been besieged by lava flows over the years. Tours depart from both Hilo and Kona. ✉ *Grand Naniloa Hotel, 93 Banyan Dr., Hilo* ☎ *808/964–1000* 🌐 *www.kapohokine.com* 🎫 *From $149.*

HORSEBACK RIDING

TOURS

Paniolo Adventures. Paniolo Adventures offers riders of all levels an open-range horseback ride on a working Kohala Mountain cattle ranch, spectacular views of three volcanoes and the coastline, and an authentic paniolo experience from 3,000 feet up. You don't ride nose-to-tail and can spread out and trot or canter if you wish. ✉ *Kohala Mountain Road (Hwy. 250), at mile marker 13.2, Waimea (Hawaii County)* ☎ *808/889–5354* 🌐 *www.panioloadventures.com* 🎫 *From $69.*

ZIP-LINE TOURS

Kohala Zipline. This tour features nine zips and five suspension bridges for a thrilling, within-the-canopy adventure in the forest. You'll bounce up to the site in a six-wheel-drive, military-style vehicle. Two certified guides accompany each small group. Designed for all ability levels, the Kohala Zipline focuses on fun and safety, offering a dual line for efficient confident braking. You'll soar more than 100 feet above the ground and feel like a pro by the last platform. A quickie lesson in rappelling is included. Zip and Dip tours (combining zip line, nature walk, lunch, snacks, and waterfall swim) are available. ✉ *54-3676 Akoni Pule Hwy., Kapaau* ☎ *808/331–3620, 800/464–1993* 🌐 *www.kohalazipline.com* 🎫 *From $185.*

5

KAUAI

WELCOME TO KAUAI

TOP REASONS TO GO

★ **Napali Coast:** On foot, by boat, or by air—explore what is unarguably one of the most beautiful stretches of coastline in all Hawaii.

★ **Kalalau Trail:** Hawaii's ultimate adventure hike will test your endurance but reward you with lush tropical vegetation, white-sand beaches, and unforgettable views.

★ **Kayaking:** Kauai is a hub for kayakers, with four rivers plus the spectacular coastline to explore.

★ **Waimea Canyon:** Dramatic, colorful rock formations and frequent rainbows make this natural wonder one of Kauai's most stunning features.

★ **Birds:** Birds thrive on Kauai, especially at the Kilauea Point National Wildlife Refuge.

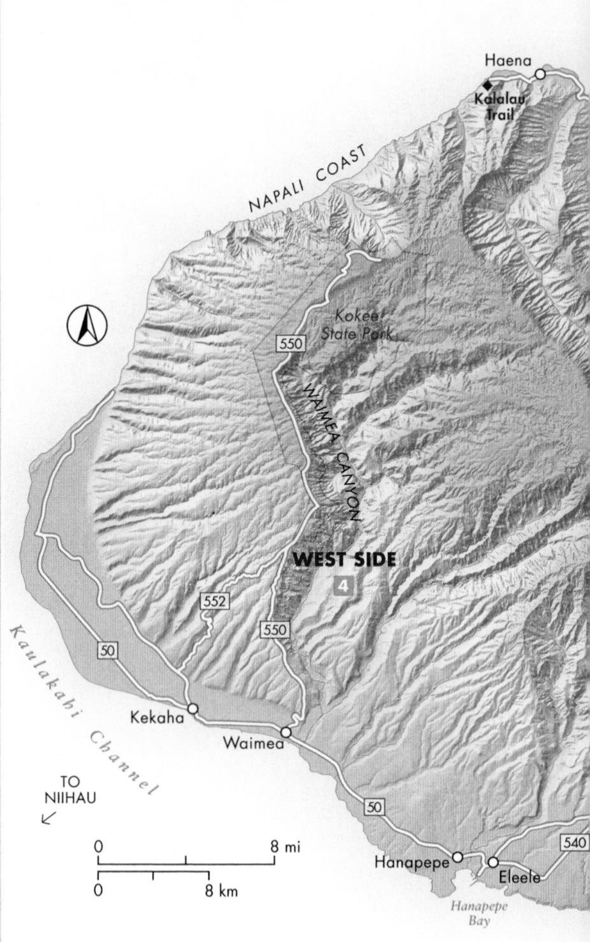

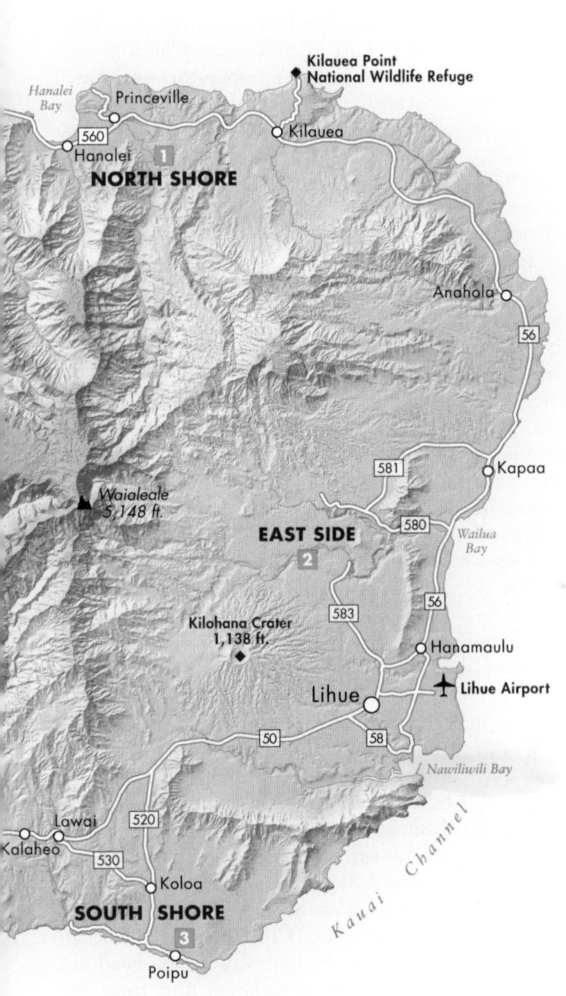

1 North Shore. Dreamy beaches, green mountains, breathtaking scenery, and abundant rain, waterfalls, and rainbows characterize the North Shore, which includes the communities of Kilauea, Princeville, and Hanalei.

2 East Side. This is Kauai's commercial and residential hub, dominated by the island's largest town, Kapaa. The airport, harbor, and government offices are found in the county seat of Lihue.

3 South Shore. Peaceful landscapes, sunny weather, and beaches that rank among the best in the world make the South Shore the resort capital of Kauai. The Poipu resort area is here, along with the small towns of Koloa, Lawai, and Kalaheo.

4 West Side. Dry, sunny, and sleepy, the West Side includes the historic towns of Hanapepe, Waimea, and Kekaha. This area is ideal for outdoor adventurers because it's the entryway to the Waimea Canyon and Kokee State Park, and the departure point for most Napali Coast boat trips.

GREAT ITINERARIES

As small as Kauai may be, you still can't do it all in one day: hiking Kalalau Trail, kayaking Wailua River, showering in a waterfall, watching whales at Kilauea Lighthouse, waking to the sunrise above Kealia, touring underwater lava tubes at Tunnels, and shopping for gifts at Koloa Town shops. Rather than trying to check everything off your list in one fell swoop, we recommend choosing your absolute favorite and devoting a full day to the experience.

A Bit of History

Hawaiian beliefs are traditionally rooted in nature. If you're interested in archaeological sites where sacred ceremonies were held, focus on the Wailua River area. Your best bet is to take a riverboat tour—it's full of kitsch, but you'll definitely walk away with a deeper understanding of ancient Hawaii. Then, head to Lihue's Kauai Museum, where you can pick up a memento of authentic Hawaiian artistry at the gift shop. End your day at Gaylord's restaurant and meander through the historic Kilohana Plantation sugar estate.

Adventure Galore

For big-time adventure, kayak Napali Coast or skydive over the ocean and island for a once-in-a-lifetime experience. For those whose idea of adventure is a good walk, take the flat, coastal trail along the East Side—you can pick it up just about anywhere starting at the southern end of Lydgate Park, heading north. It'll take you almost all the way to Anahola, if you desire. After it's all over, recuperate with a massage by the ocean—or in the comfort of your own room, so you can crash immediately afterward.

A Day on the Water

Start your day before sunrise and head west to Port Allen Marina. Check in with one of the tour-boat operators—who will provide you with plenty of coffee to jump-start your day—and cruise Napali Coast before heading across the Kaulakahi Channel to snorkel the fish-rich waters of Niihau. Slather up with sunscreen and be prepared for a long—and sometimes big—day on the water; you can enjoy a couple of mai tais on the return trip. Something about the sun and the salt air conspires to induce a powerful sense of fatigue—so don't plan anything in the evening. The trip also helps build a huge appetite, so stop at Grinds in Eleele on the way home.

Coastal Drives

If you're staying on the East Side or North Shore, the best drive for ocean vistas is, hands down, Highway 560, which begins at Princeville on the main highway where Highway 56 ends. Stop at the first lookout overseeing Hanalei River valley for a few snapshots; then head down the hill, across the one-lane bridge—taking in the taro fields—and through the town of Hanalei and on to the end of the road at Kee Beach. If you're up for it, enjoy a bit of unparalleled hiking on the Kalalau Trail, go snorkeling at Kee, or simply soak up the sun on the beach, if it's not too crowded. If you're staying on the South Shore or West Side, follow Highway 50 west. You'll start to catch distant ocean vistas from the highway as you head out of the town of Kalaheo and from the coffee fields of Kauai Coffee. Stop here for a sample. You'll come closer to the ocean—and practically reach out and touch it—after you pass through Waimea en route to Kekaha. Although this isn't great swimming water—it's unprotected, with no reef—there is a long stretch of beach here perfect for walking, running, or simply meandering. Once the paved road ends—if you're brave and your car-rental agreement allows—keep going and you'll eventually come to Polihale, a huge, deserted beach. It'll feel like the end of the world here, so it's a great place to spend a quiet afternoon and witness a spectacular sunset. Just be sure to pack plenty of food, water, and sunscreen before you depart Kekaha—and gas up the car.

Shop 'Til You Drop

You could actually see a good many of the island's sights by browsing in our favorite island shops. Of course, you can't see the entire island, but this itinerary will take you through Kapaa and north to Hanalei. A mile north of the grocery stores in Waipouli, Kela's Glass has great art pieces. From there, a leisurely drive north will reveal a rural side of Kauai. If you enjoy tea, sake, or sushi, stop at Kilauea's Kong Lung, where you can stock up on complete place settings for each. Then, head down the road to Hanalei. If you're inspired by surf, stop in Hanalei Surf Company. Our favorite for one-of-a-kind keepsakes—actually antiques and authentic memorabilia—is Yellow Fish Trading Company, and we never head into Hanalei without stopping at On the Road to Hanalei.

Relax Kauai-Style

If you're headed to Kauai for some peace and quiet, you'll want to start your day with yoga at Yoga Hanalei (🌐 *www.yogahanalei.com*) or Kapaa's Bikram Yoga House (🌐 *www.bikramyogakapaa.com*). If you're staying on the South Shore, try yoga on the beach (actually a grassy spot just off the beach) with longtime yoga instructor Joy Zepeda (🌐 *www.kauaioceanfrontyoga.com*). If it happens to be the second or last Sunday of the month, you might then head to the Lawai International Center (🌐 *www.lawaicenter.org*) for an afternoon stroll among 88 Buddhist shrines. On the North Shore, Limahuli Gardens is the perfect place to wander among native plants. Then watch the sun slip into the sea on any west-facing beach and call it a day with a glass of wine.

Have a Little Romance

We can't think of a better way to ensure a romantic vacation for two than to pop a bottle of champagne and walk the Mahaulepu shoreline at sunset, hand in hand with a loved one. Make this a Sunday and take a sunrise walk followed by brunch at the Grand Hyatt. Then spend the afternoon luxuriating with facials, body scrubs, and massage in the Hyatt ANARA Spa's Garden Treatment Village, in a private, thatched hut just for couples. That'll put you in the mood for a wedding ceremony or renewal of vows on the beach followed by a sunset dinner overlooking the ocean at the Beach House restaurant. Can it get any more romantic than this?

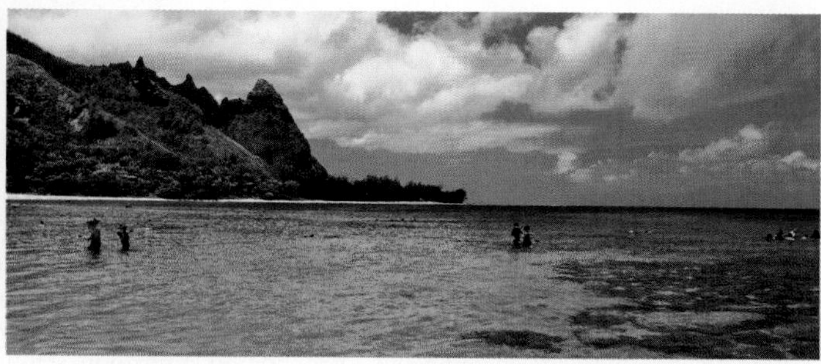

Updated by Charles E. Roessler and Joan Conrow

Even a nickname like "The Garden Island" fails to do justice to Kauai's beauty. Verdant trees grow canopies over the few roads, and brooding mountains are framed by long, sandy beaches, coral reefs, and sheer sea cliffs. Pristine trade winds moderate warm daily temperatures while offering comfort for deep, refreshing sleep through gentle nights.

The main road tracing Kauai's perimeter takes you past much more scenery than would seem possible on one small island. Chiseled mountains, thundering waterfalls, misty hillsides, dreamy beaches, lush vegetation, and small towns make up the physical landscape. Perhaps the most stunning piece of scenery is a place no road will take you—breathtakingly beautiful Napali Coast, which runs along the northwest side of the island.

For adventure seekers, Kauai offers everything from difficult hikes to helicopter tours. The island has top-notch spas and golf courses, and its beaches are known to be some of the most beautiful in the world. Even after you've spent days lazing around drinking mai tais or kayaking your way down a river, there's still plenty to do, as well as see: plantation villages, a historic lighthouse, wildlife refuges, a fern grotto, a colorful canyon, and deep rivers are all easily explored.

■ TIP→ **While exploring the island, try to take advantage of the many roadside scenic overlooks and pull over to take in the constantly changing view.** Don't try to pack too much into one day. Kauai is small, but travel is slow. The island's sights are divided into four geographic areas, in clockwise order: the North Shore, the East Side, the South Shore, and the West Side.

GEOLOGY

Kauai is the oldest and northernmost of the main Hawaiian Islands. Five million years of wind and rain have worked their magic, sculpting fluted sea cliffs and whittling away at the cinder cones and caldera that prove its volcanic origin. Foremost among these is Waialeale, one of the wettest spots on Earth. Its approximate 450-inch annual rainfall feeds the mighty Wailua River, the only navigable waterway in Hawaii. The vast Alakai Swamp soaks up rain like a sponge, releasing it slowly into the watershed that gives Kauai its emerald sheen.

FLORA AND FAUNA

Kauai offers some of the best birding in the state, due in part to the absence of the mongoose. Many nene (the endangered Hawaiian state bird) reared in captivity have been successfully released here, along with an endangered forest bird called the puaiohi. The island is also home to a large colony of migratory nesting seabirds and has two refuges protecting endangered Hawaiian waterbirds. Kauai's most noticeable fowl, however, is the wild chicken. A cross between jungle fowl (*moa*) brought by the Polynesians and domestic chickens and fighting cocks that escaped during the last two hurricanes, they are everywhere, and the roosters crow when they feel like it, not just at dawn. Consider yourself warned.

HISTORY

Kauai's residents have had a reputation for independence since ancient times. Called "The Separate Kingdom," Kauai alone resisted King Kamehameha's charge to unite the Hawaiian Islands. In fact, it was only by kidnapping Kauai's king, Kaumualii, and forcing him to marry Kamehameha's widow that the Garden Isle was joined to the rest of Hawaii. That spirit lives on today as Kauai residents try to resist the lure of tourism dollars captivating the rest of the Islands. Local building tradition maintains that no structure be taller than a coconut tree, and Kauai's capital, Lihue, is still more small town than city.

KAUAI PLANNER

GETTING HERE AND AROUND

AIR TRAVEL

On Kauai, visitors fly into Lihue Airport, on the East Side of the island. Visitor information booths are outside each baggage-claim area. Visitors will also find news- and lei stands, an HMS Host restaurant, and a Travel Traders gift shop at the airport.

Alaska Airlines has a daily Seattle–Lihue flight. American Airlines offers a daily, nonstop Los Angeles–Kauai flight, in addition to its service into Honolulu, Maui, and the Big Island. Delta has a Los Angeles–Lihue flight and also serves Oahu (Honolulu) and Maui. United Airlines provides direct service to Lihue Airport from Denver, Los Angeles, and San Francisco. The carrier also flies into Honolulu, Maui, and the Big Island. Hawaiian offers a daily, nonstop Los Angeles–Kauai flight; all other Mainland flights require a connection in Honolulu.

CAR TRAVEL

Unless you plan to stay strictly at a resort or do all of your sightseeing as part of guided tours, you'll need a rental car. There is bus service on the island, but the bumpy buses tend to run limited hours.

You most likely won't need a four-wheel-drive vehicle anywhere on the island, so save yourself the money. And although convertibles look like fun, the frequent, intermittent rain showers and intense tropical sun make hardtops a better (and cheaper) choice.

If possible, avoid the "rush" hours when the local workers go to and from their jobs. Kauai has some of the highest gas prices in the Islands.

ISLAND DRIVING TIMES

It might not seem as if driving from the North Shore to the West Side, say, would take much time, as Kauai is smaller than Oahu, Maui, and certainly the Big Island. But it will take longer than you'd expect, and Kauai roads are subject to some heavy traffic, especially going through Kapaa and Lihue.

DRIVING TIMES	
Haena to Hanalei	5 miles/15 mins
Hanalei to Princeville	4 miles/10 mins
Princeville to Kilauea	5 miles/10 mins
Kilauea to Anahola	8 miles/12 mins
Anahola to Kapaa	5 miles/10 mins
Kapaa to Lihue	10 miles/20 mins
Lihue to Poipu	13 miles/25 mins
Poipu to Kalaheo	8 miles/15 mins
Kalaheo to Hanapepe	4 miles/8 mins
Hanapepe to Waimea	7 miles/10 mins

HOTELS

If you want to golf, play tennis, or hang at a spa, stay at a resort. You'll also be more likely to find activities for children at resorts, including camps that allow parents a little time off. The island's hotels tend to be smaller and older, with fewer on-site amenities. Some of the swankiest places to stay on the island are the St. Regis Princeville Resort on the North Shore, where rooms run more than $1,000 per night in high season, and the Grand Hyatt Kauai on the South Shore for a bit less; of course, those with views of the ocean book faster than those without.

Condos and vacation rentals on Kauai tend to run the gamut from fabulous luxury estates to scruffy little dives. It's buyer-beware in this totally unregulated sector of the visitor industry. If you're planning to stay at a vacation rental, be sure it's one that is properly permitted by the county. The permit number should be prominent on the ads and signs outside the house.

Properties managed by individual owners can be found on online vacation-rental directories such as CyberRentals and Vacation Rentals By Owner, as well as on the Kauai Visitors Bureau's website. There are also several Kauai-based management companies with vacation rentals.

The island's limited bed-and-breakfasts allow you to meet local residents and more directly experience the aloha spirit. Some have oceanfront settings and breakfasts with everything from tropical fruits and juices, Kauai coffee, and macadamia-nut waffles to breads made with local bananas and mangoes. Some have pools, hot tubs, services such as *lomilomi* massage, and breakfasts delivered to your lanai. Some properties have stand-alone units on-site. *Hotel reviews have been shortened. For full information, visit Fodors.com.*

RESTAURANTS

Kauai's cultural diversity is apparent in its restaurants, which offer authentic Vietnamese, Chinese, Korean, Japanese, Thai, Mexican, Italian, and Hawaiian specialties. Less specialized restaurants cater to the tourist crowd, serving standard American fare—burgers, pizza, sandwiches, surf-and-turf combos, and so on. Kapaa offers the best selection of restaurants, with options for a variety of tastes and budgets; most fast-food joints are in Lihue.

Parents will be relieved to encounter a tolerant attitude toward children, even if they're noisy. Men can leave their jackets and ties at home; attire tends toward informal. But if you want to dress up, you can. Reservations are accepted in most places and required at some of the top restaurants.

WHAT IT COSTS

	$	$$	$$$	$$$$
Restaurants	Under $17	$17–$26	$27–$35	Over $35
Hotels	Under $180	$180–$260	$261–$340	Over $340

Restaurant prices are for a main course at dinner. Hotel prices are for two people in a standard double room in high season. Condo price categories reflect studio and one-bedroom rates. Prices do not include 13.42% hotel tax.

TOURS

Guided tours are convenient; you don't have to worry about finding a parking spot or getting admission tickets. Certified tour guides have taken special classes in Hawaiian history and lore. On the other hand, you won't have the freedom to proceed at your own pace, nor will you have the ability to take a detour trip if something else catches your attention.

Aloha Kauai Tours. You get *way* off the beaten track on these four-wheel-drive van excursions. Choose from several options, including the half-day *Backroads Tour* covering mostly haul-cane roads behind the locked gates of Grove Farm Plantation, and the four-hour *Seafun Snorkeling Tour,* which takes you to a mellow bay where you'll get an up-close experience swimming with schools of multicolor ocean fish. ✉ *3477A Weliweli Rd. (for check-in), Koloa* ☎ *808/245–6400* 🌐 *www.alohakauaitours.com.*

Roberts Hawaii Tours. The *Round-the-Island Tour*, sometimes called the *Waimea Canyon–Fern Grotto Tour,* gives a good overview of half the island, including Fort Elisabeth and Opaekaa Falls. Guests are transported in air-conditioned, 25-passenger minibuses. The $98 trip includes a boat ride up the Wailua River to the Fern Grotto and a visit to the lookouts above Waimea Canyon. They also offer a *Kauai Movie Tour* for $108. ✉ *3-4567 Kuhio Hwy., Hanamaulu* ☎ *808/245–9101, 800/831–5541* 🌐 *www.robertshawaii.com/kauai/* 🎫 *From $98.*

Waimea Historic Walking Tour. Led by a *kupuna,* a respected Hawaiian elder, this two-hour tour begins promptly at 8:30 am every Monday at the West Kauai Visitor Center. While sharing her personal remembrances, Aletha Kaohi leads an easy walk that explains Waimea's distinction as a recipient of the 2006 National Trust for Historic Preservation Award. The tour is free, but a reservation is required. ✉ *9565 Kaumualii Hwy., Waimea (Kauai County)* ☎ *808/338–1332* 🎫 *Free.*

VISITOR INFORMATION

For information about hiking and camping permits and rules and regulations for Napali Coast visit the Division of State Parks section of the 🌐 *hawaii.gov* website.

Contacts Division of State Parks. ✉ *3060 Eiwa St., Suite 306, Lihue* ☎ *808/274–3444* 🌐 *dnlr.hawaii.gov.* **West Kauai Visitor Center.** ✉ *West Kauai Technology and Visitor Center Building, 9565 Kaumualii Hwy, Waimea (Kauai County)* ☎ *808/338–1332* 🌐 *www.westkauaivisitorcenter.org.*

EXPLORING

Updated by Charles E. Roessler

The main road tracing Kauai's perimeter takes you past much more scenery than would seem possible on one small island. Chiseled mountains, thundering waterfalls, misty hillsides, dreamy beaches, lush vegetation, and small towns make up the physical landscape. Perhaps the most stunning piece of scenery is a place no road will take you—the breathtakingly beautiful Napali Coast, which runs along the northwest side of the island.

■ TIP→ **While exploring the island, try to take advantage of the many roadside scenic overlooks and pull over to take in the constantly changing view.** Don't try to pack too much into one day. Kauai is small, but travel is slow. The island's sights are divided into four geographic areas, in clockwise order: the North Shore, the East Side, the South Shore, and the West Side.

THE NORTH SHORE

The North Shore of Kauai includes the environs of Kilauea, Princeville, Hanalei, and Haena. Traveling north on Route 56 from the airport, the coastal highway crosses the Wailua River and the busy towns of Wailua and Kapaa before emerging into a decidedly rural and scenic landscape, with expansive views of the island's rugged interior mountains. As the two-lane highway turns west and narrows, it winds through spectacular scenery and passes the posh resort community of Princeville before dropping down into Hanalei Valley. Here it narrows further and becomes a federally recognized scenic roadway, replete with one-lane bridges (the local etiquette is for six or seven cars to cross at a time, before yielding to those on the other side), hairpin turns, and heart-stopping coastal vistas. The road ends at Kee, where the ethereal rain forests and fluted sea cliffs of Napali Coast Wilderness State Park begin.

In winter Kauai's North Shore receives more rainfall than other areas of the island. Don't let this deter you from visiting. The clouds drift over the mountains of Namolokama creating a mysterious mood and then, in a blink, disappear, rewarding you with mountains laced with a dozen waterfalls or more. The views of the mountain—as well as the sunsets over the ocean—from the St. Regis Bar, adjacent to the lobby of the St. Regis Princeville Resort, are fantastic.

The North Shore attracts all kinds—from celebrities to surfers. In fact, the late Andy Irons, three-time world surfing champion, along with his brother Bruce and legend Laird Hamilton grew up riding waves along the North Shore.

HANALEI, HAENA, AND WEST

Haena is 40 miles northwest of Lihue; Hanalei is 5 miles southeast of Haena.

Crossing the historic one-lane bridge into Hanalei reveals old-world Hawaii, including working taro farms, poi making, and evenings of throwing horseshoes at Black Pot Beach Park—found unmarked (as many places are on Kauai) at the east end of Hanalei Bay Beach Park. Although the current real-estate boom on Kauai has attracted mainland millionaires to build estate homes on the few remaining parcels of land in Hanalei, there's still plenty to see and do. It's *the* gathering place on the North Shore. Restaurants, shops, and people-watching here are among the best on the island, and you won't find a single brand name, chain, or big-box store around—unless you count surf brands like Quiksilver and Billabong.

The beach and river at Hanalei offer swimming, snorkeling, body boarding, surfing, and kayaking. Those hanging around at sunset often congregate at the Hanalei Pavilion, where a husband-and-wife-slack-key-guitar-playing combo makes impromptu appearances. There's an old rumor, since quashed by the local newspaper, the *Garden Island*, that says Hanalei was the inspiration for the song "Puff the Magic Dragon," performed by the 1960s singing sensation Peter, Paul & Mary. Even with the newspaper's clarification, some tours still point out the shape of the dragon carved into the mountains encircling the town.

Once you pass through Hanalei town, the road shrinks even more as you skirt the coast and pass through Haena. Blind corners, quick turns, and one-lane bridges force slow driving along this scenic stretch across the Lumahai and Wainiha valleys. ⚠ **Following extensive flooding in early 2018, areas of Haena, including the state park, are undergoing repairs. Please check before visiting to make sure places are open.**

GETTING HERE AND AROUND

There is only one road leading beyond Princeville to Kee Beach at the western end of the North Shore: Route 560. Hanalei's commercial stretch fronts this route, and you'll find parking at the shopping compounds on each side of the road. After Hanalei, parking is restricted to two main areas, Haena Beach Park and a new lot at Haena State Park, and there are few pullover areas along Route 560. Traffic and especially parking have become major concerns as the North Shore has gained popularity, so be prepared to be patient.

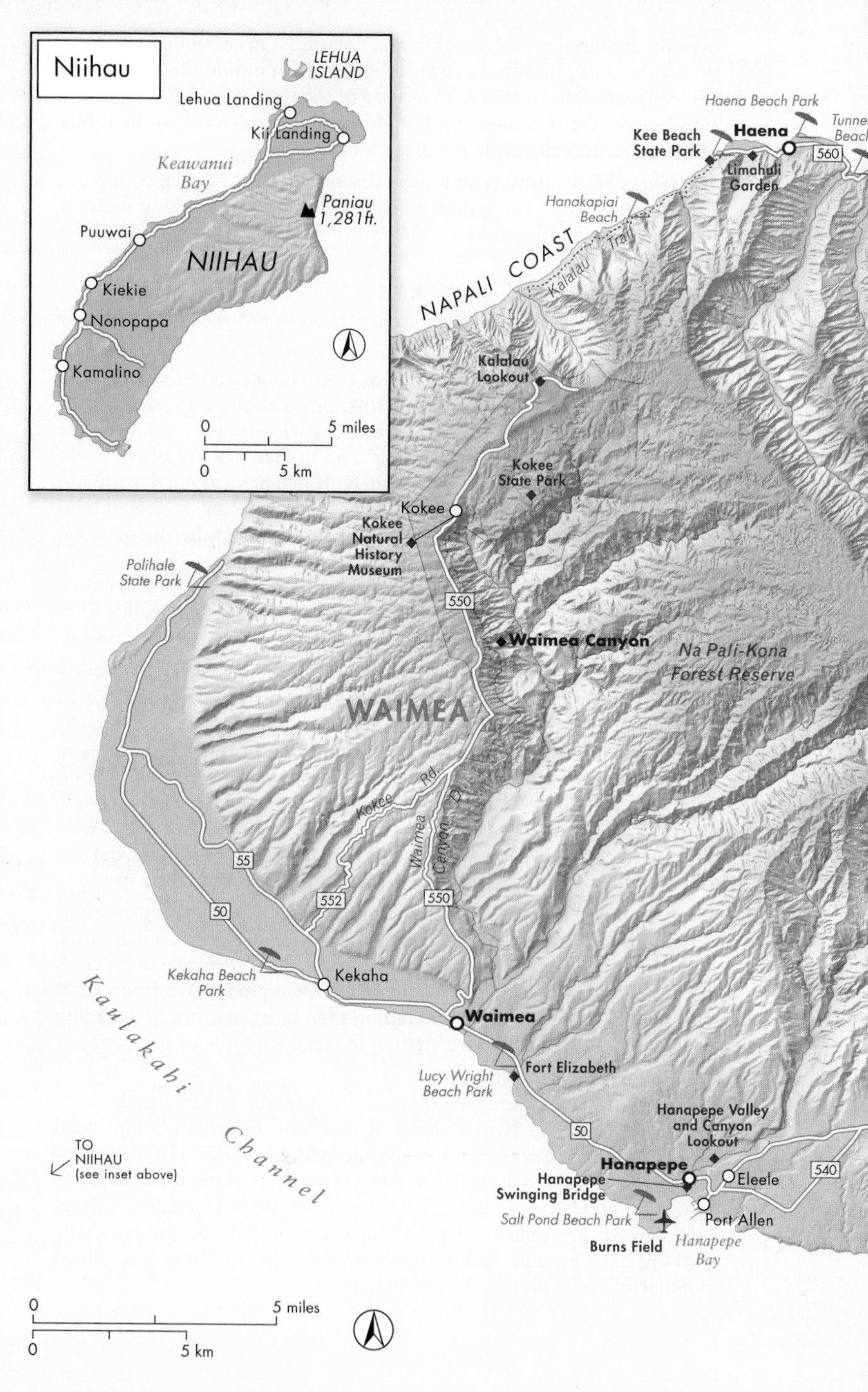

Niihau
LEHUA ISLAND
Lehua Landing
Kii Landing
Keawanui Bay
Paniau 1,281ft.
Puuwai
NIIHAU
Kiekie
Nonopapa
Kamalino
0
5 miles
0
5 km
Haena Beach Park
Tunnels Beach
Kee Beach State Park
Haena
560
Limahuli Garden
Hanakapiai Beach
NAPALI COAST
Kalalau Trail
Kalalau Lookout
Kokee State Park
Kokee
Kokee Natural History Museum
Polihale State Park
550
Waimea Canyon
Na Pali-Kona Forest Reserve
WAIMEA
Kokee Rd.
Waimea Canyon Dr.
55
552
550
50
Kekaha Beach Park
Kekaha
Kaulakahi Channel
Waimea
Fort Elizabeth
Lucy Wright Beach Park
50
Hanapepe Valley and Canyon Lookout
TO NIIHAU (see inset above)
Hanapepe
Hanapepe Swinging Bridge
Eleele
540
Salt Pond Beach Park
Port Allen
Burns Field
Hanapepe Bay
0
5 miles
0
5 km

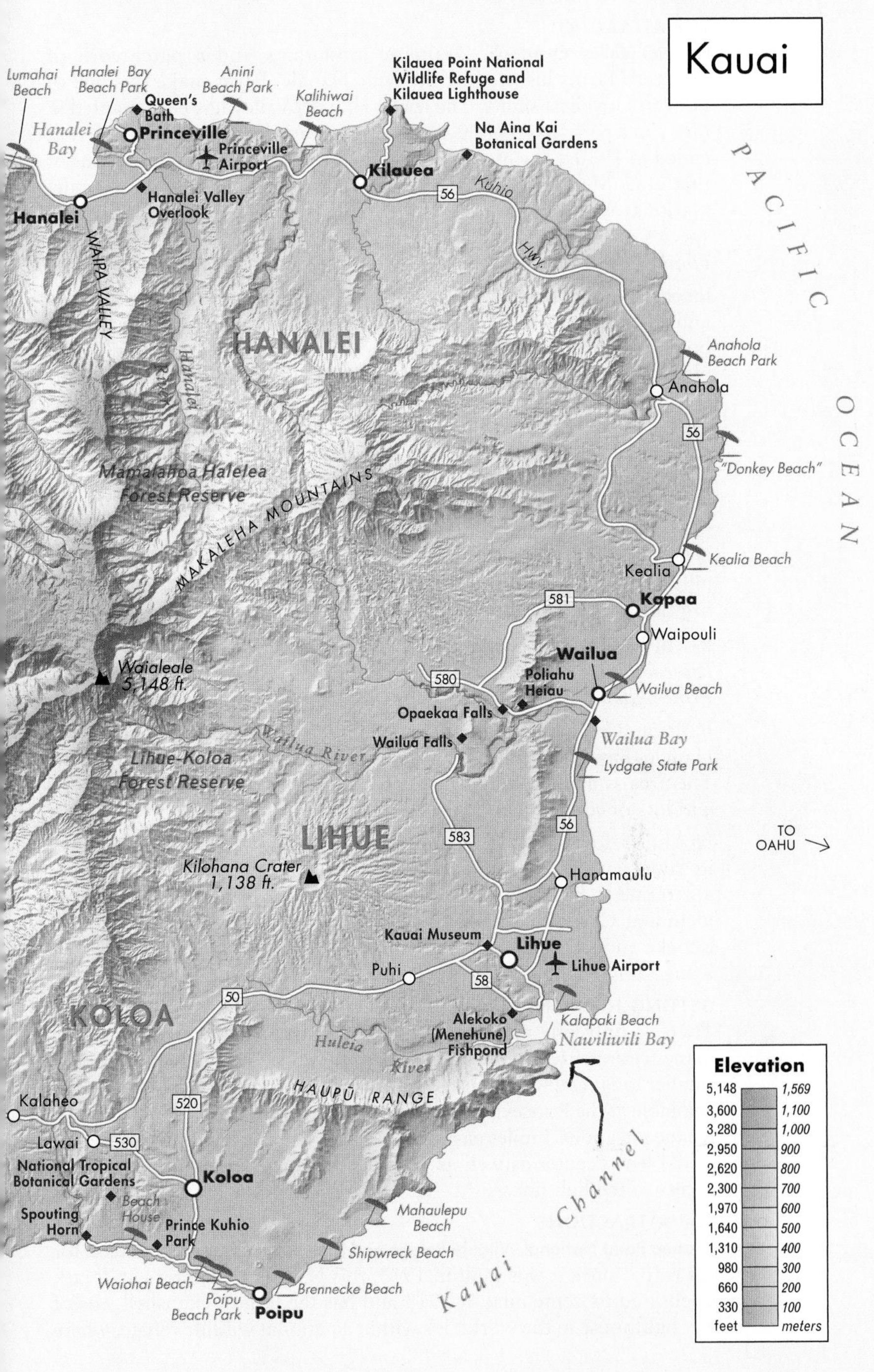
Kauai
Lumahai Beach
Hanalei Bay Beach Park
Anini Beach Park
Kalihiwai Beach
Kilauea Point National Wildlife Refuge and Kilauea Lighthouse
Na Aina Kai Botanical Gardens
Queen's Bath
Princeville
Hanalei Bay
Princeville Airport
Kilauea
56
Kuhio Hwy.
Hanalei Valley Overlook
Hanalei
WAIPA VALLEY
PACIFIC OCEAN
HANALEI
Hanalei River
Anahola Beach Park
Anahola
"Donkey Beach"
Mamalahoa Halelea Forest Reserve
MAKALEHA MOUNTAINS
Kealia Beach
Kealia
581
Kapaa
Waipouli
Wailua
Waialeale 5,148 ft.
580
Poliahu Heiau
Wailua Beach
Opaekaa Falls
Wailua Falls
Wailua River
Wailua Bay
Lihue-Koloa Forest Reserve
Lydgate State Park
LIHUE
583
TO OAHU
Kilohana Crater 1,138 ft.
Hanamaulu
Kauai Museum
Lihue
Lihue Airport
Puhi
58
50
KOLOA
Alekoko (Menehune) Fishpond
Kalapaki Beach
Nawiliwili Bay
Huleia River
HAUPŪ RANGE
Kalaheo
520
Lawai
530
National Tropical Botanical Gardens
Koloa
Beach House
Spouting Horn
Prince Kuhio Park
Mahaulepu Beach
Shipwreck Beach
Waiohai Beach
Brennecke Beach
Poipu Beach Park
Poipu
Kauai Channel
Elevation
5,148 1,569
3,600 1,100
3,280 1,000
2,950 900
2,620 800
2,300 700
1,970 600
1,640 500
1,310 400
980 300
660 200
330 100
feet meters

TOP ATTRACTIONS

Fodor's Choice ★ **Hanalei Valley Overlook.** Dramatic mountains and a patchwork of neat taro farms bisected by the wide Hanalei River make this one of Hawaii's loveliest sights. The fertile Hanalei Valley has been planted in taro since perhaps AD 700, save for a century-long foray into rice that ended in 1960. (The historic Haraguchi Rice Mill is all that remains of that era.) Many taro farmers lease land within the 900-acre Hanalei National Wildlife Refuge, helping to provide wetland habitat for four species of endangered Hawaiian waterbirds. ✉ *Rte. 56, across from Foodland, Princeville.*

Limahuli Garden. Narrow Limahuli Valley, with its fluted mountain peaks and ancient stone taro terraces, creates an unparalleled setting for this botanical garden and nature preserve. Dedicated to protecting native plants and unusual varieties of taro, it represents the principles of conservation and stewardship held by its founder, Charles "Chipper" Wichman. Limahuli's primordial beauty and strong *mana* (spiritual power) eclipse the extensive botanical collection. It's one of the most gorgeous spots on Kauai and the crown jewel of the National Tropical Botanical Garden, which Wichman now heads. Call ahead to reserve a guided tour, or tour on your own. Be sure to check out the quality gift shop and revolutionary compost toilet, and be prepared to walk a somewhat steep hillside. ✉ *5-8291 Kuhio Hwy., Haena* ☎ *808/826–1053* 🌐 *www.ntbg.org* 🎫 *Self-guided tour $20, guided tour $40 (reservations required).*

PRINCEVILLE, KILAUEA, AND AROUND

Princeville is 4 miles northeast of Hanalei; Kilauea is 5 miles east of Princeville.

Built on a bluff offering gorgeous sea and mountain vistas, including Hanalei Bay, Princeville is the creation of a 1970s resort development. The area is anchored by a few large hotels, world-class golf courses, and lots of condos and time-shares.

Five miles down Route 56, a former plantation town, Kilauea maintains its rural flavor in the midst of unrelenting gentrification encroaching all around it. Especially noteworthy are its historic lava-rock buildings, including **Christ Memorial Episcopal Church** on Kolo Road and, on Keneke and Kilauea Road (commonly known as Lighthouse Road), the Kong Lung Company, which is now an expensive shop.

GETTING HERE AND AROUND

There is only one main road through the Princeville resort area, so maneuvering a car here can be a nightmare. If you're trying to find a smaller lodging unit, be sure to get specific driving directions. Parking is available at the Princeville Shopping Center at the entrance to the resort. Kilauea is about 5 miles east on Route 56. There's a public parking lot in the town center as well as parking at the end of Kilauea Road for access to the lighthouse.

TOP ATTRACTIONS

Fodor's Choice ★ **Kilauea Point National Wildlife Refuge and Kilauea Lighthouse.** A beacon for sea traffic since it was built in 1913, this National Historic Landmark celebrated its centennial in 2013 and has the largest clamshell lens of any lighthouse in the world. It's within a national wildlife refuge, where thousands of seabirds soar on the trade winds and nest on the steep ocean cliffs. Seeing endangered nene geese, white- and red-tailed tropic birds, and more (all identifiable by educational signboards) as well as native plants, dolphins, humpback whales, huge winter surf, and gorgeous views of the North Shore are well worth the modest entry fee. The gift shop has a great selection of books about the island's natural history and an array of unique merchandise, with all proceeds benefiting education and preservation efforts. ✉ *Kilauea Lighthouse Rd., Kilauea* ☎ *808/828–1413* 🌐 *www.kilaueapoint.org, www.fws.gov/kilaueapoint* 🎟 *$5, under 15 free.*

Fodor's Choice ★ **Na Aina Kai Botanical Gardens.** Joyce and Ed Doty's love for plants and art spans 240 acres and includes many different gardens, a hardwood plantation, an ahupua'a (a Hawaiian land division), a re-created Navaho compound and an Athabascan village, a Japanese teahouse, a hedge maze, a waterfall, and access to a sandy beach. Throughout are more than 200 bronze sculptures, one of the nation's largest collections. One popular feature is a children's garden with a 16-foot-tall Jack and the Beanstalk bronze sculpture, gecko maze, tree house, kid-size train, and, of course, a tropical jungle. Located in a residential neighborhood and hoping to maintain good neighborly relations, the Gardens, a nonprofit organization, limits tours (guided only). Tour lengths vary widely, from 1½ to 5 hours. Reservations are required. ✉ *4101 Wailapa Rd., Kilauea* ☎ *808/828–0525* 🌐 *www.naainakai.org* 🎟 *From $35.*

Fodor's Choice ★ **Queen's Bath.** A tropical path tucked away in a North Shore neighborhood winds its way down to the oceanfront, where a large tide pool has been carved into the dark lava rock creating nature's version of an infinity pool. It takes some dexterity (and reef shoes) to get there, but once in you can dawdle like a regal queen, emerging only to scramble up the rocks for a short cliff dive back in. Every now and again a wave breaks the barrier, sending squealing bathers asunder. Be careful, though: October through May brings big surf, and people have been swept off the rocks and have drowned. ■ **TIP→ Look for green sea turtles swimming in the surf beyond the pool.** ✉ *Kapiolani Rd., Princeville.*

NAPALI COAST

Napali Coast is considered the jewel of Kauai, and for all its greenery, it would surely be an emerald. After seeing the coast, many are at a loss for words, because its beauty is so overwhelming. Others resort to poetry. Pulitzer Prize–winning poet W. S. Merwin wrote a book-length poem, *The Folding Cliffs,* based on a true story set in Napali. *Napali* means "the cliffs," and while it sounds like a simple name, it's quite an apt description. The coastline is cut by a series of small valleys, like fault lines, running to the interior, with the resulting cliffs seeming to bend back on themselves like an accordion-folded fan made of green velvet. More than 5 million years old, these sea cliffs rise thousands of feet above the Pacific, and every shade of green is represented in the vegetation that blankets their lush peaks and folds. At their base there are caves, secluded beaches, and waterfalls to explore.

5

Let's put this in perspective: even if you had only one day on Kauai, we'd still recommend heading to Napali Coast on Kauai's northwest side. Once you're there, you'll soon realize why no road traverses this series of folding-fan cliffs. That leaves three ways to experience the coastline—by air, by water, or on foot. We recommend all three, in this order: air, water, foot. Each one gets progressively more sensory.(⇨ *See the Napali feature in the chapter.*) A helicopter tour is your best bet if you're strapped for time. We recommend Jack Harter Helicopters or Safari Helicopters. Boat tours are great for family fun; and hiking, of course, is the most budget-friendly option.

Whatever way you choose to visit Napali, you might want to keep this awe-inspiring fact in mind: at one time, thousands of Hawaiians lived self-sufficiently in these valleys. ⚠ **Following extensive flooding in early 2018, areas of the Napali Coast, including the Kalalau Trail, are undergoing repairs. Please check before visiting to make sure places are open.**

GETTING HERE AND AROUND

Napali Coast runs 15 miles from Kee Beach, one of Kauai's more popular snorkeling spots, on the island's North Shore to Polihale State Park, the longest stretch of beach in the state, on the West Side of the island.

How do you explore this gorgeous stretch of coastline? You can't drive to it, through it, or around it. You can't see Napali from a scenic lookout. You can't even take a mule ride to it. The only way to experience its magic is from the sky, the ocean, or the trail. The Kalalau Trail can be hiked from the "end of the road" at Kee Beach where the trailhead begins in Haena State Park at the northwest end of Kuhio Highway (Route 56). There's no need to hike the entire 11 miles to get a full experience, especially if you just hike the first 2 miles into Hanakapiai Beach and another 2 miles up that valley.

TOP ATTRACTIONS

Kee Beach State Park. This stunning, and often extremely overcrowded, beach marks the start of majestic Napali Coast. The 11-mile **Kalalau Trail** begins near the parking lot, drawing day hikers and backpackers. Another path leads from the sand to a stone hula platform dedicated to **Laka,** the goddess of hula, which has been in use since ancient times. This is a sacred site that should be approached with respect; it's inappropriate for visitors to leave offerings at the altar, which is tended by students in a local hula *halau* (school). Local etiquette suggests observing from a distance. Most folks head straight for the sandy beach and its dreamy lagoon, which is great for snorkeling when the sea is calm. ✉ *Western end of Rte. 560, Haena.*

THE EAST SIDE

The East Side encompasses Lihue, Wailua, and Kapaa. It's also known as the Coconut Coast, as there was once a coconut plantation where today's aptly named Coconut Marketplace is located. A small grove still exists on both sides of the highway. *Mauka,* a fenced herd of goats keeps the grass tended; on the *makai* side, you can walk through the grove, although it's best not to walk directly under the trees—falling coconuts can be dangerous. Lihue is the county seat, and the whole East Side is the island's center of commerce, so early-morning and late-afternoon drive times (or rush hour) can get very congested. (Because there's only one main road, if there's a serious traffic accident the entire roadway may be closed, with no way around. Not to worry; it's a rarity.)

KAPAA AND WAILUA

Kapaa is 16 miles southeast of Kilauea; Wailua is 3 miles southwest of Kapaa.

Old Town Kapaa was once a plantation town, which is no surprise—most of the larger towns on Kauai once were. Old Town Kapaa is made up of a collection of wooden-front shops, some built by plantation workers and still run by their progeny today. Kapaa houses the two biggest grocery stores on the island, side by side: Foodland and Safeway. It also offers plenty of dining options for breakfast, lunch, and dinner, and gift shopping. If the timing is right, plan to cruise the town on the first Saturday evening of each month when the bands are playing and the town's wares are on display. To the south, Wailua comprises a few restaurants and shops, a few mid-range resorts along the coastline, and a housing community *mauka*. ⚠ **Following extensive flooding in early 2018, areas along the Wailua River, including the state park, are undergoing repairs. Please check before visiting to make sure places are open.**

5

GETTING HERE AND AROUND

Turn to the right out of the airport at Lihue for the road to Wailua. Careful, though—the zone between Lihue and Wailua has been the site of many car accidents. Two bridges—under which the very culturally significant Wailua River gently flows—mark the beginning of Wailua. It quickly blends into Kapaa; there's no real demarcation. Pay attention and drive carefully, always knowing where you are going and when to turn off.

TOP ATTRACTIONS

FAMILY **Opaekaa Falls.** The mighty Wailua River produces many dramatic waterfalls, and Opaekaa (pronounced oh-pie-kah-ah) is one of the best. It plunges hundreds of feet to the pool below and can be easily viewed from a scenic overlook with ample parking. Opaekaa means "rolling shrimp," which refers to tasty native crustaceans that were once so abundant they could be seen tumbling in the falls. Do not attempt to hike down to the pool. **■TIP→ Just before reaching the parking area for the waterfalls, turn left into a scenic pullout for great views of the Wailua River valley and its march to the sea.** ✉ *Kuamoo Rd., Wailua (Kauai County)* ✢ *From Rte. 56, turn mauka onto Kuamoo Rd. and drive 1½ miles.*

Fodor's Choice ★ **Poliahu Heiau.** Storyboards near this ancient *heiau* (sacred site) recount the significance of the many sacred structures found along the Wailua River. It's unknown exactly how the ancient Hawaiians used Poliahu Heiau—one of the largest pre-Christian temples on the island—but legend says it was built by the Menehune because of the unusual stonework found in its walled enclosures. From this site, drive downhill toward the ocean to *pohaku hanau*, a two-piece birthing stone said to confer

Continued on page 448

NAPALI COAST: EMERALD QUEEN OF KAUAI

If you're coming to Kauai, Napali ("the cliffs" in Hawaiian) is a major must-see. More than 5 million years old, these sea cliffs rise thousands of feet above the Pacific, and every shade of green is represented in the vegetation that blankets their lush peaks and folds. At their base, there are caves, secluded beaches, and waterfalls to explore.

The big question is how to explore this gorgeous stretch of coastline. You can't drive to it, through it, or around it. You can't see Napali from a scenic lookout. You can't even take a mule ride to it. The only way to experience its magic is from the sky, the ocean, or the trail.

FROM THE SKY

If you've booked a helicopter tour of Napali, you might start wondering what you've gotten yourself into on the way to the airport. Will it feel like being on a small airplane? Will there be turbulence? Will it be worth all the money you just plunked down?

Your concerns will be assuaged on the helipad, once you see the faces of those who have just returned from their journey: Everyone looks totally blissed out. And now it's your turn.

Climb on board, strap on your headphones, and the next thing you know the helicopter gently lifts up, hovers for a moment, and floats away like a spider on the wind—no roaring engines, no rumbling down a runway. If you've chosen a flight with music, you'll feel as if you're inside your very own IMAX movie.

Pinch yourself if you must, because this is the real thing. Your pilot shares history, legend, and lore. If you miss something, speak up: pilots love to show off their island knowledge. You may snap a few pictures (not too many or you'll miss the eyes-on experience!), nudge a friend or spouse, and point at a whale breeching in the ocean, but mostly you stare, mouth agape. There is simply no other way to take in the immensity and greatness of Napali but from the air.

(left) The Napali Coast is a breathtaking stretch of Kauai coastline lined by sea cliffs rising thousands of feet into the sky. (bottom) Helicopter tour over Napali Coast

GOOD TO KNOW	WHAT YOU MIGHT SEE
Helicopter companies depart from the north, east, and west sides of the island. Most are based in Lihue, near the airport. If you want more adventure—and air—choose one of the helicopter companies that flies with the doors off. Some companies offer flights without music. Know the experience you want ahead of time. Some even sell a DVD of your flight, so you don't have to worry about taking pictures. Wintertime rain grounds some flights; plan your trip early in your stay in case the flight gets rescheduled.	■ Nualolo Kai (an ancient Hawaiian fishing village) with its fringed reef ■ The 300-foot Hanakapiai Falls ■ A massive sea arch formed in the rock by erosion ■ The 11-mile Kalalau Trail threading its way along the coast ■ The amazing striations of aa and pahoehoe lava flows that helped push Kauai above the sea
IS THIS FOR ME?	
Taking a helicopter trip is the most expensive way to see Napali—as much as $300 for an hour-long tour. Claustrophobic? Choose a boat tour or hike. It's a tight squeeze in the helicopter, especially in one of the middle seats. Short on time? Taking a helicopter tour is a great way to see the island.	

FROM THE OCEAN

Napali from the ocean is two treats in one: spend a good part of the day on (or in) the water, and gaze up at majestic green sea cliffs rising thousands of feet above your head.

There are three ways to see it: a mellow pleasure-cruise catamaran allows you to kick back and sip a mai tai; an adventurous raft (Zodiac) tour will take you inside sea caves under waterfalls, and give you the option of snorkeling; and a daylong outing in a kayak is possible in the summer.

Any way you travel, you'll breathe ocean air, feel spray on your face, and see pods of spinner dolphins, green sea turtles, flying fish, and, if you're lucky, a rare Hawaiian monk seal.

Napali stretches from Kee Beach in the north to Polihale beach on the West Side. You'll be heading towards the lush Hanakapiai Valley, where within a few minutes, you'll see caves and waterfalls galore. About halfway down the coast just after the Kalalau Trail ends, you'll come to an immense arch—formed where the sea eroded the less dense basaltic rock—and a thundering 50-foot waterfall. And as the island curves near Nualolo State Park, you'll begin to notice less vegetation and more rocky outcroppings.

(left and top right) Kayaking on Napali Coast
(bottom right) Dolphin on Napali Coast

GOOD TO KNOW

If you want to snorkel, choose a morning rather than an afternoon tour—preferably during a summer visit—when seas are calmer.

If you're on a budget, choose a non-snorkeling tour.

If you want to see whales, take any tour, but be sure to plan your vacation for December through March.

You can only embark from the North Shore in summer. If you're staying on the South Shore, it might not be worth your time to drive to the north, so head to the West Side.

IS THIS FOR ME?

Boat tours are several hours long, so if you have only a short time on Kauai, a helicopter tour is a better alternative.

Even on a small boat, you won't get the individual attention and exclusivity of a helicopter tour.

Prone to seasickness? A large boat can be surprisingly rocky, so be prepared. Afternoon trips are rougher because the winds pick up.

WHAT YOU MIGHT SEE

- Hawaii's state fish—the humuhumunukunukuapuaa—otherwise known as the reef triggerfish
- Waiahuakua Sea Cave, with a waterfall coming through its roof
- Tons of marine life, including dolphins, green sea turtles, flying fish, and humpback whales, especially in February and March
- Waterfalls—especially if your trip is after a heavy rain

FROM THE TRAIL

If you want to be one with Napali—feeling the soft red earth beneath your feet, picnicking on the beaches, and touching the lush vegetation—hiking the Kalalau Trail is the way to do it.

Most people hike only the first 2 miles of the 11-mile trail and turn around at Hanakapiai. This 4-mile round-trip hike takes three to four hours. It starts at sea level and doesn't waste any time gaining elevation. (Take heart—the uphill lasts only a mile and tops out at 400 feet; then it's downhill all the way.) At the half-mile point, the trail curves west and the folds of Napali Coast unfurl.

Along the way you might share the trail with feral goats and wild pigs. Some of the vegetation is native; much is introduced.

After the 1-mile mark the trail begins its drop into Hanakapiai. You'll pass a couple of streams of water trickling across the trail, and maybe some banana, ginger, the native uluhe fern, and the Hawaiian ti plant. Finally the trail swings around the eastern ridge of Hanakapiai for your first glimpse of the valley and then switchbacks down the mountain. You'll have to boulder-hop across the stream to reach the beach. If you like, you can take a 4-mile, round-trip fairly strenuous side trip from this point to the gorgeous Hanakapiai Falls.

(left) Awaawapuhi mountain biker on razor-edge ridge
(top right) Feral goats in Kalalau Valley
(bottom right) Napali Coast

GOOD TO KNOW

Wear comfortable, amphibious shoes. Unless your feet require extra support, wear a self-bailing sort of shoe (for stream crossings) that doesn't mind mud. Don't wear heavy, waterproof hiking boots.

During winter the trail is often muddy, so be extra careful; sometimes it's completely inaccessible.

Don't hike after heavy rain—flash floods are common.

If you plan to hike the entire 11-mile trail (most people do the shorter hike described at left) you'll need a permit to go past Hanakapiai.

IS THIS FOR ME?

Of all the ways to see Napali (with the exception of kayaking the coast), this is the most active. You need to be in decent shape to hit the trail.

If you're vacationing in winter, this hike might not be an option due to flooding—whereas you can take a helicopter year-round.

WHAT YOU MIGHT SEE

- Big dramatic surf right below your feet
- Amazing vistas of the cool blue Pacific
- The spectacular Hanakapiai Falls; if you have a permit don't miss Hanakoa Falls, less than 1/2 mile off the trail
- Wildlife, including goats and pigs
- Zany-looking hala trees, with aerial roots and long, skinny serrated leaves known as lau hala. Early Hawaiians used them to make mats, baskets, and canoe sails.

special blessings on all children born there, and *pohaku piko,* whose crevices were a repository for umbilical cords left by parents seeking a clue to their child's destiny, which reportedly was foretold by how the cord fared in the rock. Some Hawaiians feel these sacred stones shouldn't be viewed as tourist attractions, so always treat them with respect. Never stand or sit on the rocks or leave any offerings. ✉ *Rte. 580, Kuamoo Rd., Wailua (Kauai County).*

FAMILY **Wailua Falls.** You may recognize this impressive cascade from the opening sequences of the *Fantasy Island* television series. Kauai has plenty of noteworthy waterfalls, but this one is especially gorgeous, easy to find, and easy to photograph. ✉ *Maalo Rd., off Rte. 580, Lihue.*

LIHUE

7 miles southwest of Wailua.

The commercial and political center of Kauai County, which includes the islands of Kauai and Niihau, Lihue is home to the island's major airport, harbor, and hospital. This is where you can find the state and county offices that issue camping and hiking permits and the same fast-food eateries and big-box stores that blight the mainland. The county is seeking help in reviving the downtown; for now, once your business is done, there's little reason to linger in lackluster Lihue.

GETTING HERE AND AROUND

Route 56 leads into Lihue from the north and Route 50 comes here from the south and west. The road from the airport (where Kauai's car rental agencies are) leads to the middle of Lihue. Many of the area's stores and restaurants are on and around Rice Street, which also leads to Kalapaki Bay and Nawiliwili Harbor.

TOP ATTRACTIONS

Fodor's Choice ★ **Alekoko (Menehune) Fishpond.** No one knows just who built this intricate aquaculture structure in the Huleia River. Legend attributes it to the Menehune, a mythical—or real, depending on who you ask—ancient race of people known for their small stature, industrious nature, and superb stoneworking skills. Volcanic rock was cut and fit together into massive walls 4 feet thick and 5 feet high, forming an enclosure for raising mullet and other freshwater fish that has endured for centuries. ✉ *Hulemalu Rd., Niumalu.*

Fodor's Choice ★ **Kauai Museum.** Maintaining a stately presence on Rice Street, the historic museum building is easy to find. It features a permanent display, "The Story of Kauai," which provides a competent overview of the Garden Island and Niihau, tracing the Islands' geology, mythology, and cultural history. Local artists are represented in changing exhibits in the second-floor Mezzanine Gallery. The expanded gift shop alone is worth a visit, with a fine collection of authentic Niihau shell lei, feather hatband lei, hand-turned wooden bowls, reference books, and other quality arts, crafts, and gifts—many of them locally made. ✉ *4428 Rice St., Lihue* ☎ *808/245–6931* 🌐 *www.kauaimuseum.org* 🎟 *$15.*

THE SOUTH SHORE

As you follow the main road south from Lihue, the landscape becomes lush and densely vegetated before giving way to drier conditions that characterize Poipu, the South Side's major resort area. Poipu owes much of its popularity to a steady supply of sunshine and a string of sandy beaches, although the beaches are smaller and more covelike than those on the West Side. With its extensive selection of accommodations, services, and activities, the South Shore attracts more visitors than any other area of Kauai. It also attracted developers with big plans for the onetime sugarcane fields that are nestled in this region and enveloped by mountains. There are few roads in and out, and local residents are concerned about increased traffic as well as noise and dust pollution as a result of chronic construction. If you're planning to stay on the South Side, be sure to ask if your hotel, condo, or vacation rental will be impacted by the development during your visit.

Both Poipu and nearby Koloa (site of Kauai's first sugar mill) can be reached via Route 520 (Maluhia Road) from the Lihue area. Route 520 is known locally as Tree Tunnel Road, due to the stand of eucalyptus trees lining the road that were planted at the turn of the 20th century by Walter Duncan McBryde, a Scotsman who began cattle ranching on Kauai's South Shore. The canopy of trees was ripped to literal shreds twice—in 1982 during Hurricane Iwa and again in 1992 during Hurricane Iniki. And, true to Kauai, both times the trees grew back into an impressive tunnel. It's a distinctive way to announce, "You are now on vacation," for there's a definite feel of leisure in the air here. There's still plenty to do—snorkel, bike, walk, horseback ride, take an ATV tour, surf, scuba dive, shop, and dine—everything you'd want on a tropical vacation. From the west, Route 530 (Koloa Road) slips into downtown Koloa, a string of fun shops and restaurants, at an intersection with the only gas station on the South Shore.

KOLOA

11 miles southwest of Lihue.

Hawaii's lucrative foray into sugar was born in this sleepy town, where the first sugar was milled back in 1835. You can still see the mill's old stone smokestack. Little else remains, save for the charming plantation-style buildings that have kept Koloa from becoming a tacky tourist trap for Poipu-bound visitors. The original small-town character has been preserved by converting historic structures along the main street into boutiques, restaurants, and shops. Placards describe the original tenants and life in the old mill town. Look for Koloa Fish Market, which offers poke and sashimi takeout, and Progressive Expressions, a popular local surf shop.

TOP ATTRACTIONS

Fodor's Choice ★ **Old Koloa Town.** Koloa's first sugar mill opened in 1835, ushering in an era of sugar production throughout the Islands, with more than 100 plantations established by 1885. Many of the workers came from the Philippines, Japan, China, Korea and Portugal, creating Hawaii's multiethnic mélange. Today, many of Koloa's historic buildings beneath the shade of ancient monkeypod trees have been converted into fun

"Jungle fowl were all over some of the scenic stops in Kauai. They had beautiful colors, and it was cool just to see them walking around." —jedivader

shops and restaurants. You'll just want to stroll and take it all in; favorites include Island Soap and Candleworks, Crazyshirts, and Lappert's, Hawaiian-inspired ice cream made daily in nearby Hanapepe. Try the Kauai Pie and Luau Delight flavors. ■ **TIP→ Be sure to approach Old Koloa Town via the Tree Tunnel, a romantic canopy of eucalyptus trees planted more than a century ago along a stretch of Maluhia Road.** ✉ *Koloa Rd., Koloa* 🌐 *www.oldkoloa.com.*

POIPU

2 miles southeast of Koloa.

Thanks to its generally sunny weather and a string of golden-sand beaches dotted with oceanfront lodgings, Poipu is a top choice for many visitors. Beaches are user-friendly, with protected waters for *keiki* (children) and novice snorkelers, lifeguards, restrooms, covered pavilions, and a sweet coastal promenade ideal for leisurely strolls. Some experts have even ranked Poipu Beach Park number one in the nation. It depends on your preferences, of course, though it certainly does warrant high accolades.

GETTING HERE AND AROUND

Poipu is the one area on Kauai where you could get by without a car, though that could mean an expensive taxi ride from the airport and limited access to other parts of the island. To reach Poipu by car, follow Poipu Road south from Koloa. After the traffic circle, the road curves to follow the coast, leading to some of the popular South Shore beaches.

TOP ATTRACTIONS

National Tropical Botanical Gardens (*NTBG*). Tucked away in Lawai Valley, these gardens include lands and a cottage once used by Hawaii's Queen Emma for a summer retreat. Trams depart on the half hour to transport people from the visitor center to the gardens. The rambling 252-acre McBryde Gardens has a number of exhibits to help visitors learn about biodiversity and plants collected throughout the tropics, including the Life Canoe Garden that features plants originally brought to Hawaii by early voyagers from distant Polynesian islands. It is known as a garden of "research and conservation." The 100-acre Allerton Gardens, which can be visited only on a guided tour, artfully displays statues and water features that were originally developed as part of a private estate. Reservations are required to visit both gardens. The visitor center has a high-quality gift shop with botany-theme merchandise. Besides harboring and propagating rare and endangered plants from Hawaii and elsewhere, NTBG functions as a scientific research and education center. The organization also operates gardens in Limahuli, on Kauai's North Shore, and in Hana, on Maui's east shore, as well as one in Florida. ✉ *4425 Lawai Rd., Poipu* ☎ *808/742–2623* 🌐 *www.ntbg.org* 🎫 *McBryde self-guided tour $30, Allerton guided tour $50.*

Prince Kuhio Park. A triangle of grass behind the Prince Kuhio condominiums honors the birthplace of Kauai's beloved Prince Jonah Kuhio Kalanianaole. Known for his kind nature and good deeds, he lost his chance at the throne when Americans staged an illegal overthrow of Queen Liliuokalani in 1893 and toppled Hawaii's constitutional monarchy. This is a great place to view wave riders surfing a popular break known as PKs and to watch the sun sink into the Pacific. ✉ *Lawai Rd., Poipu.*

Fodor's Choice ★ **Spouting Horn.** If the conditions are right, you can see a natural blowhole in the reef behaving like Old Faithful, shooting salt water high into the air and making a cool, echoing sound. It's most dramatic during big summer swells, which jam large quantities of water through an ancient lava tube with great force. Vendors hawk inexpensive souvenirs and collectibles in the parking lot. You may find good deals on shell jewelry, but some vendors also carry exotic Niihau-shell creations with prices up to $12,000. ✉ *End of Lawai Rd., Poipu* 🌐 *www.kauai.com/spouting-horn.*

THE WEST SIDE

Exploring the West Side is akin to visiting an entirely different world. The landscape is dramatic and colorful: a patchwork of green, blue, black, and orange. The weather is hot and dry, the beaches are long, the sand is dark. Niihau, a private island and the last remaining place in Hawaii where Hawaiian is spoken exclusively, can be glimpsed offshore. This is rural Kauai, where sugar is making its last stand and taro is still cultivated in the fertile river valleys. The lifestyle is slow, easy, and traditional, with many folks fishing and hunting to supplement their diets. Here and there modern industry has intruded into this pastoral scene: huge generators turn oil into electricity at Port Allen; seed companies cultivate experimental crops of genetically engineered plants in Kekaha and Waimea; the navy launches rockets at Mana to test the "Star Wars" missile defense system; and NASA mans a tracking station in the wilds of Kokee. It's a region of contrasts that simply shouldn't be missed.

Heading west from Lihue or Poipu, you pass through a string of tiny towns, plantation camps, and historic sites, each with a story to tell of centuries past. There's Hanapepe, whose coastal salt ponds have been harvested since ancient times; Kaumakani, where the sugar industry still clings to life; Fort Elisabeth, from which an enterprising Russian tried to take over the island in the early 1800s; and Waimea, where Captain Cook made his first landing in the Islands, forever changing the face of Hawaii.

From Waimea town you can head up into the mountains, skirting the rim of magnificent Waimea Canyon and climbing higher still until you reach the cool, often-misty forests of Kokee State Park. From the vantage point at the top of this gemlike island, 3,200 to 4,200 feet above sea level, you can gaze into the deep, verdant valleys of the North Shore and Napali Coast. This is where the "real" Kauai can still be found: the native plants, insects, and birds that are found nowhere else on Earth.

HANAPEPE

15 miles west of Poipu.

In the 1980s Hanapepe was fast becoming a ghost town, its farm-based economy mirroring the decline of agriculture. Today it's a burgeoning art colony with galleries, crafts studios, and a lively art-theme street fair on Friday nights. The main street has a new vibrancy enhanced by the restoration of several historic buildings. The emergence of Kauai coffee as a major West Side crop, and expanded activities at Port Allen, now the main departure point for tour boats, also gave the town's economy a boost.

GETTING HERE AND AROUND

Hanapepe, locally known as Kauai's "biggest little town," is just past the Eleele Shopping Center on the main highway (Route 50). A sign leads you to the town center, where street parking is easy and there's an enjoyable walking tour.

TOP ATTRACTIONS

Hanapepe Swinging Bridge. This bridge may not be the biggest adventure on Kauai, but it's enough to make your heart hop. It's considered a historic suspension bridge even though it was rebuilt in 1996 after the original was destroyed—like so much of the island—by Hurricane Iniki. What is interesting about this bridge is that it's not just for show; it actually provides the only access to taro fields across the Waimea River. If you're in the neighborhood, it's worth a stroll. ⊠ *Off Hanapepe Rd., next to Banana Patch Studios parking lot, Hanapepe.*

Hanapepe Valley and Canyon Lookout. This dramatic divide and fertile river valley once housed a thriving Hawaiian community of taro farmers, with some of the ancient fields still in cultivation today. From the lookout, you can take in the farms on the valley floor with the majestic mountains as a backdrop. ⊠ *Rte. 50, Hanapepe.*

SUNSHINE MARKETS

If you want to rub elbows with the locals and purchase fresh produce and flowers at (somewhat) reasonable prices, head for Sunshine Markets, also known as Kauai's farmers' markets. These busy markets are held throughout the week, usually in the afternoon, at locations all around the island—just ask any local person. They're good fun, and they support neighborhood farmers. Arrive a little early, bring dollar bills to speed up transactions and your own shopping bags to carry your produce, and be prepared for some pushy shoppers. Farmers are usually happy to educate visitors about unfamiliar fruits and veggies, especially when the crowd thins. For schedules and information on all of the Sunshine Markets, call ☎ *808/241-6303*; and check out Kauai's government website at 🌐 *www.kauai.gov*.

East Side Sunshine Markets
✉ *Vidinha Stadium, Lihue, ½ mile south of airport on Rte. 51*, Friday 3 pm. ✉ *Kapaa, turn mauka on Rte. 581/Olohena Rd. for 1 block*, Wednesday 3 pm.

North Shore Sunshine Markets
✉ *Waipa, mauka of Rte. 560 north of Hanalei after mile marker 3, Hanalei*, Tuesday 2 pm. ✉ *Kilauea Neighborhood Center, on Keneke St., Kilauea*, Thursday 4:30 pm. ✉ *Hanalei Community Center, 5299 Kuhio Hwy, Hanalei*, Saturday 9:30 am.

South Shore Sunshine Markets
✉ *Ballpark, Koloa, north of intersection of Koloa Rd. and Rte. 520*, Monday noon.

West Side Sunshine Markets
✉ *Kalaheo Community Center, on Papalina Rd. just off Kaumualii Hwy., Kalaheo*, Tuesday 3 pm. ✉ *Hanapepe Park, Hanapepe*, Thursday 3 pm. ✉ *Kekaha Neighborhood Center, Elepaio Rd., Kekaha*, Saturday 9 am.

WAIMEA, WAIMEA CANYON, AND AROUND

Waimea is 7 miles northwest of Hanapepe; Waimea Canyon is approximately 10 miles northeast of Waimea.

Waimea is a serene, pretty town that has the look of the Old West and the feel of Old Hawaii, with a lifestyle that's decidedly laid-back. It's an ideal place for a refreshment break while sightseeing on the West Side. The town has played a major role in Hawaiian history since 1778, when Captain James Cook became the first European to set foot on the Hawaiian Islands. Waimea was also the place where Kauai's King Kaumualii acquiesced to King Kamehameha's unification drive in 1810, averting a bloody war. The town hosted the first Christian missionaries, who hauled in massive timbers and limestone blocks to build the sturdy Waimea Christian Hawaiian and Foreign Church in 1846. It's one of many lovely historic buildings preserved by residents who take great pride in their heritage and history.

North of Waimea town, via Route 550, you'll find the vast and gorgeous Waimea Canyon, also known as the Grand Canyon of the Pacific. The spectacular vistas from the lookouts along the road culminate with an overview of Kalalau Valley. There are various hiking trails leading to the inner heart of Kauai. A camera is a necessity in this region.

You don't have to hike to see sweeping Waimea Canyon vistas. Many overlooks, like the one pictured above, are reachable by car, right off the main road.

GETTING HERE AND AROUND

Route 50 continues northwest to Waimea and Kekaha from Hanapepe. You can reach Waimea Canyon and Kokee State Park from either town—the way is clearly marked. Some pull-off areas on Route 550 are fine for a quick view of the canyon, but the designated lookouts have bathrooms and parking.

TOP ATTRACTIONS

Fort Elizabeth. The ruins of this stone fort, built in 1816 by an agent of the imperial Russian government named Anton Scheffer, are reminders of the days when Scheffer tried to conquer the island for his homeland, or so one story goes. Another claims that Scheffer's allegiance lay with King Kaumualii, who was attempting to regain leadership of his island nation from the grasp of Kamehameha the Great. The crumbling walls of the fort are not particularly interesting, but the signs loaded with historical information are. ✉ *Rte. 50, Waimea (Kauai County).*

Kalalau Lookout. At the end of the road, high above Waimea Canyon, Kalalau Lookout marks the start of a 1-mile (one-way) hike to **Puu o Kila Lookout.** On a clear day at either spot, you can see a dreamy landscape of gaping valleys, sawtooth ridges, waterfalls, and turquoise seas, where whales can be seen spouting and breaching during the winter months. If clouds block the view, don't despair—they tend to blow through fast, giving you time to snap that photo of a lifetime. You may spot wild goats clambering on the sheer, rocky cliffs, and white tropic birds. If it's very clear to the northwest, drink in the shining sands of Kalalau Beach, gleaming like golden threads against the deep blue of the Pacific. ✉ *Waimea Canyon Dr.* ✣ *4 miles north of Kokee State Park.*

Kokee State Park. This 4,345-acre wilderness park is 3,600 feet above sea level, an elevation that affords you breathtaking views in all directions and a cooler, wetter climate. You can gain a deeper appreciation of the island's rugged terrain and dramatic beauty from this vantage point. Large tracts of native ohia and koa forest cover much of the land, along with many varieties of exotic plants. Hikers can follow a 45-mile network of trails through diverse landscapes that feel wonderfully remote—until the tour helicopters pass overhead. ✉ *Hwy. 50, Kekaha* ⊕ *15 miles north of Kekaha* 🌐 *kokee.org.*

Kokee Natural History Museum. When you arrive at Kokee State Park, Kokee Natural History Museum is a great place to start your visit. The friendly staff is knowledgeable about trail conditions and weather, while informative displays and a good selection of reference books can teach you more about the unique attributes of the native flora and fauna. You may also find that special memento or gift you've been looking for. ✉ *Rte. 550, Kokee* ☎ *808/335–3353* 🌐 *kokee.org* *Donations accepted.*

5

QUICK BITES

Kokee Lodge. There's only one place to buy food and hot drinks in Kokee State Park, and that's the dining room of rustic Kokee Lodge. It's known for its Portugese bean soup and corn bread, of all things. ✉ ***Kokee State Park, 3600 Kokee Rd., mile marker 15, Kokee*** ☎ ***808/335–6061*** 🌐 ***kokeelodge.com*** ⊗ ***No dinner.***

Fodor's Choice ★

Waimea Canyon. Carved over countless centuries by the Waimea River and the forces of wind and rain, Waimea Canyon is a dramatic gorge nicknamed the "Grand Canyon of the Pacific"—but not by Mark Twain, as many people mistakenly think. Hiking and hunting trails wind through the canyon, which is 3,600 feet deep, 2 miles wide, and 10 miles long. The cliff sides have been sharply eroded, exposing swatches of colorful soil. The deep red, brown, and green hues are constantly changing in the sun, and frequent rainbows and waterfalls enhance the natural beauty. This is one of Kauai's prettiest spots, and it's worth stopping at both the **Puu ka Pele** and **Puu Hinahina** lookouts. Clean public restrooms and parking are at both lookouts. ✉ *Hwy. 550 (Kokee Rd.), Waimea (Kauai County)* ☎ *808/274–3444* 🌐 *dlnr.hawaii.gov/dsp/parks/kauai/.*

BEACHES

Updated by Joan Conrow

Kauai may be nicknamed the Garden Island, but with more sandy beaches per mile of coastline than any other Hawaiian Island, it could easily be called the Sandy Island as well. Totaling more than 50 miles, Kauai's beaches make up 44% of the island's shoreline—almost twice that of Oahu, second on this list.

It is, of course, because of Kauai's age as the eldest sibling of the inhabited Hawaiian Islands, allowing more time for water and wind erosion to break down rock and coral into sand.

But not all of Kauai's beaches are the same. Each beach is unique unto itself. Conditions and scenery can change throughout the day and certainly throughout the year, transforming, say, a tranquil, lakelike ocean setting in summer into monstrous waves drawing internationally ranked surfers from around the world in winter.

There are sandy beaches, rocky beaches, wide beaches, narrow beaches, skinny beaches, and alcoves. Generally speaking, surf kicks up on the North Shore in winter and the South Shore in summer, although summer's southern swells aren't nearly as frequent or as big as the northern winter swells that attract those surfers. Kauai's longest and widest beaches are found on the North Shore and West Side and are popular with beachgoers, although during winter's rains, everyone heads to the drier South Shore and West Side. The East Side beaches tend to be narrower and have onshore winds less popular with sunbathers, yet fishers abound. Smaller coves are characteristic of the South Shore and attract all kinds of water lovers year-round, including monk seals.

In Hawaii, all beaches are public, but their accessibility varies greatly. Some require an easy ½-mile stroll, some require a four-wheel-drive vehicle, others require boulder-hopping, and one takes an entire day of serious hiking. And then there are those "drive-in" beaches adjacent to parking areas. Kauai is not Disneyland, so don't expect much signage to help you along the way. One of the top-ranked beaches in the whole world—Hanalei—doesn't have a single sign in town directing you to the beach. Furthermore, the majority of Kauai's beaches on Kauai's vast coastline are remote, offering no facilities. It's important to note that drownings are common on Kauai, in part because many beaches have no lifeguards and tricky ocean conditions. When in doubt, stay out. ■ TIP→ **If you want the convenience of restrooms, picnic tables, lifeguards, and the like, stick to county beach parks.**

THE NORTH SHORE

If you've ever dreamed of Hawaii—and who hasn't—you've dreamed of Kauai's North Shore. *Lush, tropical,* and *abundant* are just a few words to describe this rugged and dramatic area. And the views to the sea aren't the only attraction—the inland views of velvety-green valley folds and carved mountain peaks will take your breath away. Rain is the reason for all the greenery on the North Shore, and winter is the rainy season. Not to worry, though; it rarely rains *everywhere* on the island at one time. ■ TIP→ **The rule of thumb is to head south or west when it rains in the north.**

The waves on the North Shore can be big—and we mean huge—in winter, drawing crowds to witness nature's spectacle. By contrast, in summer the waters can be completely serene. ⚠ **Following extensive flooding in early 2018, areas of Haena, including Haena Beach Park and Kee Beach, are undergoing repairs. Please check before visiting to make sure places are open.**

FAMILY **Anini Beach Park.** A great family park, Anini features one of the longest and widest fringing reefs in all Hawaii, creating a shallow lagoon that is good for snorkeling and kids splashing about. It is safe in all but the highest of winter surf. The reef follows the shoreline for some 2 miles and extends 1,600 feet offshore at its widest point. There's a narrow ribbon of sandy beach and lots of grass and shade, as well as a county campground at the western end and a small boat ramp. **Amenities:** lifeguard; parking; showers; toilets. **Best for:** sunrise; swimming; walking. ✉ *Anini Rd., off Rte. 56, Princeville.*

Fodor's Choice ★ **Haena Beach Park.** This is a drive-up beach park popular with campers year-round. The wide bay here—named Makua—is bordered by two large reef systems creating favorable waves for skilled surfers during peak winter conditions. In July and August, waters at this same beach usually are as calm as a lake. Entering the water can be dangerous in winter when the big swells roll in. ■ TIP→ **During the summer months only, this is a premier snorkeling site on Kauai.** It's not unusual to find a food vendor parked here selling sandwiches and drinks out of a converted bread van. **Amenities:** food and drink; lifeguards; parking; showers; toilets. **Best for:** snorkeling; surfing; walking. ✉ *Near end of Rte. 560, across from "Dry Cave", Haena.*

5

FAMILY Fodor's Choice ★ **Hanalei Bay.** This 2-mile crescent beach cradles a wide bay in a setting that is quintessential Hawaii. The sea is on one side, and behind you are the mountains, often ribboned with waterfalls and changing color in the shifting light. In winter, Hanalei Bay boasts some of the biggest onshore surf breaks in the state, attracting world-class surfers, and the beach is plenty wide enough for sunbathing and strolling. In summer, the bay is transformed—calm waters lap the beach, sailboats moor in the bay, and outrigger-canoe paddlers ply the sea. Pack the cooler, haul out the beach umbrellas, and don't forget the beach toys, because Hanalei Bay is worth scheduling for an entire day, maybe two. Several county beach parks, some with pavilions, can be found along the bay. **Amenities:** lifeguards; parking; showers; toilets. **Best for:** sunset; surfing; swimming; walking. ✉ *Weke Rd., Hanalei.*

Fodor's Choice ★ **Kalalau.** Located at the end of the trail with the same name, Kalalau is a remote beach in spectacular Napali Coast State Wilderness Park. Reaching it requires an arduous 11-mile hike along sea cliff faces, through steaming tropical valleys, and across sometimes-raging streams. Another option is to paddle a kayak to the beach—summer only, though; otherwise the surf is way too big. The beach is anchored by a *heiau* (a stone platform used as a place of worship) on one end and a waterfall on the other. The safest time to come is summer, when the trail is dry and the beach is wide, cupped by low, vegetated sand dunes and a large walk-in cave on the western edge. Day hikes into the valley offer waterfalls, freshwater swimming pools, and wild, tropical fruits. Though state camping permits are required, the valley often has a significant illegal crowd, which has strained park facilities and degraded much of its former peaceful solitude. Helicopter overflights are near-constant in good weather. **Amenities:** none. **Best for:** sunset; walking. ✉ *Trailhead starts at end of Rte. 560, 7 miles west of Hanalei* 🌐 *www.hawaiistateparks.org.*

Kalihiwai Beach. A winding road leads down a cliff face to picture-perfect Kalihiwai Beach, which fronts a bay of the same name. It's another one of those drive-up beaches, so it's very accessible. Most people park under the grove of ironwood trees, near the stream, where young kids

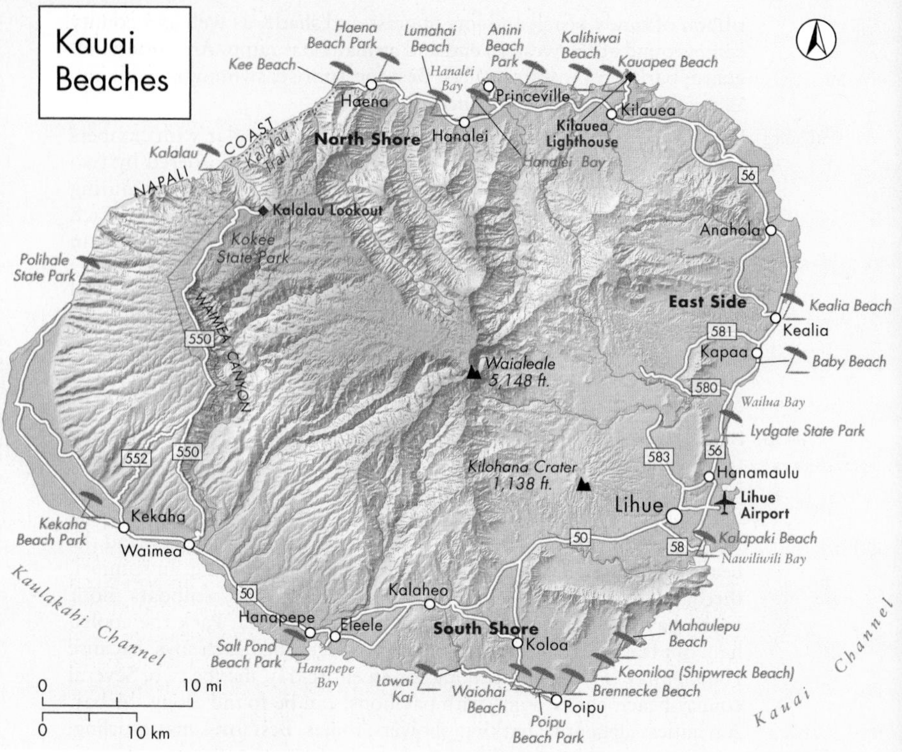

like to splash and older kids like to body board. Though do beware: the stream carries leptospirosis, a potentially lethal bacteria that can enter through open cuts. In winter months, beware of a treacherous shore break. Summer is the only truly safe time to swim. There's a local-favorite winter surf spot off the eastern edge of the beach, for advanced surfers only. The toilets here are the portable kind, and there are no showers. **Amenities:** parking; toilets. **Best for:** surfing; swimming; walking. ✉ *Kalihiwai Rd., on Kilauea side of Kalihiwai Bridge, Kilauea.*

Kauapea Beach (*Secret Beach*). This beach went relatively unknown—except by local fishermen, of course—for a long time, hence the common reference to it as "Secret Beach." You'll understand why once you stand on the coarse white sands of Kauapea and see the solid wall of rock that runs the length of the beach, making it fairly inaccessible. For the hardy, there is a steep hike down the western end. From there, you can walk for a long way in either direction in summer. During winter, big swells cut off access to sections of the beach. You may witness dolphins just offshore, and it's a great place to see seabirds, as the Kilauea Point National Wildlife Refuge and its historic lighthouse lie at the eastern end. Nudity is not uncommon, though it is illegal in Hawaii. A consistent onshore break makes swimming here typically very dangerous. **Amenities:** parking. **Best for:** solitude; sunrise; walking. ✉ *Kalihiwai Rd., just past turnoff for Kilauea, Kilauea.*

Fodor's Choice ★ **Kee Beach.** Highway 560 on the North Shore literally dead-ends at this beach, pronounced kay-eh. This is also the start of the famous Kalalau Trail, and a culturally significant area to Native Hawaiians, who still use an ancient *heiau* dedicated to hula. (It's not appropriate to hang out on the grass platform or leave offerings there.) The setting is gorgeous, with Makana (a prominent peak that Hollywood dubbed "Bali Hai" in the blockbuster musical *South Pacific*) dramatically imposing itself on the lovely coastline and lots of lush tropical vegetation. The small beach is protected by a reef—except during high surf—creating a small sandy-bottom lagoon that's a popular snorkeling spot. There can be a strong current in winter. Unfortunately, it's so heavily visited that parking is difficult, if not impossible. Expect to park quite a distance from the beach. It's a great place to watch the sunset lighting up Napali Coast. **Amenities:** lifeguards; parking; showers, toilets. **Best for:** snorkeling; sunset; swimming; walking. ⊠ *End of Rte. 560, 7 miles west of Hanalei.*

Lumahai Beach. Famous as the beach where Nurse Nellie washed that man right out of her hair in *South Pacific,* Lumahai's setting is picturesque, with a river and ironwood grove on the western end, and stands of hala (pandanus) trees and black lava rock on the eastern side. In between is a long stretch of thick olivine-flecked sand that can be wide or narrow, depending on surf. It can be accessed in two places from the highway; one involves a steep hike from the road. The ocean can be very dangerous here, with a snapping shore break year-round and monster swells in the winter. The current can be strong near the river. Parking is very limited along the road, or in a rough dirt lot near the river. **Amenities:** none. **Best for:** solitude; sunset; walking. ⊠ *On winding section of Rte. 560, near mile marker 5, Hanalei.*

THE EAST SIDE

The East Side of the island is considered the "windward" side, a term you'll often hear in weather forecasts. It simply means the side of the island receiving onshore winds. The wind helps break down rock into sand, so there are plenty of beaches here. Unfortunately, only a few of those beaches are protected, so many are not ideal for beginning ocean goers, though they are perfect for long sunrise ambles. On superwindy days, kiteboarders sail along the east shore, sometimes jumping waves and performing acrobatic maneuvers in the air.

⚠ **Following extensive flooding in early 2018, areas along the Wailua River, including Wailua Beach, are undergoing repairs. Please check before visiting to make sure places are open.**

FAMILY **Baby Beach.** There aren't many safe swimming beaches on Kauai's East Side; however, this one usually ranks highly with parents because there's a narrow, lagoonlike area between the beach and the near-shore reef perfect for small children. In winter, watch for east and northeast swells that would make this not such a safe option. There are no beach facilities—no lifeguards—so watch your babies. There is an old-time shower spigot (cold water only) along the roadside available to rinse the salt water. **Amenities:** parking; showers. **Best for:** sunrise; swimming. ⊠ *Moanakai Rd., Kapaa.*

Be sure to set aside time to catch a sunset over Napali Coast from Kee Beach on Kauai's North Shore.

FAMILY **Kalapaki Beach.** Five minutes south of the airport in Lihue, you'll find this wide, sandy-bottom beach fronting the Kauai Marriott. This beach is almost always safe from rip currents and undertows because it's around the back side of a peninsula, in its own cove. There are tons of activities here, including all the usual water sports—beginning and intermediate surfing, body boarding, bodysurfing, and swimming—plus, there are two outrigger canoe clubs paddling in the bay and the Nawiliwili Yacht Club's boats sailing around the harbor. **Kalapaki** is the only place on Kauai where double-hulled canoes are available for rent (at Kauai Beach Boys, which fronts the beach next to Duke's Canoe Club restaurant). Visitors can also rent snorkel gear, surfboards, body boards, and kayaks from Kauai Beach Boys. A volleyball court on the beach is often used by a loosely organized group of local players; visitors are always welcome. ■ TIP→ **Beware the stream on the south side of the beach, though, as it often has high bacteria counts.** Duke's Canoe Club restaurant is one of only a couple of restaurants on the island actually on a beach; the restaurant's lower level is casual, even welcoming beach attire and sandy feet, perfect for lunch or an afternoon cocktail. **Amenities:** food and drink; lifeguard; parking; showers; toilets; water sports. **Best for:** partiers; surfing; swimming; walking. ✉ *Off Rice St., Lihue* 🌐 *www.kauai.com/kalapaki-beach.*

Kealia Beach. A half mile long and adjacent to the highway heading north out of Kapaa, Kealia Beach attracts body boarders and surfers year-round. It's a favorite with locals and visitors alike. Kealia is not generally a great beach for swimming, but it's a place to sunbathe and enjoy the beach scene. The waters are usually rough and the waves crumbly due to an onshore break (no protecting reef) and northeasterly trade winds. A scenic lookout on the southern end, accessed off the highway, is a superb location for saluting the morning sunrise or spotting whales during winter. A level, paved trail with small, covered pavilions runs along the coastline here, and is very popular for walking and biking. **Amenities:** lifeguard; parking; showers; toilets. **Best for:** sunrise; surfing; swimming; walking. ✉ *Rte. 56, at mile marker 10, Kealia.*

FAMILY **Lydgate State Park.** This is by far the best family beach park on Kauai. The waters off the beach are protected by a hand-built breakwater, creating two boulder-enclosed saltwater pools for safe swimming and snorkeling most of the year. The smaller of the two pools is perfect for *keiki* (children). Behind the beach is Kamalani Playground; children of all ages—that includes you—enjoy the swings, lava-tube slides, tree house, and more. Picnic tables abound in the park, and pavilions for day use and overnight camping are available by permit. The Kamalani Kai Bridge is a second playground, south of the original. (The two are united by a bike and pedestrian path that is part of the coastal multiuse path.) ■ TIP→ **This park system is perennially popular; the quietest times to visit are early mornings and weekdays. Amenities:** lifeguards; parking; showers; toilets. **Best for:** partiers; sunrise; swimming; walking. ✉ *Leho Dr., just south of Wailua River, Wailua (Kauai County).*

THE SOUTH SHORE

The South Shore's primary access road is Highway 520, a tree-lined, two-lane, windy road. As you drive along it, there's a sense of tunneling down a rabbit hole into another world, à la Alice. And the South Shore is certainly a wonderland. On average, it rains only 30 inches per year, so if you're looking for fun in the sun, this is a good place to start. The beaches, with their powdery-fine sand, are consistently good year-round, except during high surf, which, if it hits at all, will be in summer. If you want solitude, this isn't it; if you want excitement—well, as much excitement as quiet Kauai offers—this is the place for you.

Brennecke Beach. This beach is synonymous on Kauai with board surfing and bodysurfing, thanks to its shallow sandbar and reliable shore break. Because the beach is small and often congested, surfboards are prohibited near shore. The water on the rocky eastern edge of the beach is a good place to see the endangered green sea turtles noshing on plants growing on the rocks. **Amenities:** food and drink; parking. **Best for:** sunset; surfing. ✉ *Hoone Rd., off Poipu Rd., Poipu.*

Keoniloa Beach (*Shipwreck Beach*). Few—except the public relations specialists at the Grand Hyatt Kauai Resort and Spa, which backs the beach, but is separated by water features and vegetation—refer to this beach by anything other than its common name: Shipwreck Beach. Its Hawaiian name means "long beach." Both make sense. It is a long stretch of crescent-shape beach punctuated by stunning sea cliffs on both ends, and, yes, a ship once wrecked here. With its onshore break, the waters off Shipwreck are best for body boarding and bodysurfing; however, the beach itself is plenty big for sunbathing, sand-castle building, Frisbee, and other beach-related fun. The eastern edge of the beach

BEST BEACHES

He says "to-mah-toe," and she says "to-may-toe." When it comes to beaches on Kauai, the meaning behind that axiom holds true: people are different. What rocks one person's world wreaks havoc for another's. Here are some additional tips on how to choose a beach that's right for you.

BEST FOR FAMILIES

Lydgate State Park, East Side. The kid-designed playground, the protected swimming pools, and Kamalani Bridge guarantee you will not hear these words from your child: "Mom, I'm bored."

Poipu Beach Park, Poipu, South Shore. The *keiki* (children's) pool and lifeguards make this a safe spot for kids. The near-perpetual sun isn't so bad, either.

BEST STAND-UP PADDLING

Anini Beach Park, North Shore. The reef and long stretch of beach give beginners to stand-up paddling a calm place to give this new sport a try. You won't get pummeled by waves here.

Wailua Beach, East Side. On the East Side, the Wailua River bisects the beach and heads inland 2 miles, providing stand-up paddlers with a long and scenic stretch of water before they have to figure out how to turn around.

BEST SURFING

Hanalei Bay Beach Park, North Shore. In winter, Hanalei Bay offers a range of breaks, from beginner to advanced. Surfing legends Laird Hamilton and the Irons Brothers grew up surfing the waters of Hanalei.

Waiohai Beach, South Shore. Surf instructors flock to this spot with their students for its gentle, near-shore break. Then, as students advance, they can paddle out a little farther to an intermediate break—if they dare.

BEST SUNSETS

Kee Beach, North Shore. Even in winter, when the sun sets in the south and out of view, you won't be disappointed here, because the "magic hour," as photographers call the time around sunset, paints Napali Coast with a warm gold light. But it can be tough to find parking here.

Polihale State Park, West Side. This due-west-facing beach may be tricky to get to, but it does offer the most unobstructed sunset views on the island. The fact that it's so remote means you won't have strangers in your photos, but you will want to depart right after sunset or risk getting lost in the dark.

BEST FOR CELEB SPOTTING

Haena Beach Park, North Shore. Behind those gated driveways and heavily foliaged yards that line this beach live—at least, part-time—some of the world's most celebrated music and movie moguls.

Hanalei Bay Beach Park, North Shore. We know we tout this beach often, but it deserves the praise. It's a mecca for everyone—regular joes, surfers, fishers, young, old, locals, visitors, and, especially, the famous. You may also recognize Hanalei Bay from the movie *The Descendants.*

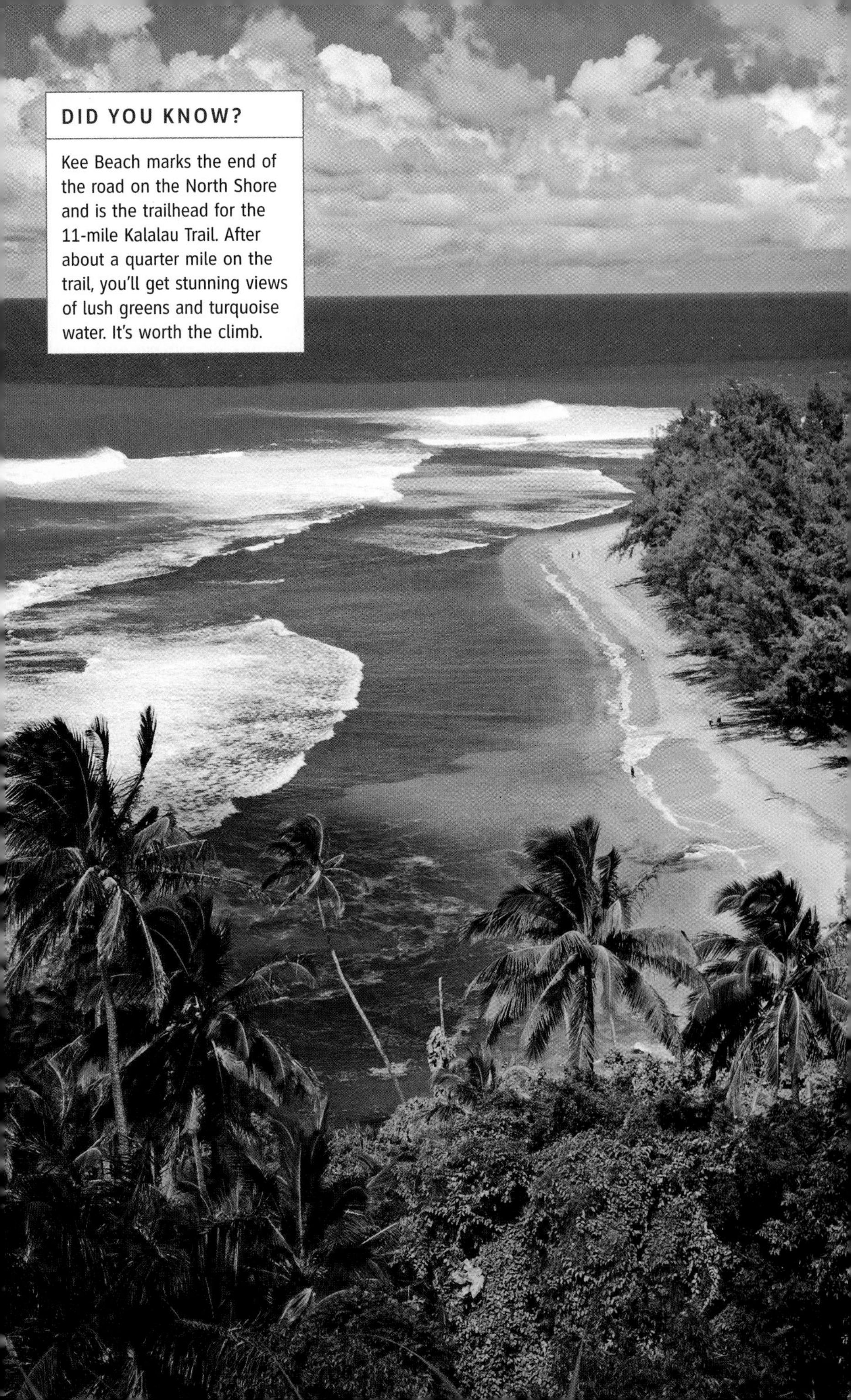

DID YOU KNOW?

Kee Beach marks the end of the road on the North Shore and is the trailhead for the 11-mile Kalalau Trail. After about a quarter mile on the trail, you'll get stunning views of lush greens and turquoise water. It's worth the climb.

is the start of an interpretive dune walk (complimentary) held by the hotel staff; check with the concierge for dates and times. **Amenities:** food and drink; parking; showers; toilets. **Best for:** sunrise; surfing; walking. ✉ *Ainako Rd., continue on Poipu Rd. past Hyatt, turn makai on Ainako Rd., Poipu.*

Fodor's Choice ★ **Lawai Kai.** One of the most spectacular beaches on the South Shore is inaccessible by land unless you tour the National Tropical Botanical Garden's Allerton Garden, which we highly recommend. On the tour, you'll see the beach, but you won't visit it. One way to legally access the beach on your own is by paddling a kayak 1 mile from Kukuiula Harbor. However, you have to rent the kayaks elsewhere and haul them on top of your car to the harbor. Also, the wind and waves usually run westward, making the in-trip a breeze but the return trip a workout against Mother Nature. ■ TIP→ **Do not attempt this beach in any manner during a south swell.** **Amenities:** none. **Best for:** solitude; sunset. ✉ *4425 Lawai Rd., off Poipu Rd.* ☎ *808/742–2433 for tour information at the National Tropical Botanical Garden's Allerton Garden* 🌐 *http://ntbg.org.*

Fodor's Choice ★ **Mahaulepu Beach.** This 2-mile stretch of coast, with its sand dunes, limestone hills, sinkholes, and caves, is unlike any other on Kauai. Remains of a large, ancient settlement, evidence of great battles, and the discovery of a now-underwater petroglyph field indicate that Hawaiians lived in this area as early as AD 700. Mahaulepu's coastline is unprotected and rocky, which makes venturing into the ocean hazardous. There are three beach areas with bits of sandy-bottom swimming; however, the best way to experience Mahaulepu is simply to roam, especially in the morning. ■ TIP→ **Access to this beach is via private property. The owner allows access during daylight hours, but be sure to depart before sunset or risk getting locked in for the night.** **Amenities:** parking. **Best for:** solitude; sunrise; walking. ✉ *Poipu Rd., past Hyatt Hotel, Poipu.*

FAMILY Fodor's Choice ★ **Poipu Beach Park.** The most popular beach on the South Shore is Poipu Beach Park. During calm seas, the snorkeling and swimming are good, and when the surf's up, the body boarding and surfing are good, too. Frequent sunshine, grassy lawns, and easy access add to the appeal, especially with families. The beach is frequently crowded and great for people-watching. Even the endangered Hawaiian monk seal often makes an appearance. **Amenities:** food and drink; lifeguards; parking; showers; toilets. **Best for:** partiers; snorkeling; sunbathing; swimming. ✉ *Hoone Rd., off Poipu Rd., Poipu* ☎ *808/742–7444.*

Waiohai Beach. The first hotel built in Poipu in 1962 overlooked this beach, adjacent to Poipu Beach Park. Actually, there's little to distinguish where one starts and the other begins other than a crescent reef at the eastern end of Waiohai Beach. That crescent, however, is important. It creates a small, protected bay—good for snorkeling and beginning surfers. If you're a beginner, this is the spot. However, when a summer swell kicks up, the near-shore conditions become dangerous; offshore, there's a splendid surf break for experienced surfers. The beach itself is narrow and, like its neighbor, gets very crowded in summer. **Amenities:** parking. **Best for:** snorkeling; sunset; surfing; swimming. ✉ *Hoone Rd., off Poipu Rd., Poipu.*

CLOSE UP

Seal-Spotting on the South Shore

When strolling on one of Kauai's lovely beaches, don't be surprised if you find yourself in the rare company of Hawaiian monk seals. These are among the most endangered of all marine mammals, with perhaps fewer than 1,200 remaining. They primarily inhabit the northwestern Hawaiian Islands, although more are showing their sweet faces on the main Hawaiian Islands, especially on Kauai. They're fond of hauling out on the beach for a long snooze in the sun, particularly after a night of gorging on fish. They need this time to rest and digest, safe from predators.

Female seals regularly birth their young on the beaches around Kauai, where they stay to nurse their pups for upward of six weeks. It seems the seals enjoy particular beaches for the same reasons we do: the shallow, protected waters.

If you're lucky enough to see a monk seal, keep your distance and let it be. Although they may haul out near people, they still want and need their space. Stay several hundred feet away, and forget photos unless you've got a zoom lens. It's illegal to do anything that causes a monk seal to change its behavior, with penalties that include big fines and even jail time. In the water, seals may appear to want to play. It's their curious nature. Don't try to play with them. They are wild animals—mammals, in fact, with teeth.

If you have concerns about the health or safety of a seal, or just want more information, contact the **Hawaiian Monk Seal Conservation Hui** (☏ *808/651-7668* 🌐 *www.kauaiseals.com*).

5

THE WEST SIDE

The West Side of the island receives hardly enough rainfall year-round to water a cactus, and because it's also the leeward side, there are few tropical breezes. That translates to sunny and hot with long, languorous, and practically deserted beaches. You'd think the leeward waters—untouched by wind—would be calm, but there's no reef system, so the beach drops off quickly and currents are common. Rivers often turn the ocean water murky. ■TIP→ **The best place to gear up for the beaches on the West Side is on the South Shore or East Side.** Although there's some catering to visitors here, it's not much.

Kekaha Beach Park. This is one of the premier spots on Kauai for sunset walks and the start of the state's longest beach. We don't recommend much water activity here without first talking to a lifeguard. The beach is exposed to open ocean and has an onshore break that can be hazardous any time of year. However, there are some excellent surf breaks—for experienced surfers only. Or, if you would like to run or stroll on a beach, this is the one—the hard-packed sand goes on for miles, all the way to Napali Coast, but you won't get past the Pacific Missile Range Facility and its post-9/11 access restrictions. Another bonus for this beach is its relatively dry weather year-round. If it's raining where you are, try Kekaha Beach Park. Toilets here are the portable kind.

Amenities: lifeguards; parking; showers; toilets. **Best for:** sunset; surfing; walking. ✉ *Rte. 50, near mile marker 27, Kekaha.*

Fodor's Choice ★ **Polihale State Park.** The longest stretch of beach in Hawaii starts in Kekaha and ends about 15 miles away at the start of Napali Coast. At Napali end of the beach is the 5-mile-long, 140-acre Polihale State Park. In addition to being long, this beach is 300 feet wide in places and backed by sand dunes 50 to 100 feet tall. It is frequently very hot, with minimal shade and scorching sand in summer. Polihale is a remote beach accessed via a rough, 5-mile haul-cane road (four-wheel drive needed in wet weather) at the end of Route 50 in Kekaha. ■ **TIP→ Be sure to start the day with a full tank of gas and a cooler filled with food and drink.** Though it's a popular camping and day-use beach location, the water here is typically rough and not recommended for recreation. No driving is allowed on the beach. The Pacific Missile Range Facility (PMRF), operated by the U.S. Navy, is adjacent to the beach and access to the coastline in front of the base is restricted. **Amenities:** parking; showers; toilets. **Best for:** solitude; sunset; walking. ✉ *Dirt road at end of Rte. 50, Kekaha* ☎ *808/587–0300.*

FAMILY **Salt Pond Beach Park.** A great family spot, Salt Pond Beach Park features a naturally made, shallow swimming pond behind a curling finger of rock where *keiki* (children) splash and snorkel. This pool is generally safe except during a large south swell, which usually occurs in summer, if at all. The center and western edge of the beach is popular with body boarders and bodysurfers. Pavilions with picnic tables offer shade, and there's a campground that tends to attract a rowdy bunch at the eastern end. On a cultural note, the flat stretch of land to the east of the beach is the last spot in Hawaii where ponds are used to harvest salt in the dry heat of summer. The beach park is popular with locals and it can get crowded on weekends and holidays. **Amenities:** lifeguard; parking; showers; toilets. **Best for:** sunset; swimming; walking. ✉ *Lolokai Rd., off Rte. 50, Hanapepe.*

WHERE TO EAT

Updated by Joan Conrow

On Kauai, if you're lucky enough to win an invitation to a potluck, baby luau, or beach party, don't think twice—just accept. The best grinds (food) are homemade, and so you'll eat until you're full, then rest, eat some more, and make a plate to take home, too.

But even if you can't score a spot at one of these parties, don't despair. Great local-style food is easy to come by at countless low-key places around the island. As an extra bonus, these eats are often inexpensive, and portions are generous. Expect plenty of meat—usually deep-fried or marinated in a teriyaki sauce and grilled *pulehu*-style (over an open fire)—and starches. Rice is standard, even for breakfast, and often served alongside potato–macaroni salad, another island specialty. Another local favorite is *poke,* made from chunks of raw tuna or octopus seasoned with sesame oil, soy sauce, onions, and pickled seaweed. It's a great *pupu* (appetizer) when paired with a cold beer.

Kauai's cultural diversity is apparent in its restaurants, which offer authentic Chinese, Korean, Japanese, Thai, Mexican, Italian, Vietnamese, and Hawaiian specialties. Less specialized restaurants cater to the tourist crowd, serving standard American fare—burgers, pizza, sandwiches, surf-and-turf combos, and so on. Poipu and Kapaa offers the best selection of restaurants, with options for a variety of tastes and budgets; most fast-food joints are in Lihue.

THE NORTH SHORE

Because of the North Shore's isolation, restaurants have enjoyed a captive audience of visitors who don't want to make the long, dark trek into Kapaa town for dinner. As a result, dining in this region has been characterized by expensive fare that isn't especially tasty, either. Fortunately, the situation is slowly improving as new restaurants open and others change hands or menus.

Still, dining on the North Shore can be pricier than other parts of the island, and not especially family-friendly. Most of the restaurants are found either in Hanalei town or the Princeville resorts. Consequently, you'll encounter delightful mountain and ocean views, but just one restaurant with oceanfront dining. ⚠ **Following extensive flooding in early 2018, areas of Haena and the Napali Coast are undergoing repairs. Please check before visiting to make sure places are open.**

$$ AMERICAN

Hanalei Gourmet. This spot in Hanalei's restored old schoolhouse offers dolphin-safe tuna, low-sodium meats, fresh-baked breads, and homemade desserts as well as a casual atmosphere where both families and the sports-watching crowd can feel equally comfortable. Lunch and dinner menus feature sandwiches, burgers, hearty salads, a variety of pupus, and nightly specials of fresh local fish. **Known for:** friendly bar; consistently good food; fresh bread. *Average main: $25* *Hanalei Center, 5-5161 Kuhio Hwy., Hanalei* *808/826–2524* *www.hanaleigourmet.com.*

$$$$ ECLECTIC Fodor's Choice ★

Kauai Grill. Savor an artful meal created by world-renowned chef Jean-Gorges Vongerichten, surrounded by a dramatic Hanalei Bay scene that's positively stunning at sunset. Located at the luxurious St. Regis Princeville Resort, Kauai Grill has dark-wood decor and an ornate chandelier, the centerpiece of the room. **Known for:** skill on the grill; Hawaii-grown ingredients; attentive service. *Average main: $50* *St. Regis Princeville, 5520 Ka Haku Rd., Princeville* *808/826–9644* *www.kauaigrill.com* *Closed Sun. and Mon. No lunch.*

$$ AMERICAN FAMILY

Kilauea Bakery and Pau Hana Pizza. Open from 6:30 am, the bakery serves coffee drinks, delicious fresh pastries, bagels, and breads in the morning. Late risers beware: breads and pastries sell out quickly. **Known for:** its starter of Hawaiian sourdough made with guava; specialty pizzas topped with eclectic ingredients; fresh chocolate chip cookies made in-house daily. *Average main: $20* *Kong Lung Center, 2484 Keneke St., Kilauea* *808/828–2020* *www.kilaueabakery.com.*

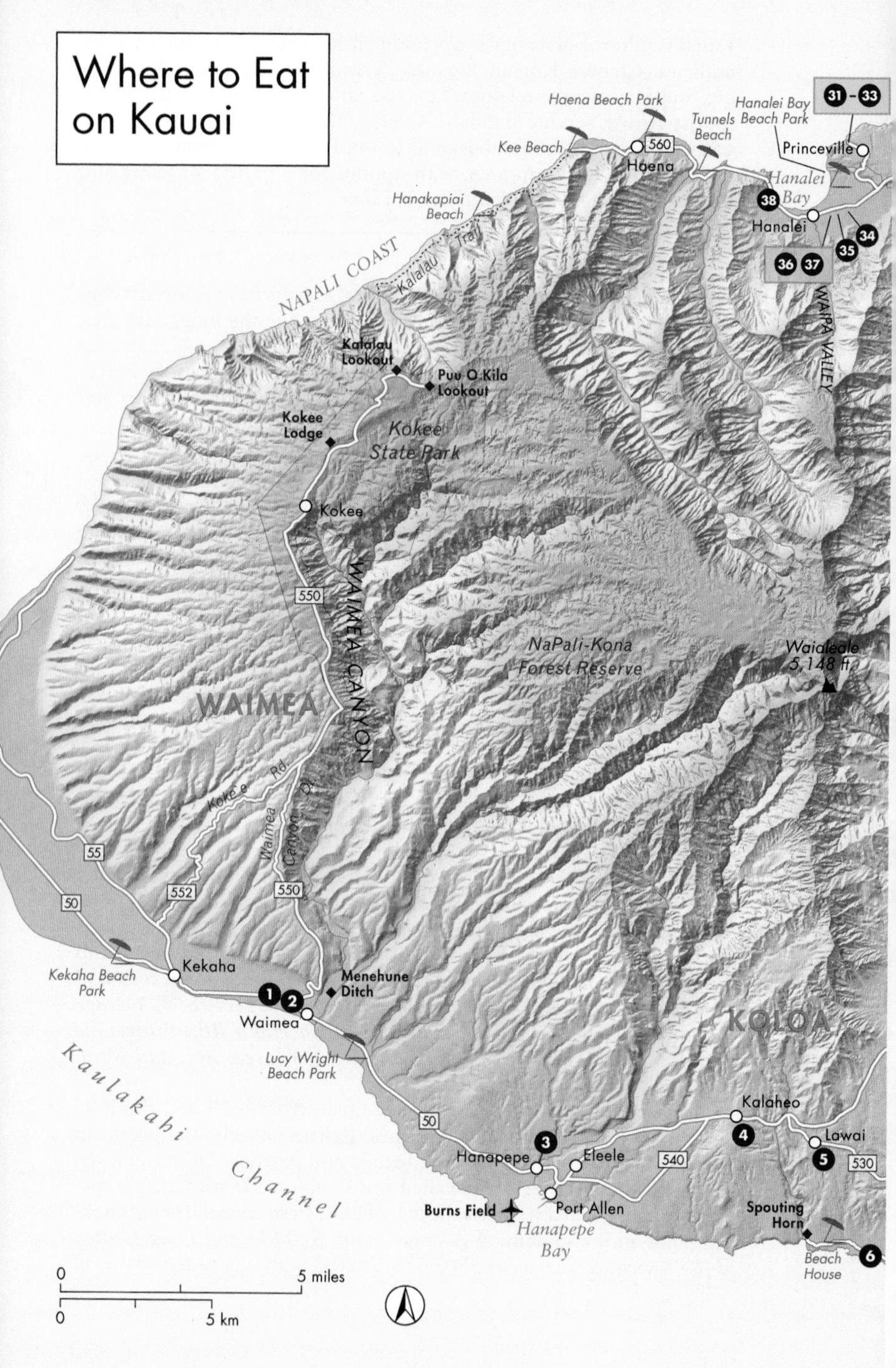

Where to Eat on Kauai
Haena Beach Park
Hanalei Bay Beach Park
31 - 33
Kee Beach
560
Tunnels Beach
Princeville
Haena
Hanalei Bay
Hanakapiai Beach
38
Hanalei
34
35
36
37
NAPALI COAST
Kalalau Trail
WAIPA VALLEY
Kalalau Lookout
Puu O Kila Lookout
Kokee Lodge
Kokee State Park
Kokee
550
WAIMEA CANYON
NaPali-Kona Forest Reserve
Waialeale 5,148 ft.
WAIMEA
Koke'e Rd.
Waimea Canyon Dr.
55
552
550
50
Kekaha
Kekaha Beach Park
1
2
Menehune Ditch
Waimea
KOLOA
Lucy Wright Beach Park
Kaulakahi Channel
50
Kalaheo
4
Lawai
5
3
530
Hanapepe
Eleele
540
Burns Field
Port Allen
Hanapepe Bay
Spouting Horn
6
Beach House
0
5 miles
0
5 km

Beach House	6
Bull Shed	23
Dani's Restaurant	18
Dondero's	14
Eat Healthy Cafe	28
Eating House 1849	7
Gaylord's	16
Hamura Saimin	17
Hanalei Gourmet	35
Hukilau Lanai	21
JJ's Broiler	19
Joe's on the Green	11
JO2 Restaurant	27
Kalaheo Café & Coffee Co.	4
Kalapaki Joe's	15
Kauai Grill	32
Kauai Pasta	25
Keoki's Paradise	8
Kilauea Bakery and Pau Hana Pizza	30
Kountry Kitchen	29
Kukui's Restaurant and Bar	20
Little Fish Coffee	3
Makai Sushi	12
Makana Terrace	31
Merriman's Fish House	9
Nanea Restaurant and Bar	33
Neide's Salsa and Samba	36
Opakapaka Grill and Bar	38
Pizzetta	5
Plantations BBQ & Bar	2
Postcards Café	34
Red Salt	10
Restaurant Bar Acuda	37
Restaurant Kintaro	22
Shivalik Indian Cuisine	24
Tidepools	13
Tiki Tacos	26
Wrangler's Steakhouse	1

$$$$ HAWAIIAN FAMILY ✕ **Makana Terrace.** There's no doubt this spot is pricey, but you're paying for the view—sit on the terrace if you can—and for an attentive staff. The menu is simple and the focus is on local dishes like taro waffles and Molokai sweet potato pancakes or island-caught fish and grilled beef tenderloin. **Known for:** breathtaking panoramic view of Hanalei Bay; local, Hawaii-grown foods; lavish daily breakfast/brunch buffet. *Average main: $42 St. Regis Princeville Resort, 5520 Ka Haku Rd., Princeville 808/826–9644 www.stregisprinceville.com Closed Tues. and Wed. No lunch.*

$$$ HAWAIIAN FAMILY ✕ **Nanea Restaurant and Bar.** This is the signature restaurant of the Westin Princeville Ocean Resort Villas, and its casual, open-air seating is the perfect compliment to an island-style menu that is sure to please a wide range of diners. The grilled rib eye is served with bacon and sour cream mashed potatoes, while the half-chicken—smoked kalua style—is accompanied by Molokai sweet potatoes. **Known for:** kids eat free; inventive cocktails; local ingredients. *Average main: $35 Westin Princeville Ocean Resort Villas, 3838 Wyllie Rd., Princeville 808/827–8808 www.westinprinceville.com.*

$$ BRAZILIAN ✕ **Neide's Salsa and Samba.** The only restaurant serving authentic Brazilian food on Kauai, Neide's Salsa and Samba is also one of the most affordable establishments on the North Shore. The first half of the menu focuses on Mexican food, but it's the Brazilian dishes here that deserve your attention. **Known for:** authentic Brazilian food; great view of the Hanalei mountains; relaxed service. *Average main: $22 5-5161 Kuhio Hwy., Hanalei 808/826–1851.*

$$ FUSION ✕ **Opakapaka Grill and Bar.** A trip to this oceanfront oasis requires a narrow, cliff-hugging ride along the exquisite North Shore coastline or a short walk from the condos at Hanalei Colony Resort. The menu features the regular choices of burgers, sandwiches, and salads for lunch, while dinner options include fresh island fish, pasta, and meats and chicken dishes, as well as a good selection of small plates. **Known for:** oceanfront setting and view; Hawaiian fusion menu; good selection of pupu (appetizers). *Average main: $26 Hanalei Colony Resort, 5-7130 Kuhio Hwy., Haena 808/826–9875 www.hcr.com/dining.*

$$$ AMERICAN ✕ **Postcards Café.** This plantation-cottage restaurant has a menu full of seafood but also offers additive-free vegetarian and vegan options. Top menu picks include taro fritters, wasabi-crusted ahi, fennel-crusted lobster tail, and baked portobello mushrooms. **Known for:** meat-free menu; cozy dining room; historic setting. *Average main: $35 5-5075A Kuhio Hwy., Hanalei 808/826–1191 postcardscafe.com No lunch.*

$$$$ TAPAS Fodor's Choice ★ ✕ **Restaurant Bar Acuda.** This hip and pricey tapas bar is a top place in Hanalei in terms of tastiness, creativity, and pizzazz. Owner-chef Jim Moffat's brief menu changes regularly: you might find grilled short rib skewers with horseradish chimichurri, or Hawaiian mahimahi with roasted shimeji mushrooms. **Known for:** sophisticated cuisine; innovative specials; eclectic menu. *Average main: $40 Hanalei Center, 5-5161 Kuhio Hwy., Hanalei 808/826–7081 www.restaurantbaracuda.com.*

THE EAST SIDE

Because the East Side is the island's largest population center, it makes sense that it should boast a wide selection of restaurants. It's also a good place to get both cheaper meals and the local-style cuisine that residents favor.

Most of the eateries are found along Kuhio Highway between Kapaa and Wailua; a few are tucked into shopping centers and resorts. In Lihue, it's easier to find lunch than dinner because many restaurants cater to the business crowd.

You'll find all the usual fast-food joints in both Kapaa and Lihue, as well as virtually every ethnic cuisine available on Kauai. Although fancy gourmet restaurants are less abundant in this part of the island, there's plenty of good, solid food, and a few stellar attractions. But unless you're staying on the East Side, or passing through, it's probably not worth the long drive from the North Shore or Poipu resorts to eat here.

KAPAA AND WAILUA

$$$ STEAKHOUSE

Bull Shed. The A-frame structure makes this popular restaurant look distinctly rustic from the outside, but inside, light-color walls and a full wall of glass highlight an ocean view that is one of the best on Kauai. The food is simple, but they know how to do surf and turf. **Known for:** views of the surf crashing on the rocks; unlimited salad bar; quiet bar. *Average main: $35* *796 Kuhio Hwy.* *808/822–3791, 808/822–1655* *www.bullshedrestaurant.com* *No lunch.*

$$ VEGETARIAN

Eat Healthy Cafe. A restored plantation cottage surrounded by tropical foliage is the casual setting for this island café. The menu emphasizes local and organic products, with many vegan, vegetarian, and gluten-free options including nori wraps and tofu-based entrées. **Known for:** outdoor seating in the vine-covered garden; delicious food with healthy ingredients; smoothies like Chocolate & Coffee Kiss and I Heart Blueberries. *Average main: $24* *4-369 Kuhio Hwy., Wailua (Kauai County)* *808/822–7990* *eathealthykauai.com* *No dinner Sun. and Mon.*

$$ AMERICAN Fodor's Choice ★

Hukilau Lanai. Relying heavily on superfresh island fish and local meats and produce, this restaurant offers quality food that is competently and creatively prepared. The nightly fish specials—served grilled, steamed, or sautéed with succulent sauces—shine here. **Known for:** nightly fish specials; gluten-free options; delicious desserts. *Average main: $25* *Kauai Coast Resort, Coconut Marketplace, 520 Aleka Loop, Wailua (Kauai County)* *808/822–0600* *www.hukilaukauai.com* *Closed Mon.*

$$$ ECLECTIC Fodor's Choice ★

JO2 Restaurant. This is the newest creation of Jean-Marie Josselin, the renowned chef who brought Hawaii regional cuisine to Kauai in 1990, and it reflects his growth as a chef. The food is very imaginative, with its French, Japanese, and Islands influences, and served with flair in a chic, yet casual, dining room that's tucked away in a nondescript strip mall. **Known for:** the $35 prix fix 5–6 pm; inventive cuisine; excellent service. *Average main: $35* *4-971 Kuhio Hwy., Kapaa* *808/212–1627* *www.jotwo.com.*

$$ ITALIAN
Kauai Pasta. This simple yet elegant establishment offers some of the best Italian food on the island at moderate prices. Their specials are delicious, and their 10-inch pizzettas make a fine meal for one. **Known for:** chocolate crème brûlée; good value; gluten-free options. *Average main: $26 ✉ 4-939B Kuhio Hwy. www.kauaipasta.com.*

$ AMERICAN FAMILY
Kountry Kitchen. If you like a hearty breakfast, try this family-friendly restaurant with its cozy, greasy-spoon atmosphere, and friendly service; it's a great spot for omelets, banana pancakes, waffles, and eggs Benedict in two sizes. Lunch selections include sandwiches, burgers, and *loco mocos* (a popular local rice, beef, gravy, and eggs concoction). **Known for:** all day breakfast; take-out options; hearty portions. *Average main: $14 ✉ 1485 Kuhio Hwy., Kapaa ☎ 808/822–3511 www.kountrystylekitchen.com No dinner.*

$$ JAPANESE
Fodor's Choice ★
Restaurant Kintaro. If you want to eat at a lively restaurant that's a favorite with locals, visit Kintaro, but be prepared to wait—or better yet, make reservations— because the dining room and sushi bar are always busy. Try the soft-shell crab roll or the unbeatable Bali Hai bomb, a roll of crab and smoked salmon, baked and topped with wasabi mayonnaise. **Known for:** local favorite; lively bar; friendly service. *Average main: $22 ✉ 4-370 Kuhio Hwy., Wailua (Kauai County) ☎ 808/822–3341 Closed Sun. No lunch.*

$ INDIAN
Shivalik Indian Cuisine. This eatery provides a refreshing alternative to the typical surf and turf offerings at most of Kauai's restaurants. Boasting no particular Indian regional style, this small-plaza hideaway turns out delectable biryani and tandoori, light and flavorful naan, many vegetarian items, as well as curries and chicken and lamb dishes. **Known for:** Wednesday and Friday night all-you-can eat buffet; tandoor oven; extensive menu. *Average main: $17 ✉ 4-771 Kuhio Hwy., Wailua (Kauai County) ☎ 808/821–2333 www.shivalikindianfood.com Closed Tues.*

$ MEXICAN
Tiki Tacos. Tiki Tacos is a notch above most Kauai taco joints, with excellent authentic Mexican food at reasonable prices. The meals are made from quality ingredients, many of them organic and locally sourced. **Known for:** large potions; good value; friendly service. *Average main: $8 ✉ 4-971 Kuhio Hwy., Kapaa ☎ 808/823–8226.*

LIHUE

You will probably find yourself in Lihue at least a few times during your stay. When it comes to restaurants, Lihue isn't especially outstanding. There are some decent restaurants and some good low-cost eateries that feed locals and the business-lunch crowd—but nothing really stellar. If you are in town for lunch, don't pass up some of the authentic local spots.

$ HAWAIIAN FAMILY
Dani's Restaurant. Kauai residents frequent this eatery near the Lihue Fire Station for hearty, local-style food at breakfast and lunch; it's a good place to try traditional luau cuisine without commercial luau prices. You can order Hawaiian-style *laulau* (pork and taro leaves wrapped in ti leaves and steamed) or kalua pig, slow roasted in an underground oven. **Known for:** local-style dining; low prices; casual setting. *Average main: $8 ✉ 4201 Rice St., Lihue ☎ 808/245–4991 Closed Sun. No dinner.*

Some of the best eats on Kauai come from the sea. Ask what the local catch of the day is for the freshest option.

$$$ **ECLECTIC** **Gaylord's.** Located in what was once Kauai's most expensive plantation estate, Gaylord's pays tribute to the elegant dining rooms of 1930s high society—candlelit tables sit on a cobblestone patio that surrounds a fountain and overlooks a wide lawn. The menu is eclectic, ranging from tender seared scallops served in a fennel cream to grilled filet mignon. **Known for:** lavish Sunday brunch buffet; quiet dining; delightful outdoor seating. *Average main: $30* *Kilohana Plantation, 3-2087 Kaumualii Hwy., Puhi* *808/245–9593* *www.gaylordskauai.com.*

$ **ASIAN** Fodor's Choice ★ **Hamura Saimin.** Folks just love this funky old plantation-style diner—locals and tourists stream in and out all day long, and neighbor islanders stop in on their way to the airport to pick up take-out orders to bring home. Their famous *saimin* soup is the big draw, and each day the Hiraoka family dishes up about 1,000 bowls of steaming broth and homemade noodles, topped with a variety of garnishes. **Known for:** classic Kauai experience; grilled chicken and beef sticks; counter-style dining. *Average main: $7* *2956 Kress St., Lihue* *808/245–3271* *No credit cards.*

$$$ **AMERICAN** **JJ's Broiler.** This spacious, low-key restaurant serves hearty fare, with dinner specials such as lobster and Slavonic steak, a broiled sliced tenderloin dipped in buttery wine sauce, and local-style kalua pig and cabbage; you can save money by ordering from the lunch menu at dinner time. On sunny afternoons, ask for a table on the lanai overlooking Kalapaki Bay and try one of the generous salads or appetizers and a drink. **Known for:** one of the best ocean views in Lihue; great place for a drink; friendly service. *Average main: $30* *Anchor Cove, 3416 Rice St., Nawiliwili* *808/246–4422* *www.jjsbroiler.com.*

$$ AMERICAN ✕ **Kalapaki Joe's.** Both locations—in Lihue's Kukui Grove and in Poipu—appeal to sports fans who like a rip-roaring happy hour as the appetizer menu is extensive. You can also choose from burgers, salads, sandwiches, fish tacos, steaks, ribs, and fresh fish specials. **Known for:** wide-ranging menu; boisterous bar; affordable, casual dining. *Average main: $20 ✉ 3-2600 Kaumualii Hwy., Lihue ☎ 808/245–6366 🌐 www.kalapakijoes.com.*

$$ ECLECTIC FAMILY ✕ **Kukui's Restaurant and Bar.** The meals at Kukui's feature Hawaiian, Asian, and contemporary American influences, and the open-air setting makes it a pleasant place to dine. It's very spacious, and not as busy and noisy as the other eateries at the Marriott, making it well suited to families and those who want a relaxed setting. **Known for:** garden setting; lavish buffets; evening entertainment. *Average main: $25 ✉ Kauai Marriott Resort & Beach Club, 3610 Rice St., Kalapaki Beach, Lihue ☎ 808/245–5050 🌐 www.marriott.com.*

THE SOUTH SHORE

Most South Shore restaurants are more upscale and located within the Poipu resorts. If you're looking for a gourmet meal in a classy setting, the South Shore is where you'll find it. Poipu has a number of excellent restaurants in dreamy settings and decidedly fewer family-style, lower-price eateries.

$$$$ ASIAN FUSION ✕ **Beach House.** This restaurant has a dreamy ocean view, making it a good setting for a romantic dinner or a cocktail and appetizer while the sun sinks into the glassy blue Pacific and surfers slice the waves. The prices have gone up, but you can still find satisfaction in the crispy crab-stuffed ahi roll, roasted duck breast, or fresh catch of the day served with lilikoi lemon grass beurre blanc. **Known for:** gluten-free and vegan options; small bar with a big view; outdoor dining. *Average main: $38 ✉ 5022 Lawai Rd., Poipu ☎ 808/742–1424 🌐 www.the-beach-house.com.*

$$$$ ITALIAN Fodor's Choice ★ ✕ **Dondero's.** With a beautiful setting, good food, stunning ocean view, and impeccable service, Dondero's is one of Kauai's better restaurants. The elegant tasting menu features Italian dishes or opt for classic dishes like grilled seafood cioppino or the tender veal osso buco. **Known for:** Italianate murals and elegant interior; wonderful outdoor dining experience; emphasis on local ingredients. *Average main: $38 ✉ Grand Hyatt Kauai Resort and Spa, 1571 Poipu Rd., Poipu ☎ 808/240–6456 🌐 kauai.grand.hyatt.com/en/hotel/dining/Donderos.html ⊙ Closed Sun. and Mon. No lunch.*

$$$ ASIAN FUSION Fodor's Choice ★ ✕ **Eating House 1849.** Hawaii's culinary superstar, Roy Yamaguchi, has moved his signature Hawaiian-fusion-cuisine restaurant on Kauai's South Shore to an updated shopping-center locale that suits the new name and creative fare. Though billed as "plantation cuisine," the hot pot rice bowl or spicy ramen bowl are about the only items that might have their roots in the days when sugar was king, otherwise, the menu is classic Asian fusion. **Known for:** innovative cuisine; use of local ingredients; lively atmosphere. *Average main: $35 ✉ Shops at Kukuiula, 2829 Ala Kalanikaumaka Rd., No. A-201, Poipu ☎ 808/742–5000 🌐 www.eatinghouse1849.com.*

$ AMERICAN ✕ **Joe's on the Green.** Located at the Kiahuna Golf Course, the casual atmosphere and generous portions at Joe's makes it a refreshing alternative to the pricier hotel brunch venues in this area. Open-air breakfasts and lunches—think tofu scramble and banana-macadamia-nut pancakes or the quarter-pound hot dog and the build-your-own-salad options—comes with an expansive vista of Poipu, and happy hour, which often features live music, offers local favorites like *manapua* dumplings and ahi poke. **Known for:** upbeat happy hour; outdoor dining; friendly service. *Average main: $14 ✉ 2545 Kiahuna Plantation Dr., Poipu ☎ 808/742–9696 🌐 www.joesonthegreen.com.*

$$ AMERICAN FAMILY ✕ **Kalaheo Café & Coffee Co.** Folks love this busy roadside café—especially for breakfast, though it's good for lunch and a simple dinner, too—for it's casual atmosphere, and it's frequently busy, especially on weekend mornings. Lots of local products are used here, including Anahola Granola, local fish, and Kauai coffee, which you can buy by the pound; it's a solid choice in an area with limited restaurants. **Known for:** fresh-baked bread; great local coffee; hearty portions like the Kahili Breakfast or the Longboard sandwich. *Average main: $22 ✉ 2-2560 Kaumualii Hwy. (Rte. 50), Kalaheo ☎ 808/332–5858 🌐 www.kalaheo.com ⏲ No dinner Sun. and Mon.*

$$$ ASIAN FAMILY ✕ **Keoki's Paradise.** Built to resemble a dockside boathouse, this active, boisterous place fills up quickly at night thanks to a busy bar and frequent live music. The day's fresh catch is available in various styles and sauces that span the tide from appetizers (Thai shrimp sticks) to mains (seafood risotto), and meat-lover options like the *imu*-roasted pork ribs; the bar serves lighter fare. **Known for:** bustling bar with live music; keiki (kids) menu; fresh fish. *Average main: $30 ✉ Poipu Shopping Village, 2360 Kiahuna Plantation Dr., Poipu ☎ 808/742–7534 🌐 www.keokisparadise.com.*

$ SUSHI Fodor's Choice ★ ✕ **Makai Sushi.** The menu is simple—poke bowls, sashimi, and four types of sushi rolls—but the freshness of the fish and attention to quality preparation set this tiny sushi bar apart from the crowd and make it a welcome addition to the Poipu Beach food scene. Tucked into a corner of Kukuiula Market, it attracts a steady stream of customers who watch owner Matthew Oliver and an assistant transform spicy ahi, blue crab, avocado, cucumber, tobiko into the Hapa Roll or mix raw ahi, ono, salmon, cucumber, avocado, and sweet Maui onion into the Gorilla Bowl. **Known for:** superfresh fish; friendly sushi chefs; take-out options. *Average main: $13 ✉ Kukuiula Market, 2728 Poipu Rd., Koloa ☎ 808/639–7218 🌐 makaisushi.com.*

$$$$ MODERN HAWAIIAN ✕ **Merriman's Fish House.** The regional food served up at chef Peter Merriman's namesake restaurant is enhanced by a sophisticated setting and lovely views from a pretty second-floor dining room. Start at the bar, where fine wines are offered by the glass, and then continue to the dinner menu, which states the origin of the fish, lamb, beef, chicken, and veggies; lunch and simple dinners of pizza and burgers are served downstairs, which has a nice outdoor eating area. **Known for:** upscale, romantic atmosphere; casual menu downstairs; locally caught fish. *Average main: $45 ✉ 2829 Ala Kalanikaumaka St., G-149, Poipu ☎ 808/742–8385 🌐 www.merrimanshawaii.com.*

$ ITALIAN FAMILY

Pizzetta. This family-style Italian restaurant has an open-air deck where hearty portions of pasta, calzones, and thin-crust pizza are served, along with kalua pork and cabbage, grilled fish, and barbecue ribs, all of which can find their way into pizza toppings. Gluten-free crust and pasta are available. **Known for:** neighborhood delivery service; attentive wait staff; fresh, house-made bread. *Average main: $17 ✉ 5408 Koloa Rd., Koloa ☎ 808/742–8881.*

$$$$ ECLECTIC Fodor's Choice ★

Red Salt. Smart, sophisticated decor, attentive and skilled service, and an exceptional menu that highlights Hawaiian seafood make Red Salt a great choice for leisurely fine dining. A breakfast buffet is also served, and the sushi bar and pool bar offer more of the kitchen's great food, at lower prices. **Known for:** dramatic presentation; $79 tasting menu; perfectly grilled meats. *Average main: $48 ✉ Koa Kea Resort, 2251 Poipu Rd., Poipu ☎ 808/742–4288 🌐 meritagecollection.com/koakea/dining-at-red-salt/.*

$$$$ SEAFOOD

Tidepools. Of the Grand Hyatt's many notable restaurants, Tidepools is definitely the most tropical and campy, with private grass-thatch huts that seem to float on a koi-filled pond beneath starry skies while torches flicker in the lushly landscaped grounds nearby. The equally distinctive food has an island flavor that comes from the chef's advocacy of Hawaii regional cuisine and extensive use of island-grown products including fresh herbs from the resort's organic garden. **Known for:** Hawaii regional cuisine; extensive use of island-grown products; excellent service. *Average main: $45 ✉ Grand Hyatt Kauai Resort and Spa, 1571 Poipu Rd., Poipu ☎ 808/240–6456 🌐 kauai.grand.hyatt.com/en/hotel/dining/Tidepools.html ⏲ No lunch.*

THE WEST SIDE

When it comes to dining on the West Side, pickings are mighty slim. Fortunately, the few eateries that are here are generally worth patronizing.

$ CAFÉ FAMILY

Little Fish Coffee. For a wholesome breakfast or lunch on the West Side, this friendly, funky, and fun—right down to the marking pens that allow you to leave your own graffiti on the bathroom wall—café is the spot. The coffee is good, with each cup individually dripped, and the fresh bagels come with house-made cream cheese. **Known for:** casual setting; emphasis on wholesome ingredients; smoothies and fresh juices. *Average main: $9 ✉ 3900 Hanapepe Rd., Eleele ☎ 808/335–5000 🌐 littlefishcoffee.com ⏲ No dinner.*

$ BARBECUE FAMILY

Plantations BBQ & Bar. This casual eatery is located in the equally laid-back Waimea Plantation Cottages; it's a great place to sit with a cocktail and watch the sun set. The fare is simple and hearty: chili fries, burgers, sandwiches, salads, and barrel-smoked BBQ chicken and beef for lunch and dinner, and the usual eggs and pancakes for breakfast. **Known for:** large portions; kid-friendly dining; great selection of sides. *Average main: $15 ✉ 9400 Kaumualii Hwy., Waimea (Kauai County) ☎ 808/338–1625.*

$$$ STEAKHOUSE FAMILY **Wrangler's Steakhouse.** Denim-covered seating, decorative saddles, and a stagecoach in a loft helped to transform the historic Ako General Store in Waimea into a West Side steak house where you can eat under the stars on the deck out back or inside the old-fashioned, wood-panel dining room. Open weekend evenings, the Saddle Room features a bar menu that includes seven styles of burgers and there's live music on Saturday night. **Known for:** special lunch (rice, beef teriyaki, and shrimp tempura with kimchi) served in a three-tier kaukau tin; campy setting; local, grass-fed beef. *Average main: $28* *9852 Kaumualii Hwy., Waimea (Kauai County)* *808/338–1218* *wranglerssteakhouse.com* *Closed Sun. No lunch Sat.*

WHERE TO STAY

Updated by Joan Conrow

5

The Garden Isle has lodgings for every taste, from swanky resorts to rustic cabins, and from family-friendly condos to romantic bed-and-breakfasts. The savvy traveler can also find inexpensive places that are convenient, safe, and accessible to Kauai's special places and activities.

Kauai may seem small on a map, but because it's circular with no through roads, it can take more time than you think to get from place to place. If at all possible, stay close to your desired activities. This way, you'll save time to squeeze in all the things you'll want to do.

Time of year is also a factor. If you're here in winter or spring, consider staying on the South Shore, as the surf on the North Shore and East Side tends to be rough, making many ocean beaches dangerous for swimming or water sports.

Before booking accommodations, think hard about what kind of experience you want to have for your island vacation. There are several top-notch resorts to choose from, and Kauai also has a wide variety of condos, vacation rentals, and bed-and-breakfasts. The Kauai Visitors Bureau provides a comprehensive listing of accommodation choices to help you decide.

THE NORTH SHORE

The North Shore is mountainous and wet, which accounts for its rugged, lush landscape. Posh resorts and condominiums await you at Princeville, a community with dreamy views, excellent golf courses, and lovely sunsets. It maintains the lion's share of North Shore accommodations—primarily luxury hotel rooms and condos built on a plateau overlooking the sea. Hanalei, a bay-side town in a broad valley, has a smattering of hotel rooms and numerous vacation rentals, many within walking distance of the beach. Prices tend to be high in this resort area. If you want to do extensive sightseeing on other parts of the island, be prepared for a long drive—one that's very dark at night. ⚠ **Following extensive flooding in early 2018, areas of Haena and the Napali Coast are undergoing repairs. Please check before visiting to make sure places are open.**

WHERE TO STAY IN KAUAI

	Local Vibe	Pros	Cons
The North Shore	Properties here have the "wow" factor with ocean and mountain beauty; laid-back Hanalei and Princeville set the high-end pace.	When the weather is good (summer) this side has it all. Epic winter surf, gorgeous waterfalls, and verdant vistas create some of the best scenery in Hawaii.	Frequent winter rain (being green has a cost) means you may have to travel south to find the sun; expensive restaurants and shopping offer few deals.
The East Side	The most reasonably priced area to stay for the practical traveler; lacks the pizzazz of expensive resorts on North and South shores; more traditional beach hotels.	The best travel deals show up here; more direct access to the local population; plenty of decent restaurants with good variety, along with delis in food stores.	Beaches aren't the greatest (rocky, reefy) at many of the lodging spots; congested traffic at times; some crime issues in parks.
The South Shore	Resort central; plenty of choices where the consistent sunshine is perfect for those who want to do nothing but play golf or tennis and read a book by the pool.	Beautiful in its own right; many enchanted evenings with stellar sunsets; summer surf a bit easier for beginners to handle.	Though resorts are lush, surrounding landscape is desertlike with scrub brush; construction can be brutal on peace of mind.
The West Side	There are few options for lodging in this mostly untouristed setting, with contrasts such as the extreme heat of a July day in Waimea to a frozen winter night up in Kokee.	A gateway area for exploration into the wilds of Kokee or for boating trips on Napali Coast; main hub for boat and helicopter trips; outstanding sunsets.	Least convenient side for most visitors; daytime is languid and dry; river runoff can ruin ocean's clarity.

$$ RESORT FAMILY **Hanalei Bay Resort.** The nicest feature of this condominium resort overlooking Hanalei Bay and Napali Coast is its upper-level pool, with authentic lava-rock waterfalls, an open-air hot tub, and a kid-friendly sand "beach." **Pros:** beautiful views; tennis courts on property with a children's program; 24-hour fitness center; tropical pool. **Cons:** steep walkways; long walk to beach; no restaurant or lounge. *Rooms from: $215 ✉ 5380 Honoiki Rd., Princeville ☎ 808/826–6522, 877/507–1428 🌐 www.hanaleibayresort.com 134 units No meals.*

$$$$ RESORT **Hanalei Colony Resort.** The only true beachfront resort on Kauai's North Shore, Hanalei Colony is a laid-back, go-barefoot kind of resort sandwiched between towering mountains and the sea. **Pros:** oceanfront setting; private, quiet property; well-maintained units with Hawaiian-style furnishings. **Cons:** poor cell-phone reception; damp in winter; isolated location. *Rooms from: $375 ✉ 5-7130 Kuhio Hwy., Haena ☎ 808/826–6235, 800/628–3004 🌐 www.hcr.com 48 units No meals.*

$ RENTAL **Hanalei Inn.** If you're looking for lodgings that won't break the bank a block from gorgeous Hanalei Bay, look no further, as this is literally the only choice among the town's pricey vacation rentals. **Pros:** quick walk to beach, bus stop, and shops; full kitchen; coin-operated laundry on-site. **Cons:** strict cancellation policy; daytime

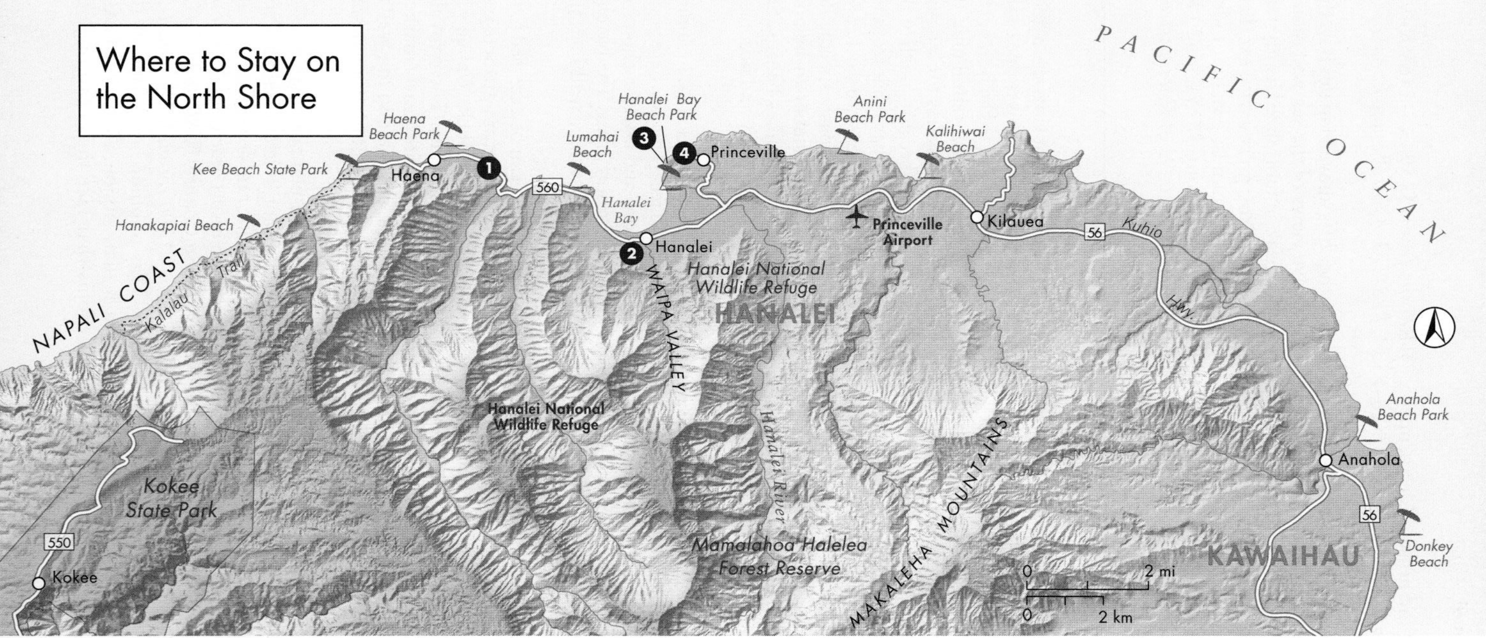

Hanalei Bay Resort **4**
Hanalei Colony Resort **1**
Hanalei Inn **2**
St. Regis Princeville Resort **3**

traffic noise; older property. [$] *Rooms from: $159* ✉ *5-5468 Kuhio Hwy., Hanalei* ☎ *808/826–9333, 888/773–4730* 🌐 *www.hanaleiinn.net* *4 studios* *No meals.*

$$$$ RESORT FAMILY Fodor's Choice ★ **St. Regis Princeville Resort.** Built into the cliffs above Hanalei Bay, this swanky Starwood resort offers expansive views of the sea and mountains, including Makana, the landmark peak immortalized as mysterious Bali Hai island in the film *South Pacific*. **Pros:** great views; excellent restaurants; attractive lobby. **Cons:** minimal grounds; beach not ideal for swimming; extremely expensive. [$] *Rooms from: $815* ✉ *5520 Ka Haku Rd., Princeville* ☎ *877/787–3447, 808/826–9644* 🌐 *www.stregisprinceville.com* *252 rooms* *No meals.*

THE EAST SIDE

Location, location, location. The East Side, or Coconut Coast, is a good centralized home base if you want to see and do it all. This is one of the few resort areas on Kauai where you can actually walk to the beach, restaurants, and stores from your condo, hotel, or vacation-rental unit. It's not only convenient, but comparatively cheap. You pay less for lodging, meals, services, merchandise, and gas here—mainly because much of the coral-reef coastline isn't as ideal as the sandy-bottom bays that front the fancy resorts. We think the shoreline is just fine. There are pockets in the reef to swim in, and the coast is uncrowded and boasts spectacular views. **TIP→ Traffic on the main highway can be bumber-to-bumper in the afternoon.** All in all, it's a good choice for families because the prices are right and there's plenty to keep everyone happy and occupied.

KAPAA AND WAILUA

Since Kapaa is the island's major population center, this area, including Waipouli and Wailua, has a lived-in, real-world feel. This is where you'll find some of the best deals on accommodations and a wider choice of inexpensive restaurants and shops than in the resort areas. The beaches here are so-so for swimming but nice for sunbathing, walking, and watching the sun- and moonrise.

The Wailua area is rather compact and much of it can be accessed from a coastal walking and biking path. The resorts here are attractive to middle-class travelers seeking a good bang for their buck. Wailua had a rich cultural significance for the ancient Hawaiians. Their royalty lived here, and ancient sacred grounds, called *heiau,* are clearly marked. ⚠ **Following extensive flooding in early 2018, areas along the Wailua River are undergoing repairs. Please check before visiting to make sure places are open.**

$$ HOTEL **Aston Islander on the Beach.** A low-rise, Hawaii-plantation-style design gives this 6-acre beachfront property a pleasant, relaxed feeling. **Pros:** convenient location; free airport shuttle; online rate deals. **Cons:** smallish pool; no restaurant on the property; no resort amenities. [$] *Rooms from: $239* ✉ *440 Aleka Pl., Wailua (Kauai County)* ☎ *808/822–7417, 866/774–2924* 🌐 *www.astonhotels.com* *200 rooms* *No meals.*

$$ RESORT **Courtyard Kauai at Coconut Beach.** This popular hotel, one of the few true oceanfront properties on Kauai, sits on a ribbon of sand in Kapaa with bright, spacious rooms that face the ocean or pool.

Pros: convenient location; close to ocean; pleasant grounds. **Cons:** coastline not conducive to swimming; small pool; high daily parking fee. *Rooms from: $249 ✉ 650 Aleka Loop, Wailua (Kauai County) ☎ 808/822–3455, 800/760–8555 🌐 www.marriott.com ⇆ 311 rooms 🍴 No meals.*

$$$ HOTEL FAMILY **Hotel Coral Reef.** This small hotel has been in business since 1956 and is something of a Kauai beachfront landmark, with clean, comfortable rooms, some with great ocean views, and a large pool that overlooks the water; expect great sunrises. **Pros:** free parking; oceanfront setting; convenient location. **Cons:** located in a busy section of Kapaa; ocean swimming is marginal; traffic noise. *Rooms from: $289 ✉ 4-1516 Kuhio Hwy., Kapaa ☎ 808/822–4481, 800/843–4659 🌐 www.hotelcoralreefresort.com ⇆ 20 rooms 🍴 Free Breakfast.*

$ RENTAL **Kapaa Sands.** An old rock etched with *kanji* (Japanese characters) reminds you that the site of this condominium gem was once occupied by a Shinto temple. **Pros:** discounts for extended stays; walking distance to shops, restaurants, and beach; turtle and monk seal sightings common. **Cons:** no-frills lodging; small bathrooms; traffic noise in rear units. *Rooms from: $179 ✉ 380 Papaloa Rd., Wailua (Kauai County) ☎ 808/822–4901, 800/222–4901 🌐 www.kapaasands.com ⇆ 24 units 🍴 No meals.*

$$ RENTAL FAMILY Fodor's Choice ★ **Kauai Coast Resort at the Beachboy.** Fronting an uncrowded stretch of beach, this three-story primarily time-share resort is convenient and a bit more upscale than nearby properties. **Pros:** central location; nice sunrises; free parking. **Cons:** beach is narrow; ocean not ideal for swimming; daily housekeeping fee. *Rooms from: $215 ✉ 520 Aleka Loop, Wailua (Kauai County) ☎ 808/822–3441, 866/678–3289 🌐 www.shellhospitality.com ⇆ 108 units 🍴 No meals.*

$ HOTEL **Kauai Shores.** This oceanfront inn has been transformed into an affordable boutique hotel, thanks to a much-needed renovation of its guest rooms and public spaces. **Pros:** convenient location; free Wi-Fi; great sunrises; discount for LGBT travelers. **Cons:** coral reef makes ocean swimming marginal; modest property; minimal amenities; daily hospitality fee. *Rooms from: $158 ✉ 420 Papaloa Rd., Wailua (Kauai County) ☎ 808/822–4951, 800/560–5553 🌐 www.kauaishoreshotel.com ⇆ 202 rooms 🍴 No meals.*

$$$ RENTAL **Outrigger at Lae Nani.** Ruling Hawaiian chiefs once returned from ocean voyages to this spot, now host to comfortable condominiums. **Pros:** nice beach; walking distance to playground; attractively furnished. **Cons:** third floor is walk-up; no Wi-Fi; cleaning fee. *Rooms from: $339 ✉ 410 Papaloa Rd., Wailua (Kauai County) ☎ 808/823–1401, 866/956–4262 🌐 www.outrigger.com ⇆ 84 units 🍴 No meals.*

LIHUE

Lihue is not the most desirable place to stay on Kauai, in terms of scenic beauty, although it does have its advantages, including easy access to the airport. Restaurants and shops are plentiful, and there's lovely Kalapaki Bay for beachgoers. Aside from the Marriott and the Kauai

5

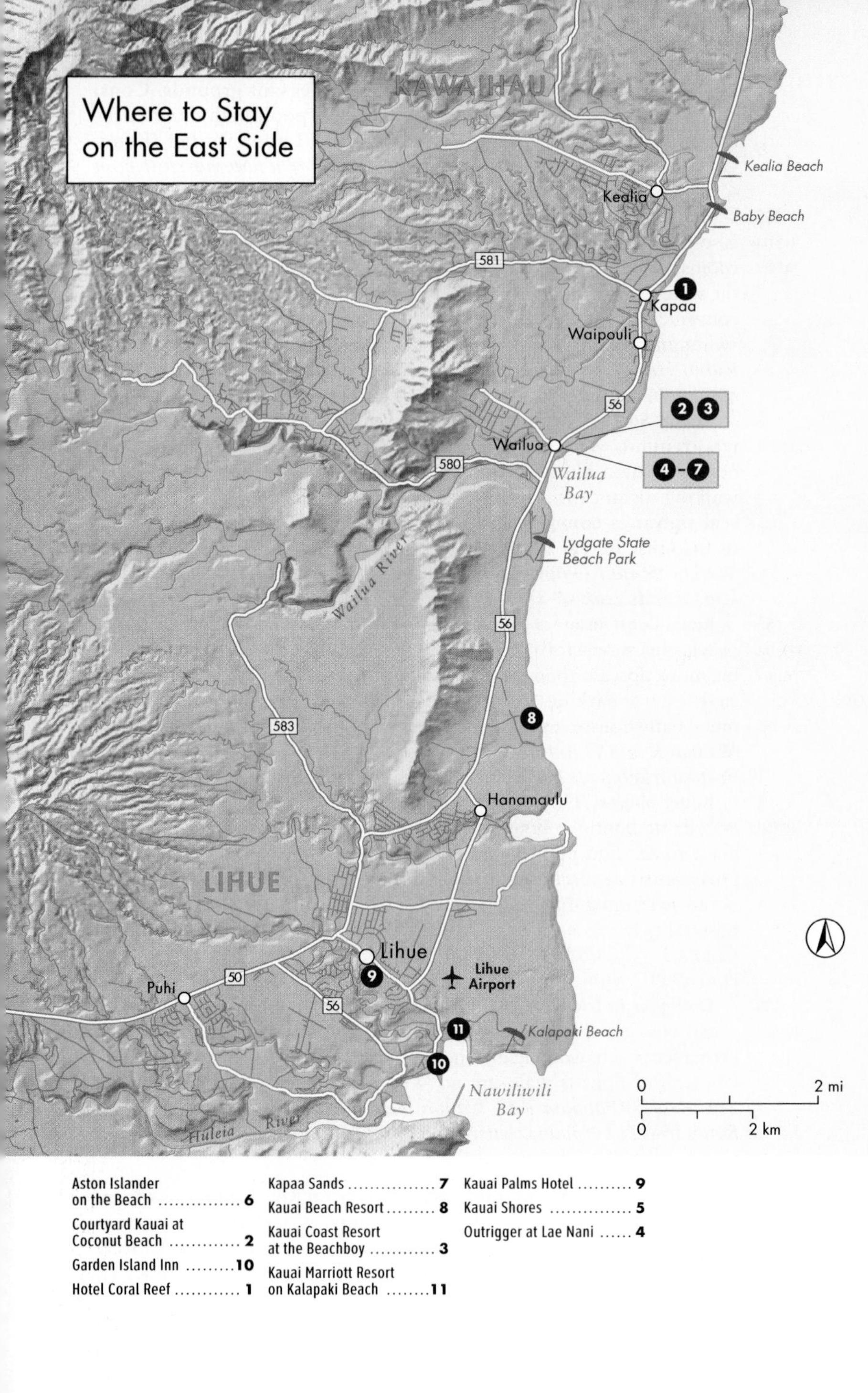
Where to Stay on the East Side
KAWAIHAU
Kealia Beach
Kealia
Baby Beach
581
1
Kapaa
Waipouli
56
2 3
Wailua
580
4-7
Wailua Bay
Lydgate State Beach Park
Wailua River
56
8
583
Hanamaulu
LIHUE
Lihue
9
Lihue Airport
Puhi
50
56
11
Kalapaki Beach
10
Nawiliwili Bay
Huleia River
0 2 mi
0 2 km
Aston Islander on the Beach 6
Courtyard Kauai at Coconut Beach 2
Garden Island Inn 10
Hotel Coral Reef 1
Kapaa Sands 7
Kauai Beach Resort......... 8
Kauai Coast Resort at the Beachboy 3
Kauai Marriott Resort on Kalapaki Beach 11
Kauai Palms Hotel 9
Kauai Shores 5
Outrigger at Lae Nani 4

Beach Resort, most of the limited lodging possibilities are smaller and aimed at the cost-conscious traveler.

$$ HOTEL **Garden Island Inn.** Budget travelers love this three-story inn near Kalapaki Bay and Anchor Cove shopping center as it's clean, offers free Wi-Fi, and the innkeepers are friendly, sharing fruit, flowers, and beach gear. **Pros:** walk to beach, restaurants, and shops; good for extended stays and budget travel; air-conditioning. **Cons:** some traffic noise; near a busy harbor; limited grounds; no pool. *Rooms from: $185* *3445 Wilcox Rd., Kalapaki Beach, Lihue* *808/245–7227, 800/648–0154* *www.gardenislandinn.com* *21 rooms* *No meals.*

$$$ RESORT **Kauai Beach Resort.** This plantation-style hotel recently came under the management of Aqua Hotels and Resorts and in 2017 completed a $14 million renovation that upgraded the amenities to provide a relaxing, upscale experience close to the airport, but without the noise. **Pros:** unique sand-bottom pool with 12-foot waterfall; shuttle service to airport; resort amenities. **Cons:** not a good swimming beach; windy at times; no nearby restaurants or resorts. *Rooms from: $329* *4331 Kauai Beach Dr., Hanamaulu* *888/805–3843* *www.kauaibeachresorthawaii.com* *357 rooms* *No meals.*

$$$ RESORT FAMILY **Kauai Marriott Resort on Kalapaki Beach.** An elaborate tropical garden, waterfalls right off the lobby, Greek statues and columns, and an enormous 26,000-square-foot swimming pool characterize the grand—and grandiose—scale of this resort on Kalapaki Beach, which looks out at the dramatic Haupu Ridge. **Pros:** oceanfront setting; numerous restaurants; convenient location; airport shuttle. **Cons:** airport noise; ocean water quality can be poor at times; located near an industrial area. *Rooms from: $339* *3610 Rice St., Kalapaki Beach, Lihue* *808/245–5050, 800/220–2925* *www.kauaimarriott.com* *367 rooms* *Free Breakfast.*

$ HOTEL **Kauai Palms Hotel.** Not only is this low-cost alternative close to the airport, but it's also a great base for day trips to all sides of the island. **Pros:** friendly staff; inexpensive; centrally located. **Cons:** bare-bones amenities; smallish rooms; traffic noise. *Rooms from: $95* *2931 Kalena St., Lihue* *808/246–0908* *www.kauaipalmshotel.com* *33 rooms* *No meals.*

THE SOUTH SHORE

Sunseekers usually head south to the condo-studded shores of Poipu, where three- and four-story complexes line the coast and the surf is generally ideal for swimming. As the island's primary resort community, Poipu has the bulk of the island's accommodations, and more condos than hotels, with prices in the moderate to expensive range. Although it accommodates many visitors, its extensive, colorful landscaping and low-rise buildings save it from feeling dense and overcrowded, and it has a delightful coastal promenade perfect for sunset strolls. Surprisingly, the South Shore doesn't have as many shops and restaurants as one might expect for such a popular resort region, but the new Kukuiula shopping plaza is doing its best to fill the gaps. **TIP→ The**

area's beaches are among the best on the island for families, with sandy shores, shallow waters, and grassy lawns adjacent to the sand.

$$$$ RESORT FAMILY Fodor's Choice ★ **Grand Hyatt Kauai Resort and Spa.** Dramatically handsome, this classic Hawaiian low-rise is built into the cliffs overlooking an unspoiled coastline; it's taken great strides to reduce its carbon footprint and boasts mouthwatering restaurants, which helps to make it Kauai's best mega-resort. **Pros:** fabulous pool; excellent restaurants; Hawaiian ambience. **Cons:** poor and somewhat dangerous swimming beach during summer swells; small balconies; $35 daily resort fee. *Rooms from: $424 ✉ 1571 Poipu Rd., Poipu ☎ 808/742–1234, 800/633–7313 🌐 www.grandhyattkauai.com 639 rooms No meals.*

$ RENTAL **Kauai Cove Cottages.** Located in a residential neighborhood, this property includes a modern studio cottage at the mouth of Waikomo Stream, about two blocks from a nice snorkeling cove, as well as a full bedroom suite and a guest room with shared bath in a larger house a few miles away in the resort community at Poipu Kai. **Pros:** clean; great snorkeling nearby; quiet neighborhood. **Cons:** not on beach; $60–$75 cleaning fee upon departure; no shops or restaurants nearby. *Rooms from: $169 ✉ 2672 Puuholo Rd., Poipu ☎ 808/742–2562, 800/624–9945 🌐 www.kauaicove.com 1 cottage, 2 rooms No meals.*

$$$ RENTAL FAMILY **Kiahuna Plantation Resort Kauai by Outrigger.** This longtime Kauai condo project consists of 42 plantation-style, low-rise buildings with individually owned one- and two-bedroom units that arc around a large, grassy field leading to a lovely beach. **Pros:** great sunset and ocean views are bonuses in some units; convenient to restaurants and shops; swimmable beach and lawn for picnics and games. **Cons:** no air-conditioning; be prepared for stairs; somewhat lackluster property. *Rooms from: $299 ✉ 2253 Poipu Rd., Poipu ☎ 808/742–6411, 800/542–4862 🌐 www.outrigger.com 333 units No meals.*

$$$$ RESORT Fodor's Choice ★ **Koa Kea Hotel and Resort.** This boutique property offers a luxurious, high-end experience without the bustle of many larger resorts, making it a great place to forget it all while relaxing at the spa or lounging by the pool. **Pros:** incredibly comfortable beds; friendly service; romantic spa; perfect romantic getaway. **Cons:** not much for children; all parking is valet, but it feels more like a convenience than a burden; the area is very busy. *Rooms from: $429 ✉ 2251 Poipu Rd., Poipu ☎ 808/828–8888, 888/898–8958 🌐 www.koakea.com 121 rooms No meals.*

$ RENTAL **Poipu Crater Resort.** Set within a nicely landscaped resort built on an extinct volcanic crater known as *Piha Keakua* , or "place of the gods," these two-bedroom condominium units are fairly spacious, with large windows and high ceilings, and full kitchens. **Pros:** attractive and generally well kept; pretty setting on the South Shore; located just 700 yards from Keoniloa Bay (Shipwreck Beach). **Cons:** beach isn't good for swimming; few resort amenities; individually owned units means upkeep and decor varies. *Rooms from: $150 ✉ 2330 Hoohu Rd., Poipu ☎ 808/742–7400 🌐 www.parrishkauai.com 30 units No meals.*

$$$ RENTAL FAMILY **Poipu Kapili Resort.** White-frame exteriors and double-pitched roofs complement the tropical landscaping at this resort, which offers spacious one- and two-bedroom condo units—with full kitchens, entertainment centers, and garden or ocean views—that are minutes from

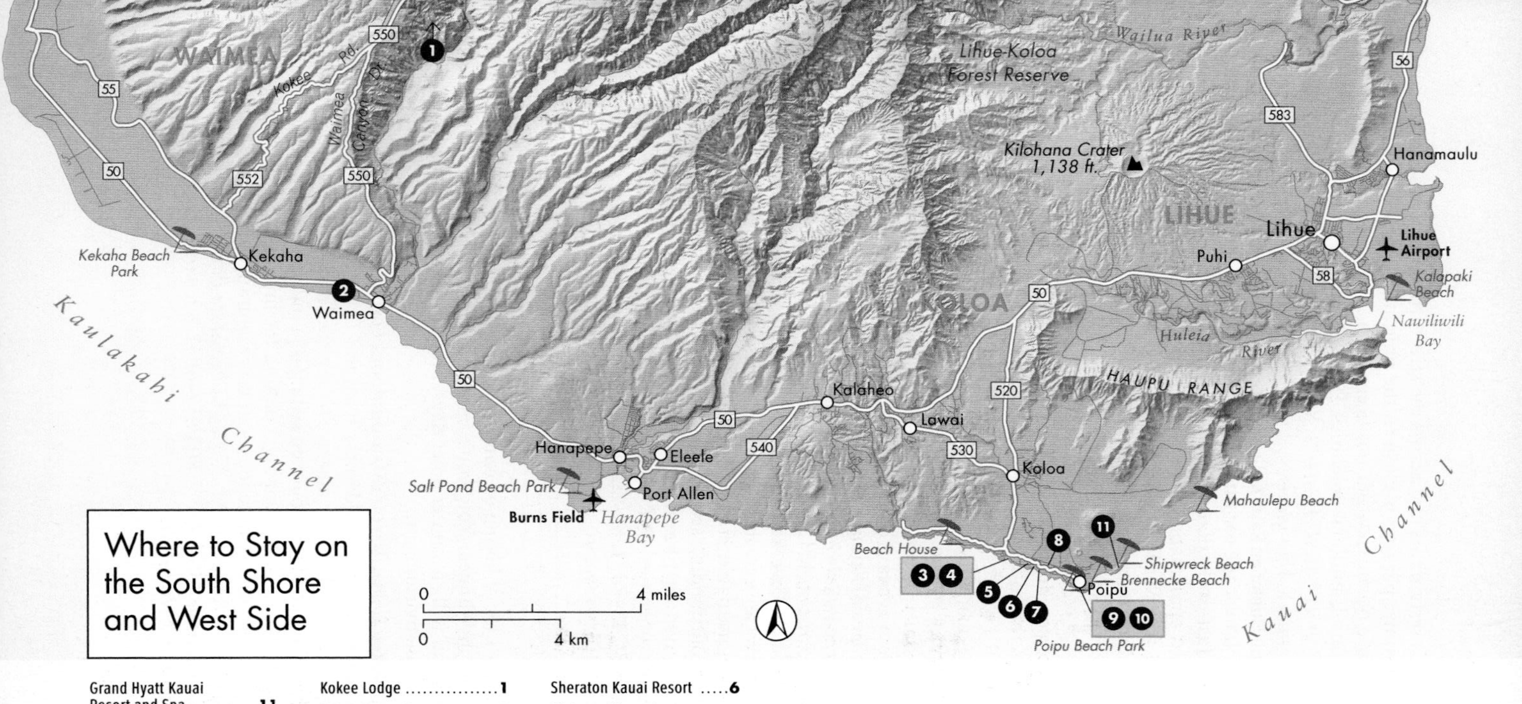

Where to Stay on the South Shore and West Side

Grand Hyatt Kauai Resort and Spa 11
Kauai Cove Cottages 3
Kiahuna Plantation Resort Kauai by Outrigger 7
Koa Kea Hotel and Resort 8
Kokee Lodge 1
Poipu Crater Resort 10
Poipu Kapili Resort 5
Poipu Plantation Resort.......................9
Sheraton Kauai Resort 6
Waimea Plantation Cottages 2
Whalers Cove Resort 4

Poipu's restaurants and across the street from a nice beach. **Pros:** units are roomy; parking is close to the unit; units are well spaced. **Cons:** units are ocean-view but not oceanfront; a three-night minimum stay is required; minimal amenities. *Rooms from: $300 ✉ 2221 Kapili Rd., Poipu ☎ 808/742–6449, 800/443–7714 🌐 www.poipukapili.com ⇨ 60 units 🍴 No meals.*

$ B&B/INN **Poipu Plantation Resort.** Plumeria, ti, and other tropical foliage create a lush landscape for this resort, which rents four suites in a bed-and-breakfast–style plantation home and nine one- and two-bedroom cottage apartments. **Pros:** attractively furnished; full breakfast at B&B; free Wi-Fi. **Cons:** three-night minimum; not on the ocean; no resort amenities. *Rooms from: $155 ✉ 1792 Pee Rd., Poipu ☎ 808/742–6757, 800/634–0263 🌐 www.poipubeach.com ⇨ 4 rooms, 9 cottages 🍴 Free Breakfast.*

$$$ RESORT Fodor's Choice ★ **Sheraton Kauai Resort.** The Sheraton is a sprawling resort with rooms that offer views of the ocean and its lovely landscaped gardens; it's worth splurging on the newly renovated ocean-wing accommodations, which are so close to the water you can practically feel the spray of the surf as it hits the rocks below. **Pros:** ocean-view pool; quiet; great restaurant with spectacular views. **Cons:** parking can be a ways from the room; some rooms feel dated; $30 daily resort fee. *Rooms from: $340 ✉ 2440 Hoonani Rd., Poipu Beach, Koloa ☎ 808/742–1661, 888/488–3535 🌐 www.sheraton-kauai.com ⇨ 405 rooms 🍴 No meals.*

$$$$ RENTAL FAMILY **Whalers Cove Resort.** Perched about as close to the water's edge as they can get, these condos are the most luxurious on the South Shore, available in one-, two-, or three-bedroom units. **Pros:** on-site staff; outstanding setting; spacious, fully equipped units. **Cons:** rocky beach not ideal for swimming; no air-conditioning; resort fee, but no resort amenities. *Rooms from: $430 ✉ 2640 Puuholo Rd., Poipu ☎ 808/742–7571, 800/225–2683 🌐 www.whalerscoveresort.com ⇨ 39 units 🍴 No meals.*

THE WEST SIDE

To do a lot of hiking or immerse yourself in the island's history, find a room in Waimea. You won't find many resorts, restaurants, or shops, but you will encounter quiet days, miles of largely deserted beach, and a rural environment.

$ RENTAL **Kokee Lodge.** If you're an outdoors enthusiast, you can appreciate Kauai's mountain wilderness from the 12 rustic cabins that make up this lodge; cabins are austere, to say the least, but more comfortable than a tent, and the mountain setting is grand. **Pros:** outstanding setting; more refined than camping; cooking facilities. **Cons:** austere accommodations in a remote location; no restaurants for dinner; $45 cleaning fee. *Rooms from: $79 ✉ Kokee State Park, 3600 Kokee Rd., at mile marker 15, Kokee ☎ 808/652–6852 🌐 www.kokeelodge.com ⇨ 12 cabins 🍴 No meals.*

$ RENTAL Fodor's Choice ★ **Waimea Plantation Cottages.** Originally built in the early 1900s, history buffs will adore these relocated and refurbished one- to five-bedroom sugar-plantation cottages, which are tucked among coconut trees along a lovely, walkable stretch of beach on the sunny West Side. **Pros:** unique lodging experience; quiet and low-key; free Wi-Fi. **Cons:** not a good swimming beach; rooms are not luxurious; minimal amenities. *Rooms from: $170 ✉ 9400 Kaumualii Hwy., Box 367, Waimea (Kauai County) ☎ 808/338–1625, 800/716–6199 ⊕ www.coasthotels.com ⇨ 61 cottages No meals.*

NIGHTLIFE AND PERFORMING ARTS

Updated by Joan Conrow

Kauai has never been known for its nightlife. It's a rural island, where folks tend to retire early, and the streets are dark and deserted well before midnight. The island does have its nightspots, though, and the after-dark entertainment scene keeps expanding, especially in areas frequented by tourists.

Most of the island's dinner and luau shows are held at hotels and resorts. Hotel lounges are a good source of live music, often with no cover charge, as are a few bars and restaurants around the island.

Check the local newspaper, the *Garden Island,* for listings of weekly happenings. Free publications such as *Kauai Gold, This Week on Kauai,* and *Essential Kauai* also list entertainment events. You can pick them up at Lihue Airport near the baggage claim area, as well as at numerous retail areas on the island.

NIGHTLIFE

For every new venue that opens on Kauai, another one closes, mainly because most island residents tend to retire early. It is, after all, a rural island. But still, there are a number of places to shake your booty, hear local music, and simply enjoy a drink. Nightclubs that stay open until the wee hours are rare on Kauai, and the bar scene is limited. The major resorts generally host their own live entertainment and happy hours. All bars and clubs that serve alcohol must close at 2 am, except those with a cabaret license, which allows them to close at 4 am.

THE NORTH SHORE

Hanalei Gourmet. The sleepy North Shore stays awake—until 10:30, that is—each evening in this small, convivial deli and bar inside Hanalei's restored old school building. There's local live Hawaiian, jazz, rock, and folk music on Sunday and Wednesday evening. *✉ Hanalei Center, 5-5161 Kuhio Hwy., Hanalei ☎ 808/826–2524 ⊕ www.hanaleigourmet.com.*

Fodor's Choice ★ **Happy Talk Lounge.** Want to sip an umbrella cocktail while you gaze at the original Bali Hai? Open on two sides, Happy Talk Lounge offers breezy views across Hanalei Bay to plush emerald mountains. If you think the scene looks familiar, maybe you've seen the film classic *South Pacific,* filmed here. The film version of Bali Hai is actually Kauai's Mount Makana. Order a tropical cocktail and *pupu* (Hawaiian hors d'oeuvres) and enjoy a truly enchanting evening as the sun sets over the sparkling waters. ■ **TIP→ Nearby Tunnels Beach (aka Haena Beach and Makua) is often called Nurses' Beach, where Mitzi Gaynor sang about washing that man right outta her hair; Hanalei Bay is where Bloody Mary sang "Bali Hai."** ✉ *Hanalei Bay Resort, 5380 Honoiki Rd., Princeville* ☎ *808/431–4084* 🌐 *www.happytalklounge.com.*

St. Regis Bar. This spacious and comfortable lounge with a gorgeous view of Hanalei Bay offers drinks daily from 3:30 to 11 and a Champagne toast at sunset. Stop by between 5:30 and 10 for *pupu* (hors d'oeuvres), with a popular Hawaiian music and hula show from 6:30 to 9 on Sunday night. ✉ *Princeville Resort, 5520 Ka Haku Rd., Princeville* ☎ *808/826–9644* 🌐 *www.stregisprinceville.com.*

Tahiti Nui. This venerable and funky institution in sleepy Hanalei still offers its famous luau at 5 on Wednesday evenings, although the bar is the big attraction. Spirits are always high at this popular hangout for locals and visitors alike, which houses live nightly entertainment and Hawaiian slack key guitar music on Friday evenings. Open until 1 am. ✉ *5-5134 Kuhio Hwy., Hanalei* ☎ *808/826–6277* 🌐 *www.thenui.com.*

THE EAST SIDE

EatHealthy Cafe. Nestled in a bamboo forest draped in bougainvillea and flowering vines and hidden from view off the Kuhio Highway is a charming little venue where local musicians perform most evenings. Previously known as Caffé Coco, it now offers vegan fare, including *pupu* (appetizers), entrées, and desserts. It may not have a liquor license, but don't let that stop you from enjoying the entertainment in a pleasant outdoor setting; just bring your own wine or beer. It's open Tuesday through Saturday until 9. ✉ *4-369 Kuhio Hwy., Kapaa* ☎ *808/822–7990* 🌐 *eathealthykauai.com.*

Duke's Barefoot Bar. This is one of the liveliest bars in Nawiliwili. Contemporary Hawaiian music is usually performed at this beachside bar and restaurant every day but Tuesday during "Aloha Hours" from 4 to 6 pm. On Thursday, Friday, and Saturday nights, live music is held from 8:30 to 10:30 pm. ✉ *Kalapaki Beach, 3610 Rice St., Lihue* ☎ *808/246–9599* 🌐 *www.dukeskauai.com.*

Fodor's Choice ★ **Hukilau Lanai.** This open-air bar and restaurant is on the property of the Kauai Coast Resort but operates independently. Trade winds trickle through the modest little bar, which looks out into a coconut grove. If the mood takes you, go on a short walk to the sea, or recline in big, comfortable chairs in Wally's Bar in the lobby while listening to mellow jazz or Hawaiian slack-key guitar. Live music plays from 6 to 9 every night, though the restaurant and bar are closed on Monday. Poolside happy hour runs from 3 to 5. Freshly infused tropical martinis—perhaps locally grown lychee and pineapple or a Big Island vanilla bean infusion—are house favorites. ✉ *520 Aleka Loop, Wailua (Kauai County)* ☎ *808/822–0600* 🌐 *www.hukilaukauai.com.*

Rob's Good Times Grill. Let loose at this popular restaurant and sports bar, which has live music Monday through Thursday from 4 to 6 pm. Tuesday offers swing dancing from 7:30 to 10 pm, Friday features live music until midnight, Saturday has late-night club dancing with DJ, while Sunday through Thursday go full-on karaoke until closing. ✉ *4303 Rice St., Lihue* ☎ *808/246–0311* 🌐 *www.kauaisportsbarandgrill.com.*

Trees Lounge. This funky bar and restaurant is popular with a middle-aged crowd. It hosts live music nightly that gets people out on the tiny dance floor. It's behind the Coconut Marketplace and next to the Kauai Coast Resort in Kapaa. Closed Sunday. ✉ *440 Aleka Pl., Kapaa* ☎ *808/823–0600* 🌐 *www.treesloungekauai.com.*

THE SOUTH SHORE

Keoki's Paradise. A young, energetic crowd makes this a lively spot on Friday and Saturday night. When the dining room clears out, there's a bit of a bar scene for singles. Live music every night and two happy hours—one 3–5 pm and the other from 9:30 until closing at 10:30 pm—keep the Bamboo Bar a happening place. ✉ *Poipu Shopping Village, 2360 Kiahuna Plantation Dr., Poipu* ☎ *808/742–7534* 🌐 *www.keokisparadise.com.*

5

PERFORMING ARTS

Although luau remain a primary source of evening fun for families on vacation, there are a handful of other possibilities. There are no traditional dinner cruises, but some boat tours do offer an evening buffet with music along Napali Coast. A few times a year, Women in Theater (WIT), a local women's theater group, performs dinner shows at the Hukilau Lanai in Wailua and the Kauai Community Players offers regular performances at its Puhi Theatrical Warehouse. Kauai Community College Performing Arts Center also draws well-known artists.

VENUES

Kauai Community College Performing Arts Center. This is a main venue for island entertainment, hosting a concert music series, visiting musicians, dramatic productions, and special events such as educational forums. ✉ *3-1901 Kaumualii Hwy., Lihue* ☎ *808/245–8311* 🌐 *www.kauai.hawaii.edu/pac.*

LUAU

Although the commercial luau experience is a far cry from the backyard luau thrown by local residents to celebrate a wedding, graduation, or baby's first birthday, they're nonetheless entertaining and a good introduction to the Hawaiian food that isn't widely sold in restaurants. With many, you can watch a roasted pig being carried out of its *imu,* a hole in the ground used for cooking meat with heated stones. Besides the feast, and free mai tais, there's often an exciting dinner show with Polynesian-style music and dancing. It all makes for a fun evening that's suitable for couples, families, and groups, and the informal setting is conducive to meeting other people. Every luau is different, reflecting the cuisine and tenor of the host facility, so compare prices, menus, and entertainment before making your reservation. Most luau on Kauai are offered only on a limited number of nights each week, so plan ahead to get the luau you want. We tend to prefer those *not* held on resort properties, because they feel a bit more authentic.

The luau shows listed below are our favorites.

Grand Hyatt Kauai Luau. Excellent food and an exciting dance performance characterize this traditional luau buffet, held in a garden setting near majestic Keoneloa Bay. ✉ *Grand Hyatt Kauai Resort and Spa, 1571 Poipu Rd., Poipu* ☎ *808/240–6456* 🌐 *kauai.grand.hyatt.com/en/hotel/dining/grand-hyatt-kauai-luau.html* 🎟 *From $113.*

Luau Kalamaku. Set on historic sugar-plantation land, this luau bills itself as the only "theatrical" luau on Kauai. The luau feast is served buffet style, there's an open bar, and the performers aim to both entertain and educate about Hawaiian culture. Guests sit at tables around a circular stage; tables farther from the stage are elevated, providing unobstructed views. Additional packages offer visitors the opportunity to watch the show only, tour the 35-acre plantation via train, or special romantic perks like a lei greeting and Champagne. ✉ *3-2087 Kaumualii St., Lihue* ☎ *877/622–1780* 🌐 *www.luaukalamaku.com* 🎟 *From $57.*

Fodor's Choice ★ **Smith's Tropical Paradise Luau.** A 30-acre tropical garden on the Wailua River provides the lovely setting for this popular luau, which begins with the traditional blowing of the conch shell and *imu* (pig roast) ceremony, followed by cocktails, an island feast, great music, and an international show in the amphitheater overlooking a torch-lighted lagoon. It's fairly authentic and a better deal than the pricier resort events. ✉ *174 Wailua Rd., Kapaa* ☎ *808/821–6895* 🌐 *www.smithskauai.com* 🎟 *$98.*

MUSIC

Check *The Garden Island,* Kauai's newspaper, for outdoor reggae and Hawaiian-music shows.

Hanalei Slack Key Concerts. Relax to the instrumental music form created by Hawaiian *paniolo* (cowboys) in the early 1800s. Shows are Wednesday in Kapaa at All Saints Church and Tuesday at the Princeville Community Center. If you're looking for a scenic setting, head to Hale Halawai Ohana O Hanalei, on Friday and Sunday; it's *mauka* (toward the mountains) down a dirt access road across from St. William's Catholic Church (Malolo Road) and then left down another dirt road. ✉ *5-5299 Kuhio Hwy., Hanalei* ☎ *808/826–1469* 🌐 *www.hawaiianslackkeyguitar.com* 🎟 *From $10.*

Kauai Concert Association. This group offers a seasonal program at the Kauai Community College Performing Arts Center that features well-known classical musicians, including soloists and small ensembles. ✉ *3-1901 Kaumualii Hwy., Lihue* ☎ *808/245–7464* 🌐 *www.kauaiconcert.org* 🎟 *From $30.*

SHOPS AND SPAS

Updated by Joan Conrow

There aren't a lot of shops and spas on Kauai, but what you will find here are a handful of places very much worth checking out for the quality of their selection of items sold and services rendered. Many shops now make an effort to sell as many locally made products as possible. When buying an item, ask where it was made or even who made it.

CLOSE UP

Kauai: Undercover Movie Star

Though Kauai has played itself in the movies, most recently starring in *The Descendants* (2011), most of its screen time has been as a stunt double for a number of tropical paradises. The island's remote valleys portrayed Venezuelan jungle in Kevin Costner's *Dragonfly* (2002) and a Costa Rican dinosaur preserve in Steven Spielberg's *Jurassic Park* (1993). Spielberg was no stranger to Kauai, having filmed Harrison Ford's escape via seaplane from Menehune Fishpond in *Raiders of the Lost Ark* (1981).

The fluted cliffs and gorges of Kauai's rugged Napali Coast play the misunderstood beast's island home in *King Kong* (1976), and a jungle dweller of another sort, in *George of the Jungle* (1997), frolicked on Kauai. Harrison Ford returned to the island for 10 weeks during the filming of *Six Days, Seven Nights* (1998), a romantic adventure set in French Polynesia. Part-time Kauai resident Ben Stiller used the island as a stand-in for the jungles of Vietnam in *Tropic Thunder* (2008) and Johnny Depp came here to film some of *Pirates of the Caribbean: On Stranger Tides* (2011). But these are all relatively contemporary movies. What's truly remarkable is that Hollywood discovered Kauai in 1933 with the making of *White Heat*, which was set on a sugar plantation and—like *South Pacific* (also filmed on Kauai)—dealt with an interracial love story.

Then, it was off to the races, as Kauai saw no fewer than a dozen movies filmed on the island in the 1950s, not all of them Oscar contenders. Rita Hayworth starred in *Miss Sadie Thompson* (1953) and no one you'd recognize starred in the tantalizing *She Gods of Shark Reef* (1956).

The movie that is still immortalized on the island in the names of restaurants, real estate offices, a hotel, and even a sushi item is *South Pacific* (1957). (You guessed it, right?) That mythical place called Bali Hai is never far away on Kauai.

In the 1960s Elvis Presley filmed *Blue Hawaii* (1961) and *Girls! Girls! Girls!* (1962) on the island. A local movie tour likes to point out the stain on a hotel carpet where Elvis's jelly doughnut fell.

Kauai has welcomed a long list of Hollywood's A-List: John Wayne in *Donovan's Reef* (1963); Jack Lemmon in *The Wackiest Ship in the Army* (1961); Richard Chamberlain in *The Thorn Birds* (1983); Gene Hackman in *Uncommon Valor* (1983); Danny DeVito and Billy Crystal in *Throw Momma from the Train* (1987); and Dustin Hoffman, Morgan Freeman, Renee Russo, and Cuba Gooding Jr. in *Outbreak* (1995).

Kauai has also appeared on a long list of TV shows and made-for-TV movies, including *Gilligan's Island, Fantasy Island, Starsky & Hutch, Baywatch Hawaii*—even reality TV shows *The Bachelor* and *The Amazing Race 3.*

For the record, just because a movie did some filming here doesn't mean the entire movie was filmed on Kauai. *Honeymoon in Vegas* filmed just one scene here, while the murder mystery *A Perfect Getaway* (2009) was set on the famous Kalalau Trail and featured beautiful Kauaian backdrops but was shot mostly in Puerto Rico.

Often you will find that a product handcrafted on the island may not be that much more expensive than a similar product made overseas. You can also look for the purple "Kauai Made" sticker many merchants display.

Along with one major shopping mall, a few shopping centers, and a growing number of big-box retailers, Kauai has some delightful mom-and-pop shops and specialty boutiques with lots of character. The Garden Isle also has a large and talented community of artisans and fine artists, with galleries all around the island showcasing their creations. You can find many island-made arts and crafts in the small shops, and it's worthwhile to stop in at crafts fairs and outdoor markets to look for bargains and mingle with island residents.

If you're looking for a special memento of your trip that is unique to Kauai County, check out the distinctive Niihau shell lei. The tiny shells are collected from beaches on Kauai and Niihau, pierced, and strung into beautiful necklaces, chokers, and earrings. It's a time-consuming and exacting craft, and these items are much in demand, so don't be taken aback by the high price tags. Those made by Niihau residents will have certificates of authenticity and are worth collecting. You often can find cheaper versions made by non-Hawaiians at crafts fairs.

Kauai is often touted as the healing island, and local spas try hard to fill that role. With the exception of the Hyatt's ANARA Spa, the facilities aren't as posh as some might want, but it's in the human element that Kauai excels. Many island residents are known for their warmth, kindness, and humility, and you can often find all these attributes in the massage therapists and technicians who work long hours at the resort spas. These professionals take their therapeutic mission seriously; they genuinely want you to experience the island's relaxing, restorative qualities. Private massage services abound on the island, and your spa therapist may offer the same services at a much lower price outside the resort, but if you're looking for a variety of health-and-beauty treatments, an exercise workout, or a full day of pampering, a spa will prove most convenient.

Though most spas on Kauai are associated with resorts, none is restricted to guests only. And there's much by way of healing and wellness to be found on Kauai beyond the traditional spa—or even the day spa. More and more retreat facilities are offering what some would call alternative healing therapies. Others would say there's nothing alternative about them; you can decide for yourself.

Open Hours. Stores are typically open daily from 9 or 10 am to 5 pm, although some stay open until 9 pm, especially those near resorts. Don't be surprised if the posted hours don't match the actual hours of operation at the smaller shops, where owners may be fairly casual about keeping to a regular schedule.

THE NORTH SHORE

The North Shore has three main shopping areas, all in towns off the highway. Hanalei has two shopping centers directly across from each other, which offer more than you would expect in a remote, relaxed town. Princeville Shopping Center is a bustling little mix of businesses, necessities, and some unique, often pricey, shops. Kilauea is a bit more sprawled out and offers a charming, laid-back shopping scene with a neighborhood feel.

SHOPPING CENTERS

Ching Young Village. This popular shopping center has its roots in the Chinese immigrants who came to Hawaii in the early 19th century. Hanalei's only full-service grocery store is here along with a number of other shops useful to locals and visitors, such as a music shop selling ukulele and CDs, jewelry stores, art galleries, a surf shop, variety store, and several restaurants. ✉ *5-5190 Kuhio Hwy., near mile marker 2, Hanalei.*

5

Hanalei Center. Once an old Hanalei schoolhouse, the Hanalei Center is now a bevy of boutiques and restaurants. You can dig through '40s and '50s vintage memorabilia, find Polynesian artifacts, or search for that unusual gift. Buy beach gear as well as island wear and women's clothing. Find a range of fine jewelry and paper art jewelry. There are a full-service salon and a yoga studio in the two-story modern addition to the center, which also houses a small natural foods grocery. ✉ *5-5161 Kuhio Hwy., near mile marker 2, Hanalei* ☎ *808/826–7677.*

Princeville Shopping Center. The big draws at this small center are a full-service grocery store and a hardware store, but there's also a fun toy store, bar, mailing service, a very nice sandal boutique, women's clothing, and an ice-cream shop. This is also the last stop for gas and banking when you're heading to the North Shore. ✉ *5-4280 Kuhio Hwy., near mile marker 28, Princeville* ☎ *808/826–9497* 🌐 *www.princevillecenter.com.*

RECOMMENDED STORES

Kong Lung Co. Sometimes called the Gump's of Kauai, this gift store sells elegant clothing, exotic glassware, ethnic books, gifts, and artwork—all very lovely and expensive. The shop is housed in a beautiful 1892 stone building in the heart of Kilauea. It's the showpiece of the pretty little Kong Lung Center, where everything from handmade soaps to hammocks can be found. A great bakery and pizzeria round out the offerings, along with an exhibit of historical photos. ✉ *2484 Keneke St., Kilauea* ☎ *808/828–1822* 🌐 *www.konglungkauai.com.*

Village Variety Store. How about a fun beach towel for the folks back home? That's just one of the gifts you can find here, along with shell lei, Kauai shirts, macadamia nuts, and other souvenirs at low prices. The store also has many small, useful items such as envelopes, housewares, and toiletries. ✉ *Ching Young Village, 5-5190 Kuhio Hwy., Hanalei* ☎ *808/826–6077.*

KAPAA AND WAILUA

Kapaa is the most heavily populated area on Kauai, so it's not surprising that it has the most diverse shopping opportunities on the island. Unlike the North Shore's retail scene, shops here are not neatly situated in centers; they are spread out along a long stretch of road, with many local retail gems tucked away that you may not find if you're in a rush.

SHOPPING CENTERS

Kauai Village Shopping Center. The buildings of this Kapaa shopping village are in the style of a 19th-century plantation town. **ABC Discount Store** sells sundries; **Safeway** carries groceries and alcoholic beverages; **Papaya's** has health foods and a minimalist café. There's also a **Ross Dress for Less** and a **UPS store.** Other shops sell jewelry, art, and home decor. Restaurants include Chinese, and Vietnamese options, and there's also a **Starbucks** and two bars. ✉ *4-831 Kuhio Hwy., Kapaa* ☎ *808/822–3777.*

Kinipopo Shopping Village. Kinipopo is a tiny little center on Kuhio Highway. **Korean Barbeque** fronts the highway, as does **Goldsmith's Kauai Gallery,** which sells handcrafted Hawaiian-style gold jewelry. **Monico's** has authentic Mexican food, and is the center's biggest draw. There's also a clothing shop, beauty salon, bakery, cake shop, and a healing-arts center. ✉ *4-356 Kuhio Hwy., Kapaa* 🌐 *www.kinipopovillage.com.*

RECOMMENDED STORES

Deja Vu Surf Hawaii: Kapaa. This family operation has a great assortment of surf wear and clothes for outdoors fanatics, including tank tops, visors, swimwear, and Kauai-style T-shirts. They also carry body boards and water-sports accessories. Good deals can be found at sidewalk sales. ✉ *4-1419 Kuhio Hwy., Kapaa* ☎ *808/822–4401* 🌐 *www.dejavusurf.com.*

Jim Saylor Jewelers. Jim Saylor and his team of jewelers have been designing beautiful keepsakes for more than 40 years on Kauai. Gems from around the world, including black pearls, diamonds, and more, appear in his unusual settings. ✉ *4-1318 Kuhio Hwy., Kapaa* ☎ *808/822–3591* 🌐 *www.jimsaylorjewelers.com* ⏲ *Closed Sun.*

Kela's Glass Gallery. The colorful vases, bowls, and other fragile items sold in this distinctive gallery, now expanded into a new, larger space, are definitely worth viewing if you appreciate quality handmade glass art. It's expensive, but if something catches your eye, they'll happily pack it for safe transport home. They also ship worldwide. ✉ *4-1400 Kuhio Hwy., Kapaa* ☎ *808/822–4527* 🌐 *www.glass-art.com.*

Vicky's Fabric Shop. This small store is packed full of tropical and Hawaiian prints, silks, slinky rayons, soft cottons, and other fine fabrics. A variety of sewing patterns and notions are featured as well, making it a must-stop for any seamstress, and a great place to buy unique island-made gifts. Check out the one-of-a-kind selection of purses, aloha wear, and other quality hand-sewn items. ✉ *4-1326 Kuhio Hwy., Kapaa* ☎ *808/822–1746* 🌐 *www.vickysfabrics.com* ⏲ *Closed Sun.*

LIHUE

Lihue is the business area on Kauai, as well as home to all the big-box stores (Costco, Home Depot, Walmart, and Big K) and the only real mall. Do not mistake this town as lacking in rare finds, however. Lihue is steeped in history and diversity while simultaneously welcoming new trends and establishments.

SHOPPING CENTERS

Kilohana Plantation. This 16,000-square-foot Tudor mansion contains art galleries, a jewelry store, and the restaurant Gaylord's. Kilohana Plantation is filled with antiques from its original owner, and the restored outbuildings house a craft shop and a Hawaiian-style clothing shop. Train rides on a restored railroad are available, with knowledgeable guides reciting the history of sugar on Kauai. The site is also now the home of Luau Kalamaku and Koloa Rum Company. ✉ *3-2087 Kaumualii Hwy., Lihue* ☎ *808/245–5608* 🌐 *www.kilohanakauai.com.*

5

Kukui Grove Center. This is Kauai's only true mall. Besides Kmart, anchor tenants are Longs Drugs, Macy's, Ross, Pier One Imports, Kukui Grove Cinemas, and Times Supermarket. The mall's stores offer women's clothing, surf wear, art, toys, athletic shoes, jewelry, a hair salon, and locally made crafts. Restaurants range from fast food and sandwiches to sushi and Korean, with a popular Starbucks and Jamba Juice. The center stage often has entertainment, especially on Friday night, and there is a farmers' market on Monday. ✉ *3-2600 Kaumualii Hwy., Lihue* ☎ *808/245–7784* 🌐 *www.kukuigrovecenter.com.*

RECOMMENDED STORES

Hilo Hattie, The Store of Hawaii. This is the big name in aloha wear for tourists throughout the Islands, and Hilo Hattie, the Store of Hawaii has only one store on Kauai. Located a mile from Lihue Airport, come here for cool, comfortable aloha shirts and muumuu in bright floral prints, as well as other souvenirs. Also, be sure to check out the line of Hawaii-inspired home furnishings. ✉ *3252 Kuhio Hwy., Lihue* ☎ *808/245–3404* 🌐 *www.hilohattie.com.*

Fodor's Choice ★ **Kapaia Stitchery.** Hawaiian quilts made by hand and machine, a beautiful selection of fabrics, quilting kits, handmade aloha shirts, and unique fabric arts fill Kapaia Stitchery, a cute little red plantation-style building. There are also many locally made gifts and quilts for sale in this locally owned store. The staff is friendly and helpful, even though a steady stream of customers keeps them busy. ✉ *3-3551 Kuhio Hwy., Lihue* ☎ *808/245–2281* 🌐 *kapaia-stitchery.com* ⏲ *Closed Sun.*

FAMILY Fodor's Choice ★ **Kauai Community Market.** This is the biggest and best farmers' market on Kauai, sponsored by the Kauai Farm Bureau at the community college in Lihue, and held on Saturday mornings. You'll find fresh produce and flowers, as well as packaged products like breads, goat cheese, pasta, honey, coffee, soaps, lotions, and more, all made locally. Seating areas are available to grab a snack or lunch from the food booths and lunch wagons set up here. ✉ *3-1901 Kaumualii Hwy., Lihue* ☎ *808/855–5429* 🌐 *www.kauaicommunitymarket.com.*

Kauai Fruit and Flower Company. At this shop near Lihue and five minutes away from the airport, you can buy fresh Hawaii Gold pineapple, sugarcane, ginger, tropical flowers, coconuts, local jams, jellies, and honey, plus papayas, bananas, and mangoes from Kauai. Some of the fruit at Kauai Fruit and Flower Company cannot be shipped out of state. ✉ *3-4684 Kuhio Hwy., Lihue* ☎ *808/245–1814* 🌐 *www.kauaifruit.com* ⏲ *Closed Sat. afternoon and Sun.*

Fodor's Choice ★ **Kauai Museum.** The gift shop at the museum sells some fascinating books, maps, and prints, as well as lovely authentic Niihau shell jewelry, handwoven *lau hala* hats, and koa wood bowls. Also featured at the Kauai Museum are tapa cloth, authentic *tikis* (hand-carved wooden figurines), as well as other good-quality local crafts and books at reasonable prices. ✉ *4428 Rice St., Lihue* ☎ *808/245–6931* 🌐 *www.kauaimuseum.org* ⏲ *Closed Sun.*

Two Frogs Hugging. At Two Frogs Hugging, you'll find lots of interesting housewares, accessories, knickknacks, and hand-carved collectibles, as well as baskets and furniture from Indonesia, the Philippines, and China. The shop occupies expansive quarters in the Lihue Industrial Park. ✉ *3094 Aukele St., Lihue* ☎ *808/246–8777* 🌐 *www.twofrogshugging.com* ⏲ *Closed Sun.*

THE SOUTH SHORE

The South Shore, like the North Shore, has convenient shopping clusters, including Poipu Shopping Village and the upscale The Shops at Kukuiula. There are many high-priced shops, but some unique clothing and gift selections.

SHOPPING CENTERS

FAMILY **Poipu Shopping Village.** Convenient to nearby hotels and condos on the South Shore, the two dozen shops at Poipu Shopping Village sell resort wear, gifts, souvenirs, and art. This complex also has a few food choices, from hot-dog stands to casual restaurants. There are a few upscale and appealing jewelry stores and fun clothing stores. Watch a traditional hula show in the open-air courtyard Monday and Thursday at 5 pm. ✉ *2360 Kiahuna Plantation Dr., Poipu* ☎ *808/742–2831* 🌐 *www.poipushoppingvillage.com.*

The Shops at Kukuiula. This is the South Shore's newest shopping center, with chic, high-end shops, exclusive galleries, several great restaurants, and a gourmet grocery store. Check out the Kauai Culinary Market on Wednesday from 3:30 to 6, to see cooking demonstrations, listen to live Hawaiian music, visit the beer and wine garden, and browse wares from local vendors. This attractive open-air, plantation-style center is just beyond the roundabout as you enter Poipu. ✉ *2829 Kalanikaumaka St., Poipu* ☎ *808/742–9545* 🌐 *www.theshopsatkukuiula.com.*

RECOMMENDED STORES

Fodor's Choice ★ **Galerie 103.** This gallery sells art, but the owners want you to experience it as well. Sparse and dramatic, the main room at Galerie 103 consists of concrete floors and walls of featured pieces, from internationally acclaimed artists and local Kauai ones. Most of the artwork is contemporary or modern with a focus on nature. ✉ *2829 Kalanikaumaka Rd., Koloa* ☎ *808/742–0103* 🌐 *www.galerie103.com* ⏲ *Closed Sun. and Mon.*

THE WEST SIDE

The West Side is years behind the South Shore in development, offering minimal, simple shops with authentic local flavor.

SHOPPING CENTERS

Eleele Shopping Center. Kauai's West Side has a scattering of stores, including those at this no-frills strip mall. It has several banks, a hardware store, laundromat, and a hair salon and it's a good place to rub elbows with local folk at Longs Drugs or Times Big Save grocery store. There's a McDonald's, Subway, and a few little local eateries. ✉ *4469 Waialo Rd., Eleele* ☎ *808/245–7238* 🌐 *www.eleeleshoppingcenter.com.*

5

Waimea Canyon Plaza. As the last stop for supplies before heading up to Waimea Canyon, Waimea Canyon Plaza has a Menehune Food Mart with limited groceries, snacks, beverages, fresh and prepared local foods, souvenirs, and island-made gifts for all ages. ✉ *8171 Kekaha Rd., at Rte. 50, Kekaha* ☎ *808/337–1335.*

RECOMMENDED STORES

Kauai Coffee Visitor Center and Museum. Kauai produces more coffee than any other island in the state. The local product can be purchased from grocery stores or here at the Kauai Coffee Visitor Center and Museum, where a sampling of the nearly two dozen coffees is available. Be sure to try some of the estate-roasted varieties. ✉ *870 Halawili Rd., off Rte. 50, Kalaheo* ☎ *808/335–0813, 800/545–8605* 🌐 *www.kauaicoffee.com.*

Talk Story Bookstore. Located in a historic building in quiet Hanapepe town, this cozy bookstore with its friendly cat is the only bookstore on Kauai. It becomes a gathering place on busy Friday evenings during the weekly art nights when local authors sign their books inside while outside there's live music and food trucks for treats. New, used, and out-of-print books are sold here. ✉ *3785 Hanapepe Rd., Hanapepe* ☎ *808/335–6469* 🌐 *www.talkstorybookstore.com.*

SPAS

THE NORTH SHORE

Fodor's Choice ★ **Halelea Spa.** This superb spa at the St. Regis Princeville Resort is indeed a House of Joy, as its Hawaiian name translates, so long as you are prepared to pay handsomely for services. Opened in 2009, the 11,000-square-foot Halelea Spa transports users to a place of tranquillity. The spa's 12 luxurious treatment rooms afford a subdued indoor setting outmatched only by the professional service. Take advantage of the dedicated couple's room and enjoy a hot *pohaku* (stone) massage. Follow that with a few hours sipping tea in the relaxation lounge, sweating in the sauna, and rinsing in an overhead rain shower. There is a qualified wellness consultant, and spa programs are inspired by Native Hawaiian healing rituals. ✉ *The St. Regis Princeville Resort, 5520 Ka*

Haku Rd., Princeville ☎ *877/787–3447, 808/826–9644* 🌐 *www.stregisprinceville.com* 🎫 *Massage from $185.*

Hanalei Day Spa. As you travel beyond tony Princeville, life slows down. The single-lane bridges may be one reason. Another is the Hanalei Day Spa, an open-air, thatched-roof, Hawaiian-style hut nestled just off the beach on the grounds of Hanalei Colony Resort in Haena. Though this no-frills day spa offers facials, waxing, wraps, scrubs, and the like, its specialty is massage: Ayurveda, Zen Shiatsu, Swedish, four-handed, and even a baby massage (and lesson for Mom, to boot). ✉ *Hanalei Colony Resort, Rte. 560, Haena* ✣ *6 miles past Hanalei* ☎ *808/826–6621* 🌐 *www.hanaleidayspa.com* 🎫 *Massage from $110* ⏲ *Closed Sun. and Mon.*

THE EAST SIDE

Alexander Day Spa & Salon at the Kauai Marriott. This sister spa of Alexander Simson's Beverly Hills spa focuses on body care rather than exercise, so don't expect any fitness equipment or exercise classes, just pampering and beauty treatments. The Alexander Day Spa & Salon at the Kauai Marriott is a sunny, pleasant facility. Massages are available in treatment rooms, your room, and on the beach, although the beach locale isn't as private as you might imagine. Wedding-day and custom spa packages can be arranged. ✉ *Kauai Marriott Resort & Beach Club, 3610 Rice St., Suite 9A, Lihue* ☎ *808/246–4918* 🌐 *www.alexanderspa.com* 🎫 *Massage from $130.*

Angeline's Muolaulani Wellness Center. It doesn't get more authentic, or rustic, than this. In the mid-1980s Aunty Angeline Locey opened her Anahola home to offer traditional Hawaiian healing practices. Though she passed on in 2017, her son and granddaughter carry on the tradition. There's a two-hour treatment ($175) that starts with a steam, followed by a sea-salt-and-clay body scrub and a four-handed massage. The real treat, however, is relaxing on Aunty's open-air garden deck. Hot-stone lomi is also available. The Center's mission is to promote a healthy body image; as such, au naturel is an option here, but if you're nudity-shy, you can wear a sarong. Detailed directions are given when you book a treatment. ■ **TIP→ This is cash only and you need to bring your own towel.** ✉ *Kamalomaloo Pl., Anahola* ☎ *808/822–3235* 🌐 *www.angelineslomikauai.com.*

THE SOUTH SHORE

Fodor's Choice ★ **ANARA Spa.** The luxurious ANARA Spa has all the equipment and services you expect from a top resort spa, along with a pleasant, professional staff. Best of all, it has indoor and outdoor areas that capitalize on the tropical locale and balmy weather, further distinguishing it from the Marriott and St. Regis spas. Its 46,500 square feet of space includes the lovely Garden Treatment Village, an open-air courtyard with private thatched-roof huts, each featuring a relaxation area, misters, and open-air shower in a tropical setting. Ancient Hawaiian remedies and local ingredients are featured in many of the treatments, such as a pineapple-papaya body hydration, and a traditional lomilomi massage. The open-air lava-rock showers are wonderful, introducing many guests to the delightful island practice of showering outdoors. The spa, which

Continued on page 502

HAWAII'S PLANTS 101

Tropical Hibiscus

Hawaii is a bounty of rainbow-colored flowers and plants. The evening air is scented with their fragrance. Just look at the front yard of almost any home, travel any road, or visit any local park and you'll see a spectacular array of colored blossoms and leaves. What most visitors don't know is that many of the plants they are seeing are not native to Hawaii; rather, they were introduced during the last two centuries as ornamental plants, or for timber, shade, or fruit.

Hawaii boasts nearly every climate on the planet, excluding the two most extreme: arctic tundra and arid desert. The Islands have wine-growing regions, cactus-speckled ranchlands, icy mountaintops, and the rainiest forests on earth.

Plants introduced from around the world thrive here. The lush lowland valleys along the windward coasts are predominantly populated by non-native trees including yellow- and red-fruited **guava**, silvery-leafed **kukui**, and orange-flowered **tulip trees.**

The colorful **plumeria flower**, very fragrant and commonly used in lei making, and the giant multicolored **hibiscus flower** are both used by many women as hair adornments, and are two of the most common plants found around homes and hotels. The umbrella-like **monkeypod tree** from Central America provides shade in many of Hawaii's parks including Kapiolani Park in Honolulu. Hawaii's largest tree, found in Lahaina, Maui, is a giant **banyan tree.** Its canopy and massive support roots cover about two-thirds of an acre. The native **ohia tree**, with its brilliant red brush-like flowers, and the **hapuu**, a giant tree fern, are common in Hawaii's forests and are also used ornamentally in gardens.

Naupaka, Limahuli Garden

Bougainvillea	 Guava	 Monkeypod
 Banyan	 Ohia Lehua*	 Tulip Tree
 Plumeria	 Pandanus	 Hibiscus
 Anthurium	 Kukui	 Hapuu

*endemic to Hawaii

DID YOU KNOW?

More than 2,200 plant species are found in the Hawaiian Islands, but only about 1,000 are native. Of these, 320 are so rare, they are endangered. Hawaii's endemic plants evolved from ancestral seeds arriving in the Islands over thousands of years as baggage with birds, floating on ocean currents, or drifting on winds from continents thousands of miles away. Once here, these plants evolved in isolation, creating many new species known nowhere else in the world.

includes a full-service salon, adjoins the Hyatt's legendary swimming pool. ✉ *Hyatt Regency Kauai Resort and Spa, 1571 Poipu Rd., Poipu* ☎ *808/240–6440* 🌐 *www.anaraspa.com* 💳 *Massages from $180.*

WATER SPORTS AND TOURS

Updated by Joan Conrow

Ancient Hawaiians were water-sports fanatics—they invented surfing, after all—and that propensity hasn't strayed far from today's mind-set. Even if you're not into water sports or sports in general, there's only a slim chance that you'll leave this island without getting out on the ocean, as Kauai's top attraction—Napali Coast—is something not to be missed.

For those who can't pack enough snorkeling, fishing, body boarding, or surfing time into a vacation, Kauai has it all—everything except parasailing, that is, as it's illegal to do it here (though not on Maui, the Big Island, or Oahu). If you need to rent gear for any of these activities, you'll find plenty of places with large selections at reasonable prices. And no matter what part of the island you're staying on, you'll have several options for choice spots to enjoy playing in the water.

One thing to note, and we can't say this enough—the waters off the coast of Kauai have strong currents and can be unpredictable, so always err on the side of caution and know your limits. Follow the tagline repeated by the island's lifeguards—"When in doubt, don't go out."

BOAT TOURS

Deciding to see Napali Coast by boat is an easy decision. Choosing the outfitter to go with is not. There are numerous boat-tour operators to choose from, and, quite frankly, they all do a good job. Before you even start thinking about whom to go out with, answer these three questions: What kind of boat do I prefer? Where am I staying? Do I want to go in the morning or afternoon? Once you settle on these three, you can easily zero in on the tour outfitter.

First, the boat. The most important thing is to match your personality and that of your group with the personality of the boat. If you like thrills and adventure, the rubber, inflatable rafts—often called Zodiacs, which Jacques Cousteau made famous and which the U.S. Coast Guard uses—will entice you. They're fast, likely to leave you drenched and windswept, and quite bouncy. If you prefer a smoother, more leisurely ride, then the large catamarans are the way to go. The next boat choice is size. Both the rafts and catamarans come in small and large. Again—think smaller, more adventurous; larger, more leisurely. **■ TIP→ Do not choose a smaller boat because you think there will be fewer people. There might be fewer people, but you'll be jammed together sitting atop strangers.** If you prefer privacy over socializing, go with a larger boat, so you'll have more room to spread out. The smaller boats will also take you along the coast at a higher rate of speed, making photo opportunities a bit more challenging. One advantage to smaller boats, however, is that—depending on ocean conditions—some may slip into a sea cave or two. If that sounds interesting to you, call the outfitter and ask their policy on entering sea caves. Some won't, no matter the conditions, because they consider the caves sacred or because they don't want to cause any environmental damage.

Boats leave from three points around the island (Hanalei, Port Allen, and Waimea), and all head to the same spot: Napali Coast. Here's the inside skinny on which is the best: if you're staying on the North Shore, choose to depart out of the North Shore. If you're staying anywhere else, depart out of the West Side. It's that easy. Sure, the North Shore is closer to Napali Coast; however, you'll pay more for less overall time. The West Side boat operators may spend more time getting to Napali Coast; however, they'll spend about the same amount of time along Napali, plus you'll pay less. Finally, you'll also have to decide whether you want to go on a morning tour, which includes a deli lunch and a stop for snorkeling, or an afternoon tour, which does not always stop to snorkel but does include a sunset over the ocean. The morning tours with snorkeling are more popular with families and those who love dolphins, as the animals enjoy the "waves" created by the front of the catamarans and might just escort you down the coast. The winter months will also be a good chance to spot some whales breaching, though surf is much rougher along Napali. You don't have to be an expert snorkeler or even have any prior experience, but if it is your first time, note that although there will be some snorkeling instruction, there might not be much. Hawaiian spinner dolphins are so plentiful in the mornings that some tour companies guarantee you'll see them, though you won't get in the water and swim with them. The afternoon tours are more popular with nonsnorkelers—obviously—and photographers interested in capturing the setting sunlight on the coast. ■ **TIP→ No matter which tour you select, book it online whenever possible.** Most companies offer Web specials, usually around $10 to $20 off per person.

5

CATAMARAN TOURS

Fodor's Choice ★ **Blue Dolphin Charters.** Blue Dolphin operates 65-foot sailing (rarely raised and always motoring) catamarans designed with three decks of spacious seating with great visibility, as well as motorized rafts. ■ **TIP→ The lower deck is best for shade seekers.** The most popular is a daylong tour of Napali Coast, which includes a detour across the channel to Niihau for snorkeling and diving. Morning snorkel tours of Napali include a deli lunch. Sunset sightseeing tours include a Hawaiian-style buffet. North Shore and South Shore rafting tours are also available, as are daily sportfishing charters of four to eight hours for no more than six guests. Blue Dolphin promises dolphin sightings and the best mai tais "off the island." Book online for cheaper deals on every tour offered. ✉ *4353 Waialo Rd., No. 2-6B7B, Eleele* ☎ *808/335–5553, 877/511–1311* 🌐 *www.kauaiboats.com* 🎫 *From $100; 2-hr whale-watching/sunset tours, winter only, $65.*

FAMILY Fodor's Choice ★ **Capt. Andy's Sailing Adventures.** Departing from Port Allen and running 55- and 60-foot sailing catamarans, as well as 24-foot inflatables out of Kikiaoloa Harbor in Kekaha, Capt. Andy's offers something for every taste, from raft expeditions to Hawaiian yachting. They have several lunch and snorkeling packages and four-hour sunset tours along Napali Coast. The Zodiac rafts have hydrophones to hear whales and other underwater sounds. The longtime Kauai company also operates a snorkel barbecue sail and dinner sunset sail aboard its *Southern Star* yacht, originally built for private charters. This boat now operates as host for two of Capt. Andy's daily sailing trips for an upgraded feel. For a shorter adventure, they have a two-hour sunset sail, embarking out of Kukuiula Harbor in Poipu along the South Shore—with live Hawaiian music—on Thursday. **TIP→ If the winds and swells are up on the North Shore, this is usually a good choice—especially if you're prone to seasickness.** This is the only tour-boat operator that allows infants on board—but only on the two-hour trip. Note, if you have reservations for the shorter tour, you'll check in at their Kukuiula Harbor office. ✉ *4353 Waiola Rd., Suite 1A-2A, Eleele* ☎ *808/335–6833* 🌐 *www.napali.com* 🎫 *From $89, discounts for online booking.*

Captain Sundown. Sundown has one of the few permits to sail from Hanalei Bay and operates the only sailing catamaran there. Captain Bob has been cruising Napali Coast since 1971—six days a week, sometimes twice a day. (And right alongside Captain Bob is his son, Captain Larry.) To say he knows the area is an understatement. Here's the other good thing about this tour: they take a maximum of 17 passengers on the 40-foot boat. The breathtaking views of the waterfall-laced mountains behind Hanalei and Haena start immediately, and then it's around Kee Beach and the magic of Napali Coast unfolds before you. All the while, the captains are trolling for fish, and if they catch any, guests get to reel 'em in. Afternoon sunset sails (summertime only) run three hours and check in around 3 pm—these are BYOB. Cancellations due to rough surf are more frequent in winter. ✉ *5-5134 Kuhio Hwy., Hanalei* ☎ *808/826–5585* 🌐 *www.captainsundown.com* 🎫 *From $165.*

Catamaran Kahanu. Hawaiian-owned and -operated, Catamaran Kahanu has been in business since 1985 and runs a 40-foot power catamaran with 18- to 20-passenger seating. It offers seasonal whale-watching, snorkeling, and sunset cruises, ranging from two to five hours, and departs from Port Allen. The five-hour Na Pali Coast tour includes snorkeling at Nualolo Kai, plus a deli lunch and soft drinks. The four-hour afternoon tour takes in the sunset and includes a hot dinner. The boat is smaller than most and may feel a tad crowded, but the tour feels more personal, with a laid-back, *ohana* (family) style. Guests can witness the ancient cultural practice of coconut weaving or other Hawaiian craft demonstrations on board. There's no alcohol allowed. ✉ *4353 Waialo Rd., near Port Allen Marina Center, Eleele* ☎ *808/645–6176, 888/213–7711* 🌐 *www.catamarankahanu.com* 🎫 *From $75.*

HoloHolo Charters. Choose between the 50-foot catamaran called *Leila* for a morning snorkel sail to Napali Coast, or the 65-foot *HoloHolo* seven-hour catamaran trip to the "forbidden island" of Niihau. Both boats have large cabins and little outside seating. HoloHolo also offers a four-hour seasonal voyage of Napali from Hanalei Bay on its rigid-hull inflatable rafts, specifically for diving and snorkeling. Originators of the Niihau tour, HoloHolo Charters built their 65-foot powered catamaran with a wide beam to reduce side-to-side motion, and twin 425 HP turbo diesel engines specifically for the 17-mile channel crossing to Niihau. It's the only outfitter running daily Niihau tours. The

If you choose to sail by yourself in Kauai, be prepared for strong currents and know your limits.

HoloHolo also embarks on a daily sunset and sightseeing tour of Napali Coast. *Leila* can hold 37 passengers, while her big brother can take a maximum of 49. Check-in is at Port Allen Marina Center. ⊠ *4353 Waialo Rd., Suite 5A, Eleele* ☎ *808/335–0815, 800/848–6130* 🌐 *www.holoholocharters.com* 🎟 *From $70.*

Kauai Sea Tours. This company operates the *Lucky Lady*, a 60-foot sailing catamaran designed almost identically to that of Blue Dolphin Charters—with all the same benefits—including great views and spacious seating. Snorkeling tours anchor near Makole (based on the captain's discretion). If snorkeling isn't your thing, try the four-hour sunset tour, with beer, wine, mai tais, *pupu* (appetizers), and a hot buffet dinner or a two-hour seasonal whale-watching cruise. Tours of Napali, one with a beach landing, are offered on inflatable rafts. Check in at Port Allen Marina Center. ⊠ *4353 Waialo Rd., Eleele* ☎ *808/335–5309, 800/733–7997* 🌐 *www.kauaiseatours.com* 🎟 *From $79.*

Liko Kauai Cruises. There are many things to like about Liko Kauai Cruises. The 49-foot powered cat will enter sea caves, ocean conditions permitting. Sometimes, even Captain Liko himself—a Native Hawaiian—still takes the captain's helm. We particularly like the layout of his boat—most of the seating is in the bow, so there's good visibility. A maximum of 32 passengers make each trip, which last five hours and include snorkeling, food, and soft drinks. Trips usually depart out of Kikiaola Harbor in Waimea, a bit closer to Napali Coast than those leaving from Port Allen. ⊠ *4516 Alawai Rd., Waimea (Kauai County)* ☎ *808/338–0333, 888/732–5456* 🌐 *www.liko-kauai.com* 🎟 *$135.*

BOAT TOUR WEATHER CANCELLATIONS

If it's raining where you're staying, that doesn't mean it's raining over the water, so don't shy away from a boat tour. Besides, it's not the rain that should concern you—it's the wind and waves. Especially from due north and south, wind creates surface chop and makes for rough riding. Larger craft are designed to handle winter's ocean swells, however, so unless monster waves are out there, your tour should depart without a hitch. If the water is too rough, your boat captain may reroute to calmer waters. It's a tough call to make, but your comfort and safety are always the foremost factor. ■ TIP→ **In winter months, North Shore departures are canceled much more often than those departing the West Side.** This is because the waves are often too big for the boats to leave Hanalei Bay. If you want the closest thing to a guarantee of seeing Napali Coast in winter, choose a West Side outfitter. Oh, and even if your tour boat says it cruises the "entire Napali," keep in mind that "ocean conditions permitting" is always implied.

RAFT TOURS

Kauai Sea Tours. This company holds a special permit from the state to land at Nualolo Kai along Napali Coast, ocean conditions permitting. Here, you'll enjoy a picnic lunch, as well as an archaeological tour of an ancient Hawaiian fishing village, ocean conditions permitting. Kauai Sea Tours operates four 24-foot inflatable rafts—maximum occupancy 14. These are small enough for checking out the insides of sea caves and the undersides of waterfalls. Four different tours are available, including snorkeling and whale-watching, depending on the season. ✉ *Port Allen Marina Center, 4353 Waialo Rd., Eleele* ☎ *800/733–7997, 800/733–7997* 🌐 *www.kauaiseatours.com* 🎟 *From $110.*

Fodor's Choice ★ **Napali Explorer.** These tours operate out of Kikialoa Harbor, a tad closer to Napali Coast than most of the other West Side catamaran tours. The company runs two different sizes of inflatable rubber raft: a 48-foot, 36-passenger craft with an onboard toilet, freshwater shower, shade canopy, and seating in the stern (which is surprisingly smooth and comfortable) and bow (which is where the fun is); and a 26-foot, 14-passenger craft for the all-out fun and thrills of a white-knuckle ride in the bow. The smaller vessel stops at Nualolo Kai and ties up onshore for a tour of the ancient fishing village. Charters are available. ✉ *9814 Kaumalii Hwy., Waimea (Kauai County)* ☎ *808/338–9999* 🌐 *www.napaliexplorer.com* 🎟 *From $99.*

Napali Riders. This tour-boat outfitter distinguishes itself in two ways. First, it cruises the entire Napali Coast, clear to Kee Beach and back. Second, it has a reasonable price because it's a no-frills tour—no lunch provided, just beverages and snacks. The company runs morning and afternoon four-hour snorkeling, sightseeing, and whale-watching trips out of Kikiaola Harbor in Waimea on a 30-foot inflatable raft with a 28-passenger maximum—that's fewer than they used to take, but can still be a bit cramped. ✉ *9600 Kaumualii Hwy., Waimea (Kauai County)* ☎ *808/742–6331* 🌐 *www.napaliriders.com* 🎟 *$119.*

Z-Tourz. What we like about Z-Tourz is that it's a boat company that makes snorkeling its priority. Its two- and three-hour tours focus solely on the South Shore's abundant offshore reefs. If you want to snorkel with Hawaii's tropical reef fish and turtles (pretty much guaranteed), this is your boat. The craft is a 26-foot rigid-hull inflatable (think Zodiac) with a maximum of 16 passengers. These snorkel tours are guided, so someone actually identifies what you're seeing. Rates include lunch and snorkel gear. ✉ *3417 Poipu Rd., Poipu* ☎ *808/742–7422, 888/998–6879* 🌐 *www.kauaiztours.com* 🎟 *From $99.*

RIVERBOAT TOURS TO FERN GROTTO

Smith's Motor Boat Services. This 2-mile trip up the lush and lovely Wailua River, the only navigable waterway in Hawaii, culminates at the infamous Fern Grotto, a yawning lava tube that is covered with fishtail ferns. During the boat ride, guitar and ukulele players regale you with Hawaiian melodies and tell the history of the river. It's a kitschy, but fun, bit of Hawaiiana and the river scenery is beautiful. Flat-bottom, 150-passenger riverboats (that rarely fill up) depart from Wailua Marina at the mouth of the Wailua River. ■ TIP→ **It's extremely rare, but occasionally after heavy rains the tour doesn't disembark at the grotto; if you're traveling in winter, ask beforehand.** Round-trip excursions take 1½ hours, including time to walk around the grotto and environs. Tours run at 9:30, 11, 2, and 3:30 daily. ✉ *5971 Kuhio Hwy., Kapaa* ☎ *808/821–6895* 🌐 *www.smithskauai.com/fern-grotto/* 🎟 *$25.*

5

BODY BOARDING AND BODYSURFING

The most natural form of wave riding is bodysurfing, a popular sport on Kauai because there are many shore breaks around the island. Wave riders of this style stand waist deep in the water, facing shore, and swim madly as a wave picks them up and breaks. It's great fun and requires no special skills and absolutely no equipment other than a swimsuit. The next step up is body boarding, also called boogie boarding. In this case, wave riders lie with their upper body on a foam board about half the length of a traditional surfboard and kick as the wave propels them toward shore. Again, this is easy to pick up, and there are many places around Kauai to practice. The locals wear short-finned flippers to help them catch waves, which is a good idea to enhance safety in the water. It's worth spending a few minutes watching these experts as they spin, twirl, and flip—that's right—while they slip down the face of the wave. Of course, all beach-safety precautions apply, and just because you see wave riders of any kind in the water doesn't mean the water is safe for everyone. Any snorkeling-gear outfitter also rents body boards.

Some of our favorite bodysurfing and body-boarding beaches are **Brennecke, Wailua, Kealia, Kalihiwai,** and **Hanalei.**

DEEP-SEA FISHING

Simply step aboard and cast your line for mahimahi, ahi, ono, and marlin. That's about how quickly the fishing—mostly trolling with lures—begins on Kauai. The water gets deep quickly here, so there's less cruising time to fishing grounds, which is nice, since Hawaii's seas are notoriously rough. Of course, your captain may elect to cruise to a hot location where he's had good luck lately.

There are oodles of charter fishermen around; most depart from Nawiliwili Harbor in Lihue, and most use lures instead of live bait. Inquire about each boat's "fish policy," that is, what happens to the fish if any are caught. Some boats keep all; others will give you enough for a meal or two, even doing the cleaning themselves. On shared charters, ask about the maximum passenger count and about the fishing rotation; you'll want to make sure everyone gets a fair shot at reeling in the big one. Another option is to book a private charter. Shared and private charters run four, six, and eight hours in length.

BOATS AND CHARTERS

Captain Don's Sport Fishing & Ocean Adventure. Captain Don is very flexible and treats everyone like family—he'll stop to snorkel or whale-watch if that's what the group (four to six) wants. Saltwater fly-fishermen (bring your own gear) are welcome. He'll even fish for bait and let you keep part of whatever you catch. The *June Louise* is a 34-foot twin diesel. ✉ *Nawiliwili Small Boat Harbor, 2494 Niumalu Rd., Nawiliwili* ☎ *808/639–3012* 🌐 *www.captaindonsfishing.com* 🎫 *From $150 (shared); from $650 (private).*

Kai Bear. The father of this father-and-son duo has it figured out: he lets the son run the business and do all the work. Or so he says. The prices are reasonable, and they share the catch. Trips run from a four-hour, shared charter (six fishermen max) up to an eight-hour, keep-all-the-fish-you-want exclusive. What's particularly nice about this company are the boats: the 38-foot Bertram, *Kai Bear*, and the 42-foot Bertram, *Grander*, which are well maintained and very roomy. ✉ *Nawiliwili Small Boat Harbor, 2900 Nawiliwili Rd., Nawiliwili* ☎ *808/652–4556* 🌐 *www.kaibear.com* 🎫 *From $175.*

KAYAKING

Kauai is the only Hawaiian island with navigable rivers. As the oldest inhabited island in the chain, Kauai has had more time for wind and water erosion to deepen and widen cracks into streams and streams into rivers. Because this is a small island, the rivers aren't long, and there are no rapids, which makes them generally safe for kayakers of all levels, even beginners, except when rivers are flowing fast from heavy rains.

For more advanced paddlers, there aren't many places in the world more beautiful for sea kayaking than Napali Coast. If this is your draw to Kauai, plan your vacation for the summer months, when the seas are at their calmest. ■ **TIP→ Tour and kayak-rental reservations are recommended at least two weeks in advance during peak summer and holiday seasons.** In general, tours and rentals are available year-round, Monday through Saturday. Pack a swimsuit, sunscreen, a hat, bug repellent, water shoes (sport sandals, aqua socks, old tennis shoes), and motion sickness medication if you're planning on sea kayaking.

RIVER KAYAKING

Tour outfitters operate on the Huleia, Wailua, and Hanalei rivers with guided tours that combine hiking to waterfalls, as in the case of the first two, and snorkeling, as in the case of the third. Another option is renting kayaks and heading out on your own. Each has its advantages and disadvantages, but it boils down as follows:

If you want to swim at the base of a remote 100-foot waterfall, sign up for a five-hour kayak (4-mile round-trip) and hiking (2-mile round-trip) tour of the **Wailua River.** It includes a dramatic waterfall that is best accessed with the aid of a guide, so you don't get lost. ■ **TIP→ Remember—it's dangerous to swim under waterfalls no matter how good a water massage may sound. Rocks and logs are known to plunge down, especially after heavy rains.**

If you want to kayak on your own, choose the **Hanalei River.** It's most scenic from the kayak itself—there are no trails to hike to hidden waterfalls. And better yet, a rental company is right on the river—no hauling kayaks on top of your car.

If you're not sure of your kayaking abilities, head to the **Huleia River;** 3½-hour tours include easy paddling upriver, a nature walk through a rain forest with a cascading waterfall, a rope swing for playing Tarzan and Jane, and a ride back downriver—into the wind—on a motorized, double-hull canoe.

As for the kayaks themselves, most companies use the two-person sit-on-top style that is quite buoyant—no Eskimo rolls required. The only possible danger comes in the form of communication. The kayaks seat two people, which means you'll share the work (good) with a guide, or your spouse, child, parent, or friend (the potential danger part). On the river, the two-person kayaks are known as "divorce boats." Counseling is not included in the tour price.

SEA KAYAKING

Kauai is the only Hawaiian island with navigable rivers. As the oldest inhabited island in the chain, Kauai has had more time for wind and water erosion to deepen and widen cracks into streams and streams into rivers. Because this is a small island, the rivers aren't long, and there are no rapids, which makes them generally safe for kayakers of all levels, even beginners, except when rivers are flowing fast from heavy rains.

For more advanced paddlers, there aren't many places in the world more beautiful for sea kayaking than Napali Coast. If this is your draw to Kauai, plan your vacation for the summer months, when the seas are at their calmest. ■ **TIP→ Tour and kayak-rental reservations are recommended at least two weeks in advance during peak summer and holiday seasons.** In general, tours and rentals are available year-round, Monday through Saturday. Pack a swimsuit, sunscreen, a hat, bug repellent, water shoes (sport sandals, aqua socks, old tennis shoes), and motion sickness medication if you're planning on sea kayaking.

EQUIPMENT AND TOURS

Kayak Kauai. This company pioneered kayaking on Kauai. It offers guided tours on the Wailua River, and sea kayak tours in Hanalei Bay, and along Napali Coast in season. It has consolidated operations, and is now conveniently located in the Wailua Marina. From there, it can launch kayaks right into the Wailua River for its five-hour Secret Falls hike-paddle tour and three-hour paddle to a swimming hole. Kayak Kauai also offers 12-hour escorted summer sea kayak tours and camping trips on Napali Coast. Stand-up paddleboard instruction and sea-kayak whale-watching tours round out its repertoire. The company will shuttle kayakers as needed, and, for rentals, it provides the hauling gear necessary for your rental car. Snorkel gear, body boards, and stand-up paddleboards also can be rented. ✉ *Wailua Marina, 3-5971 Kuhio Hwy., Wailua (Kauai County)* ☎ *808/826–9844, 888/596–3853* 🌐 *www.kayakkauai.com* 🎫 *From $85 (river tours) and $240 (sea tours); kayak rentals from $95 per day.*

Kayak Wailua. We can't quite figure out how this family-run business offers pretty much the same Wailua River kayaking tour as everyone else—except for lunch and beverages, which are BYO—for the lowest price, but it does. They say it's because they don't discount and don't offer commissions to activities and concierge desks. Their trips, a 4½-hour kayak, hike, and waterfall swim, are offered six times a day, with the last at 1 pm. With the number of boats going out, large groups can be accommodated. No tours are allowed on Wailua River on Sunday. ✉ *4565 Haleilio Rd., behind old Coco Palms hotel, Kapaa* ☎ *808/822–3388* 🌐 *www.kayakwailua.com* 🎫 *$60.*

Fodor's Choice ★ **Napali Kayak.** A couple of longtime guides ventured out on their own to create this company, which focuses solely on a 17-mile sea-kayaking paddle along Napali Coast from April to October for small groups, or private and honeymoon tours. These guys are highly experienced and still highly enthusiastic about their livelihood—so much so that REI Adventures hires them to run their multiday, multisport tours. If you're an experienced kayaker and want to try camping on your own at Kalalau (you'll need permits), Napali Kayak will provide kayaks outfitted with dry bags, extra paddles, and seat backs, while also offering transportation drop-off and pickup. They also do Napali Coast day tours from Hanalei to Polihale, with a lunch break at Milolii, and rent camping equipment and first-aid kits. ✉ *5-5075 Kuhio Hwy., next to Postcards Café, Hanalei* ☎ *808/826–6900* 🌐 *www.napalikayak.com* 🎫 *From $225.*

FAMILY **Outfitters Kauai.** This well-established tour outfitter operates year-round river-kayak tours on the Huleia and Wailua rivers, as well as sea-kayaking tours along Napali Coast in summer and the South Shore in winter. Outfitters Kauai's specialty, however, is the Kipu Safari. This all-day adventure starts with kayaking up the Huleia River and includes a rope swing over a swimming hole, a wagon ride through a working cattle ranch, a picnic lunch by a private waterfall, hiking, and two "zips" across the rain-forest canopy (strap on a harness, clip into a cable, and zip over a quarter of a mile). They then offer a one-of-a-kind Waterzip Zipline at their mountain stream–fed blue pool. The day ends with a ride on a motorized double-hull canoe. It's a great tour for the family, because no one ever gets bored. ✉ *2827-A Poipu Rd., Poipu* ☎ *808/742–9667, 888/742–9887* 🌐 *www.outfitterskauai.com* 🎫 *Kipu Safari $189.*

Wailua Kayak & Canoe. This purveyor of kayak rentals is right on the Wailua River, which means no hauling your kayak on top of your car (a definite plus). Guided waterfall tours are also offered. This outfitter promotes itself as "Native Hawaiian owned and operated." No Wailua River tours are offered on Sunday. ✉ *162 Wailua Rd., Kapaa* ☎ *808/821–1188* 🌐 *www.wailuariverkayaking.com* 🎫 *$50 for a single, $90 for a double; guided tours from $75.*

SCUBA DIVING

The majority of scuba diving on Kauai occurs on the South Shore. Boat and shore dives are available, although boat sites surpass the shore sites for a couple of reasons. First, they're deeper and exhibit the complete symbiotic relationship of a reef system, and second, the visibility is better a little farther offshore.

The dive operators on Kauai offer a full range of services, including certification dives, referral dives, boat dives, shore dives, night dives, and drift dives. ■ TIP→ **As for certification, we recommend completing your confined-water training and classroom testing before arriving on the island.** That way, you'll spend less time training and more time diving.

BEST SPOTS

The best and safest scuba-diving sites are accessed by boat on the South Shore of the island, right off the shores of Poipu. The captain selects the actual site based on ocean conditions of the day. Beginners may prefer shore dives, which are best at **Koloa Landing** on the South Shore year-round and **Makua (Tunnels) Beach** on the North Shore in the calm summer months. Keep in mind, though, that you'll have to haul your gear a ways down the beach.

For the advanced diver, the island of Niihau—across an open ocean channel in deep and crystal-clear waters—beckons and rewards, usually with some big fish. Seasport Divers, Fathom Five, and Bubbles Below venture the 17 miles across the channel in summer when the crossing is smoothest. Divers can expect deep dives, walls, and strong currents at Niihau, where conditions can change rapidly. To make the long journey worthwhile, three dives and Nitrox are included.

EQUIPMENT, LESSONS, AND TOURS

Bubbles Below. Marine ecology is the emphasis here aboard the 36-foot, eight-passenger *Kai Manu*. This longtime Kauai company discovered some pristine dive sites on the West Side of the island where white-tip reef sharks are common—and other divers are not. Thanks to the addition of a 32-foot powered catamaran—the six-passenger *Dive Rocket*—the group also runs Niihau, Napali, and North Shore dives year-round (depending on ocean conditions, of course). They're still known for their South Side trips and lead dives at the East Side walls as well, so they truly do circumnavigate the island. A bonus on these tours is the wide variety of food served between dives. Open-water certification dives, check-out dives, and intro shore dives are available upon request. ✉ *Port Allen Small Boat Harbor, 4353 Waialo Rd., Eleele* ☎ *808/332–7333* 🌐 *www.bubblesbelowkauai.com* 🎫 *$140 for 2-tank boat dive; $90 for rider/snorkeler; Niihau charter $350.*

Kauai Down Under Dive Team. This company offers boat dives, but specializes in shore diving, typically at Koloa Landing (year-round) and Tunnels (summers). They're not only geared toward beginning divers—for whom they provide a thorough and gentle certification program as well as the Discover Scuba program—but also offer night dives and scooter (think James Bond) dives. Their main emphasis is a detailed review of marine biology, such as pointing out rare dragon eel and harlequin shrimp tucked away in pockets of coral. ■ TIP→ **Hands down, we recommend Kauai Down Under for beginners, certification (all levels), and refresher dives.** One reason is that their instructor-to-student ratio never exceeds 1:4—that's true of all their dive groups. All dive gear included. ✉ *Sheraton Kauai Resort, 2440 Hoonani Rd., Koloa* ☎ *877/538–3483, 808/742–9534* 🌐 *www.kauaidownunderscuba.com* 🎫 *From $149 for a 2-tank certified dive; $550 for certification.*

Fodor's Choice ★ **Ocean Quest Watersports/Fathom Five.** This operator offers it all: boat dives, shore dives, night dives, certification dives. They pretty much do what everyone else does with a few twists. First, they offer a three-tank premium charter for those really serious about diving. Second, they operate a Nitrox continuous-flow mixing system, so you can decide the mix rate. Third, they add on a twilight dive to the standard, one-tank night dive, making the outing worth the effort. Fourth, their shore diving isn't an afterthought. Finally, we think their dive masters are pretty darn good, too. They even dive Niihau in the summer aboard their 35-foot *Force*. In summer, book well in advance. ✉ *3450 Poipu Rd., Koloa* ☎ *808/742–6991, 800/972–3078* 🌐 *www.fathomfive.com* 🎫 *From $155 for boat dives; from $100 for shore dives; $45 for gear rental, if needed.*

Seasport Divers. Rated highly by readers of *Scuba Diving* magazine, Seasport Divers' 48-foot *Anela Kai* tops the chart for dive-boat luxury. But owner Marvin Otsuji didn't stop with that. A second boat—a 32-foot catamaran—is outfitted for diving, but we like it as an all-around charter. The company does brisk business, which means it won't cancel at the last minute because of a lack of reservations, like some other companies, although they may book up to 18 people per boat. ■ TIP→ **There are slightly more challenging trips in the morning; mellower dive sites are in the afternoon.** The company runs a good-size dive shop for purchases and rentals, as well as a classroom for certification. Night dives are offered, and Niihau trips are available in summer. There's also an outlet in Kapaa. ✉ *2827 Poipu Rd., look for yellow submarine in parking lot, Poipu* ☎ *808/742–9303, 808/742–9303* 🌐 *www.seasportdivers.com* 🎫 *From $140, includes gear; $100 1-tank shore dive.*

If you get up close with a Hawaiian monk seal, consider yourself lucky—they're endangered. But look, don't touch—it's illegal.

SNORKELING

Generally speaking, the calmest water and best snorkeling can be found on Kauai's North Shore in summer and South Shore in winter. The East Side, known as the windward side, has year-round, prevalent northeast trade winds that make snorkeling unpredictable, although there are some good pockets. The best snorkeling on the West Side is accessible only by boat.

A word on feeding fish: don't. As Captain Ted with HoloHolo Charters says, fish have survived and populated reefs for much longer than we have been donning goggles and staring at them. They will continue to do so without our intervention. Besides, fish food messes up the reef and—one thing always leads to another—can eliminate a once-pristine reef environment. As for gear, if you're snorkeling with one of the Napali boat-tour outfitters, they'll provide it; however, depending on the company, it might not be the latest or greatest. If you have your own, bring it. On the other hand, if you're going out with SeaFun or Z-Tourz, the gear is top-notch. If you need to rent, hit one of the "snorkel-and-surf" shops such as Snorkel Bob's in Koloa and Kapaa, Nukumoi in Poipu, or Seasport in Poipu and Kapaa, or shop Walmart or Kmart if you want to drag it home. Typically, though, rental gear will be better quality than that found at Walmart or Kmart. ■ TIP→ **If you wear glasses, you can rent prescription masks at the rental shops—just don't expect them to match your prescription exactly.**

BEST SPOTS

Just because we say these are good places to snorkel doesn't mean that the exact moment you arrive, the fish will flock—they are wild, after all.

Beach House (Lawai Beach). Don't pack the beach umbrella, beach mats, or cooler for snorkeling at Beach House. Just bring your snorkeling gear. The beach—named after its neighbor the Beach House restaurant—is on the road to Spouting Horn. It's a small slip of sand during low tide and a rocky shoreline during high tide; however, it's right by the road's edge, and its rocky coastline and somewhat rocky bottom make it great for snorkeling. Enter and exit in the sand channel (not over the rocky reef) that lines up with the Lawai Beach Resort's center atrium. Stay within the rocky points anchoring each end of the beach. The current runs east to west. ✉ *5017 Lawai Rd., makai (ocean) side of Lawai Rd., park on road in front of Lawai Beach Resort, Koloa.*

Kee Beach. Although it can get quite crowded, Kee Beach is quite often a good snorkeling destination if the water conditions are right. Just be sure to come during the off-hours, say early in the morning or later in the afternoon, or you will have difficulty finding a parking spot. **■ TIP→ Snorkeling here in winter can be hazardous. Summer is the best and safest time, although you should never swim beyond the reef.** During peak times, a parking lot is available back down the road away from the beach. ✉ *At end of Rte. 560, Haena.*

Lydgate Beach Park. Lydgate Beach Park is typically the safest place to snorkel on Kauai, though not the most exciting. With its lava-rock wall creating a protected swimming pool, it's a good spot for beginners, young and old. The fish are so tame here it's almost like swimming in a saltwater aquarium. There is also a lifeguard, a playground for children, plenty of parking, and full-service restrooms with showers. ✉ *4470 Nalu Rd.* ✣ *Just south of Wailua River, turn makai (towards ocean) off Rte. 56 onto Lehu Dr. and left onto Nalu Rd., Kapaa.*

Fodor's Choice ★ **Niihau.** With little river runoff and hardly any boat traffic, the waters off the island of Niihau are some of the clearest in all Hawaii, and that's good for snorkeling and excellent for scuba diving. Like Nualolo Kai, the only way to snorkel here is to sign on with one of the tour boats venturing across a sometimes rough open-ocean channel: Blue Dolphin Charters and HoloHolo.

Nualolo Kai. Nualolo Kai was once an ancient Hawaiian fishpond and is now home to the best snorkeling along Napali Coast (and perhaps on all of Kauai). The only way to access it is by boat, including kayak. Though many boats stop offshore, only a few Napali snorkeling-tour operators are permitted to come ashore. We recommend Napali Explorer and Kauai Sea Tours.

Poipu Beach Park. You'll generally find good year-round snorkeling at Poipu Beach Park, except during summer's south swells (which are not nearly as frequent as winter's north swells). The best snorkeling fronts the Marriott Waiohai Beach Club. Stay inside the crescent created by the sandbar and rocky point, and within sight of the lifeguard tower. The current runs east to west. ✉ *Hoone Rd.* ✣ *From Poipu Rd., turn right onto Hoone Rd.*

Tunnels (Makua). The search for Tunnels (Makua) is as tricky as the snorkeling. Park at Haena Beach Park and walk east—away from Napali Coast—until you see a sand channel entrance in the water, almost at the point. Once you get here, the reward is fantastic. The name of this beach comes from the many underwater lava tubes, which always attract marine life. The shore is mostly beach rock interrupted by three sand channels. You'll want to enter and exit at one of these channels (or risk stepping on a sea urchin or scraping your stomach on the reef). Follow the sand channel to a drop-off; the snorkeling along here is always full of nice surprises. Expect a current running east to west. Snorkeling here in winter can be hazardous; summer is the best and safest time for snorkeling. ✉ *Haena Beach Park* ⊕ *Near end of Rte. 560, across from lava-tube sea caves, after stream crossing.*

TOURS

FAMILY Fodor's Choice ★ **SeaFun Kauai.** This guided snorkeling tour, for beginners and intermediates alike, is led by a marine expert, so there's instruction plus the guide actually gets into the water with you and identifies marine life. You're guaranteed to spot tons of critters you'd never see on your own. This is a land-based operation and the only one of its kind on Kauai. (Don't think those snorkeling cruises are guided snorkeling tours—they rarely are. A member of the boat's crew serves as lifeguard, not a marine life *guide.*) A morning or afternoon tour includes all your snorkeling gear—and a wet suit to keep you warm—and stops at one or two snorkeling locations, chosen based on ocean conditions. They will pick up customers at some of the resorts, depending on locale and destination. ✉ *3477A Weliweli Rd., Koloa* ☎ *808/245–6400, 800/452–1113* 🌐 *www.alohakauaitours.com* 🎫 *$85.*

STAND-UP PADDLING

Unlike kiteboarding, this is an increasingly popular sport that even a novice can pick up—*and* have fun doing. Technically, it's not really a new sport but a reinvigorated one from the 1950s. Beginners start with a heftier surfboard and a longer-than-normal canoe paddle. And, just as the name implies, stand-up paddlers stand on their surfboards and paddle out from the beach—no timing a wave and doing a push-up to stand. The perfect place to learn is a river (think **Hanalei** or **Wailua**) or a calm lagoon (try **Anini** or **Kalapaki**). But this sport isn't just for beginners. Tried-and-true surfers turn to it when the waves are not quite right for their preferred sport, because it gives them another reason to be on the water. Stand-up paddlers catch waves earlier and ride them longer than longboard surfers. In the past couple of years, professional stand-up paddling competitions have popped up, and surf shops and instructors have adapted to its quick rise in popularity.

EQUIPMENT

Not all surf instructors teach stand-up paddling, but more and more are, like Blue Seas Surfing School and Titus Kinimaka Hawaiian School of Surfing *(see Surfing)*.

Back Door Surf Co. Along with its sister store across the street—Hanalei Surf Shop—Back Door Surf Co. provides just about all the rentals necessary for a fun day at Hanalei Bay, along with clothing and new boards. ✉ *Ching Young Village, 5-5190 Kuhio Hwy., Hanalei* ☎ *808/826–9000* 🌐 *www.hanaleisurf.com/backdoor.htm.*

Hawaiian Surfing Adventures. This Hanalei location has a wide variety of stand-up boards and paddles for rent, with a few options depending on your schedule. Check in at the storefront and then head down to the beach, where your gear will be waiting. Lessons are also available on the scenic Hanalei River or in Hanalei Bay, and include 30 minutes of ocean safety, paddling, and wave-reading instruction and an hour in the water to practice with the board. This Native Hawaiian–owned company also offers surfboard and kayak rentals and surfing lessons. ✉ *5134 Kuhio Hwy., Hanalei* ☎ *808/482–0749* 🌐 *www.hawaiiansurfingadventures.com* 💵 *Paddleboard rental from $30; surfboard rentals from $20; lessons from $65.*

Kauai Beach Boys. This outfitter is right on the beach at Kalapaki, so there's no hauling your gear on your car. Classes are also held at Poipu Beach, at the Marriott Waiohai. In addition to stand-up paddle lessons, they offer sailing and surfing lessons, too. ✉ *3610 Rice St., Lihue* ☎ *808/246–6333, 808/742–4442* 🌐 *www.kauaibeachboys.com* 💵 *$82 for 1½-hr surf or SUP lesson.*

SURFING

Good ol' stand-up surfing is alive and well on Kauai, especially in winter's high-surf season on the North Shore. If you're new to the sport, we highly recommend taking a lesson. Not only will this ensure you're up and riding waves in no time, but instructors will provide the right board for your experience and size, help you time a wave, and give you a push to get your momentum going. ■ **TIP→ You don't need to be in top physical shape to take a lesson. Because your instructor helps push you into the wave, you won't wear yourself out paddling.** If you're experienced and want to hit the waves on your own, most surf shops rent boards for all levels, from beginners to advanced.

BEST SPOTS

Perennial-favorite beginning surf spots include **Poipu Beach** (the area fronting the Marriott Waiohai Beach Club), **Hanalei Bay,** and the stream end of **Kalapaki Beach.** More advanced surfers move down the beach in Hanalei to an area fronting a grove of pine trees known as **Pine Trees,** or paddle out past the pier. When the trade winds die, the north ends of **Wailua** and **Kealia** beaches are teeming with surfers. Breaks off **Poipu** and **Beach House/Lawai Beach** attract intermediates year-round. During high surf, the break on the cliff side of **Kalihiwai** is for experts only. Advanced riders will head to Polihale to face the heavy West Side waves when conditions are right.

EQUIPMENT AND LESSONS

Hanalei Surf Company. You can rent boards here and shop for rash guards, wet suits, and some hip surf-inspired apparel. ✉ *Hanalei Center, 5-5161 Kuhio Hwy., Hanalei* ☎ *808/826–9000* 🌐 *www.hanaleisurf.com.*

Winter brings big surf to Kauai's North Shore. You can see some of the sport's biggest celebrities catching waves at Haena and Hanalei Bay.

Nukumoi Surf Co. Owned by the same folks who own Brennecke's restaurant, this shop offers surfing lessons, board (surfing, body, and stand-up paddle), snorkel, and beach-gear rental, as well as casual clothing. Their primary surf spot is the beach fronting the Sheraton. ✉ *2100 Hoone Rd., across from Poipu Beach Park, Koloa* ☎ *808/742–8019* 🌐 *www.nukumoi.com* 🎫 *$75 for groups for 1½ hrs; $250 for private sessions.*

Progressive Expressions. This full-service shop has a choice of rental boards and a whole lotta shopping for clothes, swimsuits, and casual beach wear. ✉ *5428 Koloa Rd., Koloa* ☎ *808/742–6041* 🌐 *www.progressiveexpressions.com.*

Tamba Surf Company. This is Kauai's homegrown surf shop, and your best bet for surfboard and snorkel gear rentals, new boards, and surfing lessons on the East Side. Tamba is a big name in local surf apparel. ✉ *4-1543 Kuhio Hwy., Kapaa* ☎ *808/823–6942* 🌐 *www.tamba.com.*

Titus Kinimaka Hawaiian School of Surfing. Famed as a pioneer of big-wave surfing, this Hawaiian believes in giving back to his sport. Beginning, intermediate, and advanced lessons are available at Hanalei, with a maximum of three students. If you want to learn to surf from a living legend, this is the man. Advanced surfers can also take a tow-in lesson with a Jet Ski. **TIP→ He employs other instructors, so if you want Titus, be sure to ask for him. (And good luck, because if the waves are going off, he'll be surfing, not teaching.)** Customers are able to use the board for a while after the lesson is complete. ✉ *Quicksilver, 5-5088 Kuhio Hwy., Hanalei* ☎ *808/652–1116* 🌐 *www.hawaiianschoolofsurfing.com* 🎫 *$65, 90-min group; $250 Jet Ski surf; $65, 90-min group stand-up paddle.*

WHALE-WATCHING

Every winter North Pacific humpback whales swim some 3,000 miles over 30 days, give or take a few, from Alaska to Hawaii. Whales arrive as early as November and sometimes stay through April, though they seem to be most populous in February and March. They come to Hawaii to breed, calve, and nurse their young.

TOURS

Of course, nothing beats seeing a whale up close. During the season, any boat on the water is looking for whales; they're hard to avoid, whether the tour is labeled "whale-watching" or not. Consider the whales a benefit to any boating event that may interest you. If whales are definitely your thing, though, you can narrow down your tour-boat decision by asking a few whale-related questions, like whether there's a hydrophone on board, how long the captain has been running tours in Hawaii, and if anyone on the crew is a marine biologist or trained naturalist.

Several boat operators will add two-hour afternoon whale-watching tours during the season that run on the South Shore (not Napali). Operators include **Blue Dolphin, Catamaran Kahanu, HoloHolo,** and **Napali Explorer** *(see Boat Tours)*. Trying one of these excursions is a good option for those who have no interest in snorkeling or sightseeing along Napali Coast, although keep in mind, the longer you're on the water, the more likely you'll be to see the humpbacks.

One of the more unique ways to (possibly) see some whales is atop a kayak. For such an encounter, try **Outfitters Kauai**'s South Shore kayak trip *(see Kayaking Tours)*. There are a few lookout spots around the island with good land-based viewing: Kilauea Lighthouse on the North Shore, the Kapaa Scenic Overlook just north of Kapaa town on the East Side, and the cliffs to the east of Keoniloa (Shipwreck) Beach on the South Shore.

GOLF, HIKING, AND OUTDOOR ACTIVITIES

Updated by Charles Roessler

Kaui's outdoor recreation options extend well beyond the sand and surf, with plenty of activities to keep you busy on the ground and even in the air. You can hike the island's many trails, or consider taking your vacation into flight with a treetop zip line. You can have a backcountry adventure in a four-wheel drive, or relax in an inner tube floating down the cane-field irrigation canals.

Before booking tours, check with your concierge to find out what the forecast is for water and weather conditions. **■TIP→ Don't rely on the Weather Channel for accurate weather reports, as they're often reporting Oahu weather.** If you happen to arrive during a North Shore lull in the surf, you'll want to plan to be on the ocean in a kayak or snorkeling on the reef. If it's raining, ATV tours are the activity of choice.

For the golfer in the family, Kauai's spectacular courses are rated among the most scenic, as well as the most technical. Princeville Golf Course has garnered accolades from numerous national publications, and Poipu Bay Golf Course hosted the prestigious season-end PGA

Humpback whales arrive at Kauai in December and stick around until early April. Head out on a boat tour for a chance to see these majestic creatures breach.

Grand Slam of Golf for 13 years, although Tiger (he won a record five-straight tournaments) and company, unfortunately, now head to Bermuda for this tourney.

One of the most popular Kauai experiences is to see the island from the air. In an hour or so, you can see waterfalls, craters, and other places that are inaccessible even by hiking trails (some say that 70% or more of the island is inaccessible). The majority of flights depart from the Lihue airport and follow a clockwise pattern around the island. ■ TIP→ **If you plan to take an aerial tour, it's a good idea to fly when you first arrive, rather than saving it for the end of your trip. It will help you visualize what's where on the island, and it may help you decide what you want to see from a closer vantage point during your stay.** Be prepared to relive your flight in dreams for the rest of your life. The most popular flight is 60 minutes long.

AERIAL TOURS

If you only drive around Kauai in your rental car, you will not see *all* of Kauai. There is truly only one way to see it all, and that's by air. Helicopter tours are the favorite way to get a bird's-eye view of Kauai—they fly at lower altitudes, hover above waterfalls, and wiggle their way into areas that a fixed-wing aircraft cannot. That said, if you've already tried the helitour, how about flying in the open cockpit of a biplane—à la the Red Baron?

Air Tour Kauai. This company, which is operated by the same group that runs Skydive Kauai, can hold up to six people in its Cessna 207 plane. The flights take off from the less crowded Port Allen Airport and will last 65 to 70 minutes. ✉ *Port Allen Airport, 3441 Kuiloko Rd., Hanapepe* ☎ *808/639–3446* 🌐 *www.airtourkauai.com* 🎫 *$99 per person.*

Blue Hawaiian Helicopters. This multiisland operator flies the latest in helicopter technology, the Eco-Star, costing $1.8 million. It has 23% more interior space for its six passengers, has unparalleled viewing, and offers a few extra safety features. As the name implies, the helicopter is also a bit more environmentally friendly, with a 50% noise-reduction rate. Even though flights run a tad shorter than others (50 to 55 minutes instead of the 55 to 65 minutes that other companies tout), they feel complete. A DVD of your tour is available for an additional $25. ✉ *3651 Ahukini Rd., Heliport 8, Lihue* ☎ *808/245–5800, 800/745–2583* 🌐 *www.bluehawaiian.com* 🎫 *$239.*

Fodor's Choice ★ **Jack Harter Helicopters.** Jack Harter was the first company to offer helicopter tours on Kauai. The company flies the six-passenger ASTAR helicopter with floor-to-ceiling windows, and the four-person Hughes 500, which is flown with no doors. The doorless ride can get windy, but it's the best bet for taking reflection-free photos. Pilots provide information on the Garden Island's history and geography through two-way intercoms. The company flies out of Lihue. Tours are 60 to 65 minutes and 90 to 95 minutes. Receive a $30 discount when you book through their website. ✉ *4231 Ahukini Rd.* ☎ *808/245–3774, 888/245–2001* 🌐 *www.helicopters-kauai.com* 🎫 *From $289.*

Safari Helicopters. This company flies the "Super" ASTAR helicopter, which offers floor-to-ceiling windows on its doors, four roof windows, and Bose X-Generation headphones. Two-way microphones allow passengers to converse with the pilot. There's a 60-minute waterfall tour and a 90-minute "eco-tour," which adds a landing in Olokele Canyon. Passengers are often met by Keith Robinson of *the* Robinson family, who provides a brief tour of the Kauai Wildlife Refuge, with endangered, endemic plants. A DVD is available for $26. ✉ *3225 Akahi St., Lihue* ☎ *808/246–0136, 800/326–3356* 🌐 *www.safarihelicopters.com* 🎫 *$239; eco-tour $314.*

Sunshine Helicopter Tours. If the name of this company sounds familiar, it may be because its pilots fly on all the main Hawaiian Islands except Oahu. On Kauai, Sunshine Helicopters departs out of two different locations: Lihue and Princeville. They fly the six-passenger FX STAR from Lihue and superroomy six-passenger WhisperSTAR birds from Princeville. ■ TIP→ **Discounts can be substantial by booking online and taking advantage of the "early-bird" seating during off-hours.** ✉ *3416 Rice St., Suite 203, Lihue* ☎ *808/240–2577, 866/501–7738* 🌐 *www.sunshinehelicopters.com* 🎫 *From $244, Princeville $289.*

ATV TOURS

Although all the beaches on the island are public, much of the interior land—once sugar and pineapple plantations—is privately owned. This is really a shame, because the valleys and mountains that make up the vast interior of the island easily rival the beaches in sheer beauty. The good news is some tour operators have agreements with landowners that make exploration possible, albeit a bit bumpy, and unless you have back troubles, that's half the fun. **TIP→ If it looks like rain, book an ATV tour ASAP. That's the thing about these tours: the muddier, the better.**

Fodor's Choice ★ **Kauai ATV Tours.** This is *the* thing to do when it rains on Kauai. Consider it an extreme mud bath. Kauai ATV in Koloa is the originator of the island's all-terrain-vehicle tours. The three-hour Koloa tour takes you through a private sugar plantation and historic cane-haul tunnel. The four-hour waterfall tour visits secluded waterfalls and includes a picnic lunch. This popular option includes a hike to secret WWII bunkers and a swim in a freshwater pool at the base of the falls—to rinse off all that mud. You must be 16 or older to operate your own ATV, but Kauai ATV also offers its four-passenger "Ohana Bug" and two-passenger "Mud Bugs" to accommodate families with kids ages five and older. ✉ *3477A Weliweli Rd., Koloa* ☎ *808/742–2734, 877/707–7088* 🌐 *www.kauaiatv.com* *From $252 for 2 people.*

Kipu Ranch Adventures. This 3,000-acre property extends from the Huleia River to the top of Mt. Haupu. *Jurassic Park* and *Indiana Jones* were filmed here, and you'll see the locations for them on the three-hour Ranch Tour. The four-hour Waterfall Tour includes a visit to two waterfalls and a picnic lunch. Once a sugar plantation, Kipu Ranch today is a working cattle ranch, so you'll be in the company of bovines as well as pheasants, wild boars, and peacocks. If you're not an experienced ATV driver, they also offer guide-driven tour options. ✉ *235 Kipu Rd., off Hwy. 50, Lihue* ☎ *808/246–9288* 🌐 *www.kipu-tours.com* *From $104.*

BIKING

Kauai is a labyrinth of cane-haul roads, which are fun for exploring on two wheels. The challenge is finding roads where biking is allowed and then not getting lost in the maze. Maybe that explains why Kauai is not a hub for the sport—yet. Still, there are some epic rides for those who are interested—both the adrenaline-rush and the mellower beach-cruiser kind. If you want to grind out some mileage, you could take the main highway that skirts the coastal area, but be careful: there are only a few designated bike lanes, and the terrain is hilly. You may find that keeping your eyes on the road rather than the scenery is your biggest challenge. "Cruisers" should head to Kapaa. A new section of Ke Ala Hele Makalae, a pedestrian and bicycle trail that runs along the East Side of Kauai, was completed in the summer of 2013, extending the multiuse path to about 8 miles. You can rent bikes (with helmets) from the activities desks of certain hotels, but these are not the best quality. You're better off renting from Kauai Cycle in Kapaa, Outfitters

Kauai in Poipu, or Pedal 'n' Paddle in Hanalei. Ask for the "Go Green Kauai" map for a full description of Kauai biking options. ⚠ **Following extensive flooding in early 2018, areas of Haena and along the Wailua River are undergoing repairs. Please check before visiting to make sure places are open.**

BEST SPOTS

Fodor's Choice ★ **Ke Ala Hele Makalae** (*coastal path*). This county beach park path follows the coastline on Kauai's East Side and is perfect for cruisers. Eventually, the path is projected to run some 20 miles, but an existing 6½-mile-long stretch already offers scenic views, picnic pavilions, and restroom facilities along the way—all in compliance with the Americans with Disabilities Act. The path runs from Lydgate Beach Park to secluded Kuna Bay (aka Donkey Beach). An easy way to access the longest completed section of the path is from Kealia Beach. Park here and head north into rural lands with spectacular coastline vistas, or head south into Kapaa for a more immersive experience. ✉ *Kealia Beach, Kapaa* ✣ *Trailhead: 1 mile north of Kapaa; park at north end of Kealia Beach* 🌐 *www.kauaipath.org/kauaicoastalpath*.

Moalepe Trail. This trail is perfect for intermediate to advanced trail-bike riders. The first 2 miles of this 5-mile double-track road wind steeply through pastureland. The real challenge begins when you reach the steep and rutted switchbacks, which during a rainy spell can be hazardous. Moalepe intersects the Kuilau Trail, which you can follow to its end at the Keahua Arboretum stream. ✉ *Wailua (Kauai County)* ✣ *From Kuhio Hwy. in Kapaa drive mauka (toward mountains) on Kuamoo Rd. for 3 miles and turn right on Kamalu Rd., which dead-ends at Olohena Rd. Turn left and follow until road veers sharply to right.*

Wailua Forest Management Road. For the novice mountain biker, this is an easy ride, and it's also easy to find. From Route 56 in Wailua, turn *mauka* (toward the mountains) on Kuamoo Road and continue 6 miles to the picnic area known as Keahua Arboretum; park here. The potholed four-wheel-drive road includes some stream crossings—⚠ **stay away during heavy rains, because the streams flood**—and continues for 2 miles to a T-stop, where you should turn right. Stay on the road for about 3 miles until you reach a gate; this is the spot where the gates in the movie *Jurassic Park* were filmed, though it looks nothing like the movie. Go around the gate and down the road for another mile to a confluence of streams at the base of Mt. Waialeale. Be sure to bring your camera. ✉ *Kuamoo Rd., Kapaa.*

Waimea Canyon Road. For those wanting a very challenging road workout, climb this road, also known as Route 550. After a 3,000-foot climb, the road tops out at mile 12, adjacent to Waimea Canyon, which will pop in and out of view on your right as you ascend. From here it continues several miles (mostly level) past the Kokee Museum and ends at the Kalalau Lookout. It's paved the entire way, uphill 100%, and curvy. ⚠ **There's not much of a shoulder on either road—sometimes none—so be extra cautious.** The road gets busier as the day wears on, so you may want to consider a sunrise ride. A slightly more moderate uphill climb is Kokee Road, Route 552, from Kekaha, which intersects

Bikers who prefer a leisurely cruise can pedal along the Ke Ala Hele Makalae trail, an 8-mile, multiuse path in Kapaa.

with Route 550. Bikes aren't allowed on the hiking trails in and around Waimea Canyon and Kokee State Park, but there are miles of wonderful four-wheel-drive roads perfect for mountain biking. Check at Kokee Natural History Museum for a map and conditions. ✉ *Off Rte. 50, near grocery store, Waimea (Kauai County).*

EQUIPMENT AND TOURS

Kauai Cycle. This reliable, full-service bike shop rents, sells, and repairs bikes. Cruisers, mountain bikes (front and full suspension), and road bikes are available, with directions to trails. The Ke Ala Hele Makalae coastal path is right out the back door. ✉ *4-934 Kuhio Hwy., across from Taco Bell, Kapaa* ☎ *808/821–2115* 🌐 *www.kauaicycle.com* 🎫 *Rentals from $20 per day and $110 per wk.*

Outfitters Kauai. Hybrid "comfort" and mountain bikes (both full suspension and hardtails) as well as road bikes are available at this shop in Poipu. You can ride right out the door to tour Poipu, or get information on how to do a self-guided tour of Kokee State Park and Waimea Canyon. The company also leads sunrise and evening coasting tours (under the name **Bicycle Downhill**) from Waimea Canyon past the island's West Side beaches. Stand-up paddle tours are also available. ✉ *2827-A Poipu Rd., near turnoff to Spouting Horn, Poipu* ☎ *808/742–9667, 888/742–9887* 🌐 *www.outfitterskauai.com* 🎫 *Rentals from $25; tours $109.*

Pedal 'n' Paddle. This company rents old-fashioned, single-speed beach cruisers and hybrid road bikes. In the heart of Hanalei, this is a great way to cruise the town; the more adventuresome cyclist can head to the end of the road. Be careful, though, because there are no bike lanes on the twisting-and-turning road to Kee Beach. ✉ *Ching Young Village, 5-5190 Kuhio Hwy., Hanalei* ☎ *808/826–9069* 🌐 *www.pedalnpaddle.com* 🎫 *Rentals from $15 per day and $60 per wk.*

GOLF

For golfers, the Garden Isle might as well be known as the Robert Trent Jones Jr. Isle. Four of the island's eight courses, including Poipu Bay—onetime home of the PGA Grand Slam of Golf—are the work of Jones, who maintains a home at Princeville. Combine these four courses with those from Jack Nicklaus, Robin Nelson, and local legend Toyo Shirai, and you'll see that golf sets Kauai apart from the other Islands as much as the Pacific Ocean does. ■ TIP→ **Afternoon tee times at most courses can save you big bucks.**

Ocean Course Hokuala Golf Club. The Jack Nicklaus–designed Ocean Course Hokuala completed its latest renovation in November 2016 creating not only a superb golf experience, but a visual treat and a Hawaii educational experience as well. With an assortment of plants and tropical birds adding to the atmosphere, this course wends through dark ravines and over picturesque landscape. The 5th hole is particularly striking as it requires a drive over a valley populated by mango and guava trees. The final holes hold unmatched views of Nawiliwili Bay, including the harbor, a lighthouse, and secluded beaches. ✉ *3351 Hoolaulea Way, Lihue* ☎ *808/241–6000, 800/634–6400* 🌐 *www.hokualakauai.com/golf* 🎫 *From $160; after 2 pm $126* 🏌 *18 holes, 7156 yards, par 72.*

Anaina Hou Mini Golf & Gardens. The island's first miniature-golf course also has a small botanical garden and a new 300-seat theater/arts center. The 18-hole course was designed to be challenging, beautiful, and family-friendly. Replacing the typical clown's nose and spinning wheels are some water features and tropical tunnels. Surrounding each hole is plant life that walks players through different eras of Hawaiian history. A gift shop with local products and a concessions counter make it a fun activity for any time of day. On Saturday morning and Monday afternoon, a farmers' market is adjacent to the course with fresh Kauai produce and local goods. ✉ *5-273 Kuhio Hwy., Kilauea* ☎ *808/828–2118* 🌐 *www.kauaiminigolf.com* 🎫 *$18.*

Kiahuna Plantation Golf Course. A meandering creek, lava outcrops, and thickets of trees give Kiahuna its character. Robert Trent Jones Jr. was given a smallish piece of land just inland at Poipu, and defends par with smaller targets, awkward stances, and optical illusions. In 2003 a group of homeowners bought the club and brought Jones back to renovate the course (it was originally built in 1983), adding tees and revamping bunkers. The pro here boasts his course has the best putting greens on the island. This is the only course on Kauai with a complete set of junior's tee boxes. ✉ *2545 Kiahuna Plantation Dr., Koloa* ☎ *808/742–9595* 🌐 *www.kiahunagolf.com* 🎫 *$96, including cart* 🏌 *18 holes, 6787 yards, par 70.*

Poipu Bay Golf Course. Poipu Bay has been called the Pebble Beach of Hawaii, and the comparison is apt. Like Pebble Beach, Poipu is a links course built on headlands, not true links land. There's wildlife galore. It's not unusual for golfers to see monk seals sunning on the beach below, sea turtles bobbing outside the shore break, and humpback whales leaping offshore. From 1994 to 2006, the course (designed by Robert Trent Jones Jr.) hosted the annual PGA Grand Slam of Golf. Tiger Woods was a frequent winner here. Call ahead to take advantage of varying prices for tee times. ✉ *2250 Ainako St., Koloa* ☎ *808/742–8711* 🌐 *www.poipubaygolf.com* 🎫 *$209 before noon, $189 after* ⛳ *18 holes, 6127 yards, par 72.*

Fodor's Choice ★ **Princeville Makai Golf Club.** The 27-hole Princeville Makai Golf Club was named for its five ocean-hugging front holes. Designed by golf-course architect Robert Trent Jones Jr. in 1971, the 18-hole championship Makai Course underwent extensive renovations from 2008 to 2010, including new turf throughout, reshaped greens and bunkers, refurbished cart paths and comfort stations, and an extensive practice facility. Since the renovation the Makai Course has consistently been ranked a top golf course in the United States. ■ TIP→ **Check the website for varying rates as well as other nongolf activities at the facility like the Sunset Golf Cart Tour, where you ride the course, sans clubs, and take in the spectacular ocean views.** ✉ *4080 Lei O Papa Rd., Princeville* 🌐 *www.makaigolf.com* 🎫 *$295* ⛳ *18 holes, 7223 yards, par 72; Woods Course: 9 holes, 3445 yards, par 36.*

Wailua Municipal Golf Course. Considered by many to be one of Hawaii's best public golf courses, this seaside course provides an affordable game with minimal water hazards, but it is challenging enough to have been chosen to host three USGA Amateur Public Links Championships. It was first built as a nine-holer in the 1930s. The second nine holes were added in 1961. Course designer Toyo Shirai created a course that is fun but not punishing. The trade winds blow steadily on the East Side of the island and provide a game with challenges. An ocean view and affordability make this one of the most popular courses on the island. Tee times are accepted up to seven days in advance and can be paid in cash, traveler's checks, and some credit cards. ✉ *3-5350 Kuhio Hwy., Lihue* ☎ *808/241–6666* 🌐 *www.kauai.gov/Golf* 🎫 *$48 weekdays, $60 weekends; cart rental $20* ⛳ *18 holes, 6585 yards, par 72.*

HIKING

The best way to experience the *aina*—the land—on Kauai is to step off the beach and hike into the remote interior. You'll find waterfalls so tall you'll strain your neck looking, pools of crystal-clear water for swimming, tropical forests teeming with plant life, and ocean vistas that will make you wish you could stay forever.

■ TIP→ **For your safety wear sturdy shoes—preferably water-resistant ones.** All hiking trails on Kauai are free, so far. There's a development plan in the works that could turn the Waimea Canyon and Kokee state parks into admission-charging destinations. Whatever it may be, it will be worth it. ⚠ **Following extensive flooding in early 2018, areas of the Napali Coast, including the Kalalau Trail, are undergoing repairs. Please check before visiting to make sure places are open.**

BEST SPOTS

Hanalei-Okolehao Trail. *Okolehao* basically translates to "moonshine" in Hawaiian. This trail follows the Hihimanu Ridge, which was established in the days of Prohibition, when this backyard liquor was distilled from the roots of ti plants. The 2-mile hike climbs 1,200 feet and offers a 360-degree view of Hanalei Bay and Waioli Valley. Your ascent begins at the China Ditch off the Hanalei River. Follow the trail through a lightly forested grove and then climb up a steep embankment. From here the trail is well marked. Most of the climb is lined with hala, ti, wild orchid, and eucalyptus. You'll get your first of many ocean views at mile marker 1. ✉ *Hanalei* ✣ *Follow Ohiki Rd. (north of Hanalei Bridge) 5 miles to U.S. Fish and Wildlife Service parking area. Directly across street is small bridge that marks trailhead.*

Fodor's Choice ★ **Kalalau Trail.** Of all the hikes on the island, Kalalau Trail is by far the most famous and in many regards the most strenuous. A moderate hiker can handle the 2-mile trek to Hanakapiai Beach, and for the seasoned outdoorsman, the additional 2 miles up to the falls is manageable. But be prepared to rock-hop along a creek and ford waters that can get waist high during the rain. Round-trip to Hanakapiai Falls is 8 miles. This steep and often muddy trail is best approached with a walking stick. If there has been any steady rain, wait for drier days for a more enjoyable trek. The narrow Kalalau Trail delivers one startling ocean view after another along a path that is alternately shady and sunny. Wear hiking shoes or sandals, and bring drinking water since the creeks on the trail are not potable. Plenty of food is always encouraged on a strenuous hike such as this one. If you plan to venture the full 11 miles into Kalalau, you need to acquire a camping permit, either online or at the State Building in Lihue, for $20 per person per night. You should secure a permit well in advance of your trip. ⚠ **Following extensive flooding in early 2018, call to make sure that the trail is open and accessible.** ✣ *Drive north past Hanalei to end of road. Trailhead is directly across from Kee Beach* 🌐 *www.kalalautrail.com* 🎫 *$20 per person per night.*

Mahaulepu Heritage Trail. This trail offers the novice hiker an accessible way to appreciate the rugged southern coast of Kauai. A cross-country trail wends its way along the water, high above the ocean, through a lava field, and past a sacred *heiau* (stone structure) . Walk all the way to Mahaulepu, 2 miles north, for a two-hour round-trip. ✣ *Drive north on Poipu Rd., turn right at Poipu Bay Golf Course sign. The street name is Ainako, but sign is hard to see. Drive down to beach and park in lot* 🌐 *www.hikemahaulepu.org.*

Sleeping Giant Trail. An easily accessible trail practically in the heart of Kapaa, the moderately strenuous Sleeping Giant Trail—or simply Sleeping Giant—gains 1,000 feet over 2 miles. We prefer an early-morning—say, sunrise—hike, with sparkling blue-water vistas, up the east-side trailhead, but there are other back-side approaches. At the top you can see a grassy grove with a picnic table. It is a local favorite, with many East Siders meeting here to exercise. ✉ *Haleilio Rd., off Rte. 56, Wailua (Kauai County).*

Waimea Canyon and Kokee State Park. This park contains a 50-mile network of hiking trails of varying difficulty that take you through acres of native forests, across the highest-elevation swamp in the world, to the river at the base of the canyon, and onto pinnacles of land sticking their necks out over Napali Coast. All hikers should register at Kokee Natural History Museum, where you can find trail maps, current trail information, and specific directions.

The **Kukui Trail** descends 2½ miles and 2,200 feet into Waimea Canyon to the edge of the Waimea River—it's a steep climb. The **Awaawapuhi Trail,** with 1,600 feet of elevation gains and losses over 3¼ miles, feels more gentle than the Kukui Trail, but it offers its own huffing-and-puffing sections in its descent along a spiny ridge to a perch overlooking the ocean.

The 3½-mile **Alakai Swamp Trail** is accessed via the **Pihea Trail** or a four-wheel-drive road. There's one strenuous valley section, but otherwise it's a pretty level trail—once you access it. This trail is a birdwatcher's delight and includes a painterly view of Wainiha and Hanalei valleys at the trail's end. The trail traverses the purported highest-elevation swamp in the world via a boardwalk so as not to disturb the fragile plant and wildlife. It is typically the coolest of the hikes due to the tree canopy, elevation, and cloud coverage.

The **Canyon Trail** offers much in its short trek: spectacular vistas of the canyon and the only dependable waterfall in Waimea Canyon. The easy 2-mile hike can be cut in half if you have a four-wheel-drive vehicle. The late-afternoon sun sets the canyon walls ablaze in color. ✉ *Kokee Natural History Museum, 3600 Kokee Rd., Kekaha* ☎ *808/335–9975 for trail conditions* 🌐 *www.kokee.org.*

5

EQUIPMENT AND TOURS

Fodor's Choice ★ **Kauai Nature Tours.** Father-and-son scientists started this hiking tour business. As such, their emphasis is on education and the environment. If you're interested in flora, fauna, volcanology, geology, oceanography, and the like, this is the company for you. They offer daylong hikes along coastal areas, beaches, and in the mountains. **TIP→ If you have a desire to see a specific location, just ask. They will do custom hikes to spots they don't normally hit if there is interest.** Hikes range from easy to strenuous. Transportation is often provided from your hotel. ✉ *5162 Lawai Rd., Koloa* ☎ *808/742–8305, 888/233–8365* 🌐 *www.kauainaturetours.com* 🎟 *From $155.*

Princeville Ranch Adventures. This 4-mile hike traverses Princeville Ranch, crossing through a rain forest and to a five-tier waterfall for lunch and swimming. Moderately strenuous hiking is required. ✉ *Rte. 56, between mile markers 27 and 28, Princeville* ☎ *808/826–7669, 888/955–7669* 🌐 *www.princevilleranch.com* 🎟 *$129.*

HORSEBACK RIDING

Most of the horseback-riding tours on Kauai are primarily walking tours with little trotting and no cantering or galloping, so no experience is required. Zip. Zilch. Nada. If you're interested, most of the stables offer private lessons. The most popular tours are the ones including a picnic lunch by the water. Your only dilemma may be deciding what kind of water you want—waterfalls or ocean. You may want to make your decision based on where you're staying. The "waterfall picnic" tours are on the wetter North Shore, and the "beach picnic" tours take place on the South Side.

Fodor's Choice ★ **Princeville Ranch Adventures.** A longtime *kamaaina* (resident) family operates Princeville Ranch. They originated the waterfall picnic tour, which runs 3½ hours and includes a short but steep hike down to Kalihiwai Falls, a dramatic three-tier waterfall, for swimming and picnicking. Princeville also has shorter, straight riding tours and private rides. A popular option is the three-hour combination Ride N' Glide tour with three zip lines. ✉ *Kuhio Hwy., off Kapaka Rd., between mile markers 27 and 28, Princeville* ☎ *808/826–7669* 🌐 *www.princevilleranch.com* 🎫 *Ride only from $119; private tours from $189.*

MOUNTAIN TUBING

For the past 40 years, Hawaii's sugarcane plantations have closed one by one. In the fall of 2009, Gay & Robinson announced the closure of Kauai's last plantation, leaving only one in Maui, the last in the state. The sugarcane irrigation ditches remain, striating these Islands like spokes in a wheel. Inspired by the Hawaiian *auwai,* which diverted water from streams to taro fields, these engineering feats harnessed the rain. One ingenious tour company on Kauai has figured out a way to make exploring them an adventure: float inflatable tubes down the route.

FAMILY **Kauai Backcountry Adventures.** Both zip-line and tubing tours are offered. Popular with all ages, the tubing adventure can book up two weeks in advance in busy summer months. Here's how it works: you recline in an inner tube and float down fern-lined irrigation ditches that were built more than a century ago—the engineering is impressive—to divert water from Mt. Waialeale to sugar and pineapple fields around the island. They'll even give you a headlamp so you can see as you float through five covered tunnels. The scenery from the island's interior at the base of Mt. Waialeale on Lihue Plantation land is superb. Ages five and up are welcome. The tour takes about three hours and includes a picnic lunch and a swim in a swimming hole. ■ **TIP→ You'll definitely want to pack water-friendly shoes (or rent some from the outfitter), sunscreen, a hat, bug repellent, and a beach towel.** Tours are offered up to a dozen times daily. ✉ *3-4131 Kuhio Hwy., across from gas station, Hanamaulu* ☎ *808/245–2506, 888/270–0555* 🌐 *www.kauaibackcountry.com* 🎫 *$114 per person.*

WORD OF MOUTH

"We spotted this remote waterfall [Hanakapiai Falls] on a helicopter trip. Later we tried finding it while hiking on Napali Coast, but the trail disappeared into the jungle." —koala

ZIP-LINE TOURS

The latest adventure on Kauai is "zipping," or "zip-lining." Regardless of what you call it, chances are you'll scream like a rock star while trying it. Strap on a harness, clip onto a cable running from one side of a river or valley to the other, and zip across. The step off is the scariest part. ■ **TIP→ Pack knee-length shorts or pants, athletic shoes, and courage for this adventure.**

Fodor's Choice ★ **Just Live.** When Nichol Baier and Julie Lester started Just Live in 2003, their market was exclusively school-age children, but soon they added visitor tours. Experiential education through adventure is how they describe it. Whatever you call it, sailing 70 feet above the ground for three-plus hours will take your vacation to another level. This is the only treetop zip line on Kauai where your feet never touch ground once you're in the air: seven zips and four canopy bridges make the Tree Top Tour their most popular one. For the heroic at heart, there's the Zipline Eco Adventure, which includes three zip lines, two canopy bridges, a climbing wall, a 100-foot rappelling tower, and a "Monster Swing." If you're short on time—or courage—you can opt for the Wikiwiki Zipline Tour, which includes three zip lines and two canopy bridges in about two hours. They now have a shop with outdoor gear specifically for the island's activities, although their primary focus remains community programming. Enjoy knowing that money spent here serves Kauai's children. ✉ *Harbor Mall Shopping Center, 3501 Rice St., Lihue* ☎ *808/482–1295* 🌐 *www.zipkauai.com* 🎟 *From $79.*

Outfitters Kauai. This outfitter's most popular adventure, the Kipu Zipline Safari Tour, features an 1,800-foot tandem zip—that's right, you don't have to go it alone. You can also paddle the Wailua River or take the downhill bike ride along the Waimea Canyon road. They also offer The Flyline, the state's longest zip line, which has a "run" of 4,000 feet. ✉ *2827-A Poipu Rd., Poipu* ☎ *808/742–9667, 888/742–9887* 🌐 *www.outfitterskauai.com* 🎟 *From $116.*

Princeville Ranch Adventures. The North Shore's answer to zip-lining is a nine-zip-line course with a bit of hiking, and suspension-bridge crossing thrown in for a half-day adventure. The 4½-hour Zip N' Dip tour includes a picnic and swimming at a waterfall pool, while the Zip Express whizzes you through the entire course in 3 hours. Both excursions conclude with a 1,200-foot tandem zip across a valley. Guides are energetic and fun. This is as close as it gets to flying; just watch out for the albatross. ✉ *Rte. 56, between mile markers 27 and 28, Princeville* ☎ *808/826–7669, 888/955–7669* 🌐 *www.princevilleranch.com* 🎟 *From $139.*

6

MOLOKAI

WELCOME TO MOLOKAI

TOP REASONS TO GO

★ **Kalaupapa Peninsula:** Hike or take a mule ride down the world's tallest sea cliffs to a fascinating historic community that still houses a few former Hansen's disease patients.

★ **A waterfall hike in Halawa:** A fascinating guided hike through private property takes you past ancient ruins, restored taro patches, and a sparkling cascade.

★ **Deep-sea fishing:** Sport fish are plentiful in these waters, as are gorgeous views of several islands. Fishing is one of the island's great adventures.

★ **Closeness to nature:** Deep valleys, sheer cliffs, and the untamed ocean are the main attractions on Molokai.

★ **Papohaku Beach:** This 3-mile stretch of golden sand is one of the most sensational beaches in all of Hawaii. Sunsets and barbecues are perfect here.

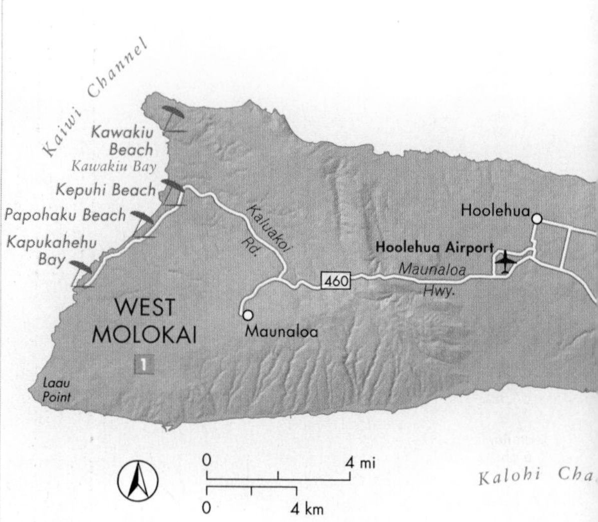

Molokai is about 10 miles wide on average and four times that long. The north shore thrusts up from the sea to form the tallest sea cliffs on Earth, while the south shore slides almost flat into the water, then fans out to form the largest shallow-water reef system in the United States. Kaunakakai, the island's main town, has most of the stores and restaurants. Surprisingly, the highest point on Molokai rises to only 4,970 feet.

1 West Molokai. The most arid part of the island, known as the west end, has two inhabited areas: the coastal stretch includes a few condos and luxury homes, and the largest beaches on the island; nearby is the fading hilltop hamlet of Maunaloa.

6

2 Central Molokai. The island's only true town, Kaunakakai, with its mile-long wharf, is here. Nearly all the island's eateries and stores are in or close to Kaunakakai. Highway 470 crosses the center of the island, rising to the top of the sea cliffs and the Kalaupapa overlook. At the base of the cliffs is Kalaupapa National Historical Park, a top attraction.

3 Kalaupapa Peninsula. The most remote area in the entire Hawaiian Islands is accessible only by air, on foot, or on a mule. It's a place of stunning beauty with a tragic history.

4 East Molokai. The scenic drive on Route 450 around this undeveloped area, also called the east end, passes through the green pastures of Puu O Hoku Ranch and climaxes with a descent into Halawa Valley. As you continue east, the road becomes increasingly narrow and the island ever more lush.

KALAUPAPA PENINSULA: TRAGEDY AND TRIUMPH

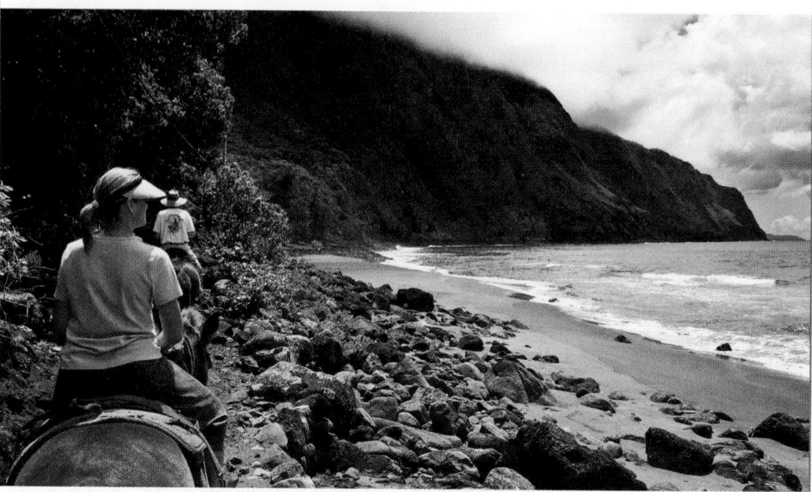

Today, it's hard to picture how for over a century Molokai's remote Kalaupapa Peninsula was "the loneliest place on earth," a feared place of exile for those suffering from leprosy (now known as Hansen's disease).

But for visitors who crave drama, there's no better destination than this remote strip, where the scenery blends with quintessential facets of small-town life.

The world's tallest sea cliffs, rain-chiseled valleys, and tiny islets dropped like exclamation points along the coast emphasize the passionate history of the Kalaupapa Peninsula. You'll likely be tugged by emotions—awe and disbelief, for starters. It's impossible to visit this stunning National Historical Park and view the evidence of human ignorance and heroism without responding.

Getting to the peninsula is still not easy, and there are only two ways: you can hike or you can fly into the small Kalaupapa Airstrip. The strenuous hike takes about an hour down and 90 minutes up; once on the ground, you must join a guided tour.

Visitors under 16 are not allowed at Kalaupapa, nor is photographing patients without their written permission. Whatever your experience is, chances are you'll return home feeling that the journey to present-day Kalaupapa is one you'll never forget.

Daily tours are offered Monday–Saturday through Damien Tours or on the Kalaupapa Guided Mule Tour; be sure to call in advance for times and reservations.

THE SETTLEMENT'S EARLY DAYS

In 1865, pressured by foreign residents, the Hawaiian Kingdom passed "An Act to Prevent the Spread of Leprosy." Anyone showing symptoms of the disease was to be permanently exiled to Kalawao, the north end of Kalaupapa Peninsula—a spot walled in on three sides by nearly impassable cliffs. The peninsula had been home to a fishing community for 900 years, but those inhabitants were evicted and the entire peninsula was declared settlement land.

The first 12 patients were arrested and sent to Kalawao in 1866. More banishments followed. People of all ages and many nationalities were taken from their homes and dumped on the isolated shore. Officials thought the patients could become self-sufficient, fishing and farming sweet potatoes in the stream-fed valleys. That was not the case. Settlement conditions were deplorable.

FATHER DAMIEN'S ARRIVAL

Belgian missionary Father Damien was one of four priests who volunteered to serve the leprosy settlement at Kalawao on a rotating basis. His turn came in 1873, and there were 600 patients on the island already. When his time was up, he refused to leave. Father Damien is credited with turning the settlement from a merciless exile into a place where hope could be heard in the voices of his recruited choir.

Sixteen years after his arrival, in 1889, he died from the effects of leprosy, having contracted the disease during his service. Renowned for his sacrifice, Father Damien was canonized in 2009.

KALAUPAPA TODAY

Kalaupapa today exudes bittersweet charm. Signs posted here and there remind residents when the bankers will be there (once monthly), when to place annual barge orders for nonperishable items, and what's happening around town. It has the nostalgic, almost naive ambience expected from a place that's essentially segregated from modern life.

About eight former patients remain at Kalaupapa (by choice, as the disease is controlled by drugs and the patients are no longer carriers), and all are now quite elderly. They never lost their chutzpah, however. Having survived a lifetime of prejudice and misunderstanding, Kalaupapa's residents haven't been willing to be pushed around any longer—in past years, several made the journey to Honolulu from time to time to testify before the state legislature about matters concerning them.

To get a feel for what residents' lives were like, visit the National Park Service website (🌐 *www.nps.gov/kala*) or buy one of several heartbreaking memoirs at the park's library-turned-bookstore.

6

Updated by Kyle Ellison

With sandy beaches to the west, sheer sea cliffs to the north, and a rainy, lush eastern coast, Molokai offers a bit of everything, including a peek at what the Islands were like 50 years ago. Large tracts of land from Hawaiian Homeland grants have allowed the people to retain much of their traditional lifestyle. A favorite expression is "Slow down, you're on Molokai." Exploring the great outdoors and visiting the historic Kalaupapa Peninsula, where Saint Damien and Saint Marianne Cope helped people with leprosy, are attractions for visitors.

Molokai is generally thought of as the last bit of "real" Hawaii. Tourism has been held at bay by the island's unique history and the pride of its predominantly native Hawaiian population. Only 38 miles long and 10 miles wide at its widest point, Molokai is the fifth-largest island in the Hawaiian archipelago. Eight thousand residents call Molokai home, nearly 60% of whom are Hawaiian.

Molokai is a great place to be outdoors. There are no tall buildings, no traffic lights, no streetlights, no stores bearing the names of national chains, and nothing at all like a resort. You will, however, find 15 parks and more than 100 miles of shoreline to play on. At night the whole island grows dark, creating a velvety blackness and a wonderful rare thing called silence.

GEOGRAPHY

Molokai was created when two large volcanoes—Kamakou in the east and Mauna Loa in the west—broke the surface of the Pacific Ocean to create an island. Afterward, a third section of the island emerged when a much smaller caldera, Kauhako, popped up to form the Kalaupapa Peninsula. But it wasn't until an enormous landslide sent much of Kauhako Mountain into the sea that the island was blessed with the sheer sea cliffs—the world's tallest—that make Molokai's north shore so spectacularly beautiful.

HISTORY

Molokai is named in chants as the child of the moon goddess Hina. For centuries the island was occupied by native people, who took advantage of the reef fishing and ideal conditions for growing taro.

When leprosy broke out in the Hawaiian Islands in the 1840s, the Kalaupapa Peninsula, surrounded on three sides by the Pacific and accessible only by a steep trail, was selected as the place to exile people suffering from the disease. The first patients were thrown into the sea to swim ashore as best they could, and left with no facilities, shelter, or supplies. In 1873 a missionary named Father Damien arrived and began to serve the peninsula's suffering inhabitants. He died in 1889 from leprosy and was canonized as a saint by the Catholic Church in 2009. In 1888, a nun named Mother Marianne Cope moved to Kalaupapa to care for the dying Father Damien and continue his vital work. Mother Marianne stayed at Kalaupapa until her death in 1918 (not from leprosy), and was canonized in 2012.

Although leprosy, known now as Hansen's disease, is no longer contagious and can be remitted, the buildings and infrastructure created by those who were exiled here still exist, and some longtime residents have chosen to stay in their homes. Today the area is Kalaupapa National Historical Park. Visitors are welcome but must prebook a tour operated by Damien Tours of Kalaupapa. You can reach the park by plane, by hiking, or by taking a mule ride down the steep Kalaupapa Trail.

THE BIRTHPLACE OF HULA

Tradition has it that, centuries ago, Lailai came to Molokai and lived on Puu Nana at Kaana. She brought the art of hula and taught it to the people, who kept it secret for her descendants, making sure the sacred dances were performed only at Kaana. Five generations later, Laka was born into the family and learned hula from an older sister. She chose to share the art and traveled throughout the Islands teaching the dance, although she did so without her family's consent. The yearly Ka Hula Piko Festival, held on Molokai in May, celebrates the birth of hula at Kaana.

PLANNING

WHEN TO GO

If you're keen to explore Molokai's beaches, coral beds, or fishponds, summer is your best bet for nonstop calm seas and sunny skies. The weather mimics that of the other Islands: low to mid-80s year-round, slightly rainier in winter. As you travel up the mountainside, the weather changes with bursts of downpours. The strongest storms occur in winter, when winds and rain shift to come in from the south.

For a taste of Hawaiian culture, plan your visit around a festival. In January, islanders and visitors compete in ancient Hawaiian games at the Ka Molokai Makahiki Festival. The Molokai Ka Hula Piko, an annual daylong event in May, draws premier hula troupes, musicians, and storytellers. Long-distance canoe races from Molokai to Oahu are in late September and early October. Although never crowded, the island is busier during these events—book accommodations and transportation six months in advance.

GETTING HERE AND AROUND

AIR TRAVEL

If you're flying in from the mainland United States, you must first make a stop in Honolulu, Oahu; Kahului, Maui; or Kailua-Kona, the Big Island. From any of those, Molokai is just a short hop away. Molokai's transportation hub is Hoolehua Airport, a tiny airstrip 8 miles west of Kaunakakai and about 18 miles east of Maunaloa. An even smaller airstrip serves the little community of Kalaupapa on the north shore.

From Hoolehua Airport, it takes about 10 minutes to reach Kaunakakai and 25 minutes to reach the west end of the island by car. There's no public bus. A taxi will cost about $27 from the airport to Kaunakakai with Hele Mai Taxi. Shuttle service costs about $25 per person from Hoolehua Airport to Kaunakakai; call Molokai Tours. Keep in mind, however, that it's difficult to visit the island without a rental car.

Airport Contacts Molokai Airport (MKK). ✉ *3980 Airport Loop, Hoolehua* ☎ *808/567–9660* 🌐 *www.airports.hawaii.gov/mkk.*

Taxi Contacts Hele Mai Taxi. ☎ *808/336–0967, 808/646–9060* 🌐 *www.molokaitaxi.com.* **Molokai Day Tours.** ☎ *808/660–3377* 🌐 *www.molokaidaytours.com.*

CAR TRAVEL

If you want to explore Molokai from one end to the other, you must rent a car. With just a few main roads to choose from, it's a snap to drive around here. The gas stations are in Kaunakakai. Ask your rental agent for a free *Molokai Drive Guide*.

Alamo maintains a counter at Hoolehua Airport. Make arrangements in advance, because the number of rental cars on Molokai is limited. Be sure to check that the vehicle's four-wheel drive is working before you depart from the agency. Off-road driving is not allowed and beware of fees for returning the car dirty. If Alamo is fully booked, check out Molokai Car Rental.

Contacts Alamo. ☎ *808/567–6381* 🌐 *www.alamo.com.* **Molokai Car Rental.** ☎ *808/336–0670* 🌐 *www.molokaicars.com.*

COMMUNICATIONS

There are many locations on the island where cell-phone reception is difficult, if not impossible, to obtain. Your best bet for finding service is in Kaunakakai.

HOTELS

Molokai appeals most to travelers who appreciate genuine Hawaiian ambience rather than swanky digs. Most hotel and condominium properties range from adequate to funky. Visitors who want to lollygag on the beach should choose one of the condos or home rentals in West Molokai. Travelers who want to immerse themselves in the spirit of the island should seek out a condo or cottage, the closer to East Molokai the better. *Hotel reviews have been shortened. For full information, visit Fodors.com.*

Kapuaiwa Coconut Grove in central Molokai is a survivor of royal plantings from the 19th century.

Destination Molokai Visitors Bureau. Ask about a brochure with up-to-date listings of vacation rentals operated by this agency's members. ✉ *2 Kamoi St., Suite 200, Kaunakakai* ☎ *808/553–5221* 🌐 *www.gohawaii.com/molokai.*

Molokai Vacation Properties. This company handles condo rentals and can act as an informal concierge, including arranging for a rental car, during your stay. There is a three-night minimum on all properties. Private rental properties, from beach cottages to large estates, are also available. ☎ *800/367–2984, 808/553–8334* 🌐 *www.molokai-vacation-rental.net.*

RESTAURANTS

Dining on Molokai is simply a matter of eating—there are no fancy restaurants, just pleasant low-key places to eat out. Paddlers' Inn and Hiro's Ohana Grill currently have the best dinner offerings. Other options include burgers, plate lunches, pizza, coffee shop–style sandwiches, and make-it-yourself fixings.

VISITOR INFORMATION

Contacts Destination Molokai Visitors Bureau. ✉ *2 Kamoi St., Suite 200, Kaunakakai* ☎ *808/553–5221* 🌐 *www.gohawaii.com/molokai.* **Maui Visitors Bureau.** ☎ *808/244–3530, 800/525–6284* 🌐 *www.gohawaii.com/maui.*

EXPLORING

The first thing to do on Molokai is to drive everywhere. It's a feat you can accomplish comfortably in two days. Depending on where you stay, spend one day exploring the west end and the other day exploring the east end. Basically you have one 40-mile west–east highway (two lanes, no stoplights) with three side trips: the nearly deserted little west-end town of Maunaloa, the Highway 470 drive (just a few miles) to the top of the north shore and the overlook of Kalaupapa Peninsula, and the short stretch of shops in Kaunakakai town. After you learn the general lay of the land, you can return to the places that interest you most. Directions on the island—as throughout Hawaii—are often given as *mauka* (toward the mountains) and *makai* (toward the ocean).

MOLOKAI VIBES

Molokai is one of the last places in Hawaii where most of the residents are living an authentic rural lifestyle and wish to retain it. Many oppose developing the island for visitors or outsiders, so you won't find much to cater to your needs, but if you take time and talk to the locals, you will find them hospitable and friendly. Some may even invite you home with them. It's a safe place, but don't interrupt private parties on the beach or trespass on private property. Consider yourself a guest in someone's house, rather than a customer.

■ TIP→ Most Molokai establishments cater to the needs of locals, not tourists, so you may need to prepare a bit more than if you were going to a more popular destination. Pick up a disposable cooler in Kaunakakai town, then buy supplies in local markets. Don't forget to carry some water, and bring sunscreen and mosquito repellent to the island with you.

WEST MOLOKAI

Papohaku Beach is 17 miles west of the airport; Maunaloa is 10 miles west of the airport.

The remote beaches and rolling pastures on Molokai's west end are presided over by Mauna Loa, a dormant volcano, and a sleepy little former plantation town of the same name. Papohaku Beach, the Hawaiian Islands' second-longest white-sand beach, is one of the area's biggest draws. *For information about Papohaku Beach, see Beaches.*

GETTING HERE AND AROUND

The sometimes winding paved road through West Molokai begins at Highway 460 and ends at Kapukahehu Bay. The drive from Kaunakakai to Maunaloa is about 30 minutes.

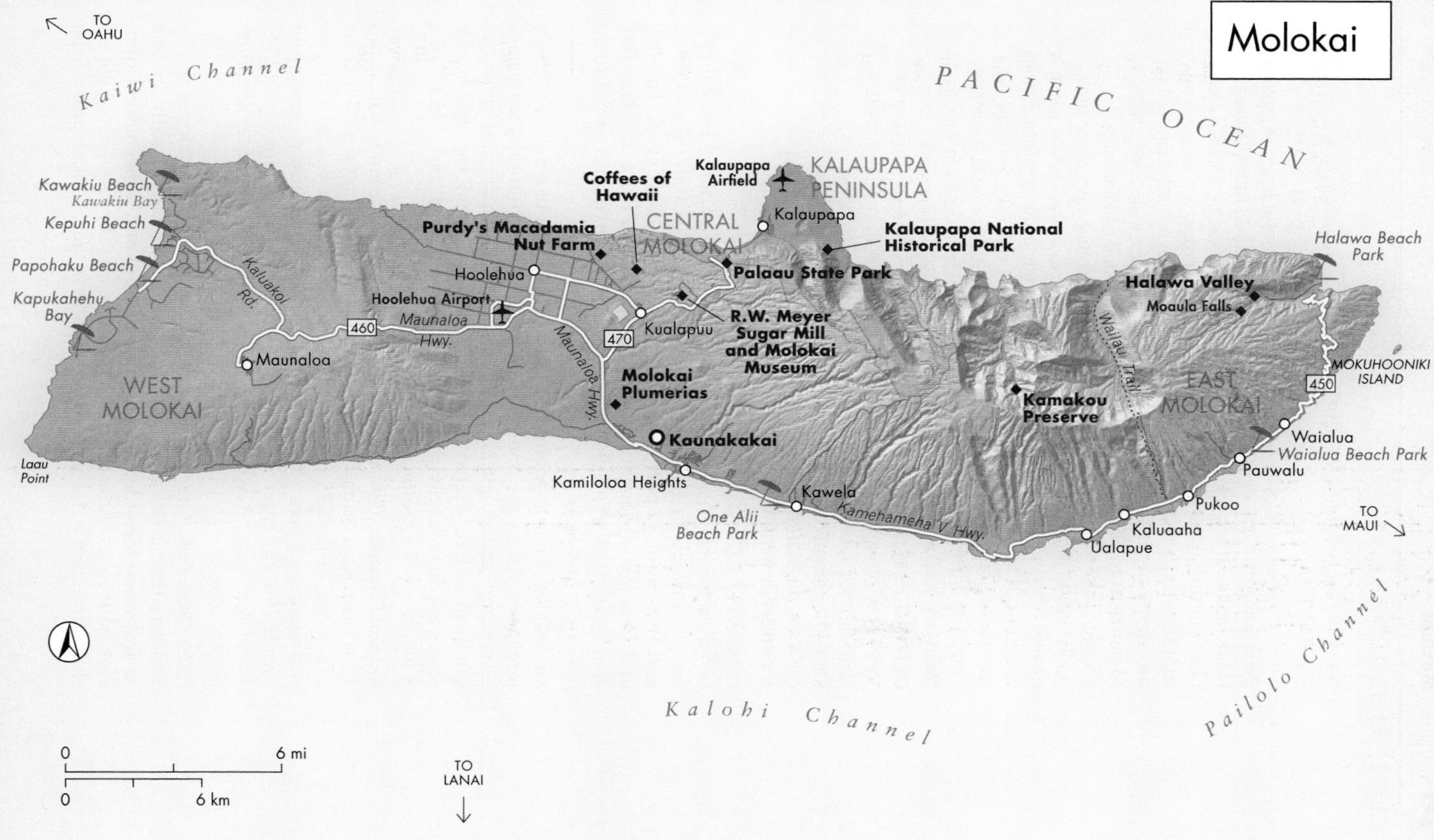
Molokai
TO OAHU
Kaiwi Channel
PACIFIC OCEAN
Kawakiu Beach
Kawakiu Bay
Kepuhi Beach
Papohaku Beach
Kapukahehu Bay
Kaluakoi Rd.
Maunaloa
WEST MOLOKAI
Laau Point
460
Maunaloa Hwy.
Hoolehua Airport
Hoolehua
Purdy's Macadamia Nut Farm
Coffees of Hawaii
CENTRAL MOLOKAI
Kalaupapa Airfield
KALAUPAPA PENINSULA
Kalaupapa
Kalaupapa National Historical Park
Palaau State Park
R.W. Meyer Sugar Mill and Molokai Museum
Kualapuu
470
Maunaloa Hwy.
Molokai Plumerias
Kaunakakai
Kamiloloa Heights
One Alii Beach Park
Kawela
Kamehameha V Hwy.
Kamakou Preserve
Wailau Trail
Halawa Valley
Moaula Falls
Halawa Beach Park
MOKUHOONIKI ISLAND
450
EAST MOLOKAI
Waialua
Waialua Beach Park
Pauwalu
Pukoo
Kaluaaha
Ualapue
TO MAUI
Pailolo Channel
Kalohi Channel
TO LANAI
0
6 mi
0
6 km

CENTRAL MOLOKAI

Kaunakakai is 8 miles southeast of the airport.

Most residents live centrally, near the island's one and only true town, Kaunakakai. It's just about the only place on the island to get food and supplies—it *is* Molokai. Go into the shops along and around Ala Malama Street. Buy stuff. Talk with people. Take your time, and you'll really enjoy being a visitor. Also in this area, on the north side, is Coffees of Hawaii, a 500-acre coffee plantation, and the Kalaupapa National Historical Park, one of the island's most notable sights.

GETTING HERE AND AROUND

Central Molokai is the hub of the island's road system, and Kaunakakai is the commercial center. Watch for kids, dogs, and people crossing the street downtown.

HAWAII'S FIRST SAINT

A long-revered figure on Molokai and in Hawaii, Father Damien, who cared for the desperate patients at Kalaupapa, was elevated to sainthood in 2009. Plans call for a small museum and bookstore in his honor in Kaunakakai, and refurbishment of the three churches in the Catholic parish is currently under way. Visitors who cannot visit Kalaupapa can find information on Saint Damien at the Damien Center in Kaunakakai, and may worship at Our Lady of Seven Sorrows (just west of Kaunakakai) or at St. Vincent Ferrer in Maunaloa.

TOP ATTRACTIONS

Coffees of Hawaii. Visit the headquarters of a 500-acre Molokai coffee plantation. There's a small gift shop that sells all things coffee, and live music is performed on the covered lanai every Tuesday and Thursday at lunchtime. ✉ *1630 Farrington Hwy., off Rte. 470, Kualapuu* ☎ *808/567–9490* 🌐 *www.coffeesofhawaii.com* ⏲ *Closed Sat. 2 pm and Sun.*

Kaunakakai. Central Molokai's main town looks like a classic 1940s movie set. Along the one-block main drag is a cultural grab bag of restaurants and shops, and many people are friendly and willing to supply directions. Preferred dress is shorts and a tank top, and no one wears anything fancier than a cotton skirt or aloha shirt. ✉ *Rte. 460, 3 blocks north of Kaunakakai Wharf, Kaunakakai.*

Molokai Plumerias. The sweet smell of plumeria surrounds you at this 10-acre orchard containing thousands of these fragrant trees. Purchase a lei to go, or for $25 owner Dick Wheeler will give you a basket, set you free to pick your own blossoms, then teach you how to string your own lei. For the latter, it's best to call first for an appointment. ✉ *1342 Maunaloa Hwy., Kaunakakai* ☎ *808/553–3391* 🌐 *www.molokaiplumerias.com.*

Palaau State Park. One of the island's few formal recreation areas, this 233-acre retreat sits at a 1,000-foot elevation. A short path through an ironwood forest leads to **Kalaupapa Lookout,** a magnificent overlook with views of the town of Kalaupapa and the 1,664-foot-high sea cliffs protecting it. Informative plaques have facts about leprosy, Saint

Damien, and the colony. The park is also the site of **Kaule O Nanahoa** (Phallus of Nanahoa), where women in old Hawaii would come to the rock to enhance their fertility; it is said some still do. Because the rock is a sacred site, be respectful and don't deface the boulders. The park is well maintained, with trails, camping facilities, restrooms, and picnic tables. ✉ *Rte. 470, Kaunakakai* ✣ *Take Hwy. 460 west from Kaunakakai and then head mauka (toward the mountains) on Hwy. 470, which ends at the park* 🎟 *Free.*

Purdy's Macadamia Nut Farm. Molokai's only working macadamia-nut farm is open for educational tours hosted by the knowledgeable and entertaining owner. A family business in Hoolehua, the farm takes up 1½ acres with a flourishing grove of 50 original trees that are more than 90 years old, as well as several hundred younger trees. The nuts taste delicious right out of the shell, home roasted, or dipped in macadamia-blossom honey. Look for Purdy's sign behind Molokai High School. ✉ *Lihi Pali Ave., Hoolehua* ☎ *808/567–6601* 🌐 *www.molokai-aloha.com/macnuts* 🎟 *Free* 🕒 *Closed Sun. and Mon.*

R.W. Meyer Sugar Mill and Molokai Museum. Built in 1877, the fully restored, three-room sugar mill has been reconstructed as a testament to Molokai's agricultural history. It is located next to the Molokai Museum and is usually included in the museum tour. Several interesting machines from the past are on display, including a mule-driven cane crusher and a steam engine. The museum contains changing exhibits on the island's early history and has a gift shop. ✉ *Rte. 470, Kualapuu* ✣ *2 miles southwest of Palaau State Park* ☎ *808/567–6436* 🎟 *$5* 🕒 *Closed Sun.*

KALAUPAPA PENINSULA

The Kalaupapa Airport is in the town of Kalaupapa.

The most remote area in the entire Hawaiian Islands is a place of stunning natural beauty coupled with a tragic past. It's here that residents of Hawaii who displayed symptoms of Hansen's disease (formerly known as leprosy) were permanently exiled beginning in 1866. Today, the peninsula is still isolated—it's accessible only by air, on foot, or on a mule. But a day spent here is, without a doubt, a profound, once-in-a-lifetime experience.

■ TIP→ Disputes continue between the land owner and the Kalaupapa Guided Mule Tour company. Call in advance to verify times and make reservations.

GETTING HERE AND AROUND

Unless you fly (through Makani Kai Air), the only way into Kalaupapa National Historical Park is to travel down a dizzying switchback trail, either on foot or by mule. Going down on foot takes at least an hour, but you must allow 90 minutes for the return; going down by mule is even slower, taking two hours and the same going back up. The switchbacks are numbered—26 in all—and descend 1,700 feet to sea level in just under 3 miles. The steep trail is more of a staircase, and most of the trail is shaded. However, the footing is uneven and there is little to keep you from pitching over the side. If you don't mind heights, you can stare straight down to the ocean for most of the way. It's strenuous regardless of which method you choose.

The Kalaupapa Trail and Peninsula are all part of Kalaupapa National Historical Park (☎ *808/567–6802* 🌐 *www.nps.gov/kala*), which is open every day but Sunday for tours only. Keep in mind, there are no public facilities (except an occasional restroom) anywhere in the park. Pack your own food and water, as well as light rain gear, sunscreen, and bug repellent.

TOURS

Damien Tours. The only way to explore Kalaupapa once you get there, this four-hour bus tour is operated by a resident family. You must bring your own snacks, lunch, and water if you travel by plane or hike in, and remain on the bus except for designated rest stops. No one may wander alone at Kalaupapa, and photographs are not allowed without prior permission of the subject. Remember this is home to the people here. No children under 16 are allowed. The tour starts at 10 am; hikers must be down in the park by then. ✉ *Kalaupapa* ☎ *808/567–6171* 🎫 *$60* 🕐 *Closed Sun.*

Fodor's Choice ★ **Kalaupapa Guided Mule Tour.** Mount a friendly, well-trained mule and wind along a thrilling 3-mile, 26-switchback trail to reach the town of Kalaupapa, which was once home to patients with leprosy who were exiled to this remote spot. The path was built in 1886 as a supply route for the settlement below. Once in Kalaupapa, you take a guided tour of the town and enjoy a light picnic lunch. The trail traverses some of the highest sea cliffs in the world, and views are spectacular. **TIP→ Only those in good shape should attempt the ride, as two hours each way on a mule can take its toll.** You must be at least 16 years old and weigh no more than 250 pounds; pregnant women are not allowed. The entire event takes seven hours. ⚠ **Disputes continue between the land owner and the tour company. Call in advance to verify times and make reservations.** The same outfit can arrange for you to hike down or fly in. No one is allowed in the park or on the trail without booking a tour. ✉ *100 Kalae Hwy., Kualapuu* ☎ *808/567–6088, 800/567–7550* 🌐 *www.muleride.com* 🎫 *$209.*

Makani Kai Air. If you plan to visit Kalaupapa National Historical Park, but want to avoid the strenuous three-hour (round-trip) hike or two-hour mule ride, Makani Kai Air provides flights into the park from the Molokai Airport. ✉ *Kalaupapa* ☎ *808/834–1111* 🌐 *www.makanikaiair.com.*

TOP ATTRACTIONS

Kalaupapa National Historical Park. For 100 years, this remote strip of land was "the loneliest place on Earth," a beautiful yet feared place of exile for those suffering from leprosy (now known as Hansen's disease). Today, visitors to Molokai's **Kalaupapa Peninsula,** open every day but Sunday, can admire the tall sea cliffs, rain-chiseled valleys, and tiny islets along the coast. The park tells a poignant human story, as the Kalaupapa Peninsula was once a community of about 1,000 people who were banished from their homes in Hawaii. It also recounts the

CLOSE UP

The Truth About Hansen's Disease

- A cure for leprosy has been available since 1941. Multidrug therapy, a rapid cure, has been available since 1981.
- With treatment, none of the disabilities traditionally associated with leprosy need occur.
- Most people have a natural immunity to leprosy. Only 5% of the world's population is even susceptible to the disease.
- There are still more than 200,000 new cases of leprosy each year; the majority are in India.
- All new cases of leprosy are treated on an outpatient basis.
- The term "leper" is offensive and should not be used. It is appropriate to say "a person is affected by leprosy" or "by Hansen's disease."

wonderful work of Father Damien, a Belgian missionary who arrived in 1873 to work with the patients. He died in 1889 from leprosy and was canonized as a saint by the Catholic Church in 2009. Mother Marianne Cope, who continued St. Damien's work after his death, was canonized in 2012.

Today there are about eight patients still living in Kalaupapa—now by choice, as the disease is treatable. Out of respect to these people, visitors must be at least 16 years old, cannot stay overnight, and must be on a guided tour or invited by a resident. Photographing patients without their permission is forbidden. Guided tours of the settlement, which start at 10 am, are available by reservation through Damien Tours if you're hiking or flying in. The Kalaupapa Guided Mule Tour can also accommodate hikers, in addition to rides on their mules. Reserve well in advance to avoid disappointment. There are no public facilities (except an occasional restroom) anywhere in the park. Pack your own food and water, as well as light rain gear, sunscreen, and bug repellent.

Unless you fly with Makani Kai Air, the only way into Kalaupapa National Historic Park is on the dizzying switchback **Kalaupapa Trail.** The switchbacks are numbered—26 in all—and descend 1,700 feet to sea level in just under 3 miles. The steep trail is more of a staircase, and most of the trail is shaded. ⚠ **Footing on the Kalaupapa Trail is uneven and there is little to keep you from pitching over the side.** Hikers should be in good physical condition. If you don't mind heights, you can stare straight down to the ocean for most of the way. There is ample parking near the end of Highway 470. You can access Kalaupapa Trail off Highway 470 near Kalaupapa Overlook. ✉ *Hwy. 470, Kualapuu* ☎ *808/567–6802* 🌐 *www.nps.gov/kala.*

EAST MOLOKAI

Halawa Valley is 36 miles northeast of the airport.

On the beautifully undeveloped east end of Molokai you can find ancient fishponds, a magnificent coastline, splendid ocean views, and a fertile valley that's been inhabited for 14 centuries. The eastern uplands are flanked by Mt. Kamakou, the island's highest point at 4,970 feet and home to the Nature Conservancy's Kamakou Preserve. Mist hangs over waterfall-filled valleys, and ancient lava cliffs jut out into the sea.

GETTING HERE AND AROUND

Driving the east end is a scenic adventure, but the road narrows and becomes curvy after the 20-mile marker. Take your time, especially in the seaside lane, and watch for oncoming traffic. Driving at night is not recommended.

TOP ATTRACTIONS

Fodor's Choice ★

Halawa Valley. The Solatorio *Ohana* (family) leads hikes through the valley, the oldest recorded habitation on Molokai. It is home to two sacrificial temples and many historic sites. Inhabitants grew taro and fished from 650 until the 1960s, when an enormous flood wiped out the taro patches and forced old-timers to abandon their traditional lifestyle. Now, a new generation of Hawaiians has begun the challenging task of restoring the taro fields. Much of this work involves rerouting streams to flow through carefully engineered level ponds called *loi*. Taro plants, with their big, dancing leaves, grow in the submerged mud of the loi, where the water is always cool and flowing. Hawaiians believe that the taro plant is their ancestor and revere it both as sustenance and as a spiritual necessity. The 3.4-mile round-trip valley hike, which goes to **Moaula Falls,** a 250-foot cascade, is rated intermediate to advanced and includes two moderate river crossings (so your feet will get wet). A $60 fee per adult supports restoration efforts. ✉ *Eastern end of Rte. 450* ☎ *808/542–1855* 🌐 *www.halawavalleymolokai.com* 🎟 *$60.*

OFF THE BEATEN PATH

Kamakou Preserve. Tucked away on the slopes of Mt. Kamakou, Molokai's highest peak, this 2,774-acre rain-forest preserve is a dazzling wonderland full of wet *ohia* forests (hardwood trees of the myrtle family, with red blossoms called *lehua*), rare bogs, and native trees and wildlife. Guided educational tours, limited to eight people, are held one Saturday each month March–October. Reserve well in advance, as these excursions fill up several months in advance. ✉ *23 Pueo Pl., Kualapuu* ☎ *808/553–5236* 🌐 *www.nature.org* 🎟 *Free.*

BEACHES

Molokai's unique geography gives the island plenty of drama and spectacle along the shorelines but not so many places for seaside basking and bathing. The long north shore consists mostly of towering cliffs that plunge directly into the sea and is inaccessible except by boat, and even then only in summer. Much of the south shore is enclosed by a huge reef, which stands as far as a mile offshore and blunts the action of the waves. Within this reef you can find a thin strip of sand, but the water here is flat, shallow, and at times clouded with silt. This reef area is best suited to wading, pole fishing, kayaking, and paddleboarding.

The big, fat, sandy beaches lie along the west end. The largest of these—the second largest in the Islands—is Papohaku Beach, which fronts a grassy park shaded by a grove of *kiawe* (mesquite) trees. These stretches of west-end sand are generally unpopulated. At the east end, where the road hugs the sinuous shoreline, you encounter a number of pocket-size beaches in rocky coves, good for snorkeling. Don't venture too far out, however, or you can find yourself caught in dangerous currents. The island's east-end road ends at Halawa Valley with its unique double bay, which is not recommended for swimming.

If you need snorkeling gear, head to Molokai Fish & Dive at the west end of Kaunakakai's only commercial strip, or rent beach chairs, surfboards, or umbrellas from Beach Break, 4 miles west of Kaunakakai. To rent kayaks contact Molokai Outdoors.

Department of Parks, Land and Natural Resources. All of Hawaii's beaches are free and public. None of the beaches on Molokai have telephones or lifeguards, and they're all under the jurisdiction of the Department of Parks, Land and Natural Resources. ☎ *808/587–0300* 🌐 *www.hawaiistateparks.org.*

WEST MOLOKAI

Molokai's west end looks across a wide channel to the island of Oahu. This crescent-shape cup of coastline holds the island's best sandy beaches as well as the sunniest weather. Remember: all beaches are public property, even those that front developments, and most have public access roads. *Beaches below are listed from north to south.*

Kawakiu Beach. Seclusion is yours at this remote, beautiful, white-sand beach, accessible by four-wheel-drive vehicle (through a gate that is sometimes locked) or a 45-minute walk. To get here, drive to Paniolo Hale off Kaluakoi Road and look for a dirt road off to the right. Park here and hike in or, with a four-wheel-drive vehicle, drive along the dirt road to beach. ⚠ **Rocks and undertow make swimming extremely dangerous at times, so use caution.** **Amenities:** none. **Best for:** solitude. ✉ *Off Kaluakoi Rd., Maunaloa.*

Kepuhi Beach. The Kaluakoi Hotel is closed, but its half mile of ivory sand is still accessible. The beach shines against the turquoise sea, black outcroppings of lava, and magenta bougainvillea blossoms. When the sea is perfectly calm, lava ridges in the water make good snorkeling spots. With any surf at all, however, the water around these rocky places churns and foams, wiping out visibility and making it difficult to avoid being slammed into the jagged rocks. **Amenities:** none. **Best for:** snorkeling; walking. ✉ *Kaluakoi Rd., Maunaloa.*

Fodor's Choice ★ **Papohaku Beach.** One of the most sensational beaches in Hawaii, Papohaku is a 3-mile-long strip of light golden sand, the longest of its kind on the island. There's so much sand here that Honolulu once purchased bargeloads of the stuff to replenish Waikiki Beach. A shady beach park just inland is the site of the Ka Hula Piko Festival, held each year in May. The park is also a great sunset-facing spot for a rustic afternoon barbecue. A park ranger patrols the area periodically. ■TIP→ **Swimming is not recommended, as there's a dangerous undertow except on exceptionally calm summer days.** **Amenities:** showers; toilets. **Best for:** sunset; walking. ✉ *Kaluakoi Rd., Maunaloa* ✣ *2 miles south of the former Kaluakoi Hotel.*

Kapukahehu Bay. The sandy protected cove is usually completely deserted on weekdays but can fill up when the surf is up. The water in the cove is clear and shallow with plenty of well-worn rocky areas. These conditions make for excellent snorkeling, swimming, and body boarding on calm days. Locals like to surf in a break called Dixie's or Dixie Maru. **Amenities:** none. **Best for:** snorkeling; surfing; swimming. ✉ *End of Kaluakoi Rd., 3½ miles south of Papohaku Beach, Maunaloa.*

BEACH SAFETY

Unlike protected shorelines like Kaanapali on Maui, the coasts of Molokai are exposed to rough sea channels and dangerous rip currents. The ocean tends to be calmer in the morning and in summer. No matter what the time, however, always study the sea before entering. Unless the water is placid and the wave action minimal, it's best to stay on shore, even though locals may be in the water. Don't underestimate the power of the ocean. Protect yourself with sunblock; cool breezes make it easy to underestimate the power of the sun as well.

CENTRAL MOLOKAI

The south shore is mostly a huge, reef-walled expanse of flat saltwater edged with a thin strip of gritty sand and stones, mangrove swamps, and the amazing system of fishponds constructed by the chiefs of ancient Molokai. From this shore you can look out across glassy water to see people standing on top of the sea—actually, way out on top of the reef—casting fishing lines into the distant waves. This is not a great area for beaches but is a good place to snorkel or wade in the shallows.

One Alii Beach Park. Clear, close views of Maui and Lanai across the Pailolo Channel dominate One Alii Beach Park (*One* is pronounced "o-nay," not "won"), the only well-maintained beach park on the island's south-central shore. Molokai folks gather here for family reunions and community celebrations; the park's tightly trimmed expanse of lawn could almost accommodate the entire island's population. Swimming within the reef is perfectly safe, but don't expect to catch any waves. Nearby is the restored One Alii fishpond (it is appropriate only for native Hawaiians to fish here). **Amenities:** playground, showers; toilets. **Best for:** parties; swimming. ✉ *Rte. 450, Kaunakakai* ✣ *east of Hotel Molokai.*

EAST MOLOKAI

The east end unfolds as a coastal drive with turnouts for tiny cove beaches—good places for snorkeling, shore fishing, or scuba exploring. Rocky little Mokuhooniki Island marks the eastern point of the island and serves as a nursery for humpback whales in winter and nesting seabirds in spring. The road loops around the east end, then descends and ends at Halawa Valley.

Halawa Beach Park. The vigorous water that gouged the steep, spectacular Halawa Valley also carved out two adjacent bays. Accumulations of coarse sand and river rock have created some protected pools that are good for wading or floating around. You might see surfers, but it's not wise to entrust your safety to the turbulent open ocean along this coast. Most people come here to hang out and absorb the beauty of Halawa Valley. The valley itself is private property, so do not wander without a guide. **Amenities:** toilets. **Best for:** solitude. ✉ *End of Rte. 450, Kaunakakai.*

Waialua Beach Park. Also known as Twenty Mile Beach, this arched stretch of sand leads to one of the most popular snorkeling spots on the island. The water here, protected by the flanks of the little bay, is often so clear and shallow that even from land you can watch fish swimming among the coral heads. Watch out for traffic when you enter the highway. ■ TIP→ **This is a pleasant place to stop on the drive around the east end.** **Amenities:** none. **Best for:** snorkeling; swimming. ✉ *Rte. 450 near mile marker 20.*

6

WHERE TO EAT

During a week's stay, you might easily hit all the dining spots worth a visit and then return to your favorites for a second round. The dining scene is fun, because it's a microcosm of Hawaii's diverse cultures. You can find locally grown vegetarian foods, spicy Filipino cuisine, or Hawaiian fish with a Japanese influence—such as tuna, mullet, and moonfish that's grilled, sautéed, or mixed with seaweed to make *poke* (salted and seasoned raw fish).

Most eating establishments are on Ala Malama Street in Kaunakakai. If you're heading to West Molokai for the day, be sure to stock up on provisions, as there is no place to eat there. If you are on the east end, stop by **Manae Goods & Grindz** (☎ *808/558–8186*) near mile marker 16 for good local seafood plates, burgers, and ice cream.

WHAT IT COSTS

	$	$$	$$$	$$$$
Restaurants	under $18	$18–$26	$27–$35	over $35

Restaurant prices are the average cost of a main course at dinner or, if dinner is not served, at lunch.

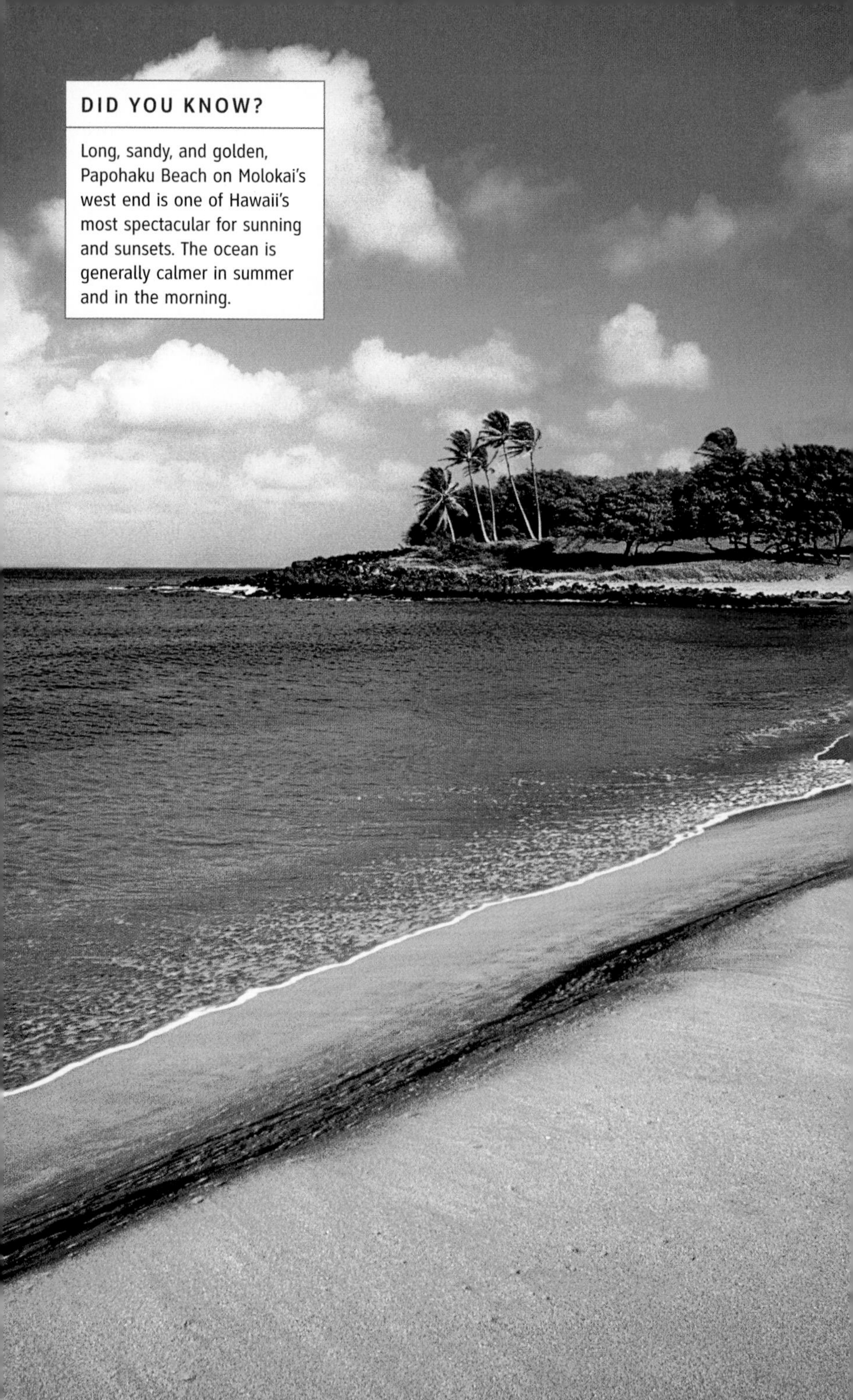
DID YOU KNOW?
Long, sandy, and golden, Papohaku Beach on Molokai's west end is one of Hawaii's most spectacular for sunning and sunsets. The ocean is generally calmer in summer and in the morning.

CENTRAL MOLOKAI

Central Molokai offers most of the island's dining options.

$$ MODERN HAWAIIAN Fodor's Choice ★ **Hiro's Ohana Grill.** Located in Hotel Molokai, the island's only oceanfront restaurant is also its fanciest and best place to grab a drink or watch the game on TV. Enjoy pasta, steak, shrimp, or fish while watching the sunset and listening to live music, and don't be surprised if the couple you saw hiking is seated at the table right next to you. **Known for:** shrimp pesto over linguini; live music and hula; whale-watching from your table in winter. *Average main: $25 Hotel Molokai, 1300 Kamehameha V Hwy., Kaunakakai 808/660–3400.*

$ AMERICAN **Kamoi Snack-n-Go.** The old school interior at this "Molokai rest stop" feels a bit like a time warp, making it the perfect place to try one (or two) of the 30 or more flavors of Dave's Hawaiian Ice Cream; it's the only place that serves it on the island. Sit in the refreshing breeze on one of the benches outside to enjoy your cone, pick up snacks, crack seed, water, and cold drinks. **Known for:** tropical flavors of Dave's Hawaiian Ice Cream; milkshakes; grab-n-go snacks and drinks. *Average main: $6 28 Kamoi St., Kaunakakai 808/553–3742.*

$ CAFÉ **Kanemitsu's Bakery and Coffee Shop.** Stop at this James Beard–nominated Molokai institution for morning coffee and some Molokai bread—a sweet, pan-style white loaf that makes excellent cinnamon toast; by night, the famous "Hot Bread Lane" is a Molokai institution. You can also try a taste of *lavash,* a pricey flatbread flavored with sesame, taro, Maui onion, Parmesan cheese, or jalapeño. **Known for:** Molokai sweet bread; evening dessert breads. *Average main: $9 79 Ala Malama St., Kaunakakai 808/553–5855.*

$ HAWAIIAN **Kualapuu Cookhouse.** Across the street from Kualapuu Market, this laid-back diner is a local favorite set in a classic, refurbished, green-and-white plantation house that's decorated with local photography and artwork and accented with a shady lanai. Typical fare at Kualapuu's only restaurant is a plate of chicken, pork, or hamburger steak served with rice, but there's also the more expensive spicy crusted ahi at dinner. **Known for:** chicken katsu; BYOB; laid-back atmosphere. *Average main: $13 Farrington Hwy., 1 block west of Rte. 470, Kualapuu 808/567–9655 No credit cards.*

$ HAWAIIAN **Manae Goods & Grindz.** The best place to grab a snack or picnic supplies is this store, 16 miles east of Kaunakakai. It's the only place on the east end where you can find essentials such as ice and bread, and not-so-essentials such as seafood plate lunches, bentos, burgers, shakes, and refreshing smoothies. **Known for:** the only place to get food on the east end; banana pancakes; loco moco and plate lunch. *Average main: $9 Rte. 450, Kaunakakai 808/558–8498, 808/558–8186 Lunch counter closed Wed.; no dinner.*

$ BURGER **Molokai Burger.** Clean and cheery, Molokai Burger offers both drive-through and eat-in options. Healthier items include breakfast sandwiches without cheese and mayonnaise, salads featuring local veggies, and whole wheat buns for your burgers. **Known for:** affordable burgers; convenient and quick; centrally located. *Average main: $7 20 W. Kamehameha V Hwy., Kaunakakai 808/553–3533 www.molokai-burger.com Closed Sun.*

$ AMERICAN ✕ **Molokai Pizza Cafe.** Cheerful and busy, this is a popular gathering spot for local families and a good place to pick up food for a picnic. Pizza, sandwiches, salads, pasta, and fresh fish are simply prepared and served without fuss. **Known for:** games for the kids; linguine alfredo; open on Sundays. *Average main: $15 ✉ 15 Kaunakakai Pl. , at Wharf Rd., Kaunakakai ☎ 808/553–3288.*

$ AMERICAN Fodor's Choice ★ ✕ **Paddlers' Restaurant and Bar.** New owners breathed new life—and a new menu—into this popular Molokai standout, and the result is a fusion of gourmet cuisine that stays true to the island's roots, with tacos carne asada and heaping plates of loco moco, in a laid-back setting. The bar has the island's only draft beer, there's live music most nights, and produce is locally sourced when available—especially with daily fish specials. **Known for:** steak and frites; Tomato Jam burger; live performance by Na Kupuna on Fridays from 4 to 6 pm. *Average main: $16 ✉ 10 N. Mohala St., Kaunakakai ☎ 808/553–3300 www.paddlersrestaurant.com Closed Sun.*

$ DELI ✕ **Sundown Deli.** A Molokai staple for more than 20 years, this small deli focuses on freshly made takeout food. Sandwiches come on a half dozen types of bread and the homemade soups are outstanding. **Known for:** homemade soups; affordable wraps. *Average main: $8 ✉ 145 Ala Malama St., Kaunakakai ☎ 808/553–3713 Closed weekends. No dinner.*

WHERE TO STAY

The coastline along Molokai's west end has ocean-view condominium units and luxury homes available as vacation rentals. Central Molokai offers seaside condominiums. The only lodgings on the east end are some guest cottages in magical settings and the cottages and ranch lodge at Puu O Hoku. Note that room rates do not include 13.42% sales tax.

Note: Maui County has regulations concerning vacation rentals; to avoid disappointment, always contact the property manager or the owner and ask if the accommodations have the proper permits and are in compliance with local ordinances. *Hotel reviews have been shortened. For full information, visit Fodors.com.*

WHAT IT COSTS

	$	$$	$$$	$$$$
Hotels	under $181	$181–$260	$261–$340	over $340

Hotel prices are the lowest cost of a standard double room in high season. Condo price categories reflect studio and one-bedroom rates.

WEST MOLOKAI

If you want to stay in West Molokai so you'll have access to unspoiled beaches, your only choices are condos or vacation homes. Note that units fronting the abandoned Kaluakoi golf course present a bit of a dismal view.

$ RENTAL **Ke Nani Kai.** These pleasant, spacious one- and two-bedroom condos—each with a washer, dryer, and a fully equipped kitchen—near the beach have ocean views and nicely maintained tropical landscaping. **Pros:** on island's secluded west end; uncrowded pool; beach is across the road. **Cons:** amenities vary from unit to unit; far from commercial center; some units overlook abandoned golf course. *Rooms from: $125* ✉ *50 Kepuhi Beach Rd., Maunaloa* ☎ *808/553–8334, 800/367–2984* 🌐 *www.molokai-vacation-rental.net* *120 units* *No meals.*

$ RENTAL Fodor's Choice ★ **Paniolo Hale.** Perched high on a ridge overlooking a favorite local surfing spot, this is Molokai's best condominium property and boasts mature tropical landscaping and a private serene setting. **Pros:** close to beach; quiet surroundings; perfect if you are an expert surfer. **Cons:** amenities vary; far from shopping; golf course units front abandoned course. *Rooms from: $125* ✉ *100 Lio Pl., Kaunakakai* ☎ *808/553–8334, 800/367–2984* 🌐 *www.molokai-vacation-rental.net* *77 units* *No meals.*

CENTRAL MOLOKAI

There are two condo properties in this area, one close to shopping and dining in Kaunakakai, and the other on the way to the east end.

$ HOTEL Fodor's Choice ★ **Hotel Molokai.** At this local favorite, Polynesian-style bungalows are scattered around the nicely landscaped property, many overlooking the reef and distant Lanai. **Pros:** five minutes to town; some units have kitchenettes; authentic Hawaiian entertainment. **Cons:** not many frills; lower-priced rooms are small and plain; evening live music can be loud. *Rooms from: $179* ✉ *1300 Kamehameha V Hwy., Kaunakakai* ☎ *808/660–3408, 877/553–5347* 🌐 *www.hotelmolokai.com* *40 rooms* *Some meals.*

$ RENTAL **Molokai Shores.** Many of the units in this three-story condominium complex have a view of the ocean and Lanai in the distance, and there's a chance to see whales in season. **Pros:** convenient location; some units upgraded; near water. **Cons:** older accommodations; units close to highway can be noisy; beach is narrow and water is too shallow for swimming. *Rooms from: $169* ✉ *1000 Kamehameha V Hwy., Kaunakakai* ☎ *808/553–8334, 800/367–2984* 🌐 *www.molokai-vacation-rental.net* *100 units* *No meals.*

$ RENTAL **Wavecrest.** This 5-acre oceanfront condominium complex is convenient if you want to explore the east side of the island—it's 13 miles east of Kaunakakai—with access to a beautiful reef, excellent snorkeling, and kayaking. **Pros:** convenient location for exploring the east end; good value; nicely maintained grounds. **Cons:** amenities vary; far from shopping; area sometimes gets windy. *Rooms from: $125* ✉ *Rte. 450, near mile marker 13, Kaunakakai* ☎ *800/367–2984, 808/553–8334* 🌐 *www.molokai-vacation-rental.net* *126 units* *No meals.*

EAST MOLOKAI

Puu O Hoku Ranch, a rental facility on East Molokai, is the main lodging option on this side of the island. The ranch is quite far from the center of the island.

$$ RENTAL FAMILY Fodor's Choice ★ **Dunbar Beachfront Cottages.** Perfect for a comfortable base in the country, think of these two oceanfront, plantation-style cottages as your own private beach home on Molokai's east end; each has a full kitchen, washer and dryer, and ocean-facing lanai. **Pros:** oceanfront location; full kitchen and amenities; convenient location to east end beaches. **Cons:** isolated and far from town; close to the highway; additional cleaning fee. *Rooms from: $190 ✉ 9916 Kamehameha V Hwy., Kaunakakai ✣ Just past the 18 mile marker www.molokai-beachfront-cottages.com 2 cottages No meals No credit cards.*

$$ B&B/INN **Puu O Hoku Ranch.** At the east end of Molokai, these ocean-view accommodations are on 14,000 isolated acres of pasture and forest—a remote and serene location for people who want to get away from it all or meet in a retreat atmosphere. **Pros:** ideal for large groups; authentic working ranch; great hiking. **Cons:** on remote east end of island; road to property is narrow and winding; area can sometimes get windy. *Rooms from: $200 ✉ Rte. 450 near mile marker 25, Kaunakakai ☎ 888/573–7775, 808/558–8109 www.puuohoku.com 3 cottages, 1 lodge No meals.*

WATER SPORTS AND TOURS

Molokai's shoreline topography limits opportunities for water sports. Sea cliffs dominate the north shore; the south shore is largely encased by a huge, taming reef. **TIP→ Open-sea access at west-end and east-end beaches should be used only by experienced ocean swimmers, and then with caution because seas are rough, especially in winter.** Generally speaking, there's no one around—certainly not lifeguards—if you get into trouble. For this reason alone, guided excursions are recommended. At least be sure to ask for advice from outfitters or residents. Two kinds of water activities predominate: kayaking within the reef area, and open-sea excursions on charter boats, most of which tie up at Kaunakakai Wharf.

BODY BOARDING AND BODYSURFING

You rarely see people body boarding or bodysurfing on Molokai, and the only surfing is for advanced wave riders. The best spots for body boarding when conditions are safe (occasional summer mornings) are the west-end beaches. Another option is to seek out waves at the east end around mile marker 20.

DEEP-SEA FISHING

For Molokai people, as in days of yore, the ocean is more of a larder than a playground. It's common to see residents fishing along the shoreline or atop South Shore Reef, using poles or lines. Deep-sea fishing by charter boat is a great Molokai adventure. The sea channels here, though often rough and windy, provide gorgeous views of several islands. Big fish are plentiful in these waters, especially mahimahi, marlin, and various kinds of tuna. Generally speaking, boat captains will customize the outing to your interests, share a lot of information about the island, and let you keep some or all of your catch.

EQUIPMENT

Molokai Fish & Dive. If you'd like to try your hand at fishing, you can rent or buy equipment and ask for advice here. ✉ *53 Ala Malama St., Kaunakakai* ☎ *808/553–5926* 🌐 *www.molokaifishanddive.com.*

BOATS AND CHARTERS

Alyce C. This 31-foot cruiser runs excellent sportfishing excursions in the capable hands of Captain Joe. Full-day and four- to five-hour trips are available upon the six-passenger boat; gear is provided. It's a rare day when you don't snag at least one memorable fish. ✉ *Kaunakakai Wharf, Kaunakakai Pl., Kaunakakai* ☎ *808/558–8377* 🌐 *www.alycec-sportfishing.com* 🎟 *From $450.*

Fun Hogs Sportfishing. Trim and speedy, the 27-foot flybridge boat named *Ahi* offers four-hour, six-hour, and eight-hour sportfishing excursions. Skipper Mike Holmes also provides one-way or round-trip fishing expeditions to Lanai, as well as sunset cruises and whale-watching trips in winter. ✉ *Kaunakakai Wharf, Kaunakakai Pl., Kaunakakai* ☎ *808/336–0047* 🌐 *www.molokaifishing.com* 🎟 *From $450.*

Molokai Action Adventures. Walter Naki has traveled (and fished) all over the globe. He will create customized fishing expeditions and gladly share his wealth of experience. He will also take you to remote beaches for a day of swimming. If you want to explore the north side under the great sea cliffs, this is the way to go. His 21-foot *Boston Whaler* is usually seen in the east end at the mouth of Halawa Valley. ✉ *Kaunakakai* ☎ *808/558–8184* 🎟 *From $300.*

KAYAKING

Molokai's south shore is enclosed by the largest reef system in the United States—an area of shallow protected sea that stretches over 30 miles. This reef gives inexperienced paddlers an unusually safe, calm environment for shoreline exploring. ■ TIP→ **Outside the reef, Molokai waters are often rough, and strong winds can blow you out to sea. Kayakers out here should be strong, experienced, and cautious.**

BEST SPOTS

South Shore Reef. This reef's area is superb for flat-water kayaking any day of the year. Get out in the morning before the wind picks up and paddle east, exploring the ancient Hawaiian fishponds. When you turn around, the wind will usually give you a push home. ■ TIP→ **For a kayak, contact Molokai Outdoors. For paddleboard lessons, contact Molokai Ocean Tours.** ✉ *Kaunakakai.*

6

EQUIPMENT, LESSONS, AND TOURS

Molokai Ocean Tours. At the west end of Kaunakakai's commercial strip, this outfitter offers paddleboard lessons inside the South Shore Reef. ✉ *40 Ala Malama St., Kaunakakai* ☎ *808/553–3290* 🌐 *www.molokai-oceantours.com* 🎫 *From $65.*

Molokai Outdoors. For guided kayak and paddleboard tours, this long-time Molokai activity company offers five-mile, guided, downwind runs along Molokai's southern coast. ✉ *Kaunakakai* ☎ *808/633–8700, 877/553–4477* 🌐 *www.molokai-outdoors.com* 🎫 *From $99 per person.*

SCUBA DIVING

Molokai Fish & Dive is the only PADI-certified dive company on Molokai. Shoreline access for divers is extremely limited, even nonexistent in winter. Boat diving is the way to go. Without guidance, visiting divers can easily find themselves in risky situations with wicked currents. Proper guidance, however, opens an undersea world rarely seen.

SNORKELING

During the times when swimming is safe—mainly in summer—just about every beach on Molokai offers good snorkeling along the lava outcroppings in the island's clean and pristine waters. Although rough in winter, Kepuhi Beach is a prime spot in summer. Certain spots inside the South Shore Reef are also worth checking out.

BEST SPOTS

During the summer, **Kepuhi Beach,** on Molokai's west end, offers excellent snorkeling opportunities. The ½-mile-long stretch has plenty of rocky nooks that swirl with sea life. Take Kaluakoi Road all the way to the west end, park at the now-closed Kaluakoi Resort, and walk to the beach. Avoid Kepuhi Beach in winter, as the sea is rough here.

At **Waialua Beach Park,** on Molokai's east end, you'll find a thin curve of sand that rims a sheltered little bay loaded with coral heads and aquatic life. The water here is shallow—sometimes so shallow that you bump into the underwater landscape—and it's crystal clear. Pull off the road near mile marker 20.

EQUIPMENT AND TOURS

Rent snorkel sets from Molokai Fish & Dive in Kaunakakai. Rental fees are nominal ($7–$10 per day). All the charter boats carry snorkel gear and include dive stops.

Fun Hogs Sportfishing. Mike Holmes, captain of the 27-foot *Ahi,* knows the island waters intimately, likes to have fun, and is willing to arrange any type of excursion—for example, one dedicated entirely to snorkeling. His two-hour snorkel trips leave early in the morning and explore rarely seen fish and turtle sites outside the reef. ✉ *Kaunakakai Wharf, Kaunakakai Pl., Kaunakakai* ☎ *808/336–0047* 🌐 *www.molokaifishing.com* 🎫 *From $70 per person.*

Bikers on Molokai can explore the north-shore sea cliffs overlooking the Kalaupapa Peninsula.

Molokai Fish & Dive. Climb aboard a 31-foot twin-hull PowerCat for a snorkeling trip to Molokai's pristine barrier reef. Trips include equipment, water, and soft drinks. ✉ *53 Ala Malama St., Kaunakakai* ☎ *808/553–5926* 🌐 *www.molokaifishanddive.com* 🎫 *From $79 per person.*

WHALE-WATCHING

Although Maui gets all the credit for the local wintering humpback-whale population, the big cetaceans also come to Molokai December–April. Mokuhooniki Island at the east end serves as a whale nursery and courting ground, and the whales pass back and forth along the south shore. This being Molokai, whale-watching here will never involve floating amid a group of boats all ogling the same whale.

BOATS AND CHARTERS

Alyce C. Although this six-passenger sportfishing boat is usually busy hooking mahimahi and marlin, the captain will gladly take you on a three-hour excursion to admire the humpback whales. ■ **TIP→ The price is based on the number of people in your group.** ✉ *Kaunakakai Wharf, Kaunakakai Pl., Kaunakakai* ☎ *808/558–8377* 🌐 *www.alycecsportfishing.com* 🎫 *From $75 per person.*

Ama Lua. The crew of this 31-foot dive boat, which holds up to 12 passengers, is respectful of the whales and the laws that protect them. A two-hour whale-watching trip departs from Kaunakakai Wharf at 7 am daily, December–April. ✉ *Molokai Fish & Dive, 53 Ala Malama St., Kaunakakai* ☎ *808/553–5926* 🌐 *www.molokaifishanddive.com* 🎫 *From $79 per person.*

Fun Hogs Sportfishing. The *Ahi,* a flybridge sportfishing boat, takes you on 2½-hour whale-watching trips in the morning, December–April. ■ **TIP→ No food or drink is provided.** ✉ *Kaunakakai Wharf, Kaunakakai Pl., Kaunakakai* ☎ *808/336-0047* 🌐 *www.molokaifishing.com* 🎫 *From $70 per person.*

GOLF, HIKING, AND OUTDOOR ACTIVITIES

Activity vendors in Kaunakakai are a good source of information on outdoor adventures on Molokai. For a mellow round of golf, head to the island's only golf course, Ironwood Hills, where you'll likely share the greens with local residents. Molokai's steep and uncultivated terrain offers excellent hikes and some stellar views. Although the island is largely wild, all land is privately owned, so get permission before hiking.

BIKING

Cyclists who like to eat up the miles love Molokai, because its few roads are long, straight, and extremely rural. You can really go for it—there are no traffic lights and (most of the time) no traffic.

Molokai Bicycle. You can rent a bike here for the day; prices depend on the model, with reductions for additional days or week-long rentals. Bike trailers (for your drinks cooler, perhaps) are also available. ✉ *80 Mohala St., Kaunakakai* ☎ *808/553–5740* 🌐 *www.mauimolokaibicycle.com* 🎫 *Bikes from $25 per day, bike trailers from $15 per day.*

GOLF

Molokai is not a prime golf destination, but the sole 9-hole course makes for a pleasant afternoon.

Ironwood Hills Golf Course. Like other 9-hole plantation-era courses, Ironwood Hills is in a prime spot, with basic fairways and not always manicured greens. It helps if you like to play laid-back golf with locals and can handle occasionally rugged conditions. On the plus side, most holes offer ocean views. Fairways are *kukuya* grass and run through pine, ironwood, and eucalyptus trees. Clubs are rented on the honor system; there's not always someone there to assist you and you should bring your own water. Access is via a bumpy unpaved road. ✉ *Kalae Hwy., Kualapuu* ☎ *808/567–6000* 🎫 *$20 for 9 holes* ⛳ *9 holes, 3088 yards, par 34.*

HIKING

Rural and rugged, Molokai is an excellent place for hiking. Roads and developments are few. The island is steep, so hikes often combine spectacular views with hearty physical exertion. Because the island is small, you can come away with the feeling of really knowing the place. And you won't see many other people around. Much of what may look like deserted land is private property, so be careful not to trespass—seek permission or use an authorized guide.

BEST SPOTS

Kalaupapa Trail. You can hike down to the Kalaupapa Peninsula and back via this 3-mile, 26-switchback route. The trail is often nearly vertical, traversing the face of the high sea cliffs. You can reach Kalaupapa Trail off Highway 470 near Kalaupapa Overlook. Only those in excellent condition should attempt it. You must have made prior arrangements with Damien Tours in order to access Kalaupapa via this trail. ✉ *Off Hwy. 470, Kualapuu* ☎ *808/567–6171 Damien Tours.*

GOING WITH A GUIDE

Fodor's Choice ★ **Halawa Valley Falls Cultural Hike.** This gorgeous, steep-walled valley was carved by two rivers and is rich in history. Site of the earliest Polynesian settlement on Molokai, Halawa is a sustained island culture with its ingeniously designed *loi,* or taro fields. Because of a tsunami in 1948 and changing cultural conditions in the 1960s, the valley was largely abandoned. The Solatorio Ohana (family) is restoring the loi and taking visitors on guided hikes through the valley, which includes two of Molokai's *luakini heiau* (sacred temples), many historic sites, and the trail to **Moaula Falls,** a 250-foot cascade. Bring water, food, a *ho'okupu* (small gift or offering), insect repellent, and wear sturdy shoes that can get wet. The 3½-mile round-trip hike is rated intermediate to advanced and includes two moderate river crossings. ☎ *808/542–1855* 🌐 *www.halawavalleymolokai.com* 🎫 *$60.*

6

SHOPS AND SPAS

SHOPPING

Molokai has one main commercial area: Ala Malama Street in Kaunakakai. There are no department stores or shopping malls, and the clothing is typical island wear. Local shopping is friendly, and you may find hidden treasures. A very few family-run businesses define the main drag of Maunaloa, a rural former plantation town. Most stores in Kaunakakai are open Monday–Saturday 9–6.

WEST MOLOKAI

ARTS AND CRAFTS

Big Wind Kite Factory and Plantation Gallery. The factory has custom-made kites you can fly or display. Designs range from Hawaiian petroglyphs to *pueo* (owls). Also in stock are paper kites, minikites, and wind socks. Ask to go on the factory tour, or take a free kite-flying lesson. The adjacent gallery carries an eclectic collection of merchandise, including locally made crafts, Hawaiian books and CDs, jewelry, handmade batik sarongs, and an elegant line of women's linen clothing. ✉ *120 Maunaloa Hwy., Maunaloa* ☎ *808/552–2364* 🌐 *www.bigwindkites.com.*

FOOD

Maunaloa General Store. Stocking meat, produce, beverages, and dry goods, this shop is a convenient stop if you're planning a picnic at one of the west-end beaches. ✉ *200 Maunaloa Hwy., Maunaloa* ☎ *808/552–2346.*

DID YOU KNOW?

A hike through the Kamakou Preserve in East Molokai, on the slopes of the island's highest peak, reveals a lush rain forest with bogs and native wildlife. Sign up well in advance for a guided hike with the Nature Conservancy.

CENTRAL MOLOKAI

ARTS AND CRAFTS

Molokai Art From the Heart. A small downtown shop, this arts and crafts co-op has locally made folk art like dolls, clay flowers, silk sarongs, and children's items. The shop also carries original art by Molokai artists and Giclée prints, jewelry, locally produced music, and Saint Damien keepsakes. ✉ *64 Ala Malama St., Kaunakakai* ☎ *808/553–8018* 🌐 *www.molokaigallery.com.*

CLOTHING AND SHOES

Imports Gift Shop. Across from Kanemitsu Bakery, this one-stop shop offers fancy and casual island-style wear, including Roxy and Quicksilver for men, women, and children. ✉ *82 Ala Malama St., Kaunakakai* ☎ *808/553–5734.*

FOOD

Friendly Market Center. The best-stocked supermarket on the island has a slogan ("Your family store on Molokai") that is truly credible. Sun-and-surf essentials keep company with fresh produce, meat, groceries, and liquor. Locals say the food is fresher here than at the other major supermarket. ✉ *90 Ala Malama St., Kaunakakai* ☎ *808/553–5595.*

6

Home Town Groceries & Drygoods. For those staying at a condo on Molokai, this store will come in handy. It is like a mini-Costco, carrying bulk items. ✉ *93 Ala Malama St., Kaunakakai* ☎ *808/553–3858* ⏲ *Closed Sun.*

Kumu Farms. This is the most diverse working farm on Molokai, and *the* place to purchase fresh produce, herbs, and gourmet farm products. ✉ *Hua Ai Rd., off Mauna Loa Hwy., near Molokai Airport, Kaunakakai* ☎ *808/567–6480* ⏲ *Closed Sat.–Mon.*

Molokai Wines 'n' Spirits. Don't let the name fool you; along with a surprisingly good selection of fine wines and liquors, the store also carries cheeses and snacks. ✉ *77 Ala Malama St., Kaunakakai* ☎ *808/553–5009.*

JEWELRY

Imports Gift Shop. You'll find soaps and lotions, a small collection of 14-karat-gold chains, rings, earrings, and bracelets, and a jumble of Hawaiian quilts, pillows, books, and postcards at this local favorite. The shop also special orders (takes approximately one week) for Hawaiian heirloom jewelry, inspired by popular Victorian pieces and crafted here since the late 1800s. ✉ *82 Ala Malama St., Kaunakakai* ☎ *808/553–5734.*

SPORTING GOODS

Molokai Bicycle. This bike shop rents and sells mountain and road bikes as well as helmets, racks, and jogging strollers. It supplies maps and information on biking and hiking and will pick up and drop off equipment nearly anywhere on the island. ✉ *80 Mohala St., Kaunakakai* ☎ *808/553–5740, 800/709–2453* 🌐 *www.mauimolokaibicycle.com.*

Molokai Fish & Dive. This is the source for your sporting needs, from snorkel rentals to free and friendly advice. This is also a good place to pick up original-design Molokai T-shirts, water sandals, books, and gifts. ✉ *53 Ala Malama St., Kaunakakai* ☎ *808/553–5926* 🌐 *www.molokaifishanddive.com.*

SPAS

Molokai Acupuncture & Massage. This relaxing retreat offers acupuncture, massage, herbal remedies, wellness treatments, and private yoga sessions by appointment only. ✉ *40 Ala Malama St., Suite 206, Kaunakakai* ☎ *808/553–3930* 🌐 *www.molokai-wellness.com.*

Molokai Lomi Massage. Allana Noury of Molokai Lomi Massage has studied natural medicine for nearly 40 years and is a licensed massage therapist, master herbalist, and master iridologist. She will come to your hotel or condo by appointment. ☎ *808/553–8034* 🌐 *www.molokaimassage.com.*

ENTERTAINMENT AND NIGHTLIFE

Local nightlife consists mainly of gathering with friends and family, sipping a few cold ones, strumming ukuleles and guitars, singing old songs, and talking story. Still, there are a few ways to kick up your heels. Pick up a copy of the weekly Molokai *Dispatch* and see if there's a concert, church supper, or dance.

The bar at the Hotel Molokai is always a good place to drink. To catch a showing of Na Kupuna, a group of accomplished *kupuna* (old-timers) with guitars and ukuleles, visit Paddlers Restaurant and Bar on Fridays from 4 to 6 pm.

For something truly casual, stop in at Kanemitsu Bakery on Ala Malama Street in Kaunakakai for the nightly hot bread sale (Tuesday–Sunday beginning at 7:30 pm). You can meet everyone in town and take some hot bread home for a late-night treat.

LANAI

WELCOME TO LANAI

TOP REASONS TO GO

★ **Seclusion and serenity:** Lanai is small; local motion is slow motion. Get into the spirit and go home rested.

★ **Keahiakawelo (Garden of the Gods):** Walk amid the eerie red-rock spires that Hawaiians still believe to be a sacred spot. The ocean views are magnificent, too; sunset is a good time to visit.

★ **A dive at Cathedrals:** Explore underwater pinnacle formations and mysterious caverns illuminated by shimmering rays of light.

★ **Dole Park:** Hang out in the shade of the Cook pines in Lanai City and talk story with the locals for a taste of old-time Hawaii.

★ **Hit the water at Hulopoe Beach:** This beach may have it all—good swimming, a shady park for perfect picnicking, great reefs for snorkeling, and sometimes schools of spinner dolphins.

1 Lanai City, Keahiakawelo (aka Garden of the Gods), and Manele Bay. Cool and serene, Upcountry is graced by Lanai City, towering Cook pine trees, and misty mountain vistas. The historic plantation village of Lanai City is inching into the modern world. Locals hold conversations in front of Dole Park shops and from their pickups on the road, and kids ride bikes in colorful impromptu parades. Six miles north of Lanai City, Keahiakawelo (nicknamed "Garden of the Gods") is a stunning rocky plateau. The more developed beach side of the island, Manele Bay is where it's happening: swimming, picnicking, off-island excursions, and boating are all concentrated in this accessible area.

2 Windward Lanai. This area is the long white-sand beach at the base of Lanaihale. Now uninhabited, it was once occupied by thriving Hawaiian fishing villages and a sugarcane plantation.

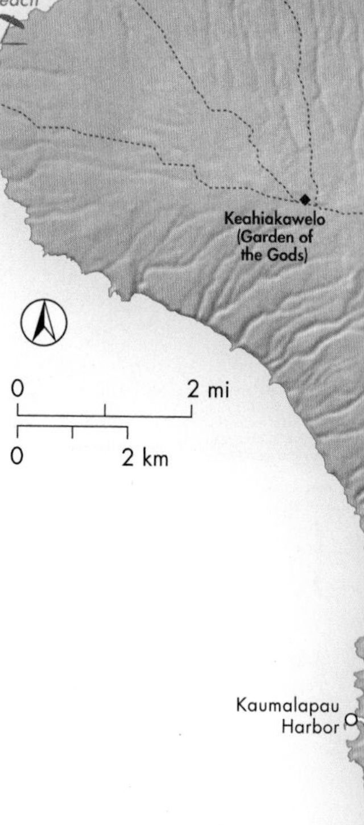

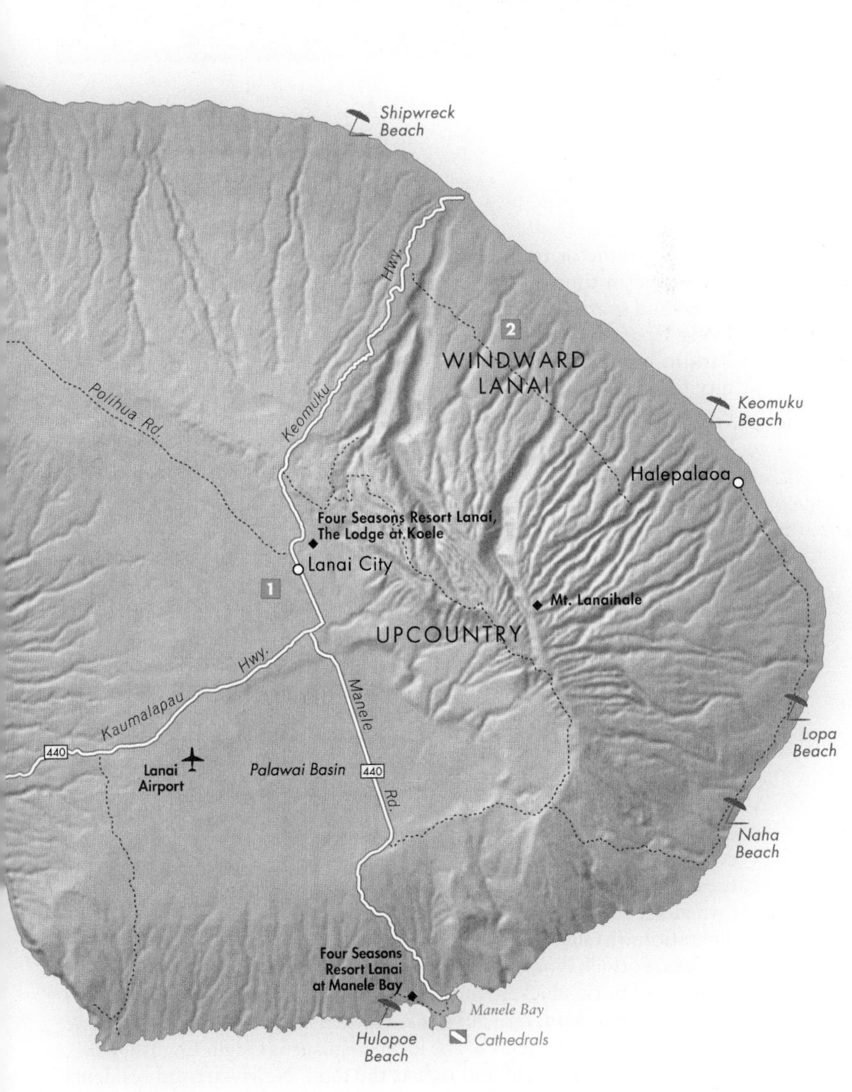
Shipwreck Beach
Hwy.
2
WINDWARD LANAI
Keomuku Beach
Polihua Rd.
Keomuku
Halepalaoa
Four Seasons Resort Lanai, The Lodge at Koele
Lanai City
1
Mt. Lanaihale
UPCOUNTRY
Hwy.
Manele
Kaumalapau
440
Lanai Airport
Palawai Basin
440
Rd.
Lopa Beach
Naha Beach
Four Seasons Resort Lanai at Manele Bay
Manele Bay
Hulopoe Beach
Cathedrals

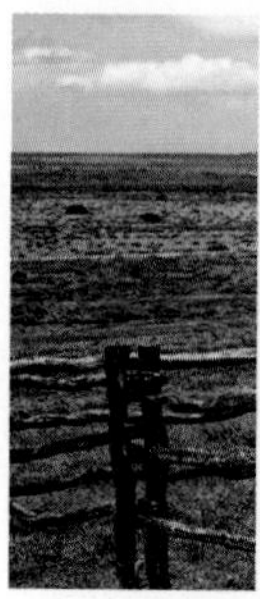

Updated by Lehia Apana

Mostly privately owned, Lanai is the smallest inhabited island in Hawaii, and is a true getaway for slowing down and enjoying serenity amid world-class comforts.

With no traffic or traffic lights and miles of open space, Lanai seems suspended in time, and that can be a good thing. Small (141 square miles) and sparsely populated, it has just 3,500 residents, most of them living Upcountry in Lanai City. An afternoon strolling around Dole Park in historic Lanai City offers shopping, dining, and the opportunity to mingle with locals. Though it may seem a world away, Lanai is separated from Maui and Molokai by two narrow channels, and is easily accessed by commercial ferry from Maui.

FLORA AND FAUNA

Lanai bucks the "tropical" trend of the other Hawaiian Islands with African kiawe trees, Cook pines, and eucalyptus in place of palm trees, and deep blue sea where you might expect shallow turquoise bays. Abandoned pineapple fields are overgrown with drought-resistant grasses, Christmas berry, and lantana; native plants *aalii* and *ilima* are found in uncultivated areas. Axis deer from India dominate the ridges, and wild turkeys lumber around the resorts. Whales can be seen November–May, and a family of resident spinner dolphins rests and fishes regularly in Hulopoe Bay.

ON LANAI TODAY

Despite its fancy resorts, Lanai still has that languid Hawaii feel. The island is 98% owned by billionaire Larry Ellison, who is in the process of revitalizing the island. Old-time residents are a mix of just about everything: Hawaiian, Chinese, German, Portuguese, Filipino, Japanese, French, Puerto Rican, English, Norwegian—you name it. When Dole owned the island in the early 20th century and grew pineapples, the plantation was divided into ethnic camps, which helped retain cultural cuisines. Potluck dinners feature sashimi, Portuguese bean soup, *laulau* (morsels of pork, chicken, butterfish, or other ingredients steamed in *ti* leaves), potato salad, teriyaki steak, chicken *hekka* (a gingery Japanese chicken stir-fry), and Jell-O. The local language is Pidgin English, a mix of words as complicated and rich as the food. Newly arrived residents have added to the cultural mix.

PLANNING

WHEN TO GO

Lanai has an ideal climate year-round, hot and sunny at the sea and a few delicious degrees cooler Upcountry. In Lanai City and Upcountry, the nights and mornings can be almost chilly when a fog or harsh trade winds settle in. Winter months are known for *slightly* rougher weather—periodic rain showers, occasional storms, and higher surf.

Because higher mountains on Maui capture the trade-wind clouds, Lanai receives little rainfall and has a near-desert ecology. Consider the wind direction when planning your day. If it's blowing a gale on the windward beaches, head for the beach at Hulopoe or check out Keahiakawelo (aka Garden of the Gods). Overcast days, when the wind stops or comes lightly from the southwest, are common in whale season. At that time, try a whale-watching trip or the windward beaches.

Whales are seen off Lanai's shores November–May (peak season January–March). A Pineapple Festival on the July 4 Saturday in Dole Park features traditional entertainment, a pineapple-eating contest, and fireworks. Buddhists hold their annual outdoor Obon Festival, honoring departed ancestors with joyous dancing, local food, and drumming, in early July. During hunting-season weekends, mid-February–mid-May and mid-July–mid-October, watch out for hunters on dirt roads even though there are designated safety zones. On Sundays, many shops and restaurants have limited hours or are closed altogether.

GETTING HERE AND AROUND

AIR TRAVEL

Hawaiian Airlines is the only commercial airline routinely serving Lanai City. Direct flights are available from Oahu; if you're flying to Lanai from any other Hawaiian island, you'll make a stop in Honolulu. Mokulele Airlines offers charter flights; guests of the Four Seasons Resort Lanai can arrange private charters from Honolulu on Lanai Air, which is operated by Mokulele Airlines.

If you're staying at the Four Seasons Resort Lanai, or renting a vehicle from Lanai City Service, you'll be met at the airport or ferry dock by a bus that shuttles between the resort and Lanai City (and there may be an additional fee).

Airline Contacts **Hawaiian Airlines.** ☎ *800/367–5320* 🌐 *www.hawaiianairlines.com.* **Mokulele Airlines.** ☎ *866/260–7070* 🌐 *www.mokuleleairlines.com.*

Airport Contacts **Lanai Airport (LNY).** ☎ *808/565–7942* 🌐 *www.airports.hawaii.gov/lny.*

CAR TRAVEL

It's always good to carry a cell phone. Lanai has only 30 miles of paved roads; its main road, Highway 440, refers to both Kaumalapau Highway and Manele Road. Keomuku Highway starts just past the Lodge at Koele and runs northeast to the dirt road that goes to Kaiolohia (aka Shipwreck Beach) and Lopa Beach. Manele Road (Highway 440) runs south down to Manele Bay, the Four Seasons Resort Lanai, and Hulopoe Beach. Kaumalapau Highway (also Highway 440) heads west to Kaumalapau Harbor. The rest of your driving takes place on bumpy dusty roads that are unpaved and unmarked. Driving in thick mud is not recommended, and the rental agency will charge a stiff cleaning fee. Watch out for blind curves on narrow roads. Take a map, be sure you have a full tank, and bring a snack and plenty of water.

Renting a four-wheel-drive vehicle is expensive but almost essential if you'd like to explore beyond the resorts and Lanai City. Make reservations far in advance of your trip, because Lanai's fleet of vehicles is limited. Lanai City Service, where you'll find a branch of Dollar Rent A Car, is open daily 7–7. Ask the rental agency or your hotel's concierge about road conditions before you set out.

Stop from time to time to find landmarks and gauge your progress. Never drive or walk to the edge of lava cliffs, as rock can give way under you. Directions on the island are often given as *mauka* (toward the mountains) and *makai* (toward the ocean).

If you're visiting for the day, Rabaca's Limousine Service will take you wherever you want to go.

Contacts Lanai City Service. ✉ *1036 Lanai Ave., Lanai City* ☎ *808/565–7227, 800/533–7808* 🌐 *www.dollarlanai.com.* **Rabaca's Limousine Service.** ✉ *552 Alapa St., Lanai City* ☎ *808/565–6670.*

FERRY TRAVEL

Ferries operated by Expeditions cross the channel five times daily between Lahaina on Maui to Manele Bay Harbor on Lanai. The crossing takes 45 minutes and costs $30. Be warned: passage can be rough, especially in winter.

Contact Expeditions. ☎ *808/661–3756, 800/695–2624* 🌐 *www.go-lanai.com.*

SHUTTLE TRAVEL

A shuttle transports you to your hotel from the harbor or the airport (a nominal fee may apply). If you're renting a vehicle from Lanai City Service, their shuttle will pick you up at the harbor or airport for a nominal fee.

RESTAURANTS

Lanai has a wide range of choices for dining, from simple plate-lunch local eateries to gourmet resort restaurants.

HOTELS

The range of lodgings is limited on Lanai. Essentially there are only a few options: the Four Seasons Lanai and the historic Hotel Lanai, which closed for renovations in May 2018. An alternative is a house rental, which will give you a feel for everyday life on the island; make sure to book far in advance. Maui County has strict regulations concerning vacation rentals; to avoid disappointment, always contact the property manager or owner and ask if the accommodation has the proper permits and is in compliance with local laws. *Hotel reviews have been shortened. For full information, visit Fodors.com.*

Ocean views provide a backdrop to the eroded rocks at Keahiakawelo (aka Garden of the Gods).

EXPLORING

LANAI CITY, KEAHIAKAWELO (AKA GARDEN OF THE GODS), AND MANELE BAY

Lanai City is 3 miles northeast of the airport; Manele Bay is 9 miles southeast of Lanai City; Keahiakawelo (aka Garden of the Gods) is 6 miles northwest of Lanai City.

A tidy plantation town, built in 1924 by Jim Dole to accommodate workers for his pineapple business, Lanai City is home to old-time residents, resort workers, and second-home owners. With its charming plantation-era shops and restaurants having received new paint jobs and landscaping, Lanai City is worthy of whiling away a lazy afternoon.

You can easily explore Lanai City on foot. **Dole Park,** in the center of Lanai City, is surrounded by small shops and restaurants and is a great spot for sitting, strolling, and talking story. Try a picnic lunch in the park and visit the **Lanai Culture & Heritage Center** in the Old Dole Administration Building to glimpse this island's rich past, purchase historical publications and maps, and get directions to anywhere on the island.

Manele Bay is an ocean lover's dream: Hulopoe Beach offers top-notch snorkeling, swimming, picnicking, tide pools, and sometimes spinner dolphins. Off-island ocean excursions depart from nearby Manele Small Boat Harbor. Take the short but rugged hike to the Puu Pehe (Sweetheart Rock) overlook, and you'll enjoy a bird's-eye view of this iconic Lanai landmark.

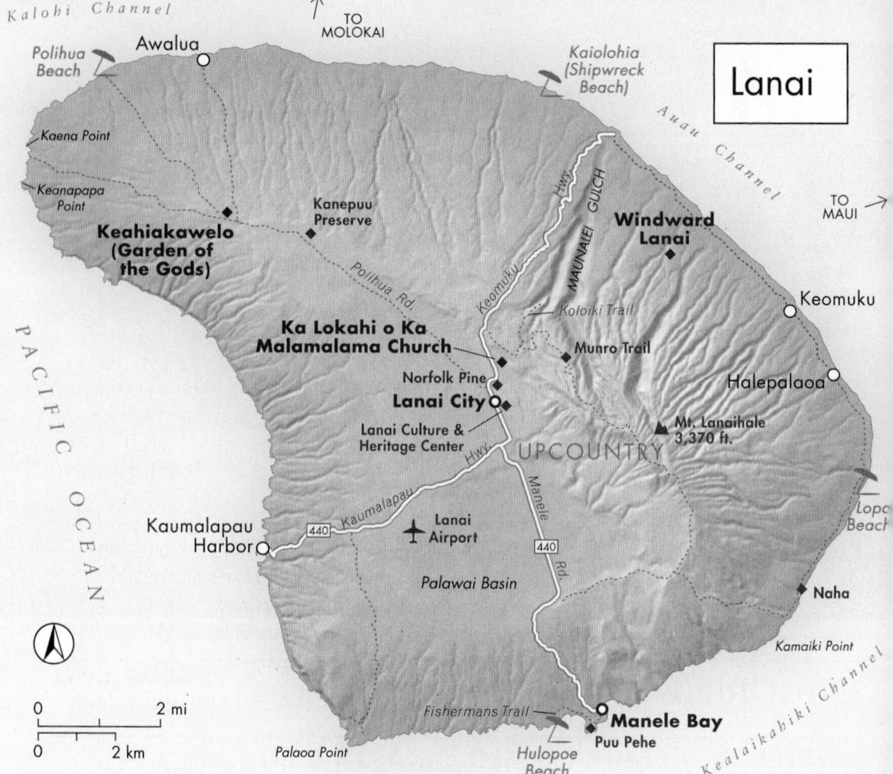

GETTING HERE AND AROUND

Lanai City serves as the island's hub, with roads leading to Manele Bay, Kaumalapau Harbor, and windward Lanai. Keahiakawelo (aka Garden of the Gods) is usually possible to visit by car, but beyond that you will need four-wheel drive.

TOP ATTRACTIONS

Kanepuu Preserve. Hawaiian sandalwood, olive, and ebony trees characterize Hawaii's largest example of a rare native dryland forest. Thanks to the efforts of volunteers at the Nature Conservancy and a native Hawaiian land trust, the 590-acre remnant forest is protected from the axis deer and mouflon sheep that graze on the land beyond its fence. More than 45 native plant species can be seen here. A short, self-guided loop trail, with eight signs illustrated by local artist Wendell Kahoohalahala, reveals this ecosystem's beauty and the challenges it faces. The reserve is adjacent to the sacred hill, Kane Puu, dedicated to the Hawaiian god of water and vegetation. ✉ *Polihua Rd., Lanai City* ✢ *4.8 miles north of Lanai City.*

Fodor's Choice ★ **Keahiakawelo (Garden of the Gods).** This preternatural plateau is scattered with boulders of different sizes, shapes, and colors, the products of a million years of wind erosion. Time your visit for sunset, when the rocks begin to glow—from rich red to purple—and the fiery globe sinks

CLOSE UP

The Story of Lanai

Rumored to be haunted by hungry ghosts, Lanai was sparsely inhabited for many centuries. Most of the earliest settlers lived along the shore and made their living from fishing the nearby waters. Others lived in the Upcountry near seasonal water sources and traded their produce for seafood. The high chiefs sold off the land bit by bit to foreign settlers, and by 1910 the island was owned by the Gay family.

When the Hawaiian Pineapple Company purchased Lanai for $1.1 million in 1922, it built the town of Lanai City, opened the commercial harbor, and laid out the pineapple fields. Field workers came from overseas to toil in what quickly became the world's largest pineapple plantation. Exotic animals and birds were imported for hunting. Cook pines were planted to catch the rain, and eucalyptus windbreaks anchored the blowing soil.

Everything was stable for 70 years, until the plantation closed in 1992. When the resorts opened their doors, newcomers arrived, homes were built, and other ways of life set in. Today, most of the island is owned by billionaire Larry Ellison, and vast areas remain untouched and great views abound. Although the ghosts may be long gone, Lanai still retains its ancient mysterious presence.

7

to the horizon. Magnificent views of the Pacific Ocean, Molokai, and, on clear days, Oahu, provide the perfect backdrop for photographs. The ancient Hawaiians shunned Lanai for hundreds of years, believing the island was the inviolable home of spirits. Standing beside the oxide-red rock spires of this strange raw landscape, you might be tempted to believe the same. This lunar savanna still has a decidedly eerie edge, but the shadows disappearing on the horizon are those of mouflon sheep and axis deer, not the fearsome spirits of lore. According to tradition, Kawelo, a Hawaiian priest, kept a perpetual fire burning on an altar here, in sight of the island of Molokai. As long as the fire burned, prosperity was assured for the people of Lanai. Kawelo was killed by a rival priest on Molokai and the fire went out. The Hawaiian name for this area is Keahiakawelo, meaning the "fire of Kawelo." ⊠ *Off Polihua Rd., Lanai City* ✣ *6 miles north of Lanai City.*

Manele Bay. The site of a Hawaiian village dating from AD 900, Manele Bay is flanked by lava cliffs hundreds of feet high. Ferries from Maui dock five times a day, and visiting yachts pull in here, as it's the island's only small boat harbor. Public restrooms, grassy lawns, and picnic tables make it a busy pit stop—you can watch the boating activity as you rest. Just offshore to the west is Puu Pehe, an isolated 80-foot-high islet steeped in romantic Hawaiian lore; it's often called Sweetheart Rock. ⊠ *Hwy. 440, Manele, Lanai City.*

Puu Pehe. Often called Sweetheart Rock, this isolated 80-foot-high islet is steeped in romantic Hawaiian lore. The rock is said to be named after Pehe, a woman so beautiful that her husband kept her hidden in a sea cave. One day, the surf surged into the cave and she drowned.

The calm crescent of Hulopoe Beach is perfect for swimming, snorkeling, or just relaxing.

Her grief-stricken husband buried her on this rock and jumped to his death. It is also believed that the enclosure on the summit is a shrine to birds, built by bird-catchers. Protected shearwaters nest in the nearby sea cliffs July–November. ✉ *Hwy. 440, Manele, Lanai City.*

WORTH NOTING

Fodor's Choice ★ **Lanai Culture & Heritage Center.** Small and carefully arranged, this historical museum features artifacts and photographs from Lanai's varied and rich history. Plantation-era clothing and tools, ranch memorabilia, old maps, precious feather lei, poi pounders, and family portraits combine to give you a good idea of the history of the island and its people. Postcards, maps, books, and pamphlets are for sale. The friendly staff can orient you to the island's historical sites and provide directions. This is the best place to start your explorations of the island. **TIP→ The Heritage Center's Lanai Guide app is a trove of information—both practical and historical—on the island's sites.** ✉ *730 Lanai Ave., Lanai City* ☎ *808/565–7177* 🌐 *www.lanaichc.org* 🎫 *Free* ⏲ *Closed Sun.*

Norfolk Pine. Considered the "mother" of all the pines on the island, this 160-foot-tall tree was planted here, at the former site of the ranch manager's house, in 1875. Almost 30 years later, George Munro, the manager, observed how, in foggy weather, water collected on its foliage, dripping off rain. This led Munro to supervise the planting of Cook pines along the ridge of Lanaihale and throughout the town in order to add to the island's water supply. This majestic tree is just in front of the south wing of the former Four Seasons Resort Lodge at Koele. ✉ *Four Seasons Resort Lodge at Koele, 1 Keomuku Hwy., Lanai City.*

WINDWARD LANAI

9 miles northeast of the Lodge at Koele to end of paved road.

The eastern shore of Lanai is mostly deserted. A few inaccessible *heiau,* or temples, rock walls and boulders marking old shrines, and a restored church at Keomuku reveal traces of human habitation. Four-wheel-drive vehicles are a must to explore this side of the isle. Pack a picnic lunch, a hat and sunscreen, and plenty of drinking water. A mobile phone is also a good idea.

GETTING HERE AND AROUND

Once you leave paved Keomuku Highway and turn left toward Kaiolohia (Shipwreck Beach) or right to Naha, the roads are dirt and sand; conditions vary with the seasons. Mileage doesn't matter much here, but figure on 20 minutes from the end of the paved road to Shipwreck Beach, and about 45 minutes to Lopa Beach.

For information about Kaiolohia (Shipwreck Beach) and Lopa Beach, see Beaches, below.

TOP ATTRACTIONS

Munro Trail. This 12.8-mile four-wheel-drive trail along a fern- and pine-clad narrow ridge was named after George Munro, manager of the Lanai Ranch Company, who began a reforestation program in the 1950s to restore the island's much-needed watershed. The trail climbs **Lanaihale** (House of Lanai), which, at 3,370 feet, is the island's highest point; on clear days you'll be treated to a panorama of canyons and almost all the Hawaiian Islands. ■ **TIP→ The road gets very muddy, and trade winds can be strong. Watch for sheer drop-offs, and keep an eye out for hikers.** You can also hike the Munro Trail, although it's steep, the ground is uneven, and there's no water. From the Four Seasons Resort Lodge at Koele (currently closed), head north on Highway 440 for 1¼ miles, then turn right onto Cemetery Road. Keep going until you're headed downhill on the main dirt road. It's a one-way road, but you may meet jeeps coming from the opposite direction. ✉ *Cemetery Rd., Lanai City.*

WORTH NOTING

Halepalaoa. Named for the whales that once washed ashore here, Halepalaoa, or the "House of Whale Ivory," was the site of the wharf used by the short-lived Maunalei Sugar Company in 1899. Some say the sugar company failed because the sacred stones of nearby **Kahea Heiau** were used for the construction of the cane railroad. The brackish well water turned too salty, forcing the sugar company to close in 1901, after just two years. The remains of the heiau, once an important place of worship for the people of Lanai, are now difficult to find through the kiawe overgrowth. There's good public-beach access here and clear shallow water for swimming, but no other facilities. Take Highway 440 (Keomuku Highway) to its eastern terminus, then turn right on the dirt road and continue south for 5½ miles. ✉ *On dirt road off Hwy. 440, Lanai City.*

Keomuku. There's a peaceful beauty about the former fishing village of Keomuku. During the late 19th century this small Lanai community served as the headquarters of Maunalei Sugar Company. After the company failed, the land was abandoned. Although there are no other signs of previous inhabitation, its church, **Ka Lanakila O Ka Malamalama,** built in 1903, has been restored by volunteers. Visitors often leave some small token, a shell or lei, as an offering. Take Highway 440 to its eastern terminus, then turn right onto a dirt road and continue south for 5 miles. The church is on your right in the coconut trees. ✉ *On dirt road off Hwy. 440.*

THE COASTAL ROAD

Road conditions can change overnight and become impassable due to rain in the Upcountry. The car-rental agency will give you an update before you hit the road. Some of the spur roads leading to the windward beaches from the coastal dirt road cross private property and are closed off by chains. Look for open spur roads with recent tire marks (a fairly good sign that they are safe to drive on). It's best to park on firm ground and walk in to avoid getting your car mired in the sand.

Naha. An ancient rock-walled fishpond—visible at low tide—lies where the sandy shore ends and the cliffs begin their rise along the island's shores. Accessible by four-wheel-drive vehicle, the beach is a frequent dive spot for local fishermen. ■ TIP→ **Treacherous currents make this a dangerous place for swimming.** Take Highway 440 to its eastern terminus, then turn right onto a sandy dirt road and continue south for 11 miles. The shoreline dirt road ends here. ✉ *On dirt road off Hwy. 440, Lanai City.*

BEACHES

Lanai offers miles of secluded white-sand beaches on its windward side, plus the moderately developed Hulopoe Beach, which is adjacent to the Four Seasons Resort Lanai. Hulopoe is accessible by car or hotel shuttle bus; to reach the windward beaches you need a four-wheel-drive vehicle. Reef, rocks, and coral make swimming on the windward side problematic, but it's fun to splash around in the shallow water. Expect debris on the windward beaches due to the Pacific convergence of ocean currents. Driving on the beach itself is illegal and can be dangerous. *Beaches in this chapter are listed alphabetically.*

FAMILY Fodor's Choice ★ **Hulopoe Beach.** A short stroll from the Four Seasons Resort Lanai, Hulopoe is one of the best beaches in Hawaii. The sparkling crescent of this Marine Life Conservation District beckons with calm waters safe for swimming almost year-round, great snorkeling reefs, tide pools, and sometimes spinner dolphins. A shady, grassy beach park is perfect for picnics. If the shore break is pounding, or if you see surfers riding big waves, stay out of the water. In the afternoon, watch Lanai High School students heave outrigger canoes down the steep shore break and race one another just offshore. To get here, take Highway 440 south to the bottom of the hill and turn right. The road dead-ends at the beach's parking lot. **Amenities:** parking (no fee); showers; toilets. **Best for:** snorkeling; surfing; swimming. ✉ *Off Hwy. 440, Lanai City.*

Kaiolohia (Shipwreck Beach). The rusting World War II tanker abandoned off this 8-mile stretch of sand adds just the right touch to an already photogenic beach. Strong trade winds have propelled vessels onto the reef since at least 1824, when the first shipwreck was recorded. Beachcombers come to this fairly accessible beach for shells and washed-up treasures, and photographers take great shots of Molokai, just across the Kalohi Channel. A deserted plantation-era fishing settlement adds to the charm. It's still possible to find glass-ball fishing floats as you wander along. Kaiolohia, its Hawaiian name, is a favorite local diving spot. Beyond the beach, about 200 yards up a trail past the Shipwreck Beach sign, are the Kukui Point petroglyphs, marked by reddish-brown boulders. ■ **TIP→ An offshore reef and rocks in the water mean that it's not for swimmers, though you can play in the shallow water on the shoreline.** To get here, take Highway 440 to its eastern terminus, then turn left onto a dirt road and continue to the end. **Amenities:** none. **Best for:** solitude; stargazing; windsurfing. ✉ *Off Hwy. 440, Lanai City.*

Lopa Beach. A difficult surfing spot that tests the mettle of experienced locals, Lopa is also an ancient fishpond. With majestic views of West Maui and Kahoolawe, this remote white-sand beach is a great place for a picnic. ⚠ **Don't let the sight of surfers fool you: the channel's currents are too strong for swimming.** Take Highway 440 to its eastern terminus, turn right onto a dirt road, and continue south for 7 miles. **Amenities:** none. **Best for:** solitude; sunrise; walking. ✉ *On dirt road off Hwy. 440.*

7

Polihua Beach. This often-deserted beach features long wide stretches of white sand and unobstructed views of Molokai. The northern end of the beach ends at a rocky lava cliff with some interesting tide pools, and sea turtles that lay their eggs in the sand. (Do not drive on the beach and endanger their nests.) However, the dirt road leading here has deep sandy places that are difficult in dry weather and impassable when it rains. In addition, strong currents and a sudden drop in the ocean floor make swimming dangerous, and strong trade winds can make walking uncomfortable. Thirsty wild bees sometimes gather around your car. To get rid of them, put out water some distance away and wait. The beach is in windward Lanai, 11 miles north of Lanai City. To get here, turn right onto the marked dirt road past Keahiakawelo (aka Garden of the Gods). **Amenities:** none. **Best for:** solitude; sunrise; walking. ✉ *East end of Polihua Rd., Lanai City.*

WHERE TO EAT

Lanai's own version of Hawaii regional cuisine draws on the fresh bounty provided by local farmers and fishermen, combined with the skills of well-regarded chefs. The upscale menus at the Four Seasons Resort Lanai encompass European- and Asian-inspired cuisine as well as innovative preparations of international favorites and vegetarian delights. All Four Seasons Resort restaurants offer children's menus. Lanai City's eclectic ethnic fare runs from construction-worker-size local plate lunches to *poke* (raw fish), pizza, and pasta. ■ **TIP→ Lanai "City" is really a small town; restaurants sometimes close their kitchens early, and only a few are open on Sunday.**

	WHAT IT COSTS			
	$	$$	$$$	$$$$
Restaurants	under $18	$18–$26	$27–$35	over $35

Restaurant prices are the average cost of a main course at dinner or, if dinner is not served, at lunch.

MANELE BAY

Dining at Manele Bay offers the range of options provided by the Four Seasons Resort Lanai, from informal poolside meals to relaxed eclectic dining.

$$$ JAPANESE **Nobu Lanai.** Chef Nobuyuki "Nobu" Matsuhisa offers his signature new-style Japanese cuisine in this open-air, relaxed luxury venue that features a lounge, teppanyaki stations, and a sushi bar. This is fine dining without the stress, as black-clad waiters present dish after dish of beautifully seasoned, raw and lightly cooked seafood from local waters, or flown in directly from Alaska and Japan. **Known for:** omakase (chef's choice) multicourse menu; pricey menu; fresh fish. *Average main: $32 Four Seasons Resort Lanai, 1 Manele Bay Rd., Manele, Lanai City 808/565–2832 www.noburestaurants.com/lanai No lunch.*

$$$$ AMERICAN **One Forty.** Named after the island's 140 square miles, prime cuts of beef and the freshest local fish are served in airy comfort on the hotel terrace, which overlooks the wide sweep of Hulopoe Bay; retractable awnings provide shade on sunny days. Comfy rattan chairs, potted palms, and tropical decor create an inviting backdrop for the ocean-view restaurant. **Known for:** steak and seafood; ocean views; suberb service. *Average main: $45 Four Seasons Resort Lanai, 1 Manele Bay Rd., Lanai City 808/565–2290 www.fourseasons.com/lanai No lunch.*

$$ AMERICAN **Views at Manele Golf Course.** A stunning view of the legendary Puu Pehe rock only enhances the imaginative fare of this open-air restaurant that has great views of frolicking dolphins from the terrace. Tuck into a Hulopoe Bay prawn BLT, the crispy battered fish-and-chips with Meyer lemon tartar sauce, or any one of the tempting salad options. **Known for:** ocean views; superb service; fish tacos. *Average main: $25 Four Seasons Resort Lanai, 1 Manele Bay Rd., Manele, Lanai City 808/565–2230 www.fourseasons.com/lanai No dinner.*

LANAI CITY AND UPCOUNTRY

In Lanai City you can enjoy everything from local-style plate lunches to upscale gourmet meals. For a small area, there are a number of good places to eat and drink, but remember that Lanai City mostly closes down on Sunday.

$ ECLECTIC **Blue Ginger Café.** Owners Joe and Georgia Abilay made this cheery place into a Lanai City institution with simply prepared, consistent, tasty food. Local paintings and photos line the walls inside, while townspeople parade by the outdoor tables. **Known for:** authentic local cuisine; comfort food; fresh-baked bread and pastries. *Average main:*

$12 ✉ 409 7th St., Lanai City ☎ 808/565–6363 🌐 www.bluegingercafelanai.com ▭ No credit cards.

$ ECLECTIC ✕ **Café 565.** Named after the oldest telephone prefix on Lanai, Café 565 is a convenient stop for plate lunches, sandwiches on freshly baked focaccia, pizza, or platters of local-style favorites to take along for an impromptu picnic. Bring your own beer or wine for lunch or dinner and request a table on the patio, which is kid-friendly. **Known for:** local-style "plate lunch" meals; friendly service; quick takeout meals. *[$] Average main: $10 ✉ 408 8th St., Lanai City ☎ 808/565–6622 ⏲ Closed Sun.*

$ AMERICAN ✕ **Coffee Works.** A block from Dole Park, this Northern California–style café offers an umbrella-covered deck where you can sip cappuccinos and get in tune with the slow pace of life. Bagels with lox, deli sandwiches, and pastries add to the caloric content, while blended espresso shakes and gourmet ice cream complete the coffeehouse vibe. **Known for:** casual atmosphere; comfortable outside seating; varied drink selection. *[$] Average main: $8 ✉ 604 Ilima St., Lanai City ☎ 808/565–6962 ⏲ Closed Sun.*

$ HAWAIIAN FAMILY ✕ **No Ka Oi Grindz Lanai.** A local favorite, this lunchroom-style café has picnic tables in the landscaped front yard where diners can watch the town drive by and five more tables in the no-frills interior. The menu includes local favorites like kimchi fried rice and massive plate lunches, plus daily specials. **Known for:** local comfort food; large portions; reasonable prices. *[$] Average main: $10 ✉ 335 9th St., Lanai City ☎ 808/565–9413 ▭ No credit cards.*

$$ ITALIAN ✕ **Pele's Other Garden.** Small and colorful, Pele's is a deli and bistro all in one. For lunch, sandwiches or daily hot specials satisfy hearty appetites; at night, it's transformed into a busy bistro, with an intimate back-room bar where entertainers often drop in for impromptu jam sessions. **Known for:** Italian cuisine; quaint atmosphere; good beer and wine selection. *[$] Average main: $19 ✉ 811 Houston St., Lanai City ☎ 808/565–9628 🌐 www.pelesothergarden.com ⏲ Closed Sun.*

WHERE TO STAY

The good news is that you're sure to escape the crowds on this quaint island. The bad news is that Lanai has limited accommodation options, including the pricey Four Seasons Resort Lanai, or the relatively budget-friendly Hotel Lanai (which closed for renovations in mid-2018). Four Seasons Resort's Lodge at Koele has also closed for renovations, though there's talk it will reopen as a destination spa in early 2019.

	WHAT IT COSTS			
	$	$$	$$$	$$$$
Hotels	under $181	$181–$260	$261–$340	over $340

Hotel prices are the lowest cost of a standard double room in high season. Condo price categories reflect studio and one-bedroom rates.

$$$$ RESORT FAMILY Fodor's Choice ★ **Four Seasons Resort Lanai.** With stunning views of Hulopoe Bay and the astonishing rocky coastline, this sublime retreat offers beachside urban chic decor with meticulously curated artwork from across Polynesia, Micronesia, and Hawaii and manicured grounds that feature an array of native Hawaiian plants and species. **Pros:** nearby beach; outstanding restaurants; newly renovated; rental vehicles available on property. **Cons:** 20 minutes from town; need a car to explore the area; not all guest rooms have coast views. *Rooms from: $1150* ✉ *1 Manele Rd., Manele, Lanai City* ☎ *808/565–2000, 800/321–4666* 🌐 *www.fourseasons.com/lanai* *258 rooms* *No meals.*

WATER SPORTS AND TOURS

The easiest way to enjoy the water on Lanai is to wade in at Hulopoe Beach and swim or snorkel. If you prefer an organized excursion, a fishing trip is a good bet (you keep some of the fish). Snorkel trips are a great way to see the island, above and below the surface, and scuba divers can marvel at one of the top cave-dive spots in the Pacific.

DEEP-SEA FISHING

Some of the best fishing grounds in Maui County are off the southwest shoreline of Lanai, the traditional fishing grounds of Hawaiian royalty. Pry your eyes open and go deep-sea fishing in the early morning, with departures from Manele Harbor. Console yourself with the knowledge that Maui anglers have to leave an hour earlier to get to the same prime locations. Peak seasons are spring and summer, although good catches have been landed year-round. Mahimahi, *ono* (a mackerel-like fish; the word means "delicious" in Hawaiian), ahi, and marlin are prized catches and preferred eating.

SCUBA DIVING

When you have a dive site such as Cathedrals—with eerie pinnacle formations and luminous caverns—it's no wonder that scuba-diving buffs consider exploring the waters off Lanai akin to a religious experience.

BEST SPOTS

Cathedrals. Just outside Hulopoe Bay, Cathedrals is the best cavern dive site in Lanai. Shimmering light makes the many openings resemble stained-glass windows. A current generally keeps the water crystal clear, even if it's turbid outside. In these unearthly chambers, large *ulua* and small reef sharks add to the adventure. Tiger sharks may appear in certain seasons. ✉ *Manele, Lanai City.*

Sergeant Major Reef. Off Kamaiki Point, Sergeant Major Reef is named for big schools of yellow- and black-striped *manini* (sergeant major fish) that turn the rocks silvery as they feed. There are three parallel lava ridges separated by rippled sand valleys, a cave, and an archway. Depths range 15–50 feet. Depending on conditions, the water may be clear or cloudy. ✉ *Lanai City.*

EQUIPMENT, LESSONS, AND TOURS

Lanai Ocean Sports. Explore the underwater lava formations and pristine coral Lanai is famous for with Lanai Ocean Sports, which offers a one-tank dive during its snorkel sail; the fee includes gear, lunch, and beverages. Serious certified divers can opt for a two-tank dive, which includes a private charter with dive masters, plus all the equipment you need; locations depend on the weather. ✉ *Manele Small Boat Harbor, Manele Rd., Manele, Lanai City* ☎ *808/866–8256* 🌐 *www.lanaioceansports.com* 🎟 *From $209 for a one-tank dive; $1,800 for a private two-tank dive.*

SNORKELING

Snorkeling is the easiest ocean sport available on the island, requiring nothing but a snorkel, mask, fins, and good sense. Borrow equipment from your hotel or purchase some in Lanai City if you didn't bring your own. Wait to enter the water until you are sure no big sets of waves are coming, and observe the activity of locals on the beach. If little kids are playing in the shore break, it's usually safe to enter. ■ TIP→ **To get into the water safely, always swim in past the breakers, and in the comparative calm put on your fins, then mask and snorkel.**

BEST SPOTS

The best snorkeling on Lanai is at **Hulopoe Beach** and **Manele Small Boat Harbor.** Hulopoe, which is an exceptional snorkeling destination, has schools of manini that feed on the coral and coat the rocks with flashing silver. You can also easily view *kala* (unicorn fish), *uhu* (parrot fish), and *papio* (small trevally) in all their rainbow colors. Beware of rocks and surging waves. At Manele Harbor, there's a wade-in snorkel spot beyond the break wall. Enter over the rocks, just past the boat ramp. ■ TIP→ **Do not enter if waves are breaking.**

EQUIPMENT, LESSONS, AND TOURS

Lanai Ocean Sports. Take in the beauty of towering sea cliffs, playful spinner dolphins, and crystal-clear waters as you sail along Lanai's coastline, before arriving at Kaunolu, where King Kamehameha challenged his Hawaiian warriors to show their courage by cliff jumping. This intimate trip includes snorkel equipment, wet-suit tops, and stand-up paddleboards, plus a gourmet picnic lunch. ✉ *Manele Small Boat Harbor, Manele Rd., Manele, Lanai City* ☎ *808/866–8256* 🌐 *www.lanaioceansports.com* 🎟 *From $149.*

SURFING

Surfing on Lanai can be truly enjoyable. Quality, not quantity, characterizes this isle's few breaks. Be considerate of the locals and they will be considerate of you—surfing takes the place of megaplex theaters and pool halls here, serving as one of the island's few recreational luxuries.

BEST SPOTS

Don't try to hang 10 at **Hulopoe Bay** without watching the conditions for a while. When it "goes off," it's a tricky left-handed shore break that requires some skill. Huge summer south swells are for experts only.

The southeast-facing breaks at **Lopa Beach** on the east side are inviting for beginners, but hard to get to. Give them a try in summer, when the swells roll in nice and easy.

EQUIPMENT AND LESSONS

Lanai Surf School & Safari. Nick Palumbo offers the only surf instruction on the island. The Lanai native is a former Hawaii State Surfing Champion, so you're in good hands. Experienced riders can rent boards overnight, which can be delivered. Palumbo also has the only paddleboard permit for Hulopoe Bay, and gives lessons and rents equipment. You can also rent skimboards, boogie boards, and kayaks. He will pick you up at your hotel or at the ferry dock. ✉ *Lanai City* ☎ *808/649–0739* 🌐 *www.surfinglanai.com* 🎫 *Lessons from $200.*

GOLF, HIKING, AND OUTDOOR ACTIVITIES

Manele Golf Course will certainly test your skill on the green. Experienced hikers can choose from miles of dirt roads and trails, but note that you're on your own—there's no water or support. Remember that Lanai is privately owned, and all land-based activities are at the owner's discretion.

BIKING

Many of the same red-dirt roads that invite hikers are excellent for biking, offering easy, flat terrain and long clear views. There's only one hitch: you will have to bring your own bike, as there are no rentals or tours available.

BEST SPOTS

A favorite biking route is along the fairly flat red-dirt road northward from Lanai City through the old pineapple fields to Keahiakawelo (Garden of the Gods). Start your trip on Keomuku Highway in town. Take a left just before the Lodge at Koele's (closed for renovation) tennis courts, and then a right where the road ends at the fenced pasture, and continue on to the north end and the start of Polihua and Awalua dirt roads. If you're really hardy, you could bike down to Polihua Beach and back, but it would be a serious all-day trip. In wet weather these roads turn to mud and are not advisable. Go in the early morning or late afternoon, because the sun gets hot in the middle of the day. Take plenty of water, spare parts, and snacks.

For the exceptionally fit, it's possible to bike from town down the Keomuku Highway to the windward beaches and back, or to bike the Munro Trail (⇨ *see Hiking*). Experienced bikers also travel up and down the Manele Highway from Manele Bay to town.

GOLF

Lanai's only golf course, located at the Four Seasons Resort Lanai, is one of the loveliest golf courses in the world—and one of the most challenging.

Some holes at the Manele Golf Course use the Pacific Ocean as a water hazard.

Manele Golf Course. Designed by Jack Nicklaus in 1993, this course sits right over the water of Hulopoe Bay. Built on lava outcroppings, it features three holes on cliffs that use the Pacific Ocean as a water hazard. The five-tee concept challenges the best golfers—tee shots over natural gorges and ravines must be precise. Unspoiled natural terrain provides a stunning backdrop, and every hole offers ocean views. Early-morning tee times are recommended to avoid the midday heat. Another reason to start early: Morning golfers can enjoy a complimentary continental breakfast at Views. ✉ *Four Seasons Resort Lanai, Challenge Dr., Manele, Lanai City* ☎ *808/565–2222* 🌐 *www.fourseasons.com/lanai* 🎫 *$275 for resort guests, $450 for nonguests* 🏌 *18 holes, 7039 yards, par 72.*

HIKING

Only 30 miles of Lanai's roads are paved, but red-dirt roads and trails, ideal for hiking, will take you to sweeping overlooks, isolated beaches, and shady forests. Take a self-guided walk through Kane Puu, Hawaii's largest native dryland forest. You can also explore the Munro Trail over Lanaihale with views of plunging canyons, hike along an old coastal fisherman trail, or head out across Koloiki Ridge. Wear hiking shoes, a hat, and sunscreen, and carry a windbreaker, cell phone, and plenty of water.

BEST SPOTS

Koloiki Ridge. This marked trail starts behind the Lodge at Koele (closed for renovations) and takes you along the cool and shady Munro Trail to overlook the windward side, with impressive views of Maui, Molokai,

Maunalei Valley, and Naio Gulch. The average time for the 5-mile round trip is two hours. Bring snacks, water, and a windbreaker; wear good shoes; and take your time. *Moderate.* ✉ *Lanai City.*

Lanai Fisherman Trail. Local anglers still use this trail to get to their favorite fishing spots. The trail takes about 1½ hours and follows the rocky shoreline below the Four Seasons Resort Lanai. The marked trail entrance begins at the west end of Hulopoe Beach. Keep your eyes open for spinner dolphins cavorting offshore and the silvery flash of fish feeding in the pools below you. The condition of the trail varies with weather and frequency of maintenance; it can be slippery and rocky. Take your time, wear a hat and enclosed shoes, and carry water. *Moderate.* ✉ *Manele, Lanai City.*

Fodor's Choice ★ **Munro Trail.** This is the real thing: a strenuous 12.8-mile trek that begins behind the Lodge at Koele (closed for renovations) and follows the ridge of Lanaihale through the rain forest. The island's most demanding hike, it has an elevation gain of 1,400 feet and leads to a lookout at the island's highest point, Lanaihale. It's also a narrow dirt road; watch out for careening four-wheel-drive vehicles. The trail is named after George Munro, who supervised the planting of Cook pine trees and eucalyptus windbreaks. Mules used to wend their way up the mountain carrying the pine seedlings. Unless you arrange for someone to pick you up at the trail's end, you have a 3-mile hike back through the Palawai Basin to return to your starting point. The summit is often cloud-shrouded and can be windy and muddy, so check conditions before you start. *Difficult.* ✉ *Keomuku Hwy., Lanai City.*

Puu Pehe Trail. Beginning to the left of Hulopoe Beach, this trail travels a short distance around the coastline, and then climbs up a sharp rocky rise. At the top, you're level with the offshore stack of Puu Pehe and can overlook miles of coastline in both directions. The trail is not difficult, but it's hot and steep. Be aware of nesting seabirds and don't approach their nests. ⚠ **Stay away from the edge, as the cliff can easily give way.** The hiking is best in the early morning or late afternoon, and it's a perfect place to look for whales in season (November–May, peak season January–March). Wear a hat and enclosed shoes, and take water so you can spend some time at the top admiring the view. *Moderate.* ✉ *Manele, Lanai City.*

HORSEBACK RIDING

GOING WITH A GUIDE

Lanai Ranch at Koele. The subtle beauty of the high country slowly reveals itself to horseback riders. Two-hour adventures traverse leafy trails with scenic overlooks. Well-trained horses take riders (must be under 200 pounds) of all skill levels. Prices are $175 for a 90-minute group ride and $225 for a two-hour private ride. A four person carriage ride is $350 an hour. Lessons are also available. Operated by Four Seasons Resort Lanai, these activities are open to anyone, although prices are slightly higher for nonguests. ✉ *1 Keomuku Hwy., Lanai City* ☎ *808/565–2072,* 🌐 *www.fourseasons.com/lanai.*

SHOPS AND SPAS

SHOPPING

A cluster of Cook pines in the center of Lanai City surrounded by small shops and restaurants, Dole Park is the closest thing to a mall on Lanai. Except for high-end resort boutiques and pro shops, it's the island's only shopping. A morning or afternoon stroll around the park offers an eclectic selection of gifts and clothing, plus a chance to chat with friendly shopkeepers. Well-stocked general stores are reminiscent of the 1920s, and galleries and a boutique have original art and fashions for everyone.

CLOTHING

Fodor's Choice ★ **The Local Gentry.** Spacious and classy, this store has clothing for every need, from casual men's and women's beachwear to evening resort wear, shoes, jewelry, and hats. There are fancy fashions for tots as well. A selection of original Lanai-themed clothing is also available, including the signature "What happens on Lanai everybody knows" T-shirts. Proprietor Jenna Gentry Majkus will mail your purchases. ✉ *363 7th St., Lanai City* ☎ *808/565–9130.*

FOOD

Pine Isle Market. One of Lanai City's two all-purpose markets, Pine Isle stocks everything from beach toys and electronics to meats and vegetables. The staff are friendly, and it's the best place around to buy fresh fish. The market is closed Sunday. ✉ *356 8th St., Lanai City* ☎ *808/565–6488* ⏲ *Closed Sun.*

Richard's Market. Along with fresh meats, fine wines, and imported gourmet items, Richard's stocks everything from camping gear to household items. ✉ *434 8th St., Lanai City* ☎ *808/565–3780.*

GALLERIES

Lanai Art Center. Local artists display their work at this dynamic center staffed by volunteers. Workshops in pottery, photography, woodworking, and painting welcome visitors. The gift shop sells Lanai handicrafts and special offerings like handmade Swarovski crystal bracelets, the sale of which underwrites children's art classes. There are occasional concerts and special events. ✉ *339 7th St., Lanai City* ☎ *808/565–7503* 🌐 *www.lanaiart.org* ⏲ *Closed Sun.*

Fodor's Choice ★ **Mike Carroll Gallery.** The dreamy, soft-focus oil paintings of award-winning painter Mike Carroll are inspired by island scenes. His work is showcased along with those of other local artists and visiting plein air painters. You can also find handcrafted jewelry and other accessories. ✉ *443 7th St., Lanai City* ☎ *808/565–7122* 🌐 *www.mikecarrollgallery.com.*

GENERAL STORES

International Food and Clothing Center. This old-fashioned emporium stocks everything from fishing and camping gear to fine wine and imported beer. It's a good place to pick up last-minute items on Sunday, when other stores are closed. ✉ *833 Ilima Ave., Lanai City* ☎ *808/565–6433* ⏲ *Closed Sat.*

Lanai City Service. In addition to being Lanai's only gas station and auto-parts store, this outfit sells resort wear, *manapua* (steamed buns with pork filling), hot dogs, beer, soda, and bottled water. The on-site Plantation Deli serves specialty or make-your-own sandwiches, salads, and soups. ✉ *1036 Lanai Ave., Lanai City* ☎ *808/565–7227.*

SPAS

Hawanawana Spa. No two experiences are alike at Hawanawana Spa, where every treatment is tailored to your individual desires. Spa and salon services—like the Ocean Ritual or Lanai Tai Signature Scrub—feature locally inspired ingredients and techniques. The spa's Zen aesthetic is complimented with soothing colors of natural sands, ocean textures, and whimsical touches from beneath the sea. Massages are available in couples' suites; limited selection available poolside. ✉ *Four Seasons Resort Lanai, 1 Manele Bay Rd., Manele, Lanai City* ☎ *808/565–2088* 🌐 *www.fourseasons.com/lanai* ☞ *$240–$360 for 60–90 min massage, Ocean Ritual $460 per person for two hours.*

NIGHTLIFE

Lanai's nightlife offerings are fairly limited. The Sports Bar at the Four Seasons Resort Lanai at Manele Bay features a lively sophisticated atmosphere in which to take in ocean views while noshing with your favorite libations. The Hale Keaka (Lanai Theater) screens recent releases five nights a week.

FAMILY **Hale Keaka (Lanai Theater).** Modern and comfortable, Hale Keaka's two 93-seat theaters and green room screen recent movie releases throughout the week. ✉ *465 7th St., Lanai City* 🌐 *www.lanai96763.com.*

Sports Bar & Grill. At the Four Seasons Resort Lanai, the oceanfront Sports Bar & Grill is an open-air lounge serving casual fare such as kiawe-smoked chicken wings, burgers, and kalbi-beef short ribs. This isn't your average sports bar food though, as an expansive menu tempts with fresh seafood appetizers, lavish salads, and healthy entrées. Pool tables, shuffleboard courts, and a 90-inch TV make for an amusing time out. An added bonus: dolphins play in the bay below. ✉ *Four Seasons Resort Lanai, 1 Manele Bay Rd., Manele, Lanai City* ☎ *808/565–2000* 🌐 *www.fourseasons.com/lanai.*

TRAVEL SMART HAWAII

GETTING HERE AND AROUND

AIR TRAVEL

Flying time to Oahu or Maui is about 10 hours from New York, 8 hours from Chicago, and 5 hours from Los Angeles.

All the major airline carriers serving Hawaii fly direct to Honolulu; some also offer nonstops to Maui, Kauai, and the Big Island, though most flights to the latter two come from the West Coast only. Honolulu International Airport, although open-air and seemingly more casual than most major airports, can be very busy. Allow extra travel time during busy mornings and afternoons.

Plants and plant products are subject to regulation by the Department of Agriculture, both on entering and leaving Hawaii. Upon leaving, you'll have to have your bags x-rayed and tagged at the airport's agricultural inspection station before you proceed to check-in. Pineapples and coconuts with the packer's agricultural inspection stamp pass freely; papayas must be treated, inspected, and stamped. All other fruits are banned for export to the U.S. mainland. Flowers pass except for gardenia, rose leaves, jade vine, and mauna loa. Also banned are insects, snails, soil, cotton, cacti, sugarcane, and all berry plants.

Bringing your dog or cat with you is a tricky process and not something to be done lightly. Hawaii is a rabies-free state and requires animals to pass strict quarantine rules, which you can find online at 🌐 *hdoa.hawaii.gov/ai/aqs/*. Most airlines do not allow pets to travel in the cabin on flights to Hawaii (though Alaska Airlines and Hawaiian Airlines are notable exceptions). If specific pre- and post-arrival requirements are met, most animals qualify for a five-day-or-less quarantine.

Air-Travel Resources in Hawaii State of Hawaii Airports Division Offices. ☎ *808/836–6413* 🌐 *www.hidot.hawaii.gov/airports.*

AIRPORTS

All of Hawaii's major islands have their own airports, but Honolulu's International Airport is the main stopover for most domestic and international flights. From Honolulu, there are flights to the Neighbor Islands almost every half-hour from early morning until evening. In addition, some carriers now offer nonstop service directly from the mainland to Maui, Kauai, and the Big Island on a limited basis.

BIG ISLAND OF HAWAII AIRPORTS

Those flying to the Big Island regularly land at one of two fields. Ellison Onizuka Kona International Airport at Keahole, on the west side, serves Kailua-Kona, Keauhou, the Kohala Coast, North Kohala, Waimea, and points south. Hilo International Airport is more appropriate for those planning visits based on the east side of the island.

Waimea-Kohala Airport, called Kamuela Airport by residents, is used primarily for private flights between islands, but has recently welcomed one commercial carrier with a single route.

Airport Information Hilo International Airport (ITO). ☎ *808/961–9300* 🌐 *hawaii.gov/ito.* **Ellison Onizuka Kona International Airport at Keahole (KOA).** ☎ *808/327–9520* 🌐 *hawaii.gov/koa.* **Waimea-Kohala Airport (MUE).** ☎ *808/887–8126* 🌐 *hawaii.gov/mue.*

HONOLULU/OAHU AIRPORT

Honolulu International Airport (HNL) is roughly 20 minutes (9 miles) west of Waikiki (40 minutes during rush hour), and is served by most of the major domestic and international carriers. To travel to other islands from Honolulu, you can depart from either the interisland terminal or the commuter-airline terminal, located in two separate structures adjacent to the main overseas terminal building. A free Wiki-Wiki shuttle bus operates between terminals.

Airport Information **Honolulu International Airport (HNL).** ☎ *808/836–6411* 🌐 *airports.hawaii.gov/hnl/.*

KAUAI

On Kauai, visitors fly into Lihue Airport, on the East Side of the island. Visitor information booths are outside each baggage-claim area. Visitors will also find news- and lei stands, an HMS Host restaurant, and a Travel Traders gift shop at the airport.

Information **Lihue Airport (LIH).** ☎ *808/274–3800* 🌐 *www.hawaii.gov/dot/airports.*

MAUI AIRPORTS

Maui has two major airports. Kahului Airport handles major airlines and interisland flights; it's the only airport on Maui that has direct service from the mainland. Kapalua–West Maui Airport is served by Hawaiian and Mokulele airlines. If you're staying in West Maui and you're flying in from another island, you can avoid the hour drive from the Kahului Airport by flying into Kapalua–West Maui Airport. Hana Airport in East Maui is small; Mokulele Airlines flies twice per day between Kahului and Hana.

Airport Information **Hana Airport (HNM).** ✉ *700 Alalele Rd., Hana* ☎ *808/248–4861* 🌐 *www.airports.hawaii.gov/hnm.* **Kahului Airport (OGG).** ✉ *1 Keolani Pl., Kahului* ☎ *808/872–3830* 🌐 *www.airports.hawaii.gov/ogg.* **Kapalua–West Maui Airport (JHM).** ✉ *4050 Honoapiilani Hwy, Lahaina* ☎ *808/665–6108* 🌐 *www.airports.hawaii.gov/jhm.*

MOLOKAI AIRPORT

Molokai's transportation hub is Hoolehua Airport, a tiny airstrip 8 miles west of Kaunakakai and about 18 miles east of Maunaloa. An even smaller airstrip serves the little community of Kalaupapa on the north shore.

Contacts **Molokai Airport (MKK).** ✉ *3980 Airport Loop, Hoolehua* ☎ *808/567–9660* 🌐 *www.airports.hawaii.gov/mkk.*

LANAI AIRPORT

Lanai's tiny airport is in Lanai City.

Contacts **Lanai Airport (LNY).** ☎ *808/565–7942* 🌐 *www.airports.hawaii.gov/lny.*

FLIGHTS

Big Island of Hawaii: Serving Kona are Air Canada, Alaska Airlines, American Airlines, Delta Airlines, Hawaiian Airlines, Japan Airlines, Mokulele, United Airlines, Virgin Atlantic, and Westjet. Hawaiian, Mokulele, and United fly also into Hilo.

Kauai: Alaska Airlines, American Airlines, Delta, Hawaiian, and United Airlines all offer nonstop flights to Kauai from the mainland U.S.; all other Mainland flights require a connection in Honolulu.

Lanai and Molokai: No airlines fly nonstop to either island from the mainland U.S. All flights to Lanai are via Honolulu; you can take local flights to Molokai from the Big Island of Hawaii, Honolulu, or Maui.

Maui: Alaska Airlines, American Airlines, Delta, Hawaiian Airlines, United offer nonstop service from the U.S. mainland.

Oahu: From the U.S. mainland, Alaska Airlines, American, Delta, Hawaiian, and United are the primary U.S. carriers to serve Honolulu. Southwest plans to add service to Hawaii in late 2018 or early 2019.

Mainland Airline Contacts **Alaska Airlines.** ☎ *800/252–7522* 🌐 *www.alaskaair.com.* **American Airlines.** ☎ *800/433–7300* 🌐 *www.aa.com.* **Delta Airlines.** ☎ *800/221–1212 for U.S. reservations, 800/241–4141 for international reservations* 🌐 *www.delta.com.* **Hawaiian Airlines.** ☎ *800/367–5320* 🌐 *www.hawaiianairlines.com.* **Southwest.** ☎ *800/435–9792* 🌐 *www.southwest.com.* **United Airlines.** ☎ *800/864–8331 for U.S. reservations* 🌐 *www.united.com.*

Interisland Airline Contacts **Hawaiian Airlines.** ☎ *800/367–5320* 🌐 *www.hawaiianairlines.com.* **Makani Kai Air.** ☎ *808/834–1111, 877/255–8532* 🌐 *www.makanikaiair.com.* **Mokulele Airlines.** ☎ *866/260–7070* 🌐 *www.mokuleleairlines.com.*

BOAT TRAVEL

There is daily ferry service between Lahaina on Maui, and Manele Bay on Lanai, with Expeditions Lanai Ferry. The 9-mile crossing costs $60 round-trip and takes about 45 minutes or so, depending on ocean conditions (which can make this trip a rough one).

There is no longer ferry service to Molokai

Ferry Contacts Expeditions Lanai Ferry. ☎ *800/695–2624* 🌐 *www.go-lanai.com.*

BUS TRAVEL

BIG ISLAND OF HAWAII

Depending on where you're staying, you can take advantage of the affordable Hawaii County Mass Transit Agency's Hele-On Bus, which travels several routes throughout the island. Mostly serving local commuters, the Hele-On Bus costs $2 per person (students and senior citizens pay $1). Just wait at a scheduled stop and flag down the bus. A one-way journey between Hilo and Kona takes about four hours. There's regular service in and around downtown Hilo, Kailua-Kona, Waimea, North and South Kohala, Honokaa, and Pahoa. However, some routes are served only once a day so if you are planning on using the bus, be sure to study up carefully before assuming the bus serves your area.

Visitors staying in Hilo can take advantage of the Transit Agency's Shared Ride Taxi program, which provides door-to-door transportation in the area. A one-way fare is $2, and a book of 15 coupons can be purchased for $30. Visitors to Kona can also take advantage of free trolleys operated by local shopping centers.

Contacts Hele-On Bus. ☎ *808/961–8744* 🌐 *www.heleonbus.org.*

KAUAI

On Kauai, the County Transportation Agency operates the Kauai Bus, which provides service between Hanalei and Kekaha. It also provides limited service to the airport and to Koloa and Poipu. The fare is $2 for adults, and frequent-rider passes are available.

Information Kauai Bus. ☎ *808/246–8110* 🌐 *www.kauai.com/kauai-bus.*

MAUI

Maui Bus, operated by the tour company Roberts Hawaii, offers 13 routes in and between various Central, South, and West Maui communities. You can travel in and around Wailuku, Kahului, Lahaina, Kaanapali, Kapalua, Kihei, Wailea, Maalaea, the North Shore (Paia), and Upcountry (including Kula, Pukalani, Makawao, Haliimaile, and Haiku). The Upcountry and Haiku Islander routes include a stop at Kahului Airport. All routes cost $2 per boarding.

Bus Contact Maui Bus. ☎ *808/871–4838* 🌐 *www.mauicounty.gov/bus.*

OAHU

Getting around by bus is an affordable option on Oahu, particularly in the most heavily touristed areas of Waikiki. In addition to TheBus and the Waikiki Trolley, Waikiki has brightly painted private buses, many of them free, that shuttle you to such commercial attractions as dinner cruises, garment factories, and the like.

You can travel around the island or just down Kalakaua Avenue for $2.75 on Honolulu's municipal transportation system, affectionately known as TheBus. It's one of the island's best bargains. Buses make stops in Waikiki every 10–15 minutes to take passengers to nearby shopping areas. Free transfers have been discontinued, but you can purchase a one-day pass for $5.50. Just ask the driver as you're boarding. Exact change is required, and dollar bills are accepted.

The Waikiki Trolley has five lines and dozens of stops that allow you to plan your own itinerary while riding on brass-trimmed, open-air buses that look like trolleys. The Historic Honolulu Tour (Red Line) travels between Waikiki and Chinatown and includes stops at the

State Capitol, Iolani Palace, and the King Kamehameha statue. The Waikiki-Ala Moana Shopping Shuttle (Pink Line) runs from the T Galleria by DFS to Eggs 'n Things, stopping at various Waikiki locations and the Ala Moana Center. The Scenic Diamond Head Sightseeing Tour (Green Line) runs through Waikiki and down around Diamond Head. There's also a south shore coastline tour (Blue Line) and a line that runs to Aloha Stadium and Pearl Harbor (Purple Line). A one-day pass costs $23 to $45, four-day passes are $36.50 to $74, and seven-day passes are $41 to $79. All passes are discounted when purchased in advance.

Contacts TheBus. ☎ *808/848–5555* 🌐 *www.thebus.org.* **Waikiki Trolley.** ☎ *808/593–2822* 🌐 *waikikitrolley.com.*

CAR TRAVEL

Technically, the Big Island of Hawaii is the only island you can completely circle by car, but each island offers plenty of sightseeing from its miles of roadways.

On Kauai, the 15-mile stretch of the Napali Coast is the only part of the island's coastline that's not accessible by car. Otherwise, one main road can get you from Barking Sands Beach on the West Side to Haena on the North Shore.

Traffic on Maui can be very bad branching out from Kahului to and from Paia, Kihei, and Lahaina. Parking along many streets is curtailed during these times, and towing is strictly practiced. Read curbside parking signs before leaving your vehicle, even at a meter.

Although Molokai and Lanai have fewer roadways, car rental is still worthwhile and will allow plenty of interesting sightseeing. A four-wheel-drive vehicle is best.

Oahu can be circled except for the roadless northwest-shore area around Kaena Point. Elsewhere, major highways follow the shoreline and traverse the island at two points. Rush-hour traffic (6:30 to 8:30 am and 3:30 to 6 pm) can be frustrating around Honolulu and the outlying areas, as many thoroughfares allow no left turns.

Asking for directions will almost always produce a helpful explanation from the locals, but you should be prepared for an Islands term or two. Instead of using compass directions, remember that Hawaii residents refer to places as being either *mauka* (toward the mountains) or *makai* (toward the ocean) from one another.

GASOLINE

National chains like 76, Chevron, 7-Eleven, and Shell are ubiquitous, and accept all major credit cards right at the pump or inside the station. Gasoline is generally more expensive than on the mainland United States (other than in California). Neighbor Islands have higher gasoline prices than Oahu.

ROAD CONDITIONS

It's difficult to get lost in most of Hawaii. Although their names may challenge a visitor's tongue, roads and streets are well marked; just watch out for the many one-way streets in Waikiki. Keep an eye open for the Hawaii Visitors and Convention Bureau's red-caped King Kamehameha signs, which mark attractions and scenic spots. Free publications containing high-quality road maps can be found on all islands. And, of course, a GPS or your passenger's smartphone are great ways to find your way around, too.

Many of Hawaii's roads are two-lane highways with limited shoulders—and yes, even in paradise, there is traffic, especially during the morning and afternoon rush hour. In rural areas, it's not unusual for gas stations to close early. If you see that your tank is getting low, don't take any chances; fill up when you see a station. In Hawaii, turning right on a red light is legal, except where noted. Use caution during heavy downpours, especially if you see signs warning of falling rocks. If you're enjoying views from the road or need to study a map, pull over to the side. Remember the aloha spirit when you are driving; allow other cars to merge, don't honk (it's considered extremely rude in the Islands), leave a comfortable distance between your car and the car ahead of you; use your headlights, especially during sunrise and sunset, and use your turn signals.

ROADSIDE EMERGENCIES

If you have an accident or car trouble, call the roadside assistance number on your rental car contract or AAA Help. If you find that your car has been broken into or stolen, report it immediately to your rental car company and they can assist you. Call 911 for any emergency.

Emergency Services AAA Help. ☎ *800/222-4357* 🌐 *www.hawaii.aaa.com.*

RULES OF THE ROAD

Be sure to buckle up, as Hawaii has a strictly enforced mandatory seat-belt law for front- and backseat passengers. Children under four must be in a car seat (available from car-rental agencies), and children ages four to seven must be seated in a booster seat or child safety seat with restraint such as a lap and shoulder belt. Hawaii also prohibits texting or talking on the phone (unless you are over 18 and using a hands-free device) while driving. The highway speed limit is usually 55 mph. In-town traffic travels 25–40 mph. Jaywalking is not uncommon, so watch for pedestrians, especially in congested areas such as Waikiki and downtown Honolulu. Unauthorized use of a parking space reserved for persons with disabilities can net you a $250–$500 fine.

Oahu's drivers are generally courteous, and you rarely hear a horn. People will slow down and let you into traffic with a wave of the hand. A friendly wave back is customary. If a driver sticks a hand out the window in a fist with the thumb and pinky sticking straight out, this is a good thing: it's the *shaka,* the Hawaiian symbol for "hang loose," and is often used to say "thanks."

CAR RENTAL

If you plan to do lots of sightseeing, it's best to rent a car. Even if all you want to do is relax at your resort, you may want to hop in the car to check out a popular restaurant. All the big national rental car agencies have locations throughout Hawaii. There also are several local rental car companies so be sure to compare prices before you book. While in the Islands, you can rent anything from an econobox to a Ferrari. On the Big Island, Lanai, and Molokai, four-wheel-drive vehicles are recommended for exploring off the beaten path. It's wise to make reservations far in advance and make sure that a confirmed reservation guarantees you a car, especially if visiting during peak seasons or for major conventions or sporting events.

Rates begin at about $30 to $40 a day for an economy car with air-conditioning, automatic transmission, and unlimited mileage, depending on your pickup location. This does not include the airport concession fee, general excise tax, rental vehicle surcharge, or vehicle license fee. When you reserve a car, ask about cancellation penalties and drop-off charges should you plan to pick up the car in one location and return it to another.

In Hawaii you must be 21 years of age to rent a car and you must have a valid driver's license and a major credit card. Those under 25 will pay a daily surcharge of $10 to $30. Your unexpired mainland driver's license is valid for rental for up to 90 days. Request car seats and extras such as GPS when you make your reservation. Car seats and boosters range from about $10 to $15 per day.

CAR RENTAL RESOURCES

Automobile Associations		
AAA	800/222-4357 for roadside assistance	www.aaa.com
National Automobile Club	650/294-7000	www.nacroadservice.com (CA residents only)
Local Agencies		
Aloha Campers (Maui)	855/671-1122	www.alohacampers.com
Discount Hawaii Car Rental	800/292-1930	www.discounthawaiicar-rental.com
Harper Car and Truck Rental (Big Island)	800/852-9993	www.harpershawaii.com
Hawaii Car Rental (Big Island, Maui, Oahu)	800/655-7989	www.hawaiicarrental.com
Hawaiian Discount Car Rentals (all but Lanai)	800/955-3142	www.hawaiidrive-o.com
JN Car and Truck Rentals (Oahu)	800/363-4180	www.jnrentalshawaii.com
Lanai City Service (Lanai)	808/565-7227	www.adventurelanai.com
Molokai Rental Car (Molokai)	808/336-0670	www.molokairentalcar.com
Major Agencies		
Alamo	888/233-8749	www.alamo.com
Avis	800/633-3469	www.avis.com
Budget	800/218-7992	www.budget.com
Dollar	800/800-5252	www.dollar.com
Enterprise	855/226-9289	www.enterprise.com
Hertz	800/654-3131	www.hertz.com
National Car Rental	888/826-6890	www.nationalcar.com
Thrifty	800/334-1705	www.thrifty.com

ESSENTIALS

ACCOMMODATIONS

Hawaii truly offers something for everyone. Are you looking for a luxurious oceanfront resort loaded with amenities, an intimate two-room bed-and-breakfast tucked away in a lush rain forest, a house with a pool and incredible views for your extended family, a condominium just steps from the 18th hole, or even a campsite at a national park? You can find all these and more throughout the Islands.

Most hotels and other lodgings require you to give your credit-card details before they will confirm your reservation. Get confirmation in writing and have a copy of it handy when you check in. Be sure you understand the hotel's cancellation policy. Some places allow you to cancel without any kind of penalty—even if you prepaid to secure a discounted rate—if you cancel at least 24 hours in advance. Others require you to cancel a week in advance or penalize you the cost of one night. Small inns and bed-and-breakfasts are most likely to require you to cancel far in advance. Most hotels allow children under a certain age to stay in their parents' room at no extra charge, but others charge for them as adults; find out the cutoff age for discounts.

Hotel reviews have been shortened. For full information, visit www.Fodors.com.

BED-AND-BREAKFASTS

For many travelers, nothing compares to the personal service and guest interaction offered at bed-and-breakfasts. There are hundreds of bed-and-breakfasts throughout the Islands; many even invite their guests to enjoy complimentary wine tastings and activities such as lei making and basket weaving. Each island's website also features a listing of member B&Bs that are individually owned.

Contacts Hawaii's Best Bed & Breakfasts. ☎ *808/885–4550* 🌐 *www.bestbnb.com.*

CONDOMINIUM AND HOUSE RENTALS

Vacation rentals are perfect for couples, families, and friends traveling together who like the convenience of staying at a home away from home. Properties managed by individual owners can be found on online vacation-rental listing directories such as HomeAway, Vacation Rentals By Owners (VRBO), and Airbnb, as well as on the visitors bureau website for each island. There also are several Islands-based management companies with vacation rentals.

Compare companies, as some offer Internet specials and free night stays when booking. Policies vary, but most require a minimum stay, usually greater during peak travel seasons.

Contacts Airbnb. ☎ *855/424–7262* 🌐 *www.airbnb.com.* **HomeAway.** ☎ *877/228–3145* 🌐 *www.homeaway.com.* **Vacation Rentals By Owner.** 🌐 *www.vrbo.com.*

COMMUNICATIONS

INTERNET

If you've brought your laptop with you to the Islands, you should have no problem connecting to the Internet. Major hotels and resorts offer high-speed access in rooms and/or lobbies. In some cases there will be an hourly or daily charge billed to your room. If you're staying at a small inn or vacation home without Internet access (a rarity these days), ask for the nearest café or coffee shop with wireless access.

EATING OUT

Whether you're looking for a dinner for two in a romantic oceanfront dining room or a family get-together in a hole-in-the-wall serving traditional Hawaiian fare like *kalua* (cooked in an underground oven) pig, you'll find it throughout the Islands. When it comes to eating, Hawaii has something for every taste bud and every budget. With chefs using locally grown fruits and vegetables, vegetarians often have many exciting choices for their meals. And because Hawaii is a popular destination for families, restaurants almost always have a children's menu. When making a reservation at your hotel's dining room, ask about free or reduced-price meals for children.

MEALS AND MEALTIMES

Breakfast is usually served from 6 or 7 am to 9:30 or 10 am.

Lunch typically runs from 11:30 am to around 1:30 or 2 pm, and will include salads, sandwiches, and lighter fare. The "plate lunch," a favorite of many locals, usually consists of an Asian protein, like shoyu chicken, seared ahi or teriyaki beef—served with two scoops of white rice and a scoop of macaroni or potato salad. The phrase "broke da mouth," often used to describe these plates, refers not only to their size, but also their tastiness.

Dinner is usually served from 5 to 9 pm and, depending on the restaurant, can be a simple or lavish affair. Stick to the chefs' specials if you can because they usually represent the best of the season. *Poke* (marinated raw tuna) is a local specialty and can often be found on *pupu* (appetizer) menus.

Meals in resort areas are pricey and only sometimes excellent. The restaurants we include are the cream of the crop in each price category. Unless otherwise noted, the restaurants listed are open daily for lunch and dinner.

For guidelines on tipping, see Tipping.

RESERVATIONS AND DRESS

Hawaii is decidedly casual. Aloha shirts and shorts or long pants for men and Islands-style dresses or casual resort wear for women are standard attire for evenings in most hotel restaurants and local eateries. T-shirts and shorts will do the trick for breakfast and lunch. We mention dress only when men are required to wear a jacket or a jacket and tie.

Regardless of where you are, it's a good idea to make a reservation if you can. In some places, it's expected. We only mention reservations specifically when they are essential or when they are not accepted. For popular restaurants, book as far ahead as you can (often a month or more), and reconfirm as soon as you arrive. Large parties should always call ahead to check the reservations policy.

WINE, BEER, AND SPIRITS

Hawaii has a new generation of microbreweries, including on-site microbreweries at many restaurants. The drinking age in Hawaii is 21 years of age, and a photo ID must be presented to purchase alcoholic beverages. Bars are open until 2 am; venues with a cabaret license can stay open until 4 am. No matter what you might see in the local parks, drinking alcohol in public parks or on the beaches is illegal. It's also illegal to have open containers of alcohol in motor vehicles.

HEALTH

Hawaii is known not only as the Aloha State, but also as the Health State. The life expectancy here is 82.4 years, the longest in the nation. Balmy weather makes it easy to remain active year-round, and the low-stress attitude seems to contribute to the general well-being. When visiting the Islands, however, there are a few health issues to keep in mind.

The Hawaii State Department of Health recommends that you drink 16 ounces of water per hour to avoid dehydration when hiking or spending time in the sun. Use sunblock, wear UV–reflective sunglasses, and protect your head with a visor or hat. If you're not acclimated to warm, humid weather, you should allow plenty of time for rest stops and refreshments. When visiting freshwater streams, be aware of the tropical disease leptospirosis, spread by animal urine and carried into streams and mud. Symptoms include fever, headache, nausea, and red eyes. If left untreated it can cause liver and kidney damage, respiratory failure, internal bleeding, and even death. To avoid this, don't swim or wade in freshwater streams or ponds if you have open sores and don't drink from any freshwater streams or ponds.

On the Islands, fog is a rare occurrence, but there can often be "vog," an airborne haze of gases released from volcanic vents on the Big Island. During certain weather conditions, such as "Kona Winds," the vog can settle over the Islands and wreak havoc with respiratory and other health conditions, especially asthma or emphysema. If susceptible, stay indoors and get emergency assistance if needed.

The Islands have their share of insects. Most are harmless but annoying, but Dengue fever, a mosquito-borne disease, has been reported in Oahu. When planning to spend time outdoors in hiking areas, wear long-sleeve clothing and pants, and use mosquito repellent containing DEET. In damp places you may encounter the dreaded local centipedes, which are brown and blue and measure up to eight inches long. Their painful sting is similar to those of bees and wasps. When camping, shake out your sleeping bag and check your shoes, as the centipedes like cozy places. When hiking in remote areas, always carry a first-aid kit.

HOURS OF OPERATION

Even people in paradise have to work. Generally local business hours are weekdays 8–5. Banks are usually open Monday–Thursday 8:30–4 and until 6 on Friday. Some banks have Saturday-morning hours.

Many self-serve gas stations stay open around the clock, with full-service stations usually open from around 7 am until 9 pm. U.S. post offices generally are open weekdays from 8 or 10 to 4:30 or 5 and Saturday from 9 to noon or 2. On Oahu, the Ala Moana post office is the only branch to stay open until 4:30 pm on Saturday. The main Honolulu International Airport facility is open until 4 pm on Saturday.

Most museums generally open their doors between 9 and 10 and stay open until 5 Tuesday to Saturday. Many museums operate with afternoon hours only on Sunday and close on Monday. Visitor-attraction hours vary, but most sights are open daily with the exception of major holidays such as Christmas. Check the local newspaper upon arrival for attraction hours and schedules if visiting over holiday periods. The local daily carries a listing of "What's Open/What's Not" for those time periods.

Stores in resort areas sometimes open as early as 8, with shopping-center opening hours varying from 9 to 10 on weekdays and Saturday, a bit later on Sunday. Bigger malls stay open until 9 weekdays and Saturday and close at between 5 and 7 on Sunday. Boutiques in resort areas may stay open as late as 11.

MONEY

⇨ *Prices for Exploring sights are given for adults.* Substantially reduced fees are almost always available for children, students, and senior citizens.

ATMS AND BANKS

ATMs, for easy access to cash, can be found at many locations throughout Oahu, including shopping centers, convenience and grocery stores, and hotels and resorts, as well as outside most bank branches.

CREDIT CARDS

It's a good idea to inform your credit-card company before you travel. Otherwise, the credit-card company might put a hold on your card owing to unusual activity—not a good thing halfway through your trip. Record all your credit-card numbers—as well as the phone numbers to call if your cards are lost or stolen—in a safe place, so you're prepared should something go wrong. Both MasterCard and Visa have general numbers you can call (collect, if you're abroad) if your card is lost, but you're better off calling the number of your issuing bank, since MasterCard and Visa usually just transfer you to your bank; your bank's number is usually printed on your card.

Reporting Lost Cards **American Express.** ☎ *800/528–4800 in the U.S.* 🌐 *www.americanexpress.com.* **Diners Club.** ☎ *800/234–6377 in the U.S.* 🌐 *www.dinersclubus.com.* **Discover.** ☎ *800/347–2683 in the U.S.* 🌐 *www.discover.com.* **MasterCard.** ☎ *800/627–8372 in the U.S.* 🌐 *www.mastercard.us.* **Visa.** ☎ *800/847–2911 in the U.S.* 🌐 *www.usa.visa.com.*

PACKING

Hawaii is casual: sandals, bathing suits, and comfortable, informal clothing are the norm. In summer, synthetic slacks and shirts, although easy to care for, can be uncomfortably warm. Only a few upscale restaurants require a jacket for dinner. The aloha shirt is accepted dress in Hawaii for business and most social occasions. Shorts are standard daytime attire, along with a T-shirt or polo shirt. There's no need to buy expensive sandals on the mainland—here you can get flip-flops for a couple of dollars and off-brand sandals for $20. Golfers should remember that many courses have dress codes requiring a collared shirt. If you're not prepared, you can pick up appropriate clothing at resort pro shops. If you're visiting in winter or planning to visit a high-altitude area, bring a sweater or light- to medium-weight jacket. A polar fleece pullover is ideal.

One of the most important things to tuck into your suitcase is sunscreen. Hats and sunglasses offer important sun protection, too. All major hotels in Hawaii provide beach towels.

SAFETY

Hawaii is generally a safe tourist destination, but it's still wise to follow common-sense safety precautions. Hotel and visitor-center staff can provide information should you decide to head out on your own to more remote areas. Don't leave any valuables in your rental car, not even in a locked trunk. Avoid poorly lighted areas, beach parks, and isolated areas after dark as a precaution.

When hiking, stay on marked trails, no matter how alluring the temptation might be to stray. Weather conditions can cause landscapes to become muddy, slippery, and tenuous, so staying on marked trails will lessen the possibility of a fall or getting lost. Be sure to heed flash flood watches or warnings. Never try to cross a stream, either on food or in a vehicle, during these weather conditions.

Ocean safety is of the utmost importance when visiting an island destination. Don't swim alone, and follow the international signage posted at beaches that alerts swimmers to strong currents, man-of-war jellyfish, sharp coral, high surf, sharks, and dangerous shore breaks. At coastal lookouts along cliff tops, heed the signs indicating that waves can climb over the ledges. Check with lifeguards at each beach for current conditions, and if the red flags are up, indicating swimming and surfing are not allowed, don't go in. Waters that look calm on the surface can harbor strong currents and undertows.

TAXES

There's a 4.17% state sales tax on all purchases, including food. A hotel room tax of 10.25%, combined with the sales tax of 4.17%, equals a 14.42% rate added onto your hotel bill. A $7.50-per-day road tax is also assessed on each rental vehicle.

TIME

Hawaii is on Hawaiian standard time, five hours behind New York, and two hours behind Los Angeles.

When the U.S. mainland is on daylight saving time, Hawaii is not, so add an extra hour of time difference between the Islands and U.S. mainland destinations. You may also find that things generally move more slowly here. That has nothing to do with your watch—it's just the laid-back way called Hawaiian time.

TIPPING GUIDELINES FOR HAWAII	
Bartender	$1 to $5 per round of drinks, depending on the number of drinks
Bellhop	$2 to $5 per bag, depending on the level of the hotel and whether you have bulky items like golf clubs, surfboards, etc.
Hotel Concierge	$10 or more, depending on the service
Hotel Doorman	$1 to $5 if he helps you get a cab or helps with bags, golf clubs, etc.
Hotel Maid	$2 to $5 a day, depending on the level of the hotel (either daily or at the end of your stay, in cash)
Hotel Room-Service Waiter	$2 to $5 per delivery, even if a service charge has been added
Porter/Skycap at Airport	$2 to $3 per bag
Spa Personnel	15% to 20% of the cost of your service
Taxi Driver	15% to 20%, but round up the fare to the next dollar amount
Tour Guide	10% of the cost of the tour
Valet Parking Attendant	$2 to $5, each time your car is brought to you
Waiter	15% to 20%, with 20% being the norm at high-end restaurants; nothing additional if a service charge is added to the bill

TIPPING

As this is a major vacation destination and many of the people who work in the service industry rely on tips to supplement their wages, tipping is not only common, but expected. Consider a tip of 18% to 20% for excellent restaurant service, even at casual eateries. It's customary to tip all service folk at hotels and resorts, from bellmen to valets to housekeepers. Keeping a stash of "singles" in your wallet or handbag makes this easy.

TOURS

ADVENTURE STUDY

A tour of Kilauea Volcano—the most active volcano on earth—is even better when led by an actual geologist, volcanologist, retired ranger, or even botanist. Mother Nature does not offer a money-back guarantee, so keep in mind that seeing active lava cannot be promised.

Contacts Friends of Hawaii Volcanoes National Park. ☎ *808/985–7373* 🌐 *fhvnp.org.* **Kapoho Kine Adventures.** ✉ *224 Kamehameha Ave., Hilo* ☎ *808/964–1000* 🌐 *www.kapohokine.com.*

BIKING

If you're a bicycling enthusiast, you've got exciting options on the Big Island. **TIP→ Most airlines accommodate bikes as luggage, provided they're dismantled and boxed.**

Contacts Bicycle Adventures. ☎ *800/443–6060* 🌐 *www.bicycleadventures.com.* **WomanTours.** ☎ *800/247–1444* 🌐 *www.womantours.com.*

BIRD-WATCHING

More than 150 species of birds live in the Hawaiian Islands. For $5,450 per person double-occupancy, Field Guides has a three-island (Oahu, Kauai, and the Big Island), 10-day, guided bird-watching trip that includes accommodations, meals, ground transportation, and interisland air.

Victor Emanuel Nature Tours, the largest company in the world specializing in birding tours, has two 10-day Fall Hawaii and Spring Hawaii trips to Oahu, Kauai, and the Big Island that cost $4,895 (fall), including double-occupancy accommodations, meals, interisland air, ground transportation, and guided excursions.

Contacts **Field Guides.** ☎ *800/728–4953* 🌐 *www.fieldguides.com.* **Hawaii Forest & Trail.** ✉ *73-5598 Olowalu St., Kailua-Kona* ☎ *800/464–1993* 🌐 *www.hawaii-forest.com.* **Victor Emanuel Nature Tours.** ☎ *800/328–8368* 🌐 *www.ventbird.com.*

HIKING

Hiking the Garden Island is the theme of a weeklong trip to Kauai sponsored by Sierra Club Outings. In addition to daylong hikes of 5 to 9 miles through many of the rain forests in Kokee State Park, participants will have opportunities for snorkeling and swimming at secluded beaches, as well as bird-watching. Hikers also will help in the maintenance of some of the trails. Accommodations are in shared cabins and, as with all Sierra Club Outings, participants are expected to help prepare some of the meals using only local, fresh ingredients. The trip costs about $1,695 per person and includes accommodations, meals, and ground transportation.

Timberline Adventures offers periodic trips to the Garden Island, including its *Kauai: Waimea Canyon and the NaPali Coast*, a six-day journey into the rain forests of Kokee State Park and Waimea Canyon. With miles of hiking trails, it's an opportunity to explore Kauai's inner beauty, including rare birds, waterfalls, and spectacular scenery. Other day trips have you hiking Sleeping Giant and kayaking the Wailua River. Perhaps the best hike is along the Kalalau Trail up into Hanakapiai Falls, with a payoff of tropical tranquility. Cost is $3,495/person for a double booking or $4,395 for a single.

Travelers must purchase their own tickets to and from their gateway city.

Contacts **Sierra Club Outings.** ☎ *415/977–5500* 🌐 *sierracluboutings.org.* **Timberline Adventures.** ☎ *800/417–2453* 🌐 *www.timberline-adventures.com.*

TRIP INSURANCE

Comprehensive trip insurance is valuable if you're booking a very expensive or complicated trip (particularly to an isolated region) or if you're booking far in advance. Comprehensive policies typically cover trip cancellation and interruption, letting you cancel or cut your trip short because of illness, or, in some cases, acts of terrorism in your destination. Such policies might also cover evacuation and medical care. Some also cover you for trip delays because of bad weather or mechanical problems, as well as for lost or delayed luggage.

Always read the fine print of your policy to make sure that you're covered for the risks that most concern you. Compare several policies to be sure you're getting the best price and range of coverage available.

Insurance Comparison Info **InsureMyTrip.** ☎ *800/487–4722* 🌐 *www.insuremytrip.com.* **Squaremouth.** ☎ *800/240–0369* 🌐 *www.squaremouth.com.*

Comprehensive Insurers **Allianz Global Assistance.** ☎ *866/884–3556* 🌐 *www.allianztravelinsurance.com.* **Generali Global Assistance (formerly CSA Travel Protection).** ☎ *800/874–2442* 🌐 *www.generalitravelinsurance.com/.* **Travel Guard.** ☎ *800/826–5248* 🌐 *mvp.travelguard.com.* **Travelex Insurance.** ☎ *800/228–9792* 🌐 *www.travelexinsurance.com.* **Travel Insured International.** ☎ *800/243–3174* 🌐 *www.travelinsured.com.*

VISITOR INFORMATION

Contacts **Hawaii Beach Safety.** 🌐 *hawaiibeachsafety.com.* **Hawaii Department of Land and Natural Resources.** 🌐 *dlnr.hawaii.gov.* **Hawaii Tourism Authority.** 🌐 *www.gohawaii.com.*

INDEX

F

G

H

I

N

O

P

Q

R

Z

PHOTO CREDITS

Front cover: Maridav/Shutterstock [Description: Napali coastline in Kaui, Hawaii] Back cover, from left to right: Drazen Vukelic/Shutterstock; Molokai Ranch; Photodisc. Spine: EpicStockMedia/iStockphoto/Thinkstock. Socrates | Dreamstime.com (1). Eddy Galeotti/Shutterstock (2, 3). Zhu_zhu | Dreamstime.com (4, 5). Swaengpic | Dreamstime.com (5). Michael DeFreitas North America / Alamy Stock Photo (5). EQRoy/Shutterstock (6). Tor Johnson/Hawaii Tourism Authority (6). Bonniemarie | Dreamstime.com (6). Shane Myers Photography/Shutterstock (6). Gardendreamer | Dreamstime.com (7). Idreamphotos | Dreamstime.com (8). Dave/Flickr, [CC BY-NC 2.0] (8). Luau Kalamaku (9). John Elk III / Alamy Stock Photo (10). Follow2find/Shutterstock (10). Dave Sansom 2015 (10). Dejjf82 | Dreamstime.com (10). Nalukai | Dreamstime.com (11). MNStudio | Dreamstime.com (11). Esusek | Dreamstime.com (12). Picturist21 | Dreamstime.com (12). Reinhard Dirscherl / age fotostock (13). Jewhyte | Dreamstime.com (14). Vacclav | Dreamstime.com (14). Hawaii Tourism Authority (HTA) / Dana Edmunds (14). Johnbronk | Dreamstime.com (14). O'ahu Visitor's Bureau (15). Jeff Whyte/Shutterstock (15). Kyrien | Dreamstime.com (16). Thediver123 | Dreamstime.com (16). Kelly Headrick/Shutterstock (16). Flyingwolf | Dreamstime.com (16). 7maru/Shutterstock (17). MNStudio | Dreamstime.com (18). Barsik | Dreamstime.com (18). Bosco1944 | Dreamstime.com (18). Schreier Fotografie / age fotostock (18). Cephotography | Dreamstime.com (19). Blakerandall81 | Dreamstime.com (19). Kikuko Nakayama/Flickr, [CC BY-SA 2.0] (21). **Chapter 1: Experience Hawaii:** ImagineGolf / iStockphoto (24, 25). Hawaii Visitors & Convention Bureau (39). HVCB (40). Thinkstock LLC (41). Linda Ching/HVCB (43). Sri Maiava Rusden/HVCB (43). Leis Of Hawaii, leisofhawaii.com (44). Polynesian Cultural Center (45). Public Domain (46). Dana Edmunds 2003 Polynesian Cultural Center's Alii Luau (46). Oahu Visitors Bureau (47). HTJ (47). **Chapter 2: Oahu:** Public Domain (49). Rory Hanrahan (53). Drazen Vukelic/Shutterstock (54). Corbis (61). Library of Congress (63). Library of Congress (65). NPS/ USS Arizona Memorial Photo Collection (65). USS Missouri Memorial Association (66). Army Signal Corps Collection in the U.S. National Archives (66). USS Bowfin Submarine Museum & Park (67). Public Domain (83). Rory Hanrahan (84, 87). Public Domain (91). Hawaii Tourism Authority (HTA) / Tor Johnson (94). Public Domain (97). Rory Hanrahan (104). Public Domain (137). Photo Resource Hawaii / Alamy (148). Photo Resource Hawaii / Alamy (154). Delamofoto | Dreamstime.com (158). Blue Hawaiian Helicopters (163). Photo Resource Hawaii / Alamy (166). **Chapter 3: Maui:** Ironrodart | Dreamstime.com (169). Public Domain (173). Joelanai | Dreamstime.com (181). Vlue | Dreamstime.com (195). 7Michael / iStockphoto (198). Laroach | Dreamstime.com (199). Estivillml | Dreamstime.com (200). Hawaii Tourism Authority (HTA) / Tor Johnson (209). Mike7777777 | Dreamstime.com (214). LukeGordon1/Flickr, [CC BY-ND 2.0] (253). Sunnyphotography.com / Alamy (275). HVCB/Ron Dahlquist (277). Shane Myers Photography/Shutterstock (278). SPrada/iStockphoto (280). Gert Vrey/iStockphoto (280). sweetlifephotos/iStockphoto (281). Michael S. Nolan / age fotostock (288). Ray Mains Photography / Wailea Emerald Course Hole #4, Wailea Golf Club, Maui, Hawaii (294). 7Michael / iStockphoto (298). **Chapter 4: The Big Island:** Walter Bibikow/Viesti Associates (301). Hawaii's Big Island Visitor Bureau (BIVB) (305). Hawaii Tourism Authority (HTA) / Tor Johnson (323). Russ Bishop / Alamy (331). NickiGgert (338). Big Island Visitors Bureau (340). Russ Bishop / age fotostock (341). Photo Resource Hawaii / Alamy (343). Cornforth Images/Alamy (344). Hawaii Tourism Authority (HTA) / Tor Johnson (345). Linda Robshaw / Alamy (345). Cornforth Images / Alamy (351). Luis Castañeda / age fotostock (352). Hawaii Tourism Authority (HTA) / Kirk Lee Aeder (390). Kushch Dmitry/Shutterstock (402, 403). Andre Seale / Alamy (411). travel192 (415). Hawaii Tourism Authority (HTA) / Kirk Lee Aeder (420). **Chapter 5: Kauai:** Karl Weatherly / age fotostock (423). Tor Johnson (428). Sergiyn | Dreamstime.com (440-443). Kikuko Nakayama/Flickr, [CC BY-SA 2.0] (444, 445). Photo Resource Hawaii / Alamy (445). Public Domain (445). Mark A. Johnson / Alamy (446). Photo Resource Hawaii / Alamy (447). Dallas & John Heaton / age fotostock (447). jedivader (450). Hawaii Tourism Authority/Ron Dahlquist (HTA) / Tor Johnson (454). Cornforth Images / Alamy (460). Junko Kubota/iStockphoto (463). Ray Kachatorian/Starwood Hotels & Resorts (473). Cphoto | Dreamstime.com (499). Kauai Visitors Bureau (500). Jack Jeffrey (501). Americanspirit | Dreamstime.com (505). David Fleetham / Alamy (513). jarvis gray/Shutterstock (517). Robert Plotz/iStockphoto (519). Hawaii Tourism Authority (HTA) / Tor Johnson (523). Koala (529). **Chapter 6: Molokai:** Molokai Visitors Association (531). Greg Vaughn / Alamy (534). Douglas Peebles Photography / Alamy (535). Public Domain (535). Michael Brake/iStockphoto (536). JS Callahan/tropicalpix/iStockphoto (539). Tony Reed / Alamy (550). Public Domain (557). Greg Vaughn / Alamy (560). **Chapter 7: Lanai:** Public Domain (563). Sheldon Kralstein/iStockphoto (566). iStockphoto (569). Superstock (572). Hawaii Tourism Japan (HTJ) (581).

About Our Writers: All photos are courtesy of the writers except for the following: Cheryl Crabtree, courtesy of Bryn Berg. Christie Leon, courtesy of Honolulu Star-Advertiser. Lehia Apana, courtesy of Brad Bayless. Trina Kudlacek, courtesy of Karin Kibby.

NOTES

ABOUT OUR WRITERS

Karen Anderson is a Kona resident who enjoys horseback riding in the hills of the Big Island. She is the managing editor of *At Home, Living with Style in West Hawaii* and has written for a variety of publications including *West Hawaii Today, Big Island Weekly, Hawaii* magazine, and the Kona-Kohala Chamber of Commerce. She's also the best-selling author of *The Hawaii Home Book, Practical Tips for Tropical Living*, which received an award of excellence from the Hawaii Book Publishers Association. Her monthly editor's column and chef/restaurant profiles are known throughout West Hawaii.

Kristina Anderson has been writing professionally for more than 25 years. After working as an advertising copywriter and creative director in Southern California for more than a decade, she moved to Hawaii in 1992, freelancing copy and broadcast for Hawaii agencies. Since 2006, she's written for national and regional publications, most notably for *At Home in West Hawaii* magazine, which profiles a variety of homes—from coffee shacks to resort mansions—and for USAToday.com Travel Tips. She also fills in here and there as a substitute teacher, which keeps her busy, as does being a single mom to two teenage boys. When there's time, she paddles outrigger canoes competitively and plays tennis very noncompetitively.

Born and raised on Maui, **Lehia Apana** is an island girl with a wandering spirit. She has lived in Chicago, Rome, and Sydney, but always finds her way back home. Lehia has been writing about Maui for more than a decade, beginning as a reporter, and later as special sections editor, at the *Maui News*. These days, when she's not flexing her writing muscles as the managing editor at *Maui Nō Ka 'Oi Magazine*, she can be found training for her next triathlon, surfing, or working on her farm.

Powell Berger lives in the heart of Honolulu's Kakaako neighborhood, where she's ever in search of the best poke bowl. Her wanderlust has taken her to more than 50 countries around the world, and her writing appears in numerous state and regional publications, AAA magazines, *The Atlantic*, and various websites, in addition to Fodor's.

Joan Conrow is an independent journalist who splits her time between Kauai and New Mexico. She has written about Hawaii politics, culture, environment, and lifestyles for many regional and national publications. She helped write the original Fodor's guide to Kauai.

Native Californian **Cheryl Crabtree** has worked as a freelance writer since 1987 and regularly travels up, down, and around California for work and fun. She has contributed to *Fodor's California* since 2003 and also contributes to the *Fodor's National Parks of the West* guide. She now has a home in Oahu, where she lives part-time.

Kyle Ellison was raised on Maui before setting out to wander the world for the better part of 10 years. After 65 countries and 49 U.S. states he returned back home to Kula's pasturelands, along with his wife and two sons. Find out more at @themauiexpert and *themauiexpert.com*.

Tiffany Hill has lived on Oahu's Leeward and Windward sides, but today she calls Honolulu home. She is a freelance writer whose work is regularly published in regional and national publications, as well as online. When she's not on assignment, you can find her playing roller derby.

Trina Kudlacek fell in love with Hawaii while on vacation 20 years ago. She now has the best of all possible worlds as she splits her time between her home in Hawaii, where she is a lecturer at the University of Hawaii, and Italy, where she is a tour guide. She updated all coverage of Beaches; Water Sports and Tours; and Golf, Hiking, and Outdoor Activities for this edition.

Christie Leon is an award-winning journalist who has covered volcanic eruptions, shark attacks, hurricanes, and all the other things not commonly written about in guidebooks. Raised in Honolulu, she lived on Maui for 30 years and works for Hawaii's largest daily newspaper. Thanks to Maria Leon, who assisted with fact-checking.

U.K.-born Chris Oliver has been a resident of Oahu for 30 years. As a reporter and travel editor for the *Honolulu Advertiser* she wrote about the Hawaiian Islands, as well as national and international destinations, with an eye for what visitors would most enjoy on a visit to Hawaii. Coming from a different country, climate, and culture has given her an enthusiasm for the exotic. She currently edits a newsletter, writes for *Hawaii* magazine, and divides her time between Hawaii and the United Kingdom.

Charles E. Roessler is a longtime Kauai resident who was an editor for the *Japan Times* and the *Buffalo News* after teaching English and journalism for 10 years. He contributes to the *New York Times* as a stringer/freelancer and loves Kauai, especially playing tennis and swimming at Anini Beach.

Writer and multimedia journalist Anna Weaver is a sixth-generation *kamaaina,* born and raised in Kailua, Oahu. She can never get enough Spam *musubi, malassadas*, or hiking time in her home state. Anna has written for *Slate,* as well as such Hawaii publications as the *Honolulu Advertiser* (now *Star-Advertiser*), *Honolulu Magazine*, and *Pacific Business News*.